California's Great Chardonnays

The Wine Spectator's Ultimate Guide for Consumers, Collectors and Investors

By James Laube

Author of *California's Great Cabernets*

Published by Wine Spectator Press
A division of M. Shanken Communications, Inc./West
Opera Plaza Suite 2014
601 Van Ness Avenue
San Francisco, CA 94102
(415) 673-2040, (415) 673-0103 (fax)

M. Shanken Communications, Inc. also publishes *The Wine Spectator, Impact, Impact International, Market Watch, Food Arts, Impact Research Reports, Leaders, Impact Yearbook, Impact International Directory, Market Watch Creative Adbook, The Wine Spectator's Wine Country Guide,* and sponsors the Impact Marketing Seminars and the California and New York Wine Experiences. Headquarters office at 387 Park Avenue South, New York, NY 10016, (212) 684-4224, (212) 684-5424 (fax).

First Edition
Book and jacket design by Kathy McGilvery
Grape cluster illustration by Dorothy Reinhardt

Distributed to the Book Trade by Sterling Publishing Co., New York, NY

Manufactured in the United States of America
ISBN 0-918076-79-X

TO DWIGHT AND MARGAUX

FOREWORD

No California wine has seen such explosive growth in such a short time as Chardonnay. Thirty years ago, consumers saw nothing inherently special about the name "Chardonnay" on a wine label. Only a handful of producers in California were making wine from this grape, and just as few growers had planted Chardonnay vines in their vineyards.

The wine boom of the 1970s opened the floodgates for California wines in general, and Chardonnay was no exception. Thousands of acres of vines were planted and hundreds of wineries began experimenting with this malleable grape. By the end of the decade, there seemed to be almost as many different styles of Chardonnay as there were producers.

Throughout the 1980s, the popularity of Chardonnay continued on an upward spiral, as did the quality of wines produced. Wineries honed their individual styles and searched for the ideal vineyard sites.

Today, with more than 500 Chardonnay producers actively pursuing the white wine consumer, Chardonnay may be the most recognized white-wine name in the world. It may also be the most variable in the world in terms of style and quality.

Despite its incredible popularity, surprisingly little has been written for the consumer on these wines. In *California's Great Chardonnays*, James Laube sets out to document the story of California's greatest white wine, and to give the consumer a definitive guide to this ever-growing wine category.

Many producers will be unhappy with the conclusions Laube draws about their wines. Many more will be surprised to see that their wines are not included. Of the hundreds of Chardonnay producers in California only 74 wineries were chosen for this book.

This is nonetheless a complete reference, covering all aspects of the greatest Chardonnay wines in California — from history to vineyards and appellations to vintage evaluations and buying strategies. But by far the most controversial part of this book is Laube's classification of the top California Chardonnays.

Here Laube takes a very hard look at the best Chardonnays and classifies them into five levels — first through fifth growths — based loosely on Bordeaux's 1855 classification. This Chardonnay classification is based on tasting evaluation and consistency of style and quality, not mere reputation. Thus some of the Chardonnays one might expect to be included in the higher ranking levels are not.

This is Laube's second book. His first, on California Cabernet, was hailed by many as one of the most controversial and comprehensive wine books ever. His role as senior editor at *The Wine Spectator* has given him years of in-depth blind-tasting experience with wines from around the world. His special concentration on the wines of California makes him ideally suited to tackle a project of this kind.

California's Great Chardonnays joins *California's Great Cabernets* and the just-published *Vintage Port*, by James Suckling, as the latest additions to *The Wine Spectator's* "Ultimate Guide" series of comprehensive guides for consumers, collectors and investors.

It is our intention to revise this book every few years, with updated tasting notes, rankings and price data, so that it continues to be the most comprehensive and current reference on the subject.

Finally, this book would not have been possible without the team spirit and commitment of members of the entire staff of *The Wine Spectator*.

Marvin R. Shanken
Editor and Publisher
The Wine Spectator
New York, NY
August 1990

ACKNOWLEDGMENTS

This is a special two pages, for it gives me the pleasure of publicly thanking the many people who contributed to this book.

At the top of this list, I owe a great debt of gratitude to Marvin Shanken, my editor and publisher, and Greg Walter, my good friend and president of *The Wine Spectator*. It was Marvin who encouraged me to write *California's Great Chardonnays* to help wine lovers better understand these magnificent wines. Greg helped me refine my ideas and organize my thoughts, and he supervised every detail of this book, keeping it on schedule through some very tight and harried deadlines.

The entire staff of *The Wine Spectator* has been highly enthusiastic and supportive. In particular a special thanks to Mark Norris for helping me keep track of all the wines, scores and tasting notes, as well as compiling and analyzing price trends, and Ray Bush, our tasting coordinator, for helping me gather many hard-to-get wines. Thanks also to Kathy McGilvery for designing the book and cover, to Donna Marianno Morris, Liza Gross and their production staff for putting it together, and to copy editor Lisa King for her attention to detail and for polishing my prose. Julie Huntsinger provided important research assistance. Thanks too to *Wine Spectator* managing editor Jim Gordon for his help in editing the book and sharing his thoughts about Chardonnay, as well as lending his encouragement and support.

Through the past decade, many vintners have shared their time and knowledge of Chardonnay with me. I am extremely grateful for that education. Much of what I know about Chardonnay is due to their teachings. Each vintner in this book, as well as dozens of others, provided wines for review and analysis. Many of them knew that some of their older vintages might not show well and could receive unflattering reviews. Nonetheless, they provided their wines anyway, in order to contribute to my education about past vintages, as well as to help build a source of reference on California Chardonnay. From that group I would like to single out and acknowledge the support of Richard Graff, Zelma Long, Richard Arrowood, Mike Grgich, Robert, Tim and Michael Mondavi, Bob Sessions, Gary Andrus, Bill Dyer, Tom Ferrell, William

Hill, Ed Sbragia, Richard Ward, David Graves, Brice Jones, Bill Bonetti, Bob Travers, Don and Rhonda Carano, George Bursick, John and Janet Trefethen, David Whitehouse, Jay Corley, Alan Phillips, Eleanor McCrea, Gil Nickel, Ric Forman, Julie Garvey, Manfred Esser, John Thacher, Jim and Bo Barrett, Stephen Kistler, Phil Woodward, Tom Burgess, Roy and Walt Raymond, Fred Fisher, Donn Chappellet, Frank Altamura, Marcus and Anne Moller-Racke, Jill Davis, Stuart and Charles Smith, Larry Brooks, Mike Richmond, John Kongsgaard, Robert Pecota, Koerner and Joan Rombauer, Warren Winiarski, Bernard Portet, John Richburg, Dan Lee, Richard Sanford, Norm de Leuze, Bryan del Bondio, Jim Allen, Charles Shaw, Stan Anderson, Chuck Carpy, John Stuart, John Hawley, Sandra MacIver, Steve Girard, Deborah Cahn, Cecil De Loach, Tom Dehlinger, John Williams, Jeffery Patterson, Jess Jackson, Jed Steele, Randle Johnson, Ted Edwards, Jerry Luper, Mike and Marty Lee, Agustin Huneeus, Greg Upton, Richard Maher and the late Myron Nightingale.

Barney and Belle Rhodes and Bob Adamson helped me find some very old and very hard-to-get Chardonnays from yesteryear; Robert Young, Rene di Rosa, André Tchelistcheff, Dennis Bowker, John Skupny, Tor Kenward, Andy Blue, Harvey Posert, Jack Daniels and Win Wilson enhanced my understanding of Chardonnay in one way or another, and wine historian William Heintz has been a great source of information, perspective and analysis.

Last but not least, a special thanks to my wife, Cheryl, for all her support and for standing by me through this summer's sequel to *California's Great Cabernets*. My children, Dwight and Margaux, both contributed what they could in their own way.

Thanks again to everyone.

James Laube
Napa, Calif.
September 1990

CONTENTS

INTRODUCTION

T his is a book for California Chardonnay lovers. Odds are that if you drink much white wine, California Chardonnay is among your favorites. In the past two decades, California Chardonnay has risen from obscurity to trendiness, making a dramatic rise in prominence in the United States and international wine markets. Today Chardonnay is the champion of white table wines in America. It is the wine most consumers and connoisseurs turn to for a truly unique drinking experience.

What is astonishing is that just 30 years ago there were only a few hundred acres of Chardonnay scattered throughout California, and only a dozen or so winemakers who took this grape seriously enough to squeeze it into wine. Since the mid-1970s all that has changed. Chardonnay has led the "white wine as a cocktail" boom, and the growing popularity of the wine among both winemakers and wine lovers has been astounding. It has become one of the most fascinating chapters in the modern history of California wine.

As varietal wines gained credibility in the United States in the 1970s, Chardonnay emerged as the natural companion to California's greatest red wine, Cabernet Sauvignon. Of California's dry white wines, Chardonnay is by far the most distinctive; not so much for its pure varietal character, which is more subdued and refined than that of any other white grape variety, but for its intensity and its ability to be shaped, styled, manipulated and coaxed into performing well in different climates, soils and at the hands of different winemakers.

When properly grown and vinified, Chardonnay is a wine of uncommon richness, complexity and depth of flavors, not to mention that it is delicious to drink, is able to stand on its own or complement a wide assortment of foods. California's great Chardonnays also are able to age and improve in the bottle for years, sometimes decades, gaining added dimensions of flavor, texture, aroma, subtlety and finesse.

Part of my fascination with Chardonnay is grounded in its recent surge in popularity and new-found celebrity status. In the mid-1970s, when I was a student, it was unusual to find Chardonnay on a restaurant wine list, and what was available generally was not very good.

At the time, I worked as a waiter in a restaurant where an expanded wine list was being introduced for customers who preferred vintage dates and corks to generic table wine poured from a spout or carafe. The new wine list featured varietal reds from Louis M. Martini and whites from Wente Bros. The Wente wines were an assortment of off-dry varietals — Riesling, Le Blanc de Blancs (a sweet Riesling-style wine) and Pinot Chardonnay, which was dry. Wente's Pinot Chardonnay did not leave an impression of particular distinction upon me, as I barely recall its character.

In those days, I preferred red wine to white, because red paired well with barbecued chicken, hamburgers, steaks and lasagna, all mainstays at our college beach-house table. When it came to white wine, I drank mostly Riesling and Gewürztraminer and occasionally Sauvignon Blanc and rosé. The Rieslings and Gewürztraminers were off-dry and refreshing, much more popular than they are today, but not wines we served regularly at the dinner table.

The era of pairing dry white wine with food may have resulted from our gradual change of diet — eating less red meat and more fish and poultry. As we ate more salmon, red snapper and shrimp, poached more chicken and tossed more salads, Chardonnay increasingly earned its rightful place at the dinner table. Its vast array of delicious fruit flavors demonstrated Chardonnay's complexity, finesse and ability to be appreciated on its own, as an enjoyble drink before dinner as well.

One of the first things I learned about buying Chardonnay was that not all of my favorite Cabernet or Zinfandel producers could work the same kind of magic with Chardonnay. As it turned out, I had accidentally stumbled on a major theme that permeates the history of California Chardonnay. For most of its life, Chardonnay has been planted in precisely the wrong locations, specifically in regions and vineyards that were too hot. You will get a strong rebuttal from old-time Stony Hill, Hanzell or Mayacamas drinkers, who will swear by those old glories, and in fact, they have the proof in the bottle to support their claims.

Nonetheless, the truth remains that most growers and winemakers in the 1960s and 1970s planted Chardonnay grapes in the warmest areas, right next to their Zinfandel and Petite Sirah vines, to ensure that the white grapes would ripen. By and large, that worked well enough to get Chardonnay started. With a few exceptions, no one bothered to plant Chardonnay in cooler coastal climates, and those who did often made poor wines. There were not many great Chardonnays produced in those days, which represented the beginning of the trial-and-error process by which so much wine-producing knowledge is sorted out, analyzed and learned.

Early on, most of the Chardonnays I drank were from red-wine specialists such as Martini, Beaulieu, Heitz and Inglenook. Those were the brands that our local wine shops stocked, and the ones that I could afford. It soon became clear that some good red-wine producers possessed a greater Chardonnay dexterity than others, so crossing over from red wine to white with Robert Mondavi, Burgess or Chateau Montelena reduced the risk and enhanced the drinking experience.

Not until I moved to Napa in 1978 did I become fully aware of how widespread the Chardonnay craze had grown. I had noticed that each time I went into a wine shop there seemed to be more new Chardonnay brands from different appellations. Some producers were getting serious, making vineyard-designated wines from different appellations and even two or more wines from one viticultural area.

I remember visiting Chateau St. Jean one summer afternoon and discovering that this Sonoma Valley winery was making five or six different Chardonnays from vineyards in disparate locations in Sonoma County. It would have taken a full day of frenetic driving to visit them all. Moreover, no two St. Jean Chardonnays tasted exactly alike. Each had a subtle distinction: One might have a touch more peach than pear or apple flavor, while the next might stand out for its crisp acidity, lush texture or toasty oak notes.

It was my St. Jean experience that triggered my interest in studying California Chardonnays. Since then I have been paying closer attention to the producers, vintages, appellations and techniques, and reading the fine print on the label, which tells me this wine came from a special vineyard, ranch, valley or mountain in a particular region. Most of my wine education has come through reading, tasting and on-the-job training — learning first-hand from wine professionals. This includes years of interviews and informal conversations with winemakers in their labs and cellars, vineyard managers among their vines, university professors, restaurateurs and chefs, and other wine journalists, authors and wine aficionados, each of whom has contributed to my understanding and appreciation of wine in general and Chardonnay in particular.

In the past decade, I have had the opportunity to taste thousands of Chardonnays and other wines, both domestic and imported. I have traveled to and written about the wines of Bordeaux, Burgundy, the Loire Valley, the Rhône Valley, Sauternes, Germany, Italy, Spain, Australia, Mexico, Oregon, Long Island and California. While Napa Valley is my home and California wines are the ones I am most familiar with, my tastes extend well beyond local appellations. One of the most fascinating things about drinking fine wine is appreciating the diversity of grapes, styles, vintages and appellations from around the world. I have personal favorites when it comes to wine, but they are not based on grape varieties or geographic boundaries. Each year at *The Wine Spectator*, we taste and review 4,000 to 5,000 of the world's greatest wines. This allows me the opportunity to examine the quality of the wines, vintages, appellations and producers on a regular basis. It is in that spirit that I have researched and written this book.

California Chardonnay has come a long way in the past three decades. Those few hundred acres of Chardonnay vines have grown to more than 48,000 acres today, producing more than 7 million cases of Chardonnay, with more than 500 different brands from dozens of appellations stretching from San Diego to Mendocino to the foothills of the Sierra Nevada. Despite its popularity, it is my belief that Chardonnay is still in its infancy in California, and that winemakers are just beginning to realize the full potential for greatness this wine has. Cabernet Sauvignon has had a long track record in California dating to the 1800s, and early winemaking pioneers were keen on identifying the best soils and climates to root those vines. There is no parallel history with Chardonnay. With few exceptions, the 1960s planted the seed of interest with Chardonnay, but it was the 1970s that proved the decade of discovery, experimentation and advancement. The 1980s not only continued those trends but amplified them, moving from generalities to specifics in the search for better grape clones, soils and the perfect climate for the cultivation of this grape variety. There also have been dramatic strides in vinification techniques with Chardonnay, with countless experiments varying fermentation temperatures and containers (from small oak barrels to stainless steel tanks), and using different yeast strains to produce faster, slower or more even-handed fermentations. Greater attention is paid now to picking grapes at precise levels of ripeness, the use or avoidance of skin contact during fermentation, and the effect of malolactic fermentation and extended lees aging on the complexity and longevity of the wines. Still, many of these and other topics are discussed in the form of questions. The answers lie somewhere ahead.

WHAT TO LOOK FOR IN A GREAT CHARDONNAY

Chardonnay is a winemaker's wine and a grape grower's delight. As a variety, Chardonnay is highly adaptable and performs well in a wide variety of climates and soils from one end of California to another. As a wine, it is extremely versatile — easy to manipulate, shape and style. No other white wine benefits as much from toasty oak barrels as Chardonnay. Part of the reason is that Chardonnay, for all its richness, intensity and concentration, is a fairly neutral-flavored wine. Riesling, with its spicy, grapy flavors, and Sauvignon Blanc, with its intensely herbal, grassy aromas, have stronger personalities and more readily identifiable varietal characteristics. They do not benefit from winemaking manipulation as much as the relatively neutral Chardonnay grape can. The principal aromas and flavors of Chardonnay are often so closely identified with oak seasoning that it is sometimes difficult to separate them. The fruit flavors most closely associated with Chardonnay are apple, pear, melon, fig, citrus (lemon and grapefruit) and spice. Sometimes the flavors are more exotic, like pineapple, guava or banana, and occasionally peach or nectarine. With age, honey and anise flavors often emerge.

Since virtually all California's finest Chardonnays are fermented and aged in small French oak barrels, descriptors like wood, toast, butter, vanilla and smoke are closely linked with the Chardonnay flavor. Chardonnay's affinity for oak, whether for additional flavor, texture or aroma, contributes to its complexity as a wine. Oak also influences the wine's color.

The finest Chardonnays demonstrate great balancing acts. They combine rich, deeply concentrated, sharply focused fruit flavors with a smooth, lush, creamy texture that is enlivened by crisp acidity and a long, lingering aftertaste. In great Chardonnays there is harmony among those elements, along with a subtle measure of delicacy, grace and finesse. Each sip allows you to discover a new marvelous flavor or aroma. When evaluating wines, one of the most important criteria is the nature of the finish, how long the appealing flavors remain on your palate. Everything leading up to the finish counts, from color and aroma to the intensity, texture and depth of flavor. Ultimately, however, what matters most are the flavors you discern lingering on the palate, once you have swallowed a sip. A great Chardonnay should continue to echo the same sharply focused, richly concentrated fruit that was tasted with the first sip. If there is oak present, it should be in balance with fruit and acidity, more like seasoning than a dominant flavor. Fine Chardonnays need lively acidity to provide structure and sustain the flavors. If the finish leaves a muddled, disjointed impression, shows too much oak and not enough acidity, or is coarse in texture, it is less desirable.

As Chardonnays age, they undergo changes in color, texture and flavor. Young Chardonnays are brilliant in color, with pale yellow or straw hues. With maturity the color gradually deepens to richer shades of yellow and gold. A deep yellow-gold color is a strong indication that the wine is fully mature and probably declining. Young wines with a deep color are usually very ripe and high in extract, a result of skin contact during fermentation and time spent in new oak. Many of the California Chardonnays of the 1970s and 1980s that matured quickly were made in this style. Chardonnay's texture also softens with age, changing from the fresh, crisp mouth-feel you find in fresh fruit to a lusher, creamier buttery sensation. When a great Chardonnay matures, the flavors change from specific fruit flavors to less precise but more complex and harmonious flavors. Mature Chardonnays often display honey, butterscotch or anise flavors, which are attractive when they are part of the flavor spectrum and not the lone flavor. Older Chardonnays often taste and feel heavier on the palate. A great Chardonnay should drink well on release, reach maturity in two to five years and age well for 10 to 12 years. Most of the wines selected for this book have that kind of aging profile.

WHAT TO EXPECT FROM THIS BOOK

In writing this book, my primary goal was to research and analyze the history of California's leading Chardonnay producers, as well as examine their top wines, vintage by vintage and appellation by appellation, providing consumers with my perspective on selecting the best wines to cellar or collect. *California's Great Chardonnays* is written with specific information and advice for consumers and collectors who regularly drink Chardonnay and want to concentrate on the state's best wines, vintages or appellations. It is also designed to provide newcomers to California Chardonnay with a perspective on this great wine.

The appreciation of wine, like that of music, art, the theater or even cuisine, is highly personal and subjective. Each of us has our own tastes and preferences. Yet even with such subjective topics as art or classical music, a consensus forms with the passage of time. Those opinions in turn are open to revision and new analysis. In the pages that follow is one critic's view of Chardonnay in California. It is the result of years of research and is intended to be a contribution to the greater knowledge and understanding of the topic, to stimulate and provoke new thought. It is not by any means intended to be the final word. This book can only be a beginning in the understanding of the tremendous changes that are taking place with California Chardonnay at this very moment.

HOW TO USE THIS BOOK

My studies of California Chardonnay have taken me throughout the state, from the heart of the Napa, Sonoma and Alexander valleys to such remote outposts as Temecula, Chalone and Anderson Valley, to discover where and how Chardonnay is grown, how and why it is vinified differently, and why it has risen from the common ranks of other California table wines to join the company of the world's finest wines.

In the pages and chapters that follow, the 951 tasting notes and evaluations of individual wineries, vintages and appellations are intended to enlighten wine lovers about California Chardonnay, and direct consumers and collectors to the finest Chardonnays California has to offer. This book is designed as an easy-to-use reference source. This chapter begins with a discussion of tasting and evaluating wines, explains how the wines were chosen, and provides tools to help you apply the information of this book in the best way.

TASTING AND EVALUATING WINE

No two people have the same taste. Each of us has our own preferences for flavor, aroma, texture, complexity and nuance in wine. The distinction of the world's expert wine tasters has less to do with talent or superior taste buds than with their repeated exposure to a broad range of wines. The world's great tasters not only taste a lot of wines and pay careful attention to what they're tasting, but possess a great taste memory — the ability to remember the unique flavor, aroma, texture and structural features of different wines. Moreover, they are highly consistent in their analysis and evaluation of wines, and are able to duplicate their conclusions. That is, if they like a particular wine, they consistently rate it highly. If they dislike a wine, they consistently mark it down.

It is possible to evaluate wines in all kinds of settings, but the most objective method is the blind tasting, where the identity of the wine is not known. The Chardonnays selected for this book were chosen primarily through years of blind tastings. The most comprehensive blind tastings I participate in are conducted at the offices of *The Wine Spectator* in San Francisco. I also taste hundreds of wines at my home office and at wineries, where winemakers can demonstrate their techniques and the characteristics of their vineyards using barrel samples, finished bottles and aged wines from their cellars. After tracking these wines and producers for years, I narrowed my list of candidates to just over 120 producers. Then I went back and re-tasted as many of these wines as possible in vertical tastings. This provided an opportunity to confirm my original opinions, as well as evaluate how consistent the style was over a period of years. I was also able to evaluate how older vintages had aged. This process eliminated nearly half the 120 producers, and focused my attention on the producers and wines chosen for this book.

The most reliable way to evaluate wines is to taste them as often as possible, or at least frequently enough to form an educated opinion of their quality and development. I have tasted most of the wines in this book on at least five occasions. In some instances, particularly with older vintages from the 1960s and 1970s, I only had the opportunity to taste a wine once or twice and sometimes not under blind conditions. In cases where my notes were inconsistent or a wine appeared to vary in quality, I attempted to retaste it at least once. It also is true that some wines and vintages are more difficult to evaluate than others. In instances where wines were particularly tough to rate, I re-tasted them until I had a good sense of their quality, in an attempt to provide the most accurate description and rating possible. Because wines can change dramatically in a matter of years, I decided to list only current tasting notes. Each of the Chardonnays in this book was tasted at least once between December 1989 and July 1990.

In researching this book I have encountered considerable bottle variation most commonly caused by poor storage conditions. Wines stored in an environment that is too warm mature much more quickly than those cellared at constant, cooler temperatures. I have also encountered widespread corkiness, especially in recent vintages, a result of defective corks. Most of the time one can tell when a wine is corky, because it smells and tastes like wet, moldy newspaper. In some cases, however, a wine can be mildly corky, a condition that is less obvious, which strips the wine of its fruitiness. In instances where bottle variation proved especially problematic, I have indicated that condition in the tasting note. In general, I have given the wine the benefit of the doubt, and printed the most complimentary review and score. Several of the wines were consistently flawed by one defect or another. I have recommended that consumers avoid these wines.

As much as I hope this book will be a useful guide, the most important wine critic is you. Use this book for information, analysis, research and opinion, but learn to trust your own taste and you won't go wrong.

HOW THE WINES WERE CHOSEN

Since the late 1970s and early 1980s, I have been both a regular drinker and keen student of California Chardonnays. Early on many of my notes were mental ones of fond remembrances of wines I loved and wished I had more of, or bad experiences with wines I wished I had avoided. Since the 1980 vintage, I have tasted virtually every major new Chardonnay released in California. In my experience, the best way to buy great wines is to concentrate on producers, appellations and vintages with the best track records for consistency and excellence. That is the method I used with this book. Each of the producers selected for *California's Great Chardonnays* has demonstrated to me that they can produce excellent Chardonnays on a consistent basis. There were other factors as well, among the most significant being the following:

Producer and overall quality: This is of paramount importance. The producer's name on the bottle is the single greatest guarantee of quality. Appellations, vineyards, vintages, winemakers and techniques are all important considerations in buying wine, but none is as crucial to the quality of the wine in the bottle as who made the wine.

Track record of excellence: This is a measure of how good the wines are from vintage to vintage within a general framework of consistency of style. Wines with track records of 10 years or more from the same vineyard under the same winemaker are your greatest assurance of excellence; they have established that they are well-made wines with continuity. Five vintages of consistently high quality also make a wine worth buying. With a few exceptions, including Altamura and Forman, all of the wineries selected for this book have a minimum of five years of producing very good to outstanding Chardonnays. Factors such as improvement or decline of a winery's quality are all crucial elements in critiquing wines. I gave high marks to wineries that made older vintages that have aged well, but did not hold it against those with wines that had not aged as gracefully. I was especially critical of the most recent vintages, from 1984 to 1988, for each was a very good to outstanding year in which most winemakers should have made high-quality wines.

Consistency of style: I also evaluated how precise, deliberate and consistent the style is from year to year. A wine, vineyard, winery or winemaker with a deliberate style ensures consistency. The key to evaluating consistency of style begins with understanding the style, that is, what the winemaker is attempting to achieve with the grapes from a specific vineyard or set of vineyards. For example, the following two Chardonnay styles are characterized by these disparate qualities: One style produces a wine that is crisp, tart and austere, with very little oak evident and no malolactic fermentation, while the other style wine is lavishly oaked in toasty barrels, undergoes full malolactic fermentation and is very ripe and lush. Both are acceptable, legitimate styles that deserve to be judged on their own merits. Moreover, there is nothing wrong with a winery changing its style to make better wine. But a consistent style renders wines that are most often affected by the quality and character of the vintage rather than by changes in grape source, winemaking technique or style. Most connoisseurs choose wines made in styles they prefer and can depend on, not those that change every other year.

Private reserve and special designations: In general, I have concentrated on each winery's top Chardonnay. Some wineries label those wines reserve or private reserve to designate superior quality, but many do not. Moreover, many producers who bottle a reserve or special-designation wine make a very fine regular bottling that deserves a try as well.

Estate bottled: This is a guarantee of authenticity and often superior quality as well, because it means the owner controls the winemaking process from the vineyard to the bottle. Increasingly this control has become more important in California, because it ensures a consistent source of grapes and offers the greatest potential for consistency in quality and style from vintage to vintage. Wineries that own their own grapes are much more capable of monitoring the quality of the vineyards. Wineries that use a different source of grapes each year face a far greater challenge in achieving uniformity of style and quality. This is not meant to denigrate all independent grape growers, but most growers are interested in producing large crops because they are paid by the ton. They use rootstock, grape clones and vineyard techniques to maximize production. Most of the wines included in this book are estate bottled or are made by vintners who have long-term contracts with first-rate growers who work with them to ensure maximum quality.

Two or more wines from one winery: Many producers make more than one Chardonnay. Chateau St. Jean usually makes four or five, and once it made nine Chardonnays from the same vintage. Wineries that produce more than one Chardonnay may or may not have the second wine included, depending on the quality.

Vineyard designations: Many wineries use vineyard designations to identify specific growers and vineyards of distinction, such as Robert Young Vineyards, Les Pierres or Dutton Ranch. In fact, these are often among the finest Chardonnays produced in California. In most instances a vineyard-designated wine is similar to one that is estate bottled. A vineyard designation is an indication that the winery and grower have a solid relation, but it also usually means that the winery does not own the vineyard. Sonoma-Cutrer Vineyards does own all three of the vineyards it bottles separately — Les Pierres, Cutrer Vineyard and Russian River Ranches. Chateau St. Jean, on the other hand, owns only the St. Jean Vineyard. All its other sources of vineyard-designated wines are independently owned.

Rare or older bottles: One of my principal goals in writing *California's Great Chardonnays* was to examine the quality of older vintages, and I have tried to include as many old wines as possible, for the historical record and the winery's track record. With wineries that produced a regular Chardonnay before a reserve or vineyard-designated bottling, I have included the earlier bottlings and then focused on the specialty wine. Sterling Vineyards, for instance, has made Chardonnay for years, but it was not until the mid 1980s that it began bottling two separate vineyard-designated wines, both of which are superior to the regular bottling. Unfortunately most wines from the 1970s and earlier are extremely rare and difficult to come by. Few wineries have these old wines in their cellars.

Vineyards: Great wines begin in the vineyard, and the quality and track record of a vineyard often predate a wine brand. Sonoma-Cutrer's Les Pierres and Cutrer Vineyard were both providing excellent grapes to other wineries before their fruit was vinified by Sonoma-Cutrer beginning in 1981. The famous Winery Lake Vineyard in Carneros sold grapes to more than a dozen different Chardonnay producers before it was bought by Sterling Vineyards' parent, Seagram Classics Wine Co. Today the only Winery Lake Chardonnay is produced by Sterling.

Winemakers: Certain winemakers have a talent for making consistently wonderful Chardonnays. Both Richard Arrowood, of Chateau St. Jean and Arrowood, and Ric Forman, of Sterling, Newton, Shaw, Merryvale and Forman, had distinguished careers making Chardonnay before they started their own wineries. Their prior experience with Chardonnay bears directly on their ability to produce outstanding wines, even when their grape sources have changed. The role of the winemaker in establishing a style is important, particularly, early in a winery's development. It usually takes between five and 10 years to establish a credible style of Chardonnay, and to know how well it will age. When a winery depends on several different vineyards as grape sources, it is the winemaker who is the arbiter of quality and style. After a winery establishes a style and constant source of grapes, there is less a winemaker must do, which is why the great European wine estates, domaines and châteaux consider a winemaker to be more of a caretaker than a creator.

How This Book Is Organized

California's Great Chardonnays is designed for easy use. It is divided into six chapters, beginning with Chapter I, Chardonnay in California; Chapter II, Chardonnay Vineyards and Appellations; and Chapter III, The Vintages: 1970 to 1989. Chapter IV, A Classification: Ranking Chardonnays, is my classification of the Chardonnays chosen for this book based on overall quality and track record. Chapter V, Chardonnay Strategies: Collecting and Investing, offers my recommendations on which are the best Chardonnays for collecting based on my collectibility rating, as well as general advice for investing in Chardonnay for resale. Chapter VI, Profiles and Tasting Notes, is the heart of this book.

About the Wineries

In this section each of the wineries and wines selected for this book is presented in alphabetical order along with the following data:

Classification: One of five categories, first through fifth growth, denoting the overall quality of the wine.

Collectibility rating: One of three ratings — AAA, AA, or A. Chardonnays with AAA ratings are the wines I believe have the best track records for excellence and are the best candidates for long-term cellaring and appreciation of value. Many of the wines in this book have not been given a rating, but this does not necessarily reflect on their quality.

Best vintages: A summary of the best vintages of the wine, listed in order by highest score.

Winery profile: A brief history of the winery, along with a description of the style and character of the producer's wines.

At a glance: Facts and figures about the winery: the owner, address and phone number, founding date, winemaker and number of years in service, first Chardonnay vintage, total Chardonnay production (as distinguished from a single specific wine chosen for this book), Chardonnay acres owned, and time and type of oak used for aging. In addition, the winemaking notes reflect whether the wines are barrel fermented, undergo malolactic fermentation or receive lees aging. Wines that are not barrel fermented are usually fermented in stainless steel tanks. Many producers employ both techniques.

Tasting notes: A description of each wine: its style and flavor, and how it compares with other wines by the same producer and with other wines from the vintage. Each wine is rated on *The Wine Spectator*'s 100-point scale.

About the Wines

For each of the individual Chardonnays tasted, this additional information is included:

Cases produced: This information is provided by the wineries. It illustrates how limited the production of the truly great California Chardonnays is, though there are always exceptions. Edna Valley Vineyards produced 45,000 cases of barrel-fermented Chardonnay in 1988, and the quality is superb, but few wineries can produce wines on that scale and still maintain high quality standards.

Release price: The wine's suggested retail price on release. This information was obtained from the wineries.

Current price: Estimated market value today, based on information provided by wineries along with data from the retail market, auctions and leading restaurants as of June 1990. The estimated value today is an approximation of what you can expect to pay for a particular wine, not what you can expect to get for selling it. Retailers typically mark up prices from 33 percent to 50 percent. For more on the topic of buying and selling older wines, see Chapter V, Chardonnay Strategies: Collecting and Investing.

Last tasted: The latest month and year that I tasted a particular wine.

Drink: My estimate of when each wine will be at its best for drinking. Most Chardonnays are ready to drink on release and will peak by the age of five, but when you prefer to drink your wines is a matter of personal taste. There is no exact moment when a young wine becomes mature, heads into its prime or begins to decline. The drink window is at best a guideline of when to drink the wine before it begins to decline. If you buy a case of Chardonnay, you should periodically open a bottle and taste it to determine how it is aging. Wines that score below 69 points are not recommended; rather than provide a drink window I use the phrase "best to avoid."

Score: A numerical rating from 50 to 100 points based on *The Wine Spectator*'s 100-point scale. The ratings indicate how good the wines are today. With newly released wines, I have factored in their potential for improvement, based on my research. Since all of the tasting notes are my own, careful readers of *The Wine Spectator* will see that many of the wines have notes or scores different from those that appeared in the magazine. This reflects my personal preferences as distinguished from *The Wine Spectator* tasting panel's, as well as my re-evaluation of the wines. As important as the score is, I consider the tasting note description to be the most accurate reflection of the wine's quality, for the notes deal with aesthetics, not numbers.

ABOUT THE RATING SYSTEM

Scores gauge how much the critic likes or dislikes a wine, but far too often the tasting note description is overlooked and consumers either dismiss a very good wine because it doesn't score 90 points or higher, or they read that a wine is given a fair or poor rating without reading the tasting note. It is important to read carefully what the following numbers indicate about the quality of a wine. The best wines to concentrate on are the ones with the highest scores and most complimentary reviews, but wines that are good are just that and should not be ignored. *The Wine Spectator* 100-point scale is as follows.

95-100 Classic, a wine of extraordinary character
90-94 Oustanding, a wine of superior quality and style
80-89 Good to very good, a wine with special qualities
70-79 Average, a decent wine that may have minor flaws
60-69 Below average, a drinkable wine but not recommended
50-59 Poor, an undrinkable wine, best to avoid

Final Thoughts on Tasting

The best way to learn about Chardonnay is to drink it regularly, so you can learn about how a wine matures and when a Chardonnay is at the right age for you. To do this, buy six bottles to a case, so you will be able to drink the wine in its youth and watch it mature. You might be surprised by how well many of the wines age.

Tasting and drinking older Chardonnays requires some adjustment if you have not had much experience. Old California Chardonnays are very rare; in general most have not aged very well. Nonetheless, there are enough exceptions to that rule for me to encourage you to use this book as a guide to some of the finer, older Chardonnays and buy a bottle to drink. It can be a magnificent experience.

CHAPTER I

CHARDONNAY IN CALIFORNIA

Chardonnay is the most popular of California's fine wines, yet the history of this noble grape variety in the Golden State has been obscure until the early 20th century. Early European settlers brought scores of different grapevine cuttings to California in the 1800s and early 1900s, but there is little substantive evidence that Chardonnay vines were among those transported. Historical records of grapevine plantings in California compiled by the state make no mention of Chardonnay until the 1960s, although it was planted in Livermore Valley in the 1920s and was produced as a wine first in the 1930s.

It is possible that Chardonnay was among the hundreds of cuttings brought to California by Agoston Haraszthy of Hungary and others who began importing vines to California in the 1850s. A controversial and dashing figure, Haraszthy has become known as the "father of California viticulture" for bringing vines to California from Europe. In 1856 he began planting a vineyard near Sonoma, and a year later he founded Buena Vista Winery. According to several accounts, Haraszthy planted 14,000 vines consisting of 165 different varieties in his vineyard. It is uncertain exactly how many different varieties he possessed, but Chardonnay was not listed among any of his records or the state's official documents of vines being grown in California at that time.

The white grape varieties Haraszthy imported included Sauvignon Blanc, Sémillon, Riesling, Sylvaner and Gewürztraminer. It is known that Haraszthy visited the great Burgundy estates as he traveled throughout Europe collecting new cuttings. He no doubt knew that the great white Burgundies were made from Chardonnay grapes, but there were no Chardonnay cuttings among his vines.

By the late 1800s, several California wineries were producing white wines they called chablis. The California wine industry was well established by then, with 75,000 to 100,000 acres of vineyard, and hundreds of wineries spread throughout the state. It is possible, though not likely, that some of the grapes used for California chablis were Chardonnay, or Pinot Chardonnay, as it was sometimes called. There is no conclusive viticultural evidence, however, to support this theory. It was a common practice among European immigrants in California to use the wine names of the old world and to copy these styles. California wines labeled champagne, claret, sauternes, burgundy and chablis are just a few examples. Champagne, for instance, was used for sparkling wines. Claret referred to Bordeaux-style reds. Sauternes were late-harvest dessert wines. When the famous Hotel del Monte resort opened its doors in Monterey in 1888, the wine list included many of the aforementioned names, including a section of California "Burgundies," under which "Chablis, White" was listed

What grapes were used to make California chablis? Probably any combination of white varieties, including Sémillon and Sauvignon Blanc. Charles Wetmore, chief executive officer of the Board of State Viticultural Commissioners of California in the 1880s, probably knew more about grape culture and winemaking in that era in California than any other single individual, according to wine historian and author William Heintz. In his *Second Annual Report of 1883-84*, Wetmore wrote, "The white and gray Pinot, which make the famous Chablis wine, are not practically known to us, although we have scattering lots of Klevner (gray Pinot) and white Pinot; I believe that a Melon Blanc in Santa Clara County, which Mr. Crabb is now using in grafting old vines, is a true white Gamay." Moreover, in the same report, he went on, "The French varieties (of imported vines), as well as the large collections made by Colonel Haraszthy from all sources, fell generally into the hands of planters, who either abandoned their enterprise before perfecting them, or were not acquainted with the relative merits and proper methods of culture. A few of those notable were Mr. Chas. Lefranc and Mr. P. Pellier, who preserved the propagated collections, now extant, which have been of recent service. The noble varieties of wine grapes of France and Germany, with few exceptions, require long pruning, special care and adaptation to soil and climate, in order to produce profitable results."

THE ERA OF CALIFORNIA CHABLIS

Heintz's own research into the origins of California chablis concluded that there is no way of determining precisely when chablis was first sold in California, but notes: "In 1889 at the Paris, France, World's Fair, 'Mont Rouge Winery,' Livermore, California, owned by Adrian Chauche, won a 'Gold Medal' for its 'Wines,' which happened to be a chablis. Chauche was not adverse to labeling and marketing his wines as 'Pure California Chablis,' " according to Heintz. State grape records show 1 acre of "chablis" grapes being grown in California at that time. In 1881 both Inglenook Winery and To-Kalon Vineyard Co. in Napa Valley were producing chablis. Inglenook's was a "Burger, Chablis-type." At the San Francisco Midwinter Fair of 1894, another chablis, produced by H.W. Crabb, claimed a first-place award in the "California white wine, Chablis type" category, but there is no mention of Chardonnay, nor are there any indications from California State Fair wine competition results that Chardonnay was being grown or made into wine. If any Chardonnay existed in the 1800s or early 1900s it would probably have been grown on a very small or experimental scale, and used in blends with other grapes. Chardonnay apparently had nothing to do with California chablis.

In the late 1800s and early 1900s, the California wine industry was in a downward spiral, and there was still no sign of Chardonnay. The outbreak of the root louse phylloxera in the 1880s and 1890s devastated Californian and European vineyards, and many wineries closed. Then came Prohibition, which outlawed the sale of alcoholic beverages from 1919 to 1933 and diminished the California wine industry. The Great Depression of the 1930s proved another blow to the wine-grape economy as it struggled to revive itself.

THE FIRST CALIFORNIA CHARDONNAYS

It is unclear which company first began producing Chardonnay in California on a commercial basis, but several signs point to Wente Bros. in Livermore Valley as being among the leaders in planting Chardonnay vines. In 1936 Wente Bros. began making Pinot Chardonnay from its vineyard, which was planted in the 1920s. By the 1940s, Wente's Pinot Chardonnay began winning awards at the state's wine competition. In 1939 Maynard Amerine, a professor of enology at the University of California at Davis, wrote that there was a strong intent among winegrowers to plant Chardonnay in California. Nonetheless, there is no evidence that any significant plantings followed his optimistic forecast. In a 1955 article entitled "California's Principal Wine Grape Varieties," Davis professor Harold Olmo made no mention of Chardonnay. As late as 1961, it is estimated that only 300 acres of Chardonnay were planted in California.

In the late 1930s and continuing to the 1950s, some vintners began to take a keener interest in Chardonnay, but on a very limited scale. Almadén, Beaulieu Vineyard, Hanzell, Inglenook, Charles Krug, Paul Masson, Mayacamas, Louis Martini, Martin Ray, Stony Hill and Weibel joined Wente Bros. in producing Chardonnay. What linked most of these producers was budwood from the Wente Chardonnay vineyard. Throughout Napa, Sonoma and Santa Clara valleys, the so-called "Wente clone" was used extensively in new plantings. There were other clones, but researchers have not determined whether they also originated from the Wente vineyard. Undoubtedly other clones were imported from Burgundy. The early Wente clone was a sporadic producer. In some years, it set well and offered a healthy crop, but in other years it set unevenly and produced a sparse crop. Growers were hesitant to plant Chardonnay that threw a good crop one year but left them empty-handed the next. There was no market for the Chardonnay anyway. Worst of all, the vine proved susceptible to viruses, spring frost, Botrytis and mildew. It did not make much sense to grow it.

In the 1950s and 1960s, the role models for California white wines were not the great white Burgundies, but the fruity wines of the Rhine and Mosel. Sweet, lush, Sauternes-style wines were popular. While California Cabernet Sauvignon producers from the 1800s on looked to Bordeaux as a model for both grape growing and winemaking with claret-style wines, Chardonnay developed at a much slower and less certain pace. Dry white table wines in general were not of much interest to producers, growers or consumers. Most of the early Chardonnays were crudely made, often flawed by bacterial defects, oxidized and unpleasant to drink. Crop yields remained a problem, as did vineyard locations. With a few notable exceptions, most growers and vintners planted Chardonnay in with other grape varieties that often resulted in planting Chardonnay next to Cabernet, Zinfandel or Petite Sirah.

THE NEW PIONEERS

In Napa Valley in the late 1940s, Fred and Eleanor McCrea began planting their Stony Hill vineyard in the hills north of St. Helena. There was no particular reason they chose Chardonnay, other than predictions from friends in the wine industry that it would grow well in their rocky soil. On weekends and holidays they would drive from San Francisco to their wine-country retreat. Each year they planted an additional acre or two of Chardonnay. If other vintners wanted a vine cutting, all they needed to do was ask, recalled Eleanor McCrea. The McCreas had obtained their clone from Wente. Meanwhile, at the other end of the valley, Fred and Mary Taylor were producing small lots of Chardonnay in their mountain hideaway they called Mayacamas. Neither winery made much Chardonnay. The McCreas' Stony Hill production consisted of fewer than 50 cases a year. By 1953 Stony Hill made enough wine (50 cases) to enter the state fair wine competition in 1955. That year Stony Hill won its first gold medal. The Taylors bottled their Chardonnay in a clear Bordeaux-style bottle. It looked like a Sauvignon Blanc.

About the same time, an important development began to take form in the hills above the city of Sonoma. James Zellerbach began planting a Chardonnay vineyard and constructed his dream winery, Hanzell Vineyards, designed after the famous Burgundian Château de Vougeot. Zellerbach, a member of the wealthy family that owned the paper products firm Crown Zeller-bach Corp., was the U.S. ambassador to Italy in the 1950s. He was fascinated by the challenge of creating a California Chardonnay that would rival the great white Burgundies. Worldly and well traveled, Zellerbach had been to Burgundy often enough to know that white Burgundies were aged in small, French oak barrels. He suspected that might be a factor in their quality and imported some to California to age his wine. It proved one of the most significant events of the era. Once winemakers and connoisseurs tasted the Hanzell Chardonnays in the late 1950s and early 1960s, with their rich, ripe fruit, toasty vanilla aromas of new oak and creamy textures, there was no turning back. Zellerbach's Hanzell Chardonnays revolutionized the way California winemakers thought about Chardonnay. The impact on the wines of the 1960s proved dramatic. It led directly to the widespread use of new oak barrels in California. It also indirectly contributed to new winemaking techniques. Once winemakers learned how oak could change the flavor, texture and aroma of Chardonnay, they examined other ways to improve their wines.

WHITE BURGUNDY AS A MODEL

As the 1960s unfolded, winemakers increasingly believed that small, French oak barrels were the missing link between good California Chardonnays and great white Burgundies. Part of that was wishful thinking, but winemakers had found a new role model for Chardonnay. Montrachet, Puligny-Montrachet, Chassagne-Montrachet, Chevalier-Montrachet, Meursault and Corton-Charlemagne became benchmarks for style and character. They were delicious demonstrations of what the Chardonnay grape could achieve when grown with the right clones in the right soils under the right climatic conditions, and made with proper vinification techniques. Increasingly, California vintners turned to Burgundy for new insights and ideas about making Chardonnay. Gradually each step of winemaking came under renewed scrutiny.

One curious winemaker who made a pilgrimage to Burgundy was Richard Graff. A U.C. Davis winemaking student, Graff had scraped together enough money to buy Chalone Vineyard in the 1960s. He had learned of Hanzell's successful experiments with aging, but not fermenting, Chardonnay in small French cooperage. That opened his mind to new ideas about winemaking and caused him to re-think the entire winemaking process. It was through experiences like this that traditional California methods for making Chardonnay were questioned, re-evaluated and changed.

The traditional California Chardonnay of the 1960s was made from very ripe grapes (24 degrees Brix) grown in warm climates. In California, it is legal to add acidity to wine, a wine that was low in acidity could be given an acid adjustment. Sulfur dioxide, a preservative, was sprinkled on grapes as soon as they were picked. Additional doses of sulfur dioxide were added as the wine aged in barrels, and again right before it was bottled. Chardonnay grapes were crushed and destemmed before pressing, and the juice was given extended skin contact, often at warm temperatures to extract flavor and color. Fermentation usually took place in old wood or large stainless steel tanks at 45 to 50 degrees Fahrenheit. Wines were cleaned up, removed from their lees and filtered before being put in barrels. The end result was often a very ripe, alcoholic, richly flavored, deeply colored wine that was high in extract, tannic, coarse, heavy and generally fast maturing. The longer those wines aged, the less attractive they were, and it became apparent that further adjustments were needed if vintners wanted to create Chardonnays of elegance, finesse and grace.

Critics of California Chardonnays denounced them as excessive, alcoholic and overblown. That led to a curious but brief "food wine" revolt in the early 1980s. Instead of letting their grapes ripen fully, vintners harvested earlier at lower sugar and ripeness levels, leading to a stream of highly acidic, austere, bland wines that lacked character. The short-lived food-wine craze proved beneficial in one way: It steered winemakers back to a middle ground and wines of greater balance.

BARRELS AND FASCINATION WITH NEW TECHNIQUES

The fascination with barrels, barrel fermentation and new techniques continued to spread. At Robert Mondavi Winery in Napa Valley, Mondavi had long used oak barrels to age his wines, and in the 1960s and 1970s he conducted extensive tests with a wide assortment of barrels, wood types, barrel staves, levels of toastiness (from charring), and barrel aging and barrel fermentation techniques. By the 1970s, Mondavi began barrel fermenting his Chardonnays and inducing partial malolactic fermentation. By the end of the 1980s, all of Mondavi's Reserve Chardonnays were barrel fermented in toasty French oak with nearly full malolactic fermentation.

Like Mondavi and others, Graff was convinced that French oak was a vital ingredient in creating complex, distinctive wines. It added smoky, toasty seasoning to a wine's aroma and flavor as well as adding texture, depth and structure. Graff started importing French oak for use at Chalone, where the Chardonnay is barrel fermented, and for sale to other winemakers. Barrel fermenting Chardonnay not only added a new dimension to the flavor and texture, it also added new costs. It is more expensive to ferment in a barrel than in stainless steel.

There were other important discoveries as well. On a trip to Burgundy in the late 1970s, Graff met with André Noblet, the winemaker at Domaine de la Romanée-Conti. DRC owns a small parcel, 1.7 acres, of the legendary 19.76-acre Montrachet vineyard, from which DRC makes just under 300 cases in a good year. During their discussion of winemaking techniques, Graff noticed that Noblet removed the bung from a barrel of wine and stirred the lees, the fine sediment that is a byproduct of fermentation and settles in the barrel. This ran contrary to Graff's Davis education, which held that all fermentations and subsequent aging of the wine should be done as cleanly as possible. Once the fermentation was completed, the wine should be racked, or removed, from the lees as soon as possible. When Graff saw Noblet stir the lees, he was startled. "You can't do that," Graff warned. "You'll ruin the wine." Noblet replied that, on the contrary, aging on the lees and regularly stirring them nourished the wine, made it more complex, added new dimensions of flavor, aroma and texture, as well as giving it additional structure. The next year Graff began aging his Chardonnays *sur lie*, on the lees, at Chalone and Mount Eden, where he was overseeing winemaking. In the 1980s, aging Chardonnay on its lees was one of the most widespread trends, although its benefits are still subject to debate. Joe Heitz, of Heitz Wine Cellar in Napa Valley, does not approve of the practice of lees aging. The basic component of lees is a "one-cell animal, and when it dies it smells just like a horse when it dies," Heitz said in an interview in 1989. He believes in the Davis doctrine that white wines should be fermented as cleanly as possible.

Another fashionable trend was toward malolactic fermentation, a secondary fermentation that converts malic acid, which is found in many fruits, most notably apples, to a less powerful lactic acid, the acid found in milk. Lactic acid is much softer, less tart and not as harsh as malic

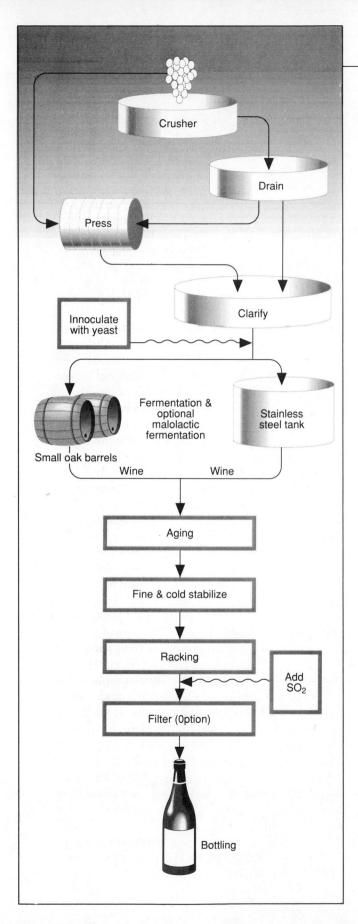

MAKING CHARDONNAY

This chart shows the more common methods currently in use to make top-quality Chardonnay in California. The options and individual style permutations are too numerous to cover here, although I have indicated the more common differences below.

1. **HARVEST:** Ripe grapes are harvested at between 22 and 24 degrees Brix, leading to wines of 12 percent to 14.5 percent alcohol.

2. **CRUSH:** Grapes are crushed and destemmed. Grapes become known as "must," while stems are removed. Wineries that press whole grapes bypass the crusher and go directly to the press.

3. **PRESS AND CLARIFY:** "Free run" juice (that which is created by the crusher without the press) is drained, separating skins and pulp. Skins and pulp are sent to the press. Juice is allowed to settle and clarify at cold temperatures. *Options:* 1. Press juice (either from whole grapes or by pressing skins and pulp) is returned to the master blend. 2. Limited skin contact with juice extracts flavor from the skins. Most excess solids settle at low temperatures leaving a small percentage of settled solids, called lees.

4. **FERMENTATION AND AGING:** Juice is innoculated with yeast in either stainless steel fermenting tanks, small oak barels or a combination of both for one week to two months or longer. Fermentation converts sugar to alcohol. Aging continues in stainless steel tanks or barrels for four to 10 months. Aging *sur lie* (on the lees) requires lees being stirred in a regular basis to nourish the wine. *Option:* Malolactic fermentation for all or part of the wine.

5. **FINING AND COLD STABILIZATION (optional):** Most Chardonnays are fined with Bentonite, which removes excess proteins and clarifies the wine. Cold stabilization at 30 degrees Fahrenheit removes excess potassium bitartrate.

6. **RACKING AND FILTRATION:** Clarification by racking, where wine is pumped off its lees. Sulfur dioxide is generally added at this point, but it can be added at most stages of winemaking. Filtration (optional), ranging from a coarse to very fine polish filter. Some Chardonnays are unfiltered.

7. **BOTTLING:** Chardonnay is bottled.

acid. Virtually all red wines undergo malolactic fermentation as a matter of course. Otherwise they would taste too sharp or acidic. White Burgundies almost always undergo full or partial malolactic fermentation, because the grapes are high in malic acid. California Chardonnays had been undergoing malolactic fermentation for years too, mostly accidentally in the bottle instead of the barrel, resulting in a flawed, unpleasant wine.

Deliberate malolactic fermentation opened new discussions about texture and complexity in young Chardonnays. Traditionally California Chardonnays did not undergo malolactic fermentation. Winemakers wanted to preserve the naturally high acidity in their wines, maintaining the wines' varietal intensity and tart, crisp apple flavors. Malolactic fermentation does alter the taste, texture and flavor spectrum of a wine. It can also give a wine added richness, depth and complexity while preserving the grape's fruitiness. There is a broad middle ground with malolactic fermentation. Many winemakers use malolactic fermentation for only part of their production. Recent studies indicate that California's Chardonnays are lower in malic acid than their French counterparts. Therefore the net effect of malolactic fermentation depends on the percentage of malic acid in a wine in a given vintage. There are vintages when malolactic fermentation is appropriate. The 1987 vintage in California produced many Chardonnays with excessively harsh or raw acidities. Some winemakers wished they had put at least a fraction of their wine through malolactic fermentation to soften it.

Historically, California Chardonnays that did not undergo malolactic fermentation have aged the longest. One can point to the wines of Hanzell, Stony Hill or Chateau Montelena and make a strong case that Chardonnays do not get much more complex and enticing. On the other hand, Chalone Reserve and Simi Reserve Chardonnays, both of which undergo full malolactic fermentation, are amazingly rich, complex and ageworthy. It is not so much the technique as the winemaker who controls the quality and style. For winemakers and consumers, it is a matter of preference. It is not easy to tell a wine that has gone through malolactic fermentation from one that has not. In very general terms, Chardonnays that do not undergo malolactic fermentation are more floral, with fruitier, grapy aromas and pear and apple flavors. Chardonnays that undergo malolactic fermentation display less of the tart fruitiness and more toasty, buttery and creamy aromas and textures. At times, the apple flavors end up tasting more like pineapple in wines that have undergone malolactic fermentation. Chardonnay is a winemaker's wine, and some winemakers can make successful wines in either style, malolactic fermentation or not, barrel fermented or not. It is much like the use of oak in Chardonnay: Some wines can stand an enormous amount of toasty, smoky oak and be better wines because of it; other wines lack sufficient concentration to stand up to the oak. They often taste like woody grape juice.

Of greater long-term significance has been a move toward planting Chardonnay in cooler climates with less vigorous rootstock and better clones. Chardonnay is a highly adaptable variety that performs well in many soils and microclimates throughout the world. Three of California's greatest Chardonnay vineyards, Stony Hill, Hanzell and Chalone, are rooted in entirely different environments and soil, and they experience different sun exposures, levels of rainfall, and so on. Yet each makes distinctive, complex, ageworthy Chardonnay. What is clear is that Chardonnay, with all its vigor, grows better in a cooler climate than a warmer one. Grapes like Cabernet Sauvignon, Zinfandel or even Sauvignon Blanc like the warmth, but Chardonnay does not need the heat. In the past 20 years, there has been a steady shift away from planting Chardonnay in the inland coastal valleys to planting in areas closer to the Pacific Ocean, or in the case of Carneros, the San Pablo Bay. The maritime climates of Carneros, the Russian River Valley, Monterey, San Luis Obispo and Anderson Valley are proving much more hospitable for Chardonnay than growers would have believed in 1960. More on the topic of vineyards, appellations and regional styles is addressed in the following chapter.

CHARDONNAY ACRES BY COUNTY 1971-1989

	Sonoma	Napa	Monterey	Mendocino	Santa Barbara	San Luis Obispo	Total	State Total
1971	481	752	424	152	14	35	1,857	3,057
1972	743	1,019	843	187	227	73	3,092	4,577
1973	1278	1413	2,182	292	613	208	5,986	7,368
1974	1,808	2,249	2,929	355	843	291	8,475	10,037
1975	2,652	2,499	2,990	364	857	288	9,650	11,500
1976	2,781	2,678	2,692	488	887	289	9,815	11,410
1977	2,947	2,765	2,762	512	975	366	10,327	11,957
1978	3,325	3,069	2,888	607	1032	444	11,365	13,486
1979	4,034	3,717	3,108	743	1,497	611	13,710	15,956
1980	4,504	4,269	3,140	901	1,514	506	14,834	17,033
1981	5,220	4,827	3,491	986	2,266	573	17,363	19,766
1982	5,629	5,652	4,087	1,251	2,081	604	19,304	22,076
1983	6,719	6,214	4,037	1,429	2,180	717	21,296	24,380
1984	7,250	6,488	4,224	1,737	2,349	847	22,895	26,143
1985	7,695	6,908	4,384	1,738	2,786	870	24,381	27,424
1986	8,002	7,312	4,104	2,154	2,837	1,381	25,790	29,319
1987	8,335	7,708	5,647	2,449	3,259	1,579	28,977	34,878
1988	9,206	8,155	8,011	2,747	4,080	1,884	34,083	41,870
1989	10,129	8,869	8,578	3,119	4,758	2,096	37,549	48,049

Note: These figures reflect total Chardonnay acreage for each county, non-bearing as well as bearing. Total and state total includes areas not listed in chart.

SOURCE: CALIFORNIA DEPARTMENT OF FOOD AND AGRICULTURE

Clonal research by Olmo in the 1950s and 1960s led to the discovery and cultivation of so-called "super clones" that were virus free. When these clones were grafted onto vigorous rootstock they were capable of producing consistently large crops. That appealed to growers, who were paid by the ton, and increasingly to winemakers, as potential markets developed.

With clonal selection, vintners have identified several different clones that provide different flavor and aroma components. One of the most common and distinctive is the "muscat" clone that offers spicy, wildflower aromas. Other clones add fruity and herbal flavors. The most recent trend in vineyards is to graft a mixture of different clones so that the grapes offer a variety of flavors, not a single, dominant characteristic. The choice of rootstock can also influence grapevine productivity, yield and ultimately quality. An overbearing vine will produce lesser quality grapes.

The full measure of the explosive growth in popularity of Chardonnay can be seen through acres planted, cases produced and the diversity of brands on the market. From 300 acres in 1960, the number of acres planted increased to 3,057 in 1971. A decade later, in 1980, nearly

17,000 acres of Chardonnay were rooted, and by 1989 some 48,000 acres were devoted to Chardonnay, more than twice as much as is planted in Burgundy.

In 1971 Napa Valley had 752 acres of Chardonnay, compared with 481 in Sonoma County, 152 in Mendocino, 424 in Monterey County, 27 in Santa Clara County and 13 in Santa Barbara County. By 1975 Sonoma County had surpassed Napa County, with 2,947 acres to 2,765. Since then the growth in new acreage in those two counties has been parallel, with Sonoma still holding an edge. The most recent statistics from 1989 show Sonoma County with 10,129 acres, while Napa County has 8,869 acres. In Sonoma County, much of the new Chardonnay planting has taken place in cooler areas like Carneros and Russian River Valley. The Carneros side of Napa Valley has also been the fastest-growing Chardonnay district in Napa Valley. Monterey County is the third-largest Chardonnay region, with 8,578 acres, followed by Santa Barbara County with 4,758, Mendocino with 3,119 and San Luis Obispo with 2,096.

The number of producers and Chardonnays on the market has also soared, although the number of truly outstanding Chardonnays is far less than may seem apparent. More than 500 different Chardonnay brands and some 7 million cases of Chardonnay were being produced in a single year in the 1980s. If all 48,000 acres of Chardonnay were devoted exclusively to table wine and not used for sparkling wine, California would have the potential to produce 11.5 million cases a year, a staggering figure and a convincing illustration of how popular Chardonnay has become.

While Chardonnay fueled the white wine boom it also, along with Cabernet Sauvignon, brought legitimacy to the ultra-premium sector of the California wine industry. Its popularity among consumers also influenced the acceptance of varietal wines in America. Moreover, the economics of Chardonnay planting, producing and marketing have made it the most important wine in America. The 1989 Chardonnay crop was valued at nearly $200 million, making it the dominant economic grape in the industry today.

CHAPTER II

CHARDONNAY
VINEYARDS AND APPELLATIONS

D umb luck," the late Fred McCrea once called his decision to plant Chardonnay on the hillside behind his humble Napa Valley retreat. No one knew for sure that Chardonnay would take hold in McCrea's rocky soil, much less that one day connoisseurs would marvel at the distinctive qualities of Stony Hill Chardonnays, and wait years just to get on the mailing list to buy a case.

Chardonnay was a latecomer to the California wine scene, and too many assumptions about what might be the best planting locations led to its being rooted in mostly the wrong places. With the benefit of hindsight, Fred and Eleanor McCrea appeared to be brilliant visionaries who knew all along that Stony Hill was the perfect nook for Chardonnay. The truth is that they took a risk and persisted with their dream, and it finally paid off after many years of hard work.

Not all of California's Chardonnay vineyards have enjoyed such good fortune. Plenty of risks have been taken, but few have prospered in the manner of Stony Hill. The initial wave of new Chardonnay plantings in the 1960s and 1970s was by growers and vintners already established in the business. Planting Chardonnay was new to them. It had a reputation for being a difficult grape to grow and a sporadic producer, so it made good sense to them to plant in warmer climates to ensure ripening. Ripen it did, often to excess, giving winemakers huge crops, 4 to 6 tons an acre, of ultraripe grapes that were suited for the blockbuster Chardonnay styles of the 1970s. These styles were typically very ripe and flavorful, but also alcoholic, creating coarse wines that aged poorly. It was not until the late 1970s and early 1980s, as Chardonnay's popularity spread, that it became apparent that the best areas to grow this variety had been overlooked. Chardonnay ripens more evenly in cooler climates, and inevitably that means closer to the Pacific Ocean or San Pablo Bay, which extends to the southern reaches of Carneros.

THE CLIMATE

While some grape varieties benefit from hot weather, Chardonnay does not. The grape, by its nature, is highly adaptable, growing well and producing bountiful crops in almost any soil. Too much heat during the growing season results in rapid maturation of the berries, which can lead to unbalanced wines with lower acidity. The moderating influence of the maritime climate prolongs the growing season, which allows the grapes to ripen at an even pace without overripening, ideally maintaining high acid levels to produce a balanced wine.

In general, the best regions for Chardonnay are the valleys and flatlands nearest the maritime climate. The greatest influence is the Pacific Ocean to the west and the San Francisco and San Pablo bays, an inlet that greatly influences Carneros and the southern end of both Napa and Sonoma valleys, as well as portions of Santa Clara Valley and Livermore Valley. The cooling influence of Pacific Ocean breezes moderates the temperature all along California's coastline. The Central Valley's hotter summer temperatures help create a vacuum that pulls the cooler coastal air inland. The farther inland from the ocean, the warmer the temperatures become during spring, summer and fall, all key seasons affecting the ripening and maturing of the grapes. Inland valleys, such as the Sonoma and Napa valleys, are less affected by the ocean breezes than are the Russian River and Carneros valleys, yet they all benefit from the marine influence, as do the counties farther south: Monterey, San Luis Obispo and Santa Barbara. Even Temecula, an inland area near the Los Angeles-San Diego County line where Callaway grows its Chardonnay, benefits from the steady coastal breezes.

APPELLATIONS

The principal Chardonnay appellations featured in this book share climates with more similarities than disparities. Anderson Valley and Santa Barbara are 600 miles apart, but they share the breezy maritime climate of the Pacific Ocean. There are also few apparent regional differences among Chardonnays grown in Napa Valley, Russian River Valley or Monterey. Within each of these appellations there are similar microclimates, soil types, rootstock and clones. Often winemakers use several different grape sources for their Chardonnays. That approach may contribute to a more complete and balanced wine, but it also virtually eliminates the distinctive quality one might find when using grapes grown exclusively in one vineyard or microclimate.

Then there is the matter of winemaking style and technique. Because Chardonnay is fairly neutral in flavor, it is highly malleable. If a Chardonnay is barrel fermented, put through malolactic fermentation and aged in toasty barrels, whatever distinctive regional characteristics it began with will almost certainly be obscured. Even two Chardonnays made from the same vineyard can taste quite different when made in different styles. Each technique, from vineyard to bottling, shapes the flavor, texture and body of a Chardonnay.

Regional characteristics may become more evident in the next decade as winemakers and growers identify the best soils, refine their vineyard techniques, identify superior clones, and settle on more deliberate and consistent styles of wine. Increasingly more sophisticated tastes will lead to more distinctive and unique Chardonnays. That day is coming. But it may take another 25 to 50 years before the best vineyard sites for Chardonnay in California have been planted and tested.

In listing the major Chardonnay appellations, I have included not only those appellations that are officially designated by the U.S. Bureau of Alcohol, Tobacco and Firearms, but also those that are unique enough to be recognized on their own. With the exception of Carneros,

I have grouped the appellations by county. Carneros overlaps both Napa and Sonoma counties, but in truth belongs in neither, possessing distinct qualities all its own. These appellation categories are Carneros, Napa Valley, Sonoma County, Mendocino County, Santa Cruz Mountains, Santa Clara County, Monterey County, San Luis Obispo County and Santa Barbara County. Under those headings, the important Chardonnay appellations and subappellations are listed in alphabetical order. Appellations that are not major Chardonnay districts are not included. A few of the wineries in this book use the California designation because their wines do not qualify as a specific appellation. Federal law requires that 95 percent of the grapes from a vineyard-designated wine comes from that vineyard. Laws pertaining to official appellations require that 75 percent is from the specified appellation.

CARNEROS

Carneros, which spreads across several thousand acres of vineyards at the southern edges of Napa and Sonoma valleys, is increasingly carving out a niche with its highly acidic, richly flavored Chardonnays. Carneros is distinguished by gently rolling hills with southerly exposures and cooling San Pablo Bay breezes. Vineyard plantings here were sparse until the 1970s. Two of the early pioneers of the region were Beaulieu Vineyard and Louis Martini, but Rene di Rosa's Winery Lake Vineyard put Carneros Chardonnay on the map to stay. In the 1970s and early 1980s, until it was sold to Sterling Vineyards in 1986, Winery Lake sold grapes to dozens of producers, big and small, with many like Acacia, Bouchaine and Kistler acknowledging the vineyard on their labels. Since then, there has been a rush to secure vineyard land in Carneros and prices have escalated, quickly catching up with those paid for prime vineyard land in Rutherford.

There are plenty of exciting new Carneros Chardonnays on the market, and even wineries that use the broader Napa Valley appellation like Robert Mondavi and Silverado Vineyards almost always supplement their blends with some Carneros grapes, because it gives their wines a flinty backbone. What distinguishes most Carneros-grown Chardonnays is their bracing acidity, as well as their rich, intense pineapple and tropical fruit flavors. At the forefront of pure Carneros Chardonnays are Cuvaison, Saintsbury, Sterling Winery Lake, Acacia, Frog's Leap and Bouchaine. Buena Vista Special Selection, grown on the Sonoma side, Clos Du Val and Sequoia Grove have also shown steady improvement. Clos Pegase is a newcomer with promise.

More than 7,000 acres of vineyards are now rooted in Carneros, more than half of which is Chardonnay, with more to come. Competition is stiff for this land as big sparkling-wine houses like Domaine Chandon, Gloria Ferrer, Domaine Carneros and others actively seek long-term growing contracts and acreage of their own.

NAPA VALLEY

This famous winegrowing region has long been California's leading Chardonnay appellation, primarily because of its Chardonnay acreage and prestigious brand-name producers. Napa Valley gained its reputation with Chardonnay in the late 1960s, with the likes of Stony Hill, Robert Mondavi and Freemark Abbey; in the 1970s, it gained further distinction through the wines of such big names as Chateau Montelena, Trefethen and Grgich Hills. As Napa Valley is carved up into smaller subappellations, the popularity of its name may wane, giving way to Carneros, home to many important new Chardonnay vineyards and increasing its profile as an appellation, and Oak Knoll, where Trefethen, Pine Ridge and Chateau Montelena farm their grapes. More than 8,500 of Napa Valley's 31,000 acres are planted to Chardonnay, making it the single largest variety grown here.

Through the years, Chardonnay has been tested in most areas of the valley, from the valley floor to mountain peaks. Gradually the movement of Chardonnay vineyards has been south, to Oak Knoll, an unofficial appellation between Yountville and Napa, Coombsville, east of Napa and Carneros. It is becoming common for vintners to get at least a portion of their grapes from one of these three areas—obviously a strong endorsement of the quality of the grapes grown there.

It is difficult to pinpoint a specific Napa Valley style, but Napa Valley Chardonnays that do not have a Carneros appellation are almost always ripe and brimming with fruit. They are also usually well endowed with oak. The three Stags Leap District Chardonnays chosen for this book, Robert Mondavi Reserve, Pine Ridge Stags Leap Vineyard and S. Anderson, usually fit that profile. The Stags Leap District remains best known and best suited for Cabernet Sauvignon and Merlot. It is not nearly as important as a Chardonnay district, despite the success of the two top producers. Silverado Vineyards is also in Stags Leap, but not all its grapes are grown within the official appellation.

DIAMOND MOUNTAIN

Diamond Mountain is not an official appellation yet, but is likely to become one some day. It is best known for Cabernets produced by Diamond Creek Vineyards and Sterling Vineyards. Sterling is making headway with very distinctive, flinty, austere Chardonnays from its Diamond Mountain Ranch Vineyards, located several hundred feet above the valley floor a bit southwest of Calistoga. Like the Cabernets from this area, the Chardonnays are tough and tight at first, and need time to soften and mellow.

HOWELL MOUNTAIN

Long unused for winegrowing but making a comeback on the shoulders of Dunn Vineyard's muscular Cabernets, Howell Mountain just now is establishing its Chardonnay credentials. The pioneer is Chateau Woltner, which planted vines here in the early 1980s and now makes four different bottlings from different sections of the vineyard. The Woltner style is austere and flinty, with designs on creating long-lived Chardonnays. Early signs are encouraging as the vineyards mature. The Woltner style is unique and distinctive.

MOUNT VEEDER

Mount Veeder is a new subappellation of Napa Valley high above the city of Napa, with vineyards reaching to the 2,000-foot level. It is the home of Mayacamas and the Hess Collection, the two best-known producers from this area. William Hill owns Chardonnay vines here, but blends their grapes with others grown near the Silverado Country Club. Mount Veeder Winery also produces a Chardonnay worth seeking, but I have found their style and quality inconsistent. Recent vintages from that producer have been more impressive. There is no deliberate or distinguishable Mount Veeder style yet, but this is a very young appellation and it may take years for a style to emerge.

OAK KNOLL

Oak Knoll is not an official appellation yet, but probably will be in the future. This area covers roughly the valley floor, with Yountville to the north, the city of Napa to the south, Big Ranch Road or Silverado Trail to the east, and the hills to the west. Oak Knoll is one of the coolest parts of the valley and highly regarded for Chardonnay. The big names that use Oak Knoll grapes include Trefethen, Pine Ridge, Chateau Montelena and Monticello, among others.

GREAT CHARDONNAY REGIONS

On the following pages are maps of the regions discussed in this chapter. Each map locates the wineries reviewed in this book, and the various estate and independent vineyards.

Briefly, the maps cover the following areas: Map 1: The Carneros Region; Map 2: Napa County: Napa-Yountville; Map 3: Napa County: Oakville-Rutherford; Map 4: Napa County: St. Helena-Calistoga; Map 5: Sonoma County: Sonoma Valley; Map 6: Sonoma County: Russian River Valley; Map 7: Sonoma County: Alexander and Dry Creek Valleys; Map 8: Mendocino County: Anderson Valley; Map 9: Santa Cruz and Santa Clara Counties; Map 10: Monterey County; Map 11: San Luis Obispo and Santa Barbara Counties.

MAP LEGEND

Winery

Independent Vineyard

Winery-Owned Vineyard

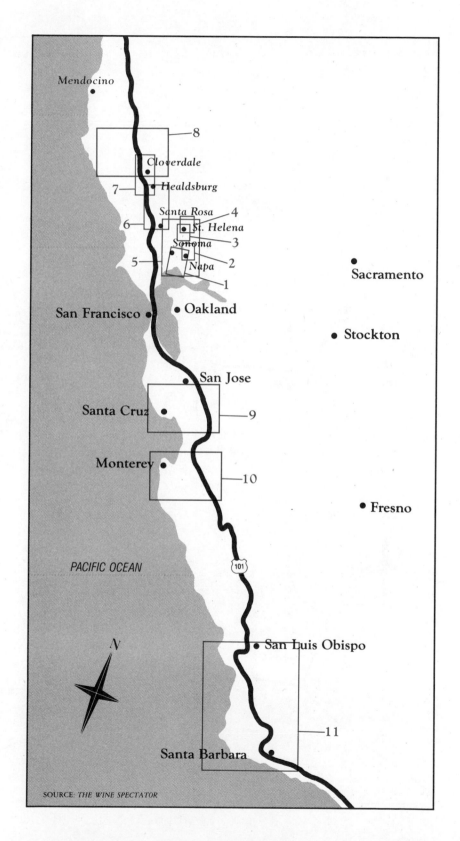

SOURCE: THE WINE SPECTATOR

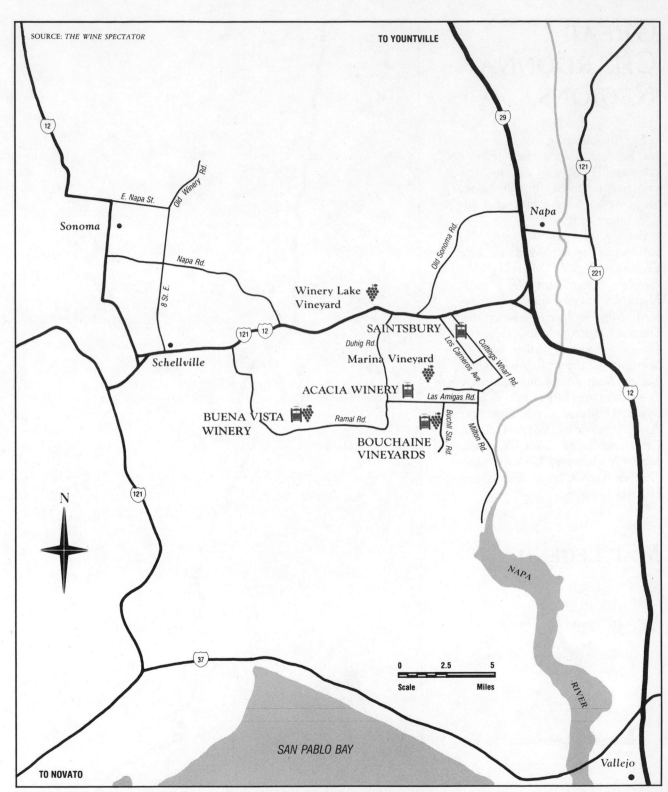

TO YOUNTVILLE

12

29

121

Napa

E. Napa St.

Old Winery Rd.

Sonoma

Napa Rd.

Old Sonoma Rd.

221

8 St. E.

Winery Lake
Vineyard

121 12

SAINTSBURY

Duhig Rd.

Schellville

Marina Vineyard

Los Carneros Ave

Cuttings Wharf Rd.

ACACIA WINERY

Las Amigas Rd.

12

BUENA VISTA
WINERY

Ramal Rd.

Buchli Sta. Rd.

Milton Rd.

BOUCHAINE
VINEYARDS

N

121

NAPA

37

0   2.5   5

Scale   Miles

RIVER

SAN PABLO BAY

TO NOVATO

Vallejo

MAP 1: CARNEROS REGION

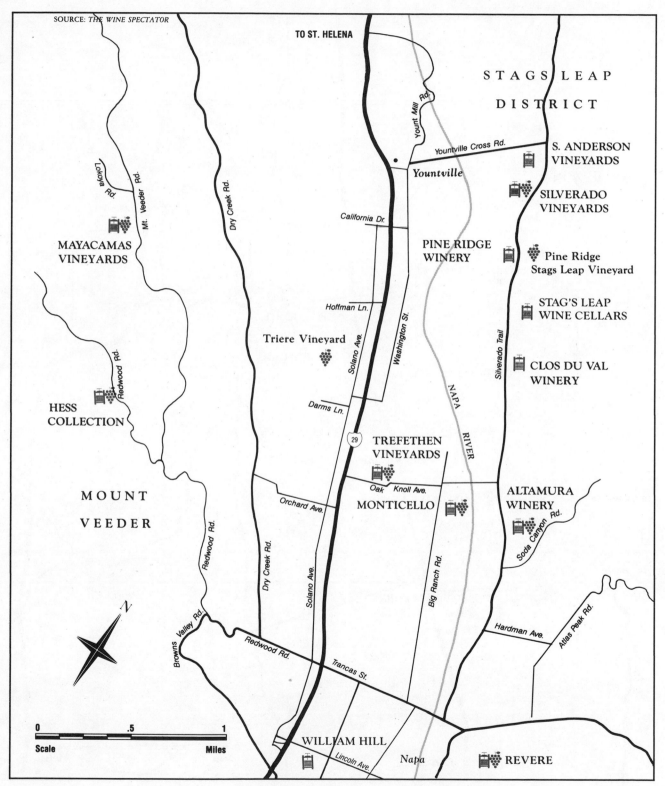

SOURCE: *THE WINE SPECTATOR*

TO ST. HELENA

S T A G S   L E A P

D I S T R I C T

Yountville Cross Rd.

S. ANDERSON
VINEYARDS

Yountville

SILVERADO
VINEYARDS

California Dr.

PINE RIDGE
WINERY

Pine Ridge
Stags Leap Vineyard

Lokoya Rd.

Mt. Veeder Rd.

Dry Creek Rd.

MAYACAMAS
VINEYARDS

Hoffman Ln.

STAG'S LEAP
WINE CELLARS

Triere Vineyard

Solano Ave.

Washington St.

Silverado Trail

CLOS DU VAL
WINERY

Redwood Rd.

HESS
COLLECTION

Darms Ln.

NAPA
RIVER

29

TREFETHEN
VINEYARDS

MOUNT

VEEDER

Oak Knoll Ave.

Orchard Ave.

MONTICELLO

ALTAMURA
WINERY

Soda Canyon Rd.

Redwood Rd.

Dry Creek Rd.

Solano Ave.

Big Ranch Rd.

Hardman Ave.

Atlas Peak Rd.

Browns Valley Rd.

Redwood Rd.

N

Trancas St.

0   .5   1

Scale   **Miles**

WILLIAM HILL

Lincoln Ave.

Napa

REVERE

MAP 2: NAPA COUNTY: NAPA—YOUNTVILLE

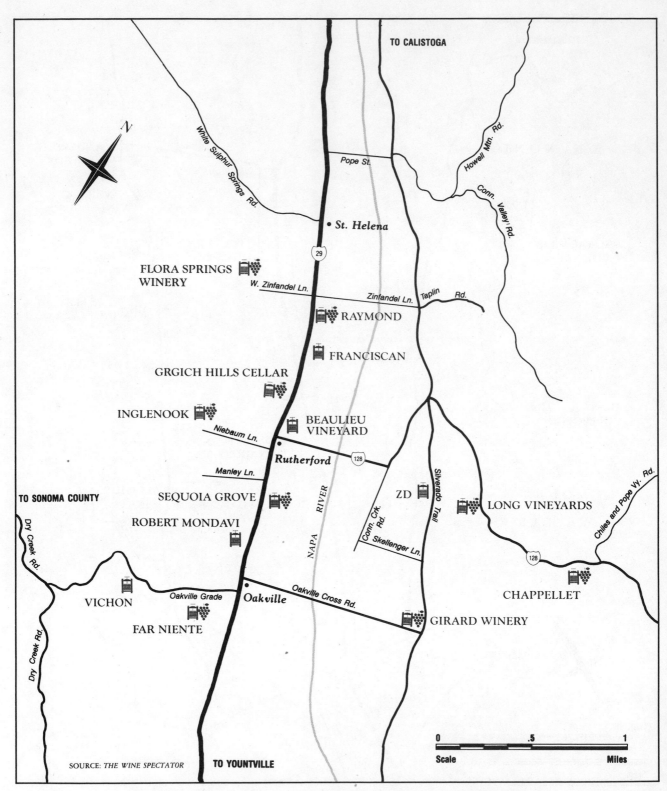

MAP 3: NAPA COUNTY: OAKVILLE—RUTHERFORD

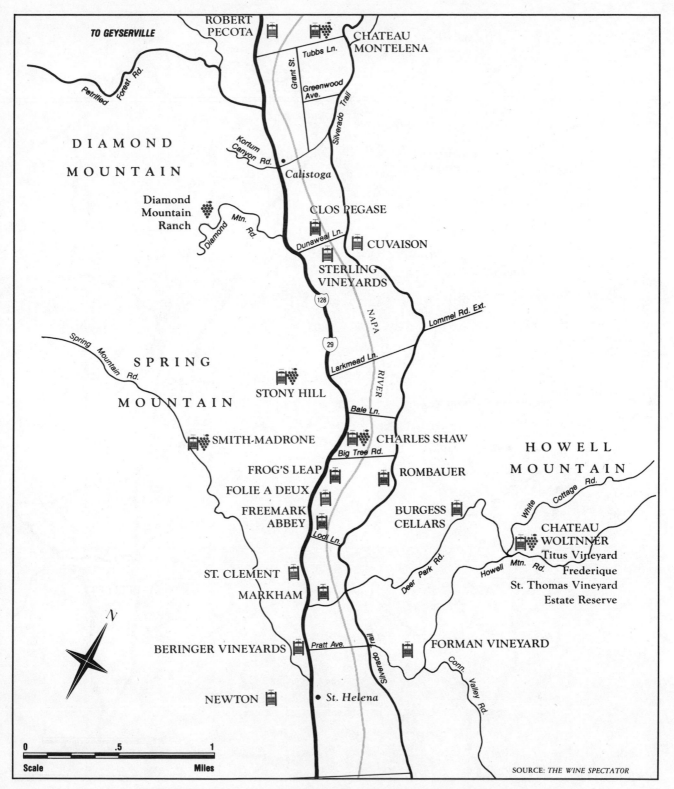

MAP 4: NAPA COUNTY: ST. HELENA–CALISTOGA

42

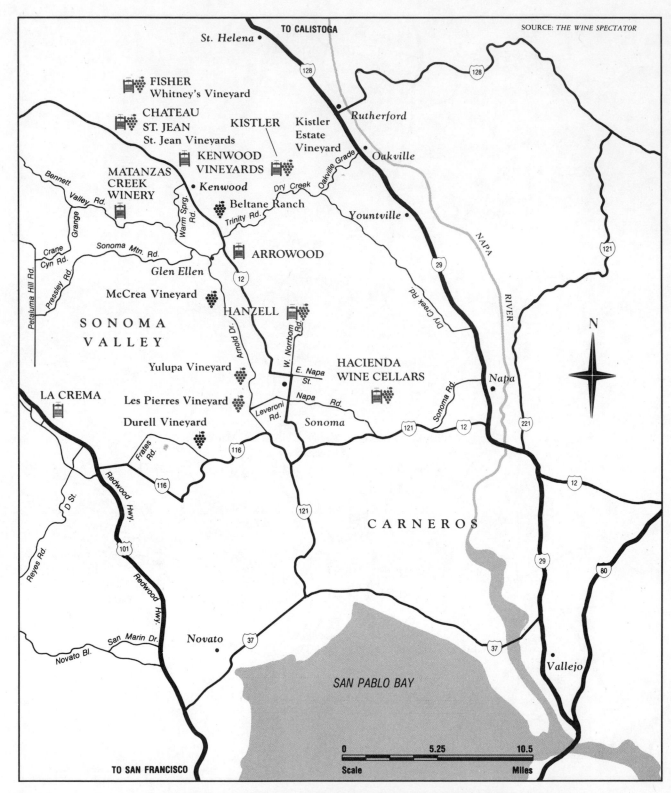

MAP 5: SONOMA COUNTY: SONOMA VALLEY

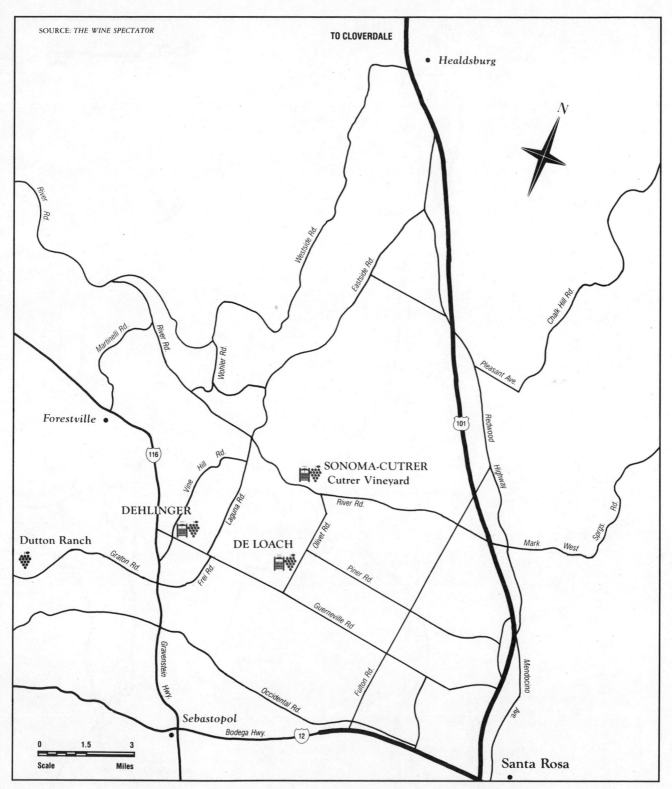

SOURCE: *THE WINE SPECTATOR*

TO CLOVERDALE

• *Healdsburg*

N

River Rd.

Westside Rd.

Eastside Rd.

Chalk Hill Rd.

Martinelli Rd.

River Rd.

Wohler Rd.

Pleasant Ave.

Forestville •

101

Redwood

Highway

116

Vine Hill Rd.

SONOMA-CUTRER
Cutrer Vineyard

DEHLINGER

River Rd.

Laguna Rd.

Olivet Rd.

Sprgs. Rd.

Dutton Ranch

DE LOACH

Mark   West

Graton Rd.

Frei Rd.

Piner Rd.

Guerneville Rd.

Mendocino   Ave.

Gravenstein   Hwy.

Occidental Rd.

Fulton Rd.

Sebastopol

Bodega Hwy.   12

Santa Rosa

0   1.5   3
Scale   **Miles**

MAP 6: SONOMA COUNTY: RUSSIAN RIVER VALLEY

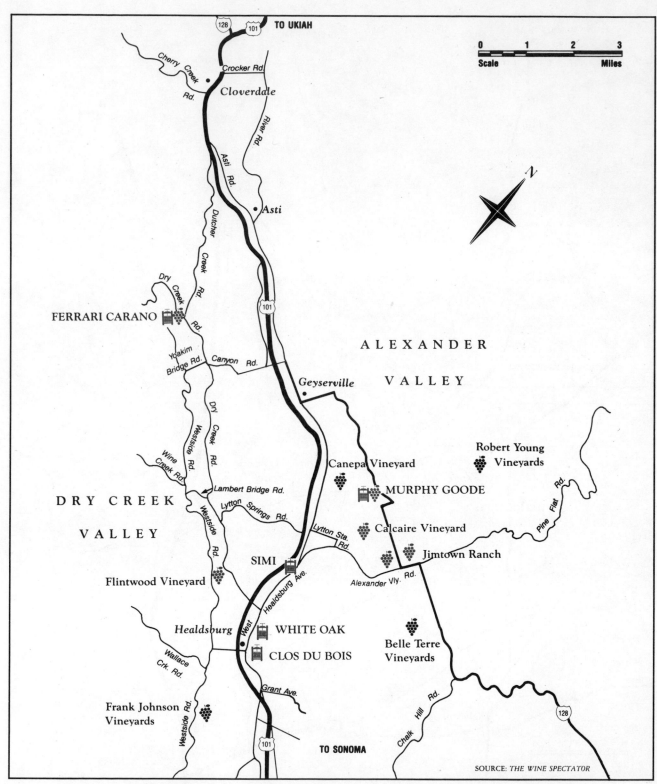

MAP 7: SONOMA COUNTY: ALEXANDER AND DRY CREEK VALLEYS

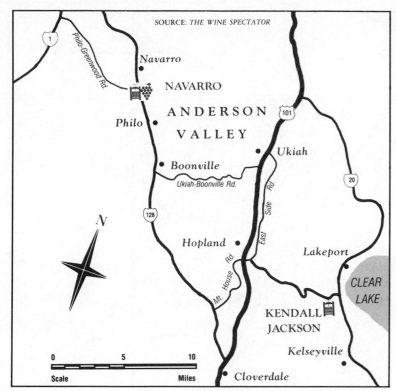

◁MAP 8: MENDOCINO COUNTY:
ANDERSON VALLEY

MAP 9: SANTA CRUZ AND
SANTA CLARA COUNTIES▽

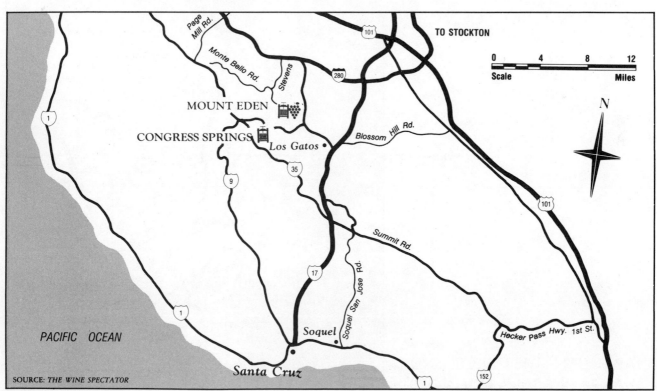

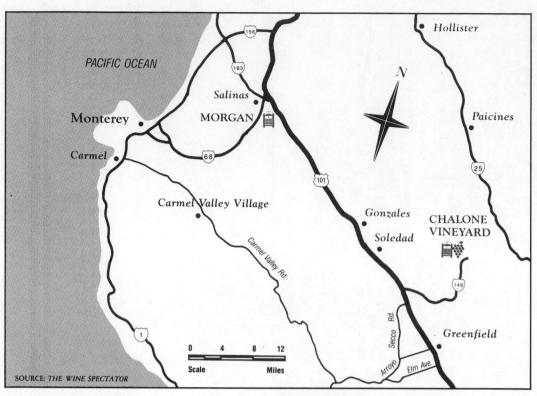

MAP 10: MONTEREY COUNTY △

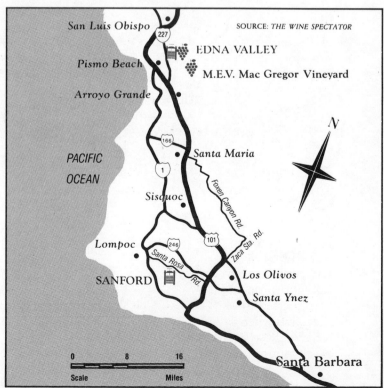

MAP 11: SAN LUIS OBISPO AND
SANTA BARBARA COUNTIES ▷

SONOMA COUNTY

Sonoma County is Chardonnay country at its biggest and increasingly at its best. Sonoma County is a political boundary split into nearly a dozen appellations, including important Chardonnay turf such as Alexander Valley, Carneros, Russian River Valley and Sonoma Valley. Most of Sonoma County's big-name producers have narrowed their focus to specific appellations, but not all. Simi, Arrowood and Matanzas Creek, to name three of the best, still use the broader appellation because they harvest grapes from several areas. At one time, Simi's Zelma Long had Chardonnay contracts with growers throughout Sonoma County. That is one way to achieve complexity in Chardonnay, though greater expertise in winemaking is necessary to achieve consistency in quality and style.

Through the excellence of its key Chardonnay districts, Sonoma County has moved to the forefront of Chardonnay production, with more than 10,000 acres in vines, but its name will never dominate the market the way Napa Valley has, because Sonoma's vintners prefer the European approach of using smaller viticultural appellations. That should not matter much to consumers, as long as they understand which appellations are best for different styles.

ALEXANDER VALLEY

Alexander Valley is a warm, slender valley in northern Sonoma County that straddles the Russian River as it heads south and then west toward the Pacific Ocean. There are many Chardonnays to admire here, but three wines stand out from the pack: Chateau Montelena, and Chateau St. Jean's Robert Young Vineyards and Belle Terre Vineyards bottlings. All three have impressive track records dating to the 1970s. The style they and other top Alexander Valley Chardonnays share is marked by ripe, sometimes openly tropical fruit flavors and a rich, lush, creamy texture. The Chateau Montelenas in particular are very long agers, and recently both Robert Young and Belle Terre have been made in somewhat tighter, more concentrated styles that should bode well for longer aging. Also distinctive and worth cellaring are Clos du Bois Calcaire and Barrel Fermented, Robert Pecota Canepa Vineyard, Chateau St. Jean Jimtown Ranch, Murphy-Goode, and the new star, Ferrari-Carano, which is making some of the most exciting new Chardonnays in California. I have also tasted some impressive Chardonnays from Jordan and newcomer deLorimier, but they are not included in this book.

DRY CREEK VALLEY

Best known for Zinfandel and Sauvignon Blanc, this narrow valley northwest of Healdsburg in northern Sonoma County features one excellent Chardonnay, Clos du Bois Flintwood Vineyard. Frank Johnson Vineyards is on the border near Russian River Valley.

RUSSIAN RIVER VALLEY

One of the most promising and fastest-growing appellations in Sonoma County, the Russian River Valley is already one of the finest for Chardonnay. Close to the ocean, often foggy and cool in the morning and evening, it has some parts where there is barely enough warm sunlight to ripen Chardonnay, while in other areas Chardonnay ripens to its fullest. One is hard-pressed to identify a Russian River style at this point because there are too many contrasts. Just when it seems that the tightly reined-in style of Sonoma-Cutrer Russian River Ranches matches closely with the flinty austerity of Dehlinger, along comes De Loach, one of the ripest, fruitiest, most opulent Chardonnays in California. The tart apple flavors of this area's Chardonnays also appeal to several sparkling-wine houses. The other stars from this region are Kistler Dutton Ranch and Sonoma-Cutrer Cutrer Vineyard.

SONOMA VALLEY

Several of California's finest and most famous Chardonnays are grown in this slender valley. On a relief map, Sonoma Valley looks like a miniature Napa Valley. It points roughly north-south, extending from the outskirts of Santa Rosa in the north to Carneros in the south. It is a good 5 miles closer to the Pacific Ocean than Napa Valley, so one would assume it is also cooler. Nonetheless, there are often days when the temperature reaches the 80s or 90s in Napa Valley and soars to 100 degrees in Sonoma. I have often watched the fog creep over Sonoma Mountain in the evenings and felt the temperatures quickly drop to much cooler levels.

The most famous Chardonnay vineyard here is Hanzell, perched on a hillside above the city of Sonoma, with a southern exposure. Hanzell's Chardonnays are big, rich and buttery, and age on and on like few others in California. Across the valley is Sonoma Cutrer's Les Pierres Vineyard, a superb vineyard that yields intensely flavored, very distinctive Chardonnays. Also worth special note for its consistently high quality is the McCrea Vineyard, which was bottled for years by Chateau St. Jean and now is bottled by Kistler. Kistler's own estate vineyard is near the top of the Mayacamas Mountains on the eastern side of the valley, and it has become a sensational source for grapes.

In recent vintages, Kenwood's two vineyard-designated Chardonnays, from Yulupa Vineyard and Beltane Ranch, have been impressive. On occasion Chateau St. Jean bottles a Chardonnay from its own estate vineyard in Kenwood. In future vintages, the label no longer will say St. Jean Vineyard, but simply "estate bottled." Worth watching is the B.R. Cohn Chardonnay from the Olive Hill Vineyard, and on occasion Haywood and Ravenswood come through with rich, complex, enduring Chardonnays.

MENDOCINO COUNTY

With 3,119 acres planted to Chardonnay, Mendocino County is expanding production, but a high proportion of grapes are devoted to sparkling-wine endeavors. The most important area to date is Anderson Valley.

ANDERSON VALLEY

This picturesque valley in Mendocino County is one of the coolest and foggiest in California. Even though it is only a few miles from the ocean, it is ideal for Chardonnay. Because of the coolness, extracting a firm acidity in the grape is not a problem. The leader here is Navarro, with its Première Reserve and other Chardonnays, which are slow to unfold but gain complexity and depth with age, and are good bets to lay down for four to five years. Kendall-Jackson also makes a fine Chardonnay from the DuPratt Vineyard. Husch makes good to very good Chardonnays on a consistent basis, but its wines did not qualify for this book.

SANTA CLARA COUNTY

This is a historic wine-producing region now largely suburbanized. It is not a major Chardonnay district, having only 224 acres planted, yet it offers a solid producer in Congress Springs, which has shown consistently high quality and steady improvement.

Santa Cruz Mountains

This is another small Chardonnay district, with 49 acres of mountaintop vines, but it is home to Mount Eden Vineyards, a producer of consistently outstanding quality. This is a very cool appellation, not too far from the Pacific Ocean, which means sufficient ripening of the grapes can be difficult in some years. Congress Springs also makes a Chardonnay from this area.

Monterey County

Increasingly this cool, coastal county is becoming a hotbed of Chardonnay. Explosive growth in planting added thousands of new Chardonnay acres in the mid-1970s before things slowed down. Early efforts with the variety were often erratic, though recently the quality has risen. Now, with more than 8,500 acres planted to Chardonnay, Monterey has approached the production levels of Sonoma and Napa counties, becoming California's third largest grower.

Within Monterey, three other important viticultural areas are recognized: Arroyo Seco, Chalone (see below) and Carmel Valley. In my tastings, the best producer is Morgan Winery, offering wines that are consistently rich and complex and age fairly well. Jekel, Durney, Ventana, J. Lohr, Robert Talbott and others have also had moments of glory and are worth following. Because Napa and Sonoma get so much attention in the market, many big-name wineries use their names, but also bottle generic "California Chardonnay" grown in Monterey. These wines are often equal to or better than higher-priced Chardonnays from loftier appellations.

Chalone

This is a tiny, single-vineyard appellation that takes its name from its only producer, Chalone Vineyards, which is named after an Indian tribe. High in the mountains of the Pinnacles National Monument, on a sloping hillside with a limestone bed beneath, Chalone has a very dry microclimate with fewer than 15 inches of rain a year. Nonetheless, it is also home to some of the most dramatic, rich and distinctive Chardonnays produced in California. and among the most ageworthy. They start out tight and austere, but gain body, richness, depth and complexity with age. Chalone makes two Chardonnays, a reserve made from the oldest vines and a regular, which is almost always as good.

San Luis Obispo County

Like most of the South Central Coast, San Luis Obispo County is widely planted to Chardonnay. The acreage has risen from 35 acres in 1971 to 2,096 acres in 1989. Edna Valley, one of the coolest Chardonnay areas in California, has the edge in quality with Edna Valley Vineyard, but Chamisal and Mount Eden are also strong. Meridian, now part of Nestlé's growing Beringer-Chateau Souverain family, should join the ranks soon with Chardonnay specialist Chuck Ortman as winemaker.

Edna Valley

Edna Valley is a small viticultural area south of San Luis Obispo where Chardonnay flourishes. The best producer to date is Edna Valley Vineyard, a winery part-owned and managed by Chalone Inc. It is too early to pinpoint an Edna Valley style, but with the Chalone tech-

EDNA VALLEY

Edna Valley is a small viticultural area south of San Luis Obispo where Chardonnay flourishes. The best producer to date is Edna Valley Vineyards; a winery part-owned and managed by Chalone Inc. It is too early to pinpoint an Edna Valley style, but with the Chalone technique — barrel fermentation, full malolactic fermentation and the use of very ripe grapes — a rich, full-bodied, complex style is emerging from this producer. Some vintages in the early 1980s were unimpressive, but this is a young viticultural area. Moreover, Edna Valley Vineyards is on its way to producing 50,000 cases of barrel-fermented Chardonnay a year, no small undertaking. Mount Eden, an established producer based in the Santa Cruz Mountains, has made wonderful Chardonnays from the MacGregor Vineyard. Chamisal Vineyards is another name worth seeking. It has also shown promise with its Chardonnays.

SANTA BARBARA COUNTY

From only 13 acres of Chardonnay in 1971, Santa Barbara County's acreage has grown to 4,758, planted primarily in the Santa Ynez and Santa Maria valleys. There are few stars in this appellation. By far the richest and most dramatic Chardonnays are Sanford's. Few Chardonnays in California can match the incredible opulence and breadth of flavor found in this producer's wines. At times Zaca Mesa has made superb, well-crafted Chardonnays, as has Byron, but they have been inconsistent and were not selected for this book. I have also given high marks to Au Bon Climat and Qupe, both of which show excellent promise. Back in 1974, Beringer's Myron Nightingale tested the grapes and produced a wonderful 1974 that is still holding up.

CHAPTER III

THE VINTAGES: 1970 TO 1989

In making decisions about buying fine wines, the most crucial factor and single greatest guarantee of quality is the producer's name. Beyond that, the vintage date, appellation and style weigh equally in determining a wine's value. The vintage date can provide a strong indication whether the wine you are contemplating is from a great year, a terrible year or somewhere in between.

California Chardonnay has enjoyed a succession of very good to excellent vintages throughout most of the past two decades. There have also been a few difficult years. Rain at harvest wreaked havoc in 1971, the drought year of 1976 yielded unbalanced and awkward wines, and rain and Botrytis plagued many wines in 1982. At no time in history have the vintages been so consistently fine as in 1984 to 1988. The 1989 vintage offers a mixed blessing for consumers. Some sensational grapes were harvested before heavy rains in the North Coast put a damper on most of the record-size crop. Nonetheless, the dramatic stylistic and quality improvements of the 1980s, along with a wealth of promising new producers, make this the greatest buying opportunity in Chardonnay history.

This chapter is devoted to summaries of the California Chardonnay vintages from 1970 to 1989. A summary is no more than an overview of some of the highlights in a given year. Most of the analysis pertains to Chardonnays grown in Napa, Sonoma and Carneros, because these appellations have longer track records and a broader selection of wines to analyze. This is not intended to short-change areas south of Napa and Sonoma, but in most instances there have not been enough wines from specific appellations or producers to make a fair analysis. I have indicated the top wines from each vintage, showing that fine wines can be made in all appellations in any year.

How much credibility should you place in vintage ratings? Many times the vintage profiles fit well. 1985 was excellent all around and the wines were ripe, rich and balanced. The 1986 vintage was also very fine, with uniformly well-balanced, flavorful wines. When the 1987s arrived, there was much enthusiasm among producers, but the wines were hard and austere, with many displaying more raw acidity and tartness than usual. The 1987s needed an extra year or two in the bottle to mellow, but the profile fit. Early on it became apparent that the 1988 vintage was in some ways the opposite of 1987, with more delicate, forward fruitiness rather than firm acidity.

Vintages are often victims of incomplete media analysis. Heavy rain at harvest certainly qualifies as legitimate news, but it is too easy to write off or hail a vintage before having tasted enough wines to form an educated opinion. It is also unfair to blame a vintage for being "off." Winemakers may also have a hand in bad wines. It is true that great wines can be made in bad vintages, and bad wines made in great vintages, but those examples are exceptions to the rule. Part of the fun of drinking wine lies in analyzing vintages, producers and appellations, and determining how the wines age, improve or disappoint, and whether they live up to or fall short of expectations.

In this section, I have divided each of the vintages into one of six categories, rating only the top wines produced in that year, using *The Wine Spectator's* 100-point scale:

95-100 Classic, a wine of extraordinary character
90-94 Outstanding, a wine of superior quality and style
80-89 Good to very good, a wine with special qualities
70-79 Average, a decent wine that may have minor flaws
60-69 Below average, a drinkable wine but not recommended
50-59 Poor, an undrinkable wine, best to avoid

For each of the vintages, I have summarized weather conditions. When possible I have indicated the styles or characteristics that make them distinctive, along with the top wines, how well they are aging and when they should be consumed. Price trends indicate how prices have escalated for some of the top wines of the vintage. Since most California Chardonnays are ready to drink on release, you can rarely go wrong opening up a bottle from a new vintage. Still, many vintages have aged very well, and mature Chardonnays can be a treat if they are well made.

1989: VERY GOOD (86)
RAINY, UNEVEN QUALITY, SOME OUTSTANDING

As summer ended, there was talk among Chardonnay specialists that 1989 would be a banner year, perhaps the top vintage of the 1980s. Those who picked early were elated with the quality and quantity, but then heavy rains fell and wiped out portions of many vineyards. The grapes in those vineyards never recovered. In Robert Young's Alexander Valley vineyard, rain ruined the crop and no 1989 Robert Young was bottled by Chateau St. Jean. Vintners have been putting the best face on this vintage, fearing it may be a bust in the minds of consumers.

Many of the Chardonnays I have tasted appear to be very promising. Behind the scenes, however, many wineries have dumped huge quantities of Chardonnay on the bulk market, which should be good for some low-priced Chardonnays, but is an indication of both poor quality and severe selections. Wineries that bottle only their best Chardonnays should have some stunning wines, but many vintners will be scrambling for bulk wine to keep their brands on the market. Expect many wines to be mediocre to good and styles to vary greatly. Despite the rainy weather at harvest, 1989 set a record as the largest crop to date in California, with more than 162 million tons, at more than 5 tons per acre.

Price trends: Expect prices for top 1989s to remain stable, with some lesser-quality bargains.

1988: OUTSTANDING (92)
DELICATE, RIPE, FORWARD, BALANCED

After years of talking about making wines of greater delicacy and finesse, many California winemakers succeeded in 1988. Both 1981 and 1984 were hotter and riper vintages, but 1988, despite being a drought year, produced wines with a greater sense of balance and proportion. There are scores of very rich, fruity, complex and charming Chardonnays to choose from, up and down the state. Some vintners prefer 1985, 1986 or 1987 to 1988, but across the board 1988 is a very successful vintage. All the forces of the past two decades came together in 1988. Vineyards were more mature, winemakers were more skilled and the harvest was ripe and easy to pick, with no threat of rain.

As dangerous as this prediction may sound, this should be a textbook vintage in style, for the 1988s are elegant and delicious to drink now and have the proper balance, weight, richness and depth to improve in the cellar. Among the many stars to choose from, the very finest include Kistler Estate, Monticello Corley Reserve, Ferrari-Carano and Ferrari-Carano Reserve, Long, Forman, Sequoia Grove Napa Valley, Saintsbury Reserve, Cuvaison, Cuvaison Carneros Reserve, Flora Springs Barrel Fermented, Sonoma-Cutrer Les Pierres and Cutrer Vineyards, Arrowood, Simi Reserve, Morgan Reserve, Sanford and Sanford Barrel Select.

Price trends: Not much movement yet, some 1988s have not been released.

1987: VERY GOOD (87)
AUSTERE, TART, CONCENTRATED, AGEWORTHY

The 1987 vintage was as distinctive as any in California. The Chardonnays up and down the coast stood out for their tartness and austerity. Early on many of these wines were crisp and firm, and did not appear to have the depth, richness and concentration found in top vintages. Time in the bottle has helped round out some of the rough edges and has produced a very impressive group of wines. 1987 was another drought year, which can often yield wines of uneven quality, but 1987 also produced some sensational bottles. Among the very best are Chateau St. Jean Robert Young Vineyards Reserve (in magnum only), Flora Springs Barrel Fermented, Simi Reserve, Ferrari-Carano, Mount Eden MacGregor Vineyards, Kistler Dutton Ranch and Kistler Durell Vineyards.

Price trends: (release price/current price)
Far Niente: $26/$30
Ferrari-Carano: $16/$23
Flora Springs Barrel Fermented: $20/$24
Kistler Dutton Ranch: $18/$24
Silverado Vineyards: $13.50/$15

1986: OUTSTANDING (91)
DEEP, RICH, CONCENTRATED, COMPLEX

A solid vintage all around, 1986 matched 1985 for richness, complexity, depth and aging ability. Sharply focused, perfectly ripe and well balanced, many 1986s were just reaching maturity in 1990 and the best appeared to have the intensity and balance to improve for another five years. It was a balanced growing season, with plenty of rain in the winter and a good-sized crop. In Napa Valley, Forman, Girard and Girard Reserve, Long, Chateau Montelena, William Hill Reserve, Grgich Hills and Franciscan Reserve were among the best wines. The two stars of the vintage were Cuvaison Reserve and Chalone, but close in quality were the superb Kistler Estate, Simi Reserve, Ferrari-Carano and Ferrari-Carano Reserve.

Price trends: (release price/current price)
Chalone: $22/$48
Ferrari-Carano: $16/$28
Forman: $18/$45
Girard: $13.50/$28
Saintsbury: $12/$17

1985: OUTSTANDING (94)
RIPE, ELEGANT, CONCENTRATED, HARMONIOUS

Considered a great vintage for many different wines and wineries, 1985 ranks narrowly ahead of 1986 and 1988 as the best vintage of the decade. Similar to 1986 in richness, focus and depth of flavor, the 1985s have a shade more elegance and finesse. Moderate temperatures led to ideal growing conditions throughout the state, producing a large crop of well-proportioned, well-balanced, harmonious Chardonnays that are just peaking now and have the ability to hold for another five years or longer. The top wines came from throughout the state, demonstrating the breadth and depth of the vintage. Chateau St. Jean Robert Young Vineyards Reserve, Chalone Reserve, Forman, Cuvaison, Sanford Barrel Select and Sonoma-Cutrer Les Pierres led the way, but not far behind were Simi Reserve, Chateau St. Jean Belle Terre, Grgich Hills, Stony Hill, Altamura, Girard, Raymond, Long and S. Anderson.

Price trends: (release price/current price)
Chateau St. Jean Belle Terre Vineyards: $16/$25
Cuvaison: $12/$20
De Loach Vineyards: $14/$23
Grgich Hills: $22/$35
Sonoma-Cutrer Les Pierres: $17.50/$30

1984: VERY GOOD (88)
VERY RIPE, BOLD, FLESHY, EARLY MATURING

Vintages like 1984 get winemakers excited. A very warm to hot year caused plenty of commotion at harvest, for in years like this grapes ripen easily and quickly. Hot years often result in wines that are ultraripe, sometimes alcoholic, and usually fast maturing, and that has been the pattern for the 1984s. They are also charming in their own way, oozing with fleshy, ripe, opulent fruit, but few of the wines have held much back for further cellaring. Monticello Cellars Corley Reserve is amazingly rich and opulent, while Saintsbury, Navarro Première Reserve and Frog's Leap Napa Valley are among the other leaders. Grgich Hills, Stony Hill, Chateau

Montelena Alexander Valley, Clos du Bois Calcaire, De Loach O.F.S., Fisher Vineyards Whitney's, Congress Springs and ZD are not far behind.

Price trends: (release price/current price)
Chateau Montelena Alexander Valley: $16/$32
Grgich Hills: $18/$33
Monticello Cellars Corley Reserve: $12.50/$25
Saintsbury: $11/$25
ZD: $15/$30

1983: GOOD (81)
AUSTERE STYLE, UNEVEN QUALITY, "FOOD WINES"

Because of rain and erratic weather patterns at harvest, the 1983 vintage has been a difficult one to characterize. The 1983 vintage was part of the "food wine" craze, and many winemakers, reacting to criticism that California Chardonnays were too ripe and overblown, over-corrected and made crisp, high-acid wines that lacked richness, flavor and charm. Luckily not everyone followed that pattern. Flora Springs Barrel Fermented, Monticello Cellars Jefferson Ranch, Grgich Hills, Chalone and Clos du Bois Calcaire were all outstanding bottles, particularly the Flora Springs. Each of these wines is drinking at its peak and a few can still hold. For most of the vintage, however, the wines have reached maturity and should be consumed or avoided.

Price trends: (release price/current price)
Chalone: $18/$50
Far Niente: $22/$38
Flora Springs Barrel Fermented: $18/$28
Grgich Hills: $17/$33
Monticello Jefferson Ranch: $10/$20

1982: AVERAGE (78)
HUGE CROP, VERY RIPE, UNBALANCED

The 1982 vintage was also part of the "food wine" era. Vintners struggled to tone down their very ripe grapes from a giant crop, but most were unsuccessful. Many 1982s also have a honey and Botrytis flavor, which made them attractive in their youth but less appealing with age. At best this was an average year affected by unpredictable weather patterns and a huge crop. Bigger-than-normal crops that are not thinned by man or nature often take longer to ripen and hang on the vine too long. When that happens, the grapes run the risk of exposure to changing weather patterns at the end of summer and the beginning of fall. For Simi Reserve,

56

Chalone and Chalone Reserve, however, it was a spectacular vintage of very rich, balanced, ageworthy Chardonnays. Far Niente Estate and Chateau Montelena Alexander Valley area also still worth seeking out, along with about a dozen others.

Price trends: (release price/current price)
Chalone: $18/$53
Chateau Montelena Alexander Valley: $14/$36
Far Niente Estate: $18/$38
Grgich Hills $17/$36
Simi Reserve: $22/$40

1981: VERY GOOD (86)
RIPE, FORWARD, FLESHY, CHARMING

The 1981 growing season was warm to hot from start to finish, with record heat in many parts of the state and an early harvest. Particularly attractive early on with their ripe opulence, the 1981s remain fleshy and forward, but they evolved quickly and are less charming now than in the first five years of their life. Most 1981s have peaked or are declining, but the stars remain Edna Valley Vineyards, Chateau Montelena Alexander Valley, Simi Reserve, Girard, Chalone, and Sonoma-Cutrer Les Pierres and Cutrer Vineyards.

Price trends: (release price/current price)
Chalone: $17/$53
Chateau Montelena Alexander Valley: $14/$36
Edna Valley Vineyards: $12/$25
Girard: $12.50/$35
Simi Reserve: $20/$40

1980: VERY GOOD (85)
HUGE CROP, VERY RIPE, FULL-BODIED

The 1980 vintage is the kind growers love. A long, cool growing season ended with a burst of heat, fully ripening a record-size crop of Chardonnay grapes. Size does not always equal quality, and the 1980 Chardonnays tended to be very ripe, full-blown, sometimes heavy and ponderous wines that aged well, but most are now in decline. Many of the wines were made in a style that featured high extract, skin contact and heavy oak. At the top of the class are Chalone Reserve and Chalone, Simi Reserve, Far Niente, Hanzell and Fisher Vineyards' Whitney's. A dozen others are worth drinking, but beyond that the list narrows quickly.

Price trends: (release price/current price)
Chalone: $17/$55
Far Niente: $16.50/$45
Grgich Hills: $17/$50
Hanzell: $17/$60
Simi Reserve: $20/$40

1979: VERY GOOD (89)
AUSTERE, ELEGANT, BALANCED, AGEWORTHY

1979 is remembered as the year when it rained on the red grapes, but most of the white grapes like Chardonnay were safely tucked away, fermenting in cool cellars. One of the top vintages of the decade, 1979 featured a mild, cool growing season that allowed Chardonnay to ripen fully but not overripen, resulting in wines of greater elegance, finesse and balance. Many 1979s from Napa Valley have aged well, particularly the incredible Grgich Hills, St. Clement, Far Niente, Smith Madrone, Flora Springs and, farther to the south, Mount Eden.

Price trends: (release price/current price)
Chalone: $14/$55
Far Niente: $15/$45
Grgich Hills: $16/$55
Mount Eden: $16/$60
St. Clement: $12/$27

1978: VERY GOOD (85)
RIPE, INTENSE, POWERFUL

The 1978 vintage for Chardonnay was not unlike that of Cabernet Sauvignon. A long, cool growing season, a huge crop, no threat of rain and plenty of heat at harvest led to very ripe grapes that were high in extract, yielding big, rich, intense wines that were showy early on but lacked the balance and grace for long-term cellaring. For Cabernet it was a great year. For Chardonnay it was only very good. The stars remain Hanzell, Grgich Hills and Trefethen. After that the list drops off quickly.

Price trends: (release price/current price)
Cuvaison: $10/$28
Grgich Hills: $13.75/$60
Hanzell: $13/$80
Matanzas Creek: $12.50/$40
Trefethen: $10/$40

1977: GOOD (84)
DROUGHT YEAR, ELEGANT, BALANCED, CHARMING

The second year of a two-year drought, 1977 generally produced some very elegant, well-balanced, attractive Chardonnays. Certainly they were better balanced and more appealing than those of 1976, the first drought year. Vintners and growers were better prepared to deal with water shortages, and the wines, while delicate in style, were reasonably concentrated and drank well early on; by now most have faded. Two in particular remain delicious, Stony Hill and Chappellet. Hanzell and Grgich Hills are also worth the extra search.

Price trends: (release price/current price)
Chappellet: $11.75/$40
Chateau Montelena Napa Valley: $15/$60
Grgich Hills: $11/$65
Hanzell: $12/$85
Stony Hill: $9/$95

1976: AVERAGE (77)
DROUGHT YEAR, VERY RIPE, UNBALANCED

The first year of a two-year drought, 1976 yielded very ripe, dehydrated and tannic Chardonnays that were high in extract and generally unbalanced. These curious wines displayed exaggerated flavors, so colors were deeper, flavors were riper and textures coarser. Not a pretty picture. Despite that, Chateau St. Jean's Robert Young Vineyards, Hanzell and Stony Hill made admirable wines.

Price trends: (release price/current price)
Chateau St. Jean Robert Young: $8.75/$25
Hanzell: $12/$90
Chateau Montelena Napa Valley: $12/$65
Mayacamas: $11/$45
Hacienda Clair de Lune: $7/$40

1975: VERY GOOD (85)
RIPE, ELEGANT, BALANCED, CHARMING

Although most of the 1975s have now faded, in their youth they were wonderful, ripe, balanced, rich and flavorful, though not overbearing like the 1976s. They were best drunk years ago, but if you come across Chateau Montelena Napa Valley, Hanzell, or either Chateau St. Jean Beltane Ranch or Belle Terre Vineyards, you won't be disappointed.

Price trends: (release price/current price)
Chateau Montelena Napa Valley: $9/$65
Chateau St. Jean Belle Terre Vineyards: $7.50/$22
Freemark Abbey: $9/$45
Hanzell: $10/$70
Trefethen: $6.50/$45

1974: VERY GOOD (88)
RIPE, RICH, BOLD, BALANCED

The 1974 vintage put California Cabernet on the map, but it was also a very fine year for Chardonnay. A long, cool growing season and just the right amount of heat at harvest led to fully ripe, richly concentrated, fairly ageworthy Chardonnays. Most of the wines are well past their primes, but the 1974s from Hanzell, Chateau Montelena Napa and Alexander Valleys, Robert Mondavi Reserve and Beringer Vineyards Santa Barbara County are still a treat.

Price trends: (release price/current price)
Beringer Santa Barbara County: $5/$45
Chateau Montelena Napa and Alexander Valleys: $8/$70
Hanzell: $9/$75
Robert Mondavi Reserve: $10/$45

1973: VERY GOOD (85)
ELEGANT, SUBTLE, BALANCED, CHARMING

After the dismal 1971 and 1972 vintages, 1973 proved a sound vintage, not as ripe as 1974, but early on the Chardonnays were rich and balanced, with good staying power throughout the decade. A few are still hanging on quite well, the best being Chateau Montelena Napa and Alexander Valleys, Chappellet, Hacienda Clair de Lune and Hanzell.

Price trends: (release price/current price)
Chappellet: $6.75/$50
Chateau Montelena Napa and Alexander Valleys: $6.50/$100
Hacienda Clair de Lune: $5/$50
Hanzell: $8/$100

1972: BELOW AVERAGE (67)
RAINY, SIMPLE, WATERY, UNINSPIRED

Great wines can be made in mediocre vintages, and 1972 for all its rain and foul weather serves to remind us of that fact. Chateau Montelena, in its first vintage, made a stunning 1972 from Napa Valley and Alexander Valley grapes that ranks as one of the finest Chardonnays ever made in California, while Hanzell's is still rich and complex. If you find either of those wines, make an offer. Otherwise it is not a year to remember.

Price trends: (release price/current price)
Chateau Montelena Napa and Alexander Valleys: $6/$110
Freemark Abbey: $6.50/$48
Hanzell: $7/$75

1971: Below Average (68)
Rainy Harvest, Poor Quality

Along with the rain-plagued 1972 vintage, 1971 was one of the worst of the decade and modern Chardonnay history. Hanzell made a very good wine that has aged well, while Stony Hill's is holding on.

Price trends: (release price/current price)
Hanzell: $7/$120
Stony Hill: $6/$110

1970: Very Good (89)
Complex, Elegant, Balanced

The 1970 Stony Hill Chardonnay remains a tribute to the excellent 1970 vintage. Severe spring frosts reduced much of the crop in Napa Valley, but the grapes that did survive were clean and concentrated and rendered excellent wines. The only other 1970 I have tasted recently that is holding up well is Hanzell.

Price trends: (release price/current price)
Hanzell: $7/$120
Stony Hill: $6/$175

CHAPTER IV

A CLASSIFICATION: RANKING THE CHARDONNAYS

This chapter features a classification of California Chardonnay. It ranks most of the Chardonnays in this book in one of five categories, from first to fifth growth. My purpose in devising this classification is to put the top California Chardonnays in historical perspective as well as to rank the wines for consumers, according to my assessment of quality.

In creating this classification, my principal criteria were overall quality and consistency of quality over time. The rankings have nothing to do with a wine's reputation or price but are based on years of research, including tasting several thousand Chardonnays from virtually every producer in California in the past decade, as well as a comprehensive review within the past nine months, during which time every wine included in this book was tasted at least once. In many instances the wines were tasted on several occasions, often in vertical flights according to producer. They were also tasted in horizontal flights, comparing wines from the same vintage.

The model for my classification is the famous 1855 classification of the Médoc, in which 61 great Bordeaux châteaux were ranked in five tiers, first through fifth growth. It is important to note that the principal criteria in the Médoc classification were prices paid for the châteaux's wines and the châteaux's reputations for quality. While those two criteria are often legitimate indications of a wine's quality and worth, they are also in my view incomplete, for they place too great a value on image without specifically addressing the issue of quality.

For all its validity in 1855, the Médoc classification is now outdated. Its principal value today for consumers is as a historical document that compares the great châteaux of that era primarily through pricing and market demand. The 1855 classification is still widely respected by the Bordeaux wine trade and by many connoisseurs. Many of the châteaux have maintained their reputations, particularly among the top growths, while many others have declined in quality. For consumers to make the most intelligent buying decisions and the most accurate appraisal of quality, a classification needs to be based primarily on quality and consistency over a period of time. It also needs to be re-evaluated and updated periodically to reflect the changes in a wine's quality.

This California Chardonnay Classification is of individual wines, not wineries, vineyards or estates. It is based on detailed criteria that include producer and overall quality, a wine's track record for excellence, consistency of style, longevity, and the history of the vineyard or vineyards and winemaker (for more details on each of these topics, see "How the Wines Were Chosen," in the chapter "How to Use This Book").

To be rated a first growth, a wine had to have at least eight consecutive vintages of very good to outstanding wines, and be distinctive in style and ageworthy. Several wines, notably Long Vineyards and Kistler Vineyards Dutton Ranch, have wine histories that would have qualified them for first-growth consideration, but I was unable to taste enough of the older vintages recently to evaluate how well they have aged. Therefore they were classified as second growths. Several other wines also have an amazing string of excellent vintages, but lacked the eight-year minimum track record. Ferrari-Carano and Sanford Barrel Select fall into this category, and they too were classified second growths. Wineries that produce more than one wine, like Chateau Montelena or Chateau St. Jean, may have wines ranked differently. Moreover, not every wine in this book is classified. If a wine is not produced on a regular basis, it may or may not be included. For more detailed information on the specific producers and wines, refer to the winery profiles and tastings notes in Chapter VI.

Finally, while I believe there is a quality and track record distinction between a first and a fifth growth, a fifth-growth Chardonnay is by no means a fifth-rate wine. Each of the wines selected for this book was chosen because of its high level of quality. There are literally hundreds of Chardonnays that were not included in this book because they did not meet my minimum standard of quality or track record. For a complete listing of all wines considered for this book, see Appendix 6.

A CLASSIFICATION OF CALIFORNIA CHARDONNAY

FIRST GROWTHS

Chalone Vineyard
Chalone Vineyard Reserve
Chateau Montelena Alexander Valley
Chateau St. Jean Robert Young Vineyards
Far Niente Winery
Flora Springs Wine Co. Barrel Fermented

Grgich Hills Cellar
Hanzell Vineyards
Simi Winery Reserve
Sonoma-Cutrer Vineyards Les Pierres
Stony Hill Vineyard

SECOND GROWTHS

Arrowood Vineyards & Winery
Chateau St. Jean Belle Terre Vineyards
Cuvaison Winery
Cuvaison Winery Reserve
Ferrari-Carano Vineyards & Winery
Ferrari-Carano Vineyards & Winery Reserve
Forman Vineyard
Girard Winery Reserve
William Hill Winery Reserve
Kistler Vineyards Durell Vineyard
Kistler Vineyards Dutton Ranch
Kistler Vineyards Estate

Long Vineyards
Matanzas Creek Winery Sonoma County
Mayacamas Vineyards
Robert Mondavi Winery Reserve
Monticello Cellars Corley Reserve
Navarro Vineyards Première Reserve
Saintsbury
Sanford Winery Barrel Select
Sequoia Grove Vineyards Napa Valley
Sonoma-Cutrer Vineyards Cutrer Vineyard
Sterling Vineyards Winery Lake Vineyard
Trefethen Vineyards

THIRD GROWTHS

Altamura Winery & Vineyards
S. Anderson Vineyard Stags Leap District
Chappellet Vineyard
Chateau Montelena Napa Valley
Chateau Woltner Estate Reserve
Clos du Bois Winery Calcaire Vineyard
Dehlinger Winery
De Loach Vineyards O.F.S.
Edna Valley Vineyards
Fisher Vineyards Whitney's Vineyard
Folie à Deux Winery
Franciscan Vineyards Cuvée Sauvage
Frog's Leap Winery Napa Valley
Hess Collection Winery

Kendall-Jackson Vineyards Durell Vineyard
Mount Eden Vineyards
Mount Eden Vineyards MacGregor
   Vineyard
Pine Ridge Winery Knollside Cuvée
Raymond Vineyard and Cellar Private
   Reserve
Sanford Winery
Sonoma-Cutrer Vineyards Russian River
   Ranches
St. Clement Vineyards
Sterling Vineyards Diamond Mountain
   Ranch

FOURTH GROWTHS

Beringer Vineyards Private Reserve
Bouchaine Vineyards Estate Reserve
Burgess Cellars Triere Vineyard
Chateau Woltner St. Thomas Vineyard
Chateau Woltner Titus Vineyard
Clos du Bois Winery Flintwood Vineyard
Clos du Bois Winery Winemaker's Reserve
Clos Pegase Carneros
Congress Springs Vineyards San Ysidro
   Reserve
De Loach Vineyards
Freemark Abbey Winery

Frog's Leap Winery Carneros
Girard Winery
Kendall-Jackson Vineyards The Proprietor's
Monticello Cellars Jefferson Ranch
Morgan Winery
Pine Ridge Winery Stag's Leap Vineyard
Saintsbury Reserve
Silverado Vineyards
Smith-Madrone Vineyard
Stag's Leap Wine Cellars Reserve
Vichon Winery
ZD Wines

64

FIFTH GROWTHS

Acacia Winery Carneros
Acacia Winery Marina
Beaulieu Vineyard Carneros Reserve
Bouchaine Vineyards Carneros
Buena Vista Winery Private Reserve
Clos du Bois Winery Barrel Fermented
Clos Du Val Wine Co. Carneros
Clos Pegase Napa Valley
Congress Springs Vineyards Monmartre
    Vineyard
Congress Springs Vineyards Santa Clara
    County
Fisher Vineyards Coach Insignia
Hacienda Winery Clair de Lune
Inglenook-Napa Valley Reserve

Kenwood Vineyards Beltane Ranch
Kenwood Vineyards Yulupa Vineyard
La Crema Reserve
Markham Vineyards
Murphy-Goode Estate Winery
Newton Vineyard
Robert Pecota Winery Canepa Vineyard
Revere Winery Reserve
Rombauer Vineyards
Rombauer Vineyards Reserve
Sequoia Grove Vineyards Carneros
Charles F. Shaw Vineyard
White Oak Vineyards & Winery
White Oak Vineyards & Winery Myers
    Limited Release

CHAPTER V

CHARDONNAY STRATEGIES: COLLECTING AND INVESTING

The major criticism of California Chardonnays is that they do not age. For the most part, this is a valid assessment. The vast majority of California's Chardonnays have not aged well. But that is an unfair indictment of the select few that have improved and matured in the bottle. This chapter is dedicated to those wines for which cellaring can be an asset.

Most California Chardonnays are drinkable as soon as they are released. They are made in a style that is suited for immediate appeal and near-term consumption. Some Chardonnays may continue to improve or maintain their quality for several years, but most fail to gain the added complexity, harmony and finesse that sets the great wines apart from the merely good ones.

With a few exceptions, it has not made much sense to stockpile cases of Chardonnay in your cellar. Most of the wines are at their peaks the moment they are released on the market. Fortunately for Chardonnay connoisseurs, this is beginning to change. More and more producers are refining their grape-growing and winemaking techniques with the specific intent of making ageworthy Chardonnays. These new wines may still taste delicious when released, but they will also improve, gaining complexity with a few years of bottle age.

This chapter is devoted to collecting and investing strategies. First, the distinctions between the two. Collectors and investors share many goals. Often their interests are parallel and overlap. Both aim to buy the best Chardonnays from the top vintages, but their motivations for purchasing wines are different. A collector buys and cellars a wine to drink at its pinnacle of quality. An investor buys and cellars a wine with the specific goal of reselling it at a future date for maximum profit. A wine's quality is important to an investor, but price appreciation is of far greater significance.

Whether you are a collector or investor, it is crucial to know which wines to concentrate on. In today's market, with more than 500 different Chardonnay brands to choose from, not only is it a challenge to keep abreast of all the new wines, it is virtually impossible for most consumers to taste them all on a regular basis. The best way to buy reliably high-quality Chardonnays consistently is to concentrate on producers with the best track records for excellence. There are often instances when new wineries produce exciting wines in their first or second vintage, but without a track record, it is impossible to know how well the wines will age. Many of the wineries considered for this book have made superb Chardonnays at one time or another, but they have not been consistent producers.

Chardonnay has not been a priority for collectors or investors. In the 1950s and 1960s, Chardonnay acreage was minimal, production was sparse and quality was often uneven. Collectors who started buying the early Chardonnays of Hanzell, Stony Hill, Chalone or Mayacamas know how fantastically well many of their vintages aged and improved over the years. They have also greatly appreciated in value, but they are exceptions to the rule.

In researching this book, I tried to taste and review as many old Chardonnays as I could to examine the different levels of quality, style and technique. Most of the vintages from the 1950s through the 1970s are long gone from retail markets. Collectors have held on to some of the wines from that era, but when it comes to buying old Chardonnays, most are very hard to find, and they are often expensive. The oldest Chardonnay tasted for this book was the 1955 Mayacamas, which was still in fine condition for a wine of its age. It cost $1 when released and now has an estimated value of $325. A 1958 Mayacamas had not survived. I was also fortunate to taste the 1957 and 1959 Hanzell Chardonnays, both of which were truly amazing wines. They too were extremely hard to come by. Released at $4, they now command prices ranging from $200 to $240, if you can find them. Occasionally a bottle shows up for sale at auction.

The Stony Hill Chardonnays from 1960 to 1975 were also exceedingly difficult to locate. Early vintages like 1960 are selling for $450 a bottle. Barney Rhodes, a Napa Valley collector, was able to provide two old Hanzell Chardonnays from the early 1960s that were bottled by Heitz Wine Cellar. These wines were bought in barrel by Heitz when Hanzell's winery was sold. They too are terribly scarce, with fewer than 300 cases made, but worth the price for such a unique tasting experience.

Because production of high-quality Chardonnay has been so limited, and its image tarnished by many mediocre wines that did not age well, there is only a very limited market for aged Chardonnay. That makes investing a high risk. There is a market for California Cabernet Sauvignon from the 1960s and 1970s, but no similar market exists for Chardonnay. Collectors may clamor for old rarities from Stony Hill, Hanzell or Chateau Montelena, but these wines are so scarce that they seldom come up for sale at auction. In the next decade, the situation may change. One reason is that, based on research compiled for this book, many Chardonnays have aged much better, in fact, than critics have claimed. The other reason is that winemakers are making superior wines that have better aging potential. Despite all that, it is still questionable how big a market will develop for aged Chardonnay. Investing in all but a few of the very choice producers will remain speculative. California Chardonnay has come of age in the 1990s, and increasingly the level of quality will continue to rise to new heights. As new vintages continue to improve with age, more and more connoisseurs will turn their attention to these wines.

In tracking prices of older vintages, it is apparent that based on comparing release prices with estimated current values for wines chosen for this book, California Chardonnays do appreciate in value. But first a word of caution. The current prices for wines in this book reflect sound estimates of what you can expect to pay for a wine at retail. What you can sell a wine for will usually be less. Don't expect to receive full retail price. A wine you bought for $10 may be estimated to sell for $20, but you will only receive $14 or $15 a bottle. Retailers typically add a 33 percent to 50 percent markup for their wines, so your gain would be much less than

CHARDONNAY PRICE APPRECIATION BY VINTAGE

Vintage	Vintage Rating	Number of Wines reviewed	Average Release Price	Average Current Price	Percent Change
1988	92	114	$18.77	$ 18.92	0.79%
1987	87	121	$18.24	$ 19.81	8.60%
1986	91	112	$17.28	$ 21.86	26.50%
1985	94	99	$16.01	$ 22.68	41.66%
1984	88	82	$15.20	$ 23.93	57.43%
1983	84	73	$14.50	$ 24.34	67.86%
1982	78	62	$14.38	$ 24.74	72.04%
1981	87	53	$14.04	$ 27.76	97.72%
1980	86	47	$14.63	$ 28.97	98.01%
1979	89	31	$13.40	$ 33.30	148.50%
1978	85	24	$12.47	$ 34.78	178.90%
1977	84	22	$11.59	$ 36.28	213.02%
1976	77	21	$ 9.42	$ 37.75	300.74%
1975	85	17	$ 9.23	$ 43.06	366.52%
1974	88	15	$ 7.26	$ 52.50	623.14%
1973	85	11	$ 7.12	$ 63.70	794.66%
1972	67	7	$ 8.91	$ 74.66	737.93%
1971	68	4	$ 6.66	$101.33	1,421.40%
1970 -	89	4	$ 6.66	$111.66	1,576.50%

you might expect. If you examine the Chardonnay price appreciation chart, figures show that the average release price for a 1980 Chardonnay chosen for this book was $14.63. Today the average price of those wines has roughly doubled to $28.97; however, if you sell your wine to a retailer, expect to receive about $20 a bottle. The potential investor in wine should ask himself if this is the best investment available to him.

COLLECTING

With a few exceptions among the older vintages, most of the Chardonnays included in this book are superb choices for buying, drinking or cellaring for five to 10 years. But clearly some Chardonnays are superior in quality to others. They age longer, gain greater depth and complexity, and have better track records. In the collectibility rating system that follows, I have singled out the Chardonnays that I believe are the best Chardonnays to concentrate on based on my research. In the rating system, three levels of collectibility are presented, using symbols used to rate bonds in the financial world — AAA, AA, A — with AAA being the highest rating and A the lowest. Many wines selected for this book have no collectibility rating.

The Chardonnays that receive the AAA rating are, in my view, the top collectibles. These are the wines that I believe will not only age the best over the longest period of time, but will also show the greatest appreciation in value. Other factors, such as production, availability, track record of excellence, vineyard location and winemaker, are also weighed in the formula for selecting these wines. Below are some guidelines to consider for collecting:

1. Concentrate on the top producers in the best vintages. In this book see Chapter IV on the Chardonnay classification, as well as Chapter III on vintages, which highlights the top vintages from 1970 to 1989. Appendix 3 lists all wines tasted by vintage; Appendix 5 ranks all vintages by score in similar fashion.

2. Focus on Chardonnays with the best track records for aging and improving in the bottle. Wineries with at least a 10-year record of excellence are the best bets. Estate-bottled Chardonnays ensure the most consistency in quality from year to year. Wineries that do not own their vineyards or have long-term agreements to buy grapes from the same vineyard are less likely to produce consistent wines. That does not mean they may not produce fine wines, but styles are more likely to change with varying grape sources. Wineries that change winemakers are also liable to modify styles, particularly if they do not own their own vineyards. The collectibility rating that follows is designed to address these issues.

3. Study the market carefully before buying, but purchase the wines as soon as you can and put them in a temperature-controlled environment. Be cautious of old vintages resting in retail shops where they may not have been stored at proper temperatures. Wine is a perishable product that, while durable when properly made and stored, is also highly susceptible to warm or well-lighted areas.

4. When buying at auction or retail, know as much as you can about the wine's prior storage history and examine the bottle carefully. Buying a five- or 10-year-old Chardonnay can be risky if you do not know how or where the wine has been stored. Check the cork for leakage or protrusion from the neck of the bottle. Also check the ullage, the space between the top of the bottle and the fill level of the wine (representing the wine lost through evaporation and seepage during shipment or storage). Examine the label to see if it is in good condition or soiled and torn. Each of those signs is a clue to its storage history. Remember that if the ullage is low, air is getting in and oxidizing the wine. If a bottle has a scuffed label, perhaps it has not been well cared for. If you notice that a bottle in your collection is leaking from the cork, it is best to drink it soon. Air is getting in and oxidizing the wine.

5. Watch for new wineries and their initial releases, particularly when a new winery is taking over an old, established vineyard, or an old, established winemaker is taking over a new winery or vineyard.

6. Oversized bottles, such as magnums, double magnums and imperials, are increasingly popular because they are rarer. Wine also tends to age more slowly in larger bottles.

7. When you find a wine or style that appeals to your taste and budget, buy six bottles to a case. That way you will have enough of the wine to enjoy it over a period of years, so you can learn more about how a wine evolves and when it reaches peak drinking condition. Buying a single bottle or two may give you pleasure, but you will probably wish you had more.

8. If you are looking for old Chardonnays recommended in this book, some may be difficult to find except at auctions. Publications like *The Wine Spectator* regularly publish auction

news and upcoming events. Also check with your wine retailer or restaurants with fine-wine lists. All may be able to help you locate the bottles you are looking for.

9. Keep a cellar book or wine-library diary. Take notes on wines you have collected, assessing the quality and when to drink them. A written memo, even a short note or score, serves as a better reminder than a mental note.

COLLECTIBILITY RATINGS FOR CALIFORNIA CHARDONNAYS

AAA

Chalone Vineyard
Chalone Vineyard Reserve
Chateau Montelena Alexander Valley
Chateau St. Jean Robert Young Vineyards
Far Niente Winery
Flora Springs Wine Co. Barrel Fermented
Grgich Hills Cellar

Hanzell Vineyards
Kistler Vineyards Dutton Ranch
Long Vineyards
Simi Winery Reserve
Sonoma-Cutrer Vineyards Les Pierres
Stony Hill Vineyard

AA

Arrowood Vineyards & Winery
Chappellet Vineyard
Chateau St. Jean Belle Terre Vineyards
Cuvaison Winery
Cuvaison Winery Reserve
Ferrari-Carano Vineyards & Winery
Ferrari-Carano Vineyards & Winery Reserve
Forman Vineyard
Girard Winery Reserve
William Hill Winery Reserve
Kistler Vineyards Durell Vineyard

Kistler Vineyards Estate
Matanzas Creek Winery Sonoma County
Mayacamas Vineyards
Robert Mondavi Winery Reserve
Monticello Cellars Corley Reserve
Saintsbury
Sanford Winery Barrel Select
Sonoma-Cutrer Vineyards Cutrer Vineyard
Sterling Vineyards Winery Lake Vineyard
Trefethen Vineyards

A

Altamura Winery & Vineyards
S. Anderson Vineyard Stags Leap District
Beringer Vineyards Private Reserve
Burgess Cellars Triere Vineyard
Chateau Montelena Napa Valley
Chateau Woltner Estate Reserve
Chateau Woltner St. Thomas Vineyard
Chateau Woltner Titus Vineyard
Clos du Bois Winery Calcaire Vineyard
Clos du Bois Winery Flintwood Vineyard
Clos du Bois Winery Winemaker's Reserve
Dehlinger Winery
De Loach Vineyards
De Loach Vineyards O.F.S.
Edna Valley Vineyard

Hess Collection Winery
Kendall-Jackson Vineyards Durell Vineyard
Monticello Cellars Jefferson Ranch
Mount Eden Vineyards
Mount Eden Vineyards MacGregor Vineyard
Navarro Vineyards Première Reserve
Pine Ridge Winery Knollside Cuvée
Pine Ridge Winery Pine Ridge Stags Leap
    Vineyard
Raymond Vineyard and Cellar
    Private Reserve
Saintsbury Reserve
Sanford Winery
Sequoia Grove Vineyards Napa Valley
Smith-Madrone Vineyard

Fisher Vineyards Whitney's Vineyard
Folie à Deux Winery
Franciscan Vineyards Cuvée Sauvage
Frog's Leap Winery Napa Valley

Sonoma-Cutrer Vineyards Russian River
    Ranches
St. Clement Vineyards
Sterling Vineyards Diamond Mountain
    Ranch

INVESTING

Investing in Chardonnay is like investing in general. There are always risks involved, and the trick is to minimize your risk and maximize the return on your money. Here are some guidelines for the Chardonnay investor:

1. Establish realistic goals for what you want to accomplish. One of the keys to investing is setting a projected price or deadline for meeting your investment goals. Once your investment reaches that price or deadline, it's time for the next move. Some wines will outperform others in appreciation. Others will struggle to keep pace with inflation.

2. Thoroughly research the subject, most importantly the wines you want to buy. Study their track records of quality and price appreciation, and evaluate the levels of demand. This book is a guide to what has happened to prices and production levels in the past 20 years.

3. As with collecting, concentrate on the best vintages, but be more cautious with high-priced or private reserve wines unless you plan to hold them for a long time. Higher-priced wines tend to appreciate in value at a slower pace. When they are rare or irreplaceable, or demand exceeds supply, people are often willing to pay huge premiums for special wines. Historically, there has always been a market for fine wines. But with California Chardonnay, no established market exists except for the very rare bottles.

4. Be aware that if you plan to resell your wine, each state has different laws. In some states it is illegal for private citizens to sell wine and a license is required. Also, don't expect to receive retail prices when you sell your wines. Retailers typically mark up prices by 33 percent to 50 percent. A wine you bought for $10 a bottle that is now retailing for $20 will probably only bring you $14 or $15, far less than the apparent gain. In the auction market, the seller usually gives up a 10 percent fee.

5. Don't hold on to a wine forever. Be prepared to sell. Remember that it is an investment and what you established as your goals. When a wine shows a substantial increase in value, it may be a good time to sell. Holding on to it might not increase or even retain its value. If the wine has reached full maturity, there is added risk in holding it.

6. Storage and insurance are important considerations that will add to your costs. If you are investing in Chardonnay for resale in five or 10 years, make sure that good temperature-controlled storage is part of your plan. If you do not have a large wine cellar, be prepared to pay for keeping your wine in a rented wine locker or warehouse. Wine needs to rest in a cool, dark environment, ideally between 55 and 65 degrees Fahrenheit. Insurance should be another factor to avoid loss from fire, theft or heat damage. In order to qualify for most insurance, you will need a detailed inventory of your wine and its estimated value.

7. Keep track of your wine's development and the market. Watch for reviews of older vintages and beware if the notes indicate your wine has peaked or is declining in quality. If

your wine has peaked, it is probably a good time to sell it. Most California Chardonnays should reach maturity within five years of their vintage; the best will peak in 10 years.

FINAL THOUGHTS ON DRINKING CHARDONNAY

There are no special rules, guidelines or glassware required to drink Chardonnay. In most instances all you need to do is open the bottle and pour. Chardonnays are often served too cold. When they are chilled like Champagne, the flavors become muted and they will not reveal as much complexity and breadth of flavor. Serving Chardonnay too warm can also detract from its quality. Cellar temperature of 55 to 65 degrees is usually fine, but don't serve Chardonnay much warmer. If it is served too cold, simply swirl it in the glass or let it warm up naturally.

Because of its richness and complexity, Chardonnay is very versatile with food. It is not surprising that Chardonnay is the top selling wine at many of the nation's top steak houses. I prefer red wines with steak, but don't be afraid to pour Chardonnay with any variety of meats, poultry, pastas, seafood or vegetables. I have found many mature Chardonnays that pair well with creamy cheeses and nuts served after dinner or before the main course. One key to enjoying any wine is determining which kinds of foods complement them. Remember, it's your taste and no two people have exactly the same preferences for the same wine and food combinations.

In some older Chardonnays you may find a fine sediment in the bottle. Usually that is no cause for concern. Wines that are old or unfiltered often throw a light sediment, and many wines that are cold stabilized and chilled may have small crystal-like tartrates attached to the cork or the bottom of the bottle. If there is sediment, it is usually a good idea to decant the wine. To decant you simply pour the wine into another clean container, until the sediment nears the lip of the bottle. When I decant a wine, I rinse the sediment out of the bottle and repour the wine back into its original bottle, with the label still attached. Some people prefer pouring wine from decanters, but I like to see the bottle and the label.

CHAPTER VI

THE WINERIES AND WINES: PROFILES AND TASTING NOTES

This chapter is the heart of *California's Great Chardonnays*. Each of the wineries chosen for this book is profiled and a tasting note is provided for each of their top Chardonnays. Most of the wines are classified from first to fifth growths denoting the overall quality of the wine, and given a collectiblity rating AAA, AA, A or no rating if the wine is new or has not yet established an adequate track record.

The best vintages are underlined. An "at a glance" box is set off for reference, providing information about who owns the winery, their address and phone number, when they began Chardonnay production, total Chardonnay case production, average vine age, time and type of oak used for aging, whether the wine is barrel fermented or lees aged, and whether it undergoes malolactic fermentation. Many producers in this book make more than one Chardonnay. For more on the topic see "How the Wines Were Chosen" in the chapter "How to Use This Book." Each of the wines is described with a tasting note and ranked on the 100-point scale. There is also information about how many cases were produced, the release price and current value, and my advice as to when to drink the wines at their best.

ACACIA WINERY
Marina Vineyard, Carneros
Carneros

CLASSIFICATION:
  Marina Vineyard: FOURTH GROWTH
  Carneros: FIFTH GROWTH

COLLECTIBILITY RATING: *Not rated*

BEST VINTAGES:
  Marina Vineyard: 1988, 1986, 1984, 1987

  Carneros: 1986, 1988

  Winery Lake Vineyard: 1984, 1983

Acacia, founded in 1979 by Michael Richmond and Jerry Goldstein, proved one of the most exciting new Burgundy-style ventures of the 1980s. As a Pinot Noir and Chardonnay specialist, this winery tapped both Carneros and Napa Valley fruit for its wines and won accolades for its elegant style and vineyard-designated wines. Through a decade the Chardonnays have been very good, consistent and appealing from year to year, a big plus for consumers seeking reliability and quality.

Acacia produced a vineyard-designated Winery Lake Chardonnay, in the best years, before that vineyard was sold to Sterling. It often stood out for its rich, deep, complex fruit flavors and good mid-range aging ability. Two characteristics of Carneros Chardonnay are its bracing acidity and presence of exotic pineapple and tropical fruit flavors. Both are results of factors in the Acacia winemaking style. In older vintages, skin contact was used to extract more flavor, and in vintages with high acidity, malolactic fermentation was employed to reduce the acidic bite. Beginning in 1985, winemaker Larry Brooks eliminated skin contact, lowered levels of sulfur dioxide additives prior to bottling, and varied the percentages of new oak and barrel fermentation. Recently up to 50 percent of the barrels used have been new. Acacia also produced a Napa Valley Chardonnay with fruit grown in the Yountville area.

Acacia ran into financial problems in 1986 when it attempted to expand into the production of Cabernet Sauvignon and Sauvignon Blanc without the blessings of all its partners. It was eventually sold to Chalone Inc., the parent firm of Chalone Vineyard and Carmenet and has a part-interest in Edna Valley Vineyards. Since then Acacia has narrowed its Chardonnay focus to its own Marina Vineyard, a 42-acre plot adjacent to the winery, and a Carneros bottling, a blend of grapes purchased from nearly a dozen Carneros District vineyards. The Marina Chardonnay can often be extremely earthy, although its recent vintages display more fruit, character and complexity, and even vintages like 1984 taste better now than on release. The 1988 Marina is the finest I have tasted. Of the older vintages, the 1983 and 1984 Winery Lake Chardonnays have aged well and are still in top condition for drinking, with bold, deep, complex flavors and a sense of elegance. Acacia's Chardonnay production is nearing 30,000 cases, with a goal of 40,000 cases a year in the next decade. The Marina Vineyard yields 6,000 to 8,000 cases, depending on the vintage.

TASTING NOTES

ACACIA WINERY, Marina Vineyard, Carneros

1988 ACACIA WINERY MARINA VINEYARD: The finest Marina vintage to date, it offers intensity with finesse, with a rich core of ripe pineapple, pear, melon and toast flavors that glide across the palate, finishing with a delicate touch. Last tasted: 1/90. Drink 1991-1996. 7,133 cases produced. Release: $20. Current: $20. **89**

1987 ACACIA WINERY MARINA VINEYARD: Fresh, intense and elegant, with crisp lemon, pear and pineapple flavors of moderate depth, tapering off on the finish. The most delicate Marina bottling to date. Last tasted: 1/90. Drink 1991-1995. 8,600 cases produced. Release: $18. Current: $19. **85**

1986 ACACIA WINERY MARINA VINEYARD: Another fine Marina bottling, offering an abundance of rich, smooth, intense, silky pear and pineapple flavors that complement the toast and earth notes. Well balanced. Last tasted: 1/90. Drink 1991-1994. 6,950 cases produced. Release: $18. Current: $22. **86**

1985 ACACIA WINERY MARINA VINEYARD: A rich, earthy wine that is showing better now than on release, when the earthiness was overpowering. It is still earthy, but offers more spicy lemon flavors to stand up to it. Texture is coarse. Tasted in magnum. Last tasted: 1/90. Drink 1991-1993. 5,000 cases produced. Release: $18. Current: $19. **80**

1984 ACACIA WINERY MARINA VINEYARD: Typical of the Marina Vineyard with its lime earthiness, the 1984 has improved considerably in the bottle, showing more fruit now than in previous tastings. Finishes with pretty honey and toast flavors. Complex. Last tasted: 1/90. Drink 1991-1994. 5,600 cases produced. Release: $16. Current: $22. **86**

1983 ACACIA WINERY MARINA VINEYARD: Earthy, with lean, crisp, simple lemon and pear flavors. Last tasted: 1/90. Drink 1991-1993. 5,300 cases produced. Release: $16. Current: $23. **79**

ACACIA WINERY, Carneros

1988 ACACIA WINERY CARNEROS: Ripe, simple fruit flavors are elegantly balanced with oak, highlighting the lemon, pear and pineapple flavors that fade on the finish. The Marina is a superior bottling. Last tasted: 1/90. Drink 1991-1993. 22,300 cases produced. Release: $16. Current: $16. **85**

1987 ACACIA WINERY CARNEROS: Elegant and fruity, with a coarse texture but plenty of ripe pear and pineapple flavors and a pretty touch of toasty oak. A shade simpler than the Marina bottling. Last tasted: 1/90. Drink 1991-1995. 17,700 cases produced. Release: $17. Current: $17. **84**

1986 ACACIA WINERY CARNEROS: Delicious, silky, rich and complex, with layers of pear, pineapple, apple and spicy oak flavors that combine to give depth and finesse. Finishes with honey and toast flavors that linger. Last tasted: 1/90. Drink 1991-1993. 11,500 cases produced. Release: $15. Current: $18. **87**

1985 ACACIA WINERY CARNEROS: Juicy fruit flavors up front but it gets oaky and dry on the finish. Simple and pleasant but lacking depth and complexity. Last tasted: 1/90. Drink 1991-1993. 10,000 cases produced. Release: $15. Current: $20. **80**

1984 ACACIA WINERY CARNEROS: Fresh, ripe, juicy flavors of pear, spice, citrus and pineapple that are smooth and supple, finishing with good length. A notch below the Winery Lake bottling. Last tasted: 1/90. Drink 1991-1993. 7,800 cases produced. Release: $14. Current: $20. **84**

ACACIA WINERY, Winery Lake Vineyard, Carneros

1985 ACACIA WINERY WINERY LAKE VINEYARD: Less obvious fruit than the 1984 bottling, with subtle, muted flavors of grapefruit, citrus and tart pineapple. Well balanced and pleasant, but less exciting. Last tasted: 1/90. Drink 1991-1994. 3,700 cases produced. Release: $18. Current: $25. **82**

1984 ACACIA WINERY WINERY LAKE VINEYARD: Bold and ripe fruit flavors with richness and depth, well-integrated grapefruit, citrus, pear and pineapple flavors that are smooth and elegant, finishing with fine length. Last tasted: 1/90. Drink 1991-1994. 2,100 cases produced. Release: $18. Current: $25. **88**

1983 ACACIA WINERY WINERY LAKE VINEYARD: Big, ripe and fruity, with a sense of elegance, still holding well, offering ripe pineapple and guava flavors, subtle oak and crisp acidity that carries the flavors. Fully mature but can stand further cellaring. Last tasted: 1/90. Drink 1991-1994. 2,460 cases produced. Release: $18. Current: $25. **87**

1979 ACACIA WINERY WINERY LAKE VINEYARD: Deep in color and mature, with rich honey, caramel and nutmeg flavors, past its prime but holding. Last tasted: 1/90. Drink 1991. 1,400 cases produced. Release: $16. Current: $25. **76**

ACACIA WINERY, Napa Valley

1986 ACACIA WINERY NAPA VALLEY: Fresh, ripe and clean, with simple, pure pear and melon flavors, moderate oak and decent length. Last tasted: 1/90. Drink 1991-1993. 6,700 cases produced. Release: $15. Current: $17. **81**

1985 ACACIA WINERY NAPA VALLEY: Fleshy and round, with simple lemon, pear and pineapple flavors that turn coarse on the finish. The least satisfying of the 1985s, but decent nonetheless. Last tasted: 1/90. Drink 1991-1992. 4,900 cases produced. Release: $12. Current: $16. **79**

1984 ACACIA NAPA VALLEY: Very ripe and rich, with layers of creamy, toasty, buttery pear and pineapple flavors that are complex and elegant, finishing with spicy nuances and good length. Complex and at its peak. Last tasted: 7/90. Drink 1991-1995. 7,000 cases produced. Release: $12. Current: $16. **87**

1983 ACACIA WINERY NAPA VALLEY: Smooth and supple, drinking well, with elegant, straightforward honey, pear, lemon and spice flavors. Simple but pleasant. Tasted in magnum. Last tasted: 1/90. Drink 1991-1993. 4,300 cases produced. Release: $12. Current: $18. **80**

1982 ACACIA WINERY NAPA VALLEY: Fully developed and a shade past its apogee, but it still offers honey, earth, spice and nutmeg flavors that are elegant and satisfying. Tasted in magnum. Last tasted: 1/90. Drink 1991-1993. 4,900 cases produced. Release: $12. Current: $20. **80**

ALTAMURA WINERY & VINEYARDS

Napa Valley

CLASSIFICATION: *THIRD GROWTH*

COLLECTIBILITY RATING: *A*

BEST VINTAGES: *1985, 1988, 1986, 1987*

Frank Altamura is a rarity — a Napa Valley native who is also a vintner. With financial backing from his family, he first grew Chardonnay grapes for wineries like Inglenook and Franciscan while learning how to make wine at Caymus Vineyards. In 1985 he founded Altamura Winery & Vineyards on the eastern side of the Silverado Trail, about halfway between the Stags Leap District and the city of Napa. This area has a relatively cool microclimate that is well suited to Chardonnay, and Altamura's goal is to make Chardonnays that need at least five years to mature.

In four vintages, Altamura has demonstrated a talent for producing rich, concentrated, deftly balanced Chardonnays that are built to age. The oldest, a 1985, is aging quite well and has not yet peaked. It features bold flavors and complex oak shadings. The 1986 is firmer, and to Altamura's mind more ageworthy, while the 1987 is typically hard and austere, like the vintage. The 1988 returns to the style of 1985, more generous, delicate and forward. Most of Altamura's Chardonnay is sold through a winery mailing list. With the 1988 vintage he began producing a Cabernet Sauvignon from his estate vineyard.

AT A GLANCE

ALTAMURA WINERY & VINEYARDS
4240 Silverado Trail
Napa, CA 94558
(707) 253-2000

Owner: Frank Altamura

Winemaker: Frank Altamura
(5 years)

Founded: 1985

First Chardonnay vintage: 1985

Chardonnay production: 2,000 cases

Chardonnay acres owned: 40

Average age of vines: 12 years

Average wine makeup: Yountville,
Napa Valley (100%)

Time in oak: 11 months

Type of oak: French
(Allier, Tronçais)

Oak age: new (75%) to 1 year old

Winemaking notes:
Barrel fermentation: 80%
Malolactic fermentation: 20%
Lees aging: 80% (11 months)

TASTING NOTES

ALTAMURA WINERY & VINEYARDS, Napa Valley

1988 ALTAMURA WINERY & VINEYARDS: Delicious apple, pear and honey aromas and flavors, with just the right kiss of French oak, resulting in a wonderfully fruity, elegant and well-balanced wine. Because the fruit is so showy, one almost misses the great intensity and vibrancy on the finish. Drink or cellar. Last tasted: 1/90. Drink 1992-1997. 2,000 cases produced. Not released. **90**

1987 ALTAMURA WINERY & VINEYARDS: Like the 1986, very tight and firm, with lean but pretty pear, lemon, apple and oak flavors that are tightly wound and in need of cellaring. Simply too young to drink now. Last tasted: 1/90. Drink 1993-1998. 1,800 cases produced. Release: $16.50. Current: $16.50. **87**

1986 ALTAMURA WINERY & VINEYARDS: A shade leaner and firmer than the 1985, with less apparent fruit, but this too is very successful in its style, displaying crisp lemon, pear and subtle honey and oak flavors that still need time to open fully. Last tasted: 1/90. Drink 1993-1997. 1,500 cases produced. Release: $15. Current: $21. **88**

1985 ALTAMURA WINERY & VINEYARDS: Altamura's first release, an excellent 1985 that combines deep, rich, complex honey, nutmeg, clove and pear flavors with toasty French oak. Tightly knit, with a creamy texture, this wine is aging exceptionally well and should hold for another five years — maybe more. Last tasted: 1/90. Drink 1991-1996. 600 cases produced. Release: $14. Current: $21. **91**

S. ANDERSON VINEYARD

Proprietor's Reserve, Stags Leap District, Napa Valley
Estate, Stags Leap District, Napa Valley

CLASSIFICATION: *THIRD GROWTH*

COLLECTIBILITY RATING: *A*

BEST VINTAGES:

Proprietor's Reserve: 1987

Estate: 1985, 1984, 1988

AT A GLANCE

S. ANDERSON VINEYARD
1473 Yountville Crossroad
Yountville, CA 94599
(707) 944-8642

Owners: Stanley and Carol
   Anderson

Winemaker: Carol Anderson
   (11 years)

Founded: 1979

First Chardonnay vintage: 1980
   Proprietor's Reserve: 1983

Chardonnay production: 4,500 cases
   Estate: 4,000 cases
   Proprietor's Reserve: 500 cases
   (in some vintages)

Chardonnay acres owned: 60

Average age of vines: 10 years

Average wine makeup: Stags Leap
   District, Napa Valley (100%)

Time in oak: 5 months

Type of oak: French (Allier, Nevers,
   François Frères)

Oak age: 1 to 6 years

Winemaking notes:
   Barrel fermentation: 60%
   Malolactic fermentation:
      Proprietor's Reserve: 75%
      Estate: none
   Lees aging: none

S. Anderson Vineyard lies at the northernmost boundary of the Stags Leap District near the intersection of Yountville Crossroad and the Silverado Trail. Founded in 1979 by Stanley and Carol Anderson, S. Anderson has been producing Chardonnays since the 1980 vintage from its 60-acre vineyard, which the family began planting in 1971. Their Chardonnays are very well made, rich and balanced, and generally underrated among Stags Leap and Napa Valley producers, considering, how well they age. For years the Andersons commuted on weekends from Pasadena in Southern California, where Stanley had his dental practice, to Napa Valley. Now they are full-time residents specializing in Napa Valley sparkling wine, producing about 8,000 cases a year, nearly double their 4,500 cases of Chardonnay. Before they began making wine, the Andersons sold Chardonnay grapes to wineries like Cuvaison, Groth and Far Niente.

Rich varietal flavors and aging ability are quite apparent in all the Andersons' Chardonnays. While the 1980 through 1982 vintages are fully mature and should be consumed, the 1983 and 1984 vintages have aged better than most California Chardonnays, showing good depth and complexity. The 1985 is the most complex and intriguing, with lush honey and butterscotch flavors echoing on the finish. The current release, the 1988, displays pure, clean pear, melon and spice notes with subtle oak shadings. While it is drinking well now, it should peak in about five years. A Proprietor's Reserve is produced in years when there is sufficient quality to warrant a special bottling. The 1987 is a deep, complex wine that rivals the wonderful 1985. The 1983 bottling, then called Proprietor's Selection, is a big, rich wine that is still holding its own.

TASTING NOTES

S. ANDERSON VINEYARD, Proprietor's Reserve, Stags Leap District, Napa Valley

1987 S. ANDERSON VINEYARD PROPRIETOR'S RESERVE: Remarkably complex, rich and creamy, with honey, butter, spice and pear flavors that are intense yet elegant, finishing with a long, smooth aftertaste. The most elegant of the Anderson Chardonnays, rivaling the 1985 for overall quality. Last tasted: 3/90. Drink 1991-1996. 480 cases produced. Release: $20. Current: $20. **89**

1983 S. ANDERSON VINEYARD PROPRIETOR'S SELECTION: A big, rich, honey-scented Chardonnay that is beginning to show signs of old age, but there is still plenty of depth and flavor, finishing with honey, spice, nutmeg and butter tones. Last tasted: 3/90. Drink 1991-1993. 100 cases produced. Release: $16. Current: $40. **87**

S. ANDERSON VINEYARD, Estate, Stags Leap District, Napa Valley

1988 S. ANDERSON VINEYARD ESTATE: Fresh, clean, ripe and delicate, another success for S. Anderson. It is young and well balanced, displaying luscious apple, pear, melon and spice notes that are vibrant and long on the finish. Last tasted: 6/90. Drink 1992-1997. 4,388 cases produced. Release: $18. Current: $18. **88**

1987 S. ANDERSON VINEYARD ESTATE: A tart, sharply acidic wine that is typical of the 1987 vintage, showing more astringency than fruit now. With time one hopes the apple, pear and citrus flavors behind the acidity will show more suppleness and a greater sense of harmony. For now it needs time or a tray of oysters. Last tasted: 6/90. Drink 1993-1998. 3,798 cases produced. Release: $16. Current: $18. **85**

1986 S. ANDERSON VINEYARD ESTATE: Less extravagant and exciting than the 1985, the 1986 is more subdued, with clean, lean and pure Chardonnay flavors, but it lacks the breadth and depth of flavor, and comes across as somewhat simple and direct. With time it may gain some depth. Last tasted: 3/90. Drink 1991-1994. 4,792 cases produced. Release: $16. Current: $18. **81**

1985 S. ANDERSON VINEYARD ESTATE: The most complex and intriguing of the S. Anderson Chardonnays, offering more character, complexity and depth than previous bottlings, with pretty, well-defined honey, pear, spice and subtle toasty oak flavors that marry well on the finish. Honey and butterscotch echo on the aftertaste. Last tasted: 3/90. Drink 1991-1995. 3,500 cases produced. Release: $14. Current: $25. **92**

1984 S. ANDERSON VINEYARD ESTATE: Delicious, ripe, rich butterscotch, spice and honey flavors are tightly knit, smooth and elegant, with a spicy honeysuckle taste that lingers on the finish. The best of

the early Anderson Chardonnays. Last tasted: 3/90. Drink 1991-1994. 1,770 cases produced. Release: $12.50. Current: $25. **89**

1983 S. ANDERSON VINEYARD ESTATE: Holding exceptionally well, displaying ripe pear, spice, honey and butter flavors of moderate depth and complexity with a pretty, elegant aftertaste. Last tasted: 3/90. Drink 1991-1993. 1,415 cases produced. Release: $12.50. Current: $25. **86**

1982 S. ANDERSON VINEYARD ESTATE: Mature and fading now, with faint pear and spice flavors that turn murky on the finish. Drinkable but unexciting. Last tasted: 3/90. Drink 1991. 1,412 cases produced. Release: $12.50. Current: $21. **72**

1981 S. ANDERSON VINEYARD ESTATE: Mature but attractive, with rich, elegant smoke, pear and citrus flavors that are very pleasant, though a bit short on the finish. A shade past its prime but still enjoyable. Last tasted: 3/90. Drink 1991-1993. 1,835 cases produced. Release: $12.50. Current: $25. **80**

1980 S. ANDERSON VINEYARD ESTATE: The first Anderson Chardonnay is fully mature, with pretty honey and butterscotch flavors of moderate depth and intensity, finishing with delicate spice and nutmeg notes. Aging well but best to drink up. Last tasted: 3/90. Drink 1991-1993. 1,545 cases produced. Release: $12.50. Current: $30. **83**

ARROWOOD VINEYARDS & WINERY
Sonoma County

CLASSIFICATION: *SECOND GROWTH*

COLLECTIBILITY RATING: *AA*

BEST VINTAGES: *1988, 1987*

In 1986, after 12 years as winemaker at Chateau St. Jean, Richard Arrowood, with his wife, Alis, founded a winery in Sonoma Valley a few miles south of St. Jean. Through the 1989 vintage Arrowood oversaw winemaking at both St. Jean and Arrowood, but in 1990 he severed ties with Suntory-owned St. Jean to devote all of his time to Arrowood, where he makes both Chardonnay and Cabernet Sauvignon.

Arrowood has created Chardonnays of great complexity through the diversity of his grape sources. He buys all his fruit from half a dozen growers spread throughout Sonoma County, including Jimtown Ranch and Russell Green Ranch in Alexander Valley, Preston Ranch and Alary Ranch in Russian River Valley, and Blasi and Chalk Hill Ranch in Chalk Hill. So far the Chardonnays have been nothing short of superb, with each vintage capturing intense, concentrated, rich and complex fruit flavors while displaying finesse and grace and the kind of intensity and depth that promise to gain in the bottle for six to eight years. The first vintage, the 1986, is still on its way up. The 1988 vintage is perhaps Arrowood's finest, although I find the Réserve Spéciale 1987, a limited bottling produced only in magnum, enormously complex and flavorful. Although Arrowood does not own any Chardonnay vineyards, he has established strong ties with experienced growers and knows Sonoma County's best Chardonnay vineyards as well as anyone.

TASTING NOTES

ARROWOOD VINEYARDS & WINERY, Sonoma County

1988 ARROWOOD VINEYARDS & WINERY: The best Arrowood Sonoma County to date, offering rich, smooth, complex and elegant Chardonnay fruit, with layers of pineapple, citrus, spice and pear flavors that are deep and concentrated, finishing with excellent length. Last tasted: 4/90. Drink 1992-1997. 6,300 cases produced. Release: $18. Current: $18. **92**

AT A GLANCE
ARROWOOD VINEYARDS & WINERY
P.O. Box 987
Glen Ellen, CA 95442
(707) 938-5170

Owners: Richard and Alis Arrowood

Winemaker: Richard Arrowood (4 years)

Founded: 1986

First Chardonnay vintage: 1986

Chardonnay acres owned: none

Chardonnay production: 6,000 cases

Average wine makeup: Alexander Valley (58%), Russian River Valley (33%), Chalk Hill (9%)

Time in oak: 9 months

Type of oak: French (Gillet, Burgundian)

Oak age: new (33%) to 2 years old

Winemaking notes:
  Barrel fermentation: 100%
  Malolactic fermentation: up to 30%
  Lees aging: 100% (9 months)

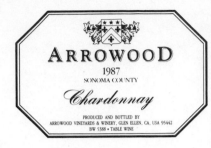

1987 ARROWOOD VINEYARDS & WINERY: Plenty of generous, forward, ripe fruit aromas, with intense yet elegant fruit flavors. Attractive for its complex pear, vanilla and spice flavors that stay with you through the finish. Last tasted: 4/90. Drink 1991-1995. 6,000 cases produced. Release: $18. Current: $18. **89**

1987 ARROWOOD VINEYARDS & WINERY RESERVE SPECIALE (IN MAGNUM ONLY): Clearly one of the two finest Arrowoods produced (the other being the 1988 Sonoma County), this is a remarkably rich, toasty, complex wine with intense pear, apple, spice and pineapple flavors and a smooth, supple texture that lets the flavors linger on the finish. A real beauty. Last tasted: 4/90. Drink 1991-1997. 57 cases produced. Release: $50. Current: $50. **92**

1986 ARROWOOD VINEYARDS & WINERY: The first Arrowood Chardonnay bottling continues to gain complexity, with mature honey, butterscotch, toast and vanilla flavors and subtle pineapple and apple notes. Long aftertaste. Last tasted: 4/90. Drink 1991-1995. 4,600 cases produced. Release: $18. Current: $25. **89**

BEAULIEU VINEYARD

Carneros Reserve, Carneros

CLASSIFICATION: *FIFTH GROWTH*
COLLECTIBILITY RATING: *Not rated*
BEST VINTAGES: *1988, 1987, 1986*

Beaulieu Vineyard, founded in 1900 in Rutherford, has been in the Chardonnay business since 1938, when the legendary André Tchelistcheff was winemaker. This historic Napa Valley winery was among the pioneers that planted Chardonnay in the cooler climate of Carneros. Throughout its history, however, BV has focused on perfecting red wines, most notably its Georges de Latour Private Reserve Cabernet Sauvignon, which was first made in 1936, and to a lesser degree Pinot Noir. Tchelistcheff once confided that in the old days BV made white wines like red wines — with skin contact, lots of sulfur, and fermentation in redwood tanks and old barrels. Chardonnay was never a priority until the late 1970s and 1980s, when it became the white wine of choice for most consumers.

I have not tried nor even seen at auction any of the old BV Chardonnays, although I am sure they appear from time to time. I have tasted a few from the 1960s, but most of my current notes date from the late 1960s through the 1970s. Those wines, bottled under the Beaufort brand, were for the most part good, sound, balanced wines, and a few have held up well over the years. Beginning with the 1981 vintage, BV began bottling a Los Carneros Chardonnay (now called Carneros Reserve), and it is a much-improved wine, showing more judicious use of French oak barrels, lees contact, and up to 25 percent malolactic fermentation. Today nearly half the barrels used are new French oak, heavy on the toast, and the wines clearly show more finesse and complexity as well as aging potential.

The 1968 through 1979 Beaufort Chardonnays and the 1981 to 1984 Carneros wines listed below are not worth seeking out, although they may still be sold at auction. I have included notes primarily to show how they have aged. The Carneros wines from 1985 to 1988 are vastly superior, each vintage showing improvement over its predecessor, with 1987 and 1988 in particular revealing a sense of elegance, grace and finesse missing in earlier bottlings. Today Beaulieu owns or controls 180 acres of Chardonnay, and under the winemaking direction of Joel Aiken, has decided to get serious and upgrade its Reserve wines. The result of these steps has been an improvement in Beaulieu's quality.

AT A GLANCE

BEAULIEU VINEYARD
P.O. Box 329
Rutherford, CA 94573
(707) 963-2411

Owner: Heublein Inc./Grand Metropolitan, Great Britain

Winemaker: Joel Aiken (5 years)

Founded: 1900

First Chardonnay vintage: 1938
   Carneros Reserve: 1981

Chardonnay production: 80,000 cases
   Carneros Reserve: 10,000 cases

Chardonnay acres owned: 180

Average age of vines: 15 years

Average wine makeup:
   Carneros, Napa Valley (100%)

Time in oak: 10 months

Type of oak: French (Allier, Limousin)

Oak age: new (50%) to 1 year old

Winemaking notes:
   Barrel fermentation: 100%
   Malolactic fermentation: 10% to 25%
   Lees aging: average, 10 months

LOS CARNEROS RESERVE
NAPA VALLEY
CHARDONNAY
PRODUCED AND BOTTLED BY BEAULIEU VINEYARD
AT RUTHERFORD, NAPA COUNTY, CALIFORNIA
ALCOHOL 13.0% BY VOLUME

TASTING NOTES

BEAULIEU VINEYARD, Carneros Reserve, Carneros

1988 BEAULIEU VINEYARD CARNEROS RESERVE: The finest Beaulieu Carneros Reserve to date, combining rich, clean, sharply defined fruit notes with elegance, grace, delicacy and finesse, and plenty of complex, ripe pear, spice, apple and butter flavors, finishing with excellent depth and length. Last tasted: 6/90. Drink 1992-1998. 10,000 cases produced. Release: $14. Current: $14. **89**

1987 BEAULIEU VINEYARD LOS CARNEROS RESERVE: One of the finest Beaulieu Chardonnays I have tasted, a rich, complex, elegant wine with a creamy smooth texture and plenty of pear and melon flavors, finishing with a hint of smoky, buttery oak. Last tasted: 5/90. Drink 1992-1998. 10,000 cases produced. Release: $14. Current: $16. **87**

1986 BEAULIEU VINEYARD LOS CARNEROS RESERVE: Better than the 1985, featuring a smoother, creamier texture to complement the ripe, rich pear, spice, melon and nutmeg flavors. Complex, balanced, gaining in the bottle. Last tasted: 6/90. Drink 1991-1996. 10,000 cases produced. Release: $12. Current: $15. **86**

1985 BEAULIEU VINEYARD LOS CARNEROS RESERVE: A significant improvement in quality for BV Chardonnays. It is aging well, with a healthy light gold color, fresh citrus and honey flavors, good balance and a pretty aftertaste. Its one drawback is a coarse texture. Last tasted: 6/90. Drink 1991-1995. 10,000 cases produced. Release: $12. Current: $16. **84**

1984 BEAULIEU VINEYARD LOS CARNEROS RESERVE: Ripe and fruity, fully mature and declining, a bit coarse and simple. Was probably better on release. Last tasted: 4/90. Drink 1991-1992. 10,000 cases produced. Release: $10. Current: $16. **79**

1983 BEAULIEU VINEYARD LOS CARNEROS RESERVE: Fully mature, with ripe but coarse pear and nutmeg flavors. Hanging on but not improving. Last tasted: 4/90. Drink 1991-1992. 5,000 cases produced. Release: $12. Current: $15. **74**

1982 BEAULIEU VINEYARD LOS CARNEROS RESERVE: Past its prime, with simple pear and spice flavors. Not going anywhere. Last tasted: 4/90. Drink 1991-1992. 5,000 cases produced. Release: $10. Current: $16. **72**

1981 BEAULIEU VINEYARD LOS CARNEROS RESERVE: Simple and plain, with blunt, one-dimensional fruit flavors. Last tasted: 4/90. Drink 1991-1992. 5,000 cases produced. Release: $18. Current: $15. **70**

BEAULIEU VINEYARD, Beaufort, Napa Valley

1979 BEAULIEU VINEYARD BEAUFORT: Aging better than most BVs, but still one-dimensional, it is fully mature and not worth cellaring. Last tasted: 4/90. Drink 1991-1992. 30,000 cases produced. Release: $6. Current: $20. **70**

1978 BEAULIEU VINEYARD BEAUFORT: Fully mature, past its prime. Not much fruit left. Last tasted: 4/90. Drink 1991. 30,000 cases produced. Release: $6. Current: $22. **70**

1977 BEAULIEU VINEYARD BEAUFORT: Oxidized, well past its prime. Last tasted: 4/90. Best to avoid. 25,000 cases produced. Release: $6. Current: $22. **62**

1976 BEAULIEU VINEYARD BEAUFORT: Deeply colored, very oxidized. Last tasted: 4/90. Best to avoid. 20,000 cases produced. Release: $6. Current: $22. **64**

1975 BEAULIEU VINEYARD BEAUFORT: Oxidized, over the hill. Last tasted: 4/90. Best to avoid. 20,000 cases produced. Release: $50. Current: $28. **61**

1974 BEAULIEU VINEYARD BEAUFORT: Well past its prime, oxidized. Last tasted: 4/90. Best to avoid. 15,000 cases produced. Release: $5. Current: $25. **62**

1973 BEAULIEU VINEYARD BEAUFORT: Oxidized, over the hill. Last tasted: 4/90. Best to avoid. 15,000 cases produced. Release: $5. Current: $30. **60**

1972 BEAULIEU VINEYARD BEAUFORT: Long gone. Last tasted: 4/90. Best to avoid. 12,000 cases produced. Release: $5. Current: $30. **60**

1971 BEAULIEU VINEYARD BEAUFORT: History. Last tasted: 4/90. Best to avoid. 10,000 cases produced. Release: $4. Current: $30. **58**

1970 BEAULIEU VINEYARD BEAUFORT: Well past its prime. Last tasted: 4/90. Best to avoid. 3,000 cases produced. Release: $4. Current: $32. **59**

1969 BEAULIEU VINEYARD BEAUFORT: Very oxidized. Last tasted: 4/90. Best to avoid. 3,000 cases produced. Release: $2. Current: $35. **57**

1968 BEAULIEU VINEYARD BEAUFORT: Deeply oxidized. Last tasted: 4/90. Best to avoid. 2,000 cases produced. Release: $2. Current: $35. **59**

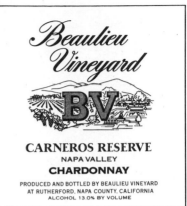

Beaulieu Vineyard
BV

CARNEROS RESERVE
NAPA VALLEY
CHARDONNAY

PRODUCED AND BOTTLED BY BEAULIEU VINEYARD
AT RUTHERFORD, NAPA COUNTY, CALIFORNIA
ALCOHOL 13.0% BY VOLUME

BERINGER VINEYARDS
Private Reserve, Napa Valley

CLASSIFICATION: *FOURTH GROWTH*
COLLECTIBILITY RATING: *A*
BEST VINTAGES: *1986, 1984, 1988, 1985,*

AT A GLANCE
BERINGER VINEYARDS
P.O. Box 111
St. Helena, CA 94574
(707) 963-7115

Owner: Wine World Inc. (Nestlé), Switzerland

Winemaker: Ed Sbragia (6 years)

Founded: 1876

First Chardonnay vintage: 1966
   Private Reserve: 1978

Chardonnay production: 108,000 cases
   Private Reserve: 8,000 cases

Chardonnay acres owned: 710

Average age of vines: 17 years

Average wine makeup: Yountville, Napa Valley (100%)

Time in oak: 6 months

Type of oak: French (Nevers, Limousin)

Oak age: New to 2 years old

Winemaking notes:
   Barrel fermentation: 93%
   Malolactic fermentation: 15%
   Lees aging: 3 months

Beringer Private Reserve Chardonnays are not shy, retiring, understated wines. They tend to be full-blown, ripe and oaky, high in extract and flavor. Yet despite their assertive style, they often display a measure of subtlety and finesse. Through a decade of Private Reserve bottlings, the wines have been inconsistent, but perhaps that is more a result of vintage variation than of stylistic changes.

Beringer has been producing Chardonnay since 1971, and in the early years the late Myron Nightingale, then winemaster, pulled out all the stops for experimentation, testing vineyard sites as far south as Santa Barbara, fiddling with barrel fermentation and malolactic fermentation, and making vineyard-specific wines. His colleague and successor Ed Sbragia has narrowed the focus and style, although on occasions he strays from the formula, most notably in 1987 when too much spicy Muscat-like flavor dominated the wine. If you taste the 1984 through 1988 vintages and toss out 1987, you will find a very steady line of rich, ripe, intense, complex Chardonnays that can age well for five to six years, maybe longer. The best of this group is the 1986. Before 1984, the wines showed very well on release, but with the exception of the 1981, which is aging quite well, they are now declining and past their primes. Further back, a 1974 from Nightingale's Santa Barbara experiments ranks as one of the finest 1974s I have ever tasted.

Beringer is one of California's oldest wineries, founded in 1876. Since 1971 the winery has been owned by Nestlé and the Labruyère family of Mâcon, France, and it has made a dramatic comeback from some tough times in the 1960s. With 710 acres of Chardonnay vines and annual production of more than 100,000 cases of Napa Valley Chardonnay, Beringer is one of the big players in ultrapremium Chardonnay. The Napa Valley bottling is often very good, rich, fruity and capable of improving in the bottle, although in the past four or five vintages the quality has dropped a bit, perhaps as a result of increased production. At any rate, the winery seems intent on keeping it stylistically different from the Private Reserve, as it should be. Beringer makes about 8,000 cases of Private Reserve. Its key Chardonnay vineyards, including Gamble Ranch, are in the Yountville area.

TASTING NOTES

BERINGER VINEYARDS, Private Reserve, Napa Valley

1988 BERINGER VINEYARDS PRIVATE RESERVE: Very ripe, rich and open, with fine depth and intensity, showing very good balance and plenty of fig, melon and pear flavors that are fresh, young and lively, although the finish loses some of its focus. Could use a year in the bottle. Last tasted: 4/90. Drink 1992-1996. 14,665 cases produced. Release: $19. Current: $19. **87**

1987 BERINGER VINEYARDS PRIVATE RESERVE: A curious Chardonnay, with more spicy, sweet Gewürztraminer and Riesling flavors than pure fig and pear, but it is pleasant. The grape, apple and melon flavors are very ripe and full, but it is decidedly different. Last tasted: 4/90. Drink 1991-1993. 12,159 cases produced. Release: $17. Current: $19. **79**

1986 BERINGER VINEYARDS PRIVATE RESERVE: The best of the current Beringer Private Reserve bottlings, remarkably rich, elegant and concentrated, with tiers of honey, pear and melon flavors and toasty, buttery oak notes that are deftly balanced and sharply focused. The finish echoes fruit and oak with fine length. Last tasted: 4/90. Drink 1991-1995. 6,747 cases produced. Release: $16. Current: $22. **90**

1985 BERINGER VINEYARDS PRIVATE RESERVE: Ripe, rich and oaky, with toasty vanilla flavors complementing the pear, lemon, honey and spice notes. Balanced, but this is a deep, high-extract wine that is best consumed soon. Last tasted: 4/90. Drink 1991-1994. 4,096 cases produced. Release: $15. Current: $24. **86**

1984 BERINGER VINEYARDS PRIVATE RESERVE: Rich, ripe and toasty, with intense, complex pear, honey, melon and spice flavors that are fully developed and aging gracefully. Plenty of acidity sustains the flavors on the finish, which is long and buttery. Last tasted: 4/90. Drink 1991-1994. 4,102 cases produced. Release: $15. Current: $24. **88**

1983 BERINGER VINEYARDS PRIVATE RESERVE: Tart, earthy and gamy, aging well, but the flavors are wide of the mark. Plenty of toasty oak underneath, with hints of pear and nutmeg. Last tasted: 4/90. Drink 1991-1993. 7,445 cases produced. Release: $15. Current: $24. **76**

1982 BERINGER VINEYARDS PRIVATE RESERVE: Mature, with tart, subdued flavors that display more oak than fruit, although hints of honey and pear peek through on the finish. Last tasted: 4/90. Drink 1991-1993. 7,077 cases produced. Release: $15. Current: $22. **74**

1981 BERINGER VINEYARDS PRIVATE RESERVE: Youthful in color but mature in flavor, with complex, moderately intense pear and spice flavors that finish with buttery oak and a touch of nutmeg. Balanced and holding, but past its prime. Last tasted: 4/90. Drink 1991-1993. 4,784 cases produced. Release: $15. Current: $28. **86**

Beringer.
1988
NAPA VALLEY
CHARDONNAY
ESTATE · BOTTLED

Winemaster Edward Sbragia produced this Private Reserve Chardonnay exclusively from Chardonnay grapes grown on our Estate Vineyards located in the cool southern end of the Napa Valley. The grapes from these cool microclimates are known for their excellent balance of flavor and acidity. Grown, Produced and Bottled by Beringer Vineyards, St. Helena, Napa Valley, California.

ESTATE BOTTLED

Beringer

1986

Napa Valley

Chardonnay

This private reserve Chardonnay was produced exclusively from Chardonnay grapes grown on the Beringer Estate Vineyards. The grapes were picked at 24.4° Brix, 1.10gm/100ml total acid. The wine was aged for seven months in Limousin and Nevers Oak barrels. Grown, produced and bottled by Beringer Vineyards, St. Helena, Napa Valley, California.

Alcohol is 13.8% by volume

1980 BERINGER VINEYARDS PRIVATE RESERVE: A full-blown, ripe, alcoholic wine that drank well on release and for the first few years of its life, but is now dropping fruit, and oak is the dominant flavor. Last tasted: 4/90. Drink 1991-1992. 4,576 cases produced. Release: $15. Current: $25. **75**

1979 BERINGER VINEYARDS PRIVATE RESERVE: Fully mature and past its prime, rich and earthy, with honey and gamy aromas; but the flavors are dry and fading despite good acidity. Drink up. Last tasted: 4/90. Drink 1991-1992. 3,228 cases produced. Release: $14. Current: $25. **78**

1978 BERINGER VINEYARDS PRIVATE RESERVE: While this wine was rich and complex on release, it is now quite mature and honeyed, well past its prime. Last tasted: 4/90. Drink 1991-1992. 1,878 cases produced. Release: $12. Current: $15. **70**

1974 BERINGER VINEYARDS CENTENNIAL CASK SELECTION: Mature, dried out, barely hanging on. Last tasted: 4/90. Drink 1991-1992. 1,000 cases produced. Release: $5. Current: $40. **70**

1974 BERINGER VINEYARDS SANTA BARBARA COUNTY: Holding up well, with pretty honey, pear and melon flavors that are still quite fresh and lively, finishing with crisp lemony acidity, complexity and harmony of flavors. Last tasted: 4/90. Drink 1991-1993. 1,000 cases produced. Release: $5. Current: $45. **88**

BOUCHAINE VINEYARDS
Estate Reserve, Carneros
Carneros

CLASSIFICATION:

Estate Reserve: **FOURTH GROWTH**

Carneros: **FIFTH GROWTH**

COLLECTIBILITY RATING: *Not rated*

BEST VINTAGES:

Estate Reserve: 1988, 1986

Carneros: 1985, 1988, 1984

Napa Valley: 1986, 1985

Bouchaine Vineyards in Carneros began as Chateau Bouchaine amidst high hopes and lofty ambitions. It was founded in 1981 by four investors — Gerret Copeland, an heir to the Du Pont estate, Richard Sutton, an attorney in Wilmington, Del.; Austin Kiplinger, publisher of the Kiplinger Washington newsletters and *Changing Times* magazine; and David Pollack, a Du Pont executive. Today Copeland owns 85 percent interest, and Pollack, a former general partner, is no longer affiliated with the winery.

Chateau Bouchaine hired Chateau Montelena's Jerry Luper as winemaker and made him a limited partner, with the goal of producing Burgundy-style Chardonnays and Pinot Noirs in the cool climate of Carneros. While some of the early Bouchaine Chardonnays made by Luper from 1982 to 1985 were very good on release, overall they were inconsistent, which was not surprising since they came from disparate vineyard sources and bore appellations ranging from Alexander Valley to Winery Lake.

A reorganization and Luper's departure to Rutherford Hill in 1986 led to the beginning of John Montero's regime and a decision to concentrate primarily on Chardonnay and less on Pinot Noir. With Chardonnay, the focus is now on Carneros, including Bouchaine's 25-acre vineyard near the winery. Several of the older Bouchaines, including the 1982 Alexander Valley and 1984 Winery Lake, are less inspiring today, although the 1985 and 1986 Napa Valley bottlings have aged very well and are impressive for their concentration of flavor and depth. The Carneros wines, including the Estate Reserve, have also shown steady improvement, particularly the string of wines from 1984 to 1988. Bouchaine's wines undergo partial malolactic fermentation and

AT A GLANCE
BOUCHAINE VINEYARDS
1075 Buchli Station Road
Napa, CA 94558
(707) 252-9065

Owners: Gerret Copeland, Austin Kiplinger, Richard Sutton

Winemaker: John Montero (4 years)

Founded: 1981

First Chardonnay vintage: 1982
Estate Reserve: 1986
Carneros: 1983

Chardonnay production: 9,000 cases
Estate Reserve: 1,600 cases
Carneros: 7,400 cases

Chardonnay acres owned: 25

Average age of vines: 8 years

Average wine makeup: Carneros (100%)

Time in oak: 9 months

Type of oak: French (Burgundian)

Oak age: new to 4 years old

Winemaking notes:
Barrel fermentation: 90%
Malolactic fermentation: 15% to 20%
Lees aging: 100% (9 months)

90 percent of the juice is barrel fermented and aged on the lees in a mixture of new and old Burgundian oak.

TASTING NOTES

BOUCHAINE VINEYARDS, Estate Reserve, Carneros

1988 BOUCHAINE VINEYARDS ESTATE RESERVE: A shade richer and more complex than the 1988 Carneros bottling, it is also smoother and creamier, with layers of vanilla, pear and melon flavors. Well balanced, with good depth and a full, lingering finish. Complex. Last tasted: 6/90. Drink 1993-1998. 1,600 cases produced. Not released. **88**

1987 BOUCHAINE VINEYARDS ESTATE RESERVE: Earthy, rich and buttery, with pear, lemon and spice flavors that are elegant and well balanced, offering moderate depth and complexity. Altogether very attractive in a subtle, reined-in style. Last tasted: 2/90. Drink 1991-1995. 1,600 cases produced. Release: $19. Current: $19. **86**

1986 BOUCHAINE VINEYARDS ESTATE RESERVE: True to the Bouchaine style of elegance and finesse, this wine is rich yet elegant, with layers of spice, pear and pineapple that offer depth of flavor without weight. Last tasted: 2/90. Drink 1991-1995. 1,500 cases produced. Release: $19. Current: $19. **88**

BOUCHAINE VINEYARDS, Carneros

1988 BOUCHAINE VINEYARDS CARNEROS: Young, rich and complex, with crisp melon, apple and spicy Muscat flavors that are moderately intense and concentrated, well balanced and tasty. Still a bit austere, best in two to four years. Last tasted: 6/90. Drink 1993-1997. 8,400 cases produced. Release: $15. Current: $15. **85**

1987 BOUCHAINE VINEYARDS CARNEROS: Ripe and fruity, with pretty, clean peach, spice and vanilla flavors that display elegance and balance and spicy nutmeg nuances on the finish. Pleasant and well made but not as sharply focused or intense as it could be. Last tasted: 2/90. Drink 1991-1994. 7,400 cases produced. Release: $14. Current: $14. **83**

1985 BOUCHAINE VINEYARDS CARNEROS: At its peak, offering elegance, finesse and delicacy, with subtle but crisp lemon, pear and spicy oak flavors, all combining to give a sense of complexity and character. Last tasted: 2/90. Drink 1991-1993. 2,250 cases produced. Release: $15. Current: $20. **87**

1984 BOUCHAINE VINEYARDS CARNEROS: Clean, elegant, fruity and balanced, with attractive pear, spice and melon flavors of moderate depth and intensity. Delicate and complex, with a pretty aftertaste. Last tasted: 2/90. Drink 1991-1993. 3,400 cases produced. Release: $14. Current: $20. **85**

1983 BOUCHAINE VINEYARDS CARNEROS: Ripe and oily, holding but not gaining, displaying exotic pineapple aromas, but less fruit is evident on the palate. Last tasted: 2/90. Drink 1991-1993. 2,200 cases produced. Release: $14. Current: $20. **77**

BOUCHAINE VINEYARDS, Various bottlings

1986 BOUCHAINE VINEYARDS NAPA VALLEY: Riper than the Carneros bottling, with rich pineapple, toast and subtle pear flavors that are lean and elegant, neatly tapered on the finish. Elegantly balanced. Last tasted: 2/90. Drink 1991-1995. 7,000 cases produced. Release: $13. Current: $17. **88**

1985 BOUCHAINE VINEYARDS NAPA VALLEY: Bold, ripe and assertive, yet maintaining a sense of elegance and finesse. Its flavors are full and rich, with pear, peach, vanilla and nutmeg nuances carrying through on the finish. Last tasted: 2/90. Drink 1991-1994. 10,100 cases produced. Release: $13. Current: $17. **87**

1984 BOUCHAINE VINEYARDS WINERY LAKE: Ripe, rich, oily and vegetal, with very ripe pineapple flavors that turn dense and earthy on the finish. Drinkable but unexciting. Last tasted: 2/90. Drink 1991. 2,200 cases produced. Release: $22. Current: $22. **71**

1984 BOUCHAINE VINEYARDS NAPA VALLEY: Ripe and earthy, slightly bitter and cloying, past its prime and turning oxidized. Marginally drinkable. Last tasted: 2/90. Best to avoid. 9,400 cases produced. Release: $12.50. Current: $15. **66**

1983 BOUCHAINE VINEYARDS NAPA VALLEY: Riper and fuller than the Carneros bottling, with butterscotch and honey flavors, but it is awkward and simple on the finish. Last tasted: 2/90. Drink 1991-1992. 10,000 cases produced. Release: $12.50. Current: $18. **75**

1982 BOUCHAINE VINEYARDS ALEXANDER VALLEY: Tart and crisp, still holding, but most of the fruit has faded, leaving it lemony and Chablis-like. Well balanced and likable, but not exciting. Last tasted: 2/90. Drink 1991-1993. 2,000 cases produced. Release: $14. Current: $18. **79**

BOUCHAINE

1986
CHARDONNAY
NAPA VALLEY

PRODUCED & BOTTLED BY BOUCHAINE VINEYARDS
LOS CARNEROS, NAPA, CALIFORNIA, U.S.A.
ALC. 13% BY VOL. • CONTAINS SULFITES

BUENA VISTA WINERY
Private Reserve, Carneros

CLASSIFICATION: *FIFTH GROWTH*
COLLECTIBILITY RATING: *Not rated*
BEST VINTAGES: *1986, 1988, 1985*

D espite extensive Chardonnay holdings in Carneros, Buena Vista has struggled more with Chardonnay than with any other major varietal it produces. Perhaps it is more than a coincidence that the winery began to improve its Chardonnays with the arrival of winemaker Jill Davis in 1983. While earlier vintages were often dense, weedy and vegetal, since 1983 the Private Reserve Chardonnays in particular have shown steady improvement. The 1983, for instance, is holding up well, showing a transition from fresh pear and melon flavors to more mature honey flavors. The 1984 is dense and pungent, not aging well, but the 1985 Reserve combines richness with delicacy. The 1986 is the finest Buena Vista I've tasted — a broad, rich, complex wine that has a tremendous burst of fruit on the finish. The 1987 is more austere, rather typical of that vintage, and may prove more generous with time. The 1988 Reserve is also intense and high in acidity, a wine that will benefit from two to three years of cellaring.

Buena Vista makes about 60,000 cases a year of its regular Chardonnay, and it too has shown considerable improvement in the past few vintages. Buena Vista, owned and operated by the Racke family of West Germany since 1979, has 238 acres of Chardonnay vineyards and a commitment to high quality from its young staff. It is reassuring to taste greater complexity and richness in the newer Private Reserve Chardonnays. The older Buena Vista Chardonnays, which date to 1965, were never very impressive on release and I have not tasted them recently. Based on my notes of older vintages dating to 1977, the wines before 1983 are not worth looking for.

AT A GLANCE
BUENA VISTA WINERY
1800 Old Winery Road
Sonoma, CA 95476
(707) 252-7117

Owner: A. Racke Co., West Germany

Winemaker: Jill Davis (7 years)

Founded: 1857; re-established: 1943

First Chardonnay vintage: 1965
Private Reserve: 1983

Chardonnay production: 65,000 cases
Private Reserve: 6,000

Chardonnay acres owned: 238

Average age of vines: 10 years

Average wine makeup: Carneros, Sonoma Valley (100%)

Time in oak: 4 to 5 months

Type of oak: French (Limousin, Nevers)

Oak age: new to 4 years old (20% each)

Winemaking notes:
Barrel fermentation: 10%
Malolactic fermentation: 20%
Lees aging: 50% (3 months)

TASTING NOTES

BUENA VISTA WINERY, Private Reserve, Carneros

1988 BUENA VISTA WINERY PRIVATE RESERVE: Intense, with bracing acidity and austere, sharply defined pear, lemon and apple

flavors that are crisp and concentrated. This is a young, ripe, balanced wine that needs another two to three years for the fruit to soften. Last tasted: 6/90. Drink 1993-1999. 6,150 cases produced. Release: $16.50. Current: $17. **86**

1987 BUENA VISTA WINERY PRIVATE RESERVE: Austere, with lean lemon, spice and pear flavors of moderate depth and intensity. Lacks the richness and flavor of the superb 1986, but it is well balanced and tasty. Last tasted: 3/90. Drink 1991-1994. 5,500 cases produced. Release: $16.50. Current: $17. **82**

1986 BUENA VISTA WINERY PRIVATE RESERVE: A considerable improvement over the previous bottlings, a richer, fuller, more complex and flavorful wine, combining ripe pear, melon and pineapple flavors that are elegant and delicate, finishing with a subtle burst of flavor that lingers on the palate. Best yet from Buena Vista. Last tasted: 3/90. Drink 1991-1996. 3,700 cases produced. Release: $16.50. Current: $17. **91**

1985 BUENA VISTA WINERY PRIVATE RESERVE: Clean and correct, offering subtle shadings of ripe pear, toast, butter and honey flavors, a delicate style that is moderately rich and intense, not a blockbuster by any means, but a very well-mannered wine that is aging gracefully. Last tasted: 3/90. Drink 1991-1995. 2,700 cases produced. Release: $16.50. Current: $17. **86**

1984 BUENA VISTA WINERY PRIVATE RESERVE: Very ripe and oily, with pungent vegetal, pear and Botrytis flavors that are dense and clumsy. Not aging very well, best to drink soon. A surprising, difficult vintage for Buena Vista. Last tasted: 6/90. Drink 1991-1992. 3,000 cases produced. Release: $14.50. Current: $15. **75**

1983 BUENA VISTA WINERY PRIVATE RESERVE: This wine from a difficult vintage is aging quite well. It is crisp and lively, with fresh, ripe pear, melon and pineapple flavors and just a hint of honey. Moderate complexity and depth, clean and pleasant on the finish, fully mature but capable of further aging. Last tasted: 3/90. Drink 1991-1994. 1,000 cases produced. Release: $14.50. Current: $18. **84**

BURGESS CELLARS
Triere Vineyard, Napa Valley

CLASSIFICATION: *FOURTH GROWTH*
COLLECTIBILITY RATING: *A*
BEST VINTAGES: *1988, 1985, 1986, 1987*

AT A GLANCE
BURGESS CELLARS
1108 Deer Park Road
St. Helena, CA 94574
(707) 963-4766

Owners: Tom and Linda Burgess

Winemaker: Bill Sorenson (18 years)

Founded: 1972

First Chardonnay vintage: 1973
  Triere Vineyard: 1986

Chardonnay production: 17,800 cases

Chardonnay acres owned: 51

Average age of vines: 14 years

Vineyard location: Yountville,
  Napa Valley

Time in oak: 8 months

Type of oak: French (J. Damy,
  Meursault, Vosges)

Oak age: new to 3 years old
  (25% each)

Winemaking notes:
  Barrel fermentation: 100%
  Malolactic fermentation: 60%
  Lees aging: up to 60%
    (8 months)

Although its wines rarely receive the attention they deserve, Burgess Cellars Chardonnays are typically very well made, rich, intense and complex, and among the most consistently fine Chardonnays produced in Napa Valley. Tom Burgess began making Chardonnay in 1973, one year after he founded his winery in the old Souverain building on Howell Mountain. Winemaker Bill Sorensen, who has presided over winemaking since 1973, is one key to the winery's consistent quality and style.

Burgess has always looked to the cooler parts of Napa Valley for its fruit. In the early years, Winery Lake Vineyard in Carneros was a source of grapes. Since 1986, Burgess' own Triere Vineyard, a 51-acre plot south of Yountville on the western side of the valley, has been its sole source of fruit and a vineyard-designated wine. Grapes from Triere Vineyard, purchased in 1979, have gone into the vintage reserve bottlings. In 1986, Triere replaced the private reserve.

Except for a string of mediocre vintages in the early 1980s, all of the Burgess Cellars Chardonnays have aged well, although some of the wines of the 1970s have faded. The 1973 is still in very good condition, with attractive smoke and butterscotch flavors. The 1974 through 1976 vintages from Winery Lake Vineyard have seen better days, but the 1975 is one of the top two or three wines from that vintage, and is holding up quite well. The 1977 through 1980 vintages reveal bolder, riper flavors in wines that are declining. The 1981 through 1984 vintages are from a most difficult phase, with 1982 and 1983 aging particularly poorly, as did most wines from those years. Beginning with the 1985 vintage, the Burgess Chardonnays return to form with a string of very fine wines that offer intense, sharply focused flavors, complexity, depth and elegance.

Burgess Chardonnays are barrel fermented and undergo varying degrees of malolactic fermentation with some lees aging. The oak is a mixture of new and old. Oak is almost always evident in the wines' aroma, flavor and texture, but it is not overdone. Production has leveled off at 18,000 cases, and with the most recent vintages, these wines look like good bets to cellar for four to six years.

TASTING NOTES

BURGESS CELLARS, Triere Vineyard, Napa Valley

1988 BURGESS CELLARS TRIERE VINEYARD: Delicious now, with fresh, clean, ripe peach, honey, toast and spice notes that are elegant, complex and well focused. This wine is made in a style that rendered it drinkable on release. Last tasted: 12/89. Drink 1991-1994. 18,000 cases produced. Release: $16. Current: $16. **88**

1987 BURGESS CELLARS TRIERE VINEYARD: Still coming together, showing plenty of oak and not much finesse, although the peach and nectarine flavors are delicate, fresh and clean. Typical of many 1987s, it is lean and understated. Last tasted: 12/89. Drink 1991-1994. 18,000 cases produced. Release: $14.50. Current: $15. **85**

1986 BURGESS CELLARS TRIERE VINEYARD: With its attractive toasty butterscotch, honey and delicate peach and nectarine flavors, it is at its peak now and should hold well for a year or so before beginning to decline. It is an elegant wine that shows fine balance with a measure of restraint. Last tasted: 12/89. Drink 1991-1994. 17,000 cases produced. Release: $14. Current: $16. **87**

BURGESS CELLARS, Various bottlings

1985 BURGESS CELLARS VINTAGE RESERVE: Delicious, fresh, clean and elegant, offering complex layers of pineapple, lemon, honey and toast flavors that are beautifully focused, long and lingering on the finish. A fine 1985 that has improved significantly in the bottle. Last tasted: 12/89. Drink 1990-1995. 17,000 cases produced. Release: $13. Current: $16. **88**

1984 BURGESS CELLARS VINTAGE RESERVE: A shade past its peak but still in good condition, displaying generous ripe, tropical fruit flavors with good depth and balance. Best to drink soon. Last tasted: 12/89. Drink 1991-1994. 17,000 cases produced. Release: $13. Current: $17. **79**

1983 BURGESS CELLARS VINTAGE RESERVE: Faded and oxidized, with Botrytis and honey notes. Last tasted: 12/89. Best to avoid. 16,000 cases produced. Release: $12. Current: $14. **69**

1982 BURGESS CELLARS VINTAGE RESERVE: Dull and waxy, with oxidized flavors. Much better in its earlier days. Last tasted: 12/89. Best to avoid. 16,000 cases produced. Release: $12. Current: $12. **68**

1981 BURGESS CELLARS: Fully mature and in decline, barely holding together, offering mature, ripe nectarine and anise flavors that are simple and shallow. Finish is alcoholic. Last tasted: 12/89. Drink 1991-1992. 15,000 cases produced. Release: $11. Current: $16. **74**

1980 BURGESS CELLARS: A big, ripe, rich wine that is in sync with the 1980 vintage, a warm year that produced very ripe, full-bodied,

BURGESS

1988
Napa Valley
Chardonnay

Triere Vineyard

GROWN, PRODUCED AND BOTTLED BY BURGESS CELLARS
ST. HELENA, CALIFORNIA   ALCOHOL 12.9% BY VOLUME

BURGESS
1978
Napa Valley
Chardonnay

Grapes picked from selected vineyards in Sept. and Oct.
with sugar average of 25.0° Brix. Alcohol 13.9% by volume.
Cellared & bottled by Burgess Cellars, St. Helena, California

deeply flavored wines that were best on release. The 1980 is fading now, showing more alcohol and less fruit than in previous years. There is a touch of creamy Chardonnay fruit lingering, but the finish is hot and coarse. Last tasted: 12/89. Drink 1991-1992. 13,000 cases produced. Release: $11. Current: $18. **75**

1979 BURGESS CELLARS: From another warm year, a very ripe and alcoholic wine that still manages to provide enough rich peach, anise and creamy oak flavors to make it attractive. Loses intensity on the finish. Last tasted: 12/89. Drink 1991-1994. 5,500 cases produced. Release: $11. Current: $18. **78**

1978 BURGESS CELLARS: From a hot vintage that produced ripe, alcoholic wines, this wine is typical of the year and style of the late 1970s, full-blown and extremely ripe (13.9 percent alcohol), with mature cream and peach flavors and a biting, alcoholic finish. Past its prime yet holding. Last tasted: 12/89. Drink 1991-1994. 4,200 cases produced. Release: $11. Current: $18. **77**

1977 BURGESS CELLARS: Still in good condition but should be consumed soon. Mature spice and nutmeg flavors and a tasty touch of butterscotch on the finish. Balanced and complex. Last tasted: 12/89. Drink 1991-1992. 4,000 cases produced. Release: $11. Current: $23. **80**

1976 BURGESS CELLARS WINERY LAKE VINEYARD: Past its prime, displaying mature pine aromas, a pronounced mintiness and not much in the way of finesse or character. It is drinkable but not exciting. Last tasted: 12/89. Drink 1991. 1,300 cases produced. Release: $10. Current: $20. **70**

1975 BURGESS CELLARS WINERY LAKE VINEYARD: A ripe, rich, unctuous wine with fully developed butterscotch, anise, peach and nectarine flavors that are very attractive and complex. A big, full-blown style that has aged well. Last tasted: 12/89. Drink 1991-1994. 770 cases produced. Release: $9. Current: $28. **84**

1974 BURGESS CELLARS WINERY LAKE VINEYARD: A mature and oxidized wine from a very ripe year, it remains palatable, although its best years are behind it. The caramel and citrus flavors fade on the finish. Last tasted: 12/89. Drink 1991. 700 cases produced. Release: $6. Current: $25. **79**

1973 BURGESS CELLARS: Mature color, with smoke and butterscotch aromas and flavors, past its prime but in fine condition considering its age. The crisp acidity carries the flavors, finishing with a touch of sweet fruit and anise. Last tasted: 12/89. Drink 1991-1993. 400 cases produced. Release: $6. Current: $30. **85**

CHALONE VINEYARD

Reserve
Estate

CLASSIFICATION: *FIRST GROWTH*

COLLECTIBILITY RATING: *AAA*

BEST VINTAGES:

Reserve: 1985, 1980, 1982, 1988, 1987, 1983

Estate: 1982, 1986, 1981, 1980, 1988, 1983

Chalone Vineyard, a single-vineyard appellation in the Gavilan Mountains near Pinnacles National Monument, is one of the world's great Chardonnay outposts. These enormously rich, deeply concentrated, wonderfully complex wines are among the most uniquely dramatic wines produced anywhere. Since 1965, when Richard Graff borrowed money from his mother to buy this isolated property, Chalone has been producing toasty, buttery, monumental Chardonnays from its vineyard at 1,800 feet among the rugged mountains east of Soledad. This remote estate, now part of the Chalone Inc. family of wineries (see Edna Valley and Acacia), deserves to be included among the legendary California Chardonnay pioneers such as Stony Hill and Hanzell. Through Graff's winemaking techniques, inspired by Burgundy, Chalone's Chardonnays are as distinctive as any in the world.

Chalone's Chardonnays, Pinot Blancs, Chenin Blancs and Pinot Noirs owe much of their character to the vineyards' unique microclimate. The soil is sparse, with substantial limestone deposits. The climate is arid; 12 to 15 inches of rainfall a year is normal, compared to about 35 inches in Napa Valley. It is typically warm during the days and cool at night, which allows grapes to ripen at an even pace. There are times when you can taste the flinty, earthy limestone flavors in a young Chalone Chardonnay — the truest expression of *goût de terroir* (taste of the soil).

A Frenchman named Tamm planted the first vineyard in the craggy hillside at the turn of the century. He liked the soil because it reminded him of Champagne. The vineyard changed ownership several times and was expanded before Graff purchased it, but all along it was a spartan operation, run out of an old converted chicken coop, 11 feet by 40 feet, with enough room for about 50 barrels. A second-hand generator provided electricity and there was no telephone line to the winery until the 1980s. Even now it is an arduous trip by car to the winery. In the early 1970s, Philip Woodward, now president of

AT A GLANCE

CHALONE VINEYARD
P.O. Box 855
Soledad, CA 93960
(415) 546-7755

Owner: Chalone Inc.

Winemaker: Michael Michaud (7 years)

Founded: 1965

First Chardonnay vintage: 1965
  Chalone Reserve: 1980

Chardonnay production: 8,500 cases
  Chalone Reserve: 500 cases
  Estate: 8,000 cases

Chardonnay acres owned: 110

Average age of vines:
  Chalone Reserve: 40 years
  Estate: 15 years

Average wine makeup: Chalone (100%)

Time in oak: 9 months

Type of oak: French

Oak age:
  Chalone Reserve: new (100%)
  Estate: new to 2 years old (33% each)

Winemaking notes:
  Barrel fermentation: 100%
  Malolactic fermentation: 100%
  Lees aging:
    Chalone Reserve: 100% (7 months)
    Estate: 100% (5 months)

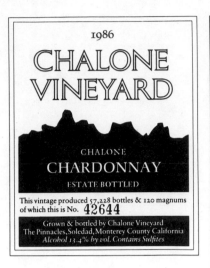

Chalone Inc., and his brother-in-law John McQuown, a Wells Fargo Bank executive, became partners with Graff and helped raise capital to plant more vines, beginning in 1973.

When he bought Chalone, named after the Indian tribe, Graff moved to a small, rustic house near the winery and lived on the estate. Graff studied winemaking at the University of California at Davis, and a visit to Burgundy exposed him to Burgundian vinification techniques with Chardonnay and Pinot Noir. He became convinced that techniques like barrel fermentation, malolactic fermentation and extended lees aging were ideally suited to the style of wines he wanted to make.

Chalone harvests its Chardonnay at optimum ripeness. It then avoids skin contact during fermentation, as did most California Chardonnay makers in California in the 1960s and 1970s. The wine goes directly into barrels for fermentation and is aged on its lees, which are stirred regularly. The wine undergoes malolactic fermentation in the barrel. Because the grapes are picked so ripe, they contain the fullest expression of Chardonnay flavor, and while they are often high in alcohol, they also have the richness and concentration to maintain a proper balance. Chalone's Chardonnay vineyard has grown to 110 acres and yields a sparse 1.5 tons per acre. Low rainfall often further reduces the crop. In 1980, Chalone began producing a Reserve Chardonnay from its oldest vines, a 20-acre section of the vineyard, so wines prior to 1980 came from the old vines. The Reserve is fermented in new oak barrels and is usually toastier than the estate bottling, though not always better.

Because of their explosive fruit, great depth and aging ability, Chalone's Chardonnays rank among the finest wines to collect and cellar. Chardonnays from the 1970s are still holding up very well, but are very hard to find. The best chance to buy these wines is at auction. The winery is sold out. My most recent notes date back to 1979, and through the 1980s the consistently high level of quality and complexity from vintage to vintage is amazing. Production of the Reserve hovers at about 500 cases a year, and the 1980, 1982 and 1985 offer uncommon richness and opulence. The current releases, from 1987 and 1988, are also excellent, although they have yet to mature fully. They are austere and tight, with all the ingredients for greatness. Since Chalone became a public company in 1984, the Reserve wines have been sold almost exclusively to shareholders.

The 1979 Estate bottling, from old vines, is still developing, while the 1980, 1982, 1983, 1986 and 1988 wines are monumental, incredibly thick, rich and hedonistic. Production is about 8,000 cases a year. The 1987 Estate is marred by serious bottle variation, apparently arising from poor cooperage, a problem the winery acknowledges. I have tried the 1987 a dozen times and only once found it satisfactory. All other tastings revealed an earthy, musty bitterness. On that basis, I would not recommend buying it. The 1987 Reserve does not suffer from this problem; it was fermented in new oak.

TASTING NOTES
CHALONE VINEYARD, Chalone Reserve

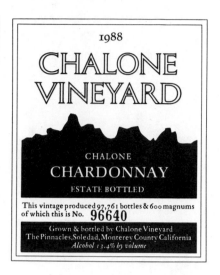

1988 CHALONE VINEYARD RESERVE: The 1988 is young and lively, with hints of smoke, flint, lime, pear and fig flavors that are a bit disjointed now, but all the ingredients are here for an excellent bottle of wine. The fruit has richness, concentration and depth, and should develop more complexity with time in the bottle. Last tasted: 5/90. Drink 1992-2000. 217 cases produced. Not released. **89**

1987 CHALONE VINEYARD RESERVE: While the 1987 regular is flawed, the Reserve is very good, with intense, sharply focused lime, pear and fig flavors that are slowly evolving and developing some depth and complexity. The flavors are balanced, elegant and well proportioned, finishing with a touch of limestone. Last tasted: 5/90. Drink 1992-2000. 727 cases produced. Not released. **87**

1986 CHALONE VINEYARD RESERVE: A touch earthy and flinty but very rich and complete, with ripe apple, pear and fig flavors that are youthful and austere, backed by firm acidity. Well balanced and well proportioned but not quite as complex as Chalone's finest. Last tasted: 5/90. Drink 1991-1995. 379 cases produced. Release: $28. Current: $38. **85**

1985 CHALONE VINEYARD RESERVE: Enormously rich and complex, deep and concentrated, with intense cream, fig, honey, pear and vanilla flavors that spread out and saturate the palate. Wonderful balance and harmony, with flavors that echo on the finish. Despite the intensity and depth of flavor, this is a graceful, elegant wine. Last tasted: 6/90. Drink 1991-1998. 308 cases produced. Release: $28. Current: $42. **94**

1983 CHALONE VINEYARD RESERVE: Complex and elegant, with youthful, vibrant, concentrated pear, honey, melon and spice notes that are backed by firm, intense acidity and a distinct earthy limestone quality that evolves into a mineral flavor on the finish. Drinking at its peak now. Last tasted: 5/90. Drink 1991-1997. 617 cases produced. Release: $25. Current: $45. **87**

1982 CHALONE VINEYARD RESERVE: At first a more elegant, refined Reserve, but with aeration it develops into quite a rich, complex and deeply concentrated wine with distinct pear, lemon, honey and butterscotch flavors. Absolutely wonderful flavors and a long, full finish. Last tasted: 5/90. Drink 1991-1996. 498 cases produced. Release: $25. Current: $48. **93**

1981 CHALONE VINEYARD RESERVE: Distinctive for its rich vanilla and butterscotch flavors, a shade more refined, with pretty pear and melon notes, not quite the breadth, richness or concentration of the 1980, but still quite complete. Finishes with good length. Last tasted: 5/90. Drink 1991-1996. 400 cases produced. Release: $20. Current: $55. **86**

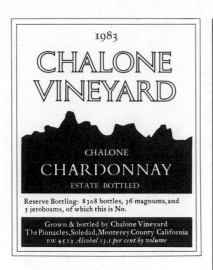

1980 CHALONE VINEYARD RESERVE: Explosively rich and creamy, with a satiny smooth texture and deep, complex and concentrated fig, honey, pear and vanilla flavors that are beautifully proportioned, finishing with great flavor and length and a sense of elegance and grace. Simply fantastic. Last tasted: 5/90. Drink 1991-1997. 166 cases produced. Release: $18. Current: $55. **94**

CHALONE VINEYARD, Estate

1988 CHALONE VINEYARD ESTATE: More forward and fruity now than the Reserve, rich and complex, with firm fig, lemon, pear and spice flavors that are elegant and well defined. Finishes with a smoky, flinty aftertaste. Last tasted: 1/90. Drink 1992-1999. 8,003 cases produced. Release: $22. Current: $27. **90**

1987 CHALONE VINEYARD ESTATE: This appears to be a seriously flawed wine that displays an "off," corky mustiness that goes well beyond earthiness. In a dozen tastings I have only encountered one bottle I thought was satisfactory. The explanation, according to the winery, is had cooperage. Not recommended. Last tasted: 1/90. Best to avoid. 5,442 cases produced. Release: $22. Current: $30. **58**

1986 CHALONE VINEYARD ESTATE: Amazingly delicious, rich, firm and complex, oozing with fresh, concentrated lemon, butterscotch, honey and toasty oak flavors that combine in perfect harmony. One of the top Chalones of the 1980s, just now beginning to show its depth and potential. Should hold up well for another five years or more. Last tasted: 1/90. Drink 1991-1996. 4,768 cases produced. Release: $22. Current: $48. **94**

1985 CHALONE VINEYARD ESTATE: This vintage has consistently been unimpressive in tastings. It is clearly a more subtle, understated style. The fruit is rather simple, with ripe pear and spice notes and hints of earth and mineral, but without the depth and richness one expects in a very good vintage, as 1985 was. Perhaps I am missing something. Last tasted: 4/90. Drink 1991-1994. 3,686 cases produced. Release: $22. Current: $45. **80**

1984 CHALONE VINEYARD ESTATE: Rich and buttery, deep and silky, with ripe pear, spice, lemon and nutmeg notes that offer supple, complex, enticing Chardonnay flavors, well balanced and harmonious, with finesse and elegance. With each sip you find a new flavor. Last tasted: 1/90. Drink 1991-1998. 2,885 cases produced. Release: $18. Current: $45. **88**

1983 CHALONE VINEYARD ESTATE: Not as rich and deep as the stunning 1982, but just as distinctive for its finesse and style. It is considerably more elegant — rich, creamy and smooth on the palate, with crisp, tart citrus, melon, honey and butterscotch flavors of moderate depth and intensity. Last tasted: 1/90. Drink 1991-1998. 6,669 cases produced. Release: $18. Current: $50. **90**

1982 CHALONE VINEYARD ESTATE: A perfect demonstration of how beautifully Chalone Chardonnays age. Simply delicious, rich, smooth and velvety, with sharply defined, complex honey, ginger, spice, butterscotch and melon flavors that glide across the palate, finishing with a long, flavorful aftertaste gathering hints of nutmeg, apple and citrus. Last tasted: 1/90. Drink 1991-1996. 5,125 cases produced. Release: $18. Current: $53. **95**

1981 CHALONE VINEYARD ESTATE: In several tastings the 1981 regular clearly surpasses the 1981 Reserve with its explosive rich, ripe, vibrant pear, honey and spicy fruit flavors. The toasty oaky aromas add complexity and depth, while the texture is smooth and creamy, finishing with a burst of flavor. Wonderful balance, harmony and finesse. Last tasted: 1/90. Drink 1991-1996. 3,545 cases produced. Release: $17. Current: $53. **93**

1980 CHALONE VINEYARD ESTATE: Absolutely delicious, rich, full, supple and complex, with a dazzling array of honey, pear, spice, toast and earth flavors that are silky smooth on the palate and echo on the finish. Amazing intensity and depth of flavor. Last tasted: 1/90. Drink 1991-1995. 3,510 cases produced. Release: $17. Current: $53. **92**

1979 CHALONE VINEYARD ESTATE: One of the most elegant Chalone Chardonnays produced, displaying plenty of flavor and finesse, depth and richness, but it is not as full blown and powerful as the 1980. The flavors are mature and attractive, with toast, honey, pear and spice notes and a satiny texture. Excellent length on the finish. Last tasted: 1/90. Drink 1991-1994. 3,728 cases produced. Release: $14. Current: $55. **89**

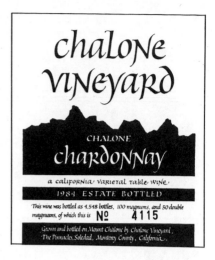

CHAPPELLET VINEYARD

Napa Valley

CLASSIFICATION: *THIRD GROWTH*

COLLECTIBILITY RATING: *AA*

BEST VINTAGES: *1973, 1986, 1977, 1988*

AT A GLANCE

CHAPPELLET VINEYARD
1561 Sage Canyon Road
St. Helena, CA 94574
(707) 963-7136

Owners: Donn and Molly
    Chappellet

Winemaker: Phillip Titus (1 year)

Founded: 1967

First Chardonnay vintage: 1970

Chardonnay production: 4,000 cases

Chardonnay acres owned: 28

Average age of vines: 16 years

Average wine makeup: Napa Valley
    (100%)

Time in oak: 8 months

Type of oak: French

Oak age: new (25%)

Winemaking notes:
    Barrel fermentation: 100%
    Malolactic fermentation:
        10% to 15%
    Lees aging: 100%
        (6 to 8 months)

Chappellet's mountain-grown Chardonnays from Pritchard Hill east of St. Helena are typically firm, austere and slow to develop, yet in good years they age very well. Because of their austerity they are often panned by critics for lacking richness and depth, though over two decades many of the estate-grown Chardonnays have aged exceptionally well. While the Chappellet style may not appeal to everyone, it is consistent from year to year, which is a big plus for consumers who prefer this reined-in style.

Donn and Molly Chappellet founded their winery in 1967, first producing Cabernet Sauvignon in 1968 and then Chardonnay beginning with the 1970 vintage. The vineyard rises 1,700 feet above a narrow fold in the mountains east of the Napa Valley floor facing north.

My recent notes date back to 1973, which was a sensational wine, rich and complex, and quite a drinking experience. The 1974 is showing its age, but the 1975 remains quite complete and delicious. The 1977 is fabulous, still a rich and delicious drink. The 1976 drought-year wine is past its prime and the 1978 and 1979 have also declined, but the 1980 is fully mature and complex. The 1980 is followed by two successful vintages in 1981 and 1982, but the 1983 is a bit thin and not likely to improve. Beginning with the 1984 vintage, Chappellet is back on its mark, and the 1988 is particularly well balanced, and a good candidate for cellaring. For the past decade Cathy Corison was winemaker, however, in 1990 she resigned to make her own brand of Cabernet Sauvignon, and Phillip Titus assumed the position of winemaker. He is familiar with the Chappellet style, having worked at the winery earlier in his career.

TASTING NOTES

CHAPPELLET VINEYARD, Napa Valley

1988 CHAPPELLET VINEYARD: Austere, but displaying a fine sense of harmony and balance, with toasty vanilla aromas and intense but delicate pear, nectarine and melon flavors that are rich and deep. More forward than the 1987, but also more complete. It should age very well for eight to 10 years. Last tasted: 6/90. Drink 1991-1998. 4,500 cases produced. Not released. **89**

1987 CHAPPELLET VINEYARD: A shade less concentrated than the 1986, fresh, tart, lively and elegant, with attractive oak that is supported by lean, crisp apple and pear flavors. Needs three to four years to soften. Last tasted: 6/90. Drink 1993-2000. 3,817 cases produced. Release: $14. Current: $14. **87**

1986 CHAPPELLET VINEYARD: The best Chappellet in years, showing richer, brighter, more concentrated fruit, with all the finesse and elegance of the best previous vintages. The pear, apple, melon and spicy oak flavors offer plenty of depth and complexity, finishing with subtlety and grace. Last tasted: 3/90. Drink 1991-1997. 4,500 cases produced. Release: $14. Current: $14. **90**

1985 CHAPPELLET VINEYARD: A pretty wine with attractive honey and wildflower aromas and rich, smooth, creamy pear, apple, lemon and spice flavors, finishing with complexity and finesse. Last tasted: 3/90. Drink 1991-1996. 3,300 cases produced. Release: $12.50. Current: $15. **87**

1984 CHAPPELLET VINEYARD: Very youthful, tight and austere, with rich honey, pear, vanilla and spice flavors that are complex and intriguing. The finish is long and clean. Well made, balanced, drinking at its peak. Last tasted: 3/90. Drink 1991-1995. 4,500 cases produced. Release: $12. Current: $20. **87**

1983 CHAPPELLET VINEYARD: Still lean and austere, tightly knit, with subtle pear, lemon and spicy oak flavors but also some chalky notes that detract from the quality. Last tasted: 3/90. Drink 1991. 6,000 cases produced. Release: $12. Current: $18. **79**

1982 CHAPPELLET VINEYARD: Very successful, still displaying rich, complex pear, toast and earth flavors that are concentrated and long on the palate. Last tasted: 3/90. Drink 1991-1993. 7,200 cases produced. Release: $12.50. Current: $20. **85**

1981 CHAPPELLET VINEYARD: Still quite austere and earthy, with lemon, pear and mineral flavors that offer their own kind of complexities. Holding its own. Last tasted: 3/90. Drink 1991. 3,947 cases produced. Release: $14. Current: $22. **80**

1980 CHAPPELLET VINEYARD: Fully mature and very distinctive, with ripe, rich honey, toast and pear flavors that are still quite opulent and complex as they unfold on the palate. Last tasted: 3/90. Drink 1991-1992. 4,000 cases produced. Release: $14. Current: $25. **84**

1979 CHAPPELLET VINEYARD: This wine has seen better days, but is still enjoyable for its ripe pear, honey and apple flavors that get simple on the finish, but this wine would be a good match for a cheese plate. Last tasted: 3/90. Drink 1991. 3,000 cases produced. Release: $12. Current: $30. **79**

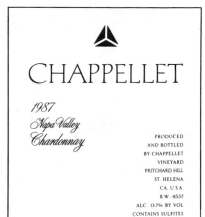

CHAPPELLET
VINEYARD
1977
Napa Valley
CHARDONNAY

PRODUCED AND BOTTLED BY CHAPPELLET VINEYARD
PRITCHARD HILL, ST. HELENA, CALIFORNIA   ALCOHOL 13½% BY VOLUME

1978 CHAPPELLET VINEYARD: Very ripe, deep yellow-gold, well past its prime but still echoing ripe fruit, honey, pineapple and butter flavors. Last tasted: 3/90. Drink 1991. 1,500 cases produced. Release: $11.75. Current: $40. **76**

1977 CHAPPELLET VINEYARD: One of the top 1977s, aging very well, with lively acidity and pear, honey and vanilla flavors that are complex and elegant, with delicacy and finesse on the finish. With its fresh fruit and crisp acidity, it still has a long life ahead. Last tasted: 6/90. Drink 1991-1998. 1,500 cases produced. Release: $11.75. Current: $40. **90**

1976 CHAPPELLET VINEYARD: Deep in color, with very ripe and oily pear and butter flavors. Past its prime. Last tasted: 3/90. Drink 1991. 1,000 cases produced. Release: $9.75. Current: $30. **71**

1975 CHAPPELLET VINEYARD: Still offering mature honey, pear, nutmeg and butterscotch flavors, but its best days are behind. Last tasted: 3/90. Drink 1991. 800 cases produced. Release: $6.75. Current: $40. **82**

1974 CHAPPELLET VINEYARD: Not quite in the class of the 1973, fully mature, with lemon and earth flavors that are now somewhat dull and fading. Last tasted: 3/90. Drink 1991. 600 cases produced. Release: $6.75. Current: $45. **72**

1973 CHAPPELLET VINEYARD: Still in superb condition, full-bodied, rich and complex, with mature honey, melon, pear and spicy apple flavors that are amazingly fresh and lively. If you have a bottle you're in for a treat. Last tasted: 3/90. Drink 1991-1994. 400 cases produced. Release: $6.75. Current: $50. **91**

CHATEAU MONTELENA WINERY

Alexander Valley
Napa Valley

CLASSIFICATION:
  Alexander Valley: FIRST GROWTH
  Napa Valley: THIRD GROWTH
COLLECTIBILITY RATING:
  Alexander Valley: AAA
  Napa Valley: A
BEST VINTAGES:
  Alexander Valley: 1982, 1988, 1986, 1985, 1981, 1984

  Napa Valley: 1988, 1986, 1985, 1984, 1981

  Napa and Alexander Valleys: 1972, 1973

AT A GLANCE
**CHATEAU MONTELENA
  WINERY**
1429 Tubbs Lane
Calistoga, CA 94515
(707) 942-5105

Owner: Montelena Associates.
  James Barrett, general partner

Winemaker: Bo Barrett (8 years)

Founded: 1882; re-established: 1972

First Chardonnay vintage: 1972
  Napa Valley: 1975
  Alexander Valley: 1981

Chardonnay production: 18,000 cases
  Napa Valley: 12,500 cases
  Alexander Valley: 5,500 cases

Chardonnay acres owned: 15

Average age of vines: 9 years

Average wine makeup:
  Napa Valley: Napa, Napa Valley
  (95%); Calistoga, Napa Valley
  (5%)
  Alexander Valley: Alexander
  Valley (100%)

Time in oak: 6 months

Type of oak: French (Limousin)

Oak age: new (5% to 7%) and
  5 years old

Winemaking notes:
  Barrel fermentation: none
  Malolactic fermentation: none
  Lees aging: none

With the exceptions of Stony Hill and Mayacamas, no one in Napa Valley has been making greater Chardonnays longer and with more consistency than Chateau Montelena. While most California Chardonnays reach their peaks in the first year or two after their release, then quickly decline, Chateau Montelenas typically need four or five years in the bottle to reveal their richness, depth and complexities. Often on release the fruit appears to be so subtle and understated that the wine is unimpressive and can be overlooked. But don't be fooled. These wines age on and on, and in the best years are good candidates for cellaring 10 to 15 years.

Montelena's first vintage, the 1972, a blend of Napa and Alexander valley grapes, was made by Mike Grgich (see Grgich Hills) and remains a stunning wine, one of the greatest ever produced in California. It should age into the next century with ease. The 1973, another blend of Napa and Alexander Valley grapes, is famous for winning top honors in the Paris Tasting of 1976, when it was tasted against a group of top white Burgundies and California Chardonnays. It too remains an amazing wine with great complexity and finesse. While the 1974 Montelena Napa-Alexander bottling is a shade less complex and intriguing than its predecessors, at age 16 it still has plenty of vibrancy and depth. Montelena made its last Napa-Alexander bottling in 1976.

In 1975 Chateau Montelena began producing a Napa Valley Chardonnay, and in 1981 introduced an Alexander Valley bottling. A small portion of the Napa Valley bottling is produced from the winery's 15-acre vineyard in Calistoga, which has a warm climate, with

most of the fruit coming from the Dry Creek area of Napa Valley, northwest of the city of Napa. This area has a cool, mild, breezy climate that is ideally suited for Chardonnay. Montelena has been buying grapes from three Dry Creek growers: John Hanna and Bill Hanna, a father and son who each own 10 acres, and Frank Takahashi, who farms 15 acres. The Napa Valley Chardonnays tend to be a shade leaner and richer than those grown in Alexander Valley at the Gauer Estate, which tend to be lusher and fruitier but just as ageworthy. Despite regional differences, which are quite apparent, both wines are elegant and impeccably balanced, and they develop exceptionally well in the bottle.

Winemaker Bo Barrett, son of general partner James Barrett, attributes Montelena's success with Chardonnay to the intense varietal character of the fruit, and to the winemaking techniques, which are based on the old style of California winemaking as exemplified by the three Chardonnay masters who have presided over Montelena winemaking, beginning with Grgich (1972 to 1975) and continuing with Jerry Luper (1976 to 1981) and Barrett (1982 to the present). Montelena's Chardonnays are not aged on the lees or barrel fermented, nor do they undergo malolactic fermentation. Barrett believes those three techniques prematurely age a wine, perhaps making it more complex and forward on release but robbing it of longer aging potential. Montelena's wines are crushed and fermented in stainless steel tanks before being aged six months in mostly five-year-old oak barrels, which are fairly neutral in flavor. Five percent to 7 percent of the oak is new. This lack of manipulation produces wines that are slow to evolve yet retain their fruitiness for more than a decade.

Both the 1975 and 1977 Napa Valley bottlings are aging quite well, while the 1976, 1978, 1979 and 1980 are declining, and in my view are the weakest Montelena Chardonnays. Beginning with 1981 and continuing through 1986, the wines returned to earlier form and are still tightly reined in, perhaps not as dramatic as the 1972 or 1973 bottlings, but still very fine wines that have not yet peaked. The 1987 is marred by a sulfur quality and is considered a failure by the winery. The 1988 Napa Valley is a young, rich, intensely fruity wine that will need until 1993 to begin opening. The Alexander Valley wines from 1981 to 1988 have been more than equal to Napa Valley in nearly every respect. The 1981, 1982, 1984, 1985, 1986 and 1988 are simply delicious wines that any serious collector should consider for his cellar. Collecting both bottlings provides a fascinating comparison between Napa Valley and Alexander Valley Chardonnays from vintage to vintage.

TASTING NOTES

CHATEAU MONTELENA WINERY, Alexander Valley

1988 CHATEAU MONTELENA WINERY ALEXANDER VALLEY: Remarkably rich and forward, offering layers of ripe, intense, supple apple, melon, pear and fig flavors that are elegant and sharply defined. Wonderful balance, long and full on the finish, this wine promises to be one of the finest Montelenas to date. Last tasted: 8/90. Drink 1992-2000. 3,100 cases produced. Release: $20. Current: $20. **91**

1987 CHATEAU MONTELENA WINERY ALEXANDER VALLEY: Continues the streak of superb Alexander Valley bottlings. It is fresh, clean, elegant and balanced, with pretty floral, pear, melon and spice flavors that are young and intense, finishing with fine length. Best to let this one develop another year or two. Last tasted: 3/90. Drink 1992-1998. 5,400 cases produced. Release: $20. Current: $24. **89**

1986 CHATEAU MONTELENA WINERY ALEXANDER VALLEY: Lush and creamy, rich and elegant, it dances across the palate, with delicate, complex apple, honey, pear and melon flavors, a pretty touch of oak and a long, fruity aftertaste that keeps you coming back for more. Last tasted: 3/90. Drink 1991-1997. 5,700 cases produced. Release: $18. Current: $26. **91**

1985 CHATEAU MONTELENA WINERY ALEXANDER VALLEY: Another highly successful Alexander Valley bottling, remarkably rich and elegant, graced with fresh, ripe, clean honey, pear and butter flavors that glide across the palate, echoing fruit along the way. Youthful and concentrated yet elegant and full of finesse. Last tasted: 3/90. Drink 1991-1997. 8,600 cases produced. Release: $16. Current: $28. **91**

1984 CHATEAU MONTELENA WINERY ALEXANDER VALLEY: Refreshingly fruity, crisp and lively, very ripe and complex, with tiers of fresh citrus, tangerine, peach and spicy apple flavors that are youthful and vibrant. At its peak now, it is elegant and well balanced, finishing with pretty fruit notes. Last tasted: 3/90. Drink 1991-1997. 5,600 cases produced. Release: $16. Current: $32. **90**

1983 CHATEAU MONTELENA WINERY ALEXANDER VALLEY: A tight, well-structured wine with pretty flavors, yet lacking the intense fruit flavors of other Alexander Valley bottlings. The pear, melon and spice notes are attractive and well balanced, but by comparison rather simple. Last tasted: 3/90. Drink 1991-1994. 5,600 cases produced. Release: $14. Current: $32. **84**

1982 CHATEAU MONTELENA WINERY ALEXANDER VALLEY: Beautiful, rich, complex honey, pear, toast and spicy oak flavors are tightly knit in a wonderfully elegant, tasty Chardonnay. Excellent depth and length, fine balance and fruit galore, one of the top 1982s. Last tasted: 3/90. Drink 1991-1996. 5,800 cases produced. Release: $14. Current: $36. **92**

1981 CHATEAU MONTELENA WINERY ALEXANDER VALLEY: Rich, clean and elegant, with intense pineapple, pear, apple and citrus flavors that echo tangerine and nectarine notes. Well balanced, sharply focused and aging quite well, this wine has a long, lingering finish that keeps you coming back for more. Last tasted: 3/90. Drink 1991-1997. 2,600 cases produced. Release: $14. Current: $36. **91**

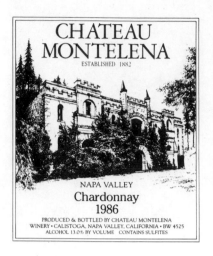

NAPA VALLEY
Chardonnay
1986
PRODUCED & BOTTLED BY CHATEAU MONTELENA
WINERY · CALISTOGA, NAPA VALLEY, CALIFORNIA · BW 4525
ALCOHOL 13.0% BY VOLUME   CONTAINS SULFITES

CHATEAU MONTELENA WINERY, Napa Valley

1988 CHATEAU MONTELENA WINERY NAPA VALLEY: Tight, firm and tannic, with well-defined pear, honey, melon and citric fruit flavors, but several years from maturity. The texture is coarse and the fruit is blunt, but this is how Montelena's Chardonnays often are in their youth. Best to cellar another three to four years. By then it may move up a notch or two. Drink 1993-2000. Last tasted: 3/90. 13,200 cases produced. Release: $20. Current: $20. **88**

1987 CHATEAU MONTELENA WINERY NAPA VALLEY: Sharp and tart, with sulfur flavors, an anomaly in the Chateau Montelena lineup. In eight tastings this wine has consistently displayed this flaw; with time the sulfur may dissipate, but for the time being it throws an unpleasant aroma and flavor. Last tasted: 3/90. Best to avoid. 12,500 cases produced. Release: $20. Current: $25. **68**

1986 CHATEAU MONTELENA WINERY NAPA VALLEY: Rivals the 1985 in quality, richer and more concentrated than the Alexander Valley bottling, showing more oak, but it is also very well balanced, with sharply focused pear and melon flavors lingering on the finish. Last tasted: 3/90. Drink 1991-1996. 12,800 cases produced. Release: $18. Current: $25. **91**

1985 CHATEAU MONTELENA WINERY NAPA VALLEY: Captures more concentrated, rich, ripe fruit flavors than earlier bottlings. It is less oaky and shows more finesse and elegance. The apple, pear and spice flavors play off each other. Last tasted: 3/90. Drink 1991-1998. 9,000 cases produced. Release: $18. Current: $25. **90**

1984 CHATEAU MONTELENA WINERY NAPA VALLEY: Firmer and more structured than the 1984 Alexander Valley, and showing a bit more wood, but consistent with the Napa Valley style. The flavors are more reined in, but finish with pretty peach, pear, melon and smoky oak flavors. Balanced, complex and drinking well now. Last tasted: 3/90. Drink 1991-1995. 8,400 cases produced. Release: $18. Current: $28. **88**

1983 CHATEAU MONTELENA WINERY NAPA VALLEY: Has a rather oaky character that dominates the delicate and pleasing ripe pear and apple flavors. Oak and fruit add harmony on the finish. Last tasted: 3/90. Drink 1991-1994. 6,600 cases produced. Release: $16. Current: $32. **85**

1982 CHATEAU MONTELENA WINERY NAPA VALLEY: Elegant and well balanced, with pear and spicy oak flavors, a clean, well-made wine not in the class of its 1982 Alexander Valley counterpart. On the finish the flavors are weaker and oakier. Best to drink soon. Last tasted: 3/90. Drink 1991-1994. 6,900 cases produced. Release: $16. Current: $32. **85**

1981 CHATEAU MONTELENA WINERY NAPA VALLEY: Shows more honey, pear and butterscotch flavors and it is a shade fuller, but very attractive and well balanced, offering complex Chardonnay flavors and good length. A notch below the 1981 Alexander Valley bottling.

Last tasted: 3/90. Drink 1991-1994. 7,900 cases produced. Release: $16. Current: $32. **88**

1980 CHATEAU MONTELENA WINERY NAPA VALLEY: An earthier wine with complex honey and pear flavors, but it is also very mature and best consumed soon. The flavors are drying out on the finish. Last tasted: 3/90. Drink 1991. 7,000 cases produced. Release: $16. Current: $38. **79**

1979 CHATEAU MONTELENA WINERY NAPA VALLEY: Mature but retaining its elegance. The rich honey, nut and spicy apricot flavors are well balanced and beginning to dry out. Last tasted: 3/90. Drink 1991. 7,800 cases produced. Release: $16. Current: $40. **78**

1978 CHATEAU MONTELENA WINERY NAPA VALLEY: Very mature in color and flavor, with rich honey, oak and pear flavors. Past its prime but still enjoyable. Last tasted: 3/90. Drink 1991. 7,100 cases produced. Release: $15. Current: $45. **77**

1977 CHATEAU MONTELENA WINERY NAPA VALLEY: Fresh, clean floral, honey and spicy pear aromas, very elegant and subtle on the palate, fully mature, a shade past its prime, but very complete and delicate. Best to drink now. Last tasted: 3/90. Drink 1991-1993. 6,000 cases produced. Release: $15. Current: $60. **85**

1976 CHATEAU MONTELENA WINERY NAPA AND ALEXANDER VALLEYS: From a difficult drought year, this wine is holding on but is past its prime and beginning to show more earthy, gluey flavors than fruit. It gains a touch of spice and grapefruit on the finish. Drink up soon. Last tasted: 3/90. Drink 1991. 2,500 cases produced. Release: $11. Current: $50. **77**

1975 CHATEAU MONTELENA WINERY NAPA VALLEY: Fully mature but holding its own, the pine, melon and honey notes are subtle and elegant, enlivened by crisp acidity and a long, lingering aftertaste. Not quite as opulent and rich as its predecessors, but exceptionally well made. Last tasted: 3/90. Drink 1991-1993. 3,300 cases produced. Release: $9. Current: $65. **87**

1974 CHATEAU MONTELENA WINERY NAPA AND ALEXANDER VALLEYS: Another excellent old Montelena, still retaining a vibrant, youthful color, with pretty, fresh, elegant melon, pear, toast and spicy oak flavors that dance on the palate. Best to drink soon, but it has the finesse, grace and flavor to last another five years. One of the top wines of the vintage. Last tasted: 3/90. Drink 1991-1996. 2,200 cases produced. Release: $8. Current: $70. **88**

1973 CHATEAU MONTELENA WINERY NAPA AND ALEXANDER VALLEYS: Amazingly fresh, young and lively, with crisp, well-defined, elegant layers of apple, pear, lemon, spicy oak and nutmeg flavors that sit softly on the palate and have great length. Remarkably complex and well preserved. Last tasted: 3/90. Drink 1991-1998. 2,000 cases produced. Release: $6.50. Current: $100. **93**

CHATEAU MONTELENA
ESTABLISHED 1882

NAPA & ALEXANDER VALLEYS
Chardonnay
1974

PRODUCED AND BOTTLED BY CHATEAU MONTELENA WINERY
CALISTOGA, NAPA VALLEY, CALIFORNIA • ALCOHOL 13.2% BY VOL.

1972 CHATEAU MONTELENA WINERY NAPA AND ALEXANDER VALLEYS: An absolutely sensational first bottling from this esteemed estate, the 1972 has retained an amazingly fruity character, with fresh, ripe honey, melon, apple and pear flavors that are crisp, elegant, rich and lively. Its vibrancy and depth will carry it for another decade. You can't ask for much more from a Chardonnay. One of the greatest ever produced in California. Last tasted: 3/90. Drink 1991-1997. 2,000 cases produced. Release: $6. Current: $110. **95**

CHATEAU ST. JEAN

Robert Young Vineyards, Alexander Valley
Belle Terre Vineyards, Alexander Valley
Frank Johnson Vineyards, Dry Creek Valley
Jimtown Ranch, Alexander Valley

CLASSIFICATION:
Robert Young Vineyards: FIRST GROWTH
Belle Terre Vineyards: SECOND GROWTH
Frank Johnson Vineyards: Not rated
Jimtown Ranch: Not rated

COLLECTIBILITY RATING:
Robert Young Vineyards: AAA
Belle Terre Vineyards: AA
Frank Johnson Vineyards: Not rated
Jimtown Ranch: Not rated

BEST VINTAGES:
Robert Young Vineyards Reserve: 1987, 1985, 1986

Robert Young Vineyards: 1986, 1976, 1988, 1987, 1985

Belle Terre Vineyards: 1985, 1987, 1988, 1986, 1983

Frank Johnson Vineyards: 1986, 1984

Jimtown Ranch: 1988

In the 1970s, as the California Chardonnay boom gained momentum, Chateau St. Jean moved ahead of the pack with a series of vineyard-designated Chardonnays. Other wineries had vineyard-designated wines, but none went to the extremes of St. Jean. At one point, winemaker Richard Arrowood had nine different Chardonnay bottlings from one vintage on the market.

The winery in Kenwood, in Sonoma Valley, was like an experimental lab for Arrowood's research with some of Sonoma County's finest Chardonnay vineyards. Names like Robert Young, Belle Terre, Les Pierres (owned by Sonoma-Cutrer), McCrea Vineyards, Beltane Ranch (Kenwood), Frank Johnson Vineyards, Jimtown Ranch and Wildwood Ranch were regulars in the St. Jean lineup, along with lesser-known names like Gauer Ranch (now Gauer Estate winery), Hunter Farms, Bacigalupi and Riverview Vineyards. The research paid off handsomely as St. Jean (pronounced the American way, "jeen") emerged

AT A GLANCE
CHATEAU ST. JEAN
P.O. Box 293
Kenwood, CA 95452
(707) 833-4134

Owner: Suntory International, Japan
Winemaker: Don Van Staaveren (1 year)
Founded: 1974
First Chardonnay vintage: 1974
 Robert Young Vineyards: 1975
 Robert Young Vineyards Reserve: 1984
 Belle Terre Vineyards: 1975
 Frank Johnson Vineyards: 1979
 Jimtown Ranch: 1980
Chardonnay production: 110,000 cases
 Robert Young Vineyards: 13,500 cases
 Robert Young Vineyards Reserve: 800 cases (in magnum only)
 Belle Terre Vineyards: 6,000 cases
 Frank Johnson Vineyards: 2,200 cases (in some vintages)
 Jimtown Ranch: 1,000 cases (in some vintages)
Chardonnay acres owned: 45
 Robert Young Vineyards: 170
 Belle Terre Vineyards: 46
 Frank Johnson Vineyards: 21
 Jimtown Ranch: 30
Average age of vines: 10 years
Vineyard locations:
 Robert Young Vineyards: Alexander Valley
 Belle Terre Vineyards: Alexander Valley
 Frank Johnson Vineyards: Dry Creek Valley
 Jimtown Ranch: Alexander Valley
Time in oak: 9 months
Type of oak: French
Oak age: new to 3 years old
Winemaking notes:
 Barrel fermentation: 100%
 Malolactic fermentation: none
 Lees aging: variable

as California's best-known Chardonnay specialist. Although there were many fine wines from the assorted vineyards, two in particular, Robert Young Vineyards and Belle Terre Vineyards, both in Alexander Valley, were the mainstays and helped to establish and maintain St. Jean's credentials. They consistently produced excellent fruit, and the resulting wines offered enormous complexity, richness and depth.

Chateau St. Jean was founded in 1974 by Central Valley table-grape growers Robert and Edward Merzoian and Ken Sheffield. The winery was named after Jean Merzoian, Ed's wife. The first person they hired was winemaker Arrowood, who stayed with the winery through the 1989 vintage, before departing to devote his time to his own venture, Arrowood Vineyards & Winery, founded in 1986. In the first St. Jean vintage, 1974, Arrowood produced a trio of Chardonnays: One each from Alexander Valley, Sonoma Valley and Mendocino County. Ironically, the first St. Jean wine to win critical acclaim was a 1974 Riesling. But soon Chardonnay became the star, riding the crest of the white-wine boom.

The early St. Jean Chardonnays typified the California style of the era. The grapes were picked very ripe and given skin contact to extract flavor, resulting in wines that were full-blown, full-bodied, oaky, often alcoholic, and very richly concentrated, sometimes with a barely perceptible trace of residual sugar. They were made in small lots, usually no more than several hundred cases, and they sold extremely well despite being relatively pricey. Critics loved the idiosyncrasies of the different vineyard appellations, but for many consumers keeping track of the wines was confusing. The 1980 vintage, with nine vineyard-designated Chardonnays, was the crescendo of Arrowood's vineyard-designation experimentations.

In 1984, Japanese drinks company Suntory bought St. Jean for $40 million, and the number of vineyard-designated Chardonnays was narrowed to five. Now the winery is concentrating on their two top vineyards, Robert Young and Belle Terre, along with Jimtown Ranch, a Sonoma County bottling, and an occasional offering from Frank Johnson Vineyards and the estate St. Jean Vineyards in Kenwood, which beginning in 1989 will carry an "Estate Bottled" designation.

Both the Robert Young and Belle Terre vineyards are family-owned and farmed. Grower Robert Young and the Dick family, owners of Belle Terre, pay special attention to their grapes, and it shows in the wines. Those who say Alexander Valley is too warm for great Chardonnays need only examine the consistently high quality and drinking charms of these two wines.

Of the two vineyards, Robert Young is the more famous. It is a large vineyard, with 170 acres planted to Chardonnay. It is tucked up against the hills on the east side of Highway 128. The St. Jean style has always emphasized the lush, ripe, creamy fruit in the Young Chardonnays. Of the earlier vintages, the 1976 is by far the finest. It is an engagingly complex, richly flavored and wonderfully textured wine that is aging exceptionally well. The first Young bottling, from 1975, is past its prime, as is the 1977. The 1978, despite being very ripe and concentrated, is holding on, with plenty of sweet fig and melon flavors showing. The 1979, 1980 and 1981 are all very ripe and true to the style of the era and are in peak drinking condition.

The 1982 has always been an earthy, awkward wine, but beginning with the 1983 and through the 1988 vintage, there is a high level of quality and consistency. The 1983 is fully mature, very attractive and aging with grace. The 1984 is ripe and full, with exotic fruit flavors. The 1985 is a shade more elegant and refined without sacrificing flavor. The 1986 is richer and smokier, a modest improvement from 1985, followed by the 1987, which succeeds with rich, elegant fruit flavors and good intensity. The 1988 is more forward, similar in style to the preceding four vintages, and may peak before the 1985 and 1986.

Beginning with the 1984 vintage, a reserve bottling of Robert Young has been released each year. It is produced from the best lots of Robert Young, aged an additional three to six months in oak, and bottled only in magnum. It also is aged longer before release. In 1990, the 1985 vintage was on the market. While I found the 1984 Reserve to be a bit oaky and ripe, the style is consistent with the 1985 Reserve, a delicious wine from a superior vintage, displaying much more complexity and finesse that most Robert Youngs, yet maintaining its rich core of ripe fruit and ample oak. The 1986 Reserve tastes more closed, but it is right in sync with the style and appears to be a wine that should age well for most of the 1990s. The 1987 Reserve is simply the most delicious Robert Young I have tasted, an incredibly rich, complex wine with toasty, smoky oak aromas and sharply focused flavors. It rates as one of the all-time greats produced in California.

The track record of the Belle Terre Chardonnays closely parallels that of the Robert Youngs. Belle Terre is southwest of Young on the west side of Highway 128. The first Belle Terre in 1975 was also the best of the 1970s. When last tasted, it still displayed wonderful fruit complexity and length. The 1976 proved more tannic and dry, while the 1977 is holding on, with a pleasant but strong honey and Botrytis quality. The 1978 is very mature, echoing the same honey and pear flavors. The 1979 is declining but still worth drinking.

The 1980 is very impressive, big, full, very ripe and deftly balanced. The 1981 is a shade lighter and tarter, while the 1982 is very successful for the vintage, very complex and mature. The 1983 has retained its youthful vitality and is one of the better Chardonnays of that year. The 1984 has improved with age, but is not one of the best Belle Terres. The 1985 is perhaps the finest Belle Terre ever produced. It is a remarkably complex and intense wine, followed by a similarly complex 1986. The 1987 has been slow to come around, but now appears outstanding, with plenty of flavor and finesse. The 1988 has a wealth of flavor and promise. It too is exceptionally fine.

From 1975 to 1987, St. Jean bottled a McCrea Vineyards Chardonnay from Sonoma Valley. Of the older vintages, the 1977 is holding on the best, followed by the vintages from 1982 to 1987, all of which

are very good. Kistler is now bottling a McCrea Vineyards Chardonnay. Of the Frank Johnson and Jimtown bottlings, my favorites have been the current vintages. Notes for these wines, along with Wildwood, are included below.

None of the St. Jean vineyard-designated Chardonnays undergoes malolactic fermentation, but they are all barrel fermented. Many of California's top Chardonnays have caught up in quality with Chateau St. Jean, but few can surpass the Robert Young and Belle Terre vineyards bottlings. The 1989 vintage is the first since 1975 in which no Robert Young was produced, as rains damaged the crop. Production of the Robert Young bottling hovers at about 13,500 cases a year, more than double the 6,000 cases of Belle Terre. The Sonoma County bottling usually contains wine left over from the special vineyard lots and can be a very fine glass of wine. I tasted through a vertical of older vintages and found many had aged well, but not as well as the vineyard-designated wines.

TASTING NOTES

CHATEAU ST. JEAN, Robert Young Vineyards Reserve, Alexander Valley

1987 CHATEAU ST. JEAN ROBERT YOUNG VINEYARDS RESERVE (IN MAGNUM ONLY): Delicious already, with fresh, youthful, vibrant citrus, melon, pear and spice, flavors and a pretty overlay of toasty, buttery, smoky oak, combining to create a wine of enormous intensity, elegance and finesse with a long, long finish. Another sensational reserve that with time will rival and best the stunning 1985. Last tasted: 7/90. Drink 1993-2000. 112 cases produced. Not released. **96**

1986 CHATEAU ST. JEAN ROBERT YOUNG VINEYARDS RESERVE (IN MAGNUM ONLY): Oakier and toastier than the 1985 Reserve, but still packing plenty of fruit, with tiers of pear, apple and melon flavors and distinctive toasty oak notes. Despite all its power and oakiness, the intensity of the fruit comes through. Showing signs of early complexity; another very well-proportioned wine that should age for years to come. Last tasted: 7/90. Drink 1992-2000. 507 cases produced. Not released. **91**

1985 CHATEAU ST. JEAN ROBERT YOUNG VINEYARDS RESERVE (IN MAGNUM ONLY): Magnificent, the finest Robert Young Chardonnay made in more than a decade. It combines a wealth of ripe, clean, rich pear, melon, lemon, honey, toast and butterscotch flavors with elegance, grace and finesse, a beautifully proportioned, delicately balanced, absolutely delicious Chardonnay that should age through the decade. Last tasted: 7/90. Drink 1992-1998. 978 cases produced. Release: $40. Current: $40. **95**

1984 CHATEAU ST. JEAN ROBERT YOUNG VINEYARDS RESERVE (IN MAGNUM ONLY): Fully mature, with rich, smoky, fruity Chardonnay aromas framed by oak and subtle layers of exotic pear, spice and pineapple flavors. Best to drink soon. Last tasted: 7/90. Drink 1991-1993. 918 cases produced. Release: $40. Current: $50. **87**

CHATEAU ST. JEAN, Robert Young Vineyards, Alexander Valley

1988 CHATEAU ST. JEAN ROBERT YOUNG VINEYARDS: Continues in the successful Robert Young tradition, offering ripe, gentle melon, pear, spice and toast flavors that are more supple and forward than the 1987, but still very pleasing. May be ready to drink before the 1985 through 1987 vintages. Last tasted: 7/90. Drink 1992-1998. 13,638 cases produced. Release: $18. Current: $18. **91**

1987 CHATEAU ST. JEAN ROBERT YOUNG VINEYARDS: Forward and alluring, with pretty scents of cedar, fig and melon, followed by rich yet elegant fruit flavors that offer complex citrus, pear, spice and apple notes. The most delicate and elegant Robert Young ever produced, this wine amazes with its finesse. Last tasted: 3/90. Drink 1992-1999. 13,108 cases produced. Release: $18. Current: $25. **91**

1986 CHATEAU ST. JEAN ROBERT YOUNG VINEYARDS: A richer, smokier Robert Young that surpasses the 1985 in complexity and depth at this stage, but in the long run both of these elegantly balanced wines will have special merits. The honey, melon, butterscotch and spicy oak flavors are all well integrated, finishing with delicacy and finesse. Last tasted: 3/90. Drink 1992-1998. 13,007 cases produced. Release: $18. Current: $25. **92**

1985 CHATEAU ST. JEAN ROBERT YOUNG VINEYARDS: Follows in the elegant style of the 1984, offering rich, sharply defined honey, toast, cream and butterscotch flavors that are impeccably balanced, revealing a measure of finesse and grace as well as restraint. Just a trace of wood tannin still showing, so let it rest until 1992. Last tasted: 3/90. Drink 1992-1998. 13,613 cases produced. Release: $18. Current: $26. **91**

1984 CHATEAU ST. JEAN ROBERT YOUNG VINEYARDS: Ripe yet crisp, with orange, citrus, melon and pear notes that are clean, rich and elegant, with a lively finish. Not quite as opulent and rich as some Robert Youngs, nonetheless it is full of flavor and very appealing. Last tasted: 3/90. Drink 1991-1995. 13,513 cases produced. Release: $20. Current: $30. **88**

1983 CHATEAU ST. JEAN ROBERT YOUNG VINEYARDS: Alluring with its rich, creamy honey, vanilla, pear, toast and spice flavors, elegant structure and fine balance, a highly successful 1983 that is aging with grace and finesse. May be a shade past its peak, but barely. Last tasted: 3/90. Drink 1991-1994. 7,697 cases produced. Release: $18. Current: $33. **88**

1982 CHATEAU ST. JEAN ROBERT YOUNG VINEYARDS: Perhaps the weakest Robert Young Chardonnay produced, this wine has always been awkward, with earthy cement aromas and hard, tart, lean fruit flavors of only moderate intensity. It is certainly drinkable, but won't remind you of most Robert Youngs. Last tasted: 3/90. Drink 1991-1993. 8,645 cases produced. Release: $18. Current: $20. **75**

1981 CHATEAU ST. JEAN ROBERT YOUNG VINEYARDS: Still fresh and lively, a bit past its prime and no longer quite as deep and flavorful as most Robert Young bottlings. The pear, apple, butter and spice flavors are more subtle and delicate than assertive. Aging well; the finish is crisp and mildly coarse. Last tasted: 3/90. Drink 1991-1993. 8,586 cases produced. Release: $18. Current: $25. **86**

1980 CHATEAU ST. JEAN ROBERT YOUNG VINEYARDS: Big, rich and ripe, fairly typical of the 1980 vintage with its fat flavors, but it is aging well, with attractive honey, pear and spicy oak flavors that are broad and full up front, tapering off on the finish. Last tasted: 3/90. Drink 1991-1993. 6,832 cases produced. Release: $18. Current: $30. **85**

1979 CHATEAU ST. JEAN ROBERT YOUNG VINEYARDS: Despite its deep gold color and maturity, there is still much to like in this rich, butterscotch-flavored wine. It is very ripe (14.5 percent alcohol) and has lost its youthful Chardonnay fruit, but what remains is easy to enjoy. Drink it with a creamy cheese. Last tasted: 3/90. Drink 1991-1994. 5,344 cases produced. Release: $17. Current: $30. **85**

1978 CHATEAU ST. JEAN ROBERT YOUNG VINEYARDS: Plenty of sweet, rich fig, melon and butter flavors that offer good depth, intensity and complexity. Shows no signs of fading into oblivion yet. Last tasted: 3/90. Drink 1991-1993. 1,099 cases produced. Release: $17. Current: $25. **84**

1977 CHATEAU ST. JEAN ROBERT YOUNG VINEYARDS: Past its prime, with oxidation overtaking the mature fruit and vegetal flavors. A curiosity. Last tasted: 3/90. Best to avoid. 1,597 cases produced. Release: $17. Current: $22. **68**

1976 CHATEAU ST. JEAN ROBERT YOUNG VINEYARDS: The best Robert Young of the 1970s, this is an amazingly ripe, very rich and complex wine. The color is deep, but the fruit is youthful and enticing, with layers of pear, apricot and creamy, buttery oak flavors. Long, long finish. Last tasted: 7/90. Drink 1991-1994. 1,400 cases produced. Release: $8.75. Current: $25. **92**

1975 CHATEAU ST. JEAN ROBERT YOUNG VINEYARDS: First Robert Young bottling, very mature and past its prime, with maderized flavors. Last tasted: 7/90. Best to avoid. 900 cases produced. Release: $7.75. Current: $22. **63**

CHATEAU ST. JEAN, Belle Terre Vineyards, Alexander Valley

1988 CHATEAU ST. JEAN BELLE TERRE VINEYARDS: Extends the Belle Terre streak of excellence, and with time may rank as one of the best. Plenty of pretty ripe apple, pear, peach, fig and spice flavors that are rich and crisp, with a measure of elegance and finesse. Still young and undeveloped, but all the elements are here for greatness. Last tasted: 3/90. Drink 1993-1998. 8,848 cases produced. Release: $16. Current: $16. **90**

1987 CHATEAU ST. JEAN BELLE TERRE VINEYARDS: A slow starter that is now revealing more depth, complexity and length than it did on release. Keeps improving in the bottle. The pretty apple, pear, spice and honey flavors are seasoned by subtle toasty oak and a long aftertaste. Has the intensity and flavor to move up a notch. Last tasted: 3/90. Drink 1992-1998. 2,590 cases produced. Release: $16. Current: $22. **91**

1986 CHATEAU ST. JEAN BELLE TERRE VINEYARDS: Rivals the superb 1985 in quality, combining rich, smoky, fruity aromas with lean, concentrated, sharply focused, earthy lemon, fig and melon flavors of elegance and finesse. Long, lingering aftertaste; still on its way up. Last tasted: 3/90. Drink 1992-1997. 3,625 cases produced. Release: $16. Current: $20. **90**

1985 CHATEAU ST. JEAN BELLE TERRE VINEYARDS: Perhaps the most successful Belle Terre to date, a bold, deep, rich wine with complexity and intensity, tiers of toasty oak, pear, fig and spice flavors, all tightly knit and slightly tannic. The finish offers pretty floral and honey notes. May be a year away from full maturity. Last tasted: 3/90. Drink 1992-1996. 3,371 cases produced. Release: $16. Current: $25. **92**

1984 CHATEAU ST. JEAN BELLE TERRE VINEYARDS: This wine has improved considerably with bottle age. It now displays more ripe, clean fig and honey aromas and flavors than in earlier tastings, and remains youthful and vibrant. Last tasted: 3/90. Drink 1991-1995. 6,384 cases produced. Release: $16. Current: $27. **85**

1983 CHATEAU ST. JEAN BELLE TERRE VINEYARDS: Youthful and in excellent condition, fully mature in a more subtle and understated style than its predecessors. The elegant honey, butter, spice, pear and melon flavors taste better with each sip. Long, smoky aftertaste. Last tasted: 3/90. Drink 1991-1995. 1,281 cases produced. Release: $16.75. Current: $30. **89**

1982 CHATEAU ST. JEAN BELLE TERRE VINEYARDS: Rich and smoky, with a touch of earthiness that is appealing without overshadowing the ripe pear, melon and spice notes. Aging well, with attractive Chardonnay flavors coming through on the finish. Last tasted: 3/90. Drink 1991-1995. 4,735 cases produced. Release: $15.50. Current: $20. **86**

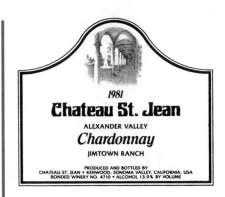

1981
Chateau St. Jean
SONOMA VALLEY
Chardonnay
HUNTER RANCH

PRODUCED AND BOTTLED BY
CHATEAU ST. JEAN • KENWOOD, SONOMA VALLEY, CALIFORNIA, USA
BONDED WINERY NO. 4710 • ALCOHOL 13.3% BY VOLUME

1981 CHATEAU ST. JEAN BELLE TERRE VINEYARDS: Tart, lean and crisp, with lemon, custard and subtle oak flavors, an appealing wine that is more austere than previous bottlings. Showing no signs of premature aging, but not quite as flavorful or rich as earlier editions. Last tasted: 3/90. Drink 1991-1995. 3,847 cases produced. Release: $15. Current: $18. **83**

1980 CHATEAU ST. JEAN BELLE TERRE VINEYARDS: Big, full and ripe, with pretty pear, spice, butter and nutmeg flavors that are broad and lush on the palate. Holding up well for this vintage, when many wines peaked early. Plenty of intensity and life left; deftly balanced. Last tasted: 3/90. Drink 1991-1994. 4,427 cases produced. Release: $15. Current: $24. **88**

1979 CHATEAU ST. JEAN BELLE TERRE VINEYARDS: Aging gracefully, a shade past its prime, but still offering richly flavored fruit, honey and butter, with some vegetal notes, but altogether pleasant, finishing with good length. Last tasted: 3/90. Drink 1991-1993. 3,668 cases produced. Release: $12. Current: $22. **84**

1978 CHATEAU ST. JEAN BELLE TERRE VINEYARDS: Still hanging on. It would pair up well with a creamy cheese. The mature honey and fig flavors are drying out. Last tasted: 3/90. Drink 1991. 2,194 cases produced. Release: $14. Current: $20. **73**

1977 CHATEAU ST. JEAN BELLE TERRE VINEYARDS: Mature and in decline but still pleasant, with honey and Botrytis notes, a touch of oak and spice and generally attractive flavors. Last tasted: 3/90. Drink 1991. 799 cases produced. Release: $12. Current: $22. **80**

1976 CHATEAU ST. JEAN BELLE TERRE VINEYARDS: Despite some attractive smoky aromas, the texture is tannic, with hard-edged pear and apricot flavors. Last tasted: 7/90. Drink 1991-1992. 1,100 cases produced. Release: $7.50. Current: $22. **77**

1975 CHATEAU ST. JEAN BELLE TERRE VINEYARDS: Very elegant, rich and smoky, with layers of intense honey, pear and apricot flavors, one of the top 1975s. Still quite delicious to drink. Best Belle Terre of the 1970s. Last tasted: 7/90. Drink 1991-1993. 750 cases produced. Release: $7.50. Current: $22. **88**

CHATEAU ST. JEAN, Frank Johnson Vineyards, Dry Creek Valley

1986 CHATEAU ST. JEAN FRANK JOHNSON VINEYARDS: Attractive, forward, toasty butterscotch, honey, pear and melon flavors that turn rich and smoky on the finish. Balanced and capable of improving for another few years. Last tasted: 7/90. Drink 1991-1995. 2,115 cases produced. Release: $14. Current: $19. **89**

1985 CHATEAU ST. JEAN FRANK JOHNSON VINEYARDS: Ripe, perfumed, Muscat aromas, with very ripe, intense, concentrated pear and apple flavors. A bold, assertive wine that is packed with flavor and lots of acidity. Last tasted: 3/90. Drink 1993-1997. 1,517 cases produced. Release: $14. Current: $14. **87**

1984 CHATEAU ST. JEAN FRANK JOHNSON VINEYARDS: At its peak, ripe, rich and mature, with honey, pear and toast flavors that are well proportioned, finishing with good length and a touch of elegance. Last tasted: 7/90. Drink 1991-1995. 3,100 cases produced. Release: $14. Current: $20. **88**

1980 CHATEAU ST. JEAN FRANK JOHNSON VINEYARDS: Plenty of ripe pear, butter, spice and fig flavors up front, but they begin to turn oaky and dry on the finish. Last tasted: 3/90. Drink 1991-1992. 1,257 cases produced. Release: $14. Current: $16. **79**

1979 CHATEAU ST. JEAN FRANK JOHNSON VINEYARDS: Very ripe and mature, with fading butter and honey flavors that gain a trace of bitterness on the finish. Last tasted: 3/90. Drink 1991. 349 cases produced. Release: $13. Current: $15. **78**

CHATEAU ST. JEAN, Jimtown Ranch, Alexander Valley

1988 CHATEAU ST. JEAN JIMTOWN RANCH: Intense and lively, with crisp lemon, earth and toast flavors dominating the pear and melon notes. Elegant, balanced, long on the finish, but it needs more time. Last tasted: 7/90. Drink 1992-1998. 700 cases produced. Not released. **88**

1987 CHATEAU ST. JEAN JIMTOWN RANCH: Tart and crisp, very lean and tight, with fresh apple and citrus notes and plenty of acidity. Young and intense, this wine needs two to three years to unwind. Last tasted: 3/90. Drink 1993-1997. 689 cases produced. Release: $15. Current: $15. **87**

1983 CHATEAU ST. JEAN JIMTOWN RANCH: Deliciously complex, with a distinct peppery-oaky quality that adds a nice dimension to the rich, intense pear and pineapple flavors. Finish picks up a nice earthy quality. Aging well. Last tasted: 7/90. Drink 1991-1996. 689 cases produced. Release: $16. Current: $20. **87**

1981 CHATEAU ST. JEAN JIMTOWN RANCH: Very ripe and fruity, aging well, with attractive pear and apple flavors and a touch of vanilla and spice on the finish. Last tasted: 3/90. Drink 1991-1995. 1,720 cases produced. Release: $14.75. Current: $22. **87**

1980 CHATEAU ST. JEAN JIMTOWN RANCH: Ripe and buttery up front, with spicy pear and vegetal notes, but it gets dry and oaky on the finish. Holding well, but in decline. Last tasted: 3/90. Drink 1991. 864 cases produced. Release: $14. Current: $16. **77**

CHATEAU ST. JEAN, McCrea Vineyards, Sonoma Valley

1987 CHATEAU ST. JEAN MCCREA VINEYARDS: Young and intense, fresh and lively, with crisp, tart apple, pear, melon and spice

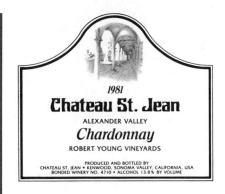

1981
Chateau St. Jean
ALEXANDER VALLEY
Chardonnay
ROBERT YOUNG VINEYARDS
PRODUCED AND BOTTLED BY
CHATEAU ST. JEAN • KENWOOD, SONOMA VALLEY, CALIFORNIA, USA
BONDED WINERY NO. 4710 • ALCOHOL 13.8% BY VOLUME

flavors. Pretty fruit flavors on the finish. Last tasted: 3/90. Drink 1992-1996. 364 cases produced. Release: $15. Current: $15. **88**

1986 CHATEAU ST. JEAN MCCREA VINEYARDS: Well balanced and fruity, with pear, apple, spice and vanilla notes that are fresh and lively. Altogether a very agreeable Chardonnay that finishes with pretty fruit flavors. Last tasted: 3/90. Drink 1992-1996. 163 cases produced. Release: $15. Current: $17. **87**

1985 CHATEAU ST. JEAN MCCREA VINEYARDS: The wildly herbaceous flavors are intriguing and complex, adding earthy, sweaty nuances to the ripe, elegant pear, melon, spice and lemon notes. Well balanced, lingering on the finish. Last tasted: 7/90. Drink 1991-1996. 1,543 cases produced. Release: $14.25. Current: $17. **86**

1984 CHATEAU ST. JEAN MCCREA VINEYARDS: Very ripe and attractive, with pure honey and butterscotch flavors that are rich, vibrant, sharply focused and stay with you through the finish. Last tasted: 3/90. Drink 1991-1995. 1,601 cases produced. Release: $14.25. Current: $17. **87**

1983 CHATEAU ST. JEAN MCCREA VINEYARDS: An earthy wine, but still pleasant, with crisp pear, apple and melon flavors that are well balanced, young and intense. Aging well for the vintage. Last tasted: 7/90. Drink 1991-1995. 1,009 cases produced. Release: $15.25. Current: $18. **85**

1982 CHATEAU ST. JEAN MCCREA VINEYARDS: Crisp, tart and lively, on the austere side. The acidity carries the crisp pear and apple flavors, and gives them excellent length. Aging very well, light in color and showing no signs of decline. Last tasted: 7/90. Drink 1991-1995. 501 cases produced. Release: $13. Current: $18. **88**

1981 CHATEAU ST. JEAN MCCREA VINEYARDS: Showing its age and drying out, but there are still faint honey and nutmeg flavors that are worth exploring. Last tasted: 3/90. Drink 1991-1992. 846 cases produced. Release: $15. Current: $18. **75**

1980 CHATEAU ST. JEAN MCCREA VINEYARDS: Oxidized honey and fruit aromas, and very dry on the palate. Fruit has faded. Last tasted: 3/90. Drink 1991-1992. 465 cases produced. Release: $15. Current: $18. **70**

1979 CHATEAU ST. JEAN MCCREA VINEYARDS: Smoky, burnt flavors override the rich honey and fig notes. The finish gets dry. Last tasted: 3/90. Drink 1991. 325 cases produced. Release: $14. Current: $18. **70**

1978 CHATEAU ST. JEAN MCCREA VINEYARDS: Almost gone but hanging on, with faint honey, spice and nectarine flavors that turn dry and oaky on the finish. At the very end of its life. Last tasted: 3/90. Drink 1991. 309 cases produced. Release: $12. Current: $20. **70**

1977 CHATEAU ST. JEAN MCCREA VINEYARDS: Still delicious, with mature butterscotch, honey, spice and tea notes that are lively and well balanced. The finish begins to fade and dry out; better drink soon. Last tasted: 3/90. Drink 1991. 346 cases produced. Release: $10. Current: $25. **85**

1976 CHATEAU ST. JEAN MCCREA VINEYARDS: Dry and losing its fruit, decent to drink, with simple pear and spice notes. Last tasted: 7/90. Drink 1991-1992. 300 cases produced. Release: $9.25. Current: $20. **75**

1975 CHATEAU ST. JEAN MCCREA VINEYARDS: Fully mature, with waxy anise and spice notes and ripe apricot flavors that dry out on the finish. Last tasted: 7/90. Drink 1991-1993. 250 cases produced. Release: $8.75. Current: $20. **78**

CHATEAU ST. JEAN, Various bottlings

1981 CHATEAU ST. JEAN HUNTER RANCH: Ripe, mature, beginning to lose its fruit, and the pear and apple flavors show signs of oxidation. Still, it is pleasant and drinkable. Last tasted: 7/90. Drink 1991-1993. 1,221 cases produced. Release: $14.75. Current: $19. **81**

1980 CHATEAU ST. JEAN GAUER RANCH: Earthy, bitter and gamy flavors detract from the ripe Chardonnay fruit, but there are still some fig and pear flavors that are pleasant. Last tasted: 7/90. Drink 1991. 2,614 cases produced. Release: $14. Current: $18. **74**

1980 CHATEAU ST. JEAN HUNTER RANCH: Oxidized honey flavors turn bitter. Last tasted: 7/90. Best to avoid. 1,355 cases produced. Release: $14. Current: $17. **67**

1980 CHATEAU ST. JEAN WILDWOOD VINEYARDS: Very ripe, mature, smoky and toasty, with very mature pear flavors that are fading. Best days are gone. Last tasted: 7/90. Drink 1990-1992. 1,853 cases produced. Release: $13. Current: $19. **71**

1979 CHATEAU ST. JEAN GAUER RANCH: Fading, with oxidized flavors replacing the very ripe pear and fig flavors. Last tasted: 7/90. Drink 1991. 2,725 cases produced. Release: $14. Current: $18. **70**

1979 CHATEAU ST. JEAN HUNTER RANCH: Deep in color, rich and complex, with honey, anise, butterscotch and oak flavors that are hot on the finish. Still holding but best consumed soon. Last tasted: 7/90. Drink 1991. 1,010 cases produced. Release: $14. Current: $20. **80**

1978 CHATEAU ST. JEAN HUNTER RANCH: Oxidized and over the hill. Last tasted: 7/90. Best to avoid. 528 cases produced. Release: $11.25. Current: $18. **65**

1978 CHATEAU ST. JEAN LES PIERRES VINEYARDS: Its best days are behind, but it still offers sweet, rich, ripe pear and spicy fig flavors that spread out on the palate. The finish is dry and oaky; 15.5 percent

1977
Chateau St. Jean
SONOMA VALLEY
Chardonnay
LES PIERRES VINEYARDS

PRODUCED AND BOTTLED BY
CHATEAU ST. JEAN • KENWOOD, SONOMA VALLEY, CALIFORNIA
BONDED WINERY NO. 4710 • ALCOHOL 13.5% BY VOLUME

alcohol. Last tasted: 7/90. Drink 1991. 729 cases produced. Release: $13.75 Current: $22. **81**

1978 CHATEAU ST. JEAN WILDWOOD VINEYARDS: Past its prime, with oxidized honey and smoke flavors. Last tasted: 7/90. Best to avoid. 480 cases produced. Release: $12. Current: $19. **65**

1977 CHATEAU ST. JEAN HUNTER RANCH: Very mature with deep yellow-gold hues, but plenty of extract and delicious, rich honey, butterscotch and butter flavors. Last tasted: 7/90. Drink 1991-1992. 482 cases produced. Release: $10.25. Current: $25. **82**

1977 CHATEAU ST. JEAN LES PIERRES VINEYARDS: Plenty of fruit and life left in this one, although it comes up short on the finish. The fig, melon and pear flavors show oxidation, but more fruit comes through. Decent. Last tasted: 7/90. Drink 1991. 308 cases produced. Release: $13.75 Current: $21. **79**

1977 CHATEAU ST. JEAN WILDWOOD VINEYARDS: Deep gold color, fading but drinkable, with rich honey and butterscotch flavors, almost like Botrytis. Drink with a creamy cheese. Last tasted: 7/90. Drink 1991. 492 cases produced. Release: $15. Current: $22. **73**

1976 CHATEAU ST. JEAN BELTANE RANCH: Very ripe nose, dry, tannic and bitter. Last tasted: 7/90. Best to avoid. 375 cases produced. Release: $7.75 Current: $18. **69**

1976 CHATEAU ST. JEAN RIVERVIEW VINEYARDS: The only Riverview Vineyards bottling ever produced by St. Jean, this is a deeply flavored, very complex wine, high in extract, with tiers of honey, pear and vanilla flavors and a powerful toasty, smoky aftertaste. Last tasted: 7/90. Drink 1991-1994. 600 cases produced. Release: $9.50 Current: $22. **88**

1976 CHATEAU ST. JEAN WILDWOOD VINEYARDS: Deep, rich and mature, with lovely cedar and sandalwood aromas, but not quite enough flavor or depth. Decent fruit coming through for this difficult vintage. Last tasted: 7/90. Drink 1991-1993. 402 cases produced. Release: $10. Current: $20. **82**

1975 CHATEAU ST. JEAN BELTANE RANCH: Impressive for its age, with sweet, ripe pear, cinnamon and apple flavors that are rich and complex, very well balanced, with ample oak showing on the finish. A sturdy wine that has held up. Last tasted: 7/90. Drink 1991-1994. 500 cases produced. Release: $12.50. Current: $21. **88**

1975 CHATEAU ST. JEAN BACIGALUPI: Wonderful harmony of flavors, rich, ripe and smoky, with deeply concentrated pear, honey and apricot flavors. Very complex, elegant and balanced. The only Bacigalupi made by St. Jean. Last tasted: 7/90. Drink 1991-1995. 800 cases produced. Release: $10. Current: $21. **86**

1975 CHATEAU ST. JEAN WILDWOOD VINEYARDS: Not showing well, with an oily, oaky, "off" component that detracts from the mature fruit flavors. Drinkable but unexciting. Last tasted: 7/90. Drink 1991. 350 cases produced. Release: $9.50. Current: $20. **70**

CHATEAU WOLTNER

Estate Reserve, Howell Mountain, Napa Valley
St. Thomas Vineyard, Howell Mountain, Napa Valley
Titus Vineyard, Howell Mountain, Napa Valley
Frederique Vineyard, Howell Mountain, Napa Valley

CLASSIFICATION:

Estate Reserve: THIRD GROWTH

St. Thomas Vineyard: FOURTH GROWTH

Titus Vineyard: FOURTH GROWTH

Frederique Vineyard: Not rated

COLLECTIBILITY RATING:

Estate Reserve: A

St. Thomas Vineyard: A

Titus Vineyard: A

Frederique Vineyard: Not rated

BEST VINTAGES:

Estate Reserve: 1986, 1987

St. Thomas Vineyard: 1986

Titus Vineyard: 1986, 1987

Frederique Vineyard: 1988

AT A GLANCE

CHATEAU WOLTNER
150 S. White Cottage Road
Angwin, CA 94508
(707) 965-2445

Owners: Francis and Françoise DeWavrin Woltner

Winemaker: Ted Lemon (5 years)

Founded: 1980

First Chardonnay vintage: 1985
  Estate Reserve: 1985
  St. Thomas Vineyard: 1985
  Titus Vineyard: 1985
  Frederique Vineyard: 1988

Chardonnay production: 2,800 cases
  Estate Reserve: 1,700 cases
  St. Thomas Vineyard: 700 cases
  Titus Vineyard: 200 cases
  Frederique Vineyard: 200 cases

Chardonnay acres owned: 55
  St. Thomas Vineyard: 9
  Titus Vineyard: 4
  Frederique Vineyard: 4

Average age of vines: 7 years

Vineyard locations:
  St. Thomas Vineyard: Howell Mountain, Napa Valley
  Titus Vineyard: Howell Mountain, Napa Valley
  Frederique Vineyard: Howell Mountain, Napa Valley

Average wine makeup:
  Estate Reserve: Howell Mountain, Napa Valley (100%)

Time in oak: 10 months

Type of oak: French (Burgundian)

Oak age: new (30%) to 3 years old

Winemaking notes:
  Barrel fermentation: 100%
  Malolactic fermentation: none
  Lees aging: 100% (10 months)

After selling Bordeaux's Château La Mission-Haut Brion in 1980, Francis and Françoise DeWavrin Woltner became partners at Conn Creek Winery in Napa Valley before starting their own winery on Howell Mountain, several hundred feet above the Napa Valley floor. As Chardonnay specialists with an emphasis on Burgundy-style wines, the owners of Chateau Woltner planted several vineyards on their property in the early 1980s. Beginning in 1985, under the supervision of consultant Ric Forman, Chateau Woltner produced wines from the Titus, St. Thomas and Estate vineyards, and in 1988, the winery introduced a Chardonnay from the Frederique Vineyard.

The Chardonnay style of Chateau Woltner is unmistakably Burgundian, with a heavy emphasis on crisp acidity, austere, tightly concentrated flavors and a generous use of oak, all designed to create wines with long-term aging potential. The 1985 Chardonnays were very controversial, not only because of their high prices, but also because the wines were produced from young vines and did not have the richness and concentration necessary to stand up to the new oak bar-

rels, purchased for the first vintage. Of the three 1985s, the Titus is the best.

Since then, Ted Lemon, who apprenticed himself with several producers in Burgundy's city of Dijon, has taken over as winemaker. Clearly the 1986s are superior in quality, showing richer flavors and less oakiness. The 1987s are tarter, typical of the vintage, but are beginning to open and reveal more complexity. The 1988s are still tight but more delicate, and may well prove to be the best wines to date.

Prices remain high and supplies are limited. The 1987 Titus Vineyard was, briefly, California's most expensive wine, selling for $54, $3 more than Opus One 1986, although it since has been surpassed by several Cabernet Sauvignons. The Titus is still the most expensive Chardonnay, a wine created for connoisseurs who appreciate the subtle differences between the closely situated vineyards and the wines they produce, and by producers who understand what the market will bear. The largest production is the Estate Reserve, with 1,700 cases, followed by St. Thomas with 700 cases, and Frederique and Titus at 200 cases each. Titus, named after the Woltners' dog, faces south and receives the greatest sun exposure. St. Thomas sits on a westerly slope, while Frederique faces north.

In several tastings I have found the wines more similar than not — austere and flinty, with lemon, pear and vanilla notes — but winemaker Lemon, who picks the grapes at around 22 degrees Brix, believes the wines will reveal more individuality as the vines mature and the wines evolve in the bottle. I gave the wines from 1986 on high marks for their deliberate and very consistent style. They will not appeal to everyone — nor to everyone's wine budget. Clearly these are luxury-priced Chardonnays designed for collectors who fully appreciate nuances, and are willing to wait as these wines evolve.

TASTING NOTES

CHATEAU WOLTNER, Estate Reserve, Howell Mountain, Napa Valley

1988 CHATEAU WOLTNER ESTATE RESERVE: Very intense and lively, with sharply focused, austere lemon, pear, apple and spice flavors that are well balanced and elegant, but right now the acidity is bracing. Best to let it age another two to four years. Last tasted: 4/90. Drink 1992-1998. 1,645 cases produced. Release: $24. Current: $24. **86**

1987 CHATEAU WOLTNER ESTATE RESERVE: Similar in style to the excellent 1986, a shade leaner but with similar honey, pear, vanilla and butterscotch flavors that gain richness and depth on the finish. Distinctive for its subtlety and elegance. Last tasted: 4/90. Drink 1991-1997. 2,151 cases produced. Release: $24. Current: $24. **88**

1986 CHATEAU WOLTNER ESTATE RESERVE: Distinctive for its elegance and finesse, rich and concentrated, with pretty, sharply defined pear, honey, toast and vanilla flavors that are silky smooth and round, finishing with smoky oak notes that linger on the palate. More delicious with every sip. Last tasted: 4/90. Drink 1991-1997. 1,228 cases produced. Release: $24. Current: $24. **91**

CHATEAU WOLTNER, St. Thomas Vineyard, Howell Mountain, Napa Valley

1988 CHATEAU WOLTNER ST. THOMAS VINEYARD: More forward than the other bottlings, with pear and peach flavors and plenty of tart, flinty lemon notes. An austere wine that will require patience, but very attractive in this style. Last tasted: 4/90. Drink 1993-1998. 617 cases produced. Release: $36. Current: $36. **86**

1987 CHATEAU WOLTNER ST. THOMAS VINEYARD: Austere and tightly structured, with flinty stone, lemon, peach and pear flavors that are very firm and concentrated, finishing with a rich, creamy texture. It avoids the hard acidity of most 1987s and is probably another few years from full maturity. Last tasted: 4/90. Drink 1993-1998. 883 cases produced. Release: $36. Current: $36. **87**

1986 CHATEAU WOLTNER ST. THOMAS VINEYARD: An intense wine that manages to provide bold and rich, yet subtle flavors, and remarkable harmony, with pretty pear, vanilla and honey notes that are smooth and polished, possessing distinctive staying power. Last tasted: 4/90. Drink 1991-1997. 747 cases produced. Release: $36. Current: $37. **89**

CHATEAU WOLTNER, Titus Vineyard, Howell Mountain, Napa Valley

1988 CHATEAU WOLTNER TITUS VINEYARD: Tight and firm, with austere, stony lemon flavors that are just now beginning to loosen a bit. Plenty of flavor and concentration and deftly balanced but one should wait on this wine. Last tasted: 4/90. Drink 1993-1999. 147 cases produced. Release: $54. Current: $54. **86**

1987 CHATEAU WOLTNER TITUS VINEYARD: Firm and lemony, with austere, flinty, toasty lemon-lime flavors and subtle, spicy vanilla notes. Balanced and closed; a very deliberate style that still needs time to blossom. Last tasted: 4/90. Drink 1992-1998. 309 cases produced. Release: $54. Current: $54. **85**

1986 CHATEAU WOLTNER TITUS VINEYARD: Tight and austere, with hard, stony, flinty lemon, herb and subtle pear shadings, plenty of oak, but very well balanced. An austere wine that is still not fully developed. May not peak for another two to three years. Last tasted: 4/90. Drink 1993-1998. 179 cases produced. Release: $54. Current: $54. **88**

CHATEAU WOLTNER, Frederique Vineyard, Howell Mountain, Napa Valley

1988 CHATEAU WOLTNER FREDERIQUE VINEYARD: Very intense and concentrated, austere, lean and sharply focused, with tight lemon, nutmeg and pear flavors that are rich but not overly ripe. The finish is almost like biting into a lemon. Last tasted: 4/90. Drink 1993-1998. 210 cases produced. Release: $54. Current: $54. **87**

CLOS DU BOIS WINERY

Calcaire Vineyard, Alexander Valley
Flintwood Vineyard, Dry Creek Valley
Winemaker's Reserve, Sonoma County
Barrel Fermented, Alexander Valley

CLASSIFICATION:

Calcaire Vineyard: THIRD GROWTH
Flintwood Vineyard: FOURTH GROWTH
Winemaker's Reserve: FOURTH GROWTH
Barrel Fermented: FIFTH GROWTH

COLLECTIBILITY RATING:

Calcaire Vineyard: A
Flintwood Vineyard: A
Winemaker's Reserve: A
Barrel Fermented: Not rated

BEST VINTAGES:

Calcaire Vineyard: 1983, 1984, 1988, 1987
Flintwood Vineyard: 1988, 1986, 1987, 1980
Winemaker's Reserve: 1987, 1988
Barrel Fermented: 1987, 1988

With four Chardonnays and more than 100,000 cases produced each year, Clos du Bois has covered most of the bases with this varietal. This Healdsburg winery has been making consistently fine Chardonnays since its founding in 1974 by Frank Woods and a group of partners. I have not recently been able to taste any of the wines prior to 1980, and cannot pass judgment on how they have aged, but more often than not, Clos du Bois has been right on target with Chardonnays that typically provide plenty of richness, flavor and character on release.

Since 1979 Clos du Bois has expanded its lineup to include two vineyard-designated Chardonnays — Calcaire Vineyard in Alexander Valley and Flintwood Vineyard in Dry Creek Valley, along with its Winemaker's Reserve, formerly called the Proprietor's Reserve, and a barrel-fermented Chardonnay with an Alexander Valley appellation.

In my tastings, the Calcaire and Flintwood have been very close in quality, with the edge going to Calcaire. This 50-acre vineyard typically produces ripe, lush, elegant wines that can age very well for up to a decade. Both the 1983 and 1984 are simply outstanding, showing wonderful depth and complexity. Anyone who has a chance to try

AT A GLANCE

CLOS DU BOIS WINERY
51 Fitch St.
Healdsburg, CA 95448
(707) 433-5576

Owner: Hiram Walker/Allied Lyons, Great Britain

Winemaker: Margaret Davenport (1 year)

Founded: 1974

First Chardonnay vintage: 1974
Calcaire Vineyard: 1979
Flintwood Vineyard: 1980
Winemaker's Reserve: 1987
Barrel Fermented: 1982

Chardonnay production: 102,000 cases
Calcaire Vineyard: 7,000 cases
Flintwood Vineyard: 5,200 cases
Winemaker's Reserve: 3,800 cases (in some vintages)
Barrel Fermented: 86,000 cases

Chardonnay acres owned: 210
Calcaire Vineyard: 50

Average age of vines: 16 years
Calcaire Vineyard: 26 years
Flintwood Vineyard: 26 years

Vineyard locations:
Calcaire Vineyard: Alexander Valley
Flintwood Vineyard: Dry Creek Valley

Average wine makeup:
Barrel Fermented: Alexander Valley (100%)

continued on next page

continued from previous page

Time in oak:
  Calcaire Vineyard: 9 months
  Flintwood Vineyard: 10 months
  Winemaker's Reserve: 10 months
  Barrel Fermented: 6 months

Type of oak:
  Calcaire Vineyard: French
    (Limousin)
  Flintwood Vineyard: French
    (Nevers)
  Winemaker's Reserve: French
    (François Frères)
  Barrel Fermented: French
    (Limousin)

Oak age:
  Calcaire Vineyard: new (100%)
  Flintwood Vineyard: new (50%)
    to 1 year old
  Winemaker's Reserve: new (100%)
  Barrel Fermented: 1 to 4 years old

Winemaking notes:
  Barrel fermentation: 100%
  Malolactic fermentation:
    Calcaire Vineyard: 40% to 80%
    Flintwood Vineyard: 33% to 60%
    Winemaker's Reserve: 100%
    Barrel Fermented: 33%

  Lees aging:
    Calcaire Vineyard: 100%
      (9 months)
    Flintwood Vineyard: 100%
      (10 months)
    Winemaker's Reserve: 100%
      (10 months)
    Barrel Fermented: 100%
      (6 months)

these wines should go out of his way to do so. The 1985 and 1986 Calcaires are a notch lower in quality, but the 1987 and 1988 are both excellent wines that offer more elegance and finesse than their predecessors.

Flintwood Vineyard covers 45 acres in Dry Creek, due west of Alexander Valley, and it too can yield enormously complex and intense wines. The 1980 in particular is aging very well. I have not tried either the 1981 or the 1982 recently, but the 1983, 1984 and 1985 were disappointing. The 1986, 1987 and 1988 vintages are all significant improvements and they appear to have the balance and intensity to improve in the bottle for up to five years.

The Winemaker's Reserve, the successor to the Proprietor's Reserve, was produced only in years when winemaker John Hawley found the right combination of fruit to create a special bottling. Hawley left Clos du Bois in late August to join Kendall Jackson Vineyards. Former assistant winemaker Margaret Davenport has replaced him as winemaker. The 1987 Winemaker's Reserve is sensational, with wonderful balance, harmony and finesse, placing it at the top for that year. The 1988 shows many of the same attributes, being silky smooth, rich and complex. The Winemaker's Reserve has undergone full malolactic fermentation, while the Calcaire, Flintwood and Barrel Fermented bottlings range from one-third to 80 percent malolactic. The Barrel Fermented, of which 86,000 cases are produced, is usually a very sound, often exceptional bottle of wine, and at around $11 it is well below the price of other Chardonnays.

Since 1988, Clos du Bois has been owned by Hiram Walker of the Allied Lyons drinks concern based in England. Ground has been broken on a new winery north of Healdsburg in the Alexander Valley.

TASTING NOTES

CLOS DU BOIS WINERY, Calcaire Vineyard, Alexander Valley

1988 CLOS DU BOIS WINERY CALCAIRE VINEYARD: Another fine success for Calcaire, offering ripe pear, citrus, melon and spice flavors in a delicate, elegant wine that is developing finesse and finishes with excellent length. Young and intense, it will need another year or two to soften. Last tasted: 6/90. Drink 1992-1997. 7,334 cases produced. Release: $17. Current: $17. **89**

1987 CLOS DU BOIS WINERY CALCAIRE VINEYARD: Similar in style, flavor and texture to the 1986 but with more suppleness and polish, featuring toasty citrus, pear, melon and honey flavors, fine balance and good length. It appears to have the depth and intensity for further cellaring. Last tasted: 6/90. Drink 1992-1996. 6,593 cases produced. Release: $20. Current: $20. **88**

1986 CLOS DU BOIS WINERY CALCAIRE VINEYARD: Distinctive for its grapefruit flavors, as well as its intensity and coarseness, it is a well-made wine that may simply need more time in the bottle to smooth out. The flavors are good, though not up to the 1983 and 1984 and the structure is fine but just a bit tannic. Last tasted: 3/90. Drink 1992-1996. 5,096 cases produced. Release: $16. Current: $22. **85**

1985 CLOS DU BOIS WINERY CALCAIRE VINEYARD: Austere, smoky and gamy, lacking the sharp fruit focus and opulence of previous vintages. Perfectly drinkable, finishing with a trace of honey. Last tasted: 3/90. Drink 1991-1994. 4,208 cases produced. Release: $18. Current: $28. **83**

1984 CLOS DU BOIS WINERY CALCAIRE VINEYARD: Lush and smooth, with delicious butterscotch, lemon and honey flavors that offer richness, depth and elegance. Not quite as concentrated as the superb 1983, but has perhaps a shade more finesse. Aging well. Last tasted: 3/90. Drink 1991-1994. 1,590 cases produced. Release: $12. Current: $30. **90**

1983 CLOS DU BOIS WINERY CALCAIRE VINEYARD: Fully mature and still retaining its richness, depth and fruit, with well-defined pear, honey, toast and spice flavors that offer excellent concentration and intensity. Crisp, lively acidity sustains the flavors on the finish. Last tasted: 3/90. Drink 1991-1996. 905 cases produced. Release: $12. Current: $30. **91**

CLOS DU BOIS WINERY, Flintwood Vineyard, Dry Creek Valley

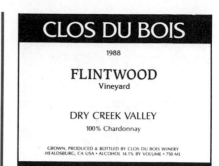

1988 CLOS DU BOIS WINERY FLINTWOOD VINEYARD: Ripe, forward, fruity and complex, delicious already, with well-defined pear, lemon, toast and honey flavors that are smooth and delicate. By far the most elegant and delicate Flintwood, it manages to maintain richness without being weighty. Last tasted: 3/90. Drink 1992-1997. 5,469 cases produced. Release: $18. Current: $18. **90**

1987 CLOS DU BOIS WINERY FLINTWOOD VINEYARD: The leanest and least opulent of the Flintwoods, tight and flinty, with ripe pear, apple and spicy oak flavors that combine to give it richness and depth. Early on this wine showed little of its potential, but in recent tastings it has revealed more breadth and complexity. Last tasted: 3/90. Drink 1992-1997. 4,217 cases produced. Release: $20. Current: $20. **87**

1986 CLOS DU BOIS WINERY FLINTWOOD VINEYARD: Tight, concentrated and focused, it will need more time to grow into its pretty pear, melon and spice flavors, but with another year or so, it should be outstanding. The finish picks up subtle lemon and oak notes, and is well balanced. Last tasted: 3/90. Drink 1992-1996. 4,911 cases produced. Release: $19.50. Current: $25. **88**

1985 CLOS DU BOIS WINERY FLINTWOOD VINEYARD: Oaky, dry and gamy, with an odd chemical note that detracts from the pear

and citrus flavors. Coarse, oaky aftertaste. Has not fared well. Last tasted: 5/90. Best to avoid. 1,535 cases produced. Release: $18. Current: $29. **69**

1984 CLOS DU BOIS WINERY FLINTWOOD VINEYARD: Flabby and losing its fruit. Last tasted: 5/90. Drink 1991-1992. 1,231 cases produced. Release: $11.25. Current: $30. **70**

1983 CLOS DU BOIS WINERY FLINTWOOD VINEYARD: Oxidized and dull, this wine has not aged well. Last tasted: 5/90. Best to avoid. 634 cases produced. Release: $10.50. Current: $30. **69** ·

1980 CLOS DU BOIS WINERY FLINTWOOD VINEYARD: Enticingly complex, very ripe and intense, with rich, concentrated layers of honey, toast, spice, pear and melon flavors that gently unfold and linger on the finish, picking up some vegetal notes along the way. The long aftertaste is very pleasant. Aging very well. Last tasted: 3/90. Drink 1991-1994. 977 cases produced. Release: $17. Current: $32. **87**

CLOS DU BOIS WINERY, Winemaker's Reserve

1988 CLOS DU BOIS WINERY WINEMAKER'S RESERVE: Deftly balanced and rich, with smoky oak, ripe pear and lemon flavors and fresh apple, subtle vanilla and earthy notes, slowly evolving into a worthy successor to the sensational 1987. It is still a bit young and raw, without the silky texture of its predecessor, but all the ingredients are here for greatness. Last tasted: 5/90. Drink 1995-1999. 3,807 cases produced. Not released. **89**

1987 CLOS DU BOIS WINERY WINEMAKER'S RESERVE: Beautifully balanced and delicious to drink now, a complex, forward wine with plenty of attractive honey, butterscotch, spice and vanilla flavors. The crisp acidity carries the flavors, but it is probably at its best now and within the next two years. Last tasted: 3/90. Drink 1991-1995. 3,565 cases produced. Release: $24. Current: $24. **92**

1986 CLOS DU BOIS WINERY PROPRIETOR'S RESERVE: Hard, oaky and gamy, with muted pear and honey flavors. A clumsy, heavily oaked wine that lacks focus and finesse. Last tasted: 5/90. Drink 1991-1994. 4,097 cases produced. Release: $22.50. Current: $23. **78**

1985 CLOS DU BOIS WINERY PROPRIETOR'S RESERVE: The best of the 1985 Clos du Bois bottlings, with crisp pea, pineapple and weedy vegetal notes. The high extract gets coarse on the finish, but it is aging well. Last tasted: 5/90. Drink 1991-1995. 1,762 cases produced. Release: $22. Current: $25. **85**

1981 CLOS DU BOIS WINERY PROPRIETOR'S RESERVE: Oxidized and losing its fruit, fading but still drinkable, with faint honey and butter notes. Last tasted: 5/90. Drink 1991-1992. 3/90 cases produced. Release: $15. Current: $22. **70**

CLOS DU BOIS WINERY, Barrel Fermented,
Alexander Valley

1988 CLOS DU BOIS WINERY BARREL FERMENTED: Clean, ripe and fruity, with pretty, fresh apple and pear flavors and subtle oak nuances, well balanced and well made; not quite as intriguing as the 1987, but very correct. Last tasted: 3/90. Drink 1991-1995. 89,600 cases produced. Release: $11. Current: $11. **85**

1987 CLOS DU BOIS WINERY BARREL FERMENTED: The best of the Barrel Fermented wines, offering more richness and depth than previous bottlings, with fresh, clean, ripe pear, apple and melon flavors of moderate depth and intensity. Flavors linger on the finish. Last tasted: 3/90. Drink 1991-1995. 81,650 cases produced. Release: $11. Current: $11. **87**

1986 CLOS DU BOIS WINERY BARREL FERMENTED: A lemony Chardonnay that is crisp and hard, with concentrated, tart apple flavors, an earthy edge and a long finish. Last tasted: 12/89. Drink 1991-1992. 81,616 cases produced. Release: $10. Current: $12. **80**

1985 CLOS DU BOIS WINERY BARREL FERMENTED: Clean and fruity, with fresh melon flavors and moderate depth and complexity. Still holding up well, but best to drink soon. Last tasted: 3/90. Drink 1991-1993. 47,082 cases produced. Release: $9. Current: $12. **84**

1984 CLOS DU BOIS WINERY BARREL FERMENTED: Aging very well, with layers of ripe pear, melon and piney oak flavors that are elegant and subtle, finishing cleanly. Not quite the depth and concentration of the other bottlings, but pleasant nonetheless. Last tasted: 3/90. Drink 1991-1994. 34,827 cases produced. Release: $8. Current: $12. **84**

Clos Du Val Wine Co.

Carneros Estate, Carneros

CLASSIFICATION: *FIFTH GROWTH*

COLLECTIBILITY RATING: *Not rated*

BEST VINTAGES:

Carneros Estate: 1987, 1988

Napa Valley: 1987, 1985, 1984

Clos Du Val began in 1972 as a red-wine specialist with a Bordeaux-trained winemaker, Bernard Portet, focusing on Cabernet Sauvignon, Merlot and Zinfandel. In 1978 this Stags Leap District winery began making Chardonnay in a tight, austere style. Today Clos Du Val has 90 acres of Chardonnay vineyards in Carneros, and another 20 acres in Yountville. The winery seems determined to succeed with this grape variety, and has moved away from the austere style to fuller, more complex wines.

Until the most recent vintages, Chardonnay had not been the winery's strength, although many of the wines have been good. While I have not tried the 1978 recently, wines from 1979 to 1984 were good, sound, pleasant wines on release, but they have not aged very well. The 1979, for instance, has lost most of its fruit and is light and simple. Chardonnays from 1980 to 1983 are lean and firm, but they are often coarse, lacking richness and finesse. The 1984 offers riper fruit and more depth, but it still could use a little more charm. The 1985 to 1988 vintages show considerable improvement, with more richness, flavor, elegance and balance; they are altogether more complete, harmonious wines that are more fun to drink and have better aging potential.

Portet attributes the changes in winemaking techniques to his visits to Burgundy and the winery's implementation of barrel fermentation and lees aging. The 1987 Clos Du Val is very well balanced, with a long, full finish. The 1988 offers rich, ripe flavors and depth. Clos Du Val also produces a Chardonnay under the Joli Val brand. It is simpler and coarser, but also lower priced. In 1988 Clos Du Val, owned by New Yorker John Goelet, acquired an interest in St. Andrews Winery, which is a few miles south of Clos Du Val. St. Andrews is a Chardonnay specialist that has on occasion excelled with this variety. In 1989 Krimo Souilah, Portet's assistant, assumed winemaking responsibilities.

AT A GLANCE

CLOS DU VAL
5330 Silverado Trail
Napa, CA 94558
(707) 252-6711

Owner: John Goelet

Winemaker: Krimo Souilah (1 year)

Founded: 1972

First Chardonnay vintage: 1978

Chardonnay production: 25,000 cases
    Carneros Estate: 13,000 cases

Chardonnay acres owned: 110

Average age of vines: 7 years

Average wine makeup:
    Carneros Estate: Carneros (100%)

Time in oak: 9 months

Type of oak: French (Nevers)

Oak age: new to 1 year old

Winemaking notes:
    Barrel fermentation: 80%
    Malolactic fermentation: 25%
       to 30%
    Lees aging: varies (3 to 6 weeks)

TASTING NOTES

CLOS DU VAL WINE CO., Carneros, Napa Valley

1988 CLOS DU VAL WINE CO. CARNEROS: May surpass the 1987 in quality with time. It shows a shade more delicacy and purity of flavor, with the pear, melon and spicy peach flavors intermingling on the palate. Fresh, clean and well balanced. Last tasted: 6/90. Drink 1992-1997. 15,000 cases produced. Release: $16. Current: $16. **88**

1987 CLOS DU VAL WINE CO. CARNEROS: The best Clos Du Val Chardonnay to date, displaying elegance, balance, flavor and finesse, with the ripe pear, melon, spice and oak flavors in harmony. The finish is long and bold. A youthful, concentrated wine. Last tasted: 6/90. Drink 1991-1995. 13,000 cases produced. Release: $13. Current: $13. **89**

1986 CLOS DU VAL WINE CO. CARNEROS: Fresh, clean and well balanced, with attractive peach, pear and vanilla flavors of moderate depth and intensity. While it is correct, showing true Chardonnay flavors, it lacks excitement and complexity. Last tasted: 6/90. Drink 1991-1995. 12,000 cases produced. Release: $12. Current: $14. **84**

CLOS DU VAL WINE CO., Various bottlings

1987 CLOS DU VAL WINE CO. NAPA VALLEY: An earthy wine, with simple melon, pear and spice notes that offer more depth and interest than previous bottlings. Still youthful and underdeveloped, but with time it may show more polish and finesse. Last tasted: 6/90. Drink 1991-1996. 9,000 cases produced. Release: $12. Current: $12. **87**

1985 CLOS DU VAL WINE CO. NAPA VALLEY: The 1985 returns to the austere style, with crisp acidity and lemony pear flavors, but it also has a measure of grace and finesse. Still developing nuances and complexity, it is ready to drink but should age well for another five to seven years. Last tasted: 6/90. Drink 1991-1997. 14,000 cases produced. Release: $11.50. Current: $17. **87**

1984 CLOS DU VAL WINE CO. NAPA VALLEY: Clearly richer, fuller and more flavorful than any previous vintages, offering ripe pear and pineapple flavors that are moderately rich and complex. Altogether more satisfying. Last tasted: 6/90. Drink 1991-1995. 12,000 cases produced. Release: $11.50. Current: $15. **85**

1983 CLOS DU VAL WINE CO. NAPA VALLEY: An improvement over earlier bottlings, still tight and acidic, but with more generous fruit flavors. Pear and spice notes come through without the bite. Last tasted: 6/90. Drink 1991-1996. 10,000 cases produced. Release: $11.50. Current: $15. **82**

1982 CLOS DU VAL WINE CO. CALIFORNIA: Lean and bitter, a hard-edged wine that shows ripe pear flavors, but the hardness of the

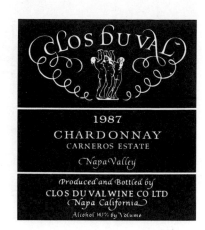

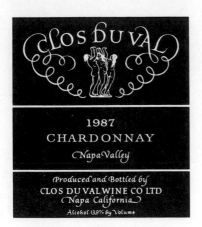

1987
CHARDONNAY
Napa Valley

Produced and Bottled by
CLOS DU VAL WINE CO LTD
Napa California
Alcohol 13.9% by Volume

acidity dominates. With time it may soften, but for now there are more edges than curves. Last tasted: 6/90. Drink 1992-1996. 4,700 cases produced. Release: $11.50. Current: $16. **78**

1981 CLOS DU VAL WINE CO. NAPA VALLEY: Despite some pleasant honey aromas, the flavors are coarse and biting. Decent and drinkable, but lacks charm and finesse. Last tasted: 6/90. Drink 1991-1994. 2,700 cases produced. Release: $12.50. Current: $18. **78**

1980 CLOS DU VAL WINE CO. NAPA VALLEY: Pungent and earthy, very lean and austere on the palate, with mouth-cleaning acidity and some faint, spicy pear flavors behind it. While it is aging well it is still quite tough and could use a little more generosity and flesh. Last tasted: 6/90. Drink 1991-1994. 2,400 cases produced. Release: $12.50. Current: $18. **80**

CLOS PEGASE

Carneros
Napa Valley

CLASSIFICATION:
  Carneros: FOURTH GROWTH
  Napa Valley: FIFTH GROWTH
COLLECTIBILITY RATING: *Not rated*
BEST VINTAGES:
  Carneros: 1987, 1988, 1986

  Napa Valley: 1988, 1987, 1986

In four vintages, Clos Pegase has established two attractive styles of Chardonnay, both made from purchased grapes: One comes from the Carneros region and a second from various Napa Valley vineyards. Under the direction of winemaker Bill Pease, the Carneros bottling has been very elegant and deftly balanced, with good intensity of fruit and lively acidity. The Napa Valley bottling is made from grapes purchased from vineyards throughout Napa Valley, and while it too is elegant and well balanced, it is a fuller, richer wine, though perhaps less complex. The first vintage, the 1985, was produced from Alexander Valley fruit while the showcase estate near Calistoga, designed by architect Michael Graves, was being designed. The 1985, made from Alexander Valley grapes, is aging very well.

While the wines to date have been made from purchased grapes, Clos Pegase's owners, Jan and Mitsuko Shrem, acquired 365 acres in 1989, including parcels in Carneros, which will be planted to Chardonnay. The Shrems' winery is ultramodern, from the postmodernist building to the winemaking equipment.

TASTING NOTES

CLOS PEGASE, Carneros

1988 CLOS PEGASE CARNEROS: Elegant and rich, with earthy Chardonnay flavors that offer ripe pear, grapefruit and citrus notes, and crisp, lively acidity that carries the flavors on the finish. Delicate. Last tasted: 3/90. Drink 1991-1997. 5,128 cases produced. Release: $16.50. Current: $16.50. **89**

AT A GLANCE

CLOS PEGASE
P.O. Box 305
Calistoga, CA 94515
(707) 942-4981

Owners: Jan and Mitsuko Shrem

Winemaker: Bill Pease (4 years)

Founded: 1985

First Chardonnay vintage: 1985
  Carneros: 1986
  Napa Valley: 1986

Chardonnay production: 18,800 cases
  Carneros: 5,100 cases
  Napa Valley: 13,700 cases

Chardonnay acres owned: 365

Average wine makeup:
  Carneros: Carneros (100%)
  Napa Valley: (100%)

Time in oak: 6 months

Type of oak: French (Tronçais, Vosges, Allier, Nevers, Limousin)

Oak age: new and old

Winemaking notes:
  Barrel fermentation: 10% to 40%
  Malolactic fermentation: 10% to 40%
  Lees aging:
    Napa Valley: 10% to 40% (3 to 6 months)

CLOS PEGASE

1985
CHARDONNAY
ALEXANDER VALLEY

PRODUCED AND BOTTLED BY CLOS PEGASE
ST. HELENA, CALIFORNIA ALCOHOL 13.6% BY VOLUME

and crisp, lively acidity that carries the flavors on the finish. Delicate. Last tasted: 3/90. Drink 1991-1997. 5,128 cases produced. Release: $16.50. Current: $16.50. **89**

1987 CLOS PEGASE CARNEROS: Creamy, smooth and elegant, with bright pineapple, vanilla, pear and lemon flavors that are braced with crisp acidity and framed by subtle oak. Wonderful balance and harmony. Last tasted: 3/90. Drink 1991-1995. 4,402 cases produced. Release: $15.50. Current: $17. **90**

1986 CLOS PEGASE CARNEROS: Crisp, smooth and elegant, with subtle pear, pineapple, lemon and nutmeg flavors that glide across the palate. Distinctive for its elegance and finesse. Last tasted: 3/90. Drink 1991-1996. 2,825 cases produced. Release: $15.50. Current: $17. **89**

CLOS PEGASE, Napa Valley

1988 CLOS PEGASE NAPA VALLEY: Wonderfully smooth and elegant, very delicate, with pretty pear, honey, toast and vanilla flavors that linger on the palate. Distinctive for its elegance and finesse. Best of the Napa Valley bottlings. Last tasted: 3/90. Drink 1991-1996. 13,681 cases produced. Release: $12. Current: $12. **88**

1987 CLOS PEGASE NAPA VALLEY: Ripe, full and flavorful, with rich pear and apple flavors, elegant and refined, finishing with a touch of earthiness and oak. Last tasted: 3/90. Drink 1991-1995. 11,131 cases produced. Release: $12. Current: $12. **86**

1986 CLOS PEGASE NAPA VALLEY: Ripe, full and elegant, with rich, creamy apple, pear and butter notes, well balanced and ready to drink. Shows some oak on the finish. Last tasted: 3/90. Drink 1991-1995. 6,689 cases produced. Release: $12. Current: $14. **85**

1985 CLOS PEGASE ALEXANDER VALLEY: Clos Pegase's first bottling is fully mature, ripe, elegant and well balanced, with plenty of rich, creamy apple, pear and vanilla flavors that are smooth and long on the palate. Last tasted: 3/90. Drink 1991-1995. 3,100 cases produced. Release: $13. Current: $15. **87**

CONGRESS SPRINGS VINEYARDS

San Ysidro Reserve, Santa Clara County
Monmartre, Santa Cruz Mountains
Santa Clara County

CLASSIFICATION:

San Ysidro Reserve: FOURTH GROWTH

Monmartre: FIFTH GROWTH

Santa Clara County: FIFTH GROWTH

COLLECTIBILITY RATING: *Not rated*

BEST VINTAGES:

San Ysidro Reserve: 1987, 1988

Monmartre: 1988, 1987, 1982

Santa Clara County: 1984, 1985, 1988

Congress Springs Vineyards has emerged as one of the top Chardonnay producers in the Santa Cruz Mountains. Founded in 1976 by winemaker Daniel Gehrs, Congress Springs has been making Chardonnay since 1982. The winery now has three separate bottlings that have consistently been very good. Gehrs began producing a Private Reserve and Santa Clara County bottling in 1982. The Private Reserve comes from the 8-acre Monmartre vineyard, located at the winery, which typically yields rich and intense yet elegant Chardonnays. The style has shifted away from bolder, riper wines to more refined and graceful ones, but not at the expense of rich fruit and toasty oak.

Both the 1987 and 1988 are beautifully balanced, with ripe, intense fruit flavors integrated with spicy oak. Gehrs dropped the Private Reserve designation in favor of the Monmartre vineyard name in 1987. The Santa Clara County bottling, from the San Ysidro vineyard near Gilroy, is made in a similar style, featuring ripe, full-bodied flavors and ample oak shadings. The best vintage so far has been the rich, creamy 1984, followed by a more delicate 1985. Beginning with the 1986 vintage, Congress Springs also added a Reserve bottling from the San Ysidro vineyard. The 1987 stands out as the finest Congress Springs Chardonnay I've tasted, combining toasty, smoky oak with sharply focused Chardonnay flavors. The 1988 is a shade more elegant and delicate, but equally impressive. This is a winery that is serious about Chardonnay and worth watching.

Gehrs departed the winery in 1990 following a buyout by his partners, Anglo-American Agriculture, owners of San Ysidro Vineyards. Ron Hendry is the new winemaker.

AT A GLANCE

CONGRESS SPRINGS VINEYARDS
23600 Congress Springs Road
Saratoga, CA 95070
(408) 741-5424

Owner: Anglo-American Agriculture

Winemaker: Ron Hendry (1 year)

Founded: 1976

First Chardonnay vintage: 1982
San Ysidro Reserve: 1986
Monmartre: 1982
Santa Clara County: 1982

Chardonnay production: 16,000 cases
San Ysidro Reserve: 2,300 cases
Monmartre: 700 cases
Santa Clara County: 13,000 cases

Chardonnay acres owned: 181
San Ysidro Vineyard: 181
Monmartre: 8

Average age of vines: 13 years
San Ysidro: 22 years
Monmartre: 14 years
Santa Clara County: 7 years

Vineyard locations:
San Ysidro: Santa Clara County
Monmartre: Santa Cruz Mountains

Average wine makeup:
Santa Clara County: Santa Clara County (100%)

Time in oak: 7 months

Type of oak: French

Oak age: new to 3 years old

Winemaking notes:
Barrel fermentation: 100%
Monmartre: 100%
San Ysidro Reserve: 100%
Santa Clara County: varies
Malolactic fermentation: usually none
Lees aging: 100% (7 months)

TASTING NOTES

CONGRESS SPRINGS VINEYARDS, San Ysidro Reserve, Santa Clara County

1988 CONGRESS SPRINGS VINEYARDS SAN YSIDRO RESERVE: A shade more delicate and fruity than the 1987 San Ysidro bottling, but very close in style, with subtle pear, melon and citrus flavors that are deftly balanced. Not quite as rich as the 1987, but elegant and stylish. Last tasted: 4/90. Drink 1991-1994. 2,682 cases produced. Release: $20. Current: $20. **86**

1987 CONGRESS SPRINGS VINEYARDS SAN YSIDRO RESERVE: One of the best Congress Springs bottlings yet, combining rich, toasty, spicy French oak with austere, sharply focused pear, citrus, pineapple and honey flavors, altogether a wonderful display of fruit and oak in a complex, elegant package. Last tasted: 4/90. Drink 1991-1995. 2,000 cases produced. Release: $16. Current: $23. **90**

1986 CONGRESS SPRINGS VINEYARDS SAN YSIDRO RESERVE: Combines rich, smooth pear and pineapple flavors with firmness and intensity. Good aftertaste. Still developing. Last tasted: 4/90. Drink 1991-1994. 2,275 cases produced. Release: $15. Current: $22. **85**

CONGRESS SPRINGS VINEYARDS, Monmartre, Santa Cruz Mountains

1988 CONGRESS SPRINGS VINEYARDS MONMARTRE: Rich, full-bodied and creamy, with pretty pear, apple, melon and pineapple flavors and gentle toasty oak seasoning, this is an elegant, subtle Chardonnay with flavors that offer nuance and depth. Last tasted: 4/90. Drink 1991-1996. 224 cases produced. Release: $30. Current: $30. **88**

1987 CONGRESS SPRINGS VINEYARDS MONMARTRE: Ripe, full-bodied and well balanced, with pretty lemon, pear, pineapple and spice notes that are moderately rich and intense, finishing with apple flavors that echo on the finish. Last tasted: 4/90. Drink 1991-1995. 770 cases produced. Release: $28. Current: $30. **87**

1986 CONGRESS SPRINGS VINEYARDS PRIVATE RESERVE: Firm and oaky but well structured, with a tight core of intense yet elegant pear, melon, spice and mint notes that offer a measure of elegance and delicacy. Just peaking now. Last tasted: 4/90. Drink 1991-1994. 552 cases produced. Release: $20. Current: $23. **85**

1985 CONGRESS SPRINGS VINEYARDS PRIVATE RESERVE: A big, rich, flavorful wine with ripe, intense pear and pineapple flavors flanked by toasty oak shadings. Balanced, mature and ready to drink. Last tasted: 4/90. Drink 1991-1994. 431 cases produced. Release: $16. Current: $27. **84**

1984 CONGRESS SPRINGS VINEYARDS PRIVATE RESERVE: Another big, rich, boldly flavored Chardonnay with intense oak, pear and pineapple flavors, but in this vintage the Private Reserve seems overblown and overly mature when tasted with the Santa Clara County bottling. It does not have the finesse and grace of its sibling. Last tasted: 4/90. Drink 1991-1992. 420 cases produced. Release: $16. Current: $27. **80**

1983 CONGRESS SPRINGS VINEYARDS PRIVATE RESERVE: Strives for a big, rich, toasty style, but does not have the fruit concentration, complexity or depth to achieve it. Finish gets dry and earthy, bordering on mossy. Last tasted: 4/90. Drink 1991-1992. 328 cases produced. Release: $15. Current: $28. **74**

1982 CONGRESS SPRINGS VINEYARDS PRIVATE RESERVE: Aging gracefully although past its apogee, offering rich, intense, well-balanced pear, toast, earth and spice notes that are still quite engaging, with attractive, mature Chardonnay flavors that are persistent and lingering. Last tasted: 4/90. Drink 1991-1994. 310 cases produced. Release: $15. Current: $28. **87**

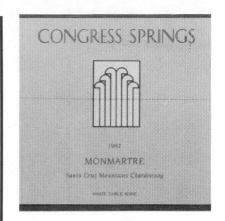

CONGRESS SPRINGS VINEYARDS, Santa Clara County

1988 CONGRESS SPRINGS VINEYARDS SANTA CLARA COUNTY BARREL FERMENTED: Smoky and toasty from barrel fermentation, but underneath those aromas is an elegant, pretty core of pear, apple, melon and pineapple flavors that are well proportioned and enlivened by crisp acidity. Last tasted: 4/90. Drink 1991-1995. 13,431 cases produced. Release: $14. Current: $14. **86**

1987 CONGRESS SPRINGS VINEYARDS SANTA CLARA COUNTY: Offers sharply focused, austere lemon, pear and spicy oak flavors that are elegantly balanced but not quite as opulent and previous bottlings. The finish picks up a trace of honey and pineapple. Last tasted: 4/90. Drink 1991-1994. 12,500 cases produced. Release: $12. Current: $18. **84**

1986 CONGRESS SPRINGS VINEYARDS SANTA CLARA COUNTY: A more elegant wine for Congress Springs, a shade lighter and more refined, with spice, pear, vanilla and toast notes that are not quite as dense as previous vintages. This wine offers deft balance and plenty of flavor. Last tasted: 4/90. Drink 1991-1994. 4,900 cases produced. Release: $12. Current: $18. **83**

1985 CONGRESS SPRINGS VINEYARDS SANTA CLARA COUNTY: A very ripe, rich, exotic wine with intense, complex pear and honey flavors that turn dry and oaky, but provide plenty of flavor from start to finish. Best now. Last tasted: 4/90. Drink 1991-1994. 2,500 cases produced. Release: $12. Current: $20. **87**

1984 CONGRESS SPRINGS VINEYARDS SANTA CLARA COUNTY: Rich, smooth and creamy, with sharply focused, mouthwatering honey, pear and butterscotch flavors that are quite attractive and beautifully integrated, gaining complexity and finesse on the finish, with subtle

Congress Springs

1984
Santa Clara County
CHARDONNAY

BY CONGRESS SPRINGS VINEYARDS, SARATOGA, CA BW

smoky, toasty flavors that add depth. Last tasted: 4/90. Drink 1991-1994. 2,053 cases produced. Release: $11. Current: $25. **90**

1983 CONGRESS SPRINGS VINEYARDS SANTA CLARA COUNTY BARREL FERMENTED: Deep in color, fully evolved and stylish, very rich and toasty, almost more woody oak, earth and butterscotch flavors than fruit, but displaying alluring, exotic, rich pear and pineapple notes to capture the imagination. Last tasted: 4/90. Drink 1991-1994. 1,102 cases produced. Release: $10. Current: $25. **85**

1982 CONGRESS SPRINGS VINEYARDS SANTA CLARA COUNTY: Mature and fading, with faint pear and melon flavors of only moderate intensity and depth. Better in its prime. Last tasted: 4/90. Drink 1991-1992. 957 cases produced. Release: $10. Current: $20. **79**

CUVAISON WINERY

Reserve, Carneros
Carneros

CLASSIFICATION: *SECOND GROWTH*

COLLECTIBILITY RATING: *AA*

BEST VINTAGES:

Reserve: 1986, 1988, 1987

Carneros: 1985, 1988, 1987

Few Napa Valley wineries better illustrate the dramatic shift toward Carneros-grown Chardonnay than Cuvaison. This winery, owned by the Schmidheiny family of Switzerland, is based near Calistoga at the northern end of Napa Valley, yet increasingly through the years the winery has looked farther south to cooler climates for better grapes. Today Cuvaison's investment in Carneros includes 200 acres of Chardonnay, and its two Chardonnay wines, a regular bottling and a new reserve, have moved to the upper echelon of Napa Valley producers.

Founded in 1969, Cuvaison made its first Chardonnay in 1970, at which time the grapes came from various parts of the valley, including the mountains. I have not recently tasted any wines older than the 1978, which is still in very good condition albeit a bit coarse and alcoholic. The 1979 and 1980 are also aging well. Both are mature, very ripe and intense, but true to the style of that era, when the wines were made by Philip Togni. The 1981 is hard and tight and the 1982 was a disappointing wine from a mixed vintage, while the 1983 always has shown an "off," tanky quality. The 1984 is an improvement over the previous two vintages, but still biting on the finish. Starting with the 1985 vintage, Cuvaison entered a new era, creating vastly superior wines. Much of the credit is due to John Thatcher, winemaker since 1983, and his efforts to bring greater elegance and grace to the wines. The 1985 Cuvaison is a dramatic example, very ripe and rich, with deeply concentrated fruit flavors, but still very refined and elegant. It ranks among the top wines of the vintage. The 1986 is less opulent, but continues to improve with bottle age, and it still has a few years before peaking. The 1987 defines elegance and finesse. It is a tightly structured wine with graceful balance and a long finish. The 1988 follows a similar pattern, with sharply focused flavors and fine depth. Production in 1988 reached 34,000 cases.

Beginning with the 1986 vintage, Cuvaison introduced a Carneros Reserve Chardonnay that offers a style different from the

AT A GLANCE

CUVAISON WINERY
P.O. Box 384
Calistoga, CA 94515
(707) 942-6266

Owner: The Schmidheiny family, Switzerland

Winemaker: John Thatcher (7 years)

Founded: 1969

First Chardonnay vintage: 1970
  Carneros: 1970
  Reserve: 1986

Chardonnay production: 35,000 cases
  Reserve: 2,000 cases
  Carneros: 33,000 cases

Chardonnay acres owned: 200

Average age of vines: 8 years

Average wine makeup: Carneros (100%)

Time in oak: 5 months

Type of oak: French (Nevers, Allier, Limousin)

Oak age:
  Reserve: new (30% to 80%) to 3 years old
  Carneros: new to 3 years old (25% each)

Winemaking notes:
  Barrel fermentation:
    Reserve: 90%
    Carneros: 70%
  Malolactic fermentation:
    Reserve: 5% to 50%
    Carneros: 5% to 20%
  Lees aging: 70% (5 months)

regular Carneros bottling. The Carneros Reserve is deliberately more subtle and complex, with a shade more oakiness and less of the ripe, opulent fruit found in the regular Carneros bottling. Winemaker Thatcher believes it will age longer than the regular bottling. Either way, both are very fine examples of their type, different expressions of Chardonnay that appear to have the intensity and depth to cellar for eight to 10 years. In 1988, 2,400 cases of the Reserve were produced. Both Chardonnays undergo partial malolactic fermentation, from 5 percent to 20 percent, and are primarily barrel fermented.

TASTING NOTES

CUVAISON WINERY, Reserve, Carneros

1988 CUVAISON WINERY RESERVE: Young and vibrant, its intense pear, pineapple and citrus flavors are rich and concentrated yet elegant and graceful, with subtle pear and honey notes lingering on the finish. This wine will need three to four years to reach maturity, but by then it could rate with Cuvaison's finest. Last tasted: 6/90. Drink 1992-2001. 2,400 cases produced. Not released. **92**

1987 CUVAISON WINERY RESERVE: Firm and delicious, with a tight core of richly concentrated pear, lemon, fig and melon flavors that are graced by smoky, toasty oak that adds complexity. Beautifully balanced, ready now but can hold for five to seven years. Last tasted: 7/90. Drink 1992-1998. 1,260 cases produced. Release: $22. Current: $22. **91**

1986 CUVAISON WINERY RESERVE: Cuvaison's first Reserve, a deceptively rich, elegant, deeply concentrated wine with tightly focused pear, pineapple, citrus and melon flavors that are framed by subtle oak shadings and structured with bracing acidity. Impressive for its balance, depth and character, as well as its grace and finesse. Last tasted: 6/90. Drink 1992-1999. 1,800 cases produced. Release: $20. Current: $28. **94**

CUVAISON WINERY, Various bottlings

1988 CUVAISON WINERY CARNEROS: Remarkably complex and dramatic, rivaling the stunning 1985 in complexity, finesse and depth. It is made entirely from Cuvaison's Carneros vineyards and features rich, sharply focused pineapple, pear and lemon flavors that linger on the finish. Last tasted: 4/90. Drink 1993-1999. 34,000 cases produced. Release: $15. Current: $15. **91**

1987 CUVAISON WINERY NAPA VALLEY: Very tight and reined in, but packed with gorgeous apple, pear, melon and spicy citrus notes that are complex and elegant, finishing with a touch of oak and crisp acidity. For all its fruity allure now, it should only get better once the texture softens. Last tasted: 4/90. Drink 1993-1998. 31,000 cases produced. Release: $13.50. Current: $16. **90**

1986 CUVAISON WINERY NAPA VALLEY: Improving in the bottle, it is still a tight, compact, richly flavored wine with great intensity and sharply focused flavors. The ripe pineapple, citrus, apple and oak flavors are youthful and well knit, lingering on the finish. Still needs time. Last tasted: 4/90. Drink 1992-1998. 22,000 cases produced. Release: $12.75. Current: $18. **89**

1985 CUVAISON WINERY NAPA VALLEY: A star of the 1985 vintage, offering enormous richness, intensity and concentration of fruit, with layers of ripe, full-bodied pineapple, pear, apple and spice flavors framed by subtle, toasty vanilla and oak. Always deliciously complex, it keeps getting better, with smoky, buttery notes on the finish. Last tasted: 4/90. Drink 1991-1996. 6,000 cases produced. Release: $12. Current: $20. **93**

1984 CUVAISON WINERY NAPA VALLEY: A considerable improvement over the previous two bottlings. It is lean and fruity, with ripe pear and melon flavors and very lively acidity though rather sharp and biting on the palate. Last tasted: 4/90. Drink 1991-1995. 5,000 cases produced. Release: $12. Current: $20. **82**

1983 CUVAISON WINERY NAPA VALLEY: Marred by tanky, lean, earthy flavors that are not very pleasant. Last tasted: 4/90. Best to avoid. 21,000 cases produced. Release: $12. Current: $17. **62**

1982 CUVAISON WINERY NAPA VALLEY: This wine has never offered much appeal, with its heavy, dull, sulfur aromas and flavors. It tasted the same way the last time around. Last tasted: 4/90. Best to avoid. 14,000 cases produced. Release: $12. Current: $17. **61**

1981 CUVAISON WINERY NAPA VALLEY: Lean, tart, tough and angular, a coarse wine that's difficult to warm up to, but there are some decent pear, apple and spice notes that perhaps with time will taste smoother. Last tasted: 4/90. Drink 1991-1995. 10,000 cases produced. Release: $12. Current: $18. **75**

1980 CUVAISON WINERY NAPA VALLEY: Very ripe, intense and concentrated, with rich pineapple, apple and spicy oak flavors, a big, broad, oaky wine that makes no pretense toward delicacy or finesse and is holding up well. Last tasted: 4/90. Drink 1991-1995. 10,000 cases produced. Release: $11. Current: $26. **87**

1979 CUVAISON WINERY NAPA VALLEY: Fully mature and drinking well, with pretty spice, pine and mature Chardonnay flavors; better balanced than the 1978, but the fruit flavors seem muted. Still, there is plenty to like; and it shows no serious signs of fatigue. Last tasted: 4/90. Drink 1991-1995. 10,000 cases produced. Release: $10. Current: $26. **84**

1978 CUVAISON WINERY NAPA VALLEY: Intense, ripe and alcoholic, but the mature, buttery pear and apple flavors are still a touch coarse and tannic. With time it may soften, but the alcohol will probably always stick out. Last tasted: 4/90. Drink 1991-1995. 10,000 cases produced. Release: $10. Current: $28 **81**

DEHLINGER WINERY
Russian River Valley

CLASSIFICATION: *THIRD GROWTH*
COLLECTIBILITY RATING: *A*
BEST VINTAGES: *1988, 1987, 1986*

T he Russian River Valley Chardonnays of Tom Dehlinger are almost the exact opposite of those produced by neighbor Cecil De Loach. While the latter's Chardonnays offer ripe, explosive, exotic fruit flavors, Dehlinger's are distinct for their elegance, subtlety and tightly reined-in fruit. At times they share those wonderful mouthwatering pineapple, honey and butter notes, while in other vintages Dehlinger's wines are clearly less showy, seemingly holding back for further time in the bottle.

Even though Dehlinger has been making Chardonnay in this cool coastal climate for more than a decade, his wines are often overlooked. In tasting back to his 1982 vintage, one has to admire the consistently high quality of the Chardonnays he has produced. Dehlinger's wines feature firm, crisp, sometimes hard acidity that bodes well for aging, for the wines have the core of concentrated fruit to last and gain in the bottle. The 1983, for instance, is still crisp, youthful and evolving, and the 1984's ripe pear, honey and butterscotch flavors are held in focus by tart acidity. The 1985 is just maturing and has the fruit concentration to age another decade. The 1986 tastes more evolved than the 1985, but the 1987 and 1988 reach new heights for Dehlinger, revealing more richness and depth of flavor without sacrificing the austerity and tension created by firm acidity and the judicious use of oak.

TASTING NOTES

DEHLINGER WINERY, Russian River Valley

1988 DEHLINGER WINERY: Another highly successful vintage for Dehlinger, full-bodied, with a wonderful harmony of rich honey, pear, apple and melon flavors that are complex and well integrated. Only moderately oaky, this 1988 is well balanced, with a lingering aftertaste

---

AT A GLANCE

DEHLINGER WINERY
6300 Guerneville Road
Sebastopol, CA 95472
(707) 823-2378

Owner: Thomas Dehlinger

Winemaker: Thomas Dehlinger (15 years)

Founded: 1975

First Chardonnay vintage: 1975

Chardonnay production: 4,500 cases

Chardonnay acres owned: 14

Average age of vines: 13 years

Average wine makeup: Russian River Valley (100%)

Time in oak: 10 months

Type of oak: French (Limousin, Tronçais, Allier)

Oak age: new to 2 years old (33% each)

Winemaking notes:
  Barrel fermentation: 100%
  Malolactic fermentation: 67%
  Lees aging: 100% (10 months)

that highlights the toast and honey notes. Last tasted: 4/90. Drink 1991-1996. 4,000 cases produced. Release: $12. Current: $12. **91**

1987 DEHLINGER WINERY: Combines rich, deep, complex honey, pear, melon and spicy oak flavors that are silky smooth and glide across the palate, finishing with excellent length and plenty of fruit. Last tasted: 4/90. Drink 1991-1996. 4,900 cases produced. Release: $11. Current: $12. **90**

1986 DEHLINGER WINERY: Intense and concentrated, with rich, creamy butterscotch, citrus and pineapple flavors that offer fine depth and complexity, with crisp acidity on the finish. Complete and well balanced, drinking very well now. Last tasted: 4/90. Drink 1991-1995. 3,200 cases produced. Release: $11. Current: $14. **87**

1985 DEHLINGER WINERY: Elegant and understated, featuring ripe apple, pear and melon flavors with subtle oak shadings, a wine of charm and harmony that is clean and refreshing. Well balanced; should age another six to eight years. Last tasted: 5/90. Drink 1991-1998. 2,000 cases produced. Release: $10. Current: $14. **86**

1984 DEHLINGER WINERY: Rich yet elegant, with pretty honey, pear, spice and butterscotch flavors that are braced by crisp, mouthwatering acidity. Fine balance, good depth, aging very well. Last tasted: 4/90. Drink 1991-1996. 2,300 cases produced. Release: $10. Current: $14. **86**

1983 DEHLINGER WINERY: A crisp, tart wine with lean lemon and pear flavors of moderate depth and intensity and a full, fruity finish. Well balanced and showing some complexity, it is still youthful and aging quite well, perhaps lacking only in dramatics. Tasted in magnum. Last tasted: 4/90. Drink 1991-1995. 1,400 cases produced. Release: $10. Current: $15. **85**

1982 DEHLINGER WINERY: Deep gold color. It is oxidized and oily. Last tasted: 4/90. Best to avoid. 1,400 cases produced. **62**

AT A GLANCE

DE LOACH VINEYARDS
1791 Olivet Road
Santa Rosa, CA 95401
(707) 526-9111

Owners: Cecil and Christine
De Loach

Winemaker: Cecil De Loach
(15 years)

Founded: 1975

First Chardonnay vintage: 1980
O.F.S.: 1984

Chardonnay production: 28,000 cases
O.F.S.: 3,000 cases
Russian River Valley: 25,000 cases

Chardonnay acres owned: 27

Average age of vines: 9 years

Average wine makeup: Russian River
Valley (100%)

Time in oak:
O.F.S.: 9 months
Russian River Valley: 3 months

Type of oak: French

Oak age:
O.F.S.: 2 years old
Russian River Valley: 2.5 years old

Winemaking notes:
Barrel fermentation:
O.F.S.: 100%
Russian River Valley: 50%
Malolactic fermentation:
O.F.S.: 100%
Russian River Valley: 50%
Lees aging:
O.F.S.: 100% (9 months)
Russian River Valley: 50%
(2 months)

DE LOACH VINEYARDS
O.F.S., Russian River Valley
Russian River Valley

CLASSIFICATION:
O.F.S.: *THIRD GROWTH*
Russian River Valley: FOURTH GROWTH

COLLECTIBILITY RATING: A

BEST VINTAGES:
O.F.S.: *1988, 1987, 1984*

Russian River Valley: 1986, 1985, 1984

The great appeal of De Loach Chardonnays is their early drinking charm. They are typically big, rich, lush and fruity, showing an impeccable balance of wildly exotic tropical fruit and subtle, spicy vanilla oak. This Santa Rosa winery is owned and operated by former San Francisco fireman Cecil De Loach and his wife, Christine. They have been making voluptuous Chardonnays since 1980. Though their grapes come from the cool Russian River Valley, often lacking the benefit of warm, sunny days, they never seem to have any problems getting their grapes to ripen fully.

Since 1984 De Loach has also bottled a rich yet somewhat more reined-in Chardonnay called O.F.S., for Our Finest Selection. There is clearly a difference in styles. While the early O.F.S. bottlings seemed a bit shy, the most recent vintages have been sensational, offering a broad array of flavors, including a wealth of complex fruit with a structure built for better aging potential. The O.F.S. is fully barrel fermented and undergoes malolactic fermentation, while only half the Russian River Valley wines undergo these processes. The O.F.S. spends up to nine months in oak, while the Russian River Valley spends only three months in used oak.

It is tempting to drink the De Loach Chardonnays on release or soon after, and because they tend to mature quickly this is the best strategy. The 1980, 1981 and 1982 Russian River Valley Chardonnays are well past their primes despite being exceptional wines on release. The 1984 to 1988 vintages are all excellent wines with a wealth of flavor and finesse. The 1984 O.F.S. bottling is still going strong; the 1985 has been somewhat disappointing in recent tastings. The 1986 is rich and full-bodied and the 1987 and 1988 vintages are the best De Loach has produced to date.

TASTING NOTES

DE LOACH VINEYARDS, O.F.S., Russian River Valley

1988 DE LOACH VINEYARDS O.F.S.: Youthful, rich, intense and fruity, with attractive peach, melon, apple and pear flavors that are lightly shaded by spicy vanilla and oak. Well balanced and elegant, it is showing early signs of complexity. Last tasted: 5/90. Drink 1991-1995. 3,200 cases produced. Release: $22. Current: $22. **92**

1987 DE LOACH VINEYARDS O.F.S.: Another deliciously complex Chardonnay that is rich, smooth and round, with layers of peach, pear, apple and spicy oak notes that all contribute to this wine's wonderful array of flavors. It is drinking exceptionally well now but should hold for another five years. Last tasted: 5/90. Drink 1991-1995. 2,400 cases produced. Release: $22. Current: $25. **92**

1986 DE LOACH VINEYARDS O.F.S.: Very ripe, with tart peach, earth and toast flavors, more reined-in and elegant than most De Loaches. It is aging very well, its crisp acidity carrying the flavors a long way on the finish. As tasty as this wine is now, it should continue to hold for another three to five years. Last tasted: 5/90. Drink 1991-1995. 1,800 cases produced. Release: $22. Current: $26. **86**

1985 DE LOACH VINEYARDS O.F.S.: More elegant but less impressive than the 1985 regular bottling, it is lean and earthy, with toasty pear flavors that turn woody and almost bitter on the finish. Seems out of sync with the De Loach style. Last tasted: 5/90. Drink 1991-1995. 1,200 cases produced. Release: $20. Current: $22. **79**

1984 DE LOACH VINEYARDS O.F.S.: Deliciously rich, smooth and complex, with intense yet elegant pear, vanilla, apple and subtle peach flavors that offer great finesse and harmony, finishing with crisp, lively acidity and excellent length. Last tasted: 5/90. Drink 1991-1995. 600 cases produced. Release: $20. Current: $28. **90**

DE LOACH VINEYARDS, Russian River Valley

1988 DE LOACH VINEYARDS RUSSIAN RIVER VALLEY: A delicious wine with fresh, ripe peach, pear, apple and nectarine flavors, crisp acidity and pretty, vanilla oak shadings. This is a classic De Loach, with plenty of flavor and finesse. Last tasted: 5/90. Drink 1992-1996. 26,000 cases produced. Release: $15. Current: $15. **87**

1987 DE LOACH VINEYARDS RUSSIAN RIVER VALLEY: Impressive for its elegance, abundance of fruit, fresh, ripe pear, melon and spice flavors and wonderful balance. Lacks the finish of the 1985 but has all the flavor of the finest De Loaches. Last tasted: 5/90. Drink 1991-1995. 24,000 cases produced. Release: $15. Current: $20. **87**

1986 DE LOACH VINEYARDS RUSSIAN RIVER VALLEY: Another delicious De Loach fruit bowl, with fresh, crisp, lively pear, apple, melon

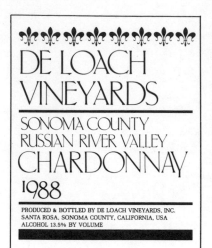

and buttery oak flavors in an elegant, stylish package. Fine length on the finish; more delicate than the 1985. Last tasted: 5/90. Drink 1991-1994. 18,000 cases produced. Release: $14. Current: $20. **89**

1985 DE LOACH VINEYARDS RUSSIAN RIVER VALLEY: Combines a wealth of flavor with a sense of elegance and finesse. The ripe pear, apple, melon and spice flavors are complemented by honey and toast notes on the finish. Fruit galore, with a long, toasty aftertaste. Last tasted: 5/90. Drink 1991-1994. 12,000 cases produced. Release: $14. Current: $23. **90**

1984 DE LOACH VINEYARDS RUSSIAN RIVER VALLEY: Still at its peak, very ripe and fruity, with rich apple, pear, melon and buttery oak flavors that are intense and lively, finishing with a burst of pear and spice. Last tasted: 5/90. Drink 1991-1994. 8,000 cases produced. Release: $12.50. Current: $24. **88**

1983 DE LOACH VINEYARDS RUSSIAN RIVER VALLEY: Aging well but beginning to decline, the ripe pear, honey and butter flavors are still rich and attractive carrying through on the finish. Last tasted: 5/90. Drink 1991-1993. 8,000 cases produced. Release: $12. Current: $22. **83**

1982 DE LOACH VINEYARDS RUSSIAN RIVER VALLEY: Dense, vegetal and honeyed, mature and past its prime. It has lost much of its fruit. Last tasted: 5/90. Drink 1991. 3,900 cases produced. Release: $12. Current: $20. **74**

1981 DE LOACH VINEYARDS RUSSIAN RIVER VALLEY: Richly flavored but vegetal and tired on the palate. A big wine that offered considerably more charm when younger. Last tasted: 5/90. Drink 1991. 2,800 cases produced. Release: $10. Current: $18. **72**

1980 DE LOACH VINEYARDS RUSSIAN RIVER VALLEY: Badly oxidized, nowhere near its younger, fruitier self. Last tasted: 5/90. Best to avoid. 2,000 cases produced. Release: $10. Current: $18. **62**

EDNA VALLEY VINEYARD

Edna Valley

CLASSIFICATION: *THIRD GROWTH*

COLLECTIBILITY RATING: *A*

BEST VINTAGES: *1981, 1987, 1988, 1986*

Edna Valley Vineyard, a part of the Chalone Inc. wine family, makes some of the boldest, richest, ripest and toastiest Chardonnays in California. This deliberate style was first developed and perfected at Chalone Vineyard.

The winery's 305 acres of Chardonnay are rooted in Edna Valley in San Luis Obispo County, which has a cool climate moderated by westerly breezes off the Pacific Ocean. Grapes grown there ripen fully only after a long growing season, which suits winemaster Richard Graff and winemaker Stephen Dooley fine. They prefer ripe berries to maximize flavor and richness. At Edna Valley Vineyard, like Chalone, the wines are highly manipulated, They undergo full malolactic fermentation, 100 percent barrel fermentation and lees aging, and spend a fair amount of time in new toasty oak barrels. For Edna Valley, these techniques create wines of enormous complexity, texture and ageworthiness.

In a decade of winemaking, there have been many great successes, most notably the explosively rich and buttery 1981 that is the finest Chardonnay produced so far at Edna Valley Vineyard. When the weather is patchy, the wines often suffer as well, as seen in 1982 and 1983. The winery is back on track with the 1984 and 1985, but returns to new heights with the 1986 through 1988 vintages. The 1987 and 1988 vintages in particular are fine examples of the Edna Valley Vineyard style. They display plenty of flavor while still maintaining a sense of elegance and finesse without weight. In 1988 some 46,500 cases were produced. The winery is part-owned by Paragon Vineyard, an independent grower in the Edna Valley area that supplies the winery's grapes.

AT A GLANCE

EDNA VALLEY VINEYARD
Route 3, Box 255
San Luis Obispo, CA 93401
(805) 544-9594

Owners: Chalone Inc., Paragon Vineyard

Winemaker: Stephen Dooley (3 years)

Founded: 1980

First Chardonnay vintage: 1980

Chardonnay production: 46,000 cases

Chardonnay acres owned: 305

Average age of vines: 17 years

Average wine makeup: Edna Valley (100%)

Time in oak: 9 months

Type of oak: French (Sirigue, François Frères)

Oak age: new to 2 years old (33% each)

Winemaking notes:
  Barrel fermentation: 100%
  Malolactic fermentation: 100%
  Lees aging: 100% (5 months)

TASTING NOTES

EDNA VALLEY VINEYARD, Edna Valley

1988 EDNA VALLEY VINEYARD: Elegant, rich and fruity, with fresh, ripe pear, melon, spice and subtle oak flavors, a more forward and fruity style, moving away from the heavy toastiness of the early

152

EDNA VALLEY
VINEYARD

1987

Edna Valley

Chardonnay

Estate Bottled

Produced and bottled by
Edna Valley Vineyard
San Luis Obispo California USA
Alcohol 13.4% by vol. Contains Sulfites

vintages. Showing signs of complexity and depth, but it is youthful and still developing. Last tasted: 3/90. Drink 1992-1997. 46,500 cases produced. Release: $14.75. Current: $16. **89**

1987 EDNA VALLEY VINEYARD: Distinctive for its richness, intensity, concentration and elegance, the finest Edna Valley since 1981, offering layers of pretty toast, vanilla, pear, honey and smoke flavors that glide across the palate, repeating the flavors on the finish. Last tasted: 3/90. Drink 1991-1996. 41,000 cases produced. Release: $14. Current: $20. **91**

1986 EDNA VALLEY VINEYARD: Very youthful and attractive, with intense, ripe pear, spice, lemon and toasty oak flavors, but not nearly as toasty as some earlier bottlings. A fine balance of fruit and oak and excellent length. Last tasted: 3/90. Drink 1991-1995. 36,000 cases produced. Release: $13.50. Current: $20. **88**

1985 EDNA VALLEY VINEYARD: More elegant than most Edna Valleys, showing a shade more oak and less concentration and extract than previous bottlings. That style may appeal to some more than others, and while it is aging well, with smoke, leather, toast and ripe pear flavors, it is not quite as dramatic as the best from this producer. Last tasted: 3/90. Drink 1991-1994. 31,000 cases produced. Release: $13. Current: $25. **85**

1984 EDNA VALLEY VINEYARD: A bold, rich and flavorful wine that is a touch coarse, but it offers plenty of ripe fig, melon, honey and butter flavors and it is well balanced with good depth. Aging quite well, though short of outstanding. Last tasted: 6/90. Drink 1991-1995. 23,800 cases produced. Release: $12.50. Current: $24. **86**

1983 EDNA VALLEY VINEYARD: Fully evolved, coarse and astringent, with mature earth, pear and rich oak flavors. Best to drink soon. Last tasted: 3/90. Drink 1991-1993. 15,500 cases produced. Release: $12.50. Current: $20. **76**

1982 EDNA VALLEY VINEYARD: Heavily oxidized now, with hints of pear and butter, not much fruit and the finish turns bitter. May have limited interest. Last tasted: 3/90. Drink 1991. 17,400 cases produced. Release: $12. Current: $22. **71**

1981 EDNA VALLEY VINEYARD: In magnificent condition, bold and complex, with great richness, depth and concentration, with layers of honey, pear, toast and buttery oak flavors that offer power, intensity and finesse. Smoky aftertaste. Last tasted: 3/90. Drink 1991-1995. 11,000 cases produced. Release: $12. Current: $25. **94**

1980 EDNA VALLEY VINEYARD: Deep gold, with pretty, complex toast, smoke, earth, pear and honey flavors that still offer plenty of intensity and depth, with a finish that echoes the tiers of flavor with a touch of butterscotch. Last tasted: 3/90. Drink 1991-1994. 5,200 cases produced. Release: $12. Current: $25. **87**

FAR NIENTE WINERY
Napa Valley

CLASSIFICATION: *FIRST GROWTH*
COLLECTIBILITY RATING: *AAA*
BEST VINTAGES: *1980, 1979, 1988, 1987, 1985*

In a decade of making Chardonnay, Far Niente Winery in Oakville has proved to be a consistently excellent producer of complex, ageworthy wines. Not many California wineries with this many vintages can boast that none of their Chardonnays has gone over the hill, yet Far Niente has demonstrated that its Chardonnays age exceptionally well from vintage to vintage. The winery's first vintage, the 1979, has evolved into an amazingly rich, smooth, complex wine that is at its peak but has the depth and firmness to hold together another five to 10 years. The 1980 is also in magnificent condition, distinct for its elegance and flavor.

Owner Gil Nickel began as a Chardonnay specialist and has spent millions of dollars renovating this stately old stone winery, buying the finest winemaking equipment available and setting high standards. The winemaking, under the direction of Dirk Hampson since 1983, has shown a commitment to excellence, creating wines that feature crisp acidity, firm, deep, concentrated flavors, subtle oak shadings and impeccable balance.

Part of the longevity of these Chardonnays stems from their origins in cool climates, where the grapes do not get overripe and acidity is high. The wine does not go through malolactic fermentation, which creates its firm, sometimes austere texture, although it is barrel fermented in a mixture of new and used oak, one and two years old. The grapes are grown at the winery's estate vineyard, Stelling Vineyard in Oakville, and in two key vineyards in the Coombsville area, a cool region east of the city of Napa that is increasingly gaining a reputation as a prime area for Chardonnay.

Far Niente (Italian for "without a care") is almost always near the top in each vintage. In 1981 Far Niente produced an excellent wine that is holding up very well, and in 1982 and 1983 produced two Chardonnays, including one from its estate vineyard, both of which were exceptionally fine and among the top wines of those vintages. The 1984 is very good, and drinking well now, while the 1985 has been slow to evolve and is showing better now than on release, with its rich and silky texture. The 1986 is also coming around in the bottle, revealing more fruit and complexity, while both the 1987 and 1988 vintages are showing more forward fruit and delicacy. Both wines should benefit

AT A GLANCE
FAR NIENTE WINERY
P.O. Box 327
Oakville, CA 94562
(707) 944-2861

Owner: Gil Nickel

Winemaker: Dirk Hampson
(7 years)

Founded: 1979

First Chardonnay vintage: 1979

Chardonnay production: 24,000 cases

Chardonnay acres owned: 100

Average age of vines: 12 years

Average wine makeup:
Napa Valley: Oakville (45%),
Coombsville (55%)

Time in oak: 7 months

Type of oak: French (Limousin,
Allier, Burgundian)

Oak age: new to 2 years old
(33% each)

Winemaking notes:
Barrel fermentation: 100%
Malolactic fermentation: none
Lees aging: 10% to 40% (1 to
17 months)

from cellaring another two to three years and will be good candidates for aging more than a decade. Production has reached 24,000 cases.

TASTING NOTES

FAR NIENTE WINERY, Napa Valley

1988 FAR NIENTE WINERY: A very successful vintage at Far Niente, youthful and fruity, with attractive peach, pear and nectarine flavors that are rich and concentrated while maintaining elegance and finesse. It has a long aftertaste. Last tasted: 3/90. Drink 1992-1998. 24,000 cases produced. Release: $26. Current: $28. **91**

1987 FAR NIENTE WINERY: Ripe and full, with a lush, creamy texture and rich fig, lemon, melon and apple flavors that are elegant and sharply focused, gaining intensity and depth on the finish. Wonderful balance, excellent aging potential. Last tasted: 3/90. Drink 1992-1998. 20,000 cases produced. Release: $26. Current: $30. **91**

1986 FAR NIENTE WINERY: Has improved considerably in the bottle, offering ripe apple, pear, melon and fig flavors that are intense and concentrated, with superb depth and complexity. Very slow to evolve, elegant in style. Last tasted: 3/90. Drink 1991-1997. 18,000 cases produced. Release: $24. Current: $31. **88**

1985 FAR NIENTE WINERY: Much more impressive now than on release, the 1985 has been slow to evolve, with rich, lush fruit flavors that add a measure of elegance and finesse on the palate. The pear, melon, spice and apple notes are understated, but linger on the finish. Last tasted: 3/90. Drink 1992-1998. 14,300 cases produced. Release: $24. Current: $33. **90**

1984 FAR NIENTE WINERY: Plenty of fresh, ripe fruit from a very warm vintage, showing generous, lively peach, pear and nectarine flavors and a touch of spicy vanilla and oak. Last tasted: 3/90. Drink 1991-1996. 11,000 cases produced. Release: $22. Current: $36. **86**

1983 FAR NIENTE WINERY: Very ripe and appealing, with peach, honey, apple and melon flavors that offer fine depth and intensity, gaining a creamy texture that adds nuances to the finish. Not quite as complex as in previous showings, but aging very well. Last tasted: 3/90. Drink 1991-1995. 8,000 cases produced. Release: $22. Current: $38. **87**

1983 FAR NIENTE WINERY ESTATE: Drinking at its peak and aging well, a shade more complex than the regular bottling, with full, ripe melon, pear and butter notes that turn to butterscotch on the finish. Long and lingering. Last tasted: 3/90. Drink 1991-1995. 2,000 cases produced. Release: $22. Current: $38. **89**

1982 FAR NIENTE WINERY: Spicy and peppery on the nose, an earthier wine with intense pear, melon and apple flavors that sit well on the palate, finishing with good length. A successful wine from a difficult vintage. Last tasted: 3/90. Drink 1991-1996. 7,000 cases produced. Release: $18. Current: $38. **86**

1982 FAR NIENTE WINERY ESTATE: Remarkably complex, rich and creamy, with pretty pear, earth and spicy oak flavors that offer great elegance and finesse. A wine of great harmony that is in peak drinking condition now, finishing with a long, delicate aftertaste. Last tasted: 3/90. Drink 1991-1996. 2,000 cases produced. Release: $18. Current: $38. **91**

1981 FAR NIENTE WINERY: Plenty of rich, complex honey, vanilla and oak flavors, excellent depth and intensity, with some leafy apple notes, very fine balance and an overall impression of youthful vitality. Not quite as complex as some of its predecessors. Last tasted: 3/90. Drink 1991-1996. 7,000 cases produced. Release: $16.50. Current: $40. **88**

1980 FAR NIENTE WINERY: Amazingly elegant, rich and smooth, with tart peach, pear, honey and melon flavors that offer uncommon depth and intensity, with impeccable balance and finesse. Clearly one of the top 1980s produced. Shows no sign of fatigue. Last tasted: 3/90. Drink 1991-1997. 6,500 cases produced. Release: $16.50. Current: $45. **93**

1979 FAR NIENTE WINERY: Far Niente's first vintage is aging remarkably well, with lovely, rich honey, spice, nutmeg and butter flavors, a smooth, creamy texture and pear, peach and nectarine notes on the long aftertaste. Simply wonderful. Last tasted: 3/90. Drink 1991-1996. 3,700 cases produced. Release: $15. Current: $45. **92**

FERRARI-CARANO VINEYARDS & WINERY

Reserve, Carneros
Alexander Valley

CLASSIFICATION: *SECOND GROWTH*

COLLECTIBILITY RATING: *AA*

BEST VINTAGES:

Reserve: 1988, 1986

Alexander Valley: 1987, 1988, 1986, 1985

AT A GLANCE

**FERRARI-CARANO
VINEYARDS & WINERY**
P.O. Box 1549
Healdsburg, CA 95448
(707) 433-6700

Owners: Don and Rhonda Carano

Winemaker: George Bursick (5 years)

Founded: 1985

First Chardonnay vintage: 1985
  Reserve: 1986

Chardonnay production: 23,000 cases
  Reserve: 1,000 cases
  Alexander Valley: 22,000 cases

Chardonnay acres owned: 118

Average age of vines: 8 years

Average wine makeup:
  Reserve: Carneros (95%),
  Alexander Valley: (5%)

Time in oak: 11 months

Type of oak: French

Oak age: new (60%) to 3 years old

Winemaking notes:
  Barrel fermentation: 85%
  Malolactic fermentation:
    15% to 25%
  Lees aging:
    Reserve: 100% (12 months)
    Alexander Valley: 80% (12 months)

Ferrari-Carano is a Chardonnay drinker's delight. California has enjoyed its share of splashy Chardonnay debuts, but few wineries have followed through with such consistently excellent and stylistically pleasing Chardonnays.

This winery in Sonoma County's Dry Creek Valley is the ambitious undertaking of hoteliers Don and Rhonda Carano. Owners of the Eldorado Hotel in Reno, Nev., they have spent several million dollars acquiring and planting vineyards and building a state-of-the-art winery. Founded in 1985, Ferrari-Carano is now headed toward production of 40,000 cases of Chardonnay, most of it from the owners' 118 acres of vines in Sonoma County. Ferrari-Carano also makes several hundred cases of reserve Chardonnay from its vineyards in Carneros.

What is most impressive about the Ferrari-Carano Chardonnays is how consistent the style has been from vintage to vintage. Winemaker George Bursick creates wines of wonderful complexity and subtle oak seasoning through a variety of techniques, using Ferrari-Carano's high-tech vinification equipment to perfection. It is a winery within a winery, capable of producing several lots of wine in different styles. Bursick utilizes different yeast strains, fermentation strategies and oak barrels, along with varying degrees of malolactic and barrel fermentation. They all contribute to the complex Ferrari-Carano style.

The wines feature very ripe, rich, sharply focused and complex fruit flavors that are deftly balanced with elegance and finesse. The first vintage, the 1985, has maintained its rich fruitiness and excellent length. It has a touch of residual sugar, but it has the depth and concentration to benefit from another three to five years' cellaring. The 1986 is tightly knit, with delicious flavor. The 1987 is one of the top wines of that vintage, displaying great complexity and elegance. The

1988 extends the streak of outstanding wines, with wonderful, complex fruit, fine balance and excellent length.

The reserve Chardonnays come primarily from Carneros grapes and have been more austere and reined in, a style that winemaker Bursick believes will allow the wines to age even longer. To date the 1986 shows that kind of aging potential, while the 1987 is a shade leaner, although it was opening up the last time I tasted it, and with time it may surprise by how much it gains in the bottle. The 1988 shows wonderfully complex aromas and flavors to match. This winery needs only a longer track record to move up in the classification.

TASTING NOTES

FERRARI-CARANO VINEYARDS & WINERY,
Reserve, California

1988 FERRARI-CARANO VINEYARDS & WINERY RESERVE: Wonderful aromas of fresh melon, apple, pear and honey, with rich, deep, complex, elegant flavors to match, another delicious reserve bottling that is smooth, supple, fragrant and long on the finish, with just the right touch of creamy, buttery oak. Still youthful and evolving, it can only get better. Last tasted: 6/90. Drink 1992-1998. 1,200 cases produced. Not released. **93**

1987 FERRARI-CARANO VINEYARDS & WINERY RESERVE: Austere and understated, but with time it may evolve into something more dramatic. It has an attractive hazelnut flavor to complement the ripe, rich pear, honey and fruit notes. Balanced, elegant, delicate and well proportioned. Last tasted: 5/90. Drink 1992-1998. 780 cases produced. Release: $28. Current: $28. **89**

1986 FERRARI-CARANO VINEYARDS & WINERY RESERVE: A shade richer and more concentrated than the 1986 Alexander Valley, this is a tightly knit, sharply focused wine with ripe pear, spice, lemon-lime and toasty butter notes that show a measure of delicacy and grace. Can stand some cellaring, but all the ingredients are there for greatness. Last tasted: 5/90. Drink 1991-1997. 300 cases produced. Release: $28. Current: $42. **93**

FERRARI-CARANO VINEYARDS & WINERY,
Alexander Valley

1988 FERRARI-CARANO VINEYARDS & WINERY ALEXANDER VALLEY: Enormous concentration of fruit, with layers of melon, apple, pear, spice, nutmeg and subtle honey and toast flavors that add a pleasant dimension to the gorgeous fruit. The texture is silky smooth

and the flavors echo long and full. Last tasted: 5/90. Drink 1991-1997. 22,000 cases produced. Release: $18. Current: $18. **93**

1987 FERRARI-CARANO VINEYARDS & WINERY ALEXANDER VALLEY: One of the stars of the 1987 vintage, combining deep, rich, intense and complex pear, lemon, spice, apple and honey flavors with elegance and finesse and a creamy texture. Best from this producer so far. Amazingly complex and elegant. Last tasted: 5/90. Drink 1991-1997. 14,000 cases produced. Release: $16. Current: $23. **94**

1986 FERRARI-CARANO VINEYARDS & WINERY ALEXANDER VALLEY: This sharply focused wine has rich, ripe pear, apple, melon and spice flavors, is tightly knit and beautifully balanced, with delicious flavors and just the right touch of acidity and oak to add depth to the flavors. Finishes with a touch of buttery oak. Drinking well now. Last tasted: 5/90. Drink 1991-1996. 7,200 cases produced. Release: $16. Current: $28. **92**

1985 FERRARI-CARANO VINEYARDS & WINERY ALEXANDER VALLEY: Ferrari-Carano's first Chardonnay is aging exceptionally well, still displaying a wealth of rich, ripe, exotic tropical fruit, honey, pear and butterscotch flavors that are deep, complex and concentrated, finishing with great length and a long, fruity aftertaste. Wonderful balance and proportion, despite the trace of residual sugar. Drinking at its peak. Last tasted: 5/90. Drink 1991-1996. 2,500 cases produced. Release: $14. Current: $30. **91**

FISHER VINEYARDS
Whitney's Vineyard, Sonoma County
Coach Insignia, Sonoma County

CLASSIFICATION:
Whitney's Vineyard: THIRD GROWTH
Coach Insignia: FIFTH GROWTH

COLLECTIBILITY RATING:
Whitney's Vineyard: A
Coach Insignia: Not rated

BEST VINTAGES:
Whitney's Vineyard: 1980, 1984, 1988

Coach Insignia: 1986

The mountainside vineyard of Fred and Juelle Fisher straddles the Napa-Sonoma county line about halfway between Calistoga and Santa Rosa. From this spectacular setting the Fishers produce two Chardonnays. Coach Insignia, named after the Fishers' "Body by Fisher" automotive company, is made with grapes from the vineyard at the winery in the mountains and from the Fishers' Napa Valley vineyard on Silverado Trail near Dunaweal Lane, and purchased grapes from Dry Creek Valley, Sonoma Mountain and Sonoma Valley. In a typical vintage, 35 percent to 50 percent of the grapes are grown by the Fishers.

Each year the winery also sets aside a barrel or two of Chardonnay from Whitney's Vineyard, named after the Fishers' eldest daughter. While production of this wine is now up to 65 cases, its minuscule supply makes it difficult to find. It is often served at parties hosted by the Fishers. Of the two wines, the Whitney's Vineyard is usually superior, coming from the finest barrels of wine from the home vineyard and showing more richness and flavor than the Coach Insignia. The two wines are made in a similar style under the supervision of winemaker Henryk "Max" Gasiewicz. They are tight and austere early on but age well. Both wines from the 1980 and 1981 vintages, for instance, are still drinking well; the Whitney's 1980 is one of the top wines of the vintage. Both wines were successful in 1984, but the Whitney's is a bold, rich, engagingly complex wine. The 1985s are close in quality but slow to evolve; they are backward and missing the elegance of the best wines from that vintage. The 1986 Coach Insignia is the best bottling since 1980. No Whitney's was produced that year. Both wines were tight and focused in 1987, but a shade more generous and forward in 1988. Case production of Coach Insignia has

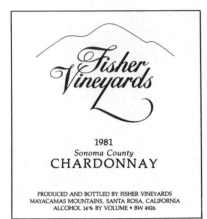

1981
Sonoma County
CHARDONNAY

PRODUCED AND BOTTLED BY FISHER VINEYARDS
MAYACAMAS MOUNTAINS, SANTA ROSA, CALIFORNIA
ALCOHOL 14% BY VOLUME • BW 4926

climbed to 10,000 in the 1988 vintage, but should creep upward to 12,000 in the future. In recent vintages a greater percentage of the wine has been barrel fermented, and malolactic fermentation has increased to about 40 percent.

TASTING NOTES

FISHER VINEYARDS, Whitney's Vineyard, Sonoma County

1988 FISHER VINEYARDS WHITNEY'S VINEYARD: Elegant and lively, with fresh, ripe, rich pear, tangerine, melon and spice notes that offer complexity, finesse and richness without weight. Delicately balanced, picking up smoky oak on the finish. Has room to grow. Last tasted: 4/90. Drink 1992-1997. 65 cases produced. Not released. **88**

1987 FISHER VINEYARDS WHITNEY'S VINEYARD: Attractive for its elegance and finesse, with sharply focused pear, apple, melon and toast flavors, offering length and finesse on the finish. Well balanced, drinking well now. Last tasted: 4/90. Drink 1991-1995. 48 cases produced. Release: $24. Current: $24. **86**

1985 FISHER VINEYARDS WHITNEY'S VINEYARD: Intense and concentrated, with rich pear, apple and spicy oak flavors, but it is still coarse and tannic, with a tough edge. Balanced, with plenty of flavor, but missing the finesse and elegance of the best bottlings. Last tasted: 4/90. Drink 1991-1994. 48 cases produced. Release: $24. Current: $30. **84**

1984 FISHER VINEYARDS WHITNEY'S VINEYARD: Rich yet elegant, with sharply focused honey, pear, toast and nutmeg flavors that glide across the palate. Very complex and enticing, finishing with flavors that fan out on the palate, picking up a pretty butterscotch note. Last tasted: 4/90. Drink 1991-1995. 48 cases produced. Release: $20. Current: $30. **90**

1983 FISHER VINEYARDS WHITNEY'S VINEYARD: Better than the regular bottling, but still somewhat coarse and tannic. It is aging well but not showing much complexity. The toast, pear, citrus and honey notes are correct but the finish gets rough. Last tasted: 4/90. Drink 1991-1993. 24 cases produced. Release: $20. Current: $30. **78**

1982 FISHER VINEYARDS WHITNEY'S VINEYARD: Brilliant yellow-gold, fully mature, with spicy oak, honey and tangerine flavors, this elegant, full-bodied wine is fully mature and should be consumed. The finish is short and drying. Last tasted: 6/90. Drink 1991-1993. 24 cases produced. Release: $20. Current: $25. **78**

1981 FISHER VINEYARDS WHITNEY'S VINEYARD: A shade less exciting than the 1980 Whitney's, with a leafy, ripe apple flavor that while rich and attractive is rather one-dimensional. Finish picks up a trace of oakiness. Aging well, but not likely to improve. Last tasted: 4/90. Drink 1991-1994. 24 cases produced. Release: $20. Current: $25. **85**

1980 FISHER VINEYARDS WHITNEY'S VINEYARD: An elegant, graceful wine that is aging amazingly well, with rich, toasty, earthy lemon, pear, spice and butter flavors that are complex and sharply focused, finishing with great length, intensity and finesse. Last tasted: 4/90. Drink 1991-1996. 24 cases produced. Release: $20. Current: $30. **92**

FISHER VINEYARDS, Coach Insignia, Sonoma County

1988 FISHER VINEYARDS COACH INSIGNIA: The best Coach Insignia since 1986, smooth and rich, with fresh, ripe pear, nectarine, peach and apple flavors that are complex and enticing. Elegant and balanced, with delicacy and grace, drinking well now. Last tasted: 4/90. Drink 1991-1996. 6,000 cases produced. Release: $18. Current: $18. **87**

1987 FISHER VINEYARDS COACH INSIGNIA: Ripe and balanced, but also firm and tannic, with rich apple, melon, honey and pear flavors that are neatly framed by oak but dry out on the finish. Nearing maturity. Last tasted: 4/90. Drink 1991-1995. 5,000 cases produced. Release: $18. Current: $18. **84**

1986 FISHER VINEYARDS COACH INSIGNIA: Rich, smooth, creamy and buttery, with ripe pear, spice, apple and melon flavors that are deceptively intense and concentrated, with a sense of elegance and finesse and a long finish. Youthful and flavorful now, it should only get better for the next two to five years. Last tasted: 4/90. Drink 1991-1997. 3,000 cases produced. Release: $17. Current: $20. **90**

1985 FISHER VINEYARDS COACH INSIGNIA: Hard, tannic and somewhat coarse, lacking the grace and finesse of the best Coach Insignias, yet still offering ripe, rich, perfumed honey and pear flavors; a wine that is holding its own. Last tasted: 4/90. Drink 1991-1993. 33,000 cases produced. Release: $16. Current: $20. **84**

1984 FISHER VINEYARDS COACH INSIGNIA: This first Coach Insignia bottling is ripe and flavorful, with honey, toast and pear flavors that are elegant and well balanced. Only moderately complex, it should be consumed soon. Last tasted: 4/90. Drink 1991-1994. 2,500 cases produced. Release: $15. Current: $20. **82**

FISHER VINEYARDS, Various bottlings

1983 FISHER VINEYARDS SONOMA AND NAPA COUNTIES: Elegant and well balanced for a 1983, with pretty lemon, pear and honey flavors that are moderately rich and intense and finishing with crisp acidity. A shade past its prime, but still drinking well. Last tasted: 4/90. Drink 1991-1994. 3,000 cases produced. Release: $14. Current: $18. **82**

1982 FISHER VINEYARDS SONOMA COUNTY: Fully mature, with full-bodied, well-defined honey and pear flavors that are coarse and

162

tannic. Best to drink soon. Last tasted: 4/90. Drink 1991-1993. 2,200 cases produced. Release: $14. Current: $22. **81**

1981 FISHER VINEYARDS SONOMA COUNTY: Fully mature and aging well, with toasty vanilla notes adding complexity to the ripe, rich, elegant pear and apple flavors. The finish picks up a pretty, complex smoky oak flavor that is quite attractive. Last tasted: 4/90. Drink 1990-1993. 2,000 cases produced. Release: $14. Current: $25. **88**

1980 FISHER VINEYARDS SONOMA COUNTY: Mature and toasty, a shade past its prime, with earthy pineapple, pear and spicy oak flavors that are rich and smooth. Fully evolved, drink now. Last tasted: 4/90. Drink 1990-1993. 1,200 cases produced. Release: $14. Current: $22. **85**

FLORA SPRINGS WINE CO.
Barrel Fermented, Napa Valley

CLASSIFICATION: *FIRST GROWTH*
COLLECTIBILITY RATING: *AAA*
BEST VINTAGES: *1987, 1983, 1988, 1979*

With recent vintages Flora Springs Wine Co., halfway between St. Helena and Rutherford, has begun to receive the recognition it deserves for its rich, complex, toasty Barrel Fermented bottling, one of the state's most distinctive Chardonnays. Flora Springs is owned by the Komes and Garvey families, and its 82 acres of Chardonnay are in two vineyards. The 26-acre P. & J. Vineyard is at the east end of Zinfandel Lane near the Napa River-Oakville area, while the 56-acre Crossroads Ranch straddles the Oakville Crossroad near Conn Creek. Since 1980 Flora Springs has barrel fermented its Chardonnays in 100 percent new oak, but the wines do not undergo malolactic fermentation.

The Barrel Fermented Chardonnay is usually very rich, with toasty, oaky flavors and a smooth, complex, satiny texture along with ripe honey, pear, melon and vanilla flavors. Some vintages of this wine are slow to evolve and others are showy early on, but either way they age exceptionally well, gaining tremendous depth and complexity. In tasting back through the older vintages, I found that the 1979 remains a stunning wine, amazingly rich and complex and capable of further aging. The 1980, bottled under the "Special Select" designation, was the first under winemaker Ken Deis, and it is nearly as intriguing and complex, while the 1981 is among the top wines of the vintage. The 1982 has been disappointing in several tastings, uneven in quality, but I have not tasted it recently. The 1983 is simply fantastic and the star of the vintage. The 1984 features a good dose of toasty oak, but the delicate fruit underneath manages to match the intensity of the wood. The 1985 has been slow to develop and is not up to the quality of the vintage's top wines, but it is showing better now than on release. The 1986 is similar in style, fairly oaky and slow to mature.

With the 1987 and 1988 vintages, Flora Springs began to age its Barrel Fermented wines on the lees, with half the 1988 being made with that technique, bringing it back to the top of the class of Chardonnay producers. The 1987 is one of the greatest Chardonnays I've tasted from California, with its satiny smooth, creamy texture and beautifully defined flavors. A 200-case lot of lees-aged Chardonnay was also produced, and while scarce, it is truly a sensational wine. The 1988 is showing signs that it too will rival the 1987. It's more forward and

AT A GLANCE
FLORA SPRINGS WINE CO.
1978 W. Zinfandel Lane
St. Helena, CA 94574
(707) 963-5711

Owners: The Komes and Garvey families
Winemaker: Ken Deis (10 years)
Founded: 1978
First Chardonnay vintage: 1979
  Barrel Fermented: 1982
Chardonnay production: 10,000 cases
  Barrel Fermented: 4,500 cases
Chardonnay acres owned: 92
Average age of vines: 13 years
Average wine makeup: Oakville, Napa Valley (100%)
Time in oak: 6 months
Type of oak: French (Nevers, Limousin, Tronçais)
Oak age: new (100%)
Winemaking notes:
  Barrel fermentation: 100%
  Malolactic fermentation: none
  Lees aging: 100% (6 months)

Flora Springs also makes a non-barrel-fermented Napa Valley Chardonnay, and while it is often very good, it is not in the same class as the Barrel Fermented.

Flora Springs Winery is on Zinfandel Lane in an old stone winery once owned by Louis M. Martini.

TASTING NOTES

FLORA SPRINGS, Barrel Fermented, Napa Valley

1988 FLORA SRINGS BARREL FERMENTED: Young and fruity, displaying pretty, forward pear, vanilla, toast and honey flavors that are delicate, concentrated and well defined. This wine has all the ingredients for greatness, but needs a year or two of bottle development. Last tasted: 4/90. Drink 1993-1997. 4,700 cases produced. Release: $24. Current: $24. **92**

1987 FLORA SRINGS BARREL FERMENTED: A stunning Flora Springs, amazingly rich and complex, offering more depth and nuance. Along with the fabulous 1983, it is one of the finest Chardonnays I've tasted. This is a seamless wine that displays beautiful flavors of spice, toast, pear and smoke in great harmony. Last tasted: 4/90. Drink 1992-1997. 3,400 cases produced. Release: $20. Current: $24. **95**

1986 FLORA SRINGS BARREL FERMENTED: This wine continues to improve, though it's still oaky. Underneath that toasty veneer is a rich core of pear, pineapple and toasty spice flavors that are very well balanced. Give it another year or two. Last tasted: 4/90. Drink 1992-1996. 2,800 cases produced. Release: $20. Current: $24. **87**

1985 FLORA SRINGS BARREL FERMENTED: Just misses the mark. It has consistently shown more dry oakiness on the palate than fruit. There are plenty of concentrated pear and spice flavors, and with further aging the wood may soften, giving the wine more harmony and finesse. Last tasted: 4/90. Drink 1992-1996. 2,100 cases produced. Release: $18. Current: $27. **85**

1984 FLORA SRINGS BARREL FERMENTED: True to the Flora Springs style, rich and toasty, but also quite woody. The oak rivals but does not overshadow the ripe pear and spicy fruit flavors. Last tasted: 4/90. Drink 1991-1994. 1,800 cases produced. Release: $18. Current: $28. **88**

1983 FLORA SRINGS BARREL FERMENTED: An absolutely sensational 1983 and one of Flora Springs' finest, this is amazingly complex and flavorful, with rich honey, pear, butter, toast, smoke and spice flavors that are deliciously fresh and vibrant and a long, lingering aftertaste. Still in pristine condition. Last tasted: 4/90. Drink 1991-1996. 1,200 cases produced. Release: $18. Current: $28. **94**

1982 FLORA SRINGS BARREL FERMENTED: A disappointing wine from a difficult vintage, it is uneven in quality, at times decent, but more often very lean and austere. Last tasted: 4/90. Drink 1991-1992. 700 cases produced. Release: $15. Current: $15. **70**

1981 FLORA SRINGS SPECIAL SELECT: One of the stars of the excellent 1981 vintage, offering a rich array of fresh fruit, complex pear, apple, spice and nutmeg flavors that are young and concentrated, long and full on the finish. Perhaps a shade past its prime, but not by much. Impressive. Last tasted: 4/90. Drink 1991-1995. 1,500 cases produced. Release: $12. Current: $25. **89**

1980 FLORA SRINGS SPECIAL SELECT: Holding up well for a 1980, fully mature and well developed, with intriguing, rich pear, smoke, butterscotch and toasty oak flavors that linger on the finish. Best to drink it now, but can hold a year or two. Last tasted: 4/90. Drink 1991-1993. 300 cases produced. Release: $12. Current: $25. **88**

1979 FLORA SRINGS: Delicious, with rich, toasty, buttery flavors that are fully mature, yet it is aging very well, displaying more complex, developed Chardonnay flavors than pure fruit, but that's what you expect with an 11-year-old. Pretty toasty aftertaste. Last tasted: 4/90. Drink 1991-1994. 200 cases produced. Release: $9. Current: $25. **91**

Folie a Deux Winery

Napa Valley

CLASSIFICATION: *THIRD GROWTH*
COLLECTIBILITY RATING: *A*
BEST VINTAGES: *1987, 1986, 1985*

Despite two difficult vintages at the outset, Folie à Deux (in French, "a shared fantasy") Winery in St. Helena has settled on an impressive style of austere, ageworthy Chardonnays that are remarkably consistent from year to year. The winery, owned by Evie and Larry Dizmang, two mental health professionals (the label is a parody of the Rorschach test), was founded in 1981. The first two Chardonnays from 1982 and 1983 were unimpressive, but since 1984 the wines have displayed a very deliberate and successful house style.

Typically the wines early on are austere and crisp, with bracing acidity and sharply focused flavors, offering intensity and concentration that hold up and improve in the bottle. The 1984 has matured into an elegant, richly flavored wine that has just reached maturity. The 1985 provides more subtlety and finesse, without the ripe richness of the 1984, but some may find it more suited to their tastes. The 1986 is right on target, walking a tightrope between lean, compact fruit flavors and subtle oak shadings. The 1987, made in a vintage in which some wines displayed raw acids, is the best Folie à Deux to date, offering more fruit, oak and complexity. The 1988 is right in sync with the winery's style, perhaps more forward and supple, but built to age for up to a decade.

The Dizmangs own 7 acres of Chardonnay at their winery and supplement that with grapes from Yountville and Carneros. They picked their grapes at 22.5 Brix for 1988, which gives them ripe but not overripe fruit, and plenty of citrus and lemon notes from acidity. Rick Tracy has been winemaker since 1987.

At a Glance

FOLIE A DEUX WINERY
3070 St. Helena Highway
St. Helena, CA 94574
(707) 963-1160

Owners: Larry and Evie Dizmang

Winemaker: Rick Tracy (3 years)

Founded: 1981

First Chardonnay vintage: 1982

Chardonnay production: 7,000 cases

Chardonnay acres owned: 7

Average age of vines: 5 years

Average wine makeup: Carneros, Napa Valley (40%); Yountville (40%); St. Helena (20%)

Time in oak: 9 months

Type of oak: French (Limousin, Nevers)

Oak age: new (40%) to 1 year old

Winemaking notes:
  Barrel fermentation: 40%
  Malolactic fermentation: none
  Lees aging: 40% (5 months)

Tasting Notes

FOLIE A DEUX WINERY, Napa Valley

1988 FOLIE A DEUX WINERY: Young and underdeveloped now, with firmly structured, tight pear and apple flavors and crisp acidity. Needs another year or two in the bottle to soften and mature, but fits in snugly with the winery style. Last tasted: 7/90. Drink 1991-1997. 6,900 cases produced. Release: $16. Current: $16. **87**

1987 FOLIE A DEUX WINERY: Remarkably elegant and refined, perhaps the best yet from Folie à Deux, with intense, concentrated pear, melon, fig and citrus flavors framed by toasty, smoky oak notes. Well balanced, youthful and alive, with firm acidity. Last tasted: 7/90. Drink 1992-1997. 5,300 cases produced. Release: $15. Current: $16. **90**

1986 FOLIE A DEUX WINERY: Ripe and intense, with rich pear, citrus and fig flavors and subtle toasty oak shadings, combining to give complexity and finesse. On the finish the acidity is bracing. A youthful wine that can stand cellaring. Last tasted: 7/90. Drink 1991-1997. 2,600 cases produced. Release: $15. Current: $18. **88**

1985 FOLIE A DEUX WINERY: Showing more subtlety and finesse than the 1984, but similar in style, with intense citrus, pear, apple and spice flavors. Not quite the richness and depth of the 1984, but some may find it more appealing. Last tasted: 7/90. Drink 1991-1995. 1,200 cases produced. Release: $14. Current: $18. **88**

1984 FOLIE A DEUX WINERY: Elegant and lively, with crisp, sharply focused apple, pear, melon, fig and spice notes that are intense and concentrated, rich without being heavy and very clean and delicate on the finish. Youthful and just reaching maturity. Last tasted: 7/90. Drink 1991-1996. 1,100 cases produced. Release: $14. Current: $18. **87**

1982 FOLIE A DEUX WINERY: Folie à Deux's first vintage is quite mature now, with a deep gold color and ripe, full-bodied honey and apricot flavors that turn heavy and tannic on the finish. Showed better earlier on. Last tasted: 6/90. Drink 1991-1992. 500 cases produced. Release: $12.50. Current: $17. **78**

FORMAN VINEYARD

Napa Valley

CLASSIFICATION: *SECOND GROWTH*
COLLECTIBILITY RATING: *AA*
BEST VINTAGES: *1985, 1986, 1988*

With five vintages under his belt and his own label, Ric Forman has proved he has not lost his touch with Chardonnay, but in fact is getting better. In 1970 Forman first produced Chardonnay at Sterling Vineyards, and later worked at Newton. Since 1984 he has been making Chardonnay at his small, château-style winery nestled in the forested hills near the Meadowood Country Club off Silverado Trail.

Each of the five Forman vintages has been excellent, with intense, concentrated, complex fruit flavors and judicious use of toasty oak. Forman's Chardonnays are barrel fermented but do not undergo malolactic fermentation, resulting in crisp, firmly structured wines that age well. The 1984 is fully mature, rich, ripe and creamy; the 1985 is one of the top wines of the vintage, showing great complexity of flavor and depth. The 1986 is similar in style, very complex and enticing, while the 1987 is fruitier. The 1988 is impressive for its fruit and delicacy. This quality lineup makes Forman a candidate for advancing in the classification ratings.

TASTING NOTES

FORMAN VINEYARD, Napa Valley

1988 FORMAN VINEYARD: Impressive for its pure, rich, concentrated layers of fruit and flavor. The toasty oak, peach, vanilla and pear flavors intermingle on the palate, and the crisp acidity carries them on the finish. More delicate and subtle than 1985 or 1986, it is like the 1987 but better. Last tasted: 3/90. Drink 1991-1994. 1,400 cases produced. Release: $20. Current: $27. **92**

1987 FORMAN VINEYARD: The 1987 is fruitier and less oaky than its two predecessors, but it is still highly successful with its delicacy and finesse. Plenty of fresh, ripe pear, spice, butter and toast notes that are long and tasty on the finish. Last tasted: 3/90. Drink 1991-1994. 1,400 cases produced. Release: $18. Current: $35. **89**

1986 FORMAN VINEYARD: Showing more toasty, smoky French oak than the 1985, but similar in style, with great richness, depth and intensity with a smooth, silky texture that allows the ripe fruit to come through and glide over the palate. Finish echoes the lemon, pear, butterscotch and smoke notes. Last tasted: 3/90. Drink 1991-1994. 1,000 cases produced. Release: $18. Current: $45. **92**

1985 FORMAN VINEYARD: Amazing for its depth, intensity and sheer elegance, offering great complexity of flavor, with tiers of rich, toasty butterscotch, honey, citrus and spice flavors that are beautifully focused, long and full on the finish. At its peak now but has the depth and concentration for another three to five years. Last tasted: 3/90. Drink 1991-1995. 800 cases produced. Release: $15. Current: $45. **93**

1984 FORMAN VINEYARD: Forman's first Chardonnay is a ripe, rich, tasty wine that is fully mature, with a smooth, creamy texture and plenty of toast, butter, honey and spice flavors that are long and lingering. Last tasted: 3/90. Drink 1991-1994. 400 cases produced. Release: $15. Current: $45. **86**

FRANCISCAN VINEYARDS
Cuvée Sauvage, Oakville, Napa Valley

CLASSIFICATION: *THIRD GROWTH*
COLLECTIBILITY RATING: *A*
BEST VINTAGES: *1988, 1986, 1987*

A lthough Franciscan Vineyards Chardonnays have until recently been decent at best, with the past few vintages they've been quite spectacular, particularly the new Cuvée Sauvage, a stunning Chardonnay fermented on its own wild yeasts. Founded in 1972, Franciscan has changed ownership several times. There was a period in the 1970s when it was owned and operated by Justin Meyer and Ray Duncan, owners of Silver Oak Cellar. Its turnaround in quality came after a takeover by the Eckes Corp. of West Germany in 1979, and the addition of Agustin Huneeus as president and Greg Upton as winemaker in the mid-1980s.

The early Franciscan Reserve wines, first made in 1982, were very ripe and showy early on. The 1984 is fairly typical of that style, with ripe, bold, assertive flavors, but it is not quite as complete as the wines that have followed. No 1985 Reserve was produced, but the 1986 Reserve is much more generous and lively. The last Reserve bottling was 1987, and it too is quite delicious, rich, complex and intriguing.

Beginning with the 1987 vintage, Franciscan introduced its Cuvée Sauvage, an enormously complex and beautifully proportioned wine that replaces the Reserve starting in 1988. The 1988 is one of the stars of the vintage. Franciscan owns 60 acres of mature Chardonnay vines in Oakville. Production is 19,000 of the Napa Valley bottling, but only 300 cases of Cuvée Sauvage in 1988, although that figure was expected to increase with the 1989 vintage.

AT A GLANCE
FRANCISCAN VINEYARDS
1178 Galleron Road
St. Helena, CA 94574
(707) 963-7111

Owners: Agustin Huneeus,
  Eckes Corp.

Winemaker: Greg Upton (5 years)

Founded: 1972

First Chardonnay vintage: 1972
  Cuvée Sauvage: 1987

Chardonnay production: 19,000 cases
  Cuvée Sauvage: 400 cases

Chardonnay acres owned: 60

Average age of vines: 17 years

Average wine makeup: Oakville,
  Napa Valley (100%)

Time in oak:
  Cuvée Sauvage: 13 months

Type of oak: French (Burgundian)

Oak age:
  Cuvée Sauvage: new (100%)

Winemaking notes:
  Barrel fermentation: 100%
  Malolactic fermentation: 100%
  Lees aging:
    Cuvée Sauvage: 100%
    (13 months)

TASTING NOTES

FRANCISCAN VINEYARDS, Cuvée Sauvage, Oakville, Napa Valley

1988 FRANCISCAN VINEYARDS CUVEE SAUVAGE: The finest Franciscan Chardonnay ever produced. It is a wonderfully seductive wine that combines intense, rich, deeply concentrated pear and honey flavors with a creamy, buttery texture. All silk and polish, lively, fresh, complex and enticing, with a long, full finish. Last tasted: 7/90. Drink 1991-1996. 300 cases produced. Release: $20. Current: $20. **94**

1987 FRANCISCAN VINEYARDS CUVEE SAUVAGE: Wonderfully complex aromas, with tiers of honey, pear, spice and subtle toasty oak flavors, an intriguing and impeccably well-made wine that has a creamy, smooth texture in a vintage of hard acidities. Butterscotch and melon linger on the finish. Last tasted: 6/90. Drink 1991-1996. 400 cases produced. Release: $20. Current: $20. **91**

FRANCISCAN VINEYARDS, Reserve

1987 FRANCISCAN VINEYARDS RESERVE: Seductive, rich, toasty and buttery, with ripe pear, melon and spice flavors, but there's a hard edge to the acidity. Best to cellar another year or two to let it mellow, but the finish provides complex flavors already. Last tasted: 6/90. Drink 1992-1997. 600 cases produced. Release: $15. Current: $15. **86**

1986 FRANCISCAN VINEYARDS RESERVE: Generous, with plenty of lush, rich, supple pear, melon, pineapple and fig flavors, just a touch of toasty, smoky oak and the kind of lively acidity that keeps the flavors dancing on your palate. Complex, intense and balanced, just reaching its peak. Last tasted: 4/90. Drink 1991-1997. 3,000 cases produced. Release: $14. Current: $15. **91**

1984 FRANCISCAN VINEYARDS RESERVE: A bold, rich and flavorful wine, packed with generous pear, spicy oak, pineapple and citrus flavors. Balanced and elegant with good length, but a bit shy in mid-palate. Last tasted: 4/90. Drink 1991-1995. 2000 cases produced. Release: $12. Current: $16. **86**

1983 FRANCISCAN VINEYARDS RESERVE: Elegant and buttery, with subtle pear, honey and citrus notes, fully mature and well balanced. Last tasted: 4/90. Drink 1991-1996. 1,500 cases produced. Release: $12. Current: $14. **82**

1982 FRANCISCAN VINEYARDS RESERVE CARNEROS: More austere and tightly knit than the regular bottling, with not quite the breadth of flavor, but still well made and aging well. It's tarter, more typical of Carneros fruit, with shades of pear and pineapple flavors. Last tasted: 4/90. Drink 1991-1994. 2,000 cases produced. Release: $12. Current: $20. **84**

FREEMARK ABBEY WINERY
Napa Valley
Carpy Ranch, Napa Valley

CLASSIFICATION:
Napa Valley: FOURTH GROWTH
Carpy Ranch: Not rated
COLLECTIBILITY RATING: *Not rated*
BEST VINTAGES: *1988, 1984*

AT A GLANCE

FREEMARK ABBEY WINERY
P.O. Box 410
St. Helena, CA 94574
(707) 963-9694

Owner: Freemark Abbey. Charles Carpy, managing partner

Winemaker: Ted Edwards (5 years)

Founded: 1935; re-established: 1967

First Chardonnay vintage: 1968
    Carpy Ranch: 1988

Chardonnay production: 19,500 cases
    Napa Valley: 19,000 cases
    Carpy Ranch: 500 cases

Chardonnay acres owned: 74

Average age of vines: 12 years

Vineyard locations:
    Carpy Ranch: Rutherford, Napa Valley

Average wine makeup:
    Napa Valley: Rutherford, Napa Valley

Time in oak: 5.5 months

Type of oak: French (Nevers)

Oak age: new (12% to 20%) to 7 years old

Winemaking notes:
    Barrel fermentation:
    Napa Valley: none
    Carpy Ranch: 100%
    Malolactic fermentation: none
    Lees aging:
    Napa Valley: none
    Carpy Ranch: 100% (8 months)

Through two decades Freemark Abbey has enjoyed many successes with Chardonnay. Although the wines are usually sound, complex and pleasing, marked by bold, rich, full-blown flavors, they are sometimes inconsistent. Freemark Abbey Chardonnay is made in a traditional California style; the wines do not go through malolactic fermentation and receive only partial barrel fermentation, so they possess firm acidity and adequate oak flavors, but wood is not a predominant flavor. The wines ferment in stainless steel tanks with three to eight hours of skin contact before aging in mostly used oak (20 percent new barrels) for five months and typically need two to three years in the bottle to peak.

Many of the early vintages from the late 1960s, called Pinot Chardonnay and made under the direction of partner and winemaker Brad Webb (see Hanzell), were excellent wines in their time, but they are past their primes, with deep golden colors and oxidized honey aromas. Most of the wines of the 1970s are also slowly declining, although the 1975 has aged well and is now perhaps showing as the best wine of the decade. In the 1980s, only the difficult 1982 and 1985 vintages are letdowns. The 1980, 1981, 1983, 1984, 1986, 1987 and 1988 bottlings are all very good, and the latest vintage is the best Freemark Abbey Chardonnay I have tasted in years.

With the 1988 vintage, Freemark Abbey introduced a new 500-case lot of Carpy Ranch Chardonnay from partner Chuck Carpy's Rutherford vineyard. It represents a departure in style, for it is barrel fermented on its lees for eight months. The result is a crisper wine that at least in the first vintage is not quite up to the standard of the regular 1988 Freemark Abbey. Ted Edwards, who has been winemaker for five years, seems intent on improving Freemark Abbey's quality while working within the winery's traditional style and exploring possibilities through the Carpy Ranch bottling.

TASTING NOTES

FREEMARK ABBEY WINERY, Napa Valley

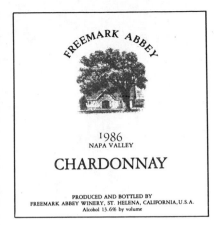

1988 FREEMARK ABBEY WINERY: A highly successful 1988 and the best Freemark Abbey bottling in years, displaying ripe, opulent flavors, pretty fig, melon, pear and spice aromas, a rich, silky smooth texture, supple viscosity and a pretty lemon and clove aftertaste. Last tasted: 3/90. Drink 1991-1997. 19,200 cases produced. Release: $15. Current: $15. **89**

1987 FREEMARK ABBEY WINERY: A leaner, more refined wine with crisp, subtle apple, pear and spice notes of moderate depth. Oak dominates the finish. May need time for the fruit and oak to knit. Last tasted: 3/90. Drink 1992-1996. 16,500 cases produced. Release: $15. Current: $15. **84**

1986 FREEMARK ABBEY WINERY: A very successful 1986, with delicious, fresh, ripe honey, apple, pineapple and toasty oak flavors that combine to give richness and complexity along with a pretty honey aftertaste. Last tasted: 3/90. Drink 1991-1996. 16,997 cases produced. Release: $15. Current: $15. **86**

1985 FREEMARK ABBEY WINERY: Youthful and fresh but somewhat simple, with pleasant spice, pear and apple flavors that offer only moderate depth and richness. Not nearly as complex as its two predecessors. Last tasted: 3/90. Drink 1991-1995. 15,787 cases produced. Release: $14. Current: $16. **80**

1984 FREEMARK ABBEY WINERY: Ripe, fruity and opulent, with fresh pear, honey, butter and spice flavors that are deep, rich and concentrated. The finish is long and full, picking up the buttery wood flavors. Last tasted: 3/90. Drink 1991-1994. 15,500 cases produced. Release: $14. Current: $17. **87**

1983 FREEMARK ABBEY WINERY: Attractive, with rich honey and spice notes, holding well, with toast, nutmeg and butterscotch flavors that are complex and long on the finish. Best now. Last tasted: 3/90. Drink 1991-1995. 13,000 cases produced. Release: $14. Current: $18. **85**

1982 FREEMARK ABBEY WINERY: From a difficult vintage, the 1982 has gamy and earthy flavors on top of the ripe pear and butter notes. The finish has a slight bitterness and is cloying. Last tasted: 3/90. Drink 1991-1993. 13,085 cases produced. Release: $12.75. Current: $18. **72**

1981 FREEMARK ABBEY WINERY: Subtle and elegant for Freemark Abbey, showing fewer ripe, opulent flavors than most vintages. The pear, spice and nutmeg flavors are youthful and in balance; holding well. Last tasted: 3/90. Drink 1991-1994. 13,183 cases produced. Release: $13.50. Current: $20. **81**

1980 FREEMARK ABBEY WINERY: Ripe, opulent and juicy, with rich butter, pear, nectarine and honey flavors that still taste delicious.

FREEMARK ABBEY

1983
NAPA VALLEY
CHARDONNAY

PRODUCED AND BOTTLED BY
FREEMARK ABBEY WINERY, ST. HELENA, CALIFORNIA, U.S.A.
Alcohol 13.7% by volume

It is drying and losing its intensity on the finish, but it has held up well. Last tasted: 3/90. Drink 1991-1993. 10,771 cases produced. Release: $13.50. Current: $24. **84**

1979 FREEMARK ABBEY WINERY: Holding together but barely, with very mature nutmeg, honey and butter flavors along with toasty oak and mint. Last tasted: 3/90. Drink 1991. 10,935 cases produced. Release: $13.25. Current: $25. **76**

1978 FREEMARK ABBEY WINERY: Still hanging together, with mature Chardonnay, nutmeg and some maderized flavors. Marginal at best. Last tasted: 3/90. Drink 1991. 9,894 cases produced. Release: $10. Current: $26. **70**

1977 FREEMARK ABBEY WINERY: Gamy and oxidized. Last tasted: 3/90. Best to avoid. 10,901 cases produced. Release: $10. Current: $36. **58**

1976 FREEMARK ABBEY WINERY: Overly mature and fading, deep gold, with heavily maderized Chardonnay flavors. Last tasted: 3/90. Best to avoid. 4,802 cases produced. Release: $9.75. Current: $26. **62**

1975 FREEMARK ABBEY WINERY: Showing more life than the 1974, but still past its prime, with mature nutmeg, butter and honey flavors that are attractive in their own right. Last tasted: 3/90. Drink 1991. 7,100 cases produced. Release: $9. Current: $45. **82**

1974 FREEMARK ABBEY WINERY: Pretty butter, honey and mint aromas, but much less fruit on the palate, where the flavors turn dry. Drinkable but past its prime. Last tasted: 3/90. Drink 1991. 4,110 cases produced. Release: $7.95. Current: $42. **74**

1973 FREEMARK ABBEY WINERY: Tart and crisp, with anise, lemon, honey and custard flavors that are fully mature and pleasant. Last tasted: 3/90. Drink 1991. 6,117 cases produced. Release: $6.50. Current: $32. **77**

1972 FREEMARK ABBEY WINERY: Youthful for its age, fully developed, with mature custard and lemon flavors along with a touch of spearmint on the finish. Last tasted: 3/90. Drink 1991-1993. 3,984 cases produced. Release: $6.50. Current: $48. **77**

1971 FREEMARK ABBEY WINERY: Healthy golden-yellow, with tart butter and lemon flavors that are crisp and decent. Last tasted: 3/90. Drink 1991. 3,959 cases produced. Release: $7. Current: $40. **70**

1970 FREEMARK ABBEY WINERY: Past its prime, high in volatile acidity. Last tasted: 3/90. Best to avoid. 2,698 cases produced. Release: $7. Current: $40. **55**

1969 FREEMARK ABBEY WINERY: Maderized and aldehydic. Last tasted: 3/90. Best to avoid. 2,307 cases produced. Release: $6. Current: $37. **60**

1968 FREEMARK ABBEY WINERY: Fully mature, with a yellow-amber color and rich walnut, apricot, honey, anise and old Chardonnay flavors. Decent, but its best years are behind it. Last tasted: 3/90. Drink 1991. 996 cases produced. Release: $5. Current: $40. **73**

FREEMARK ABBEY WINERY, Carpy Ranch, Napa Valley

1988 FREEMARK ABBEY WINERY CARPY RANCH: A shade leaner than the Freemark Abbey regular, it has a leesy aroma and a crisp, tight framework with hints of apple and pear. Last tasted: 3/90. Drink 1991-1996. 566 cases produced. Release: $20. Current: $20. **86**

FROG'S LEAP WINERY

Napa Valley
Carneros

CLASSIFICATION:
Napa Valley: THIRD GROWTH
Carneros: FOURTH GROWTH

COLLECTIBILITY RATING:
Napa Valley: A
Carneros: Not rated

BEST VINTAGES:
Napa Valley: 1984, 1986, 1987

Carneros: 1988, 1986

Frog's Leap Winery takes its name from the old creek-side farm north of St. Helena that was once a breeding ground for frogs to supply San Francisco restaurants. Owned by winemaker John Williams, his wife, Julie, and physician Larry Turley, Frog's Leap succeeds with two distinctly different styles of Chardonnay. The Napa Valley bottling, first produced in 1982 and made from grapes grown in the Rutherford area, features a typical Napa Valley character, with ripe pear, honey, apple and toasty oak flavors. The Carneros bottling showcases the crisp acidity and lemony citrus flavors found in grapes from that region, as well as the fresh pineapple and melon notes.

The Napa Valley Chardonnay, best in 1984, 1986 and 1987, is bolder and somewhat harder than the more elegant Carneros bottling. The 1984 Napa Valley is one of the vintage's top wines. The winery does not own any Chardonnay acreage, so it must rely on purchased grapes, which works fine as long as the supply is consistent. So far the quality of the grapes for both wines has been high, rendering reliable and attractive wines.

TASTING NOTES

FROG'S LEAP WINERY, **Napa Valley**

1988 FROG'S LEAP WINERY NAPA VALLEY: Youthful, rich, intense, lively and full-bodied, with tiers of apple, pear, honey and toasty oak flavors. Not quite together, it still needs time to soften and smooth out, but it has all the ingredients for excellence. Last tasted: 6/90. Drink 1991-1996. 2,500 cases produced. Release: $15. Current: $15. **87**

1987 FROG'S LEAP WINERY NAPA VALLEY: Big, full, rich and lively, a well-focused, well-defined Chardonnay with ripe pear, melon and apple flavors that offer intensity and depth, with pretty flavors on the aftertaste. While it is drinkable now, it should be best in a year. Last tasted: 6/90. Drink 1991-1995. 1,800 cases produced. Release: $14. Current: $16. **88**

1986 FROG'S LEAP WINERY NAPA VALLEY: A wonderful, rich, ripe, creamy, buttery texture with pretty pear and apple flavors coming through. Well balanced, full-bodied, and framed by toasty oak, with a powerful honey finish that carries the flavors. Last tasted: 6/90. Drink 1991-1995. 1,500 cases produced. Release: $12. Current: $18. **90**

1985 FROG'S LEAP WINERY NAPA VALLEY: Firm and mature, with strong mint and oak notes overshadowing the ripe pear and melon flavors, but with aeration it shows better balance and harmony. Nearing its peak. Last tasted: 6/90. Drink 1991-1995. 1,100 cases produced. Release: $12. Current: $16. **84**

1984 FROG'S LEAP WINERY NAPA VALLEY: Aging exceptionally well and one of the top 1984s, still displaying rich, intense, ripe and full-bodied fruit that echoes honey, pear, toast, nectarine and butter notes that fan out and linger on the palate. Drinking at its peak now. Last tasted: 6/90. Drink 1991-1995. 1,100 cases produced. Release: $12. Current: $23. **91**

FROG'S LEAP WINERY, Carneros

1988 FROG'S LEAP WINERY CARNEROS: Amazingly complex, rich and toasty, the 1988 Carneros rivals the 1984 Napa Valley as Frog's Leap's finest, offering uncommon complexity and depth while maintaining a sense of elegance and finesse. Finish echoes spicy pineapple, melon and oak flavors. Last tasted: 6/90. Drink 1992-1997. 1,200 cases produced. Release: $16. Current: $16. **91**

1987 FROG'S LEAP WINERY CARNEROS: Effusively fruity, with crisp, rich pineapple, lemon and ripe pear flavors that are well balanced and intense. Still a touch coarse and the oak comes through in force; best to cellar another year. Last tasted: 6/90. Drink 1991-1996. 1,500 cases produced. Release: $15. Current: $17. **86**

1986 FROG'S LEAP WINERY CARNEROS: Big, rich, toasty and buttery, a full-blown wine that packs in plenty of flavor, with intense fig, pineapple and citrus notes to play off the earthy, oaky flavors. Despite its size and weight, it is well balanced and complex and finishes with a sense of elegance and grace. Last tasted: 6/90. Drink 1991-1995. 1,300 cases produced. Release: $14. Current: $18. **87**

GIRARD WINERY

Reserve, Oakville, Napa Valley
Estate, Oakville, Napa Valley

CLASSIFICATION:
Reserve: SECOND GROWTH
Estate: FOURTH GROWTH

COLLECTIBILITY RATING:
Reserve: AA
Estate: Not rated

BEST VINTAGES:
Reserve: 1986, 1988, 1985

Estate: 1986, 1985, 1981, 1988

This family-owned and operated winery on the east side of Oakville on the Silverado Trail has made tremendous strides with Chardonnay in the past few vintages. All the Chardonnay grapes are grown in Girard's vineyards adjacent to the winery. Except for a rough patch between 1982 and 1984, when the Chardonnays are off the mark, the lineup is very impressive, particularly the new Reserve wines, which Girard introduced with the 1985 vintage. Three of the four Reserve bottlings have been outstanding, defining a style of richness and finesse, with sharply focused flavors and the kind of intensity that bodes well for aging up to a decade. The 1987 Reserve is a bit more austere, but generally fits in with the winery and vintage style.

The Napa Valley Estate bottling has mirrored the quality of the Reserve wines and sells for considerably less. It has been exceptionally fine in 1988, 1986 and 1985, though a bit lean in 1987. The 1980 is past its prime, but is still quite tasty. The 1981 ranks as one of the best wines of that vintage and should hold up for another five to seven years. A small portion of each Chardonnay undergoes malolactic fermentation and the wines succeed in making oak a seasoning, not a dominating flavor. Mark Smith became the winemaker in 1989, and Stephen Girard Jr. manages the business.

TASTING NOTES

GIRARD WINERY, Reserve, Oakville, Napa Valley

1988 GIRARD WINERY RESERVE: This has the potential to be one of Girard's finest Chardonnays to date, combining deep, rich, complex, toasty pear, lemon, melon and spicy oak flavors with a sense of elegance and finesse. Youthful and still developing, it won't peak for another two to three years. Wonderful fruit complexity on the finish. Last tasted: 6/90. Drink 1992-2000. 700 cases produced. Not released. **91**

1987 GIRARD WINERY RESERVE: Firm and hard now, typical of the 1987 vintage, but with good depth and concentration and well-defined pear and lemon flavors, finishing with a touch of tannic astringency. This a very youthful, understated wine that will benefit from another two to three years' cellaring. Last tasted: 6/90. Drink 1993-1999. 700 cases produced. Release: $25. Current: $25. **87**

1986 GIRARD WINERY RESERVE: Amazingly elegant and distinctive for its richness and finesse, the sharply focused and complex pear, lemon, spice and toasty oak flavors are in wonderful harmony, finishing with excellent length that echoes the pear and spice notes. Last tasted: 3/90. Drink 1991-1996. 701 cases produced. Release: $25. Current: $25. **92**

1985 GIRARD WINERY RESERVE: One of the top 1985s, this defines the Girard style of richness, elegance and finesse, with beautiful toasty oak, ripe pear and melon flavors and nutmeg and honey notes that glide across the palate. As good as it is now, it is still tight and concentrated, with youthful, intense flavors. Last tasted: 3/90. Drink 1991-1995. 242 cases produced. Release: $25. Current: $35. **91**

GIRARD WINERY, Estate, Oakville, Napa Valley

1988 GIRARD WINERY ESTATE: Wonderful balance and harmony of flavors, with smooth, rich, supple pear and melon flavors graced by spicy vanilla and oak notes and a creamy texture. Impeccable balance, very good depth and intensity, ideal for drinking or cellaring. Last tasted: 6/90. Drink 1991-1997. 4,800 cases produced. Release: $16. Current: $16. **88**

1987 GIRARD WINERY ESTATE: Tart, hard and somewhat coarse, a step down in quality from the previous two vintages. It does not display the pure Chardonnay fruit or sheer elegance of its predecessors. With time it may become more generous. Last tasted: 3/90. Drink 1992-1996. 5,757 cases produced. Release: $14.50. Current: $16. **81**

1986 GIRARD WINERY ESTATE: One of the stars of the vintage, this is a remarkably rich, smooth, elegant and beautifully balanced Chardonnay, offering ripe pear, spice, honey and toasty nutmeg flavors that echo on the finish. Drinks exceptionally well time after time, youthful and vibrant on the finish. Last tasted: 3/90. Drink 1991-1996. 5,297 cases produced. Release: $13.50. Current: $28. **92**

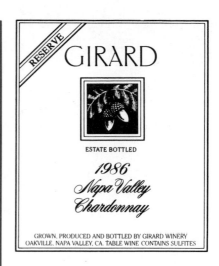

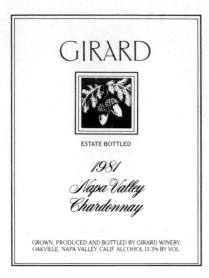

1985 GIRARD WINERY ESTATE: From the exceptional 1985 vintage, this wine is distinctively elegant and smooth, with rich, sharply defined pear, lemon, nutmeg, toast and honey flavors that are impeccably balanced and silky smooth, lingering long and full on the finish with a touch of creaminess. Drinking at its peak. Last tasted: 3/90. Drink 1991-1996. 4,740 cases produced. Release: $13.50. Current: $25. **90**

1984 GIRARD WINERY ESTATE: A lean wine from a hot vintage, not as fruity or opulent as the top 1984s. The pear and spice notes come across as simple and lacking in character. Best to drink soon. Last tasted: 3/90. Drink 1991-1993. 7,123 cases produced. Release: $13.50. Current: $22. **80**

1983 GIRARD WINERY ESTATE: Earthy and gamy, with ripe pear and spice notes, but not as rich and full-bodied as most Girards. It gets coarse and simple on the finish. Last tasted: 3/90. Drink 1991. 5,741 cases produced. Release: $12.50. Current: $22. **76**

1982 GIRARD WINERY ESTATE: Past its prime but holding, showing mature pear and honey notes. Finishes with a touch of oxidized apple cider flavors. Last tasted: 3/90. Drink 1991. 4,228 cases produced. Release: $12.50. Current: $21. **76**

1981 GIRARD WINERY ESTATE: Exquisite, rich, full and beautifully balanced, with well-focused pear, lemon, toast and earth flavors that are complex and compelling, finishing with a pretty touch of citrus. Fine length. Last tasted: 3/90. Drink 1991-1995. 4,736 cases produced. Release: $12.50. Current: $35. **90**

1980 GIRARD WINERY ESTATE: Fully mature and drinking well but past its prime, with some of the earthy pear, melon and spice flavors beginning to dry out. Best to drink soon. Last tasted: 3/90. Drink 1991-1994. 2,100 cases produced. Release: $11. Current: $25. **85**

GRGICH HILLS CELLAR

Napa Valley

CLASSIFICATION: *FIRST GROWTH*
COLLECTIBILITY RATING: *AAA*
BEST VINTAGES: *1979, 1988, 1985, 1983, 1978, 1986, 1987*

If I were forced to choose only one California Chardonnay to drink and cellar each year, it would probably be Grgich Hills Cellar. Since 1976 winemaker Miljenko "Mike" Grgich has produced the most consistently excellent and ageworthy Chardonnays in California. Stony Hill, Hanzell, Mayacamas and Chateau Montelena, where Grgich was the first winemaker in 1972, have longer track records of excellence, but when comparing vintages since 1976 side by side, Grgich comes out a slight favorite. The style — tight, austere, sharply focused and richly complex fruit flavors with subtle oak seasoning — is amazingly consistent from year to year, almost regardless of vintage vagaries. Moreover, Grgich's Chardonnays, including the 1972 to 1975 vintages made at Montelena, age incredibly well. His first Chardonnay, made under the Hills Cellars label in 1976, is still holding on despite being a difficult vintage for Chardonnay. Each of the wines since has been superb and worth waiting for.

Grgich Hills is a partnership formed in 1977 between Grgich, a native of Croatia, Yugoslavia, where his family made wine, and Austin Hills, the Hills Bros. coffee heir and a Napa Valley grape grower. One vintage, the 1976, was produced before the partnership was finalized and it was bottled under Hills' name.

Grgich has long been a Chardonnay master. He worked at Beaulieu Vineyard under André Tchelistcheff and at the Robert Mondavi Winery before signing on as winemaker during the rejuvenation of Chateau Montelena in 1972. The 1973 Montelena Chardonnay won international acclaim at the Paris Tasting of 1976, where it vanquished a group of prestigious French white Burgundies and helped establish both Montelena's and California's credentials for Chardonnay.

Since the beginning, Grgich Hills Cellar in Rutherford has gone from one strength to another. The 1977, from Sonoma, is one of the top wines of the vintage, a big, rich, flavorful wine that still is aging well. The 1978 is deep, with powerful fruit flavors that are rich and complex. The 1979 is a monumental wine, one of the 10 greatest Chardonnays I have ever tasted. The 1980 has aged exceptionally well. It is still deeply flavored and very concentrated. The 1981 provides a wonderful balance between fresh, ripe fruit and toasty oak, while the

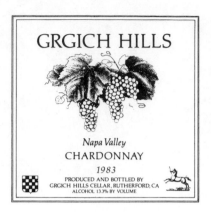

1982 is highly successful for this difficult vintage. The 1983 is one of the stars of the vintage, with great flavor, intensity and length, followed by the 1984, which shows off the bold, ripe fruit flavors of the vintage. The 1985 is just reaching full maturity, and is deftly balanced, full of fruit flavors and crisp acidity. The 1986 is young and elegant, very rich and balanced, followed by a tight, concentrated, austere 1987. The 1988, the current release, is more forward, offering subtle, fresh, complex fruit flavors that resemble the 1985. Both can stand cellaring for five to seven years.

Grgich Hills owns 165 acres of Chardonnay: 20 acres adjacent to the winery in Rutherford, 25 in Yountville, 30 near Napa and 90 in Carneros. This variety of grape sources gives Grgich the ingredients to maintain both balance and consistency in his wines. Since 1980 the Chardonnays have been at least partially barrel fermented. The 1988 is nearly 100 percent barrel fermented. Production has risen to 30,000 cases without sacrificing quality.

TASTING NOTES

GRGICH HILLS CELLAR, Napa Valley

1988 GRGICH HILLS CELLAR: Another sensational Chardonnay from Grgich that may rank as the best in time. Beautifully proportioned, it is rich, lush and elegant with intense, sharply focused pear, vanilla, honey, lemon and nutmeg flavors that are deep and concentrated yet smooth and lively with a long finish. Last tasted 3/90. Drink 1992-1999. 20,000 cases produced. Release: $22. Current: $22. **93.**

1987 GRGICH HILLS CELLAR: Just beginning to come around, this youthful 1987 offers clean, fresh apple, pear and spicy nutmeg flavors in a style that is a shade leaner and more refined than previous vintages, but has plenty of depth and intensity. With time it too will blossom into a superlative wine. Last tasted: 3/90. Drink 1992-1997. 33,000 cases produced. Release: $22. Current: $28. **90**

1986 GRGICH HILLS CELLAR: One of the most elegant and subtle of Grgich Hills' Chardonnays, but still packed with broad, rich fig, spice, citrus and butter flavors that are silky smooth, picking up nutmeg and toasty oak nuances on the finish. Last tasted: 3/90. Drink 1991-1996. 25,000 cases produced. Release: $22. Current: $33. **91**

1985 GRGICH HILLS CELLAR: Plenty of generous ripe fig, oak, spice and pear aromas and flavors, but the finish trails off, leaving a pleasant smoky, oaky aftertaste. Fully mature but has fruit that is youthful enough to develop further. Last tasted: 3/90. Drink 1991-1995. 25,000 cases produced. Release: $22. Current: $33. **92**

1984 GRGICH HILLS CELLAR: A big, rich, bold, fruity wine, typical of the 1984 vintage, with plenty of concentrated fig, pear, spice, vanilla and butter flavors that are beautifully balanced, framed by toasty French oak, finishing with a broad assertive aftertaste. Delicious. Last tasted: 3/90. Drink 1991-1995. 24,000 cases produced. Release: $18. Current: $33. **90**

1983 GRGICH HILLS CELLAR: One of the stars of the 1983 vintage, an incredibly flavorful wine, rich with fresh, ripe pear, spice, honey and oak flavors that are remarkably elegant and fleshy, with great intensity yet a measure of finesse. Flavors linger on the finish. Last tasted: 3/90. Drink 1991-1995. 15,000 cases produced. Release: $17. Current: $33. **92**

1982 GRGICH HILLS CELLAR: A big, rich, full-blown wine, packed with honey, toast, pear and spice flavors that are mature and velvety but holding up quite well, finishing with a bite of oak and tannin. Very successful for this difficult vintage. Last tasted: 3/90. Drink 1991-1994. 15,000 cases produced. Release: $17. Current: $36. **87**

1981 GRGICH HILLS CELLAR: Delicious balance between rich, ripe honey aromas and flavors and toasty oak, silky smooth on the palate, with traces of honey and spice on the finish. Very complex. Last tasted: 3/90. Drink 1991-1995. 16,000 cases produced. Release: $17. Current: $45. **88**

1980 GRGICH HILLS CELLAR: Another very ripe, intense and concentrated wine, the 1980 packs rich pineapple, pear, spice and toasty French oak flavors into a delicious mouthful of wine. Long, full aftertaste. Last tasted: 3/90. Drink 1991-1994. 15,000 cases produced. Release: $17. Current: $50. **88**

1979 GRGICH HILLS CELLAR: Perhaps the finest wine ever produced by Grgich Hills, combining all the richness, intensity and complexity of California's finest Chardonnays with a measure of elegance, depth and finesse. Layers of lush, ripe fig, pear, honey, butterscotch and spice flavors are all in delicious harmony. Last tasted: 3/90. Drink 1991-1994. 10,000 cases produced. Release: $16. Current: $55. **95**

1978 GRGICH HILLS CELLAR: Very ripe, with explosive, exotic pineapple, pear, honey and spice flavors that are rich, deep and complex, combining intensity with finesse and a measure of elegance, finishing with a flavor of toasty caramel. Holding up incredibly well. Last tasted: 3/90. Drink 1991-1996. 6,000 cases produced. Release: $13. Current: $60. **92**

1977 GRGICH HILLS CELLAR SONOMA: A mouthful of Chardonnay, big, rich and oaky, with intense honey, spice, pear and nutmeg flavors that are deep and complex. This producer's only Sonoma bottling has aged very well. Last tasted: 3/90. Drink 1991-1993. 6,000 cases produced. Release: $11. Current: $65. **89**

1976 HILLS CELLARS NAPA VALLEY: Fully mature, with rich, slightly oxidized honey, pear and nutmeg flavors that gain a smooth, buttery quality on the finish. Last tasted: 3/90. Drink 1991-1993. 2,500 cases produced. Release: $8. Current: $50. **85**

HACIENDA WINERY
Clair de Lune, Sonoma County

CLASSIFICATION: *FIFTH GROWTH*
COLLECTIBILITY RATING: *Not rated*
BEST VINTAGES: *1973, 1986, 1984*

In 1941, as the U.S. headed into World War II, newspaperman and United Press International war correspondent Frank Bartholomew bought, sight unseen, a property just east of the town of Sonoma. Upon arriving in the area to inspect the property, Bartholomew discovered several old stone buildings, apparently abandoned and in ruins for decades. As it turned out, this property was once Agoston Haraszthy's original Buena Vista Winery, founded in 1857, one of the oldest wineries in California.

Bartholomew and his wife, Antonia, revived the winery and vineyards, but when he became president of UPI and was based on the East Coast, he had little time to devote to Buena Vista. In 1968 Bartholomew sold the Buena Vista winery property, but kept the estate's vineyard. In 1973 he refitted an old hacienda-style building as a winery, and Hacienda was born. Crawford Cooley joined the business in 1976, and is its current president. Bartholomew died in 1985.

Hacienda's first vintage of Clair de Lune Chardonnay was the 1973. The wine was named after a French folk tune and the Valley of the Moon, a name by which Sonoma Valley is also known. It is a sensational wine, very complex and elegant, and one of the top wines of the vintage. The 1974 and 1976 are aging well, but the 1977 and 1978 are losing their intensity. The 1979 remains delicious. The 1980 is very ripe and a bit clumsy, and the 1981 through 1983 vintages are declining. The 1984 is very elegant and complex, drinking in peak form, as are the 1985 and 1986. The 1987 has an odd, leafy, minty quality and lacks the fruit definition of the best Haciendas. With the 1988, the winery is back on track with a very fine, elegant, well-balanced effort.

The Clair de Lune is a blend of Sonoma County grapes. Roughly half the grapes are purchased from the Sangiacomo Ranch in Carneros-Sonoma Valley, while 20 percent are estate-grown in Sonoma Valley, 20 percent are from Alexander Valley, and 10 percent are from Bennett Valley at the northern edge of Sonoma Valley southeast of Santa Rosa. Eric Laumann has been winemaker since 1986, succeeding Steve MacRostie, who departed after a decade to launch his own brand, MacRostie. With the exception of the 1987 vintage, Hacienda has made some very good, elegant and flavorful wines, though I am not sure the current releases are as fine or ageworthy as the sensational 1973. Production is at 10,500 cases with the 1988 vintage.

TASTING NOTES

HACIENDA WINERY, Clair de Lune, Sonoma County

1988 HACIENDA WINERY CLAIR DE LUNE: Firm and minty, with earthy, buttery flavors that complement the ripe pear and spice notes. Balanced, moderately rich and deep, it will benefit from another year or two of cellaring. Last tasted: 6/90. Drink 1992-1996. 10,500 cases produced. Release: $15. Current: $15. **85**

1987 HACIENDA WINERY CLAIR DE LUNE: Unusual flavors of leaves and mint turn tannic and dry in this wine. I have tasted it more than a dozen times and have consistently found it to possess a bizarre flavor and texture. It is drinkable but the style will not appeal to many. Last tasted: 4/90. Drink 1991-1993. 9,600 cases produced. Release: $12. Current: $15. **72**

1986 HACIENDA WINERY CLAIR DE LUNE: The finest Clair de Lune in years, it combines rich, deeply concentrated fruit with a flair of elegance and finesse, displaying pretty honey, pear, melon and spice flavors that are well integrated and lively, finishing with richness and depth. Delicious now. Last tasted: 4/90. Drink 1991-1995. 7,000 cases produced. Release: $12. Current: $18. **89**

1985 HACIENDA WINERY CLAIR DE LUNE: Similar in style to the excellent 1984, lean, elegant and complex, with youthful, lively lemon, pear, honey and toast flavors that hang together quite nicely. Well balanced and stylish, with pretty flavors lingering on the finish. Last tasted: 4/90. Drink 1991-1995. 7,000 cases produced. Release: $11. Current: $20. **87**

1984 HACIENDA WINERY CLAIR DE LUNE: Elegant and complex, with ripe, rich, mature honey, peach, toast, pear and spice flavors that fan out on the palate, finishing with good length and a clean, delicate aftertaste. Impressive for its length and creamy flavors. Last tasted: 4/90. Drink 1991-1994. 4,285 cases produced. Release: $10. Current: $18. **88**

1983 HACIENDA WINERY CLAIR DE LUNE: Fully mature and past its prime, rich and buttery, with earthy pear flavors that pick up a touch of anise and spice on the finish. Complex but drying out; best to drink up soon. Last tasted: 4/90. Drink 1991-1993. 4,200 cases produced. Release: $10. Current: $22. **83**

1982 HACIENDA WINERY CLAIR DE LUNE: Aging well, fully mature, with mint, pear and spice notes that turn frail and begin to fade on the finish. Past its prime, but still pleasant to drink. Last tasted: 4/90. Drink 1991-1993. 7,200 cases produced. Release: $9. Current: $20. **78**

1978
Sonoma Valley
Chardonnay
"Claire de Lune"
PRODUCED AND BOTTLED BY
HACIENDA WINE CELLARS, SONOMA, CALIFORNIA
BONDED WINERY NO. 4623   ALCOHOL 13.8% BY VOLUME

1981 HACIENDA WINERY CLAIR DE LUNE: Deep yellow-gold, with very mature honey, pear and butter flavors, bordering on oxidized. Best to drink soon, very drying on the finish. Last tasted: 4/90. Drink 1991-1992. 4,600 cases produced. Release: $12. Current: $20. **74**

1980 HACIENDA WINERY CLAIR DE LUNE: A big, rich, full-blown wine, high in extract and flavor, with intense pineapple, pear and toasty melon flavors that begin to dry out on the finish. A bit alcoholic, in sync with the vintage, somewhat disjointed on the finish. Last tasted: 4/90. Drink 1991-1993. 3,400 cases produced. Release: $10. Current: $22. **80**

1979 HACIENDA WINERY CLAIR DE LUNE: Attractive, well balanced, and still quite pleasant, offering rich, elegant pear, toast, butter, melon and spice flavors that are complex and enticing. Beginning its descent, but gracefully. Last tasted: 4/90. Drink 1991-1993. 2,900 cases produced. Release: $9. Current: $25. **86**

1978 HACIENDA WINERY CLAIR DE LUNE: Very dry and mature, losing its pizzazz, with ripe pear and honey notes that dry out on the finish. Borderline quality. Last tasted: 4/90. Drink 1991. 3,000 cases produced. Release: $9. Current: $25. **73**

1977 HACIENDA WINERY CLAIR DE LUNE: Beginning to dry out, with ripe pear and melon flavors of moderate depth. Well past its prime but holding. Last tasted: 4/90. Drink 1991-1993. 1,000 cases produced. Release: $8. Current: $30. **76**

1976 HACIENDA WINERY CLAIR DE LUNE: Ripe and mature, a touch earthy and dry, but still possessing plenty of rich honey and melon flavors that are quite tasty. Past its prime but very enjoyable. Last tasted: 4/90. Drink 1991-1994. 750 cases produced. Release: $7. Current: $50. **85**

1974 HACIENDA WINERY CLAIR DE LUNE: Elegant, fully mature and declining, but still displaying enough leafy apple and citrus flavors to make it interesting. More than a curiosity, but drink soon. Last tasted: 4/90. Drink 1991-1992. 675 cases produced. Release: $5. Current: $40. **80**

1973 HACIENDA WINERY CLAIR DE LUNE: Aging very gracefully, fully mature and quite delicious, with pretty, soft, smooth honey, melon and spice flavors that are rich, elegant and long on the finish. Very complete and impressive. Last tasted: 4/90. Drink 1991-1994. 495 cases produced. Release: $5. Current: $50. **91**

HANZELL VINEYARDS

Sonoma Valley

CLASSIFICATION: *FIRST GROWTH*

COLLECTIBILITY RATING: *AAA*

BEST VINTAGES: *1978, 1966, 1976, 1968, 1988, 1987,*

1985, 1980, 1972, 1969, 1957

There is little mistaking what James Zellerbach had in mind when he built Hanzell Vineyards in the 1950s in the sloping hills overlooking the town and valley of Sonoma. This tiny jewel of a winery is a miniature replica of the famous Burgundian Château de Vougeot in Clos de Vougeot. Zellerbach, the U.S. ambassador to Italy and a member of the family that owned the paper products firm Crown Zellerbach Corp., sought to duplicate Burgundian winemaking techniques with hopes of making California-style red and white "Burgundies."

In 1952 Zellerbach began planting the first of 14 acres to Chardonnay and Pinot Noir. Four years later he had built his winery and named it after himself and his wife, Hanna, combining her first name with his last name. In an era when California's finest wines sold for as little as $1 to $3 a bottle, Zellerbach spared no expense in building and equipping his new winery. The first vintage was the 1956, but there was apparently only enough Chardonnay to fill a demijohn, which holds five gallons. The first vintage that produced enough Chardonnay to bear the Hanzell label was 1957, but that wine, produced with part Napa Valley grapes and bearing a "California" appellation, is extremely rare because Zellerbach kept most of the bottles to drink himself and serve to his friends in Europe.

Zellerbach, a great admirer of French Burgundies, knew the importance of oak seasoning. Moreover, he could afford to buy the new barrels. Perhaps his single greatest contribution to California wine was the use of temperature-controlled stainless steel tanks for fermentation and new small French oak barrels for aging. California winemakers were using old American oak and whiskey barrels to age their wines, because they were stronger than redwood, but before Hanzell, no one had introduced the smoky, toasty flavor of new French oak to their wines.

The Hanzell Chardonnays, made under the direction of Brad Webb, were not exact copies of white Burgundies. Hanzell's Chardonnays were not barrel fermented and did not undergo malolactic fermentation, two common practices in the Côte d'Or. The fact that they

AT A GLANCE

HANZELL VINEYARDS
18596 Lomita Ave.
Sonoma, CA 95476
(707) 996-3860

Owner: Barbara de Brye, Great Britain

Winemaker: Bob Sessions (17 years)

Founded: 1957

First Chardonnay vintage: 1957

Chardonnay production: 1,000 cases

Chardonnay acres owned: 15

Average age of vines: 8 years

Average wine makeup: Sonoma Valley (100%)

Time in oak: 11 to 12 months

Type of oak: French (Sirugue)

Oak age: new (25%) to 4 years old

Winemaking notes:
  Barrel fermentation: 10%
  Malolactic fermentation: 25% to 35%
  Lees aging: 10% (5 months)

did not undergo malolactic fermentation may account in part for these wines' amazing longevity, for in my experience with California Chardonnays, Hanzells age as well as any, including Stony Hill.

When Zellerbach died in 1963, his wife Hanna sold the entire bottle inventory of Hanzell at auction, including two vintages of Chardonnay in barrel to Heitz Wine Cellar in Napa Valley, leaving none in the wine library. Fred Holmes and Barney Rhodes, two Napa Valley collectors, bought the new vintages of Chardonnay and Pinot Noir still in barrel in a deal with Joe Heitz, who sold both vintages under his own label. Rhodes recalled that the Heitz winery, then in cramped quarters on Highway 29 south of St. Helena where the tasting room is today, was so crowded that the wines had to be aged at Stony Hill. No 1963 or 1964 was produced, but beginning in 1965, with new owners Douglas and Mary Day, Hanzell resumed production. In every vintage since all the Chardonnay has been estate grown. Since 1973 Robert Sessions has been winemaker and general manager. Barbara de Brye of Great Britain has owned the winery since 1976.

The Hanzell vineyard is rooted on a gently graded and terraced hillside that faces south, so the grapes receive full sun exposure and rarely have difficulty ripening. Inside, the winery looks like a doll house, with small stainless steel fermenting tanks that each hold a ton of grapes (about 300 gallons). The Hanzell style has always featured fully ripened grapes with great flavor, intensity, power and personality. Because of their ripeness, the wines are often high in alcohol (at 13.5 percent to 14.5 percent), but with their enormous fruit concentration, achieved through skin contact during fermentation, and generous oak shadings, they are very well balanced and capable of aging for decades. The early Hanzell Chardonnays were a blend of grapes from Napa and Sonoma valleys because the Hanzell Vineyard did not produce enough grapes. Hanzell's grapes were supplemented by grapes grown in Oakville at Ivan Schoch's Vineyard (now called Stelling Vineyard) adjacent to what is now Far Niente Winery. In 1962 there were apparently two bottlings of Hanzell Chardonnay, one from Napa Valley and one from Sonoma Valley.

In the 1970s, the Hanzell style of full-blown, ripe and concentrated Chardonnay set a trend among California winemakers, some of whom interpreted the Hanzell style as "bigger is better." Increasingly many California Chardonnays were made fuller, riper and more alcoholic, blockbuster wines that did not age anywhere near as well as Hanzell's. Under Sessions, the emphasis has been on maintaining the integrity of the Hanzell Chardonnay style. The wines are still made from ultraripe grapes, are high in alcohol and sometimes heady, clearly not wines that will suit everyone's taste, but they are massive, powerful, intense and ageworthy. Most of all they are distinctive. Production has risen to nearly 1,000 cases a year, a small portion of which is barrel fermented, put through malolactic fermentation and aged on its lees.

Looking back at three decades of Hanzell Chardonnays, from 1957 to 1988, one is awed by how incredibly well these wines age and how remarkably complex and enduring they are. None of the wines has expired. The 1957 displays a wonderful wealth of fruit with a smooth, creamy texture. The 1959 is in fine condition, with complex honey and butter flavors. I have not tasted the 1958 or 1960, but both the 1961 and 1962 from Heitz Cellar are in superb condition and capable of aging for years to come. The 1965 is the least impressive of the 1960s decade, but the 1966 is incredibly fine, barely overshadowing the 1967, 1968 and 1969 vintages. In the 1970s decade, there are several terrific wines, most notably the 1972, 1974, 1976, 1977 and 1978. In the 1980s, the 1980 has enormous depth and concentration, while the 1982 is highly successful for that vintage. The 1983 and 1984 are sound, but not as exciting as the 1985, which is youthful and still years from peaking. The 1986, 1987 and 1988 are also excellent, showing great fruit concentration, depth and balance. All are good candidates for cellaring a decade or more.

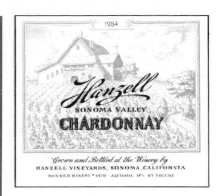

TASTING NOTES

HANZELL VINEYARDS, Sonoma Valley

1988 HANZELL VINEYARDS: Fresh, youthful and aromatic, with tight pear, lemon, fig and melon flavors that are rich yet elegant, very well balanced and integrated, a full-bodied wine with finesse and concentration. Excellent length; should develop into a beauty. Last tasted: 5/90. Drink 1993-2000. 750 cases produced. Release: $24. Current: $24. **90**

1987 HANZELL VINEYARDS: Youthful and intense, with lots of fresh pineapple, pear, citrus and melon flavors that are rich and elegant, finishing with finesse and subtlety. Approachable, but best in a few years. Last tasted: 1/90. Drink 1993-2000. 1,050 cases produced. Release: $24. Current: $28. **90**

1986 HANZELL VINEYARDS: Very ripe and forward, quite woody, with pretty pineapple, pear, apple and spice flavors of great intensity and depth. Needs several years to soften. Last tasted: 1/90. Drink 1993-1998. 1,070 cases produced. Release: $22. Current: $35. **87**

1985 HANZELL VINEYARDS: Excellent balance, intensity and depth; may become a classic. It combines ripe, rich pineapple, pear, spice and citrus notes that show remarkable finesse and elegance at this stage in its development. Smoky aftertaste. Last tasted: 1/90. Drink 1991-1999. 830 cases produced. Release: $22. Current: $40. **90**

1984 HANZELL VINEYARDS: Very ripe and fruity, a forward wine that comes across as having good intensity and depth, with pear, honey and citrus notes that build on the finish. Last tasted: 1/90. Drink 1991-1996. 980 cases produced. Release: $20. Current: $39. **84**

1983 HANZELL VINEYARDS: Light and simple by Hanzell standards, with less flavor and intensity, but still well made. It has pretty pine, pear and pineapple flavors that are perhaps more elegant than most Hanzells. Last tasted: 1/90. Drink 1991-1996. 930 cases produced. Release: $20. Current: $43. **84**

1982 HANZELL VINEYARDS: Elegant and stylish, with pretty honey, lemon, pear and spice flavors and a wonderful balance of fruit and oak. More subtle than many Hanzells. Last tasted: 1/90. Drink 1991-1996. 940 cases produced. Release: $19. Current: $45. **89**

1981 HANZELL VINEYARDS: Forward and fruity, with lemon, pear and pineapple flavors that are fresh and lively with good intensity and depth. Last tasted: 1/90. Drink 1991-1997. 650 cases produced. Release: $18. Current: $37. **86**

1980 HANZELL VINEYARDS: Enormous depth and concentration, very ripe and rich, with fig, pear and honey flavors, a big, full-blown wine with hints of pineapple, spice and butterscotch that are intense and lingering on the finish. Last tasted: 1/90. Drink 1991-1998. 740 cases produced. Release: $17. Current: $44. **90**

1979 HANZELL VINEYARDS: Elegant and spicy, with the pear and melon flavors beginning to dry out, becoming somewhat coarse. Still, there is plenty to like in this wine. Last tasted: 1/90. Drink 1991-1995. 460 cases produced. Release: $16. Current: $44. **85**

1978 HANZELL VINEYARDS: Incredibly rich, ripe and buttery, with intense fig, pear, spice and lemon flavors, finishing with lovely honey notes and a long, creamy aftertaste. One of the all-time greats. Last tasted: 1/90. Drink 1991-1998. 310 cases produced. Release: $13. Current: $40. **95**

1977 HANZELL VINEYARDS: Beginning its descent after a lofty run, the 1977 has always been one of Hanzell's greats. It still offers pretty honey, pear and spice flavors and more elegance and finesse than many vintages. Best to drink soon. Last tasted: 1/90. Drink 1991-1994. 260 cases produced. Release: $12. Current: $45. **88**

1976 HANZELL VINEYARDS: Very ripe and intense, with layers of honey, butter, pear and spice flavors. A big, full-blown wine that manages to retain a measure of elegance and finesse. Delicious. Last tasted: 1/90. Drink 1991-1995. 210 cases produced. Release: $12. Current: $55. **91**

1975 HANZELL VINEYARDS: Ripe citrus and grapefruit flavors, but not as complex as most Hanzells. Plenty of flavor and aging quite gracefully. Fine structure. Last tasted: 1/90. Drink 1991-1994. 310 cases produced. Release: $10. Current: $55. **86**

1974 HANZELL VINEYARDS: A big, ripe, unctuous wine redolent of custard, smoke, fig and pear flavors that are drying out yet still long on the finish. Aging well, still showing intensity and depth of flavor. Last tasted: 1/90. Drink 1991-1995. 300 cases produced. Release: $9. Current: $55. **88**

1973 HANZELL VINEYARDS: Another lively, youthful wine with plenty of fruit, but it is beginning to dry out a bit. Pretty honey, peach and pear flavors carry well through the finish. Better a few years ago, but still very pleasing. Last tasted: 1/90. Drink 1991-1995. 310 cases produced. Release: $8. Current: $65. **85**

1972 HANZELL VINEYARDS: Like a bowl of fruit, with fig, honey, pear, lemon and custard flavors, very elegant and well balanced, silky smooth texture and fine length. Aging quite gracefully, though a shade past its prime. Last tasted: 1/90. Drink 1991-1995. 170 cases produced. Release: $7. Current: $70. **90**

1971 HANZELL VINEYARDS: Ripe and intense yet also woody and coarse. Has not mellowed with age, but still retains a strong personality. The pear and apple flavors are showing maturity. Last tasted: 1/90. Drink 1991-1994. 160 cases produced. Release: $7. Current: $80. **85**

1970 HANZELL VINEYARDS: Plenty of fresh fruit aromas, but much drier on the palate, suggesting that this wine is slowly fading. There are some aldehydic flavors creeping in around the fruit. Last tasted: 1/90. Drink 1991-1994. 220 cases produced. Release: $7. Current: $80. **84**

1969 HANZELL VINEYARDS: Amazingly rich yet elegant, with mature honey, pear and spice flavors that linger on the palate. Fully mature, past its prime, but still providing a unique drinking experience. Last tasted: 1/90. Drink 1991-1995. 220 cases produced. Release: $6. Current: $90. **90**

1968 HANZELL VINEYARDS: A big, rich, ripe and full-blown Chardonnay packed with fig, lemon, pear and spice flavors that are very intense and buttery. Excellent balance despite the enormous ripeness of the fruit. Last tasted: 1/90. Drink 1991-1995. 240 cases produced. Release: $6. Current: $90. **91**

1967 HANZELL VINEYARDS: Plenty of ripe fig, pear and oak flavors, not quite the depth and concentration of the magnificent 1966, but complex and fine nonetheless. Last tasted: 1/90. Drink 1991-1994. 330 cases produced. Release: $6. Current: $90. **89**

1966 HANZELL VINEYARDS: Still a wealth of fruit remaining, with deep fig, lemon, honey and pear flavors that are amazingly well preserved. Crisp acidity sustains the flavors on a long, long finish. Incredibly fine. Last tasted: 1/90. Drink 1991-2000. 260 cases produced. Release: $6. Current: $115. **94**

1965 HANZELL VINEYARDS: Well preserved and minty, with tart apple flavors; drying out, but hanging on. Flavors fade on the finish. Best to drink it soon. Last tasted: 1/90. Drink 1991-1995. 190 cases produced. Release: $6. Current: $115. **84**

1962 HEITZ WINE CELLAR NAPA VALLEY: The second of two Heitz bottlings of Hanzell Chardonnays. More mature than the 1961 but holding quite well, very ripe, rich and deep, with blunt honey and

butterscotch flavors. Not quite as complex as the 1961, but on its own quite complete and rewarding. Last tasted: 6/90. Drink 1991-1995. 100 cases produced. Release: $6. Current: $100. **87**

1961 HEITZ WINE CELLAR NAPA VALLEY: A rare bottling by Heitz Wine Cellar in Napa Valley. Yellow-gold in color, healthy for a wine this age, with big, bold, rich flavors of honey, lemon and nutmeg, complex and deep, fine balance, and aging incredibly well. May last another decade. Last tasted: 6/90. Drink 1991-1995. 100 cases produced. Release: $6. Current: $125. **93**

1959 HANZELL VINEYARDS CALIFORNIA: In very fine condition despite low ullage, with wonderful, buttery honey aromas and honey, butter and lemon flavors that are very elegant and superbly balanced. Plenty of intensity and length. Last tasted: 1/90. Drink 1991-1995. 120 cases produced. Release: $4. Current: $180. **88**

1957 HANZELL VINEYARDS CALIFORNIA: An amazing amount of fruit for a wine this age, with waxy honey aromas and honey, butter and custard flavors that are still well defined and long on the finish. Last tasted: 1/90. Drink 1991-1993. 240 cases produced. Release: $4. Current: $220. **90**

HESS COLLECTION WINERY
Napa Valley

CLASSIFICATION: *THIRD GROWTH*

COLLECTIBILITY RATING: *A*

BEST VINTAGE: <u>*1987*</u>

The Hess Collection Winery on Mount Veeder is one of the bright new names in Chardonnay. Although the winery, owned by Swiss entrepreneur Donald Hess, has released only three vintages of its estate-grown Chardonnay, the wines have shown a remarkably consistent style of understated elegance, deft balance and rich concentration of fruit. The winery owns 120 acres of Chardonnay, of which 110 are bearing.

The first vintage of Chardonnay in 1986 produced a wonderfully complex and elegant wine that is now in peak drinking condition. The 1987 is similar in style, but with more polish and finesse. The 1988 has been slow to develop but is now showing more intensity and flavor. All three wines are good candidates to cellar for six to eight years. Randle Johnson is winemaker, and production has reached 10,000 cases. The winery is housed in the old Christian Brothers Mont La Salle winery. It has been beautifully restored and now also houses Hess' art collection. A second label called Hess Select bears a California appellation and comes from Hess-owned vineyards in Monterey County. The 1988 at $9 was superb.

TASTING NOTES
HESS COLLECTION WINERY, Napa Valley

1988 HESS COLLECTION WINERY: A rich and elegant wine with subtlety and intensity. The rich pear, buttery oak, nutmeg and lemon notes all combine to give it a spectrum of flavors. The finish allows each flavor to emerge with elegance and style. Last tasted: 4/90. Drink 1992-1998. 10,000 cases produced. Release: $13.75. Current: $13.75. **88**

1987 HESS COLLECTION WINERY: Another elegant, stylish wine, rich, smooth and subtle, with pretty pear, vanilla, nutmeg and apple flavors that combine to give it complexity. Fine balance, long aftertaste. Last tasted: 4/90. Drink 1991-1997. 4,100 cases produced. Release: $13.25. Current: $15. **91**

AT A GLANCE
HESS COLLECTION WINERY
P.O. Box 4140
Napa, CA 94558
(707) 255-1144

Owner: Donald Hess, Switzerland

Winemaker: Randle Johnson (7 years)

Founded: 1983

First Chardonnay vintage: 1986

Chardonnay production: 10,000 cases

Chardonnay acres owned: 120

Average age of vines: 10 years

Average wine makeup: Mount Veeder, Napa Valley (65%); Carneros (35%)

Time in oak: 11 months

Type of oak: French (Allier, Nevers, Tronçais, Vosges)

Oak age: new to 2 years old (33% each)

Winemaking notes:
  Barrel fermentation: 65%
  Malolactic fermentation: 30%
  Lees aging: 65% (11 months)

THE HESS COLLECTION
NAPA VALLEY CHARDONNAY
1986
PRODUCED & BOTTLED BY THE HESS COLLECTION WINERY
NAPA, CALIFORNIA USA
ALCOHOL 13% BY VOLUME

1986 HESS COLLECTION WINERY: Hess' first vintage is classy and elegant, with finesse and bright, pretty honey, vanilla and butterscotch flavors that are youthful and lively, finishing with spice, pear and apple notes. Rich, complex and well balanced. Last tasted: 4/90. Drink 1991-1996. 4,285 cases produced. Release: $12.75. Current: $16. **88**

WILLIAM HILL WINERY

Reserve, Napa Valley

CLASSIFICATION: *SECOND GROWTH*
COLLECTIBILITY RATING: *AA*
BEST VINTAGES: *1987, 1986, 1985*

In the decade he has been producing Chardonnay, William Hill has moved from ripe, full-blown, lavishly oaked wines that didn't age well to wines of greater finesse, elegance and complexity. In this transition, winemaker Hill has not sacrificed intensity, complexity or flavor, but merely harnessed it, giving his wines greater focus and aging potential. The results have been quite impressive. The most recent vintages, dating back to the 1984 Reserve, clearly are sound, sharply focused, ageworthy Chardonnays that need three to five years to develop fully. Once mature, they possess the intensity and depth of flavor to sustain them another three to five years. Hill is a strong advocate of mountain-grown grapes and he has invested heavily in vineyards on Mount Veeder. He also owns vineyards south of the Stags Leap District, north of Napa, along the Silverado Trail near the Silverado Country Club.

Hill's first major commercial release was the 1980. It was a richly flavored, enormously complex wine early on, but it is now past its prime. I have not tried the 1981 recently, but the 1982 is aging quite well and is fully mature. The 1983 Reserve is the first special-designation bottling, made in a crisp, austere style that required three to four years' bottle age to evolve. The 1984 Reserve is ripe and concentrated, with excellent depth. The 1985 Reserve is amazingly youthful and intense, with gobs of fruit. The 1986 Reserve shows even finer elegance and finesse without sacrificing flavor. The 1987 is similar in style, with a shade more hard acidity, but with balanced, complex honey and butter flavors. The 1988 is just now evolving, with youthful Chardonnay flavors of apple and melon, but it too is deftly balanced and should drink well through the 1990s. Construction of a winery began in 1990 near the William Hill Vineyards north of Napa. Production has soared to 30,000 cases of the Reserve, very impressive considering the quality is better than ever. A Silver Label Chardonnay, made in a crisper, more austere style, is also improving.

AT A GLANCE
WILLIAM HILL WINERY
P.O. Box 3989
Napa, CA 94558
(707) 224-6565

Owner: William Hill, general partner
Winemaker: William Hill (14 years)
Founded: 1976
First Chardonnay vintage: 1980
  Reserve: 1982
Chardonnay production: 60,000 cases
  Reserve: 30,000 cases
Chardonnay acres owned: 170
Average age of vines: 6 years
Average wine makeup: Mount Veeder, Napa Valley (100%)
Time in oak: 6 months
Type of oak: French
Oak age: 1 to 3 years old (33% each)
Winemaking notes:
  Barrel fermentation: 100%
  Malolactic fermentation: 100%
  Lees aging: 100% (4 months)

RESERVE

William Hill

1986

Napa Valley
Chardonnay

PRODUCED AND BOTTLED BY
WILLIAM HILL WINERY
NAPA, CALIFORNIA
CONTAINS SULFITES · TABLE WINE

TASTING NOTES

WILLIAM HILL WINERY, Reserve, Napa Valley

1988 WILLIAM HILL WINERY RESERVE: Very youthful and lively in the newer Hill style of elegance and finesse. The rich pear, apple, spice and melon flavors are just beginning to show, but the toasty oak and complexity are quite apparent. If it is like other recent Hill Chardonnays, it should be a magnificent wine. Last tasted: 3/90. Drink 1992-1998. 30,088 cases produced. Release: $18. Current: $18. **88**

1987 WILLIAM HILL WINERY RESERVE: Another intense, complex, flavorful Chardonnay from Hill, combining rich pear, butter, honey and spicy oak flavors with a silky smooth texture and a long aftertaste that keeps repeating the honey, butter and smoke flavors. Stylistically a step up in elegance, like the 1986. Last tasted: 3/90. Drink 1992-1998. 21,042 cases produced. Release: $18. Current: $18. **91**

1986 WILLIAM HILL WINERY RESERVE: Surpasses the superb 1985 in elegance and finesse, showing a mouthful of complex pear, spice and butterscotch flavors that are already silky smooth. Despite its early-drinking allure, this wine can be cellared for four to five more years; the finish echoes smoky oak. Last tasted: 3/90. Drink 1991-1995. 18,228 cases produced. Release: $17. Current: $20. **91**

1985 WILLIAM HILL WINERY RESERVE: Amazingly youthful and intense, offering a broad array of fresh, ripe peach, pear, apple and spicy oak flavors, all well proportioned and finishing with a pretty aftertaste that echoes the complex fruit flavors. Last tasted: 3/90. Drink 1991-1997. 16,313 cases produced. Release: $16. Current: $24. **90**

1984 WILLIAM HILL WINERY RESERVE: The 1984 is ripe and full-blown, with rich, intense pear, oak, spice and melon flavors that are very well balanced. Drinking well now, but appears to have the depth and concentration for another four to five years of cellaring. Last tasted: 3/90. Drink 1991-1996. 652 cases produced. Release: $20. Current: $24. **88**

1983 WILLIAM HILL WINERY RESERVE: Intense, clean, crisp and lean, still tightly wound and just beginning to soften, with subtle pear, apple and spice flavors that build on the finish. Last tasted: 3/90. Drink 1991-1994. 1,428 cases produced. Release: $22. Current: $28. **85**

1982 WILLIAM HILL WINERY RESERVE: Aging well, showing more complexity now than earlier on, fully mature, with earthy pear, honey and butter notes that are well balanced and showing fine depth. Plenty of length on the aftertaste. Last tasted: 3/90. Drink 1991-1995. 1,427 cases produced. Release: $24. Current: $28. **86**

1980 WILLIAM HILL WINERY GOLD LABEL: Hill's first major commercial release was a rich, creamy charmer on release and for its first few years of life, but it matured quickly and is now fairly oxidized and not worth seeking out, although it is drinkable. Last tasted: 3/90. Drink 1991. 775 cases produced. Release: $16. Current: $30. **70**

INGLENOOK-NAPA VALLEY
Reserve, Napa Valley

CLASSIFICATION: *FIFTH GROWTH*

COLLECTIBILITY RATING: *Not rated*

BEST VINTAGES: *1988, 1986*

While generally thought of as a fine producer of Cabernet Sauvignon, Inglenook-Napa Valley has been producing Chardonnay since 1946. I have not tried or even seen any of the old Inglenook Chardonnays from the John Daniel Jr. era of the 1940s to early 1960s, but some old-time collectors insist they were very good wines for their time.

The old Chardonnays were produced from Daniel's Napanook Vineyard, west of Rutherford and the current home of Dominus, the Cabernet Sauvignon-based red wine made by Christian Moueix of Château Pétrus in partnership with Daniel's two daughters. Inglenook's records on Chardonnay are incomplete and the wine library no longer contains any of the older bottles. The oldest Inglenook Chardonnays I have tasted are from the 1970s, but I have not tried them in several years and I do not have current notes. Since the late 1960s and early 1970s, after Heublein acquired Inglenook, Chardonnay has not been a top priority, but one can see progress with some of the newer wines.

In the 1980s, the Reserve Chardonnay, made under the direction of winemaker John Richburg, has been clearly a first-class wine, elegant, deep, rich and concentrated. In some cases, most recently in 1985, the wine seems overly oaky and heavy-handed, but perhaps it is just going through a phase and needs more time. The 1983 is tough and coarse but holding, while the 1984 is oaky but with attractive fruit flavors to complement the wood. The 1986 achieves a greater balance between fruit and oak. The 1987 continues that balancing act despite the hard acids of that vintage. The 1988 appears to be a worthy successor to the fine 1986 and may with time be the best to date. The winery owns 25 acres in the Yountville area and produces 2,000 to 6,000 cases of the Reserve each year. Based on the track record being re-established each year, collectors who come across any of the Inglenook Chardonnays of yesteryear may be in for a treat.

AT A GLANCE
INGLENOOK-NAPA VALLEY
P.O. Box 402
Rutherford, CA 94573
(707) 967-3300

Owner: Heublein Inc./Grand Metropolitan

Winemaker: John Richburg (11 years)

Founded: 1879; re-established: 1933

First Chardonnay vintage: 1946

Reserve: 1983

Chardonnay production: 20,000 cases
  Reserve: 4,000 cases

Chardonnay acres owned: 25

Average age of vines: 12 years

Average wine makeup: Yountville, Valley (100%)

Time in oak: 5 months

Type of oak: French (Limousin, Nevers, Allier)

Oak age: new (50%)

Winemaking notes:
  Barrel fermentation: 75%
  Malolactic fermentation: none
  Lees aging: partial (3 months)

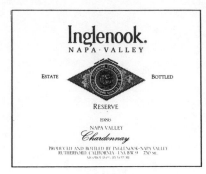

INGLENOOK-NAPA VALLEY, Reserve, Napa Valley

1988 INGLENOOK-NAPA VALLEY RESERVE: Rivals the quality of the 1986 as the best Inglenook Reserve to date. It combines ripe, rich, complex fruit with a restrained hand, allowing the pretty pear, apple, spice and melon flavors a measure of texture and grace. Well balanced, youthful and intense, best in a year or two. Last tasted: 4/90. Drink 1992-1998. 2,000 cases produced. Not released. **88**

1987 INGLENOOK-NAPA VALLEY RESERVE: Lean and intense, in sync with the vintage and Inglenook's style, featuring tightly reined-in, concentrated pear, lemon, vanilla and nutmeg flavors that are still hard and firm. Best in a year or two. Last tasted: 4/90. Drink 1992-1997. 6,000 cases produced. Release: $14. Current: $14. **86**

1986 INGLENOOK-NAPA VALLEY RESERVE: Impressive for its intensity, richness, balance and flavor, the tiers of pear, lemon, apple and melon are well integrated with the toasty French oak. The finish is long, clean and lively. Clearly one of the best of the Reserve bottlings. Last tasted: 4/90. Drink 1991-1996. 6,135 cases produced. Release: $14.50. Current: $14.50. **88**

1985 INGLENOOK-NAPA VALLEY RESERVE: Hard and oaky in my most recent tastings, with woody intensity dominating the fresh, ripe fruit. Lacking finesse and elegance, dry and woody on the finish. Disappointing for a 1985. Last tasted: 4/90. Drink 1991-1994. 2,500 cases produced. Release: $14.50. Current: $15. **78**

1984 INGLENOOK-NAPA VALLEY RESERVE: A dramatic display of rich, concentrated layers of pear, apple, melon, nutmeg and oak flavors, altogether well balanced, intense and somewhat oaky on the finish, and a step up in quality from the 1983. Butterscotch and oak come through on the finish. Could use a little more finesse. Last tasted: 4/90. Drink 1991-1995. 2,200 cases produced. Release: $12.50. Current: $18. **86**

1983 INGLENOOK-NAPA VALLEY RESERVE: Inglenook's first Reserve bottling is somewhat coarse and tannic, showing plenty of intensity and concentration of tart pear and pineapple flavors, but it tastes tart and lacks the smoothness one hopes for with a wine this age. On the finish the flavors show ripe, rich characteristics as well as some dullness. Last tasted: 4/90. Drink 1991-1994. 1,400 cases produced. Release: $16. Current: $19. **82**

KENDALL-JACKSON VINEYARDS

The Proprietor's, California
Durell Vineyard, Sonoma Valley
Dennison Vineyard, Anderson Valley
DuPratt, Anderson Valley
Lolonis Vineyard, Redwood Valley

CLASSIFICATION:

The Proprietor's: THIRD GROWTH

Durell Vineyard: THIRD GROWTH

Dennison Vineyard: Not rated

DuPratt Vineyard: Not rated

Lolonis Vineyard: Not rated

COLLECTIBILITY RATING:

The Proprietor's: Not rated

Durell Vineyard: A

Dennison Vineyard: Not rated

DuPratt Vineyard: Not rated

Lolonis Vineyard: Not rated

BEST VINTAGES:

The Proprietor's: 1987

Durell Vineyard: 1986

DePatie Vineyard: 1987

Lolonis Vineyard: 1988

I n 1982 Kendall-Jackson Vineyards in rural Lake County burst onto the scene with its Vintner's Reserve Chardonnays, wines that were ripe, opulent and juicy, but also a little sweet, with a trace of residual sugar. It was a legitimate style that proved enormously popular with consumers, and production of that wine, made from a blend of grapes from Mendocino County to the Central Coast, has soared to more than 400,000 cases a year. It is one of the great marketing success stories of the 1980s.

As appealing as the Vintner's Reserve style is for immediate consumption, those wines have not aged very well. What many consumers overlook are Kendall-Jackson's excellent, hand-crafted, single-vineyard Chardonnays from the Durell (Sonoma Valley), Dennison (Anderson Valley, Mendocino County), DePatie-DuPratt (Anderson Valley) and Lolonis (Redwood Valley, Mendocino County) vineyards. Most of those

---

AT A GLANCE
KENDALL-JACKSON VINEYARDS
640 Mathews Road
Lakeport, CA 95453
(707) 263-5299

Owner: Jess Jackson

Winemaker: Jed Steele (8 years)

Founded: 1982

First Chardonnay vintage:
The Proprietor's: 1983
Durell Vineyard: 1985
Dennison Vineyard: 1984
DuPratt Vineyard: 1987
Lolonis Vineyard: 1988

Chardonnay production: 400,000 cases
The Proprietor's: 25,000 cases
Durell Vineyard: 500 cases
Dennison Vineyard: 200 cases
DuPratt Vineyard: 200 cases
Lolonis Vineyard: 100 cases

Chardonnay acres owned: 1,000 acres

Average age of vines: 10 years

Vineyard locations:
Durell Vineyard: Sonoma Valley
Dennison Vineyard: Anderson Valley
DuPratt Vineyard: Anderson Valley
Lolonis Vineyard: Redwood Valley

Average wine makeup:
The Proprietor's: California

Time in oak:
The Proprietor's: 8 months
Durell Vineyard: 8 months
Dennison Vineyard: 8 months
DuPratt Vineyard: 8 months
Lolonis Vineyard: 8 months

continued on next page

200

Kendall-Jackson makes 25,000 cases a year of its Proprietor's brand Chardonnay, a very well-made, rich, fruity, deftly balanced wine. Each year winemaker Jed Steele pieces together the best lots of Chardonnay from all over California to achieve a wine of wonderful suppleness, richness and depth. The Proprietor's, like the other Kendall-Jackson wines, is barrel fermented and undergoes malolactic fermentation. The 1987 vintage in particular is enormously complex, brimming with fresh, ripe fruit and layers of flavor. The 1986 and 1988 vintages are less showy, but still impressive wines that won't shortchange you on flavor. Of the single-vineyard bottlings, the Durell (Kistler also makes a wine from this vineyard) is the most impressive for its rich, creamy fruit flavors, followed by the DuPratt (once named DePatie), which is firmer but just as delicious.

Proprietor Jess Jackson, a lawyer by profession, owns vineyards throughout California. His biggest holding is the former Tepusquet Vineyard in Santa Maria, with nearly 1,000 acres of Chardonnay, which he bought in the late 1980s along with Robert Mondavi. Jackson also buys on the open market but has contracts to secure grapes from the vineyards he uses for his vineyard-designated wines. In 1988 Jackson bought Cambria Vineyards in Santa Maria and launched a new brand under that name, focusing on Chardonnay.

TASTING NOTES

KENDALL-JACKSON VINEYARDS, The Proprietor's, California

1988 KENDALL-JACKSON VINEYARDS THE PROPRIETOR'S: Rich, toasty, smoky and elegant, with delicate pear, citrus, honey and spice flavors of moderate depth and intensity. Drinking well now and should hold for another three to five years. Last tasted: 4/90. Drink 1991-1995. 25,000 cases produced. Release: $24.50. Current: $25. **87**

1987 KENDALL-JACKSON VINEYARDS THE PROPRIETOR'S: Remarkable complexity, harmony and finesse, this is the best bottling of The Proprietor's, brimming with rich toast, pear, honey, butter and butterscotch flavors and laced with crisp, lively acidity that lends a feel of elegance and grace. Finish echoes flavors that keep you coming back for another sip. Last tasted: 4/90. Drink 1991-1995. 11,000 cases produced. Release: $20. Current: $20. **92**

1986 KENDALL-JACKSON VINEYARDS THE PROPRIETOR'S: An elegant, understated wine with toasty oak and vanilla flavors complemented by fresh pear, peach and apple notes. Well balanced, delicate and creamy, it is ready to drink now. Last tasted: 4/90. Drink 1991-1994. 5,000 cases produced. Release: $17. Current: $20. **86**

continued from previous page

Type of oak:
The Proprietor's: French
Durell Vineyard: French
Dennison Vineyard: French
DuPratt Vineyard: French
Lolonis Vineyard: French

Oak age:
The Proprietor's: new (50%) to 2 years old
Durell Vineyard: new (50%) to 2 years old
Dennison Vineyard: new (50%) to 2 years old
DuPratt Vineyard: new (50%) to 2 years old
Lolonis Vineyard: new (50%) to 2 years old

Winemaking notes:
Barrel fermentation:
The Proprietor's: 100%
Durell Vineyard: 100%
Dennison Vineyard: 100%
DuPratt Vineyard: 100%
Lolonis Vineyard: 100%
Malolactic fermentation:
The Proprietor's: 70% to 100%
Durell Vineyard: 70% to 100%
Dennison Vineyard: 70% to 100%
DuPratt Vineyard: 70% to 100%
Lolonis Vineyard: 70% to 100%
Lees aging:
The Proprietor's: varies (25% to 33%)
Durell Vineyard: varies (75% to 100%)
Dennison Vineyard: varies (75% to 100%)
DuPratt Vineyard: varies (75% to 100%)
Lolonis Vineyard: varies (75% to 100%)

KENDALL-JACKSON VINEYARDS, Durell Vineyard, Sonoma Valley

1987 KENDALL-JACKSON VINEYARDS DURELL VINEYARD: Complex aromas of honey, pear, toast and vanilla give way to rich, smooth, soft fruit flavors that are clean and refreshing, albeit somewhat simple on the finish. Soft enough to drink now. Last tasted: 4/90. Drink 1991-1994. 500 cases produced. Release: $14. Current: $14. **86**

1986 KENDALL-JACKSON VINEYARDS DURELL VINEYARD: Smoky, toasty, rich and elegant, with well-focused, smooth, concentrated pear, butter and creamy oak flavors that are complex and well balanced. Each sip reveals another layer of depth and flavor. Last tasted: 6/90. Drink 1991-1996. 500 cases produced. Release: $14. Current: $16. **91**

1985 KENDALL-JACKSON VINEYARDS DURELL VINEYARD: Remarkably elegant and refined, with creamy smooth honey, pear, vanilla and spice notes that are lively and well integrated, finishing with crisp acidity and fine length. Attractive from start to finish. Last tasted: 4/90. Drink 1991-1995. 500 cases produced. Release: $14. Current: $20. **87**

KENDALL-JACKSON VINEYARDS, Dennison Vineyard, Anderson Valley

1987 KENDALL-JACKSON VINEYARDS DENNISON VINEYARD: The Dennison is a touch coarse and a bit rough, with simple pear and nectarine flavors that are soft and pleasant, but not nearly as complex or elegant as Kendall-Jackson's best. Last tasted: 4/90. Drink 1991-1993. 200 cases produced. Release: $14. Current: $14. **82**

1985 KENDALL-JACKSON VINEYARDS DENNISON VINEYARD: Rich, ripe, elegant and well balanced, fully mature and still holding on, with layers of apple, melon, honey and nutmeg flavors, simple but pleasant. Last tasted: 4/90. Drink 1991-1993. 200 cases produced. Release: $14. Current: $20. **85**

KENDALL-JACKSON VINEYARDS, DuPratt Vineyard, Anderson Valley

1988 KENDALL-JACKSON VINEYARDS DUPRATT VINEYARD: Soft and smooth but with an earthy, mossy quality that detracts from the lushness of the pear and apple flavors. Elegant, well balanced, ready to drink now. Last tasted: 4/90. Drink 1991-1994. 200 cases produced. Release: $14. Current: $14. **85**

1987 KENDALL-JACKSON VINEYARDS DEPATIE VINEYARD: Wonderful complexity and depth, rich, smooth and creamy, with complex, well-integrated toast, vanilla, honey, pear and butterscotch flavors that are broad and deep, finishing with fine depth and length. Last tasted: 4/90. Drink 1991-1995. 200 cases produced. Release: $14. Current: $14. **89**

KENDALL-JACKSON VINEYARDS, Lolonis Vineyard, Redwood Valley

1988 KENDALL-JACKSON VINEYARDS LOLONIS VINEYARD: Complex, elegant and well balanced, with tiers of pear, lemon, apple, creamy vanilla and oak flavors, this vineyard-designated wine is sold only at the winery. Decent length, right in sync with the Kendall-Jackson style of elegance and softness. Last tasted: 4/90. Drink 1991-1994. 100 cases produced. Not released. **85**

KENWOOD VINEYARDS

Beltane Ranch, Sonoma Valley
Yulupa Vineyard, Sonoma Valley

CLASSIFICATION: *FIFTH GROWTH*
COLLECTIBILITY RATING: *Not rated*

BEST VINTAGES:
Beltane Ranch: 1988, 1987
Yulupa Vineyard: 1988, 1983

U ntil the mid-1980s, Chardonnay was not one of Kenwood's strengths. The early Chardonnays, dating back to 1977, were ripe and tannic, high in extract and flavor, but lacking in finesse. These Chardonnays appeared especially awkward when compared with those of Kenwood's neighbor to the north, Chardonnay specialist Chateau St. Jean. But this Sonoma Valley winery has turned things around in the past few vintages with two separate vineyard-designated Chardonnay bottlings from Sonoma Valley vineyards, one from Beltane Ranch and one from the winery's own 55-acre Yulupa Vineyard.

Kenwood has been producing the Beltane Ranch Chardonnay since the 1978 vintage, and despite a few rough spots early on, the most recent vintages have been quite impressive, showing better balance, integration of flavor, concentration of fruit and use of oak, and that extra measure of finesse that separates the best Chardonnays from the rest. The 1988 vintage in particular has the fruit, depth, richness and concentration to stand up to the French oak. The 1987 Beltane Ranch is tart and firm, like most 1987s, but has the intensity to age for four or five years. The 1986 and 1985 are both concentrated and firm, ready to drink, but they could use more time to soften.

The 1988 is also the best year for Chardonnay produced from the Yulupa Vineyard. The first vintage, the 1983, is drinking well, but shows the riper, older style of Kenwood Chardonnay and is a good example of why winemaker Michael Lee has concentrated on raising the level of quality. Kenwood's Chardonnay output is now 30,000 cases, most of it with a Sonoma Valley appellation, and it is usually a good to very good wine. About 3,000 cases each of the Beltane Ranch and Yulupa are bottled annually.

AT A GLANCE
KENWOOD VINEYARDS
9592 Sonoma Highway
Kenwood, CA 95452
(707) 833-5891

Owners: The Lee, Sheela and
   Knott families

Winemaker: Michael Lee (9 years)

Founded: 1970

First Chardonnay vintage: 1977
   Beltane Ranch: 1978
   Yulupa Vineyard: 1983

Chardonnay production: 30,000 cases
   Beltane Ranch: 3,000 cases
   Yulupa Vineyard: 3,000 cases

Chardonnay acres owned: 55

Average age of vines:
   Beltane Ranch: 18 years
   Yulupa Vineyard: 17 years

Vineyard locations:
   Beltane Ranch: Sonoma Valley
   Yulupa Vineyard: Sonoma Valley

Time in oak: 5 months

Type of oak: French (Nevers, Allier)

Oak age: new to 4 years old

Winemaking notes:
   Barrel fermentation: 100%
   Malolactic fermentation: 100%
   Lees aging: 100% (5 months)

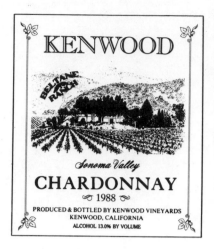

TASTING NOTES

KENWOOD VINEYARDS, Beltane Ranch, Sonoma Valley

1988 KENWOOD VINEYARDS BELTANE RANCH: The best of the Beltane Ranch bottlings, a deftly balanced wine that plays ripe, rich, concentrated pear and citrus flavors off firm, solid, smoky, toasty oak. Youthful and firm, it needs two to three years to mature fully, but all the ingredients are there for excellence. Last tasted: 7/90. Drink 1992-1998. 3,000 cases produced. Release: $15. Current: $15. **89**

1987 KENWOOD VINEYARDS BELTANE RANCH: Tart and lemony, but with attractive pear and melon flavors, elegantly balanced, smooth and supple for a 1987, but still tart from acidity. Better in a year or so. Last tasted: 7/90. Drink 1992-1997. 3,000 cases produced. Release: $15. Current: $17. **87**

1986 KENWOOD VINEYARDS BELTANE RANCH: Ripe and full-bodied, with layers of rich pineapple, melon and apple flavors and smooth oak textures, a well-balanced, forward, concentrated wine that is ready to drink. Last tasted: 7/90. Drink 1991-1995. 2,500 cases produced. Release: $14. Current: $18. **85**

1985 KENWOOD VINEYARDS BELTANE RANCH: Fully mature, elegant and graceful, with tart apple, melon and pear flavors that, while attractive, lack the complexity and breadth of flavor of the top wines from this vintage. Last tasted: 7/90. Drink 1991-1995. 2,200 cases produced. Release: $14. Current: $18. **84**

KENWOOD VINEYARDS, Yulupa Vineyard, Sonoma Valley

1988 KENWOOD VINEYARDS YULUPA VINEYARD: An elegant, concentrated wine that offers pretty, ripe peach, fig and vanilla flavors that are intense but well balanced, with a crisp, clean finish. Drink 1991-1996. 3,000 cases produced. Release: $14. Current: $14. **87**

1987 KENWOOD VINEYARDS YULUPA VINEYARD: Firm and crisp, with tart lemon, pineapple and melon flavors that are moderately rich and well balanced, but a bit on the austere side. Maybe another year in the bottle will soften it. Last tasted: 7/90. Drink 1992-1996. 3,000 cases produced. Release: $14. Current: $16. **85**

1986 KENWOOD VINEYARDS YULUPA VINEYARD: Decidedly oaky and heavy-handed, with very ripe pineapple and citrus notes dominating. Less appealing than most Yulupa bottlings; the grapes seem a shade overripe. Last tasted: 7/90. Drink 1991-1995. 6,000 cases produced. Release: $12. Current: $17. **82**

1985 KENWOOD VINEYARDS YULUPA VINEYARD: Ripe, with intense pear and pineapple flavors that are smooth and creamy. A wine that is one-dimensional in flavor yet well balanced and easy to drink.

Last tasted: 7/90. Drink 1991-1994. 3,000 cases produced. Release: $12. Current: $17. **84**

1983 KENWOOD VINEYARDS YULUPA VINEYARD: Intensely varietal, with ripe pear and pineapple flavors that are fully mature. The texture is still coarse and somewhat tannic, but the fruit is concentrated and is holding its own. Last tasted: 7/90. Drink 1991-1994. 1,000 cases produced. Release: $11. Current: $18. **85**

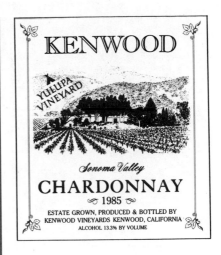

AT A GLANCE

KISTLER VINEYARDS
Nelligan Road
Glen Ellen, CA 95442
(707) 996-5117

Owners: The Kistler family

Winemaker: Stephen Kistler (11 years)

Founded: 1978

First Chardonnay vintage: 1979
　Dutton Ranch: 1979
　Kistler Estate Vineyard: 1986
　Durell Vineyard: 1986
　McCrea Vineyard: 1988

Chardonnay production: 8,500 cases
　Dutton Ranch: 4,600 cases
　Kistler Estate Vineyard: 600 cases
　Durell Vineyard: 2,300 cases
　McCrea Vineyard: 1,000 cases

Chardonnay acres owned: 22
　Kistler Estate Vineyard: 22

Average age of vines: 10 years

Vineyard locations:
　Dutton Ranch: Russian River Valley
　Kistler Estate Vineyard: Sonoma
　　Valley
　Durell Vineyard: Sonoma Valley
　McCrea Vineyard: Sonoma
　　Valley

Time in oak: 10 months

Type of oak: French (Allier)

Oak age:
　Dutton Ranch: new (33%) to
　　2 years old
　Kistler Estate Vineyard: new
　　(100%)
　Durell Vineyard: new (33%) to
　　2 years old
　McCrea Vineyard: new (75%) to
　　1 year old

Winemaking notes:
　Barrel fermentation: 100%
　Malolactic fermentation: 100%
　Lees aging: 100% (10 months)

KISTLER VINEYARDS

Dutton Ranch, Russian River Valley
Kistler Estate Vineyard, Sonoma Valley
Durell Vineyard, Sonoma Valley
McCrea Vineyard, Sonoma Valley

CLASSIFICATION:
　Dutton Ranch: SECOND GROWTH
　Kistler Estate Vineyard: SECOND GROWTH
　Durell Vineyard: SECOND GROWTH
　McCrea Vineyard: Not rated

COLLECTIBILITY RATING:
　Dutton Ranch: AAA
　Kistler Estate Vineyard: AA
　Durell Vineyard: AA
　McCrea Vineyard: Not rated

BEST VINTAGES:
　Dutton Ranch: 1987, 1988
　Kistler Estate Vineyard: 1988, 1986
　Durell Vineyard: 1987, 1988
　McCrea Vineyard: 1988

Kistler Vineyards is back on top of the California Chardonnay scene, producing some of the richest and most complex, elegant and exciting wines made today. This family-owned winery in Sonoma Valley, founded in 1979 by Stephen Kistler, emerged in the 1980s as one of California's bright new Chardonnay stars.

Kistler's first trio of wines from the 1979 vintage came from three promising Chardonnay vineyards, Dutton Ranch in Green Valley (Russian River Valley), Sonoma-Cutrer's Cutrer Vineyard (Russian River Valley) and Winery Lake (Carneros-Napa Valley, now owned by Seagram). These wines were an immediate hit, with their rich, creamy textures and wealth of complex fruit and toasty oak flavors. The 1980 wines, however, were flawed by a bad-smelling mercaptan compound that developed in the bottle. Kistler acknowledged the problem and recalled the wines at a substantial financial loss, but suffered an even greater image problem in subsequent years even though the wines from 1981 on were not only sound but often exceptional.

The driving force behind Kistler Vineyards is winemaker Stephen

Kistler, a Stanford University graduate who aspired to a career as a fiction writer before pursuing winemaking. He studied winemaking at the University of California at Davis, and worked at Ridge Vineyards before convincing his family to finance the winery. His partner from the outset was Mark Bixler, who handles the winery's marketing. The winery sits near the top of the Mayacamas Mountains on the eastern ridge of Sonoma Valley at the 1,800-foot level.

Kistler Vineyards has been a study in identifying first-rate Chardonnay vineyards and creating wines that display individualistic character. Kistler's longest association has been with the Dutton Ranch vineyard, near Graton in Sonoma County, which has been bottled separately since 1979. Kistler has also produced Chardonnays from Les Pierres and Winery Lake (1979 through 1983 and 1985). The most recent vintages have included the Kistler Estate Vineyard, which is 22 acres of Chardonnay; Durell Vineyard in Sonoma Valley, adjacent to Sonoma-Cutrer's Les Pierres; and newcomer McCrea Vineyard in Sonoma Valley, which once sold Chardonnay to Chateau St. Jean. Kistler prefers shy-bearing vineyards that yield intensely flavored fruit, and the quality of these vineyards shows in the wines.

Despite different locations, the four vineyard-designated wines share in common the Kistler style of complex flavors and smooth texture. All of the wines are barrel fermented, undergo full malolactic fermentation and are aged on their lees. Kistler is a big fan of different yeast strains and uses them to achieve the broadest range of flavors possible. He prefers his wines to have a doughy, hazelnut flavor, a character sometimes found in great white Burgundies, and part of this is achieved through his vinification techniques. The wines typically display a bold, rich, creamy texture, tiers of fruit and spice, and remarkably long finishes.

The 1988 vintage proved just how deliberate and consistent the style is, as all four wines are outstanding. The 1988 Kistler Vineyards provides an uncommon display of finesse and harmony, and this vineyard may well emerge as Kistler's best. The Dutton Ranch is typically leaner, more compact and elegant, coming from a cooler climate, while the McCrea shows more ripeness and pronounced Chardonnay flavors, and is more powerful and alcoholic (see notes from Chateau St. Jean McCrea Vineyards Chardonnays). The Durell is a shade less ripe than the McCrea but with plenty of flavor and depth.

Production ranges from about 600 cases of Kistler Estate to 4,600 of Dutton Ranch, for a total Chardonnay production of about 8,500 cases. I have not tasted any of the older Kistler Chardonnays recently, but certainly the Dutton Ranch bottlings I have tasted have usually been wonderful wines and I would go out of my way to try one. One has to be impressed by the overall high level of quality achieved by Kistler Vineyards. My only regret is I have not been able to review the older wines to see how they have aged in bottle. But this much is certain: Few producers make better Chardonnays in California today. These wines appear destined to move up in the classification.

Kistler

California Chardonnay

48,240 Bottles Produced

No.   1987

DUTTON RANCH   RUSSIAN RIVER VALLEY

TASTING NOTES

KISTLER VINEYARDS, Dutton Ranch, Russian River Valley

1988 KISTLER VINEYARDS DUTTON RANCH: Forward and fruity, with fresh, ripe, delicate pear, peach, apple and spice flavors and a subtle oak seasoning in the background. Fine balance, approaching full maturity, but it should age well for another five years or more. Last tasted: 2/90. Drink 1991-1995. 4,987 cases produced. Release: $22. Current: $22. **92**

1987 KISTLER VINEYARDS DUTTON RANCH: Offers amazing richness and depth without weight. The rich, smooth, sharply focused butterscotch, lemon, pear and honey flavors spread out on the palate and fan out on the finish, which is remarkably long and tasty. Last tasted: 2/90. Drink 1991-1993. 4,020 cases produced. Release: $18. Current: $24. **93**

1986 KISTLER VINEYARDS DUTTON RANCH: Wonderful aromas and flavors, rich, smooth and creamy, with intense, elegant honey, toast and butterscotch flavors that linger on the palate. Still developing but very close to its apogee. Fine balance. Last tasted: 2/90. Drink 1991-1997. 3,151 cases produced. Release: $16.50. Current: $28. **90**

1985 KISTLER VINEYARDS DUTTON RANCH-WINERY LAKE: Ripe, rich, smooth and creamy, with elegant pear, toast, lemon and melon flavors that are very attractive, long and fruity on the finish. Drinking at its peak. Last tasted: 2/90. Drink 1991-1994. 5,251 cases produced. Release: $15. Current: $30. **88**

1984 KISTLER VINEYARDS DUTTON RANCH: Fully mature, rich and smooth, with ripe pear, melon, honey and butter flavors that are generous and lively from start to finish. Fruit echoes on the finish. Last tasted: 2/90. Drink 1991-1995. 3,911 cases produced. Release: $15. Current: $30. **89**

KISTLER VINEYARDS, Kistler Estate Vineyard, Sonoma Valley

1988 KISTLER VINEYARDS KISTLER ESTATE VINEYARD: One of the greatest California Chardonnays I've ever tasted, a true masterpiece, richer and more concentrated than any of the wines before it, providing a wonderful orchestration of beautiful pear, vanilla and creamy butterscotch flavors that are sharply focused and linger on the palate. Amazing aftertaste keeps echoing honey, pear and butterscotch. Last tasted: 2/90. Drink 1991-1996. 507 cases produced. Release: $26. Current: $26. **95**

1987 KISTLER VINEYARDS KISTLER ESTATE VINEYARD: Similar in character to the 1986, rich and creamy, with a smooth texture that highlights the ripe pear, honey and toasty oak flavors, finishing with elegance and subtle flavors that linger on the palate. Last tasted: 2/90. Drink 1991-1996. 866 cases produced. Release: $22. Current: $26. **90**

1986 KISTLER VINEYARDS KISTLER ESTATE VINEYARD: A wine of great harmony and finesse, with creamy vanilla flavors that gently unfold, leading to ripe, rich pear, honey and citrus notes that are full-bodied, deep and complex, finishing with elegance and grace and a seductive honey and butterscotch flavor. Delicious. Last tasted: 2/90. Drink 1991-1997. 397 cases produced. Release: $18. Current: $35. **92**

KISTLER VINEYARDS, Durell Vineyard, Sonoma Valley

1988 KISTLER VINEYARDS DURELL VINEYARD: A shade more elegant and delicate than the 1987, beautifully focused, with attractive pear, honey, apple and butterscotch flavors that fan out on the palate, finishing with lovely floral and fruity notes. Last tasted: 2/90. Drink 1992-1998. 2,337 cases produced. Release: $17. Current: $17. **91**

1987 KISTLER VINEYARDS DURELL VINEYARD: Provides more richness and depth than the 1986, with uncommon depth and intensity of fruit and tiers of sharply focused pear, honey and butterscotch flavors that are amazingly smooth and elegant. Absolutely delicious. Last tasted: 2/90. Drink 1991-1997. 1,300 cases produced. Release: $16. Current: $20. **93**

1986 KISTLER VINEYARDS DURELL VINEYARD: Deep, rich, smooth and creamy, with crisp, lively acidity that gives an added dimension to the pretty honey and butterscotch flavors before picking up subtle pear and lemon notes on the finish. Very fine length. Last tasted: 2/90. Drink 1991-1997. 620 cases produced. Release: $16. Current: $25. **89**

KISTLER VINEYARDS, McCrea Vineyard, Sonoma Valley

1988 KISTLER VINEYARDS MCCREA VINEYARD: Delicious, rich and deeply concentrated, with sharply defined pear, lemon, toast and butter flavors and a rich, supple texture, finishing long and full. Perhaps the finest bottling ever from the McCrea Vineyard. Last tasted: 2/90. Drink 1991-1996. 1,010 cases produced. Release: $24. Current: $24. **92**

LA CREMA
Reserve, California

CLASSIFICATION: *FIFTH GROWTH*
COLLECTIBILITY RATING: *Not rated*
BEST VINTAGES: *1988, 1984*

L a Crema's Chardonnays are complex from the word go. The grapes are purchased from vineyards in Sonoma County, Santa Maria Valley and Mendocino County. They receive full malolactic fermentation in the barrel and are typically rich, ripe, creamy wines with plenty of fruit and buttery oak flavors. The winery began as La Crema Viñera in 1979, operating out of a warehouse in Petaluma. It has since dropped the Viñera and is now owned by Jason Korman of New York, who bought the winery in 1985.

Through the years La Crema Chardonnays have always been distinctive and well made. My most recent experience dates to the 1984 vintage of the Reserve bottling, which is complex and drinking at its peak. The 1985 is a touch earthy and tastes of lees, but is pleasant to drink. The 1986 is for fans of toasty, oaky Chardonnays; it turns a bit gamy on the finish. The 1987 shifts toward a more austere style and is heavily oaked. The 1988, however, pulls it all together in a stunning package, bringing more fruit forward to balance the buttery oak, a complex and delicious wine. Production of La Crema Reserve is about 5,000 cases, and Korman has planted 25 acres of Chardonnay in Sonoma. Korman also makes 25,000 cases of La Crema Chardonnay. Both wines carry the "California" appellation.

AT A GLANCE
LA CREMA
4940 Ross Road
Sebastopol, CA 95472
(707) 829-2609

Owner: Jason Korman

Winemaker: Dan Goldfield (1 year)

Founded: 1979

First Chardonnay vintage: 1979
   Reserve: 1984

Chardonnay production: 30,000 cases
   Reserve: 5,000 cases

Chardonnay acres owned: 25

Average age of vines: 15 years

Average wine makeup: Sonoma
   County (42%), Santa Maria
   Valley (33%), Mendocino
   County (25%)

Time in oak: 12 months

Type of oak: French, American

Oak age: new to 10 years old

Winemaking notes:
   Barrel fermentation: 100%
   Malolactic fermentation: 100%
   Lees aging: 100% (12 months)

TASTING NOTES

LA CREMA, Reserve, California

1988 LA CREMA RESERVE: Youthful, rich and attractive, with intense, complex apple, pear and buttery oak flavors tightly woven together, this wine will need another two to three years to mature fully, but it's well balanced and concentrated and has all the right ingredients for greatness. Last tasted: 6/90. Drink 1993-1999. 5,000 cases produced. Release: $22. Current: $22. **91**

1987 LA CREMA RESERVE: Austere, even hard, like 1987s in general, but with a solid core of apple and pear flavors that will take a few more years for the rough edges to smooth out. Quite oaky too, with a piney aftertaste. Last tasted: 6/90. Drink 1993-1999. 2,900 cases produced. Release: $22. Current: $22. **83**

1986 LA CREMA RESERVE: Distinctive rich, toasty aromas and flavors, complex and flavorful, with ripe pear, nutmeg and spice notes that are well integrated and balanced. Fully mature and ready to drink, although the finish turns a bit gamy. Last tasted: 6/90. Drink 1991-1996. 1,200 cases produced. Release: $18. Current: $22. **85**

1985 LA CREMA RESERVE: A touch earthy and leesy but has plenty of ripe pear and apple flavors. A shade leaner than the 1984 and not quite as complex, but altogether elegant and complete. Some may prefer this crisper style. Aging well. Last tasted: 6/90. Drink 1991-1995. 1,200 cases produced. Release: $18. Current: $22. **86**

1984 LA CREMA RESERVE: Complex and enticing, fully mature now and drinking at its peak, with a wonderful array of pear, honey, melon and toasty butterscotch flavors that are silky smooth and long on the finish. Balanced, rich and elegant. From Ventana Vineyard in Monterey. Last tasted: 6/90. Drink 1991-1998. 2,000 cases produced. Release: $18. Current: $22. **88**

LONG VINEYARDS
Napa Valley

CLASSIFICATION: *SECOND GROWTH*
COLLECTIBILITY RATING: *AAA*
BEST VINTAGES: *1988, 1986, 1985, 1987*

Long Vineyards, in the hills east of St. Helena, is owned by Bob and Zelma Long. It was founded in 1977 while they were married, and despite their divorce they remain business partners in this family-owned winery. Today Bob runs the winery and Zelma is president and chief executive officer of Simi Winery in Sonoma County, where she was winemaker from 1979 to 1989.

The first vintage for Long Vineyards was 1977, from grapes grown in the Longs' hillside vineyard that faces north, allowing for a cooler climate and wonderfully elegant and delicate Chardonnays. Production remains small at about 900 cases, and most of the wine is sold through a winery mailing list, but these are wines worth seeking out.

I have always been highly impressed by the sheer elegance and finesse of these Chardonnays. The 7 acres of vines are very mature, having been planted nearly 30 years ago. The 1977 and 1979 vintages were sensational wines early on, but I have not tasted them in several years. I have tasted most of the vintages, but I have only recent notes from 1984 to 1988. The 1988 in particular may be the best Long Chardonnay produced to date. It offers ripe, forward fruit, richness and concentration, depth and intensity without weight, and impeccable balance. The 1987 is a shade leaner, but still provides a wonderful display of fruit. The 1986 is an outstanding vintage, with a touch of earthiness to add to the complexity, while the 1985 is in peak condition now. The 1984 is forward and ripe, loaded with flavor and very well balanced. Most of the Long Chardonnays are good candidates to cellar for four to eight years. With a few more vintages like these, Long should move up in the classification.

TASTING NOTES

LONG VINEYARDS, Napa Valley

1988 LONG VINEYARDS: Ripe and forward like most 1988s, perhaps the most seductive Long Vineyards Chardonnay yet, with beautifully defined pear, apple, citrus and melon flavors and subtle vanilla and spicy oak seasoning, impeccable balance and a long, delicious after-taste. Last tasted: 4/90. Drink 1991-1998. 900 cases produced. Release: $27.50. Current: $30. **93**

1987 LONG VINEYARDS: Another great success, just beginning to open up, displaying a wealth of complex pear, honey and vanilla flavors that are well defined and well focused. Youthful and still on its way up. Last tasted: 4/90. Drink 1991-1998. 900 cases produced. Release: $27.50. Current: $35. **90**

1986 LONG VINEYARDS: On the quality level of the two previous bottlings, offering amazing complexity and flavor, a pretty earthiness to complement the fresh, ripe pear, apple, vanilla and nutmeg flavors. It is also deeper and richer, with flavors that echo on the finish. Last tasted: 4/90. Drink 1991-1997. 800 cases produced. Release: $27.50. Current: $45. **92**

1985 LONG VINEYARDS: Shows a shade more richness and finesse than the 1984, offering pure apple, pear, spice, honey and vanilla flavors that are beautifully balanced, finishing with remarkable elegance and subtlety. Terrific now and should hold up through the decade. Last tasted: 4/90. Drink 1991-1996. 850 cases produced. Release: $27.50. Current: $45. **91**

1984 LONG VINEYARDS: Elegant, complex and stylish, with intense pear, lemon, honey and spice flavors, a subtle touch of oak and a rich yet silky smooth texture that lets the flavors glide across the palate. Remarkably elegant and impeccably balanced. Mature now but aging quite gracefully. Last tasted: 4/90. Drink 1991-1995. 600 cases produced. Release: $27.50. Current: $45. **88**

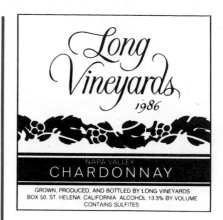

MARKHAM VINEYARDS
Yountville, Napa Valley

CLASSIFICATION: *FIFTH GROWTH*
COLLECTIBILITY RATING: *Not rated*
BEST VINTAGES: <u>*1988, 1987*</u>

AT A GLANCE
MARKHAM VINEYARDS
2812 N. St. Helena Highway
St. Helena, CA 94574
(707) 963-5292

Owner: Sanraku Inc., Japan
Winemaker: Robert Foley (12 years)
Founded: 1978
First Chardonnay vintage: 1979
Chardonnay production: 8,000 cases
Chardonnay acres owned: 63
Average age of vines: 8 years
Vineyard locations: Yountville
Time in oak: 9 months
Type of oak: French (Tronçais, Allier)
Oak age: new to 4 years old (20% each)
Winemaking notes:
  Barrel fermentation: 95%
  Malolactic fermentation: none
  Lees aging: 95% (7 months)

Consistently underrated if not overlooked, Markham Chardonnays have shown steady improvement, with each vintage showing more elegance and grace than its predecessor.

Markham Vineyards, founded by advertising man Bruce Markham, has 63 acres of Chardonnay planted in the Oak Knoll area between Napa and Yountville. Bruce Markham bought the winery on Highway 29 north of St. Helena in 1977, refurbished it, and in 1988 sold it to Japan's Sanraku Inc. Robert Foley, a University of California at Davis graduate, is the winemaker. Production has leveled off at 8,000 cases.

I have not recently tasted the 1979 to 1981 vintages, but from 1982 to 1988 there is noticeable progress. The most recent Chardonnays are fresh and lively, elegant and well balanced, with complex flavors and good aging potential. The 1988 vintage is the most impressive, bringing together rich, well-defined fruit flavors in an elegant framework. The 1987 is also highly successful, well balanced and graceful. The 1986 is a fuller, richer wine that offers more power than grace, but it is well balanced. The 1985 is also very intense but lacks the subtlety of later vintages. The 1984, 1983 and 1982 vintages share a rough, unrefined character; they are not unpleasant by any means, but they are cruder.

TASTING NOTES

MARKHAM VINEYARDS, Napa Valley

1988 MARKHAM VINEYARDS: Markham's best to date, amazingly fresh and lively, with rich, beautifully defined pear, earth, lemon, grapefruit and melon flavors that provide a complex, elegant framework and a long, lingering aftertaste. Last tasted: 2/90. Drink 1991-1997. 8,026 cases produced. Release: $12. Current: $12. **89**

1987 MARKHAM VINEYARDS: A superb bottling displaying elegance and finesse, with complex pear, earth, toast and melon flavors that are full and lively, finishing with complex flavors that stay with you. Last tasted: 2/90. Drink 1991-1996. 4,760 cases produced. Release: $12. Current: $12. **87**

1986 MARKHAM VINEYARDS: Very ripe and full-bodied, with rich fig, melon and pear flavors and a good dose of oak, it is nonetheless well balanced and provides plenty of power and flavor. Last tasted: 2/90. Drink 1991-1994. 4,649 cases produced. Release: $12. Current: $14. **84**

1985 MARKHAM VINEYARDS: Intense yet elegant, with sharply defined and well-focused pear, lemon, apple and spicy oak flavors, all combining to give complexity and finesse. Flavors linger on the aftertaste. Last tasted: 2/90. Drink 1991-1995. 2,843 cases produced. Release: $12. Current: $16. **86**

1984 MARKHAM VINEYARDS: Ripe, fruity and elegant, with pretty pear, honey, butter and butterscotch flavors that glide across the palate, finishing with a lively burst of fruit and flavor. Aging well. Last tasted: 2/90. Drink 1991-1995. 2,955 cases produced. Release: $12. Current: $16. **85**

1983 MARKHAM VINEYARDS: An earthier wine with rich pear, oak and spice flavors, fully mature, but despite the lively acidity the flavors are drying out on the finish. Last tasted: 2/90. Drink 1991-1992. 860 cases produced. Release: $11.50. Current: $16. **81**

1982 MARKHAM VINEYARDS: Fully mature, with rich, ripe pear, fig and honey flavors. There is some oxidation, but it is still quite drinkable, finishing with spice, oak and complex fruit flavors. Last tasted: 2/90. Drink 1991-1993. 531 cases produced. Release: $12. Current: $17. **83**

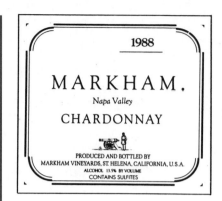

MATANZAS CREEK WINERY

Sonoma County

CLASSIFICATION: *SECOND GROWTH*

COLLECTIBILITY RATING: *AA*

BEST VINTAGES:

Sonoma County: 1987, 1988, 1986, 1984

Estate: 1982

AT A GLANCE

MATANZAS CREEK WINERY
6097 Bennett Valley Road
Santa Rosa, CA 95404
(707) 528-6464

Owners: Sandra and Bill MacIver

Winemakers: Susan Reed and Bill Parker (1 year)

Founded: 1978

First Chardonnay vintage: 1978

Chardonnay production: 15,000 cases

Chardonnay acres owned: 30

Average age of vines: 11 years

Average wine makeup: Sonoma Valley (100%)

Time in oak: 9 months

Type of oak: French

Oak age: 1 to 4 years

Winemaking notes:
  Barrel fermentation: 100%
  Malolactic fermentation: 100%
  Lees aging: 100% (9 months)

Matanzas Creek Winery has always produced rich, complex, stylish Chardonnays. The early wines, from the first vintage in 1978 to 1982, were made by Merry Edwards. These wines featured ultraripe grapes and were often high in alcohol, very rich, fairly oaky and weighty. They were also often delicious, packed with ripe fruit and buttery oak flavors that were wonderful to drink on release. But they did not gain in the bottle and were built on a fast aging curve.

Since the early 1980s owners Sandra and Bill MacIver have been gradually shifting the style toward wines of more elegance, grace and restraint without sacrificing the broad, complex range of flavors. Increasingly the winery has shopped for grapes in much cooler climates, such as Carneros, as well as harvesting grapes at lower sugar and ripeness levels. In 1984 they hired David Ramey from Simi to reshape the style, introducing full malolactic and barrel fermentations, and not only did the wines improve considerably in quality, but they have aged better in the bottle. Ramey departed before the 1988 vintage.

The 1984 Sonoma County bottling is a big, ripe wine with a rich, creamy texture, but it's aging very well. The 1985, 1986, 1987 and 1988 vintages maintain that high level of quality and consistency of style even though production has increased from 6,000 to more than 17,000 cases. Matanzas Creek also bottled an Estate Chardonnay in some vintages, but in my tastings it is almost always less complex and enticing than the Sonoma County bottling. The 1982 Estate is an exception, for it is still drinking very well, with deep, rich flavors despite being rather heavy. The winemaking responsibilities are now shared by Susan Reed and Bill Parker.

TASTING NOTES

MATANZAS CREEK WINERY, Sonoma County

1988 MATANZAS CREEK WINERY SONOMA COUNTY: Deliciously rich and fruity yet elegant, delicate and refined, with pretty melon, pear, apple and spice flavors, all in a forward, well-focused style that sustains the flavors through the finish. Ready now but should hold five years. Last tasted: 2/90. Drink 1991-1996. 17,165 cases produced. Release: $18.75 Current: $19. **89**

1987 MATANZAS CREEK WINERY SONOMA COUNTY: Wonderfully rich and elegant, with melon, spice, pear and honeysuckle flavors that are delicate and complex, finishing with lush fruit flavors and just a hint of oak. It tastes better with every sip. Last tasted: 2/90. Drink 1991-1996. 13,506 cases produced. Release: $18. Current: $20. **90**

1986 MATANZAS CREEK WINERY SONOMA COUNTY: A turning point in terms of complexity and finesse, the 1986 is rich and flavorful, with pear, melon and spicy oak flavors that maintain a sense of elegance on a long finish. Manages to combine richness and depth without weight. Last tasted: 2/90. Drink 1991-1994. 8,817 cases produced. Release: $17.50 Current: $22. **89**

1985 MATANZAS CREEK WINERY SONOMA COUNTY: Close in quality to the 1985 Estate Bottled, offering rich, deep citrus, pineapple and spicy oak flavors with great intensity and vibrancy and a pretty aftertaste. Fully mature but with the balance and depth of flavor to hold another three to five years without suffering. Last tasted: 2/90. Drink 1991-1994. 6,221 cases produced. Release: $16.50 Current: $28. **88**

1984 MATANZAS CREEK WINERY SONOMA COUNTY: Big, ripe and fruity, with grapefruit, apple, pear and melon flavors that offer fine depth and intensity and linger on the finish. The texture is rich and creamy. Last tasted: 2/90. Drink 1991-1994. 3,717 cases produced. Release: $15. Current: $28. **89**

1983 MATANZAS CREEK WINERY SONOMA COUNTY: Its attractive fresh, clean, spicy pear flavors of moderate depth and intensity, finish with lemon nuances. While aging well, it is not especially complex or dramatic, but succeeds with its delicacy and finesse. Last tasted: 2/90. Drink 1991-1993. 1,788 cases produced. Release: $15. Current: $28. **85**

1982 MATANZAS CREEK WINERY SONOMA COUNTY: Still plenty of ripe pear, melon and spicy fruit flavors, but past its prime and drying out on the finish. Last tasted: 2/90. Drink 1991. 1,735 cases produced. Release: $15. Current: $25. **78**

1981 MATANZAS CREEK WINERY SONOMA COUNTY: The best of the older Matanzas Creeks, still displaying pear, melon and honey flavors. Lighter in color than previous bottlings. Better in its youth, it

1987

SONOMA COUNTY

CHARDONNAY

PRODUCED AND BOTTLED BY MATANZAS CREEK WINERY
SANTA ROSA, CA ALCOHOL 13% BY VOLUME CONTAINS SULFITES

1982

Estate Bottled

SONOMA VALLEY

CHARDONNAY

A TABLE WINE PRODUCED AND BOTTLED BY
MATANZAS CREEK WINERY, SANTA ROSA, CALIF., BW-CA-4848.

it still remains attractive. Last tasted: 2/90. Drink 1991-1993. 1,925 cases produced. Release: $15. Current: $28. **85**

1980 MATANZAS CREEK WINERY SONOMA COUNTY: Rich, ripe, alcoholic (14.5 percent) and past its prime, yet showing pretty honey, toast and butterscotch flavors that finish with some heat. Better four to five years ago, so drink up. Last tasted: 2/90. Drink 1991-1992. 1,700 cases produced. Release: $15. Current: $25. **82**

1979 MATANZAS CREEK WINERY SONOMA-NAPA: A blend of Sonoma (73 percent) and Napa Valley (27 percent) fruit, this wine has gone beyond its peak but still offers plenty of attractive pear, honey, spice and butter flavors that begin to dry out on the finish. It's also hot and alcoholic. Last tasted: 2/90. Drink 1991. 1,650 cases produced. Release: $14.50 Current: $40. **80**

1978 MATANZAS CREEK WINERY SONOMA COUNTY: Matanzas Creek's first vintage is very deep in color and fully mature, with rich honey and butterscotch flavors that are hot and dry on the finish. Better in its youth, but it remains pleasant; best with a creamy cheese. Last tasted: 2/90. Drink 1991. 1,230 cases produced. Release: $12.50 Current: $40. **79**

MATANZAS CREEK WINERY, Estate, Sonoma Valley

1985 MATANZAS CREEK WINERY ESTATE: In peak drinking condition, with fresh, ripe peach, pear and spicy oak flavors that are rich and elegant on the palate, gaining a toasty oak flavor on the aftertaste. For current drinking, a very complete and elegant wine. Last tasted: 2/90. Drink 1991-1994. 380 cases produced. Release: $18. Current: $31. **86**

1984 MATANZAS CREEK WINERY ESTATE: Light and elegant for Matanzas Creek, with simple but pleasant pear and spice flavors of moderate depth and intensity that taper off on the finish. Last tasted: 2/90. Drink 1991-1993. 830 cases produced. Release: $18. Current: $28. **80**

1983 MATANZAS CREEK WINERY ESTATE: A tart, gamy quality on the finish detracts from otherwise fresh, clean fruit flavors. The cloying, almost sour finish is unpleasant. Last tasted: 2/90. Best to avoid. 516 cases produced. Release: $18. Current: $18. **68**

1982 MATANZAS CREEK WINERY ESTATE: Holding up remarkably well for 1982, with rich, mature honey, toast, butter and spicy oak flavors, all combining to give this wine an extra measure of depth and complexity. Crisp acidity still carries the flavors. Last tasted: 2/90. Drink 1991-1994. 700 cases produced. Release: $18. Current: $25. **88**

1980 MATANZAS CREEK WINERY ESTATE: Dry and oxidized, showing less fruit and flavor than the other 1980 bottling. Barely passable. Last tasted: 2/90. Drink 1991. 85 cases produced. Release: $18. Current: $18. **70**

MAYACAMAS VINEYARDS
Napa Valley

CLASSIFICATION: *SECOND GROWTH*

COLLECTIBILITY RATING: *AA*

BEST VINTAGES: *1964, 1985, 1988, 1955, 1984*

The remarkable thing about Mayacamas Chardonnays is that while they are elegant and subtle, they can age almost as well as the Mayacamas Cabernet Sauvignons. One night before dinner, I uncorked a bottle of 1955 Mayacamas that winemaker Bob Travers had sent to me for review. It came in a clear glass Sauvignon Blanc-style bottle with the ullage at mid-shoulder. I expected it to be nothing more than a curiosity and I had my doubts about whether there would be any life left in the wine, but it proved to be quite complex and elegant, with a wonderful bouquet of wildflowers, anise and butterscotch and subtle flavors to match. It continued to unfold for the next two hours and was quite amazing. It is the oldest California Chardonnay I've tasted and proof that when properly made, California Chardonnays can age for decades.

Few people are aware that Mayacamas, high atop Mount Veeder above the city of Napa, has been producing Chardonnays since 1950, predating both Stony Hill and Hanzell. Production has always been small, just a few hundred cases a year in the 1950s and 1960s, and even today the winery production is only 2,600 cases. Not all the old vintages I tasted have held up as well as the 1955. You would have to skip ahead to the fabulous 1964 to find the next great Mayacamas; it remains a tremendously fresh and lively wine, with crisp citrus and mature Chardonnay flavors. It can age another 10 years or more.

Chardonnays from the 1970s showed better earlier in their lives. The 1974 is hanging on, but should be consumed, as should the 1976, 1977, 1978, 1979, 1980 and 1981 vintages. The 1982 is fully mature and slow to unfold, an austere wine with clean pear and spice notes. The 1983 is also on a slow aging curve, drinking well. The 1984 is very ripe and full, drinking in peak condition now, followed by the 1985, which is the best of the current vintages. The 1986, 1987 and 1988 are all true-to-form Mayacamas Chardonnays, understated and delicate, with subtle pear, spice and nutmeg flavors and crisp, firm acidity. Under winemaker Travers, who has owned the winery since 1968, the wines do not undergo malolactic fermentation, nor are they barrel fermented, so their acidity remains high, the fruit is fresh and the wines are not overly oaky. A mixture of new to five-year-old oak barrels is used for

AT A GLANCE
MAYACAMAS VINEYARDS
1155 Lokoya Road
Napa, CA 94558
(707) 224-4030

Owner: Mayacamas Vineyards. Robert Travers, president

Winemaker: Robert Travers (22 years)

Founded: 1889; re-established: 1941

First Chardonnay vintage: 1950

Chardonnay production: 2,000 cases

Chardonnay acres owned: 24

Average age of vines: 20 years

Average wine makeup: Mount Veeder, Napa Valley (100%)

Time in oak: 12 months

Type of oak: French (various types)

Oak age: new to 5 years old

Winemaking notes:
  Barrel fermentation: none
  Malolactic fermentation: none
  Lees aging: none

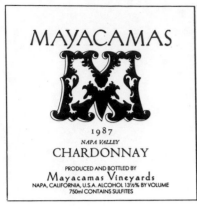

aging up to 12 months. Mayacamas owns 24 acres of Chardonnay on Mount Veeder. The appellation listed on the label has changed from California to Napa County to Napa Valley.

TASTING NOTES

MAYACAMAS VINEYARDS, Napa Valley

1988 MAYACAMAS VINEYARDS: Tight and austere, with a firm, oaky edge and plenty of rich, concentrated pear, lemon, melon and spice notes that are well defined, youthful and untamed, but extremely well balanced, showing a woody aftertaste. Just what you'd expect from a young Mayacamas, an exceptionally well-integrated wine. Last tasted: 6/90. Drink: 1992-1997. 1,447 cases produced. Release: $20. Current: $20. **89**

1987 MAYACAMAS VINEYARDS: Fresh and youthful, with ripe pear, peach and spice notes, showing moderate depth, richness and concentration. A clean, well-made, balanced wine that at this point lacks only excitement. With time it may possess more pizzazz. Last tasted: 1/90. Drink 1991-1996. 2,640 cases produced. Release: $20. Current: $20. **87**

1986 MAYACAMAS VINEYARDS: Tight and understated, typical of Mayacamas Chardonnays early on, the spicy pear and oaky vanilla flavors gain intensity with each sip. Well balanced, it appears to have the ingredients for aging another decade. Last tasted: 3/90. Drink 1991-1996. 1,860 cases produced. Release: $20. Current: $20. **87**

1985 MAYACAMAS VINEYARDS: The best Mayacamas in years, rich, deep and packed with fresh, ripe lemon, pear, nutmeg and spice flavors that are woven together with a beam of crisp acidity that carries the flavors. Long and delicious. Last tasted: 1/90. Drink 1991-1998. 1,415 cases produced. Release: $20. Current: $25. **90**

1984 MAYACAMAS VINEYARDS: From a very warm vintage, the 1984 is very ripe and concentrated, loaded with generous, juicy pear, lemon, anise and toasty oak flavors that explode on the palate. The crisp acidity carries the flavors on the finish. Last tasted: 1/90. Drink 1991-1998. 1,715 cases produced. Release: $18. Current: $25. **88**

1983 MAYACAMAS VINEYARDS: True-to-form Mayacamas, subtle and understated, with toasty oak and gamy aromas and delicate pear and spice notes. Slow to develop, showing no signs of age or fatigue. Last tasted: 1/90. Drink 1991-1996. 1,775 cases produced. Release: $16. Current: $25. **86**

1982 MAYACAMAS VINEYARDS: Toasty and earthy, a lean, understated wine that begins to open up with the characteristic pear and spice notes that are mellow and well balanced, seemingly unaffected by age. Not a great vintage, but surprisingly satisfying. Last tasted: 1/90. Drink 1991-1997. 2,215 cases produced. Release: $16. Current: $30. **85**

1981 MAYACAMAS VINEYARDS: Elegant and pleasant, fully mature, with a silky texture and citrus, honey and anise notes that are subtle and slightly alcoholic. Last tasted: 1/90. Drink 1991-1994. 1,955 cases produced. Release: $16. Current: $35. **78**

1980 MAYACAMAS VINEYARDS: Fat, ripe, oily and gamy, not showing much fruit and not aging particularly well. Drink up. Last tasted: 1/90. Drink 1991. 1,480 cases produced. Release: $16. Current: $35. **74**

1979 MAYACAMAS VINEYARDS: Declining, with a hint of honey and fruit remaining. Last tasted: 1/90. Drink 1991. 1,220 cases produced. Release: $15. Current: $35. **70**

1978 MAYACAMAS VINEYARDS: Fading, having lost its rich, buttery texture and mature honey and fruit flavors. Just a trace of fruit remains; best to drink it soon. Last tasted: 1/90. Drink 1991. 1,233 cases produced. Release: $13. Current: $30. **75**

1977 MAYACAMAS VINEYARDS: Beginning to turn, with very mature fruit flavors and a bitter finish. Best to drink soon. Last tasted: 1/90. Drink 1991. 1,520 cases produced. Release: $12. Current: $35. **70**

1976 MAYACAMAS VINEYARDS: Still holding together despite its age, with mature honey, butterscotch and anise flavors that are fully developed and long on the finish. Last tasted: 1/90. Drink 1991-1994. 1,255 cases produced. Release: $11. Current: $45. **81**

1975 MAYACAMAS VINEYARDS: Mature and past its prime but still showing attractive pear, spice and anise notes in an elegant style. Last tasted: 1/90. Drink 1991. 1,464 cases produced. Release: $9. Current: $50. **78**

1974 MAYACAMAS VINEYARDS: A faint hint of fruit remains, but it should be consumed immediately. Last tasted: 1/90. Drink 1991. 1,257 cases produced. Release: $7. Current: $50. **70**

1973 MAYACAMAS VINEYARDS: Oxidized. Last tasted: 1/90. Best to avoid. 1,082 cases produced. Release: $7. Current: $50. **60**

1972 MAYACAMAS VINEYARDS: Oxidized. Last tasted: 1/90. Best to avoid. 704 cases produced. Release: $7. Current: $50. **59**

1965 MAYACAMAS VINEYARDS: Oxidized. Last tasted: 1/90. Best to avoid. 500 cases produced. Release: $2.50. Current: $125. **58**

1964 MAYACAMAS VINEYARDS: Amazingly well preserved. Brilliant yellow, with crisp, clean, elegant honey, citrus and subtle mature Chardonnay flavors, excellent length and a pretty aftertaste that echoes the citrus flavors. Can still age another decade — maybe longer. Last tasted: 1/90. Drink 1991-1994. 500 cases produced. Release: $1.75. Current: $200. **92**

1963 MAYACAMAS VINEYARDS: Oxidized. Last tasted: 1/90. Best to avoid. 400 cases produced. Release: $1.75. Current: $150. **58**

1962 MAYACAMAS VINEYARDS: Oxidized. Last tasted: 1/90. Best to avoid. 400 cases produced. Release: $1. Current: $150. **58**

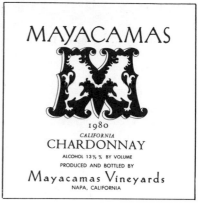

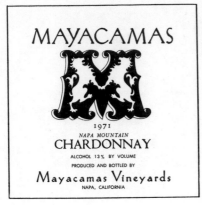

1958 MAYACAMAS VINEYARDS: Oxidized. Well past its prime. Last tasted: 1/90. Best to avoid. 500 cases produced. Release: $1. Current: $200. **60**

1955 MAYACAMAS VINEYARDS: Despite low ullage, this old wine is still very attractive and enjoyable, with butterscotch, wildflower and anise aromas and smooth, complex honey and nutmeg flavors that linger pleasantly on the finish. Extremely rare, but if you find one that's filled to the cork and has been well stored, you're in for a real treat. Last tasted: 1/90. Drink 1991-1995. 250 cases produced. Release: $1. Current: $325. **88**

ROBERT MONDAVI WINERY
Reserve, Stags Leap District, Napa Valley

CLASSIFICATION: SECOND GROWTH
COLLECTIBILITY RATING: AA
BEST VINTAGES: 1987, 1988, 1986, 1985, 1983, 1974

The Robert Mondavi Winery has often been at the forefront of research and experimentation with different vinification and growing techniques and different grape sources. This philosophy of innovation has lead the winery through a number of stylistic swings throughout the years. Critics of the Mondavi Reserve Chardonnays argue that there is no Mondavi style, that it changes with each vintage and new winemaking technique. The truth is that there has been an evolution of styles since this famous vintner began making Napa Valley Chardonnay at Charles Krug Winery in the 1950s, but much less was known back then about growing and making fine Chardonnays in California.

In the early years after founding his winery in 1966, Robert Mondavi concentrated more on upgrading the quality of his Cabernet Sauvignon and Cabernet Reserve wines, selecting his Reserve as the vehicle to raise the esteem of California wines in the eyes of the wine world. With Chardonnay, Mondavi has attempted to do the same thing, with equally impressive results, helping make it California's finest white wine. Robert's son Tim, a University of California at Davis graduate, has led much of the research since the late 1970s, with experiments in cold fermentation, malolactic fermentation and barrel fermentation, different grape clones, yeast strains, and levels of toast in oak barrels. In general the Mondavi Reserve Chardonnays are typically bolder, richer, more concentrated and more complex than the Mondavi regular bottling, and they age well for three to five years, but they are not as complex as California's finest, nor do they age with the best.

The grapes for the Mondavi Reserve Chardonnays are grown in family-owned vineyards in the Stags Leap District, which is a warm area for Chardonnay. There the Mondavis farm some 89 acres of Chardonnay on the west side of Silverado Trail across the highway from Clos Du Val, in vineyards below the hillside homes of Robert and his sons Tim and Michael. The warmth of the Stags Leap District leads to very ripe, lush, rich, sometimes voluptuous Chardonnays that have a smooth, creamy texture. Mondavi adds a layer of smoky, toasty oak, and a high percentage of his recent vintages has gone through malolactic fermentation and barrel fermentation. The result is Reserve Chardonnays that are very rich and complex, with layers of fruit, oak and spice

AT A GLANCE
ROBERT MONDAVI WINERY
7801 St. Helena Highway
Oakville, CA 94562
(707) 963-9611

Owners: The Robert Mondavi family
Winemaker: Tim Mondavi (14 years)
Founded: 1966
First Chardonnay vintage: 1966
　Reserve: 1973
Chardonnay production: 100,000 cases
　Reserve: 12,000 cases
Chardonnay acres owned: 120
Average age of vines: 15 years
Average wine makeup: Stags Leap District, Napa Valley (100%)
Time in oak: 8 to 10 months
Type of oak: French
Oak age: new (95%)
Winemaking notes:
　Barrel fermentation: 100%
　Malolactic fermentation: 95%
　Lees aging: 100% (7 months)

1987
Napa Valley
CHARDONNAY
ALCOHOL 13.5% BY VOLUME
PRODUCED AND BOTTLED BY
ROBERT MONDAVI WINERY
OAKVILLE, CALIFORNIA

flavors, but also a measure of elegance and finesse.

The most recent vintages, 1988 and 1987, are both lavishly oaked, but with firm fruit concentration underneath. They are ready to drink now and should improve for another four or five years. The 1986 and 1985 vintages are also very fine, drinking well now, as are the 1984 and 1983 vintages. The 1982 is a bit heavy, with a touch of honey and butterscotch, while the 1981 was an exceptional vintage that drank well for years. It is now declining and should be consumed soon. The 1980 showed a very deep, heavy quality the last time I tried it and appears to be well past its prime. Vintages from 1979 to 1977 are also disappointing. Both the 1976 and 1975 are curiosities, drinkable but probably not worth going out of your way to try. The 1974, however, remains in tip-top condition, probably at this point the best 1974 I've tried in several years. It still has plenty of life ahead. The oldest Reserve is from the 1973 vintage, and I have not tried it. Total production of Chardonnay at Mondavi has exceeded 100,000 cases, of which approximately 12,000 are selected for the Reserve bottling. The winery recently planted several hundred acres of new Chardonnay vines in the Carneros District.

TASTING NOTES

ROBERT MONDAVI WINERY, Reserve, Stags Leap District, Napa Valley

1988 ROBERT MONDAVI WINERY RESERVE: Ripe and fresh, with complex pear, melon and spice flavors that are elegant and polished, leaving the flavors to fan out on the finish. From a vintage that offers subtlety and finesse, this is one of the best. Last tasted: 6/90. Drink 1992-1997. 12,000 cases produced. Release: $26. Current: $26. **91**

1987 ROBERT MONDAVI WINERY RESERVE: Continues in the style of the 1985 and 1986 Reserves, a lean, rich, elegant and wonderfully flavored wine that combines toasty, earthy notes with ripe pear, melon and grapefruit flavors that are complex and tasty yet subtle and refined. Last tasted: 6/90. Drink 1991-1997. 10,000 cases produced. Release: $26. Current: $26. **92**

1986 ROBERT MONDAVI WINERY RESERVE: Elegant and delicate, with subtle pear, melon, smoke and spicy citrus notes that are complex and long on the finish. A deliberate style that follows the 1985 in reshaping the Reserve character. Clearly more elegant and restrained. Last tasted: 3/90. Drink 1991-1995. 11,000 cases produced. Release: $25. Current: $28. **89**

1985 ROBERT MONDAVI WINERY RESERVE: A distinctively elegant and subtle wine that offers attractive, ripe, well-balanced pear, earth and lemon notes that are gentle and enticing, finishing with a touch of smokiness. Last tasted: 3/90. Drink 1991-1995. 13,000 cases produced. Release: $25. Current: $27. **88**

1984 ROBERT MONDAVI WINERY RESERVE: Tart and fresh, with smoke, earth, lemon and pear flavors of good depth and intensity, this is an elegant, well-balanced wine that continues to develop on the finish. Better with every sip. Last tasted: 3/90. Drink 1991-1994. 9,000 cases produced. Release: $22. Current: $24. **87**

1983 ROBERT MONDAVI WINERY RESERVE: Rich, smooth, creamy and lively, aging very well and drinking in peak condition. Harmonious in flavor and balance, with ripe pear and melon flavors and hints of citrus, anise and spicy nutmeg on the finish. Last tasted: 3/90. Drink 1991-1995. 7,800 cases produced. Release: $20. Current: $25. **88**

1982 ROBERT MONDAVI WINERY RESERVE: Heavy honey and butterscotch flavors that turn dry on the finish. Very mature color, best to drink soon. Last tasted: 3/90. Drink 1991. 6,000 cases produced. Release: $20. Current: $25. **81**

1981 ROBERT MONDAVI WINERY RESERVE: Long one of my favorites, the 1981 Reserve is aging gracefully. It's rich, smooth and creamy, with honey, pear and vanilla flavors that are elegant and pleasant. No point in waiting much longer. Last tasted: 3/90. Drink 1991-1993. 6,800 cases produced. Release: $20. Current: $24. **86**

1980 ROBERT MONDAVI WINERY RESERVE: Past its prime, very deep color, very mature flavors. Last tasted: 3/90. Best to avoid. 3,500 cases produced. Release: $20. Current: $30. **69**

1979 ROBERT MONDAVI WINERY RESERVE: Past its prime, but still displaying intriguing rich honey, pear and vanilla flavors and good length. Last tasted: 3/90. Drink 1991. 8,700 cases produced. Release: $20. Current: $27. **79**

1978 ROBERT MONDAVI WINERY RESERVE: Very deep brassy gold, drying out, with honey and Botrytis flavors. Past its prime. Last tasted: 3/90. Best to avoid. 5,100 cases produced. Release: $20. Current: $24. **69**

1977 ROBERT MONDAVI WINERY RESERVE: Deep gold, with some aldehydic notes; past its prime. Last tasted: 3/90. Best to avoid. 2,600 cases produced. Release: $14. Current: $32. **68**

1976 ROBERT MONDAVI WINERY RESERVE: Dry, minty and elegant but dropping its fruit. Last tasted: 3/90. Drink 1991. 1,450 cases produced. Release: $12. Current: $32. **78**

1975 ROBERT MONDAVI WINERY RESERVE: Earthy, dry, green and leafy, not showing much fruit or flavor, but not over the hill, either. Last tasted: 3/90. Drink 1991. 1,500 cases produced. Release: $10. Current: $35. **75**

1974 ROBERT MONDAVI WINERY RESERVE: Youthful with lemon, grass and pear aromas that are fresh, clean and elegant, crisp, with moderate depth and intensity, echoing pear and spicy vanilla notes on the finish. Aging remarkably well; still has plenty of life. Last tasted: 3/90. Drink 1991-1994. 1,000 cases produced. Release: $10. Current: $45. **88**

MONTICELLO CELLARS

Corley Reserve, Yountville, Napa Valley
Jefferson Ranch, Yountville, Napa Valley

CLASSIFICATION:
  Corley Reserve: SECOND GROWTH
  Jefferson Ranch: FOURTH GROWTH

COLLECTIBILITY RATING:
  Corley Reserve: AA
  Jefferson Ranch: A

BEST VINTAGES:
  Corley Reserve: 1988, 1984, 1986

  Jefferson Ranch: 1983, 1988

Monticello Cellars, just north of the city of Napa, is a tribute to Thomas Jefferson, one of America's most famous wine drinkers and collectors. Founded in 1980 by Jay and Marilyn Corley, the winery is an elegant replica of Jefferson's Virginia estate, Monticello.

Corley, who has lived in Virginia and Southern California, first planted Chardonnay in Napa Valley in 1970 and was a grape grower before becoming a vintner. Alan Phillips, a University of California at Davis graduate, is winemaker and president.

Monticello concentrates on two Chardonnays made in different styles: a Corley Reserve, which at times can be sensational, and a Jefferson Ranch bottling, which is lower priced but often very impressive. The Corley Reserve began as a brand called "Barrel Fermented" and it is made in a fuller, richer style than the Jefferson Ranch. Despite its richness and concentration, in years like 1984 and 1988 it is amazingly graceful and elegant and ranks with the very best Chardonnays produced in California. Grapes for the Corley Reserve come from the western portion of the winery's estate vineyards in the Oak Knoll area of Napa Valley, due north of the Napa city limits. The Jefferson Ranch bottling comes from grapes grown on the eastern side of the vineyard. It is not barrel fermented and the style is more delicate. Both wines have aged well. The 1983 Jefferson Ranch is enormously rich and complex, and the 1980 is still holding on. The 1986 Jefferson Ranch still needs more time to mature, while the 1988 is the best since the stunning 1983. Monticello owns 92 acres of Chardonnay in the Oak Knoll area. Production of Corley Reserve is about 4,000 cases, about half as much as the 7,500 cases of Jefferson Ranch.

TASTING NOTES

MONTICELLO CELLARS, Corley Reserve, Yountville, Napa Valley

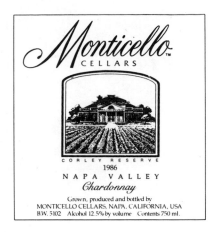

1988 MONTICELLO CELLARS CORLEY RESERVE: Magnificent richness, elegance, depth and finesse, a great success in a fine vintage, graced with beautifully defined pear, honey, butter and toast flavors that offer uncommon complexity and refinement. Should improve for the next three to five years. Last tasted: 2/90. Drink 1991-1997. 4,000 cases produced. Release: $17.25. Current: $17.25. **94**

1987 MONTICELLO CELLARS CORLEY RESERVE: Austere and firm but has all the right ingredients, with plenty of fresh, rich pear, melon and honey flavors, gentle oak seasoning and firm acidity that will probably make this wine best in two to three years. Last tasted: 6/90. Drink 1992-1997. 4,400 cases produced. Release: $17.25. Current: $18. **88**

1986 MONTICELLO CELLARS CORLEY RESERVE: Rich and intense yet elegant, with fine balance and sharply focused pear, lemon, toast and anise notes framed by spicy oak, with a wonderful finish that accents the flavors. Last tasted: 2/90. Drink 1991-1996. 3,200 cases produced. Release: $16.50. Current: $18. **89**

1985 MONTICELLO CELLARS CORLEY RESERVE: Ripe, clean, elegant and well balanced, but not as rich and dramatic as the sensational 1984 bottling. Comes across as more subdued and understated, satisfying but not nearly as distinctive. Last tasted: 2/90. Drink 1991-1994. 2,200 cases produced. Release: $14. Current: $20. **85**

1984 MONTICELLO CELLARS CORLEY RESERVE: Delicious, rich and concentrated, with flavors built on a silky smooth texture that glide across the palate. Remarkably elegant and tasty, with lots of fruit on the aftertaste. Drinking in superb condition. Last tasted: 2/90. Drink 1991-1995. 860 cases produced. Release: $12.50. Current: $25. **94**

1983 MONTICELLO CELLARS BARREL FERMENTED: Like the 1982, it's leafy and earthy but at the same time complex, with lemon, pear and spice flavors that are narrowly focused, finishing with crisp acidity and fine length. Last tasted: 2/90. Drink 1991-1993. 720 cases produced. Release: $12.50. Current: $20. **80**

1982 MONTICELLO CELLARS BARREL FERMENTED: Coarse and earthy, but there's plenty of smoky complexity and hints of pear, apple and spice that are quite distinct and intriguing. Last tasted: 2/90. Drink 1991-1992. 800 cases produced. Release: $14. Current: $20. **84**

MONTICELLO CELLARS, Jefferson Ranch, Yountville, Napa Valley

1988 MONTICELLO CELLARS JEFFERSON RANCH: Rich, clean and elegant, impeccably balanced, with ripe, delicate pear, toast, vanilla and

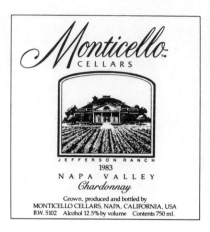

apple flavors that are youthful and lively, finishing with complex fruit, pretty citrus notes and excellent length. Last tasted: 2/90. Drink 1991-1997. 7,500 cases produced. Release: $12.25. Current: $12.25. **90**

1987 MONTICELLO CELLARS JEFFERSON RANCH: Elegant and well balanced, with more delicacy and finesse than previous bottlings but also not quite the opulence. The pear, vanilla and spice flavors are more subdued yet they fan out on the finish. Last tasted: 2/90. Drink 1991-1995. 8,100 cases produced. Release: $12.25. Current: $13. **86**

1986 MONTICELLO CELLARS JEFFERSON RANCH: Smoky and toasty, with perfumed aromas and flavors that add complexity to the ripe pear and apple flavors. Tastes youthful and vibrant, as if it still needs another year or two to develop fully. Not quite the sharp fruit definition of the best Monticellos but still very good. Last tasted: 2/90. Drink 1991-1995. 5,700 cases produced. Release: $11. Current: $14. **86**

1985 MONTICELLO CELLARS JEFFERSON RANCH: Somewhat earthier and oakier than its predecessors, elegant and well balanced but without the bright, rich, concentrated flavors evident in the other wines. Less impressive than in earlier tastings. Last tasted: 2/90. Drink 1991-1993. 4,000 cases produced. Release: $11. Current: $16. **82**

1984 MONTICELLO CELLARS JEFFERSON RANCH: Very ripe and full flavored, with rich, high-extract pear, apple, spice and earth notes, a big, deep, complex wine that still has plenty of power and intensity, lacking only the complexity of its predecessor. Drinking at its peak now. Last tasted: 2/90. Drink 1991-1994. 2,450 cases produced. Release: $10. Current: $18. **86**

1983 MONTICELLO CELLARS JEFFERSON RANCH: Enormous richness and concentration, packed with flavor, one of the top wines of this vintage, still displaying intensity and rich flavors that echo pear, honey, toast and butterscotch, finishing with a touch of anise and smoke. Complex. Last tasted: 2/90. Drink 1991-1995. 1,200 cases produced. Release: $10. Current: $20. **93**

1982 MONTICELLO CELLARS: Fully mature but hanging on, with tasty pear, honey and nectarine flavors of moderate richness and depth and flavors that linger on the finish. Better a few years ago, it remains an attractive wine. Last tasted: 2/90. Drink 1991-1993. 4,000 cases produced. Release: $13.50. Current: $20. **82**

1981 MONTICELLO CELLARS: Past its prime, offering faint, leafy pear and lemon flavors of moderate intensity. Drink up soon. Last tasted: 2/90. Drink 1991. 2,700 cases produced. Release: $12. Current: $20. **76**

1980 MONTICELLO CELLARS: Monticello's first Chardonnay is still aging gracefully. It's past its prime, but still displays pretty honey, pear and toast flavors that are rich and elegant, echoing honey and toast on the aftertaste. Last tasted: 2/90. Drink 1991-1993. 1,250 cases produced. Release: $12. Current: $20. **86**

MORGAN WINERY
Monterey Reserve
Monterey

CLASSIFICATION: *FOURTH GROWTH*
COLLECTIBILITY RATING: *Not rated*
BEST VINTAGES:

   Monterey Reserve: 1988

   Monterey: 1982, 1986, 1988

Morgan Winery is one of Monterey County's most promising Chardonnay producers. It is owned and operated by Dan Lee and his family. Lee is the former winemaker at Jekel Vineyard and Durney Vineyard, both in Monterey, and he has a knack for producing rich, complex, multidimensional Chardonnays. Morgan Winery was founded in 1982, and since 1986 Lee has devoted full time to his endeavor.

Overall I have been quite impressed with the quality of the Morgan Chardonnays. Most are rich, well-defined, concentrated wines that are complex and well balanced. The first vintage, the 1982, is still deep, flavorful and complex. The 1983 is a shade earthier, while the 1984 is fully mature, with very ripe flavors. The 1985 has been problematic for me in tastings, showing a high degree of bottle variation, and in several recent tastings I have found a troublesome musty, corky character that did not show up earlier. Others have rated the 1985 very highly and I have sometimes found it exceptional, so either it has changed or I have not seen a good bottle recently. The 1986 returns to form, with layers of fruit and rich concentration, while the 1987 is more elegant. The 1988 falls between the 1986 and 1987 stylistically, with rich fruit and a sense of elegance.

With the 1987 vintage, Morgan introduced a Monterey Reserve, and the 1988 is by far the most compelling Morgan made to date, with astonishing richness, depth and breadth of flavor. The 1987 is a little richer and more complex than the 1987 regular. The Morgans do not own any Chardonnay vineyards. Their wines are all barrel fermented and undergo malolactic fermentation.

AT A GLANCE
MORGAN WINERY
1 Calera Canyon
Salinas, CA 93908
(408) 484-1533

Owners: The Lee family

Winemaker: Daniel Lee (8 years)

Founded: 1982

First Chardonnay vintage: 1982
   Reserve: 1987

Chardonnay production: 10,000 cases
   Reserve: 1.500 cases
   Monterey: 8,500 cases

Chardonnay acres owned: none

Average wine makeup: Monterey
   (100%)

Time in oak:
   Reserve: 11 months
   Monterey: 10 months

Type of oak: French (Allier, Vosges, Tronçais)

Oak age: new (40%) to 2 years

Winemaking notes:
   Barrel fermentation: 100%
   Malolactic fermentation: 40% to 80%
   Lees aging:
      Reserve: 100% (11 months)
      Monterey: 100% (10 months)

TASTING NOTES

MORGAN WINERY, Monterey Reserve, Monterey

1988 MORGAN WINERY MONTEREY RESERVE: Youthful, deep, rich and complex, it may be Morgan's best to date, combining lavish pear, apple, toast and honey flavors that are concentrated yet elegant, finishing with great length and finesse, with flavors that keep on unfolding. Delicious now. Last tasted: 6/90. Drink 1991-1997. 1,500 cases produced. Release: $20. Current: $20. **92**

1987 MORGAN WINERY MONTEREY RESERVE: Richer, deeper and more complex than the 1987 regular bottling, with well-defined toast, apple, spice and nutmeg notes that are well balanced and linger on the finish. Last tasted: 6/90. Drink 1991-1994. 1,500 cases produced. Release: $19. Current: $19. **85**

MORGAN WINERY, Monterey

1988 MORGAN WINERY: Remarkably elegant, complex and graceful, rich and flavorful, with apple, pear, honey and toast flavors, showing greater finesse and delicacy than previous bottlings. The texture is smooth and creamy and the flavors are long and lively on the finish. Last tasted: 5/90. Drink 1991-1996. 8,500 cases produced. Release: $15. Current: $16. **89**

1987 MORGAN WINERY: Elegant and well balanced, with a shade less richness and concentration than previous bottlings, offering spicy toast and apple flavors of moderate complexity. Clearly a notch below the 1986 and 1982 bottlings, but holding together. Last tasted: 5/90. Drink 1991-1994. 8,500 cases produced. Release: $15. Current: $16. **84**

1986 MORGAN WINERY: Deliciously rich, elegant and complex, with concentrated pear, citrus, pineapple and honey flavors that are bold and well defined, offering excellent depth of flavor and a long, tasty finish. Very complete and well balanced, aging very well. Last tasted: 5/90. Drink 1991-1995. 6,000 cases produced. Release: $14. Current: $20. **89**

1985 MORGAN WINERY: Elegant, complex and mature, offering ripe pear, spice and earthy mushroom flavors that come through on the finish. Well balanced, full-bodied, complex and tasty. Last tasted: 7/90. Drink 1991-1996. 5,000 cases produced. Release: $14. Current: $25. **86**

1984 MORGAN WINERY: Fully mature, with lovely, creamy honey, pear and melon flavors that are delicate and well balanced, rich without being weighty. Ready now but can age. Last tasted: 5/90. Drink 1991-1995. 5,000 cases produced. Release: $12. Current: $25. **86**

1983 MORGAN WINERY: Not quite up to the exceptional 1982, but still very good, a shade earthier, with tart, leafy, green apple flavors that finish short. Best to drink now. Last tasted: 5/90. Drink 1991-1993. 3,000 cases produced. Release: $12. Current: $25. **80**

1982 MORGAN WINERY: Morgan's first bottling still displays deep, rich, concentrated and complex tiers of pineapple, honey, apple, pear, butter and spice flavors that fill out on the palate and finish with a trace of honey. Aging exceptionally well, especially for the vintage. Last tasted: 5/90. Drink 1991-1995. 2,000 cases produced. Release: $12. Current: $28. **89**

MOUNT EDEN VINEYARDS

Estate, Santa Cruz Mountains
MacGregor Vineyards, Edna Valley

CLASSIFICATION: **THIRD GROWTH**
COLLECTIBILITY RATING: **A**
BEST VINTAGES:

> *Estate: 1987, 1979, 1981, 1988, 1986*

> *MacGregor Vineyards: 1987*

AT A GLANCE

MOUNT EDEN VINEYARDS
22020 Mount Eden Road
Saratoga, CA 95070
(408) 867-5832

Owner: MEV Corp.

Winemaker: Jeffrey Patterson (9 years)

Founded: 1972

First Chardonnay vintage: 1972
  Estate: 1972
  MacGregor Vineyards: 1985

Chardonnay production: 2,300 cases
  Estate: 800 cases
  MacGregor Vineyards: 1,500 cases

Chardonnay acres owned: 12

Average age of vines: 35 years

Vineyard locations:
  MacGregor Vineyards: Edna
  Valley

Average wine makeup:
  Estate: Santa Cruz Mountains
  (100%)

Time in oak: 9 months

Type of oak: French (Center
  of France)

Oak age:
  Estate: new (100%)
  MacGregor Vineyards: new to
  5 years old

Winemaking notes:
  Barrel fermentation: 100%
  Malolactic fermentation
  Estate: 100%
  MacGregor Vineyards: 75%
  Lees aging: 100% (2 months)

Mount Eden Vineyards in the Santa Cruz Mountains developed a cult following in the 1970s for its ripe, rich, deeply concentrated Chardonnays. This winery high in the mountains above Saratoga was built by the late Martin Ray in the 1950s. Today MEV Corp., a group of investors, is the owner. Early in the 1970s Ray was influenced by winemakers Richard Graff of Chalone and Merry Edwards (later of Matanzas Creek), and strove to emulate their full-blown, powerful, sometimes elegant Chardonnays.

Mount Eden Chardonnays succeed with that style. The 1972 and 1973 vintages are still holding, although a shade past their primes, but they are good examples of the Mount Eden style. The 1974, 1975, 1977 and 1978 vintages are also faded, but the 1976 is worth drinking. Beginning with the 1979 vintage, however, one sees a string of rich, firmly structured, delicious Chardonnays. The 1979 and 1981 in particular are sensational wines. The 1982 to 1984 vintages should be consumed soon, while the 1985 is well balanced, with a touch of elegance and finesse, followed by a very fine 1986, which is a shade richer, fuller and more complex. The 1987 is beautifully balanced, with well-integrated flavors and texture, but it could use another year of cellaring. The 1988 is similar in style, youthful and elegant, a good candidate for cellaring through the decade.

Under winemaker Jeffrey Patterson, the style in the 1980s has shifted away from the ultraripe Chardonnays of the 1970s to wines of greater elegance and complexity. A new label, M.E.V., made with grapes purchased from MacGregor Vineyards in Edna Valley, was launched in 1985 and it too shows great promise. The 1987 M.E.V. is the finest Chardonnay I've tasted from Mount Eden. The MacGregor production is about 1,500 cases, nearly double the Mount Eden output of 800 cases. Mount Eden's 12-acre Chardonnay vineyard is 35 years old, ancient by California standards.

TASTING NOTES

MOUNT EDEN VINEYARDS, Estate, Santa Cruz Mountains

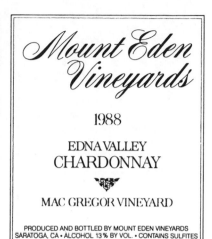

1988 MOUNT EDEN VINEYARDS ESTATE: A very promising young wine, elegant and balanced, with youthful, intense yet subtle flavors that echo pear, melon, apple and butterscotch. Crisp acidity carries the flavors on the finish. Should only get better from here. Last tasted: 4/90. Drink 1992-1997. 715 cases produced. Release: $30. Current: $30. **88**

1987 MOUNT EDEN VINEYARDS ESTATE: Young, elegant and beautifully balanced, with subtle pear, apple, nutmeg and toasty oak flavors. Needs another year or two to fill out, but it has all the ingredients to be an outstanding wine. Flavors stay with you a long time. Last tasted: 4/90. Drink 1992-1997. 1,348 cases produced. Release: $28. Current: $32. **90**

1986 MOUNT EDEN VINEYARDS ESTATE: A shade richer and more complex than the 1985, it is also very elegant and subtle, with pear, lemon, honey and spicy oak adding delicate flavor notes that linger on the palate. Last tasted: 4/90. Drink 1991-1996. 677 cases produced. Release: $25. Current: $42. **88**

1985 MOUNT EDEN VINEYARDS ESTATE: Elegant and refined, impeccably balanced, with pretty pear, lemon, honey and subtle toast notes, a youthful wine that while drinking well now can still age. Finish is elegant and delicate. Last tasted: 4/90. Drink 1991-1996. 540 cases produced. Release: $25. Current: $40. **87**

1984 MOUNT EDEN VINEYARDS ESTATE: Ripe, intense and balanced, with pretty, elegant pear and butterscotch flavors. Not too weighty or rich, but well mannered and balanced, finishing with pretty fruit flavors. Last tasted: 4/90. Drink 1991-1995. 756 cases produced. Release: $23. Current: $45. **85**

1983 MOUNT EDEN VINEYARDS ESTATE: Distinctive pine and wood flavors, but plenty of intensity and fresh, crisp fruit too. The pear, apple, lemon and spice flavors are well defined, finishing with a touch of oakiness. Last tasted: 4/90. Drink 1991-1994. 455 cases produced. Release: $20. Current: $35. **84**

1982 MOUNT EDEN VINEYARDS ESTATE: Intensely earthy, with rich, somewhat sour pineapple, pear and lemon notes. It may be going through a transitional phase where it's less attractive; an "off" bottle? Last tasted: 4/90. Drink 1991-1994. 500 cases produced. Release: $18. Current: $40. **76**

1981 MOUNT EDEN VINEYARDS ESTATE: In superb condition, fresh, rich and lively, with intense, concentrated pear, lemon, apple and toasty earth notes that add complexity. Fine flavors on the aftertaste. Last tasted: 4/90. Drink 1991-1995. 445 cases produced. Release: $18. Current: $60. **89**

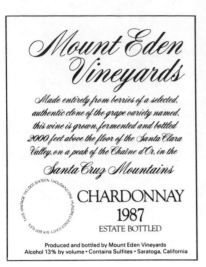

1980 MOUNT EDEN VINEYARDS ESTATE: Rich, ripe and full-bodied, plenty of flavor and extract, with opulent pear, pineapple, nutmeg and apple flavors that spread out on the palate. Well balanced, drinking perhaps a shade past its peak, but showing no signs of fading. Last tasted: 4/90. Drink 1991-1995. 245 cases produced. Release: $30. Current: $60. **87**

1979 MOUNT EDEN VINEYARDS ESTATE: Aging amazingly well, with a wonderful bouquet, rich, elegant, complex flavors and impeccable balance. It's light in color, and the mature pear, nutmeg, honey and lemon notes dance on the palate, finishing with excellent length. An absolute joy to drink. Last tasted: 4/90. Drink 1991-1996. 495 cases produced. Release: $16. Current: $60. **90**

1978 MOUNT EDEN VINEYARDS ESTATE: Strong oxidized pear and apple flavors that I found too aggressive; some might find it palatable. Tasted in magnum. Last tasted: 4/90. Best to avoid. 400 cases produced. Release: $16. Current: $60. **66**

1977 MOUNT EDEN VINEYARDS ESTATE: Fully mature, aromatically fresh and lively with anise, pear and butterscotch flavors that are rich, tart and firm. Well balanced with crisp acidity on the finish that carries the flavors. Holding very well. Last tasted 8/90. Drink 1991-1994. 150 cases produced. Release: $16. Current: $30. **85**

1976 MOUNT EDEN VINEYARDS ESTATE: Tart and lively for its age, the apple, pear and spice notes are fully mature but attractive. Best to drink soon. Last tasted: 4/90. Drink 1991. 200 cases produced. Release: $16. Current: $50. **78**

1975 MOUNT EDEN VINEYARDS ESTATE: Tart, sour, past its prime. Last tasted: 4/90. Best to avoid. 108 cases produced. Release: $14. Current: $45. **60**

1974 MOUNT EDEN VINEYARDS ESTATE: Flat, gamy, oxidized. Last tasted: 4/90. Best to avoid. 170 cases produced. Release: $14. Current: $45. **59**

1973 MOUNT EDEN VINEYARDS ESTATE: Still alive despite its age, with faint pear, apple and spice flavors that turn dry on the finish, picking up some attractive honey and butterscotch notes. Very enjoyable. Last tasted: 4/90. Drink 1991. 281 cases produced. Release: $12. Current: $55. **82**

1972 MOUNT EDEN VINEYARDS ESTATE: Past its prime but still packing plenty of rich, ripe fruit, with pear, honey and butterscotch flavors. The flavors show a trace of oxidation on the finish. Last tasted: 4/90. Drink 1991-1993. 210 cases produced. Release: $20. Current: $50. **80**

MOUNT EDEN VINEYARDS, MacGregor Vineyards, Edna Valley

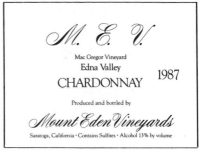

1988 MOUNT EDEN VINEYARDS MACGREGOR VINEYARDS: Distinct for its rich butter and butterscotch flavors, this is a smooth, fruity, elegant wine with pretty pear, lemon, mango and melon notes that are complex and intriguing. Delicious now, it should age well and improve for another five years or more. Last tasted: 6/90. Drink 1991-1996. 1,551 cases produced. Release: $14. Current: $14. **88**

1987 MOUNT EDEN VINEYARDS M.E.V. MACGREGOR VINEYARDS: The finest Mount Eden Chardonnay I've tasted from either appellation, this is an incredibly delicious, rich and unctuous wine, loaded with ripe pear, melon, honey, apple and butterscotch flavors and a satiny smooth texture that lets the flavors glide across the palate. Great concentration and crisp acidity sustain the finish. Last tasted: 4/90. Drink 1991-1997. 1,500 cases produced. Release: $14. Current: $18. **94**

1986 MOUNT EDEN VINEYARDS M.E.V. MACGREGOR VINEYARDS: Distinctive for its orange and citrus notes, but beyond those flavors it's rather simple, with only moderate depth and concentration. Last tasted: 4/90. Drink 1991-1995. 1,200 cases produced. Release: $13. Current: $16. **81**

1985 MOUNT EDEN VINEYARDS M.E.V. MACGREGOR VINEYARDS: Intense and concentrated, with very rich, ripe pineapple and earth flavors that give it a strong personality. Well balanced, with excellent depth and focus; some herbal notes creep in on the aftertaste. Last tasted: 4/90. Drink 1991-1995. 1,100 cases produced. Release: $12.50. Current: $14. **87**

MURPHY-GOODE ESTATE WINERY
Estate Vineyard, Alexander Valley

CLASSIFICATION: *FIFTH GROWTH*
COLLECTIBILITY RATING: *Not rated*
BEST VINTAGES: *1988, 1987*

Murphy Goode is one of the promising new Chardonnay producers from Alexander Valley. The four vintages it has released show ripe, deep, concentrated fruit flavors with good richness, fine balance, ample oak and very good aging potential. Murphy Goode uses purchased grapes and those grown by partners Tim Murphy, Dale Goode and Dave Ready, who have planted 75 of their 350 acres of vineyard to Chardonnay.

It's too early to tell how well these wines will age, but the 1985 offers plenty of ripe, rich fruit flavors that are full-bodied and holding; its only fault is the coarseness on the finish. The 1986 is a slight improvement, again in an openly fruity style. The 1987 is a shade more complex and has the potential to age another four or five years. The 1988 is very intense and well balanced, the best of the four vintages, consistent with the house style. Production is now 12,000 cases, and the Chardonnays remain very reasonably priced at $11.50 a bottle in 1990. The 1987 was called the Premier Vineyard, even though it came from the Estate Vineyard.

TASTING NOTES

MURPHY-GOODE ESTATE WINERY, Estate Vineyard, Alexander Valley

1988 MURPHY-GOODE ESTATE WINERY ESTATE VINEYARD: Intense and forward, with generous and elegant pear, apple, pineapple and citrus notes and just the right amount of oak, rendering a full-bodied, well-balanced, flavorful Chardonnay that is ready to drink now. Last tasted: 4/90. Drink 1991-1995. 12,000 cases produced. Release: $11.50. Current: $11.50. **88**

1987 MURPHY-GOODE ESTATE WINERY PREMIER VINEYARD: More complex and distinctive than the previous two bottlings, the 1987 has evolved slowly in the bottle, now showing more fresh, crisp apple, pear and pineapple flavors with a pretty touch of butterscotch on the finish. Just a bit coarse on the finish. Last tasted: 4/90. Drink 1991-1996. 7,000 cases produced. Release: $11. Current: $11. **87**

1986 MURPHY-GOODE ESTATE WINERY ESTATE VINEYARD:
Continues in the openly fruity style, with fresh, rich apple, pear and melon notes that are complex and refreshing. Full-bodied and well balanced, it is ready to drink now. Last tasted: 4/90. Drink 1991-1995. 7,000 cases produced. Release: $10. Current: $12. **86**

1985 MURPHY-GOODE ESTATE WINERY ESTATE VINEYARD: A very ripe, opulent, richly fruity wine with tiers of fresh apple, pear and pineapple flavors that are well integrated, full-bodied and aging quite well. A touch of coarseness on the finish. Last tasted: 4/90. Drink 1991-1995. 5,000 cases produced. Release: $9. Current: $12. **85**

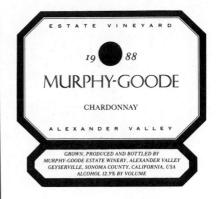

NAVARRO VINEYARDS
Première Reserve, Anderson Valley

CLASSIFICATION: SECOND GROWTH
COLLECTIBILITY RATING: A
BEST VINTAGES: 1988, 1984, 1985

From the cool, picturesque Anderson Valley in Mendocino County, Navarro Vineyards Première Reserve is the cream of the Chardonnay crop. The climate of Anderson Valley is wet and damp through the winter months and vines are slow to open in the spring. A mild, breezy climate is shaped by the Pacific Ocean 15 miles to the west. In this environment Chardonnay grows slowly and evenly and often struggles to ripen before the fall weather brings cooler temperatures again.

Navarro Vineyards Première Reserve is a classy wine, very consistent from year to year, rich, round, smooth and creamy, very well balanced and capable of aging up to a decade or more. It is also typically very ripe, evidence that Chardonnay can ripen fully even in this climate. The winery was founded near the town of Philo in 1974 by Edward "Ted" Bennett, founder of the Pacific Stereo chain of retail electronics stores, and his wife, Deborah Cahn. The first Première Reserve was produced in 1980, but I have only recently tasted the 1984 to 1988 vintages. The 1984 is a surprisingly big, bold, rich wine with plenty of vanilla and buttery oak flavors, yet for all its ripeness it's elegant too. The 1985 offers a shade more elegance and finesse without sacrificing flavor. The 1986 moves toward an even more subtle style, with well-defined flavors and a lovely finish. The 1987 is young and hard, not quite as forward or flavorful as its predecessors, but it should be more forthcoming with further bottle age. The 1988 combines bold, rich, concentrated flavors with elegance and grace, and is the best since 1984. Production of the Prémiere Reserve has climbed to 3,000 cases, and at $14 for the 1988 vintage represents an excellent value.

AT A GLANCE

NAVARRO VINEYARDS
P.O. Box 47
Philo, CA 95466
(707) 895-3686

Owners: Ted Bennett and Deborah Cahn

Winemakers: Ted Bennett (16 years) and Tom Lane (5 years)

Founded: 1974

First Chardonnay vintage: 1976
    Première Reserve: 1980

Chardonnay production: 7,000 cases
    Première Reserve: 3,000 cases

Chardonnay acres owned: 15

Average age of vines: 10 years

Average wine makeup: Anderson Valley (100%)

Time in oak: 9 months

Type of oak: French (Nevers, Allier)

Oak age: 1 to 5 years old

Winemaking notes:
    Barrel fermentation: 100%
    Malolactic fermentation: varies
    Lees aging: 100% (2 months)

TASTING NOTES

NAVARRO VINEYARDS, Première Reserve, Anderson Valley

1988 NAVARRO VINEYARDS PREMIERE RESERVE The best Navarro since 1984, a bold, rich, complex yet elegant wine brimming with pear, spice, melon, honey and toasty vanilla flavors that are interwoven, creating a wine of great harmony and finesse. The flavors linger long and full on the finish. Delicious. Last tasted: 5/90. Drink 1991-1998. 3,596 cases produced. Release: $14. Current: $14. **91**

1987 NAVARRO VINEYARDS PREMIERE RESERVE Youthful and firm in the Navarro style, not showing quite the flavor and depth of its predecessors, but with more time it may. The pear, vanilla, spicy oak, butter and nutmeg flavors are subtle yet well defined. Last tasted: 3/90. Drink 1992-1996. 1,813 cases produced. Release: $14. Current: $14. **87**

1986 NAVARRO VINEYARDS PREMIERE RESERVE Like the 1984 and 1985, a study in subtlety and finesse, offering pretty pear, honey, vanilla and spice flavors in an elegant, understated style that allows the flavors to fan out gently on the palate. Last tasted: 3/90. Drink 1991-1996. 1,555 cases produced. Release: $14. Current: $18. **87**

1985 NAVARRO VINEYARDS PREMIERE RESERVE Fully mature and elegantly balanced, with ripe pear, honey, vanilla and toasty oak flavors that offer a delicate measure of elegance and finesse, finishing with a touch of creamy butterscotch. Ready now or can age. Last tasted: 3/90. Drink 1991-1995. 1,331 cases produced. Release: $12. Current: $18. **89**

1984 NAVARRO VINEYARDS PREMIERE RESERVE Rich, round, smooth and creamy, a ripe, complex wine with pretty vanilla, pear, honey and subtle spice notes that linger on the finish. For all its full-bodied flavor, it is elegant, very well balanced and long on the finish. Last tasted: 3/90. Drink 1991-1995. 856 cases produced. Release: $12. Current: $22. **91**

NEWTON VINEYARD

Napa Valley

CLASSIFICATION: *FIFTH GROWTH*
COLLECTIBILITY RATING: **Not rated**
BEST VINTAGES: *1983, 1987, 1988*

AT A GLANCE

NEWTON VINEYARD
P.O. Box 540
St. Helena, CA 94574
(707) 963-9000

Owners: Peter and Su Hua Newton

Winemaker: John Kongsgaard (7 years)

Founded: 1979

First Chardonnay vintage: 1981

Chardonnay production: 5,400 cases

Chardonnay acres owned: none

Average wine makeup: Carneros (75%), Napa Valley (25%)

Time in oak: 10 months

Type of oak: French

Oak age: new (50%) to 1 year old

Winemaking notes:
  Barrel fermentation: 100%
  Malolactic fermentation: 100%
  Lees aging: 100% (10 months)

One of the more pleasant surprises in tasting older California Chardonnays came with Newton Vineyards. Early on, most of these wines seemed too oaky and lacking in fruit concentration ever to develop into anything special. Initially I attributed that to stylistic preferences, and in fact Newton uses mostly new and one-year-old barrels from an exclusive Burgundian cooper. I still think owners Peter and Su Hua Newton prefer a healthy dose of toasty oak in their wines, but I'm now more impressed by how well they age and improve after three to five years in the bottle. This hillside winery above St. Helena, founded in 1979 by the Newtons after Peter Newton and his partners sold Sterling Vineyards to Coca-Cola Co., first employed Ric Forman, the former winemaker at Sterling, as winemaker. He departed after the 1982 vintage to found his own winery.

The Newtons do not own any Chardonnay vineyards, but have relied on buying grapes from Napa Valley growers since their first Chardonnay vintage in 1981. Today 75 percent of their grapes are bought from the Carneros region. The Chardonnays are made by winemaker John Kongsgaard, a Napa native and University of California at Davis graduate.

I have not tried the 1981 or 1982 recently, but the 1983 is holding quite nicely, developing into a rich, complex wine with great flavor and finesse. It appears to have the depth and concentration to age through the decade. The 1984 has an attractive earthy note to complement the complex pear and honey flavors and it is aging better than most 1984s. The 1985 is intense, concentrated and very youthful, but it lacks complexity. Perhaps with time it will gain it. The 1986 is hard and tight, in need of cellaring, but it too is showing signs of complexity. Both the 1987 and 1988 vintages appear more forward, although I think they will age just fine for another six to eight years.

At Su Hua Newton's urging, winemaker Kongsgaard is experimenting with extended lees and barrel aging of their Chardonnays. A 1988 sample I tried was pulled from a barrel after 18 months in oak. It was scheduled to spend two full years in barrel before bottling, and while it was very oaky, it also had an enormous amount of fruit concentration and tasted like a very worthy stylistic experiment.

TASTING NOTES

NEWTON VINEYARD, Napa Valley

1988 NEWTON VINEYARD: Rivals the fine 1987 in quality, showing plenty of rich fruit concentration, ripe pear, melon, fig and apple flavors and a pretty touch of smoky oak. Fine balance and a long, full aftertaste that lingers. Last tasted: 3/90. Drink 1991-1997. 5,546 cases produced. Release: $14.50. Current: $14.50. **88**

1987 NEWTON VINEYARD: One of the finest Newtons I've tasted, clearly more complex, deep and concentrated, with layers of rich, ripe pear, melon, spice and toasty oak flavors, impeccably balanced and echoing flavors on the finish. Last tasted: 3/90. Drink 1991-1997. 6,000 cases produced. Release: $14. Current: $14. **88**

1986 NEWTON VINEYARD: Hard and intense, with ripe pear, apple and melon flavors and a balanced dose of oak. The impression is of firm fruit that still needs time to soften and evolve. The finish shows hints of complexity, with citrus and lemon notes. Last tasted: 3/90. Drink 1992-1997. 5,000 cases produced. Release: $14. Current: $14. **85**

1985 NEWTON VINEYARD: Intense and concentrated, youthful and assertive, tastes much younger than it is. The ripe pear, melon and apple flavors are framed by smoky oak, but for all its flavor and balance it lacks complexity. With time it may be more intriguing. Last tasted: 3/90. Drink 1991-1996. 3,100 cases produced. Release: $12.75. Current: $19. **85**

1984 NEWTON VINEYARD: Earthy and stylish, with ripe pear, honey and citrus notes that are still austere although beginning to open and reveal more fleshiness. Consistent with the Newton style of complexity and structure, this is showing much better now than most 1984s. Last tasted: 5/90. Drink 1991-1998. 3,900 cases produced. Release: $11.50. Current: $18. **86**

1983 NEWTON VINEYARD: One of the top wines of the vintage, the 1983 has evolved into a wonderfully complex and enticing Chardonnay with both richness and finesse, allowing the pretty honey, pear and nutmeg flavors to play off the firm acidity. Shows no sign of premature aging. Fine length. Last tasted: 5/90. Drink 1991-1998. 2,000 cases produced. Release: $12. Current: $19. **89**

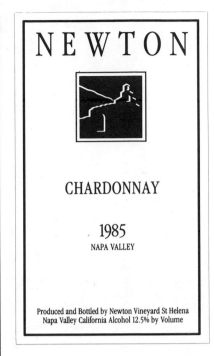

ROBERT PECOTA WINERY
Canepa Vineyard, Alexander Valley

CLASSIFICATION: *FIFTH GROWTH*
COLLECTIBILITY RATING: *Not rated*
BEST VINTAGES: *1987, 1985, 1980*

W ith grapes grown in the warm Alexander Valley, Robert Pecota has achieved a very consistent style of Chardonnay that offers layers of rich, creamy fruit flavors, often with a subtle, complex herbal and vegetal character that I find adds complexity to the wine and does not detract from the overall quality. Vintner Robert Pecota's winery is north of Calistoga in Napa Valley, but since 1980 he has bought grapes from the Canepa Vineyard on the Russian River near Jimtown.

That first vintage produced a wonderfully rich, lush wine with sweet pear and pineapple flavors and a broad, silky texture that is still aging well today. The 1981 is fully mature, and I have not tried the 1982 recently. The 1983 is past its prime, with hints of honey and Botrytis flavors. The 1984 is also ripe and forward, followed by the 1985, which is remarkably smooth and elegant. The 1986 is tasting better now than on release and the 1987 is the finest Chardonnay yet, with a broad array of ripe, rich, smooth fruit flavors and excellent length. The 1988 lacks the concentration of the 1987, but offers plenty of ripe fruit. Production hovers around 800 to 900 cases. All the Chardonnay is barrel fermented.

TASTING NOTES

ROBERT PECOTA WINERY, Canepa Vineyard, Alexander Valley

1988 ROBERT PECOTA WINERY CANEPA VINEYARD: Young and lively, with delicate pear, apple, melon and pineapple notes that are lush and smooth. Not quite the concentration and breadth of flavor of the 1987, but more elegant and understated and likely to evolve more quickly. Last tasted: 4/90. Drink 1991-1995. 800 cases produced. Release: $16. Current: $16. **87**

1987 ROBERT PECOTA WINERY CANEPA VINEYARD: A wonderfully deep, lush, supple texture, rich with honey, pear, apple, spice and creamy vanilla flavors that are concentrated and spread out on the palate, finishing with a smoky, toasty aftertaste. Impeccably balanced, with just

---

AT A GLANCE
ROBERT PECOTA WINERY
3299 Bennett Lane
Calistoga, CA 94515
(707) 942-6625

Owner: Robert Pecota

Winemaker: Robert Pecota (12 years)

Founded: 1978

First Chardonnay vintage: 1980

Chardonnay production: 800 cases

Chardonnay acres owned: none
   Canepa Vineyard: 15

Average age of vines: 12 years

Vineyard location:
   Canepa Vineyard: Alexander Valley

Time in oak: 6 months

Type of oak: French (Nevers)

Oak age: new (50%) to 2 years old

Winemaking notes:
   Barrel fermentation: 100%
   Malolactic fermentation: none
   Lees aging: 100% (6 months)

the right touch of acidity, this wine is one of the better 1987s and should be consumed within the next three to five years. Last tasted: 4/90. Drink 1991-1996. 800 cases produced. Release: $16. Current: $18. **91**

1986 ROBERT PECOTA WINERY CANEPA VINEYARD: Showing better now than on release, it has filled out, displaying more body and depth, echoing honey, pear and spicy apple flavors. Good balance, moderate richness and concentration, it is drinking well now. Last tasted: 4/90. Drink 1991-1995. 800 cases produced. Release: $16. Current: $19. **85**

1985 ROBERT PECOTA WINERY CANEPA VINEYARD: A deliciously smooth and elegant wine with tiers of honey, pear, nectarine, citrus and vanilla flavors that glide across the palate. Long, clean, lingering finish. Last tasted: 7/90. Drink 1991-1996. 800 cases produced. Release: $16. Current: $18. **89**

1984 ROBERT PECOTA WINERY CANEPA VINEYARD: From a warm, ripe vintage, the 1984 has ripe pear, apple, honey and butterscotch flavors that are well balanced and quite tasty. Drinking about as well as it will. Last tasted: 4/90. Drink 1991-1993. 600 cases produced. Release: $14. Current: $18. **83**

1983 ROBERT PECOTA WINERY CANEPA VINEYARD: Fully evolved and past its apogee, showing a hint of honey and Botrytis on the nose and palate along with anise, honey and butterscotch flavors. Last tasted: 4/90. Drink 1990-1991. 600 cases produced. Release: $14. Current: $18. **79**

1981 ROBERT PECOTA WINERY CANEPA VINEYARD: Mature in color and flavor, past its prime, with some vegetal notes creeping into the vanilla and butterscotch flavors. Best to drink soon. Last tasted: 4/90. Drink 1990-1991. 425 cases produced. Release: $12. Current: $20. **75**

1980 ROBERT PECOTA WINERY CANEPA VINEYARD: Pecota's first Chardonnay is aging well but is past its prime, revealing lush honey, vanilla, sweet pineapple and weedy herbal notes that add up to complexity. The texture is smooth and rich and there's just the right touch of acidity to carry the flavors. One of the better 1980s at this point. Last tasted: 4/90. Drink 1990-1994. 325 cases produced. Release: $12. Current: $20. **89**

PINE RIDGE WINERY

Knollside Cuvée, Napa Valley
Pine Ridge Stags Leap Vineyard, Stag's Leap District, Napa Valley

CLASSIFICATION:
   Knollside Cuvée: THIRD GROWTH
   Pine Ridge Stags Leap Vineyard: FOURTH GROWTH
COLLECTIBILITY RATING:
   Knollside Cuvée: A
   Pine Ridge Stags Leap Vineyard: A
BEST VINTAGES:
   Knollside Cuvée: 1987, 1988, 1986, 1983

   Pine Ridge Stags Leap Vineyard: 1987, 1986, 1988

Pine Ridge Winery makes some of the most consistent and well-proportioned Chardonnays in Napa Valley. The Stags Leap District winery, owned by Gary and Nancy Andrus since 1978, produces two Chardonnays each year, one from their Pine Ridge Stags Leap Vineyard across the Silverado Trail from their winery, and a Knollside Cuvée (earlier called Oak Knoll Cuvée), which is a blend of grapes from several vineyards in the area known as Oak Knoll south of Yountville and north of the city of Napa.

The Pine Ridge Stags Leap Vineyard wines tend to be riper, fuller and lusher, with a wealth of rich, ripe, creamy fruit flavors. Andrus' Chardonnays always show a measure of toasty oak, but it blends in well with the fruit, resulting in a wine of harmony and finesse. The best vintages have been the most recent, particularly the 1986, 1987 and 1988, although 1981 and 1983 have held up well. The 1987 in particular offers broad, rich, complex fruit with hints of creamy melon and butterscotch flavors. The 1988 suffers from bottle variation.

The Knollside Cuvée grapes come from a slightly cooler portion of Napa Valley and produce complex, fruity wines that are a shade firmer and less ripe than the Pine Ridge Stags Leap Vineyard. The 1985, 1986, 1987 and 1988 vintages are all very well made, my favorite being the 1987, which unfolds with a complex array of flavors and a wonderfully delicate texture. The 1988 shows bottle variation, marked by an "off" filter pad character. Both Pine Ridge Chardonnays drink well on release and hold up well for four to five years, but they have yet to demonstrate that they should be cellared much longer. Both wines are barrel fermented, undergo malolactic fermentation and are aged on the lees. I give them high marks for year-to-year consistency.

TASTING NOTES

PINE RIDGE WINERY, Knollside Cuvée, Napa Valley

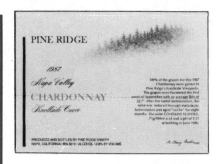

1988 PINE RIDGE WINERY KNOLLSIDE CUVEE: Beautiful, ripe, up-front fruit, with layers of honey, vanilla, spice, pear and apple flavors, delicate and well proportioned, carrying the flavors on the finish. Right in sync with the house style but plagued by bottle variation with a filter pad flavor. Last tasted: 7/90. Drink 1991-1995. 11,062 cases produced. Release: $15. Current: $15. **88**

1987 PINE RIDGE WINERY KNOLLSIDE CUVEE: The best Knollside Cuvée to date, with beautiful honey, spice, pear and apple flavors and a creamy vanilla texture that carries the flavors a long way on the finish. Wonderful balance, ripe and elegant, deep without being weighty. Last tasted: 4/90. Drink 1991-1995. 9,854 cases produced. Release: $15. Current: $16. **90**

1986 PINE RIDGE WINERY KNOLLSIDE CUVEE: Smokier on the nose, tarter on the palate than other bottlings, with well-defined pear, honey, butter and spice flavors, all elegantly packaged and well structured. Long finish. Last tasted: 4/90. Drink 1991-1995. 7,918 cases produced. Release: $14. Current: $16. **88**

1985 PINE RIDGE WINERY KNOLLSIDE CUVEE: Remarkably rich and complex, with spice, nutmeg, honey and pear flavors combining to give this wine uncommon depth and flavor. It's big and round, oozing with fruit. Last tasted: 4/90. Drink 1991-1995. 6,869 cases produced. Release: $14. Current: $16. **87**

1984 PINE RIDGE WINERY OAK KNOLL CUVEE: Ripe and full like the vintage, with pretty peach, pear and spice flavors that are direct and forward, well balanced and pleasing. Finish gains a measure of delicacy, picking up oaky nuances. Lacks the finesse and finish of the best Pine Ridge Chardonnays. Last tasted: 4/90. Drink 1991-1995. 4,285 cases produced. Release: $14. Current: $17. **85**

1983 PINE RIDGE WINERY OAK KNOLL CUVEE: Rich, lush and creamy, with mature, complex honey, butter and juicy pear flavors that are tightly knit and in peak drinking condition. Picks up honey and butterscotch notes on the finish. At its peak. Last tasted: 4/90. Drink 1991-1994. 3,685 cases produced. Release: $13. Current: $18. **88**

1982 PINE RIDGE WINERY OAK KNOLL CUVEE: Lean and elegant without the breadth of flavors, but the lemon, citrus and butter flavors are attractive. Beginning to lose its fruit. Last tasted: 4/90. Drink 1991-1993. 2,026 cases produced. Release: $13. Current: $19. **78**

1981 PINE RIDGE WINERY OAK KNOLL DISTRICT: Deliciously rich and buttery up front but beginning to dry out on the finish. At its peak, full of pretty Chardonnay flavors, but drink soon. Last tasted: 4/90. Drink 1991-1994. 1,168 cases produced. Release: $13. Current: $20. **84**

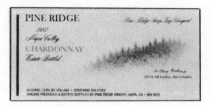

PINE RIDGE WINERY, Pine Ridge Stags Leap Vineyard, Stags Leap District, Napa Valley

1988 PINE RIDGE WINERY PINE RIDGE STAGS LEAP VINEYARD: Openly fruity, fresh and young, showing a broad array of attractive peach, pear, melon and spice flavors as well as a touch of elegance and finesse. Picks up traces of honey and orange on the finish, but I have encountered bottle variation with this wine. Last tasted: 7/90. Drink 1991-1996. 2,063 cases produced. Release: $20. Current: $20. **88**

1987 PINE RIDGE WINERY PINE RIDGE STAGS LEAP VINEYARD: Loads of fruit are evident in both aroma and flavor. The melon, pear, honey and butterscotch flavors are rich, deep, complex and sharply focused, yet silky smooth in texture. Surpasses the 1986 in quality; has shown tremendous improvement since its release. Excellent length. Last tasted: 4/90. Drink 1991-1996. 2,765 cases produced. Release: $20. Current: $20. **91**

1986 PINE RIDGE WINERY PINE RIDGE STAGS LEAP VINEYARD: Better than previous vintages, with greater intensity and fruit. The style remains elegant and understated, but there are simply more fruit flavors, with ripe, rich pear, lemon and spice notes and a hint of honey on the finish. Has the concentration for another five years' cellaring. Last tasted: 4/90. Drink 1991-1996. 2,215 cases produced. Release: $19. Current: $23. **88**

1985 PINE RIDGE WINERY PINE RIDGE STAGS LEAP VINEYARD: Continues to gain in the bottle, offering more ripe fruit and complexity than previous bottlings. The honey, melon, butterscotch, pear and vanilla flavors are subtle and delicate. Still on its way up. Last tasted: 4/90. Drink 1991-1995. 1,793 cases produced. Release: $18. Current: $23. **85**

1984 PINE RIDGE WINERY PINE RIDGE STAGS LEAP VINEYARD: Ripe, full and oaky but well balanced, with attractive honey, citrus and vanilla notes that are moderately complex and gaining on the finish. Last tasted: 4/90. Drink 1991-1994. 1,405 cases produced. Release: $18. Current: $25. **84**

1983 PINE RIDGE WINERY PINE RIDGE STAGS LEAP VINEYARD: The first of this vineyard designation is delicious for its smooth, round texture and elegant, understated honey, butterscotch and vanilla flavors. It is well balanced and holding very well. Good length on the finish. Last tasted: 4/90. Drink 1991-1994. 1,199 cases produced. Release: $16. Current: $25. **86**

1982 PINE RIDGE WINERY STAG'S LEAP CUVEE: Honey and orange blossom aromas with flavors to match, tart and lemony, well focused, with crisp acidity and good length. Not quite the breadth of flavor of other bottlings, but well made and pleasant. Last tasted: 4/90. Drink 1991-1994. 780 cases produced. Release: $15. Current: $27. **82**

1981 PINE RIDGE WINERY STAGS LEAP DISTRICT: Fully mature, rich and balanced, a subtle wine with attractive fig, vanilla and spice flavors that gain intensity on the finish. Last tasted: 4/90. Drink 1991-1994. 1,114 cases produced. Release: $15. Current: $31. **86**

1979 PINE RIDGE WINERY STAGS LEAP DISTRICT: Pretty cinnamon and nutmeg aromas lead to lean, elegant, mature honey and spice flavors that offer complexity and finesse. A wine that's reached its peak, but appears balanced enough to sustain another couple of years. Drink 1991-1992. 588 cases produced. Release: $9.50. Current: $32. **82**

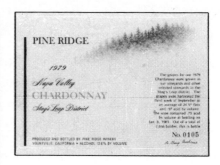

RAYMOND VINEYARD AND CELLAR
Private Reserve, Napa Valley

CLASSIFICATION: **THIRD GROWTH**
COLLECTIBILITY RATING: **A**
BEST VINTAGES: **1985, 1988**

AT A GLANCE
RAYMOND VINEYARD AND CELLAR
3849 Zinfandel Lane
St. Helena, CA 94574
(707) 963-3141

Owners: Roy and Walter Raymond, Kirin Brewery, Japan

Winemaker: Walter Raymond (16 years)

Founded: 1974

First Chardonnay vintage: 1976
   Private Reserve: 1982

Chardonnay production: 112,000 cases
   Private Reserve: 4,400 cases

Chardonnay acres owned: 40

Average age of vines: 14 years

Average wine makeup: Napa Valley (100%)

Time in oak: 6 months

Type of oak: French (Allier, Limousin)

Oak age: new to 4 years old (20% each)

Winemaking notes:
   Barrel fermentation:
      Private Reserve: 100%
   Malolactic fermentation: none
   Lees aging: none

Few California Chardonnays are as rich, lush, opulent and hedonistic as the Raymond Private Reserves. Raymond Vineyard in Rutherford is a big-volume, high-quality producer of Chardonnay, making more than 112,000 cases a year, but the cream of the crop is the effusively fruity, deeply complex Private Reserve bottling, with annual production of about 4,000 cases.

The Raymonds are old hands at winemaking. Roy Raymond Sr., the patriarch of the family, has more than 50 years of winemaking experience in Napa Valley, dating to the 1930s when the Raymonds owned Beringer Vineyards. His two sons, Roy Jr. and Walter, founded the Raymond winery with their father in 1974 after selling their interest in Beringer. The two sons manage the vineyards and make the wine, including Chardonnays with Napa Valley and California appellations, both of which are less expensive than the Private Reserve. In 1988 part-interest in the winery was sold to the Japanese brewer Kirin.

The seductive Raymond Private Reserve Chardonnays are best consumed within the first few years of release. They are not wines built for long-term aging. All of the fresh, ripe, complex fruit and oak flavors are designed for consumption within the first five years from the vintage date. The 1985, for example, is drinking exceptionally well now, with delicious fruit and layers of flavor, but it will probably not get much better. The 1986 is intense and concentrated, more subtle than the 1985. The 1987 is fresh and lively, less opulent than previous bottlings, while the 1988 is right on target, rich and buttery, with excellent fruit intensity. I have not seen all of the older Private Reserves lately, although the 1981 was well past its prime. The 1984 was from a very ripe year and was best consumed early on. I give the Raymonds very high marks for their deliberate and consistent style.

Tasting Notes

Raymond Vineyard and Cellar, Private Reserve, Napa Valley

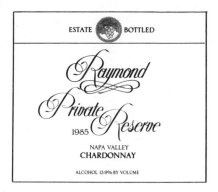

1988 Raymond Vineyard and Cellar Private Reserve: Rich and buttery, the best Private Reserve since 1985, combining deep, rich, concentrated pear, lemon, apple and pineapple flavors with toasty, buttery oak notes that are remarkably well balanced, finishing with fine length and a measure of elegance and finesse. Last tasted: 5/90. Drink 1991-1997. 4,434 cases produced. Not released. **90**

1987 Raymond Vineyard and Cellar Private Reserve: Fresh, intense and lively, with rich yet elegant pear, apple, citrus and grapefruit flavors that are sharply focused and complex. Perhaps less opulent than the 1984 or 1985 bottlings, but it is nonetheless ripe and full-bodied, finishing with plenty of fruit flavors. Last tasted: 5/90. Drink 1991-1996. 4,404 cases produced. Release: $22. Current: $22. **88**

1986 Raymond Vineyard and Cellar Private Reserve: Intense and slow to evolve, showing better now than on release, with fresh, crisp, full-bodied pear and pineapple flavors that stick with you from start to finish, where the pear and butter flavors are more subtle and delicate. Not quite the quality of the superb 1985, but still a lot to like. Last tasted: 5/90. Drink 1991-1995. 1,842 cases produced. Release: $18. Current: $21. **87**

1985 Raymond Vineyard and Cellar Private Reserve: Absolutely delicious, rich and buttery, with a silky smooth texture and layers of butter, pear, melon, spice and honey flavors that simply glide across the palate. Marvelous harmony, elegance, richness and depth, still holding quite well, with a wonderful aftertaste that keeps repeating the complex fruity flavors with a touch of butterscotch. Last tasted: 5/90. Drink 1991-1995. 1,842 cases produced. Release: $18. Current: $21. **91**

1981 Raymond Vineyard and Cellar Private Reserve: Over the hill now, very ripe and oaky. Better years ago. Still drinkable, but not worth seeking out. Last tasted: 6/90. Drink 1991. 500 cases produced. Release: $15. Current: $25. **70**

REVERE WINERY
Reserve, Napa Valley
Napa Valley

CLASSIFICATION:
   Reserve: FIFTH GROWTH
   Napa Valley: Not rated
COLLECTIBILITY RATING: Not rated
BEST VINTAGES:
   Reserve: 1988, 1986

   Napa Valley: 1985

Revere Winery is a family-owned Chardonnay specialist, producing 2,000 cases a year from 11 acres of winery-owned vineyards in the Coombsville area east of the city of Napa. Coombsville is not an official subappellation of Napa Valley, although it may be someday. There are about 300 acres planted to Chardonnay in Coombsville, owned by such esteemed producers as Grgich Hills, Silverado Vineyards, Far Niente, William Hill and Robert Mondavi Winery. Coombsville has a cool climate that is ideal for Chardonnay.

The first regular bottling by owners John and Anne Kirlin was the 1985 and it is still in very good condition, with intense acidity and firm structure. Beginning in 1986, Revere added a Reserve line, selecting superior lots of wine. Several hundred cases are made each year. The Revere Reserve wines are firm, crisp and austere, but also very concentrated and complex. The 1986 Reserve has well-defined Chardonnay flavors and needs another year or two to reach full maturity. The 1987 Reserve has more raw acidity and is coarser, but with plenty of concentrated fruit. It needs cellaring. The 1988 Reserve shows more elegance and finesse. Winemaker John Kirlin advocates Burgundian vinification techniques; his wines undergo barrel fermentation but not malolactic fermentation.

TASTING NOTES

REVERE WINERY, Reserve, Napa Valley

1988 REVERE WINERY RESERVE: A rich, smoky wine with complex pear, nectarine and butterscotch flavors that grow on you. Balanced, with good depth and intensity, but not overpowering, an elegant wine

AT A GLANCE
REVERE WINERY
2456 Third Ave.
Napa, CA 94558
(707) 224-7620

Owners: John and Anne Kirlin

Winemaker: John Kirlin (5 years)

Founded: 1985

First Chardonnay vintage: 1985
   Reserve: 1986

Chardonnay production: 2,000 cases
   Reserve: 300 cases

Chardonnay acres owned: 11

Average age of vines: 10 years

Average wine makeup: Coombsville, Napa Valley (100%)

Time in oak: 8 months

Type of oak: French (François Frères, Sirugue)

Oak age: new (20% to 30%)

Winemaking notes:
   Barrel fermentation: 100%
   Malolactic fermentation: none
   Lees aging: 100% (5 months)

that is just beginning to blossom. Last tasted: 4/90. Drink 1992-1998. 366 cases produced. Not released. **87**

1987 REVERE WINERY RESERVE: Hard and austere, with attractive honey and spice notes coming through on the finish. Overall it's typical of the 1987 vintage and needs time to mellow. Last tasted: 4/90. Drink 1991-1995. 101 cases produced. Release: $25. Current: $25. **83**

1986 REVERE WINERY RESERVE: Intense yet elegant, with a smooth, creamy texture and well-defined honey, pear, citrus and smoky oak flavors that are rich and delicate on the finish. Balanced and drinking well now. Last tasted: 4/90. Drink 1991-1996. 206 cases produced. Release: $22. Current: $25. **87**

REVERE WINERY, Napa Valley

1986 REVERE WINERY: Fresh and lively, with elegant, concentrated pear, honey and vanilla flavors that are moderately rich and well focused. Drinking at its peak now but showing no signs of declining soon. Finishes with subtlety and finesse. Last tasted: 4/90. Drink 1991-1996. 1,375 cases produced. Release: $15. Current: $15. **85**

1985 REVERE WINERY: A rich and flavorful wine from a superb vintage that is at its peak and can age for another two to four years. The complex honey, pear, toast and citrus flavors are woven together in a sharply focused style. Plenty of acidity and depth to sustain the flavors. Last tasted: 4/90. Drink 1991-1995. 1,052 cases produced. Release: $15. Current: $20. **85**

ROMBAUER VINEYARDS
Reserve, Napa Valley
Napa Valley

CLASSIFICATION: **FIFTH GROWTH**
COLLECTIBILITY RATING: *Not rated*
BEST VINTAGES:
  Reserve: 1988, 1987

  Napa Valley: 1988

D espite some austere and uneven vintages early on, Rombauer Vineyards has shown significant improvement recently and now offers a Reserve Chardonnay that merits attention. In the early vintages some of the Chardonnays were too austere for my taste. Clearly, the 1986 to 1988 Chardonnays have more fruit character, brighter flavors and better balance, while remaining true to their style of very crisp, sometimes tart, acidity.

The 1988 Napa Valley and 1988 Reserve are the best two bottlings this winery has produced. The Reserve is richer and toastier than the Napa Valley bottling. The winery also bottled for several vintages a French Vineyard Chardonnay that was highly acidic and extremely tart. Owners Joan and Koerner Rombauer buy all their Chardonnay grapes, about 50 percent coming from Carneros and the other half from vineyards near the Silverado Country Club northeast of the city of Napa. Rombauer Vineyards is north of St. Helena off the Silverado Trail. Rombauer produces 4,300 cases a year, 300 under the Reserve designation. A number of wineries custom-crush and barrel age their wines in that facility.

AT A GLANCE
ROMBAUER VINEYARDS
3522 Silverado Trail
St. Helena, CA 94574
(707) 963-5170

Owners: Koerner and Joan Rombauer

Winemaker: Greg Graham (2 years)

Founded: 1982

First Chardonnay vintage: 1982
  Reserve: 1986

Chardonnay production: 4,300 cases
  Reserve: 300 cases
  Napa Valley: 4,000 cases

Chardonnay acres owned: none

Average wine makeup: Carneros,
  Napa Valley (50%), Napa
  Valley (50%)

Time in oak:
  Reserve: 17 months
  Napa Valley: 10 months

Type of oak: French (Burgundian)

Oak age: new (25%) to 3 years

Winemaking notes:
  Barrel fermentation: 100%
  Malolactic fermentation: 1 to 10%
  Lees aging: 100% (8 months)

TASTING NOTES

ROMBAUER VINEYARDS, Reserve, Napa Valley

1988 ROMBAUER VINEYARDS RESERVE: The finest and most complex of the Rombauer wines, managing to combine rich, bold, concentrated pear, melon and apple flavors with elegant smoky, toasty oak notes. Can stand a year in the bottle to come together. Last tasted: 6/90. Drink 1992-1997. 330 cases produced. Not released. **89**

1987 ROMBAUER VINEYARDS RESERVE: True to the Reserve style, a bolder, richer version of the 1987, with a shade more depth and concentration of the pear, apple, melon and spice notes. Balanced and attractive, it is ready to drink. Last tasted: 6/90. Drink 1991-1995. 200 cases produced. Release: $25. Current: $25. **87**

1986 ROMBAUER VINEYARDS RESERVE: A bigger, fuller, richer and toastier wine, putting more depth and intensity into the Rombauer style while still maintaining its elegance and finesse. Near its peak. Last tasted: 6/90. Drink 1991-1995. 200 cases produced. Release: $24. Current: $26. **86**

ROMBAUER VINEYARDS, Napa Valley

1988 ROMBAUER VINEYARDS: The most forward and fruity of the Rombauers, offering fresh, rich, focused apple, melon and pear flavors with a measure of delicacy and finesse. Creamy texture and brighter flavors. Last tasted: 6/90. Drink 1991-1996. 4,014 cases produced. Release: $15. Current: $15. **88**

1987 ROMBAUER VINEYARDS: An oakier wine than its predecessors, still rather austere, with flinty melon, pear and apple flavors of moderate depth and intensity, finishing with crispness and a touch of stone. Could use a little more depth and richness. Last tasted: 6/90. Drink 1991-1996. 4,300 cases produced. Release: $14.50. Current: $15. **86**

1986 ROMBAUER VINEYARDS: Ripe and fruity, with fresh apple, melon, pear and spice flavors, the richest and fullest of the early Rombauers, and it's also the best balanced. Last tasted: 6/90. Drink 1991-1995. 3,815 cases produced. Release: $14.50. Current: $16. **85**

1985 ROMBAUER VINEYARDS: The 1985 has always been tight and austere, but it is now beginning to open and offer more apple, pear and toasty oak flavors. It's well balanced and holding its own, but it could use a shade more richness and depth. Last tasted: 6/90. Drink 1991-1994. 1,337 cases produced. Release: $14.50. Current: $18. **84**

1984 ROMBAUER VINEYARDS: Austere, with tightly reined-in apple and pear flavors and tart acidity, offering only a modest dose of fruit, in contrast to most of the wines from this year, which were rich, fruity and full-bodied. Last tasted: 6/90. Drink 1991-1994. 1,337 cases produced. Release: $14.50. Current: $20. **78**

1983 ROMBAUER VINEYARDS: Fully mature but aging well for a 1983, rich and viscous, with intense honey and pineapple flavors that are well proportioned and full-bodied all the way to the finish. Last tasted: 6/90. Drink 1991-1995. 1,010 cases produced. Release: $14.50. Current: $25. **87**

1982 ROMBAUER VINEYARDS: From a mediocre vintage, the 1982 has aged better than most, still offering rich, full-bodied mint, melon, apple and fig flavors that are fresh and lively, finishing with a touch of toasty oak. Last tasted: 6/90. Drink 1991-1994. 382 cases produced. Release: $14.50. Current: $30. **84**

SAINTSBURY
Carneros
Carneros Reserve

CLASSIFICATION:
Carneros: SECOND GROWTH
Carneros Reserve: FOURTH GROWTH
COLLECTIBILITY RATING:
Carneros: AA
Carneros Reserve: A
BEST VINTAGES:
Carneros: 1984, 1988, 1987, 1985

Carneros Reserve: 1988

Saintsbury Chardonnays, all produced with Carneros grapes, have aged exceptionally well. The winery's first vintage in 1981 is still a delicious wine, with rich, smooth, creamy fruit flavors. The 1982 and 1983 vintages are now less charming, but those were difficult years for many producers. But from 1984 to 1988, including three vintages of Carneros Reserve Chardonnay, one tastes a highly consistent and appealing house style of broad, ripe, complex and fruity wines that are tasty on release and improve in the bottle. The 1984 is a big, full-blown wine with wonderful depth and complexity. The 1985 is young and lively, with impeccable balance. The 1986 is a shade more austere, but may simply need more time in the bottle. Both the 1987 and 1988 vintages are very successful, classy wines.

Beginning in 1986, general partners David Graves and Richard Ward introduced a Carneros Reserve Chardonnay that is oakier and more concentrated than the regular bottling. The 1986 is fairly oaky, and in the two subsequent vintages the winery has backed off with oak and produced better-balanced wines, although so far the regular bottlings have had more appeal. The Carneros region is renowned for producing grapes with bracing acidity.

Saintsbury, which takes its name from George Saintsbury, author of *Notes on a Cellar Book*, puts its Chardonnays through full malolactic fermentation, which creates an additional level of flavor and texture without sacrificing the firm backbone of acidity. Saintsbury does not own any Chardonnay vineyards but buys from growers in Carneros on both sides of the Napa-Sonoma county line. The 1981 and 1982 vintages are called Sonoma County because Carneros had not yet been approved as an appellation.

TASTING NOTES

SAINTSBURY, Carneros

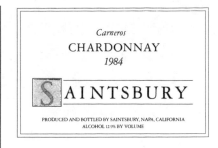

1988 SAINTSBURY CARNEROS: Another winner from Saintsbury, with plenty of ripe, rich fig, apple, pear and melon flavors and a gentle touch of spicy oak, perhaps the most delicate of the bottlings. Finish carries pretty honey flavors. Last tasted: 4/90. Drink 1992-1997. 14,750 cases produced. Release: $14. Current: $14. **90**

1987 SAINTSBURY CARNEROS: Reminds me of the 1984, with its bright, rich, vivid flavors of honey, vanilla, pear and spice that are lush and silky smooth and carry a long way on the finish, but it's a shade more elegant and refined. Last tasted: 4/90. Drink 1992-1997. 13,150 cases produced. Release: $13. Current: $15. **90**

1986 SAINTSBURY CARNEROS: Lean yet rich and full flavored, with ripe vanilla, pear, melon and spice flavors in a complex and deftly balanced style. Not as opulent and fleshy as the 1984 or 1985, but similar in style and flavor. May need longer to unfold. Last tasted: 4/90. Drink 1992-1997. 10,075 cases produced. Release: $12. Current: $17. **88**

1985 SAINTSBURY CARNEROS: Another simply delicious Chardonnay, rich, elegant and impeccably balanced, with lean yet sharply focused lemon, pear, pineapple, spice and melon flavors that are youthful and vibrant, finishing with crisp acidity and excellent length. May be best in 1992. Last tasted: 4/90. Drink 1991-1996. 6,600 cases produced. Release: $11. Current: $19. **90**

1984 SAINTSBURY CARNEROS: The best of the early Saintsburys, rich, full and very ripe, with pretty honey, custard, vanilla and spice flavors that offer depth and complexity. Still youthful and developing, with a long, lingering aftertaste. Last tasted: 4/90. Drink 1991-1994. 6,400 cases produced. Release: $11. Current: $25. **92**

1983 SAINTSBURY CARNEROS: Lean, crisp and earthy, with lemon and pear flavors of moderate depth and intensity. It's well balanced and correct, finishing with subtle flavors. Last tasted: 4/90. Drink 1991-1994. 6,550 cases produced. Release: $11. Current: $20. **80**

1982 SAINTSBURY SONOMA COUNTY: Earthy, dirty and oxidized, with honey and lemon flavors and a cardboard aftertaste. Past its prime. Last tasted: 4/90. Best to avoid. 3,750 cases produced. Release: $11. Current: $14. **65**

1981 SAINTSBURY SONOMA COUNTY: Saintsbury's first Chardonnay is still aging quite gracefully, with smooth, rich vanilla, honey and butterscotch flavors that are fully mature. Fine length echoing lemon and nutmeg flavors. Last tasted: 4/90. Drink 1991-1994. 950 cases produced. Release: $10. Current: $25. **87**

SAINTSBURY, Carneros Reserve, Carneros

1988 SAINTSBURY CARNEROS RESERVE: The fruitiest and to my taste the best of the three Reserves, with more concentrated melon, pear and spicy pineapple flavors to stand up to the oak. The finish echoes fruit and oak, but the fruit wins out this time. Last tasted: 4/90. Drink 1992-1998. 1,800 cases produced. Release: $20. Current: $20. **92**

1987 SAINTSBURY CARNEROS RESERVE: Extends the Reserve style of more oak, but this one is showing more ripe pear and pineapple flavors. The fruit competes with oak on the finish. A better Reserve than the 1986. Last tasted: 4/90. Drink 1992-1997. 1,450 cases produced. Release: $20. Current: $20. **89**

1986 SAINTSBURY CARNEROS RESERVE: Showing more oak and intensity than the 1986 Carneros, but not quite the pretty fruit. What you taste is more pine, toast and subtle pear flavors, a style that may appeal to some more than others. Altogether pleasing, but I prefer the regular in this vintage. Last tasted: 4/90. Drink 1992-1996. 1,015 cases produced. Release: $20. Current: $25. **84**

SANFORD WINERY

Barrel Select, Santa Barbara County
Santa Barbara County

CLASSIFICATION:
  Barrel Select: SECOND GROWTH
  Santa Barbara County: THIRD GROWTH
COLLECTIBILITY RATING:
  Barrel Select: AA
  Santa Barbara County: A
BEST VINTAGES:
  Barrel Select: 1988, 1985, 1987

  Santa Barbara County: 1988, 1987, 1985

E xotic is the first word that comes to mind when tasting the richly seductive Chardonnays of Sanford Winery in Buellton, Santa Barbara County. While many of the wines from this area tend to be heavily herbal and vegetal — red and white alike — Sanford is proof positive that some very dramatic, enormously complex and exciting Chardonnays can be produced there.

The more I taste Sanford's Chardonnays, both the regular Santa Barbara County bottling and the reserve-style Barrel Select, the more impressed I am by the broad array of tropical fruit and oak flavors and by the depth and richness of these wines. Because the style is so extreme, with toasty, buttery oak and tiers of wildly exotic tropical fruit flavors, these highly stylized wines tend to polarize people — either you love them or are overwhelmed by their power and intensity. There is nothing subtle or shy about the style, although they are incredibly well made and very well balanced, capable of providing both elegance and finesse.

The first vintages produced by Richard Sanford carried the Santa Maria Valley appellation. Both the 1981 and 1982 vintages are past their primes. Beginning with the 1983 vintage, Central Coast is the appellation, and the 1983 is a sensational drink. The 1984 is less showy and a touch bitter, but beginning with the 1985 Sanford narrows his focus and begins a run of wonderful wines that extends through the 1988 vintage. Both the 1987 and 1988 are textbook examples of the smooth, deep, creamy texture and beautifully defined pear, melon and spice notes that echo through his wines. The Barrel Select Chardonnays are even richer, deeper, oakier and more full-blown, yet gorgeously proportioned. Sanford does not own any bearing Chardonnay vines, but has planted a vineyard that will soon provide him with grapes of his own. Production has climbed to 19,000 cases, of which 1,000 are Barrel Select.

AT A GLANCE

SANFORD WINERY
7250 Santa Rosa Road
Buellton, CA 93427
(805) 688-3300

Owners: Richard and Thekla Sanford

Winemaker: Bruno D'Alfonso (7 years)

Founded: 1981

First Chardonnay vintage: 1981

Chardonnay production: 19,000 cases
  Barrel Select: 1,000 cases
  Santa Barbara County: 18,000 cases

Chardonnay acres owned: none

Average wine makeup: Santa Barbara
  County (100%)

Time in oak:
  Barrel Select: 16 months
  Santa Barbara County: 9 months

Type of oak: French (Allier)

Oak age:
  Barrel Select: new (100%)
  Santa Barbara County: new
  (20%) to 5 years old

Winemaking notes:
  Barrel fermentation: 100%
  Malolactic fermentation: 100%
  Lees aging: 100% (8 months)

TASTING NOTES

SANFORD WINERY, Barrel Select, Santa Barbara County

1988 SANFORD WINERY BARREL SELECT: A big, deep, rich and enormously concentrated wine with heaps of pear, pineapple, melon and spice notes, all gorgeously proportioned, with intensity and finesse. The best Sanford ever produced, a wine of incredible flavor and grace. Last tasted: 6/90. Drink 1991-1997. 1,000 cases produced. Release: $25. Current: $25. **94**

1987 SANFORD WINERY BARREL SELECT: Elegant and refined, rich and concentrated, with layers of honey, pear, vanilla and toasty oak flavors all in harmony, offering intensity, depth, finesse and grace. Ready now, but can age. Last tasted: 2/90. Drink 1991-1997. 300 cases produced. Release: $24. Current: $30. **91**

1985 SANFORD WINERY BARREL SELECT: Distinctive for its rich earthiness, complexity and sharply focused butterscotch, pear, spice and honey flavors that linger on the finish. Impeccably well balanced and fully mature, yet in this size bottle capable of aging another three to five years with ease. Tasted in magnum. Last tasted: 2/90. Drink 1991-1996. 150 cases produced. Release: $20. Current: $30. **92**

SANFORD WINERY, Santa Barbara County

1988 SANFORD WINERY SANTA BARBARA COUNTY: Amazingly rich and elegant, with pretty pear, pineapple, guava and spicy oak flavors all sharply focused and beautifully defined, a wine with great harmony and grace and a long, lingering finish. Last tasted: 6/90. Drink 1991-1997. 18,000 cases produced. Release: $16. Current: $16. **92**

1987 SANFORD WINERY SANTA BARBARA COUNTY: Wonderfully rich, creamy texture and beautifully defined pear, melon, apple and spice flavors with just the right touch of toasty vanilla and oak. Deep, complex, penetrating flavors follow through on the finish. Last tasted: 2/90. Drink 1991-1996. 18,000 cases produced. Release: $15. Current: $16. **92**

1986 SANFORD WINERY SANTA BARBARA COUNTY: Creamy, rich and buttery, a ripe, full-bodied wine with intense, concentrated butter, pear, honey and spicy oak flavors that are attractive but not quite as complex and intriguing as the 1985. Still quite impressive. Last tasted: 2/90. Drink 1991-1995. 6,000 cases produced. Release: $14. Current: $16. **88**

1985 SANFORD WINERY SANTA BARBARA COUNTY: Rich, elegant and lively, with complex earth, pear, pineapple and toasty oak flavors that are remarkably enticing. Fully mature, concentrated and deep, with a long, full finish. Last tasted: 2/90. Drink 1991-1997. 5,000 cases produced. Release: $13.50. Current: $20. **90**

1984 SANFORD WINERY CENTRAL COAST: Very ripe and in sync with the vintage, offering plenty of pear, pineapple, toast and vanilla flavors that come across as attractive but one-dimensional. Finish gets earthy and bitter. Last tasted: 2/90. Drink 1991-1993. 4,000 cases produced. Release: $12.50. Current: $15. **78**

1983 SANFORD WINERY CENTRAL COAST: Deep yellow, rich and mature, with opulent citrus, oak, vanilla and spicy honey flavors that are round and silky smooth on the palate. Wonderful harmony of flavors, fine depth and balance, in fine condition. Tasted in magnum. Last tasted: 2/90. Drink 1991-1995. 3,000 cases produced. Release: $12. Current: $15. **88**

1982 SANFORD WINERY SANTA MARIA VALLEY: Rich, buttery and gamy, a wine past its prime that turns oxidized and bitter on the finish. Much better years ago. Last tasted: 2/90. Best to avoid. 2,500 cases produced. Release: $12. Current: $20. **68**

1981 SANFORD WINERY SANTA MARIA VALLEY: Fully mature and quite caramelized, with toast, chocolate and vanilla flavors and just a hint of very ripe pear. Limited appeal, but drinkable. Last tasted: 2/90. Drink 1991. 1,000 cases produced. Release: $11. Current: $20. **74**

AT A GLANCE

SEQUOIA GROVE VINEYARDS

P.O. Box 449
Rutherford, CA 94573
(707) 944-2945

Owners: James and Barbara Allen

Winemaker: James Allen (10 years)

Founded: 1980

First Chardonnay vintage: 1980
    Carneros: 1985

Chardonnay production: 10,000 cases
    Napa Valley Estate: 4,000 cases
    Carneros: 6,000 cases

Chardonnay acres owned: 12

Average age of vines: 12 years

Average wine makeup:
    Napa Valley Estate: Rutherford,
    Napa Valley (100%)
    Carneros: Carneros (100%)

Time in oak: 7 months

Type of oak: French (Limousin,
    Tronçais)

Oak age: 3 years old (average)

Winemaking notes:
    Barrel fermentation: 50%
    Malolactic fermentation: none
    Lees aging:
       Napa Valley Estate: 50%
       (6 months)
       Carneros: none

SEQUOIA GROVE VINEYARDS

Napa Valley Estate
Carneros

CLASSIFICATION:
   Napa Valley Estate: SECOND GROWTH
   Carneros: FIFTH GROWTH

COLLECTIBILITY RATING:
   Napa Valley Estate: A
   Carneros: Not rated

BEST VINTAGES:
   Napa Valley Estate: 1988, 1985, 1987, 1986, 1981

   Carneros: 1985

The Sequoia Grove Chardonnays of Jim Allen combine authoritative flavors with finesse and grace. This small, family-owned winery in Rutherford makes its best Chardonnay from Rutherford grapes, with their ripe, rich and complex flavors. A second Chardonnay from Carneros-grown grapes, from vineyards managed by the Allen family, was introduced in 1985. It showcases the crisper acidity of Carneros grapes, but so far has not matched the quality of the Napa Valley bottling. Sequoia Grove was founded in 1980, the first year the Allens produced Chardonnay from their estate. They have also produced Chardonnays from Sonoma-Cutrer's vineyard, but all along the goal has been to concentrate on making wines from their own vineyards.

The 1980 Napa Valley is still opulent, with rich, toasty pear flavors. It's past its prime but still quite enjoyable. The 1981 is aging very well, while the 1982 is fading, turning coarse and dull. The 1983 returns to form, a fully developed wine with elegant, graceful flavors and excellent length. The 1984 to 1988 vintages are all remarkably consistent and impressive. The 1984 is riper and fuller than the 1983, with sharply focused flavors, followed by the delicious 1985, which combines power with finesse. The 1986 is distinctive for its elegance and flavor, while the 1987 offers complexity and smoky oak flavors. The 1988 is the finest I've tasted from the Allen family, a deeply concentrated and complex wine that should age for up to a decade. With the Carneros bottling, the 1985 shows the potential of that vineyard. It offers an intriguing array of flavors that gain with each sip. The 1986 shows more oak and a slight "off" quality that detracts from the flavors. The 1987 has less intensity and depth, but with the 1988 there's greater fruit and complexity to the flavors.

Both Sequoia Grove Chardonnays are 50 percent barrel fermented but do not undergo malolactic fermentation. Wood is always present in the Sequoia Grove Chardonnays, but most of the time it's in the background, letting the fruit show through, clean and pure.

TASTING NOTES

SEQUOIA GROVE VINEYARDS, Napa Valley Estate

1988 SEQUOIA GROVE VINEYARDS NAPA VALLEY ESTATE: The finest Sequoia Grove I've tasted, amazingly fresh and concentrated, with intense pear, pineapple, apple and melon flavors, a touch of smoky, toasty oak and a silky smooth texture that lets the flavors glide across your palate. The finish echoes fruit and oak on and on. Beautifully balanced. Last tasted: 5/90. Drink 1991-1996. 4,228 cases produced. Release: $16. Current: $16. **92**

1987 SEQUOIA GROVE VINEYARDS NAPA VALLEY ESTATE: Another rich yet elegant wine with sharply focused, vivid pear, vanilla and honey flavors that offer intensity without weight. The finish picks up a touch of smoky oak, which adds complexity to the fruity flavors. Last tasted: 5/90. Drink 1991-1996. 2,167 cases produced. Release: $16. Current: $16. **88**

1986 SEQUOIA GROVE VINEYARDS NAPA VALLEY ESTATE: Distinctive for its elegance, balance and finesse, combining deep, rich, concentrated pear, honey and vanilla flavors with a sense of delicacy and finesse. Finishes with subtle notes of complex fruit and oak. Last tasted: 5/90. Drink 1991-1994. 2,064 cases produced. Release: $15. Current: $18. **88**

1985 SEQUOIA GROVE VINEYARDS NAPA VALLEY ESTATE ALLEN FAMILY VINEYARD: In excellent condition, a rich, lively, smooth and concentrated wine that displays power and finesse, with intense pear and pineapple flavors that pick up a touch of toasty vanilla on a long finish. Last tasted: 5/90. Drink 1991-1995. 4,981 cases produced. Release: $16. Current: $20. **89**

1984 SEQUOIA GROVE VINEYARDS NAPA VALLEY ESTATE: A wonderful glass of Chardonnay, ripe, rich and loaded with fresh pineapple, pear, vanilla and toasty oak flavors that round out on the palate, finishing with excellent length and sharply focused flavors. Last tasted: 5/90. Drink 1991-1994. 1,808 cases produced. Release: $14. Current: $20. **87**

1983 SEQUOIA GROVE VINEYARDS NAPA VALLEY ESTATE: Fully mature, elegant and aging gracefully, offering plenty of ripe, rich pear and pineapple flavors, with subtle oak and citrus shadings, finishing with crisp acidity and good length. Holding up well for a 1983. Last tasted: 5/90. Drink 1991-1996. 1,639 cases produced. Release: $12. Current: $20. **87**

1982 SEQUOIA GROVE VINEYARDS NAPA VALLEY ESTATE: Mature and past its prime, losing its intensity and fruit. The pear and vanilla flavors are coarse and dull. Drink up soon; it's rapidly declining. Last tasted: 5/90. Drink 1991. 880 cases produced. Release: $12. Current: $20. **72**

1981 SEQUOIA GROVE VINEYARDS NAPA VALLEY ESTATE: Aging very well, deep, rich and concentrated, with well-integrated honey, pear, citrus and nutmeg flavors that are well balanced, finishing with a touch of tannin and good length. Last tasted: 7/90. Drink 1991-1995. 952 cases produced. Release: $12. Current: $20. **88**

1980 SEQUOIA GROVE VINEYARDS NAPA VALLEY ESTATE: While fully mature and past its prime, this remains a rich, opulent, deliciously concentrated wine with intense, complex toast, pear, vanilla and spice notes that finish with a sense of elegance. Best to enjoy it soon. Last tasted: 5/90. Drink 1991-1994. 1,500 cases produced. Release: $10. Current: $20. **87**

SEQUOIA GROVE VINEYARDS, Carneros

1988 SEQUOIA GROVE VINEYARDS CARNEROS: Showing ripe, clean, rich pineapple and pear flavors with ample oak seasoning and more fruit coming through on the finish, where the honey and smoke flavors add complexity. Last tasted: 5/90. Drink 1991-1996. 6,978 cases produced. Release: $14. Current: $14. **86**

1987 SEQUOIA GROVE VINEYARDS CARNEROS: An improvement over the 1986, showing riper, more focused fruit flavors and less oakiness. The pear and pineapple flavors are clean and rich but with only moderate depth and intensity. Well balanced, ready to drink. Last tasted: 5/90. Drink 1991-1995. 5,530 cases produced. Release: $14. Current: $14. **83**

1986 SEQUOIA GROVE VINEYARDS CARNEROS: Despite the intensity and richness of the pineapple and pear flavors, the oak notes border on gluey and seem to stand apart from the fruit. Stylistically distinct from the Napa Valley bottling, and somewhat less impressive. Last tasted: 5/90. Drink 1991-1995. 4,880 cases produced. Release: $13. Current: $16. **78**

1985 SEQUOIA GROVE VINEYARDS CARNEROS: Complex and intriguing, with deep, rich, complex pear, smoke and toasty vanilla flavors that gently unfold on the palate, revealing more flavor and complexity with each sip. Well balanced, aging very well. Last tasted: 5/90. Drink 1991-1995. 4,976 cases produced. Release: $12. Current: $16. **88**

CHARLES F. SHAW VINEYARD

Napa Valley

CLASSIFICATION: *FIFTH GROWTH*
COLLECTIBILITY RATING: *Not rated*

BEST VINTAGES: *1985, 1983, 1988*

The Napa Valley Chardonnays of Charles F. Shaw are delicate and understated, with moderate richness, depth and concentration and subtle oak shadings. It's not a dramatic style that grabs your attention, but its gentleness grows on you. The Shaw winery is north of St. Helena, where about half the winery's 49 acres of vines are situated. Another vineyard near Rutherford is part-owned with Ric Forman, who has been Shaw's winemaker and consultant. The winery was founded in 1978 as a Gamay specialist.

Shaw's first Chardonnay vintage, the 1983, is aging very well, still offering plenty of flavor and vitality. The 1984 is riper and beginning to decline. The 1985 is the best Chardonnay to date, very elegant, with understated flavors that are well knit and narrowly focused. The 1986 continues in the style of delicacy and balance, while the 1987 is true to the vintage, more austere and harder around the edges. The 1988 is fresh and lively, with a shade more richness and concentration than the 1987 and with time it may rival the 1985 as Shaw's best. The winery now produces 12,000 cases under the direction of current winemaker Scott McLeod. About 40 percent of the wine is barrel fermented, with the remainder fermented in stainless steel, and none of the wine undergoes malolactic fermentation, which accounts for the crisp, steely, austere style. While some might want more generosity and flavor in their Chardonnays, others will appreciate it for its austerity and consistency.

AT A GLANCE

CHARLES F. SHAW VINEYARD
1010 Big Tree Road
St. Helena, CA 94574
(707) 963-5459

Owner: Limited partnership. Charles Shaw, general partner

Winemaker: Scott McLeod (3 years)

Founded: 1978

First Chardonnay vintage: 1983

Chardonnay production: 12,000 cases

Chardonnay acres owned: 49

Average age of vines: 15 years

Average wine makeup: Rutherford, Napa Valley (60%); St. Helena, Napa Valley (40%)

Time in oak: 9 months

Type of oak: French (François Frères, Allier, Tronçais)

Oak age: new to 2 years old (33% each)

Winemaking notes:
Barrel fermentation: 40%
Malolactic fermentation: none
Lees aging: 100% (6 months)

TASTING NOTES

CHARLES F. SHAW VINEYARD, Napa Valley

1988 CHARLES F. SHAW VINEYARD: Fresh and lively, with more flavor than previous vintages, showing pear, pineapple, citrus and butterscotch flavors and a shade more richness and concentration. Finish is delicate and soft. Last tasted: 5/90. Drink 1991-1995. 10,500 cases produced. Release: $11. Current: $11. **86**

1987 CHARLES F. SHAW VINEYARD: Crisp, lean and elegant, with pretty lemon, pear and spice notes that are clean and well balanced,

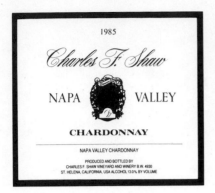

with moderate depth and intensity. Youthful and just beginning to show its potential. Last tasted: 5/90. Drink 1992-1997. 7,500 cases produced. Release: $11. Current: $11. **85**

1986 CHARLES F. SHAW VINEYARD: Elegant and stylish, well balanced and delicate, with spicy pear, melon and citrus notes that are delicate and subtle, consistent with the Shaw style. Fully mature and drinking well. Last tasted: 5/90. Drink 1991-1995. 7,500 cases produced. Release: $11. Current: $11. **85**

1985 CHARLES F. SHAW VINEYARD: The best of the Shaws, consistent with the winery's elegant, understated style, with fresh, ripe pear, melon, honey and toasty spice flavors that are well integrated and balanced. Last tasted: 5/90. Drink 1991-1994. 5,000 cases produced. Release: $12. Current: $15. **87**

1984 CHARLES F. SHAW VINEYARD: Ripe, full-bodied and mature, drinking well now, but perhaps a shade past its peak, with delicate pear, spice, lemon and oak flavors. It's a mild-mannered, pleasant wine that lacks dramatic flair. Last tasted: 5/90. Drink 1991-1993. 5,000 cases produced. Release: $12. Current: $15. **82**

1983 CHARLES F. SHAW VINEYARD: Shaw's first Chardonnay is fully evolved and aging better than most from this vintage, with ripe pear and melon flavors and a touch of spice and oak, rendering a smooth, mellow, well-balanced wine. Last tasted: 5/90. Drink 1991-1993. 5,000 cases produced. Release: $12. Current: $16. **86**

SILVERADO VINEYARDS

Napa Valley
Limited Reserve, Napa Valley

CLASSIFICATION:
Napa Valley: FOURTH GROWTH
Limited Reserve: Not rated
COLLECTIBILITY RATING: *Not rated*
BEST VINTAGES:
Napa Valley: 1986, 1988, 1987

Limited Reserve: 1987, 1986

The Chardonnays of Silverado Vineyards have always been very attractive and well made, with an abundance of rich, elegant fruit, deft oak flavors and fine balance. The winery in the Stags Leap District is owned by Lillian Disney, the widow of cartoonist and Disneyland founder Walt Disney, and her daughter and son-in-law, Diane Disney Miller and Ron Miller.

Silverado owns 89 acres of bearing Chardonnay vines at the winery and just south of the winery near Yountville. Another 22 acres are planted in Coombsville, northeast of the city of Napa, and there are 30 more in Carneros. Production is now at 41,000 cases, including a new Limited Reserve bottling that is richer, fuller and oakier than the regular bottling, a departure in style that is appropriate for a Reserve bottling. The winemaker is John Stuart.

The early Silverado Chardonnays, while delicious to drink on release, have not aged especially well. The 1981 and 1982 vintages in particular are well past their primes, while the 1983 and 1984 should both be consumed soon. Beginning with the 1985 vintage, however, there is a step up in quality. This vintage is drinking exceptionally well now, with layers of intense fruit flavors and pretty, toasty oak. The 1986 is seductive and impeccably balanced, with broad flavors that fan out on the finish. The 1987 is another highly successful vintage, with elegance and complexity. The 1988 is deliciously fruity, with intense fruit flavors and fine length. The 1986 Limited Reserve adds more flavor and concentration, as does the 1987 Limited Reserve. Clearly Silverado's Chardonnays in the past five vintages have shown tremendous improvement and aging ability. The wines are 80 percent barrel fermented, with 40 percent undergoing malolactic fermentation.

AT A GLANCE

SILVERADO VINEYARDS
6121 Silverado Trail
Napa, CA 94558
(707) 257-1770

Owners: Lillian Disney, Diane Disney Miller, Ron Miller

Winemaker: John Stuart (9 years)

Founded: 1981

First Chardonnay vintage: 1981
Limited Reserve: 1986

Chardonnay production: 40,000 cases
Limited Reserve: 1,300 cases

Chardonnay acres owned: 89

Average age of vines: 6 years

Average wine makeup: Yountville, Napa Valley (40%); Carneros (25%); Stags Leap District, Napa Valley (15%); other Napa Valley (20%)

Time in oak: 4 to 8 months

Type of oak: French (Burgundian)

Oak age: new (25%) to 5 years old

Winemaking notes:
Barrel fermentation: 80%
Malolactic fermentation: 40%
Lees aging: 100% (4 to 8 months)

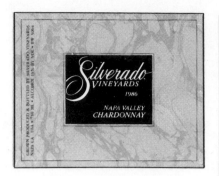

SILVERADO VINEYARDS, Napa Valley

1988 SILVERADO VINEYARDS: Deliciously fruity and complex, with elegant honey, vanilla, pear and butterscotch flavors that are well defined and sharply focused. Another superbly made wine. Last tasted: 3/90. Drink 1991-1996. 41,000 cases produced. Release: $14. Current: $14. **88**

1987 SILVERADO VINEYARDS: Another elegant, well-balanced Chardonnay with pretty fig, honey, melon, pear and butterscotch flavors that are rich and full-bodied, yet showing a measure of finesse and harmony. Last tasted: 3/90. Drink 1991-1996. 30,000 cases produced. Release: $13.50. Current: $15. **88**

1986 SILVERADO VINEYARDS: A real charmer, showing more harmony and finesse than previous bottlings, with rich, toasty honey, pear, fig and melon flavors built on an elegant framework. Finish fans out and lingers. Last tasted: 3/90. Drink 1991-1996. 22,000 cases produced. Release: $12. Current: $16. **90**

1985 SILVERADO VINEYARDS: In peak drinking condition, the 1985 is the best balanced of the early Silverados, offering rich, ripe, concentrated fig, melon, grapefruit and pear flavors and a touch of toasty oak. Aging well. Last tasted: 3/90. Drink 1991-1995. 17,000 cases produced. Release: $11.50. Current: $17. **87**

1984 SILVERADO VINEYARDS: Fully mature, with rich honey, butter, pear and apricot flavors that are broad and spread out on the palate. Finish gets a bit coarse and oaky and it lacks finesse. Last tasted: 3/90. Drink 1991-1994. 11,000 cases produced. Release: $11. Current: $18. **81**

1983 SILVERADO VINEYARDS: Ripe, rich and full-bodied, aging better than its predecessors, but best consumed soon, before the pear, honey and butter flavors gain more maturity. Last tasted: 3/90. Drink 1991-1993. 5,000 cases produced. Release: $11. Current: $20. **84**

1982 SILVERADO VINEYARDS: Ripe, fully mature and in decline, the pear and citrus flavors are losing their vitality. Last tasted: 3/90. Drink 1991. 4,500 cases produced. Release: $10. Current: $20. **73**

1981 SILVERADO VINEYARDS: Past its prime and not showing much fruit. The peach and pear flavors are oxidized. Last tasted: 3/90. Drink 1991. 1,800 cases produced. Release: $10. Current: $20. **70**

SILVERADO VINEYARDS, Limited Reserve, Napa Valley

1987 SILVERADO VINEYARDS LIMITED RESERVE: A shade more forward than the 1986, but similar in character and style, with pretty honey, pear and toasty, buttery oak flavors that are very rich and complex, long and full on the finish. Deftly balanced. Last tasted: 7/90. Drink 1993-2000. 1,300 cases produced. Not released. **92**

1986 SILVERADO VINEYARDS LIMITED RESERVE: Firm and oaky at first, but there's a deep, rich, explosive core of ripe pear and pineapple flavors underneath that's amazingly complex and lively, a wonderfully proportioned wine that has the body and intensity to improve for another three to five years and age even longer. Toasty oak lingers on the finish. Last tasted: 7/90. Drink 1992-1997. 650 cases produced. Release: $25. Current: $25. **90**

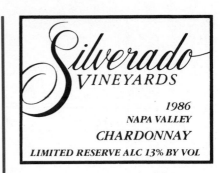

AT A GLANCE

SIMI WINERY
16275 Healdsburg Ave.
Healdsburg, CA 95448
(707) 433-6981

Owner: Moët-Hennessy/Louis
 Vuitton, France

Winemaker: Paul Hobbs (1 year)

Founded: 1876

First Chardonnay vintage: 1970
 Reserve: 1980

Chardonnay production: 55,000 cases
 Reserve: 2,000 cases

Chardonnay acres owned: 146

Average age of vines: 3 years

Average wine makeup:
 Reserve: Sonoma County: (80%),
 Mendocino County (10%),
 Napa County (10%)

Time in oak: 7 months

Type of oak: French (François Frères)

Oak age: new (75% to 100%) to
 1 year old

Winemaking notes:
 Barrel fermentation:
 Reserve: 100%
 Malolactic fermentation: 100%
 Lees aging:
 Reserve: 90% to 100%

SIMI WINERY
Reserve

CLASSIFICATION: *FIRST GROWTH*
COLLECTIBILITY RATING: *AAA*
BEST VINTAGES: *1987, 1982, 1980, 1986, 1988, 1985, 1981*

Since 1980, Zelma Long's first complete vintage at Simi Winery, the Reserve Chardonnays have been consistently sensational and among the very finest produced in California. Even now, at 10 years old, the 1980 Reserve is a bold, rich, deeply flavored Chardonnay that is sharply focused and tightly knit, capable of improving for another six to eight years and maybe longer.

Chardonnay is Long's speciality. In a decade at this Healdsburg winery she's mastered Cabernet Sauvignon and Sauvignon Blanc as well, but it has been with Simi's Reserve Chardonnay that she has made her most dramatic statements with wine so far.

Simi's first Chardonnay vintage came in 1970, but I have not tasted any of those older vintages recently. In 1980 Long began the Reserve program, modeled after the one at the Robert Mondavi Winery, where she worked as a winemaker before moving to Simi in the fall of 1979. The Reserve wines represent a richer, more intense, more concentrated and complex style than the regular bottling. In tasting the vintages from 1980 to 1988, one is impressed not only by the consistently high quality of the Simi Reserves, but also by the deliberate style of the wines. The Reserves are all barrel fermented and undergo full malolactic fermentation, resulting in bold, rich, intense and sharply focused fruit flavors, broad, creamy, layered textures, and a wealth of flavor and complexities. They are also elegant and stylish wines of beautiful proportion. The 1981 is a shade riper and perhaps less elegant than the 1980, but still among the top wines of the vintage. The 1982 is sensational on its own merits, but all the more impressive considering the difficulties many vintners faced in this vintage. The 1983 and 1984 Reserves dip a notch in quality, but with time the 1984 may improve a point or two. More importantly, both are delicious wines. The 1985 and 1986 vintages are both outstanding; with each sip you find another flavor to hang on to. The 1987 and 1988 Simi Reserves offer uncommon richness, depth and complexity. These are two sensational wines that showcase Long's talents.

The Simi Reserves are created from a mixture of grapes grown primarily in Sonoma County, ranging from Carneros to Sonoma Valley, Russian River Valley and Alexander Valley, including a Simi-owned vineyard in Chalk Hill, along with smaller percentages of grapes from

Mendocino and Napa counties. The 1988 Reserve is mostly Sonoma County; it does not include Mendocino grapes but uses a small percentage of Napa Valley grapes. The 1980 Reserve was made entirely from the Mendocino County vineyard owned by grower Andy Beckstoffer.

As great as the Simi Reserves have been, the winery, under Long's encouragement, has planted more than 100 acres of its own Chardonnay vineyards and plans to add more in the Russian River Valley. While the focus here is on the Reserve Chardonnays, Simi's regular bottling is often exceptional, differing primarily in that it is still roughly a 50-50 blend of Sonoma and Mendocino grapes and is only 50 percent barrel fermented. Long is now president and chief executive officer of Simi, but keeps her hand in winemaking at both Simi and Long Vineyards in Napa Valley, where she is a part-owner with her former husband, Bob Long. Paul Hobbs is the new winemaker. Simi produces 55,000 cases a year but only 2,000 are under the Reserve label.

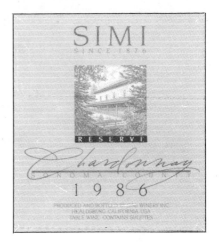

TASTING NOTES

SIMI WINERY, Reserve, Sonoma County

1988 SIMI WINERY RESERVE: Another stunning Reserve bottling, youthful and forward, in sync with the vintage, displaying a wealth of rich, creamy, smooth, buttery and intense pear, melon, apple and spicy oak flavors that linger on the finish. Wonderful. Last tasted: 4/90. Drink 1992-1998. 2,300 cases produced. Not released. **91**

1987 SIMI WINERY RESERVE: Quite possibly the finest Simi Reserve ever produced, offering a great sense of richness and concentration, intensity and depth without weight. The fruit is ripe, rich, pure and elegant, sharply focused on the honey, pear, apple, toast and spice notes, and the finish is long and graceful. Last tasted: 4/90. Drink 1991-1997. 2,000 cases produced. Not released. **94**

1986 SIMI WINERY RESERVE: The 1986 vintage was an excellent one and this wine is slowly evolving into one of its stars. It's tightly structured, very deep and concentrated, displaying subtlety and finesse, with pretty pear, toast, vanilla and apple flavors. With each sip you find another flavor to latch on to. Last tasted: 4/90. Drink 1991-1998. 1,600 cases produced. Release: $28. Current: $32. **92**

1985 SIMI WINERY RESERVE: Wonderfully complex, subtle and elegant, with fresh, ripe, rich pear, lemon and buttery toast flavors that are impeccably balanced, long and full on the finish. Drinking at its peak now; not quite the concentration of some of the earlier Reserves. Last tasted: 4/90. Drink 1991-1996. 1,200 cases produced. Release: $28. Current: $32. **91**

1984 SIMI WINERY RESERVE: Tight, rich and complex, with layers of toast, pear, lemon and honey flavors that are very sharply focused

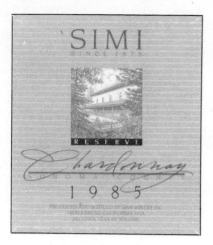

and intense. Still quite oaky on the finish, it may need another year to begin to soften. Has all the ingredients for greatness, including a long, full finish. Last tasted: 4/90. Drink 1991-1996. 1,100 cases produced. Release: $28. Current: $32. **89**

1983 SIMI WINERY RESERVE: Elegant and lively, fully mature, with subtle pear, honey and butterscotch flavors that glide across the palate. Finish offers good length and complexity. Last tasted: 4/90. Drink 1991-1995. 1,000 cases produced. Release: $22. Current: $32. **88**

1982 SIMI WINERY RESERVE: Enticing with its elegance and sharply defined pear, lemon, citrus and toast flavors, it packs plenty of fruit flavor yet it's extremely well mannered, smooth and creamy, displaying a measure of restraint. The finish is particularly attractive with its toast and pear flavors. Best wine of the vintage. Last tasted: 4/90. Drink 1991-1995. 1,000 cases produced. Release: $22. Current: $40. **94**

1981 SIMI WINERY RESERVE: Yellow-gold, deep, rich and ripe, with intense pear, butter, pineapple and oak flavors that combine to give this wine excellent intensity and flavor, yet for all its concentration and assertiveness there's a silky smooth texture and a sense of elegance. One of the best 1981s. Last tasted: 4/90. Drink 1991-1996. 1,600 cases produced. Release: $20. Current: $40. **91**

1980 SIMI WINERY RESERVE MENDOCINO COUNTY: A shade richer and more intense than the regular bottling, offering plenty of tightly reined-in flavors of pear, lemon, pineapple and toast that are still a bit hard on the palate. The finish extends the complex intensity of the flavors. Last tasted: 4/90. Drink 1991-1997. 1,100 cases produced. Release: $20. Current: $40. **94**

SMITH-MADRONE VINEYARD
Spring Mountain, Napa Valley

CLASSIFICATION: *FOURTH GROWTH*
COLLECTIBILITY RATING: *A*
BEST VINTAGES: *1979, 1987, 1986, 1988*

Brothers Stuart and Charles Smith moved to Napa Valley in the early 1970s and selected a mountaintop vineyard site a few hundred feet above the famous Stony Hill estate. They figured if Stony Hill could make magnificent Chardonnays in this soil and climate, so could they. In a decade of producing Chardonnays, Smith-Madrone has yet to pose a serious threat to Stony Hill, yet there are some striking similarities in their styles, most notably in their wines' austerity and ability to age. With the exception of a "food wine" experiment gone bad, two vintages in which the grapes were picked underripe and produced very tart, thin wines, the Smith-Madrone Chardonnays have a very respectable track record.

The vineyard is at the 2,000-foot elevation on Spring Mountain, planted in 1972 in a once forested area that the Smiths cleared. The first vintage, 1978, is aging beautifully, at its peak but with the concentration to withstand most of the 1990s decade. The 1979 is absolutely stunning, one of the top wines of the vintage and the best ever from Smith-Madrone. The 1980 is very ripe, higher in extract, packed with flavor and holding on. The 1981 is from a fast-maturing vintage and is losing its fruit. The 1982 is holding its own, surprisingly rich and enduring on the palate, with a stony, flinty aftertaste the comes through in many of the wines. The 1983 is the first of the food wines, extremely tart and unappetizing; it's for those who love high acidity in their Chardonnays. The 1984 moves away from the sharpness of the 1983 just enough to provide a glimmer of tart lemon, pear and nectarine flavors.

With the 1985, the Smiths get back on track, with a very elegant, well-integrated wine, followed by an even better 1986 and a 1987 to top that. The 1987 is clearly the best since 1979, a tight, flinty, deeply concentrated wine that should age through the decade. The 1988 continues on that track, very delicate but firm, tempting now but a good bet to improve for four to six more years. The Smith-Madrone Chardonnays are barrel fermented, but do not undergo malolactic fermentation. Production hovers at about 2,000 cases.

AT A GLANCE
SMITH-MADRONE VINEYARD
4022 Spring Mountain Road
St. Helena, CA 94574
(707) 963-2283

Owners: The Smith family

Winemakers: Charles and Stuart Smith (13 years)

Founded: 1977

First Chardonnay vintage: 1978

Chardonnay production: 2,100 cases

Chardonnay acres owned: 13

Average age of vines: 17 years

Average wine makeup: Spring Mountain, Napa Valley (100%)

Time in oak: 10 months

Type of oak: French (Nevers)

Oak age: 4 to 5 years

Winemaking notes:
Barrel fermentation: 100%
Malolactic fermentation: none
Lees aging: 100% (10 months)

ESTATE BOTTLED

1985

SMITH·MADRONE

NAPA VALLEY
CHARDONNAY

PRODUCED AND BOTTLED BY SMITH·MADRONE
4022 SPRING MOUNTAIN ROAD, ST. HELENA, CALIFORNIA
ALCOHOL 13.2% BY VOLUME

TASTING NOTES

SMITH·MADRONE VINEYARD, Spring Mountain, Napa Valley

1988 SMITH·MADRONE VINEYARD: A worthy successor to the superb 1987, a shade more forward and delicate but nonetheless tight and austere, with pear, melon and honey flavors that are well integrated and just beginning to evolve. The flinty, stony flavors are crisp and clean on the finish. Last tasted: 5/90. Drink 1993-2000. 1,980 cases produced. Release: $13. Current: $13. **88**

1987 SMITH·MADRONE VINEYARD: The best wine since the fabulous 1979, austere, flinty, rich and complex, with tart pear, nectarine, spice and toast notes that are very well balanced and integrated. Still needs two to three years — maybe more — to peak, but the flavors and style ring true for Smith-Madrone. Last tasted: 5/90. Drink 1993-2000. 2,542 cases produced. Release: $13. Current: $13. **91**

1986 SMITH·MADRONE VINEYARD: Similar in style to the 1985, this is a rich, complex, tightly reined-in wine that features crisp pear, peach and pine flavors that are full-bodied and flinty, just now reaching maturity. Appears to have the structure and depth for another decade. Last tasted: 5/90. Drink 1990-1998. 2,375 cases produced. Release: $12.50. Current: $16. **89**

1985 SMITH·MADRONE VINEYARD: Best balanced since 1980, this is an elegant, complete, well-integrated Chardonnay with a complex arrangement of pear, peach, toast and nectarine flavors that are tight and subtle. The flinty nectarine flavors cleanse the palate on the finish and it shows more austerity than when released. Last tasted: 5/90. Drink 1990-1996. 1,832 cases produced. Release: $12.50. Current: $16. **87**

1984 SMITH·MADRONE VINEYARD: Austere, with tightly reined-in pear, lemon and nectarine flavors, unusual for a vintage in which most wines are very ripe and fleshy. Underdeveloped now and in need of another two to three years, but it's balanced and well made. Stony, flinty aftertaste. Last tasted: 5/90. Drink 1991-1996. 1,606 cases produced. Release: $12. Current: $16. **80**

1983 SMITH·MADRONE VINEYARD: Highly acidic, tart and awkward, a "food wine" experiment gone bad. Simply too much acidity and not enough rich fruit to stand up to it. Might work with oysters, but most will find it way too tart. Last tasted: 5/90. Drink 1991-1994. 1,473 cases produced. Release: $12. Current: $15. **71**

1982 SMITH·MADRONE VINEYARD: Aging surprisingly well for a 1982, offering tightly focused honey, pear and citrus notes that are complex and engaging, finishing with a flinty, stony edge. Fully mature now but holding. Last tasted: 5/90. Drink 1990-1998. 1,004 cases produced. Release: $12. Current: $18. **86**

1981 SMITH-MADRONE VINEYARD: Beginning to lose its fruit. Although the honey and pear flavors are intense, they lose their depth and fade on the finish. Last tasted: 5/90. Drink 1990-1993. 650 cases produced. Release: $12. Current: $18. **81**

1980 SMITH-MADRONE VINEYARD: Very ripe and full-bodied, high in extract, with rich honey, pear and butter flavors that are broad and deep. Aging well but a shade past its prime, finishing with a hint of bitterness and oak. Last tasted: 5/90. Drink 1990-1995. 450 cases produced. Release: $11. Current: $20. **85**

1979 SMITH-MADRONE VINEYARD: One of the top wines of the vintage and Smith-Madrone's finest Chardonnay, a remarkably rich, smooth and complex wine with toast, pear, honey and nectarine flavors elegantly balanced and well integrated, finishing with a touch of clove and toasty, smoky notes. Just peaking. Last tasted: 5/90. Drink 1990-2000. 580 cases produced. Release: $10. Current: $28. **92**

1978 SMITH-MADRONE VINEYARD: Smith Madrone's first bottling is typical of the vintage but aging better than most, very ripe and full-bodied, with rich, deep honey, tangerine, fig and spice flavors, fine balance and lively acidity, finishing with a touch of clove. Last tasted: 5/90. Drink 1990-1997. 375 cases produced. Release: $10. Current: $30. **86**

SONOMA-CUTRER VINEYARDS

Les Pierres, Sonoma Valley
Cutrer Vineyard, Russian River Valley
Russian River Ranches, Russian River Valley

CLASSIFICATION:
   Les Pierres: FIRST GROWTH
   Cutrer Vineyard: SECOND GROWTH
   Russian River Ranches: THIRD GROWTH

COLLECTIBILITY RATING:
   Les Pierres: AAA
   Cutrer Vineyard: AA
   Russian River Ranches: A

BEST VINTAGES:
   Les Pierres: 1981, 1988, 1987, 1985

   Cutrer Vineyard: 1988, 1987, 1981

   Russian River Ranches: 1988, 1987, 1985

Chardonnay specialist Sonoma-Cutrer Vineyards was founded in 1972 as a grape-growing concern headed by Brice Cutrer Jones, with more than 400 acres of vines in Sonoma County. In 1981 Sonoma-Cutrer began producing three different Chardonnays in a new, ultramodern, state-of-the-art winemaking facility west of Windsor in Russian River Valley.

To call Sonoma-Cutrer a specialist is almost an understatement. "Perfectionist" is more appropriate, for I know of no winery that goes to such lengths to preserve the quality of its grapes from the vineyard to the bottle. For instance, along the way from the vineyard, the grapes are moved into a cooling tunnel to lower the temperature to around 45 degrees Fahrenheit and minimize oxidation before they're crushed.

Winemaker Bill Bonetti is a master of Chardonnay. A veteran of Charles Krug Winery in the 1960s and Souverain in the 1970s, he has been in charge at Sonoma-Cutrer from the beginning. Sonoma-Cutrer produces three Chardonnays each year. All are close in style yet distinctive. The star of the line-up is Les Pierres, a 100-acre vineyard that sits at the base of Sonoma Mountain near where the borders of Carneros and Sonoma Valley meet. Les Pierres, "the stones" in French, takes its name from the stony, rocky soil that usually shows up in the wines as a stony, flinty, mineral character. The grapes share the bracing acidity and firm austerity of Carneros-grown fruit, and because of the resulting wines' deep concentration, they take time to come around. Not everyone will find their tart, rich, austere flavors appealing. Others won't be patient enough for them to evolve.

The 1981, an extremely tart and concentrated wine, took nearly a decade to begin to shed its austerity, but it is now an amazingly complex and intriguing wine. The 1982 is also very fine, on an earlier aging curve, as is the 1983. The 1984 is riper and fuller, characteristic of a warmer vintage, and ready to enjoy. The 1985 is more like the 1981, wonderfully elegant and complex, with an excellent marriage of fruit and oak. The 1986 is very tart and concentrated, unyielding now but likely to reveal more flavor and nuances with time. The 1987 offers more flavor and complexity without sacrificing intensity, while the 1988 may rival the 1981. It's still very tightly wrapped in acidity and firm fruit concentration.

The Cutrer Vineyard, also 100 acres, is not far off Les Pierres' pace. While it's in a somewhat cooler district, its wines tend to be a bit riper and fuller than Les Pierres. The 1988 appears to be the most complete vintage to date, with great fruit flavors and impeccable balance and depth. The 1987 is not far behind, with rich, smooth, creamy flavors and plenty of length. The 1986 Cutrer overshadows Les Pierres at this point, with more generous flavors. The 1985, 1984, 1983 and 1982 vintages are all aging well, but the best of the early wines is the 1981.

The Russian River Ranches bottling comes from a trio of winery-owned vineyards and often has a dollop of wine from the other two vineyards added into the blend. The Russian River Ranches bottling in 1988 is by far the best to date. In general this wine matures more rapidly than the other two, but the 1985 is holding up very well and the 1987 promises more of the same.

Production at Sonoma-Cutrer is now at 70,000 cases, with about 11,000 each of Les Pierres and Cutrer Vineyard. Bonetti occasionally puts the wines through malolactic fermentation. In 1988, 40 percent of Les Pierres went through malolactic, while 100 percent of Cutrer did. New and used oak is used to barrel ferment all the wines, but it doesn't show up as a dominant flavor, just background seasoning.

TASTING NOTES

SONOMA-CUTRER VINEYARDS, Les Pierres, Sonoma Valley

1988 SONOMA-CUTRER VINEYARDS LES PIERRES: The finest Les Pierres since 1981, a wine that will still need another two or three years to mature. It's tart, crisp, lean and elegant, with lively, flinty pear, mineral, lemon and spice notes enlivened by bracing acidity and subtle smoky oak shadings in the background. Already showing signs of complexity and grace. Last tasted: 7/90. Drink 1992-2001. 11,075 cases produced. Not released. **93**

1987 SONOMA-CUTRER VINEYARDS LES PIERRES: Intense, lively and concentrated yet very elegant and refined, with a creamy texture and pretty, well-defined lemon, pear, toast and honey flavors that offer uncommon finesse and complexity. Lingers on the finish. Last tasted: 3/90. Drink 1992-1997. 11,510 cases produced. Release: $22.50. Current: $26. **92**

1986 SONOMA-CUTRER VINEYARDS LES PIERRES: Tart, lean, intense and concentrated, packed with toast, pear, nutmeg and lemon flavors that are still a bit hard and closed. Needs another year or two to soften. Last tasted: 3/90. Drink 1992-1997. 9,125 cases produced. Release: $19.50. Current: $27. **88**

1985 SONOMA-CUTRER VINEYARDS LES PIERRES: Amazingly complex and elegant, with pretty, well-defined honey, toast, pear and spicy oak flavors all combining to give finesse and intrigue. Flavors keep echoing on the finish. Last tasted: 3/90. Drink 1991-1997. 8,500 cases produced. Release: $17.50. Current: $30. **92**

1984 SONOMA-CUTRER VINEYARDS LES PIERRES: Ripe, full, rich and opulent, with honey and butterscotch flavors and subtle pear and citrus notes, a big, full-blown wine from a very ripe vintage. Aging quite well. Last tasted: 3/90. Drink 1991-1995. 7,000 cases produced. Release: $16.50. Current: $30. **89**

1983 SONOMA-CUTRER VINEYARDS LES PIERRES: Intense and concentrated yet fully mature, with layers of honey, vanilla, pear and butterscotch flavors that are complex and still somewhat tannic. Last tasted: 3/90. Drink 1991-1994. 7,000 cases produced. Release: $15.50. Current: $30. **86**

1982 SONOMA-CUTRER VINEYARDS LES PIERRES: Aging remarkably well, offering an array of intense, youthful, fresh peach, pear, pineapple and spice flavors that stay with you. Last tasted: 3/90. Drink 1991-1994. 2,500 cases produced. Release: $15. Current: $35. **88**

1981 SONOMA-CUTRER VINEYARDS LES PIERRES: Incredibly complex, deep and elegant, it has aged amazingly well and with its crisp acidity and lively flavors shows no signs of fading. The pear, lemon, honey and creamy butterscotch flavors are simply lovely. Last tasted: 3/90. Drink 1991-1997. 850 cases produced. Release: $14.50. Current: $40. **94**

SONOMA-CUTRER VINEYARDS, Cutrer Vineyard, Russian River Valley

1988 SONOMA-CUTRER VINEYARDS CUTRER VINEYARD: The best Cutrer Vineyard bottling to date, combining ripe, clean, lush, elegant flavors with bright lemon, pear, melon and spice notes that are richly concentrated and sharply focused, picking up smoky, toasty notes on the finish. Beautifully proportioned, long and complex. Last tasted: 7/90. Drink 1992-2000. 10,010 cases produced. Release: $17.50. Current: $17.50. **92**

1987 SONOMA-CUTRER VINEYARDS CUTRER VINEYARD: Rich, smooth, creamy and supple, with well-defined pear, lemon, honey and vanilla flavors that glide across the palate, finishing with excellent depth and intensity; wonderful body, complexity and finesse. Last tasted: 3/90. Drink 1991-1996. 9,840 cases produced. Release: $17.50. Current: $18. **91**

1986 SONOMA-CUTRER VINEYARDS CUTRER VINEYARD: Intense and concentrated yet elegant, with plenty of ripe pear, pineapple, lemon and toast flavors that pick up a touch of smoke and butterscotch on the finish. Still has not peaked. Tremendous acidity and concentration. Last tasted: 3/90. Drink 1992-1997. 7,100 cases produced. Release: $16. Current: $20. **89**

1985 SONOMA-CUTRER VINEYARDS CUTRER VINEYARD: A shade earthier and oakier, with plenty of intensity and mature flavors that turn elegant on the finish, with hints of smoke, fig, pear and nutmeg echoing on the finish. Last tasted: 3/90. Drink 1991-1996. 6,000 cases produced. Release: $14.75. Current: $23. **87**

1984 SONOMA-CUTRER VINEYARDS CUTRER VINEYARD: Ripe, opulent and complex, with pretty honey, pear and butterscotch flavors that are very attractive, full and lush. Drinking at its peak now. Last tasted: 3/90. Drink 1991-1995. 6,000 cases produced. Release: $14.25. Current: $25. **87**

1983 SONOMA-CUTRER VINEYARDS CUTRER VINEYARD: Ripe and mature, with honey, pear, melon and butterscotch flavors and a touch of juniper, finishing with mineral and flinty stone nuances. Well balanced, full flavored, ready to drink. Last tasted: 3/90. Drink 1991-1994. 3,000 cases produced. Release: $13.75. Current: $25. **86**

1982 SONOMA-CUTRER VINEYARDS CUTRER VINEYARD: Mature and earthy, declining but still showing plenty of earth, pear, toast and nutmeg flavors that are complex and pleasing. Last tasted: 3/90. Drink 1991-1994. 5,000 cases produced. Release: $13. Current: $25. **87**

1981 SONOMA-CUTRER VINEYARDS CUTRER VINEYARD: Still very attractive, elegant, complex and youthful, with fresh pear, peach, honey and vanilla flavors that glide across the palate, showing a silky texture. Remarkably complex and ageworthy. Last tasted: 3/90. Drink 1991-1995. 2,500 cases produced. Release: $12.50. Current: $30. **91**

SONOMA-CUTRER VINEYARDS, Russian River Ranches, Russian River Valley

1988 SONOMA-CUTRER VINEYARDS RUSSIAN RIVER RANCHES: Wonderful, youthful, fruity aromas, well balanced, with sharply defined pear, lemon, citrus and spice notes that are crisp and lively, finishing with excellent length. Tempting now but probably will not peak for a year or two. Last tasted: 3/90. Drink 1992-1998. 51,900 cases produced. Release: $13.25. Current: $14. **91**

1987 SONOMA-CUTRER VINEYARDS RUSSIAN RIVER RANCHES:
Ripe, full and opulent, with complex pear, earth, toast and vanilla flavors that are rich and well balanced, finishing with good length. Concentrated and intense. Last tasted: 3/90. Drink 1991-1995. 53,055 cases produced. Release: $12. Current: $16. **88**

1986 SONOMA-CUTRER VINEYARDS RUSSIAN RIVER RANCHES:
Clean, elegant, well balanced and at its peak, tight and sharply focused on the tart lemon and pear flavors, finishing with earthiness. High acidity, but not quite the opulence and attractiveness of the 1988 and 1987. Last tasted: 3/90. Drink 1992-1996. 41,725 cases produced. Release: $12. Current: $18. **86**

1985 SONOMA-CUTRER VINEYARDS RUSSIAN RIVER RANCHES:
Lovely honey, pear, vanilla and butterscotch flavors and firm, crisp acidity, remarkably well balanced, clean and lively on the finish. Last tasted: 3/90. Drink 1991-1995. 28,256 cases produced. Release: $11.50. Current: $22. **88**

1983 SONOMA-CUTRER VINEYARDS RUSSIAN RIVER RANCHES:
Earthy and very mature, with rich honey, pear and butter flavors, this is best consumed now. It won't shortchange you on flavor. Last tasted: 3/90. Drink 1991-1994. 9,900 cases produced. Release: $10.50. Current: $22. **85**

1982 SONOMA-CUTRER VINEYARDS RUSSIAN RIVER RANCHES:
Mature, rich and complex, with layers of pear, toasty oak, nutmeg and vanilla flavors that are concentrated and still a bit coarse. Best paired with food. Good length on the aftertaste. Last tasted: 3/90. Drink 1991-1994. 5,200 cases produced. Release: $10. Current: $24. **87**

1981 SONOMA-CUTRER VINEYARDS RUSSIAN RIVER RANCHES:
Fully mature, past its prime but aging well, with mature honey, pear and toast flavors that show a touch of oxidation on the finish. Best to drink up. Last tasted: 3/90. Drink 1991-1994. 1,250 cases produced. Release: $9.35. Current: $30. **82**

ST. CLEMENT VINEYARDS

Napa Valley

Abbott's Vineyard, Carneros, Napa Valley

CLASSIFICATION:

Napa Valley: THIRD GROWTH

Abbott's Vineyard: Not rated

COLLECTIBILITY RATING:

Napa Valley: A

Abbott's Vineyard: Not rated

BEST VINTAGES:

Napa Valley: 1979, 1986, 1988, 1984

Abbott's Vineyard: 1987

St. Clement Chardonnays are typically made in a lean, austere, tightly concentrated style, and with a few exceptions have aged very well. Founded in 1975 by William Casey, St. Clement has purchased Chardonnay grapes from vineyards throughout Napa Valley for most of its vintages. Winemaker Dennis Johns has concentrated on grapes grown in the cooler portions of Napa Valley, from Yountville south to Carneros, but he has also purchased grapes from Pope Valley for his blend. Today the winery, owned since 1987 by Sapporo USA, owns the 15-acre Abbott's Vineyard in Carneros and bottles a separate Chardonnay from those grapes.

The first Chardonnay came in 1975, but I have not tasted that wine recently. Of my current notes, 1979 is the oldest and it is a fabulous wine, very rich and full-bodied, with youthful, intense fruit flavors. It is clearly one of the top wines of the vintage. The 1980 is riper and lusher, past its prime, as are the 1981, 1982 and 1983 vintages. With 1984, St. Clement produced another highly successful wine that is aging well. The 1985 has been slow to mature, and lacks the finish of the 1984. The 1986 is right in sync with the St. Clement style, a sharply focused, reined-in wine that offers intense fruit flavors. The 1987 is very firm, but offers plenty of flavor. It should be better in a year or two. The 1988 is more elegant and forward, but well balanced and true to the St. Clement style.

The best St. Clement Chardonnays may come from the Abbott's Vineyard. The only bottling produced so far is the 1987, and it is a fuller, richer, creamier wine than the St. Clement Napa Valley. No 1988 was produced, but in 1989 it was bottled separately. St. Clement produces about 4,000 cases of Chardonnay a year, with about 500 coming from Abbott's Vineyard in 1987.

AT A GLANCE

ST. CLEMENT VINEYARDS
P.O. Box 261
St. Helena, CA 94574
(707) 963-7221

Owner: Sapporo USA, Japan

Winemaker: Dennis Johns (10 years)

Founded: 1975

First Chardonnay vintage: 1975
Abbott's Vineyard: 1987

Chardonnay production: 4,000 cases
Napa Valley: 3,600 cases
Abbott's Vineyard: 500 cases

Chardonnay acres owned: 15

Average age of vines: 15 years

Vineyard locations:
Abbott's Vineyard: Napa Valley
Carneros

Average wine makeup:
Napa Valley: Carneros,
Napa Valley (67%); Yountville,
Napa Valley (33%)

Time in oak: 8 months

Type of oak: French (Nevers, Tronçais)

Oak age: new to 2 years old

Winemaking notes:
Barrel fermentation: 75%
Malolactic fermentation: none
Lees aging:
Napa Valley: 67% (6 months)
Abbott's Vineyard: 100%
(6 months)

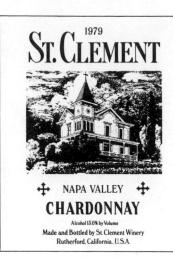

ST. CLEMENT VINEYARDS, Napa Valley

1988 ST. CLEMENT VINEYARDS: Remarkably elegant and bursting with fresh, ripe pear and pineapple flavors that are intense yet well mannered, displaying complexity and finesse, with flavors that linger on the finish. Just the right touch of oak in the background. Last tasted: 3/90. Drink 1992-1998. 3,683 cases produced. Release: $15. Current: $15. **88**

1987 ST. CLEMENT VINEYARDS: Wonderful peach, pear and butterscotch flavors in a tight, concentrated and well-balanced wine with elegant, well-defined fruit flavors that are crisp and lively. Last tasted: 3/90. Drink 1992-1997. 3,500 cases produced. Release: $15. Current: $15. **86**

1986 ST. CLEMENT VINEYARDS: Very tight and lean, firmly concentrated, with pretty honey, toast, pear and nutmeg flavors that are well balanced, finishing with good length. Still needs a year to reach its peak. Last tasted: 3/90. Drink 1992-1997. 1,450 cases produced. Release: $15. Current: $15. **89**

1985 ST. CLEMENT VINEYARDS: Slow to evolve but fully mature now, offering rich, ripe pear, apple and pineapple flavors with subtle toasty, buttery notes that are diverse yet not quite knit, and the finish tails off, lacking intensity and definition. Last tasted: 3/90. Drink 1991-1995. 3,700 cases produced. Release: $14.50. Current: $16. **85**

1984 ST. CLEMENT VINEYARDS: Plenty of ripe, rich, generous pineapple, pear, lemon and melon flavors that are supported by crisp, lively acidity and the kind of elegance and finesse that keeps you coming back for another sip. Last tasted: 3/90. Drink 1991-1996. 4,000 cases produced. Release: $14.50. Current: $17. **88**

1983 ST. CLEMENT VINEYARDS: Very mature and losing fruit, best to drink soon. Tasted in magnum. Last tasted: 3/90. Drink 1991. 4,500 cases produced. Release: $14.50. Current: $17. **76**

1982 ST. CLEMENT VINEYARDS: Deep, rich and very mature, with ripe pear and honey flavors that turn oxidized on the finish. Tasted in magnum. Last tasted: 3/90. Drink 1991. 4,600 cases produced. Release: $14.50. Current: $20. **73**

1981 ST. CLEMENT VINEYARDS: Fully mature and declining, with mature citrus and lemon flavors that offer little in the way of interest. Last tasted: 3/90. Drink 1991. 3,000 cases produced. Release: $13.50. Current: $25. **75**

1980 ST. CLEMENT VINEYARDS: Lush, ripe, rich and mature, and while it still shows plenty of mature pear and pineapple flavors and crisp acidity, it has begun to decline. Tasted in magnum. Last tasted: 3/90. Drink 1991-1992. 3,200 cases produced. Release: $12. Current: $25. **83.**

1979 ST. CLEMENT VINEYARDS: Beautifully preserved, rich, buttery and complex, with lovely honey, pear, lemon and vanilla flavors that glide across the palate. Clearly one of the best 1979s, finishing with great length and vitality, echoing fruit, oak and anise. Last tasted: 3/90. Drink 1991-1996. 3,000 cases produced. Release: $12. Current: $27. **93**

ST. CLEMENT VINEYARDS, Abbott's Vineyard, Carneros, Napa Valley

1987 ST. CLEMENT VINEYARDS ABBOTT'S VINEYARD: Richer, fuller and creamier than the regular St. Clement, the Abbott's Vineyard is also more complex, with tiers of pear, vanilla, honey and pineapple flavors that offer both intensity and finesse. Long aftertaste. Can stand some cellaring. Last tasted: 3/90. Drink 1992-1997. 500 cases produced. Release: $17. Current: $17. **91**

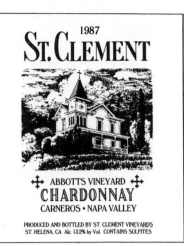

STAG'S LEAP WINE CELLARS

Reserve, Napa Valley
Napa Valley

CLASSIFICATION:
Reserve: FOURTH GROWTH
Napa Valley: Not rated
COLLECTIBILITY RATING: *Not rated*
BEST VINTAGES:
Reserve: 1988, 1987, 1986

Napa Valley: 1987, 1988, 1986

The reputation of Stag's Leap Wine Cellars is built around its rich, supple, dramatic Cabernet Sauvignons and deservedly so. They are among the finest California has to offer. Proprietor Warren Winiarski, who founded his winery in 1972, has not enjoyed anywhere near as much success with Chardonnay, although in recent vintages a new Reserve wine, made in a rich, smooth, elegant style, has shown tremendous improvement.

Winiarski does not own any Chardonnay vines, and early vintages, beginning with 1976, were palatable at best. Of the older vintages in the 1970s, only the Haynes Vineyard bottling from 1979 is worth trying. In the 1980s, the 1981 is holding up, but after that you have to skip ahead to the 1985 vintage and the 1985 Reserve where the turnabout in quality begins. With the 1986 vintage, both the regular and Reserve show considerable improvement, with more richness, elegance, balance and judicious use of oak. The 1987 and 1988 bottlings are both fine examples of their type. Production of the regular Napa Valley bottling is now 15,300 cases, while the Reserve has jumped from 480 cases in 1986 to 1,172 in 1987 and back to 335 in 1988.

TASTING NOTES

STAG'S LEAP WINE CELLARS, Reserve, Napa Valley

1988 STAG'S LEAP WINE CELLARS RESERVE: Amazingly rich, smoky and forward now, with appealing apple, pear, citrus and smoky oak flavors, a smooth, velvety texture and honey and butterscotch flavors that linger on the finish. Last tasted: 3/90. Drink 1993-1998. 335 cases produced. Release: $28. Current: $28. **90**

1987 STAG'S LEAP WINE CELLARS RESERVE: Showing more oak than the regular 1987, and will need more time to evolve. For now the smoky oak and butterscotch flavors overshadow the tight pear, lemon, nutmeg and apple notes. Last tasted: 3/90. Drink 1992-1997. 1,172 cases produced. Release: $28. Current: $28. **89**

1986 STAG'S LEAP WINE CELLARS RESERVE: Ripe, supple and elegant, with rich pear, honey, melon and toasty oak flavors combining to give this wine depth and complexity. Well balanced, delicious to drink now, finishing with crisp lemon-lime flavors. Last tasted: 6/90. Drink 1991-1994. 480 cases produced. Release: $26. Current: $26. **88**

1985 STAG'S LEAP WINE CELLARS RESERVE: A modest improvement over the 1985 regular, with a shade more depth and richness to the spicy pear flavors, but the wood stands out and is somewhat cloying on the finish. Last tasted: 3/90. Drink 1991-1995. 1,214 cases produced. Release: $22. Current: $26. **85**

STAG'S LEAP WINE CELLARS, Napa Valley

1988 STAG'S LEAP WINE CELLARS: Plenty of attractive ripe pear and apple flavors in a tight, compact style. Youthful and intense, it is a year or two away from peaking, but the balance and flavor are right and it has very good potential. Last tasted: 3/90. Drink 1993-1997. 15,500 cases produced. Release: $18. Current: $18. **87**

1987 STAG'S LEAP WINE CELLARS: Attractive for its elegance and finesse, surpasses the excellent 1986, with a narrow beam of ripe pear, melon and apple flavors and spicy vanilla and oak nuances. Flavors are well integrated, finishing with a burst of citrus. Last tasted: 3/90. Drink 1992-1997. 17,710 cases produced. Release: $18. Current: $18. **89**

1986 STAG'S LEAP WINE CELLARS: Showing a finer balance of rich, supple, concentrated fruit and oak than previous bottlings. The spicy pear and apple flavors are tart and crisp, with a gentle overlay of oak. Last tasted: 3/90. Drink 1991-1995. 8,166 cases produced. Release: $17. Current: $20. **86**

1985 STAG'S LEAP WINE CELLARS: Ripe, delicate and elegant, but perhaps too light for some. The apple, pear and spice flavors are attractive but lacking richness and concentration. Still pleasant enough. Last tasted: 3/90. Drink 1991-1994. 7,002 cases produced. Release: $16. Current: $18. **83**

1984 STAG'S LEAP WINE CELLARS: Fully mature and slightly oxidized, but with decent pear, melon and oak flavors that are balanced but blunt, with a trace of bitterness. Better earlier on, it should be consumed soon. Last tasted: 6/90. Drink 1991-1992. 5,861 cases produced. Release: $14. Current: $17. **77**

1983 STAG'S LEAP WINE CELLARS: Oxidized and fading, not much fruit left. Last tasted: 3/90. Best to avoid. 4,582 cases produced. Release: $13.50. Current: $17. **62**

1982 STAG'S LEAP WINE CELLARS: Coarse and leafy, with honey and Botrytis flavors that turn vegetal on the finish. A difficult vintage that was best drunk early. Last tasted: 3/90. Drink 1991. 3,874 cases produced. Release: $13.50. Current: $17. **70**

1981 STAG'S LEAP WINE CELLARS: Tart and lean, with a leafy spearmint quality. Never an exceptional wine, but it is still holding up well. Last tasted: 3/90. Drink 1991-1993. 4,760 cases produced. Release: $13.50. Current: $17. **79**

1980 STAG'S LEAP WINE CELLARS: Ripe and full blown like most 1980s, still retaining ripe pear and spicy apple flavors, but it's past its peak and losing intensity on the finish. Last tasted: 3/90. Drink 1991-1992. 2,194 cases produced. Release: $10.50. Current: $17. **78**

1977 STAG'S LEAP WINE CELLARS: Like the 1976, it is badly maderized. Last tasted: 3/90. Best to avoid. 2,452 cases produced. Release: $8. Current: $17. **59**

1976 STAG'S LEAP WINE CELLARS: Badly oxidized, well past its prime. Last tasted: 3/90. Best to avoid. 335 cases produced. Release: $8. Current: $17. **58**

STAG'S LEAP WINE CELLARS, Various bottlings

1982 STAG'S LEAP WINE CELLARS MIRAGE NAPA VALLEY: Tasting rather bizarre now, with earthy, woody, piney aromas dominating the honey and butterscotch flavors. Unbalanced, past its prime. Last tasted: 3/90. Drink 1991. 3,564 cases produced. Release: $11.50. Current: $18. **70**

1979 STAG'S LEAP WINE CELLARS HAYNES VINEYARD NAPA VALLEY: Smooth and creamy, with pretty honey and vanilla flavors that are rich and soft. Fully mature and beginning to dry out on the finish. Drink up. Last tasted: 3/90. Drink 1991-1992. 2,000 cases produced. Release: $12.50. Current: $20. **82**

1978 STAG'S LEAP WINE CELLARS HAYNES VINEYARD NAPA VALLEY: Very mature, with honey and butterscotch flavors that fade on the palate, finishing dry and oaky. Last tasted: 3/90. Drink 1991. 1,815 cases produced. Release: $10. Current: $20. **74**

1977 STAG'S LEAP WINE CELLARS HAYNES VINEYARD NAPA VALLEY: Dull, bitter and oxidized, with only faint fruit remaining. Last tasted: 3/90. Best to avoid. 1,752 cases produced. Release: $9. Current: $20. **67**

STERLING VINEYARDS
Winery Lake Vineyard, Carneros
Diamond Mountain Ranch, Napa Valley

CLASSIFICATION:
Winery Lake Vineyard: SECOND GROWTH
Diamond Mountain Ranch: THIRD GROWTH

COLLECTIBILITY RATING:
Winery Lake Vineyard: AA
Diamond Mountain Ranch: A

BEST VINTAGES:
Winery Lake Vineyard: 1988, 1987, 1986

Diamond Mountain Ranch: 1988, 1987, 1985

AT A GLANCE
STERLING VINEYARDS
P.O. Box 365
Calistoga, CA 94515
(707) 942-5151

Owner: Seagram Classics Wine Co.

Winemaker: Bill Dyer (5 years)

Founded: 1964

First Chardonnay vintage: 1969
Winery Lake Vineyard: 1986
Diamond Mountain Ranch: 1983

Chardonnay production: 50,000 cases
Winery Lake Vineyard: 8,000 cases
Diamond Mountain Ranch: 7,000 cases

Chardonnay acres owned: 270
Winery Lake Vineyard: 95
Diamond Mountain Ranch: 43

Average age of vines: 15 years
Winery Lake Vineyard: 25 years
Diamond Mountain Ranch: 13 years

Vineyard locations:
Winery Lake Vineyard: Carneros
Diamond Mountain Ranch: Diamond Mountain, Napa Valley

Time in oak: 6 months

Type of oak: French (Allier, Nevers, Tronçais)

Oak age: new (50%) to 2 years old

Winemaking notes:
Barrel fermentation: 100%
Malolactic fermentation:
Winery Lake: none
Diamond Mountain Ranch: 50%
Lees aging: 100% (6 months)

Sterling Vineyards is one of Napa Valley's Chardonnay old-timers. This winery near Calistoga, founded in 1964 by Peter Newton (now of Newton Vineyards) and a group of investors, has been making Chardonnay since 1969, when Ric Forman was the winemaker. The Sterling Vineyards Chardonnays have long been highly regarded for their austere style and ageability. Tasting through the older vintages, however, shows that most of the wines from the 1970s and into the early 1980s have barely hung on and are not particularly memorable at this point in their lives.

Beginning with the 1983 vintage, Sterling introduced the first of two new vineyard-designated Chardonnays, and they are clearly superior to the earlier wines. In 1983 Sterling began making a Diamond Mountain Chardonnay from its 43-acre vineyard high on Diamond Mountain, west of Calistoga and the winery. This wine is amazingly consistent in quality and style each year, with its tight, firm, austere structure and complex, flinty pear and mineral flavors. Because it is so lean and firm, it needs a good three to four years' cellaring after release to begin to open and reveal its complexities. I give it very high marks for its deliberate style and consistently high quality. The 1988 vintage is the most forward and complex of the wines so far, a good candidate for cellaring.

In 1986 Sterling, through its new parent company, Seagram Classics Wine Co., acquired the prestigious Winery Lake Vineyard in Carneros, and began bottling a wine under that designation. It too has firm, sometimes bracing acidity, but offers a wealth of rich, complex, often exotic tropical fruit flavors, and works as a perfect contrast to the Diamond Mountain style. It too has been very consistent from year to year, a tribute to the skills of winemaker Bill Dyer and vineyardist Tucker Catlin.

The two vineyard-designated wines are treated differently, with the Diamond Mountain Ranch wine undergoing partial malolactic fermentation. The Winery Lake does not undergo malolactic. The Estate bottling is produced primarily from Sterling's vineyards in Napa Valley, but typically gets a boost from small portions of both Winery Lake and Diamond Mountain Ranch wines that don't make the final blends in those bottlings.

If you want to experience the difference between a mountain-grown and a Carneros-grown Chardonnay, open up a bottle of the Diamond Mountain alongside a Winery Lake and you'll see what I mean. Production of Sterling Chardonnay has topped 50,000 cases, with 8,000 cases of Winery Lake and about 7,000 of Diamond Mountain.

TASTING NOTES

STERLING VINEYARDS, Winery Lake, Carneros

1988 STERLING VINEYARDS WINERY LAKE: Young and concentrated, offering tight acidity and firm apple, pear and nutmeg flavors, but it needs time to develop and soften. At this stage it appears to be in sync with the two previous vintages. Last tasted: 4/90. Drink 1992-1996. 8,000 cases produced. Release: $20. Current: $20. **90**

1987 STERLING VINEYARDS WINERY LAKE: Another very successful Winery Lake bottling, a shade more austere and lean than the 1986, but with just as much flavor tightly packed in. The ripe pear, pineapple and citrus notes are compelling and linger on the finish. Last tasted: 4/90. Drink 1991-1996. 7,000 cases produced. Release: $20. Current: $20. **89**

1986 STERLING VINEYARDS WINERY LAKE: The first Winery Lake bottling is a ripe, opulent, complex wine with layers of pear, apple, pineapple, spicy nutmeg and oak flavors, with bracing acidity and a full aftertaste that lingers. Last tasted: 4/90. Drink 1991-1994. 3,000 cases produced. Release: $20. Current: $23. **89**

STERLING VINEYARDS, Diamond Mountain Ranch, Napa Valley

1988 STERLING VINEYARDS DIAMOND MOUNTAIN RANCH: The finest Diamond Mountain Ranch Chardonnay to date, oakier and toastier, but those flavors add complexity and texture to the flinty, stony pear, apple, melon and spice flavors. Wonderfully proportioned, long and full on the finish. Last tasted: 7/90. Drink 1993-2000. 2,000 cases produced. Not released. **91**

1987 STERLING VINEYARDS DIAMOND MOUNTAIN RANCH: Although very austere and concentrated, it is showing fruit flavors and complexity early on, with hints of lemon and spice creeping in with the ripe pear and apple notes. The wildflower aromas are enticing, the finish is long and sturdy. Last tasted: 7/90. Drink 1993-1999. 6,000 cases produced. Not released. **88**

1986 STERLING VINEYARDS DIAMOND MOUNTAIN RANCH: Typically austere and tight, just beginning to unfold its flavors. The tart pear, mineral and oak flavors are well balanced and showing signs of complexity. Best to wait another year. Last tasted: 4/90. Drink 1991-1996. 7,500 cases produced. Release: $15. Current: $15. **86**

1985 STERLING VINEYARDS DIAMOND MOUNTAIN RANCH: Firm and tight, with stony, flinty pear and apple flavors that are tight and concentrated. Well balanced, elegant and refined, a tasty Diamond Mountain Chardonnay. Last tasted: 7/90. Drink 1993-1999. 5,400 cases produced. Release: $15. Current: $17. **87**

1984 STERLING VINEYARDS DIAMOND MOUNTAIN RANCH: Austere, tight and lemony, with firm apple, nutmeg and flinty mineral flavors, this wine is just beginning to reach full maturity. It does not have the breadth of flavor of the top 1984s, but the structure is excellent and it's aging well. Last tasted: 4/90. Drink 1991-1995. 3,000 cases produced. Release: $15. Current: $17. **86**

1983 STERLING VINEYARDS DIAMOND MOUNTAIN RANCH: Still firm and austere, but the flinty mineral notes marry well with the tart pear, honey, toast and vanilla flavors, creating a remarkably complex and well-preserved wine. Last tasted: 4/90. Drink 1991-1994. 1,400 cases produced. Release: $15. Current: $18. **86**

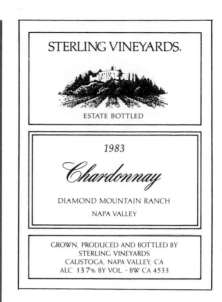

STERLING VINEYARDS, Estate, Napa Valley

1982 STERLING VINEYARDS ESTATE: Tart, earthy and gamy, the fruit is rapidly dropping out of this one. Drinkable but uninspiring. Last tasted: 4/90. Drink 1991. 10,000 cases produced. Release: $14. Current: $17. **73**

1981 STERLING VINEYARDS ESTATE: Fading, with dull, simple, flat Chardonnay flavors, and the hints of toast and honey aromas don't come through on the palate. Last tasted: 4/90. Drink 1991. 4,000 cases produced. Release: $14. Current: $17. **71**

1980 STERLING VINEYARDS ESTATE: Green, tart and very lean, almost unripe, it has shed most of its fruit, leaving a lemony flavor and some gamy notes on the finish. Decent but unexciting. Last tasted: 4/90. Drink 1991. 4,000 cases produced. Release: $13. Current: $17. **70**

1979 STERLING VINEYARDS ESTATE: Tart, lean and losing its fruit, a decent wine but at this stage there is much less to get excited about. Last tasted: 4/90. Drink 1991. 2,800 cases produced. Release: $13. Current: $17. **73**

1977 STERLING VINEYARDS ESTATE: Tart, earthy, very mature, past its prime but drinkable, with gamy pear and apple flavors. Last tasted: 4/90. Drink 1991. 4,000 cases produced. Release: $10. Current: $20. **70**

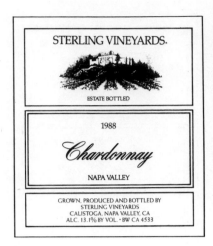

1976 STERLING VINEYARDS ESTATE: Extremely earthy and gamy. Last tasted: 4/90. Best to avoid. 2,600 cases produced. Release: $5.25. Current: $18. **59**

1974 STERLING VINEYARDS ESTATE: Tart and green, with ripe pear and green apple flavors, past its prime but enjoyable. Still crisp, with good length on the finish. Last tasted: 4/90. Drink 1991-1993. 3,000 cases produced. Release: $4.75. Current: $35. **78**

STONY HILL VINEYARD
St. Helena, Napa Valley

CLASSIFICATION: *FIRST GROWTH*
COLLECTIBILITY RATING: *AAA*
BEST VINTAGES: *1964, 1962, 1968, 1985, 1970, 1977, 1966, 1988,*
1984, 1965

Stony Hill Chardonnays are legendary among connoisseurs of California wine. They are truly magnificent wines, impeccably balanced, rich, intense and perfumed, able to age on and on as if trapped in a time warp that allows them to retain their youthful vitality and amazing fruit complexity. Production of Stony Hill Chardonnay has always been small and the wines hard to come by, but they are among the most prized possessions of seasoned wine collectors.

This tiny vineyard and winery estate, founded by Eleanor and Fred McCrea of San Francisco, is north of St. Helena in the eastern hills near Napa Valley-Bothe State Park. The McCreas bought their property in 1943 as a summer vacation home and weekend retreat. They named the estate after what it was, a stony hill. As they spent more time in Napa Valley, they became more interested in making wine. The McCreas chose to plant Pinot Chardonnay, then a relatively scarce grape variety in California, on a hunch that it would grow well in their soil. They hedged their bets against a crop failure by planting Riesling and Pinot Blanc. Later they added Gewürztraminer, Sémillon and a few dozen Pinot Noir vines.

They began planting their Chardonnay vineyard in 1946, usually 1 or 2 acres a year. The vines are planted on a north-facing hillside slope, so they receive less sun than they would with southern exposure. The McCreas took winemaking courses at the University of California at Davis, and they also learned winemaking techniques and tricks from fellow winemakers in the valley. Their first Chardonnay grapes were harvested in 1950, with the first commercial release following in 1952, but production was very small, with only a few barrels and often fewer than 100 cases. Winemaking was primitive by current standards: The McCreas picked grapes when they tasted ripe and used old brandy barrels for aging in a small stone winery, which effectively limited the amount of wine they could produce. To all appearances it was a mom-and-pop hobby winery, but the McCreas took it seriously and built slowly, always paying the greatest attention to quality and detail.

The Stony Hill style of Chardonnay has been extremely consis-

AT A GLANCE
STONY HILL VINEYARD
P.O. Box 308
St. Helena, CA 94574
(707) 963-2636

Owner: Eleanor McCrea
Winemaker: Mike Chelini (16 years)
Founded: 1952
First Chardonnay vintage: 1952
Chardonnay production: 2,400 cases
    Estate: 1,200 cases
Chardonnay acres owned: 27
Average age of vines: 10 years
Average wine makeup: St. Helena, Napa Valley (100%)
Time in oak: 10 months
Type of oak: French, Yugoslavian
Oak age: new to 28 years old
Winemaking notes:
    Barrel fermentation: 70%
    Malolactic fermentation: none
    Lees aging: none

tent through the years, although in the past decade, from 1978 to 1988, the wines are a bit more forward and less steely than they were early on. Fred McCrea was a strong believer in non-interventionist winemaking — letting the vintages dictate the character of the wines and staying out of the way of Mother Nature. Terms that typically describe Stony Hill Chardonnays are delicacy, subtlety and finesse. Vintage after vintage, these are characteristics that show up in the wines. The other element that sets these Chardonnays apart from the field is their ability to age for decades. Wines from the 1960s are still in pristine condition, light yellow-straw in color, with the balance, flavor, richness and depth to develop and age for years to come.

I'm sure there are many reasons why these wines age so exceptionally well: the shy-bearing clone that produces small, intense berries, and the north-facing hillside vineyard, which allows the grapes to ripen slowly and evenly but limits the vines' productivity to about 1 ton an acre and prevents overripeness or huge crops. The wine is rarely aged in new oak barrels, which prevents oxidation and premature aging. I also believe they are exceptionally well-made, hand-crafted wines that are given great attention. The last time I tasted through most of the older wines, I picked up a good whiff of sulfur. It was not enough to detract from the quality of the wines, but it reminded me that in the 1950s through the 1970s, it was as a common winemaking practice to sulfur grapes when they were picked, when they were crushed and barreled and before they were bottled. Sulfur is a preservative, but it also strips the color in wines, which may account for some of the lighter colors found in older Stony Hill Chardonnays. It may well have contributed to their longevity.

Stony Hill Chardonnays of the 1950s and 1960s were notoriously slow starters, often unimpressive and closed on release and typically in need of six to eight years' cellaring. While my experience tasting the older vintages is limited, the new releases I've tasted from the 1970s and 1980s show ripe, mature, subtle flavors that improve considerably in the glass. I often find a flinty, stony, mineral quality on the finish, not surprising considering the stony nature of the soil. In the 1960s, the 1960 is still quite rich and complex, with a long finish. The 1962 is stunning, amazingly complex and delicious, while the 1963 is a shade less complex but still holding. The 1964 is the greatest California Chardonnay I've ever tasted, a deeply concentrated, enormously complex and intriguing wine that still has a decade or more of life. The 1965 pales only by comparison, but offers a wealth of fruit. The 1966 is right on target, more elegant and refined, but gaining depth and intensity. The last time I tried the 1967 it was showing the wrinkles of old age, but perhaps it was just a bad bottle. The 1968 is a deep, profound, richly concentrated wine that appears still to be on its way up. It ranks with 1962 and 1964 as the stars of the decade. The 1969 was showing its age the last time I saw it.

There were some glorious wines in the 1970s, beginning with the wonderful 1970 vintage. The 1971 to 1975 vintages are often described by collectors as outstanding wines, but my limited experience indicates they are a step down in quality. Surely not all Stony Hills can go 30 years, so these wines may have been much better in their youth. Michael Chelini joined the winery as winemaker for the 1974 vintage. The last time I tried the 1974 it was dominated by a heavy sulfur quality, but perhaps that was just a poor bottle. The 1976 is rich and bold, while the 1977 is crisp and austere, aging quite gracefully. The 1978 was on a fast aging curve and is beginning to lose its fruit, as is the 1979. In the 1980s, the 1980, 1981, 1982 and 1983 vintages are similar in style, lush and elegant, rich and forward. The 1984 is very ripe, with gorgeous fruit, followed by the delicious 1985. The 1986 and 1987 are youthful and unevolved, but the 1988 is more forward and a step up from the previous two vintages.

Most of Stony Hill's Chardonnay is sold through the winery's mailing list. Portions of the original vineyard have been replanted with more vigorous vines, and in 1988 the winery added a second label, SHV, blending wines from its young estate vines with Chardonnay grapes grown across the valley at the Bancroft Vineyard on Howell Mountain. One bright note: The 1989 vintage appears very successful and production is expected to climb from the usual 1,800 to 2,000 cases to about 3,000 cases.

Collectors have long been keen on Stony Hill. The wines are incredibly hard to find, but still reasonably priced at $18 a bottle for new releases. Wines from the early 1960s are another matter. They sold for $3 to $4 a bottle, but now sell for $450 a bottle at auction. Fred McCrea died in 1977, and the winery is now run by Eleanor, who is in her 80s and still spry and active.

TASTING NOTES

STONY HILL VINEYARD, Estate, Yountville, Napa Valley

1988 STONY HILL VINEYARD ESTATE: Wonderfully rich, ripe and elegant, with tiers of pure pear, honey and melon flavors and a charming touch of spicy nutmeg and oak seasoning. Terrific balance, excellent depth of flavor and concentration, long and lingering on the finish. Last tasted: 6/90. Drink 1992-2002. 960 cases produced. Release: $18. Current: $18. **90**

1987 STONY HILL VINEYARD ESTATE: Elegant and understated, with fresh, well-defined pear, citrus, melon and toast flavors of moderate depth and intensity, a youthful, undeveloped wine that is just beginning to blossom. It's drinkable now but has the depth and balance to improve. Last tasted: 5/90. Drink 1991-1997. 1,195 cases produced. Release: $18. Current: $35. **87**

1986 STONY HILL VINEYARD ESTATE: Ripe, rich and full of fresh pear, honey, nutmeg and oak flavors, this is a very youthful wine that

needs time to fill out. The flavors are well focused, not as ripe or complex yet as most recent vintages, but very well balanced, with all the ingredients to move up a notch or two. Last tasted: 7/90. Drink 1992-1999. 1,420 cases produced. Release: $16. Current: $55. **87**

1985 STONY HILL VINEYARD ESTATE: A highly successful vintage for Stony Hill, very ripe and rich, packed with intense, sharply focused pear, honey, toast, melon and nutmeg flavors that are remarkably elegant and smooth, finishing with a rich, creamy aftertaste that lingers on and on. Last tasted: 5/90. Drink 1991-2000. 1,947 cases produced. Release: $16. Current: $61. **92**

1984 STONY HILL VINEYARD ESTATE: Very ripe and forward, with generous pear, melon, spice and subtle pine and oak shadings, the richest and most flavorful Stony Hill in years. I have tasted this wine more than half a dozen times, and it is holding quite well, gaining complexity with age. Perfect now. Last tasted: 5/90. Drink 1991-1998. 1,820 cases produced. Release: $13. Current: $70. **90**

1983 STONY HILL VINEYARD ESTATE: Intense and full-bodied, lush yet elegant, with subtle nutmeg, pear and melon flavors that are tightly knit and fully evolved. Drinking very well now and should continue for another six to eight years. Last tasted: 5/90. Drink 1991-1996. 1,934 cases produced. Release: $13. Current: $70. **85**

1982 STONY HILL VINEYARD ESTATE: Quite successful for this troubled vintage, it has with age became more pleasing, with elegant, delicate, creamy pear and melon flavors and fine balance, finishing with good length. At its apogee. Last tasted: 5/90. Drink 1991-1994. 2,747 cases produced. Release: $12. Current: $66. **85**

1981 STONY HILL VINEYARD ESTATE: Typical of the vintage, very ripe, rich and forward, big and full, with spice, honey, pear, vanilla and nutmeg flavors that glide across the palate with a creamy smooth texture. At its peak. Last tasted: 5/90. Drink 1991-1996. 2,137 cases produced. Release: $12. Current: $68. **86**

1980 STONY HILL VINEYARD ESTATE: Rich, full-bodied and ripe, with intense honey, pear, spice and vanilla flavors all neatly knit and balanced, fully developed and ready to drink, but it appears to have the depth and richness to gain for another decade. Last tasted: 5/90. Drink 1991-1998. 2,220 cases produced. Release: $12. Current: $75. **86**

1979 STONY HILL VINEYARD ESTATE: Deep mature color, with toasty hazelnut, spice and fig flavors, but in decline and beginning to lose its fruit. Best to drink soon. Last tasted: 5/90. Drink 1991-1994. 2,250 cases produced. Release: $12. Current: $108. **81**

1978 STONY HILL VINEYARD ESTATE: Fully mature, yellow-gold, a bit alcoholic but holding up well, with rich, ripe pear, lemon, honey, spice and cocoa flavors and a soft, smooth texture. Not likely to improve. Last tasted: 5/90. Drink 1991-1996. 1,750 cases produced. Release: $10. Current: $90. **85**

1977 STONY HILL VINEYARD ESTATE: Almost opposite in style from the 1976, high in acidity and austere in character, with fresh, vibrant pear, citrus and melon notes that are clean and refreshing. Delicate, with excellent balance, it still has years of life ahead. Last tasted: 6/90. Drink 1991-1999. 1,032 cases produced. Release: $9. Current: $95. **91**

1976 STONY HILL VINEYARD ESTATE: Very rich, bold and ripe, with layers of honey, pear, toast and butter flavors that offer excellent depth. With aeration it develops further complexities and subtleties. One of the few successes of the 1976 vintage. Last tasted: 6/90. Drink 1991-1997. 670 cases produced. Release: $9. Current: $120. **88**

1975 STONY HILL VINEYARD ESTATE: A sulfur quality is evident in this wine. It has a strong flavor and aroma, and it is coarse on the palate. At 15 years of age, it has developed a charm of its own, but some may not be able to look past the sulfur character. Last tasted: 5/90. Drink 1991-1993. 855 cases produced. Release: $9. Current: $125. **75**

1974 STONY HILL VINEYARD ESTATE: Appears to have more oak and sulfur than fruit, giving the wine a slight rubbery sulfur flavor. Altogether pleasant but those especially sensitive to sulfur may find that quality distracting. Last tasted: 5/90. Drink 1991-1993. 1,280 cases produced. Release: $7. Current: $110. **73**

1973 STONY HILL VINEYARD ESTATE: Fading now, but early on it was quite lovely. Delicate, with pretty pear and melon flavors. Last tasted: 5/90. Drink 1991-1992. 1,250 cases produced. Release: $7. Current: $120. **79**

1972 STONY HILL VINEYARD ESTATE: Elegant and delicate, with pear, anise and spice notes that are a bit blunt, a very good wine from a difficult vintage in most of Napa Valley. Last tasted: 5/90. Drink 1991-1992. 645 cases produced. Release: $7. Current: $110. **83**

1971 STONY HILL VINEYARD ESTATE: Fresh and open when first poured, but not quite as full in the glass, where the ginger, pear and vanilla flavors are delicate and light. Past its prime but still enjoyable. Last tasted: 5/90. Drink 1991-1992. 580 cases produced. Release: $6. Current: $110. **80**

1970 STONY HILL VINEYARD ESTATE: Ripe, rich, smooth and complex, drinking in peak condition, distinctive with its creamy vanilla flavors and texture, hints of pear, spice and honey, each pure enough to capture your attention. Remarkable persistence of flavor. Last tasted: 5/90. Drink 1991-1996. 685 cases produced. Release: $6. Current: $175. **92**

1969 STONY HILL VINEYARD ESTATE: Oxidized the last time I tasted it, but in previous tastings it was right in step with the classics of the 1960s, rich, flavorful, delicate and complex. Last tasted: 5/90. Drink 1991-1993. 750 cases produced. Release: $5. Current: $175. **85**

1968 STONY HILL VINEYARD ESTATE: A wine of great concentration and depth that curiously may still be a few years from peaking. It offers intense honey, pear, spice and vanilla flavors that are rich and elegant, very sharply focused, long and satisfying on the finish. In sync

with the 1962 and 1964 vintages, but perhaps still holding back just a little. Last tasted: 5/90. Drink 1991-1996. 750 cases produced. Release: $5. Current: $250. **93**

1967 STONY HILL VINEYARD ESTATE: More mature in color than most Stony Hills of the 1960s, perhaps an oxidized sample, but with enough earth, honey, pear and butter flavors to provide complexity and intrigue. On its way down. Last tasted: 5/90. Drink 1991-1992. 700 cases produced. Release: $4.50. Current: $250. **83**

1966 STONY HILL VINEYARD ESTATE: At first seemingly lighter and not very concentrated, but with aeration it develops a wonderful concentration of pear, spice, vanilla and nutmeg flavors that each gain prominence and then blend into the background. Wonderful interplay of flavors and textures. Last tasted: 5/90. Drink 1991-1995. 150 cases produced. Release: $4.50. Current: $300. **91**

1965 STONY HILL VINEYARD ESTATE: Forward and fruity, with a silky smooth texture and a wealth of honey, pear, melon and spice nuances that are amazingly persistent, elegant and impeccably balanced. Acidity carries the flavors on and on. Last tasted: 5/90. Drink 1991-1994. 300 cases produced. Release: $4. Current: $400. **90**

1964 STONY HILL VINEYARD ESTATE: The greatest Stony Hill ever produced and the finest California Chardonnay I've ever tasted, the 1964 opens up to reveal rich, intense, deeply concentrated fruit flavors that echo earth, mushroom, honey, toast and pear notes before developing a creamy butterscotch aftertaste. Continued to develop and hold up in the glass for several hours. A sensational wine. Last tasted: 5/90. Drink 1991-2000. 300 cases produced. Release: $4. Current: $450. **98**

1963 STONY HILL VINEYARD ESTATE: Very ripe, with complex fruit and vanilla notes, tiers of intense yet subtle pear and pineapple flavors that are beginning to lose their vitality on the finish, but this is still a very complete wine that has aged incredibly well. Last tasted: 5/90. Drink 1991-1993. 160 cases produced. Release: $4. Current: $450. **87**

1962 STONY HILL VINEYARD ESTATE: Absolutely wonderful, complex and elegant, with subtlety and finesse and a broad array of sharply focused pear, honey, butterscotch and nutmeg flavors that fan out on the palate, finishing with intensity and great length. Chardonnay doesn't get much better. In spite of its age, this wine shows no sign of losing its vitality. Last tasted: 5/90. Drink 1991-1998. 275 cases produced. Release: $3.25. Current: $450. **96**

1960 STONY HILL VINEYARD ESTATE: Remarkably youthful and lively for a 30-year-old Chardonnay, still quite rich, with delicate pear and spice flavors and a touch of pineapple, deftly balanced, with a creamy vanilla texture and a long, lingering finish. Last tasted: 5/90. Drink 1991-1995. 200 cases produced. Release: $3. Current: $430. **88**

TREFETHEN VINEYARDS
Yountville, Napa Valley

CLASSIFICATION: *SECOND GROWTH*
COLLECTIBILITY RATING: *AA*
BEST VINTAGES: *1988, 1978, 1987, 1985*

With 196 acres of mature Chardonnay vines in the heart of the Oak Knoll area, Trefethen Vineyards has come to symbolize the style of fruity, elegant, ageworthy Chardonnays grown in this cool part of Napa Valley. Trefethen Vineyards was founded and planted in 1968 by the Trefethen family, five years before their first Chardonnay vintage in 1973. The winery is owned by the Trefethen family and managed by Janet and John Trefethen. An integral part of their winemaking team is David Whitehouse, winemaker since the 1975 vintage, and vineyard manager Tony Baldini. The Trefethens only use a portion of their Chardonnay grapes for their own wines. Early on they were major Chardonnay growers for Domaine Chandon, the French-owned sparkling wine producer, and they still sell to Cakebread and Joseph Phelps Vineyards.

The Oak Knoll area is not an official appellation, but it is likely to become one at some future date. This area is about halfway between the city of Napa and Yountville and cuts a wide band across the valley, roughly from the Silverado Trail on the east to the western foothills west of Highway 29. Trefethen is right in the middle of this area, which is one of the cooler spots in the valley and ideally suited for Chardonnay. On many days the low fog hangs along the Napa River as the sun shines on the surrounding vineyards. In the evenings it's also breezy. It's not quite as cool as Carneros, but it is close. In this climate Chardonnay grapes ripen slowly and evenly, with good natural acidities and plenty of ripe flavors. The Trefethen style emphasizes ripe, rich, clean apple, pear and citrus flavors. Only rarely, in very hot vintages, do the grapes get overripe. Trefethen's wines are not put through malolactic fermentation, nor are they barrel fermented, so they remain pure expressions of Chardonnay fruit.

The oldest vintage, the 1973, is still in very fine condition, youthful for its age, with honey and melon flavors. The 1974 is fully mature and beginning to lose its fruit, but there is still much to admire in this wine. The 1975 tasted gamy and earthy the last time around, less showy than in earlier years. The 1976, from a drought year, is very elegant but showing its age. The 1977 was a classy wine for its first decade, but it is now drying out and should be consumed. The 1978 remains one of my favorites, from a huge, very ripe crop. It is a deep, rich, powerful wine with layers

AT A GLANCE
TREFETHEN VINEYARDS
1160 Oak Knoll Ave.
Napa, CA 94558
(707) 255-7700
Owner: Trefethen Vineyards Inc.
Winemaker: David Whitehouse (15 years)
Founded: 1968
First Chardonnay vintage: 1973
Chardonnay production: 28,000 cases
Chardonnay acres owned: 196
Average age of vines: 15 years
Average wine makeup: Yountville, Napa Valley (100%)
Time in oak: 6 months (65%)
Type of oak: French (Limousin)
Oak age: 1 to 7 years old
Winemaking notes:
  Barrel fermentation: none
  Malolactic fermentation: none
  Lees aging: none

of flavor and a long, full finish. The 1979 was also rather racy early on, but is now drying out. The 1980 has aged well and offers a wealth of fruit. The 1981 was showy early on but it too is declining and should be consumed. The 1982 and 1983 have followed a similar pattern. While they were lovely in their youth, they are now dry and losing their charm. From 1984 to 1988, the wines are all very good and bordering on outstanding, although I think they're missing that extra dimension of complexity and finesse to push them into the class of California's finest. Perhaps with bottle time, wines like the excellent 1985, 1987 and 1988 will gain that added dimension. Certainly this winery has the commitment and the grapes to achieve wines of even greater richness and depth. Production has reached 28,000 cases with the 1988 vintage.

TASTING NOTES

TREFETHEN VINEYARDS, Yountville, Napa Valley

1988 TREFETHEN VINEYARDS: Another delicious young Trefethen Chardonnay that is a couple of years away from maturity. The crisp, fresh apple, pear and citrus flavors are youthful and vibrant, with lively, mouthwatering acidity that carries the flavors on the finish. Last tasted: 3/90. Drink 1992-1997. 28,000 cases produced. Not released. **90**

1987 TREFETHEN VINEYARDS: Continues a streak of excellent wines, fresh, ripe, clean and elegant, with subtle, ripe pear, melon and citrus notes. Youthful and tight, it needs another year or so to mature fully, then it should hold well for another five. Last tasted: 3/90. Drink 1992-1996. 29,115 cases produced. Release: $16. Current: $16. **88**

1986 TREFETHEN VINEYARDS: Similar in quality and style to the 1985, a lean, crisp, tightly wound wine with pretty apple, pear and subtle oak seasoning. Well balanced and elegant, with a delicate aftertaste, a very deliberate and successful wine. Last tasted: 3/90. Drink 1992-1996. 26,595 cases produced. Release: $16. Current: $19. **87**

1985 TREFETHEN VINEYARDS: Offers a lovely bouquet of fruit and flowers, with tart, clean, crisp apple, pear and melon flavors that linger. An elegant, subtle, complex wine, at its peak and capable of aging another three to five years. Last tasted: 3/90. Drink 1991-1995. 23,016 cases produced. Release: $15. Current: $24. **88**

1984 TREFETHEN VINEYARDS: At its peak, with plenty of fresh, ripe, generous layers of apple, melon, peach and spicy oak flavors, all well balanced and carrying through on the finish. Last tasted: 3/90. Drink 1991-1993. 20,291 cases produced. Release: $14. Current: $25. **86**

1983 TREFETHEN VINEYARDS: Smoky, earthy and very gamy, this wine appears to be turning in the bottle, losing its earlier fruity charm. Best to drink up. Last tasted: 3/90. Drink 1991. 18,942 cases produced. Release: $13. Current: $27. **77**

1982 TREFETHEN VINEYARDS: Early on extremely rich and fruity, one of the top wines from the vintage. My most recent tasting showed that it's slowly oxidizing and drying out on the finish. Last tasted: 3/90. Drink 1991. 15,318 cases produced. Release: $13. Current: $28. **73**

1981 TREFETHEN VINEYARDS: While a shade past its prime, it still offers attractive pineapple, apple, pear and melon flavors that begin to taper off on the finish. Last tasted: 3/90. Drink 1991-1992. 12,933 cases produced. Release: $13. Current: $28. **83**

1980 TREFETHEN VINEYARDS: Another very ripe and full-bodied Chardonnay that has aged exceptionally well, displaying rich tropical fruit, pineapple, lemon, pear and melon notes that hold up well and linger on the finish. In the style of the 1978, holding on. Last tasted: 3/90. Drink 1991-1993. 9,369 cases produced. Release: $13. Current: $30. **86**

1979 TREFETHEN VINEYARDS: Not quite as showy as the 1978, the 1979 has drunk well most of its life, but is now in decline and drying out. Last tasted: 3/90. Drink 1991. 9,486 cases produced. Release: $12. Current: $30. **73**

1978 TREFETHEN VINEYARDS: Big, rich and deep, a very ripe wine from a warm, ripe vintage, packing a lot of lively flavor, with layers of peach, pear, melon, butter and spice flavors that gain intensity and breadth on the finish. Clearly one of the top 1978s. Last tasted: 3/90. Drink 1991-1994. 6,352 cases produced. Release: $10. Current: $40. **90**

1977 TREFETHEN VINEYARDS: Elegant and stylish, with pretty honey, pear, toast and nutmeg flavors that are beginning to dry out. Still, there's enough flavor to like in this wine and there's a tasty finish. Last tasted: 3/90. Drink 1991. 3,966 cases produced. Release: $8. Current: $40. **81**

1976 TREFETHEN VINEYARDS: Elegant and refined but showing its age, with decent ripe pear and vanilla flavors. Best to drink it soon. Last tasted: 3/90. Drink 1991. 3,358 cases produced. Release: $7. Current: $40. **74**

1975 TREFETHEN VINEYARDS: Gamy, earthy mushroom notes cloud the smooth, creamy butterscotch flavors. Beginning to unravel, but still drinkable. Last tasted: 3/90. Drink 1991. 1,449 cases produced. Release: $6. Current: $45. **73**

1974 TREFETHEN VINEYARDS: Past its peak but still alive, with rich, deep, concentrated fruit flavors and gamy juniper notes, but it is smooth, creamy and buttery. Last tasted: 3/90. Drink 1991-1993. 1,294 cases produced. Release: $5. Current: $50. **80**

1973 TREFETHEN VINEYARDS: Trefethen's first vintage is still quite youthful for its age. It carries a 16 percent alcohol level, which may account for part of its longevity, but it also shows some pretty honey, pear and melon flavors. Very little evidence of oxidation. Last tasted: 3/90. Drink 1991-1993. 643 cases produced. Release: $6. Current: $50. **85**

VICHON WINERY
Napa Valley

CLASSIFICATION: *FOURTH GROWTH*
COLLECTIBILITY RATING: *Not rated*
BEST VINTAGES: *1986, 1988, 1985*

Despite owning no Chardonnay vineyards, Vichon has made consistent Chardonnays through the years, with well-defined fruit flavors and subtle oak shadings, resulting in wines of elegance, grace and complexity. This Napa Valley winery was founded in 1980 by a trio of partners, George Vierra, Peter Brucher and Doug Watson, who took letters from their last names to come up with the French-sounding Vichon.

Under Vierra, Vichon was at the forefront of the "food wine" craze of the early 1980s, with a style that featured crisp acidity, lees aging, barrel fermentation and partial malolactic fermentation.

While many producers made very tart, highly acidic Chardonnays during this period, Vichon's show good balance, particularly the 1980, which is still drinking well. The 1981, 1982 and 1983 vintages are not in as good shape, but the wines since 1984 are aging well. The 1985 is very elegant and well balanced, with plenty of flavor. The 1986 is the best of the group, a deep, rich and complex wine that can stand further aging. The 1987 offers ripe, creamy fruit flavors, and the 1988 is well balanced and harmonious. Since 1984 the winery has been owned by the Robert Mondavi family. The grapes are purchased from vineyards around Napa, including vineyards in Big Ranch Road, Coombsville, Carneros and the Oakville-Yountville areas. Karen Culler is winemaker.

TASTING NOTES

VICHON WINERY, Napa Valley

1988 VICHON WINERY: A wonderful harmony of ripe, rich honey, butter and pear flavors that are well focused and framed by pretty toasty oak, leaving a hint of clove on the aftertaste. Youthful and intense, yet elegant. Last tasted: 3/90. Drink 1991-1996. 25,800 cases produced. Release: $17. Current: $17. **88**

1987 VICHON WINERY: Highly successful, with plenty of fresh, ripe, creamy layers of pear, apple and subtle oak flavors that are coming together. Delicious now but can age up to five years. Slow to develop.

Last tasted: 3/90. Drink 1991-1996. 13,500 cases produced. Release: $16. Current: $16. **87**

1986 VICHON WINERY: Vichon's finest to date, a full, deep, rich and complex wine with well-defined fruit flavors and toasty oak. The ripe pear, apple, nutmeg and spice flavors gain a honey note on the finish. Impeccable balance. Last tasted: 3/90. Drink 1991-1996. 8,000 cases produced. Release: $15. Current: $17. **90**

1985 VICHON WINERY: A wonderfully elegant and balanced wine with fresh, clean, crisp apple, pear and toasty oak flavors, all in harmony and finishing with fine length. Youthful and aging well. Last tasted: 3/90. Drink 1991-1995. 20,900 cases produced. Release: $15. Current: $17. **88**

1984 VICHON WINERY: Delicious, with fresh, ripe, rich apple, pear, spice and honey flavors in a full-blown yet elegant style, finishing with delicate toast and spicy fruit flavors. Last tasted: 3/90. Drink 1991-1994. 17,600 cases produced. Release: $15. Current: $17. **86**

1983 VICHON WINERY: Overly mature, with oxidized apple, honey and caramel flavors that may have limited appeal. Last tasted: 3/90. Drink 1991. 14,900 cases produced. Release: $15. Current: $18. **71**

1982 VICHON WINERY: Heavily oxidized, with very mature honey and earth flavors. From a troubled vintage, this one's barely alive. Last tasted: 3/90. Best to avoid. 9,500 cases produced. Release: $15. Current: $20. **66**

1981 VICHON WINERY: Fully mature, with a touch of oxidation and a juniper berry note, past its prime but still enjoyable for its honey and butterscotch flavors. Better a few years back. Last tasted: 3/90. Drink 1991-1993. 7,000 cases produced. Release: $15. Current: $25. **76**

1980 VICHON WINERY: Vichon's first Chardonnay is aging more gracefully than most 1980s; this is still a fresh, crisp, fruity wine with flinty pear, pineapple and apple flavors that are sharply focused, finishing with good length and lively acidity. Last tasted: 3/90. Drink 1991-1995. 3,800 cases produced. Release: $15. Current: $30. **87**

AT A GLANCE

WHITE OAK VINEYARDS AND WINERY
208 Haydon St.
Healdsburg, CA 95448
(707) 433-8429

Owner: Bill Myers, general partner

Winemaker: Paul Brasset (7 years)

Founded: 1981

First Chardonnay vintage: 1981
    Myers Limited Release: 1985

Chardonnay production: 7,000 cases
    Myers Limited Release: 1,000 cases
    Sonoma County: 6,000 cases

Chardonnay acres owned: 45

Average age of vines: 21 years

Average wine makeup:
    Myers Limited Release: Alexander Valley (60%), Russian River Valley (40%)
    Sonoma County: Alexander Valley (50%), Russian River Valley (50%)

Time in oak:
    Myers Limited Release: 9 months
    Sonoma County: 4 months (50%), 8 months (50%)

Type of oak: French (Limousin, Nevers)

Oak age:
    Myers Limited Release: New (100%)
    Sonoma County: 1 to 3 years

Winemaking notes:
    Barrel fermentation:
        Myers Limited Release: 100%
        Sonoma County: 50%
    Malolactic fermentation:
        Myers Limited Release: none
        Sonoma County: 20%
    Lees aging:
        Myers Limited Release: none
        Sonoma County: 30% (4 months)

WHITE OAK VINEYARDS AND WINERY

Myers Limited Release, Sonoma County
Sonoma County

CLASSIFICATION: *FIFTH GROWTH*

COLLECTIBILITY RATING: *Not rated*

BEST VINTAGES:

Myers Limited Release: 1985, 1988

Sonoma County: 1988, 1985

A specialist with two different styles of Chardonnay, White Oak Vineyards and Winery in Sonoma County is one of California's most underrated producers. Founded in 1981 by Bill Myers, this winery in Healdsburg owns 45 acres of Chardonnay and makes about 7,000 cases a year, 1,000 under the Myers Limited Release designation.

While the Myers Limited Release is the better of the two wines, the White Oak Sonoma County also has special merit. The Sonoma County Chardonnay is a blend of grapes grown in Alexander Valley and Russian River Valley. It is 50 percent barrel fermented, and 20 percent undergoes malolactic fermentation.

The Chardonnays since 1984 have been consistently very good, particularly the 1985, which is a delicious wine with intense yet elegant fruit flavors. The 1984 and 1986 vintages are maturing more quickly than the 1985, but the 1987 is coarse and will need time to soften. The 1988 is fresh and forward in a delicate style. The Myers Limited Release is more austere and usually more oaky. It is 100 percent barrel fermented, but does not undergo any malolactic fermentation. The 1985, the first offering, is fairly toasty and intense, but beautifully proportioned. The 1986 offers a shade more subtlety and grace, with lively acidity. The 1987 is even more subtle and understated, without the richness of other bottlings. The 1988 is big, ripe and intense, with smoky, toasty flavors.

TASTING NOTES

WHITE OAK VINEYARDS AND WINERY, Myers
Limited Release, Sonoma County

1988 WHITE OAK VINEYARDS AND WINERY MYERS LIMITED RELEASE: Big, rich, ripe and intense, loaded with spicy pear and pineapple flavors that are youthful and undeveloped. Plenty of vanilla and oak flavors too, but it's balanced and concentrated, finishing with a pretty smoky, toasty flavor. Last tasted: 5/90. Drink 1992-1997. 988 cases produced. Release: $18. Current: $20. **88**

1987 WHITE OAK VINEYARDS AND WINERY MYERS LIMITED RELEASE: Subtle and understated, with fresh vanilla and butter notes and ripe, moderately rich pear and honey flavors, elegantly balance. Not as austere as many 1987s, but also not as rich and flavorful as the best. Last tasted: 5/90. Drink 1991-1994. 843 cases produced. Release: $18. Current: $20. **81**

1986 WHITE OAK VINEYARDS AND WINERY MYERS LIMITED RELEASE: A shade more subtlety and grace than the 1985 Reserve, but quite complete, with fresh honey, pear and vanilla flavors that are deftly balanced and displaying plenty of crisp, lemony acidity on the finish. Last tasted: 5/90. Drink 1991-1996. 621 cases produced. Release: $16. Current: $20. **87**

1985 WHITE OAK VINEYARDS AND WINERY MYERS LIMITED RELEASE ALEXANDER VALLEY: Showing considerable toasty oak and vanilla flavors but it also has intense, concentrated lemon and pear notes to stand up to them. Altogether a very appealing wine that plays intense oak off austere, tightly reined-in fruit. Last tasted: 5/90. Drink 1991-1996. 237 cases produced. Release: $14.50. Current: $22. **90**

WHITE OAK VINEYARDS AND WINERY,
Sonoma County

1988 WHITE OAK VINEYARDS AND WINERY: Fresh and forward, with exotic pear, pineapple and guava flavors that are rich and ripe. Well balanced and delicate in texture, but still providing plenty of flavor, finishing with crisp acidity and excellent length. Last tasted: 5/90. Drink 1991-1996. 6,000 cases produced. Release: $12. Current: $12. **88**

1987 WHITE OAK VINEYARDS AND WINERY: Austere, with a coarse texture but plenty of subtle pear, apple and melon flavors that render it complex and well balanced, finishing with a combination of fruit and oak that is well focused. Last tasted: 5/90. Drink 1991-1996. 4,000 cases produced. Release: $11. Current: $16. **85**

1986 WHITE OAK VINEYARDS AND WINERY: Ripe and forward, oozing with fresh pear, honey and butterscotch flavors that spread out and finish with more subtlety and finesse. Balanced and delicate, should

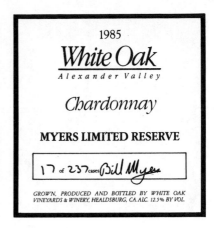

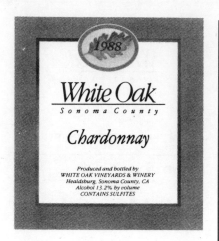

be consumed soon. Last tasted: 5/90. Drink 1991-1995. 3,500 cases produced. Release: $11. Current: $16. **86**

1985 WHITE OAK VINEYARDS AND WINERY: Deliciously rich and elegant, with intense, concentrated pear, apple, melon and spice flavors along with a pretty seasoning of vanilla and toasty oak. Sharply focused, well-integrated flavors, youthful and lively, still on its way up. Very impressive for its balance and finesse. Last tasted: 5/90. Drink 1991-1996. 3,000 cases produced. Release: $10.50. Current: $16. **89**

1984 WHITE OAK VINEYARDS AND WINERY: Graceful and elegant, with ripe, mature honey and pear flavors and vanilla and toasty oak shadings, aging very well and drinking in peak condition now. Not quite as opulent as on release, but perhaps more subtle and complex. Last tasted: 5/90. Drink 1991-1996. 3,000 cases produced. Release: $10. Current: $16. **86**

ZD WINES
California

CLASSIFICATION: *FOURTH GROWTH*
COLLECTIBILITY RATING: *Not rated*
BEST VINTAGES: *1985, 1984, 1988, 1981*

Without any Chardonnay vineyards of its own, Napa Valley-based ZD Wines has searched up and down the state of California, from Napa Valley to Sonoma County to Santa Barbara and Monterey counties, buying grapes for its wines. Despite disparate grape sources, ZD almost always manages to create Chardonnays that offer very ripe, rich, full-blown and often exotic fruit flavors that are lavishly oaked and well proportioned. The winery was founded in 1969 by the families of Norman de Leuze and Gino Zepponi, who used the initials ZD for their brand. The first vintage was the 1971, and for years the winery was based in Sonoma County, but I have not recently tasted any of the older wines.

The winery has been owned by the de Leuze family since Zepponi's death in 1985. Robert de Leuze, son of founder Norm de Leuze, has been winemaker since 1983. Increasingly, as vineyards like Tepusquet Vineyard in Santa Maria have been lost as grape sources, ZD has focused more on Napa Valley grapes, but still carries the California appellation. The 1988 vintage is 64 percent Napa Valley, 17 percent Monterey County, 10 percent Santa Barbara County and 9 percent Sonoma County.

Of the wines from 1980 on, both the 1980 and 1981 are still holding well, while the 1984 is sensational, with classic ZD flavors and proportion. The 1985 is also magnificent, with tiers of fruit in a gentler style, but still packing plenty of fruit and power. The 1986 has been less showy in recent tasting, but may simply be a slow developer. The 1987 is a shade more austere and will need more time to soften. The 1988 offers layers of fresh, ripe fruit, with intense pear and apple flavors and bracing acidity. Production of ZD Chardonnay is at 18,000 cases.

AT A GLANCE

ZD WINES
8383 Silverado Trail
Napa, CA 94558
(707) 963-5188

Owners: Norman and Rosa Lee de Leuze

Winemaker: Robert de Leuze (7 years)

Founded: 1969

First Chardonnay vintage: 1971

Chardonnay production: 17,000 cases

Chardonnay acres owned: none

Average wine makeup: Napa Valley (64%); Monterey County (17%); Santa Barbara County (10%); Sonoma County (9%)

Time in oak: 10 months

Type of oak: French, American

Oak age: new (33%) to 3 years old

Winemaking notes:
    Barrel fermentation: 100%
    Malolactic fermentation: none
    Lees aging: none

TASTING NOTES

ZD WINES, California

1988 ZD WINES: Plenty of delicious, ripe fruit up front, with tiers of peach, pear and apple flavors and just the right amount of oak and crisp,

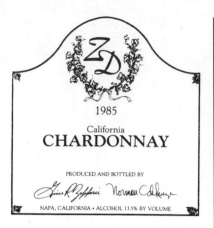

mouthwatering acidity to carry the flavors. Needs another year or so. Last tasted: 3/90. Drink 1992-1996. 18,418 cases produced. Release: $20. Current: $20. **89**

1987 ZD WINES: Ripe and well made, with pretty pear and spice flavors of moderate depth and richness, but like many 1987s not particularly exciting and too understated. More wood than fruit shows on the finish. Last tasted: 3/90. Drink 1991-1995. 15,203 cases produced. Release: $18.50. Current: $24. **85**

1986 ZD WINES: Firm, young, tight and hard, with plenty of melon, lemon, pear and spice notes that are well balanced with oak and supported by crisp, firm acidity. Still a year or two from maturity, it appears to have the balance and intensity to warrant short-term cellaring. Last tasted: 3/90. Drink 1992-1997. 15,773 cases produced. Release: $18. Current: $25. **85**

1985 ZD WINES: Slow to develop, now showing better than ever. It is more understated than the opulent 1984, but some may prefer this, with its well-defined pear, honey, pineapple and butterscotch flavors easing onto the palate. Last tasted: 3/90. Drink 1992-1996. 9,639 cases produced. Release: $16. Current: $28. **90**

1984 ZD WINES: A gorgeous 1984 and one of the best ZD I've tasted, big, full, rich and deep, with layers of complex pear, peach, honey and pineapple flavors and just the right amount of oak, finishing with a rich butterscotch flavor. This wine has improved significantly since its release. Delicious now. Last tasted: 3/90. Drink 1991-1995. 7,631 cases produced. Release: $15. Current: $30. **90**

1983 ZD WINES: Hard, lean and unfriendly, overly woody, without the fruit to stand up to the oak. Still well preserved as 1983s go, but it's doubtful this one will get much better. Last tasted: 3/90. Drink 1991-1994. 5,369 cases produced. Release: $14. Current: $28. **74**

1982 ZD WINES: Pungent and earthy, with dense, vegetal notes overpowering the ripe pineapple flavors. A difficult wine from a tough vintage. It's drinkable, but not everyone's cup of Chardonnay. Last tasted: 3/90. Drink 1991-1993. 5,506 cases produced. Release: $14. Current: $25. **76**

1981 ZD WINES: Mature but aging gracefully, showing ripe yet subtle flavors of honey, spice and pineapple that are complex and well focused. The finish picks up woody nuances, but altogether it's impressive at nine years old. Last tasted: 3/90. Drink 1991-1994. 5,742 cases produced. Release: $13. Current: $28. **87**

1980 ZD WINES: Earthy, rich and vegetal, typical of the vintage, very ripe, opulent and full-bodied, yet for all its flavor it lacks grace and finesse, but is still boldly displaying its intense flavors. Last tasted: 3/90. Drink 1991-1994. 4,005 cases produced. Release: $13. Current: $28. **81**

APPENDICES

APPENDIX 1
All Wines Tasted, Listed Alphabetically by Winery

Score	Vintage	Appellation/Vineyard	Case Production	Release Price	Current Price	Drink	Last Tasted
ACACIA WINERY							
89	1988	Carneros Marina Vineyard	7,133	$20	$20	1991-1996	1/90
85	1987	Carneros Marina Vineyard	8,600	18	19	1991-1995	1/90
86	1986	Carneros Marina Vineyard	6,950	18	22	1991-1994	1/90
80	1985	Carneros Marina Vineyard	5,000	18	19	1991-1993	1/90
86	1984	Carneros Marina Vineyard	5,600	16	22	1991-1994	1/90
79	1983	Carneros Marina Vineyard	5,300	16	23	1991-1993	1/90
85	1988	Carneros	22,300	16	16	1991-1993	1/90
84	1987	Carneros	17,700	17	17	1991-1995	1/90
87	1986	Carneros	11,500	15	18	1991-1993	1/90
80	1985	Carneros	10,000	15	20	1991-1993	1/90
84	1984	Carneros	7,800	14	20	1991-1993	1/90
82	1985	Carneros Winery Lake Vineyard	3700	18	25	1991-1994	1/90
88	1984	Carneros Winery Lake Vineyard	2,100	18	25	1991-1994	1/90
87	1983	Carneros Winery Lake Vineyard	2,460	18	25	1991-1994	1/90
76	1979	Carneros Winery Lake Vineyard	1,400	16	25	1991	1/90
81	1986	Napa Valley	6,700	15	17	1991-1993	1/90
79	1985	Napa Valley	4,900	12.50	16	1991-1992	1/90
89	1984	Napa Valley	7,000	12.50	16	1991-1996	7/90
80	1983	Napa Valley	4,300	12	18	1991-1993	1/90
80	1982	Napa Valley	4,900	12	20	1991-1993	1/90
ALTAMURA WINERY & VINEYARDS							
90	1988	Napa Valley	2,000	NR		1992-1997	1/90
87	1987	Napa Valley	1,800	16.50	16.50	1993-1998	1/90
88	1986	Napa Valley	1,500	15	21	1993-1997	1/90
91	1985	Napa Valley	600	14	21	1991-1996	1/90
S. ANDERSON VINEYARD							
89	1987	Stags Leap District Proprietor's Reserve	480	20	20	1991-1996	3/90
87	1983	Stags Leap District Proprietor's Selection	100	16	40	1991-1993	3/90
88	1988	Stags Leap District Estate	4,388	18	18	1992-1997	3/90
85	1987	Stags Leap District Estate	3,798	16	18	1993-1998	6/90
81	1986	Stags Leap District Estate	4,792	16	18	1991-1994	3/90
92	1985	Stags Leap District Estate	3,500	14	25	1991-1995	3/90
89	1984	Stags Leap District Estate	1,770	12.50	25	1991-1994	3/90
86	1983	Stags Leap District Estate	1,415	12.50	25	1991-1993	3/90
72	1982	Stags Leap District Estate	1,412	12.50	21	1991	3/90
80	1981	Stags Leap District Estate	1,835	12.50	25	1991-1993	3/90
83	1980	Stags Leap District Estate	1,545	12.50	30	1991-1993	3/90
ARROWOOD VINEYARDS & WINERY							
92	1988	Sonoma County	6,300	18	18	1992-1997	4/90
89	1987	Sonoma County	6,000	18	18	1991-1995	4/90
89	1986	Sonoma County	4,600	18	25	1991-1995	4/90
92	1987	Sonoma County Réserve Spéciale 1.5L	57	50	50	1991-1997	4/90

NR — Not released.

Score	Vintage	Appellation / Vineyard	Case Production	Release Price	Current Price	Drink	Last Tasted
BEAULIEU VINEYARD							
89	1988	Carneros Carneros Reserve	10,000	$14	$14	1992-1998	6/90
87	1987	Carneros Los Carneros Reserve	10,000	14	16	1992-1998	5/90
86	1986	Carneros Los Carneros Reserve	10,000	12	15	1991-1996	6/90
84	1985	Carneros Los Carneros Reserve	10,000	12	16	1991-1995	6/90
79	1984	Carneros Los Carneros Reserve	10,000	10	16	1991-1992	4/90
74	1983	Carneros Los Carneros Reserve	5,000	10	15	1991-1992	4/90
72	1982	Carneros Los Carneros Reserve	5,000	10	16	1991-1992	4/90
70	1981	Carneros Los Carneros Reserve	5,000	10	18	1991-1992	4/90
70	1979	Napa Valley Beaufort	30,000	6	20	1991-1992	4/90
70	1978	Napa Valley Beaufort	30,000	6	22	1991	4/90
64	1977	Napa Valley Beaufort	25,000	6	22	Avoid	4/90
62	1976	Napa Valley Beaufort	20,000	6	22	Avoid	4/90
61	1975	Napa Valley Beaufort	20,000	5	28	Avoid	4/90
62	1974	Napa Valley Beaufort	15,000	5	25	Avoid	4/90
60	1973	Napa Valley Beaufort	15,000	5	30	Avoid	4/90
60	1972	Napa Valley Beaufort	12,000	5	30	Avoid	4/90
58	1971	Napa Valley Beaufort	10,000	4	30	Avoid	4/90
59	1970	Napa Valley Beaufort	3,000	4	32	Avoid	4/90
57	1969	Napa Valley Beaufort	3,000	2	35	Avoid	4/90
59	1968	Napa Valley Beaufort	2,000	2	35	Avoid	4/90
BERINGER VINEYARDS							
87	1988	Napa Valley Private Reserve	14,665	19	19	1992-1996	4/90
79	1987	Napa Valley Private Reserve	12,159	17	19	1991-1993	4/90
90	1986	Napa Valley Private Reserve	6,747	16	22	1991-1995	4/90
86	1985	Napa Valley Private Reserve	4,096	15	24	1991-1994	4/90
88	1984	Napa Valley Private Reserve	4,102	15	24	1991-1994	4/90
76	1983	Napa Valley Private Reserve	7,445	15	24	1991-1993	4/90
74	1982	Napa Valley Private Reserve	7,077	15	22	1991-1993	4/90
86	1981	Napa Valley Private Reserve	4,784	15	28	1991-1993	4/90
75	1980	Napa Valley Private Reserve	4,576	15	25	1991-1992	4/90
78	1979	Napa Valley Private Reserve	3,228	14	25	1991-1992	4/90
70	1978	Napa Valley Private Reserve	1,878	12	15	1991	4/90
70	1974	Napa Valley Centennial Cask Selection	1,000	5	40	1991-1992	4/90
88	1974	Santa Barbara County	1,000	5	45	1991-1993	4/90
BOUCHAINE VINEYARDS							
88	1988	Carneros Estate Reserve	1,600	NR		1993-1998	6/90
86	1987	Carneros Estate Reserve	1,600	19	19	1991-1995	2/90
88	1986	Carneros Estate Reserve	1,500	19	19	1991-1995	2/90
85	1988	Carneros	8,400	15	15	1993-1997	6/90
83	1987	Carneros	7,400	14	14	1991-1994	2/90
87	1985	Carneros	2,250	15	20	1991-1993	2/90
85	1984	Carneros	3,400	14	20	1991-1993	2/90
77	1983	Carneros	2,200	14	20	1991-1993	2/90
88	1986	Napa Valley	7,000	13	17	1991-1995	2/90
87	1985	Napa Valley	10,100	13	17	1991-1994	2/90
71	1984	Carneros Winery Lake	2,200	22	22	1991	2/90
66	1984	Napa Valley	9,400	12.50	15	Avoid	2/90
75	1983	Napa Valley	10,000	12.50	18	1991-1992	2/90
79	1982	Alexander Valley	2,000	14	18	1991-1993	2/90
BUENA VISTA WINERY							
86	1988	Carneros Private Reserve	6,150	16.50	17	1993-1999	6/90
82	1987	Carneros Private Reserve	5,500	16.50	17	1991-1994	3/90
91	1986	Carneros Private Reserve	3,700	16.50	17	1991-1996	3/90
86	1985	Carneros Private Reserve	2,700	16.50	17	1991-1995	3/90
75	1984	Carneros Private Reserve	3,000	14.50	16	1991-1992	6/90
84	1983	Carneros Private Reserve	1,000	14.50	18	1991-1994	3/90

NR — Not released.

Score	Vintage	Appellation/Vineyard	Case Production	Release Price	Current Price	Drink	Last Tasted
BURGESS CELLARS							
88	1988	Napa Valley Triere Vineyard	18,000	$16	$16	1991-1996	12/89
85	1987	Napa Valley Triere Vineyard	18,000	14.50	15	1991-1996	12/89
87	1986	Napa Valley Triere Vineyard	17,000	14	16	1991-1994	12/89
88	1985	Napa Valley Vintage Reserve	17,000	13	16	1990-1995	12/89
79	1984	Napa Valley Vintage Reserve	17,000	13	17	1991-1994	12/89
69	1983	Napa Valley Vintage Reserve	16,000	12	14	Avoid	12/89
68	1982	Napa Valley Vintage Reserve	16,000	12	12	Avoid	12/89
74	1981	Napa Valley	15,000	11	16	1991-1992	12/89
75	1980	Napa Valley	5,500	11	18	1991-1992	12/89
78	1979	Napa Valley	5,500	11	18	1991-1994	12/89
77	1978	Napa Valley	4,200	11	18	1991-1994	12/89
80	1977	Napa Valley	4,000	11	23	1991-1992	12/89
70	1976	Carneros Winery Lake Vineyard	1,300	10	20	1991	12/89
84	1975	Carneros Winery Lake Vineyard	770	9	28	1991-1994	12/89
79	1974	Carneros Winery Lake Vineyard	700	6	25	1991	12/89
85	1973	Napa Valley	400	6	30	1991-1993	12/89
CHALONE VINEYARD							
89	1988	Chalone Reserve	217	NR	NR	1992-2000	6/90
87	1987	Chalone Reserve	727	NR	NR	1992-2000	5/90
85	1986	Chalone Reserve	379	28	38	1991-1995	5/90
94	1985	Chalone Reserve	308	28	42	1991-1998	6/90
87	1983	Chalone Reserve	617	25	45	1991-1997	5/90
93	1982	Chalone Reserve	498	25	48	1991-1996	5/90
86	1981	Chalone Reserve	400	20	55	1991-1996	5/90
94	1980	Chalone Reserve	166	18	55	1991-1997	5/90
90	1988	Chalone	8,003	22	27	1992-1999	6/90
58	1987	Chalone	5,442	22	30	Avoid	1/90
94	1986	Chalone	4,768	22	48	1991-1998	1/90
80	1985	Chalone	3,686	22	45	1991-1994	4/90
88	1984	Chalone	2,885	18	45	1991-1998	1/90
90	1983	Chalone	6,669	18	50	1991-1998	1/90
95	1982	Chalone	5,125	18	53	1991-1996	1/90
93	1981	Chalone	3,545	17	53	1991-1996	4/90
92	1980	Chalone	3,510	17	53	1991-1995	1/90
89	1979	Chalone	3,728	14	55	1991-1994	1/90
CHAPPELLET VINEYARD							
89	1988	Napa Valley	4,500	NR	NR	1991-1998	6/90
87	1987	Napa Valley	3,817	14	14	1993-2000	3/90
90	1986	Napa Valley	4,500	14	14	1991-1997	3/90
87	1985	Napa Valley	3,300	12.50	15	1991-1996	3/90
87	1984	Napa Valley	4,500	12	20	1991-1995	3/90
79	1983	Napa Valley	6,000	12	18	1991	3/90
85	1982	Napa Valley	7,200	12.50	20	1991-1993	3/90
80	1981	Napa Valley	3,947	14	22	1991	3/90
84	1980	Napa Valley	4,000	14	25	1991-1992	3/90
79	1979	Napa Valley	3,000	12	30	1991	3/90
76	1978	Napa Valley	1,500	11.75	40	1991	3/90
90	1977	Napa Valley	1,500	11.75	40	1991-1998	6/90
71	1976	Napa Valley	1,000	9.75	30	1991	3/90
82	1975	Napa Valley	800	6.75	40	1991	3/90
72	1974	Napa Valley	600	6.75	45	1991	3/90
91	1973	Napa Valley	400	6.75	50	1991-1994	3/90

NR — Not released.

Score	Vintage	Appellation / Vineyard	Case Production	Release Price	Current Price	Drink	Last Tasted
CHATEAU MONTELENA WINERY							
91	1988	Alexander Valley	3,100	$20	$20	1992-2000	2/90
89	1987	Alexander Valley	5,400	20	24	1992-1998	2/90
91	1986	Alexander Valley	5,700	18	26	1991-1997	2/90
91	1985	Alexander Valley	8,600	16	28	1991-1997	2/90
90	1984	Alexander Valley	5,600	16	32	1991-1997	2/90
84	1983	Alexander Valley	5,600	14	32	1991-1994	2/90
92	1982	Alexander Valley	5,800	14	36	1991-1996	2/90
91	1981	Alexander Valley	2,600	14	36	1991-1997	2/90
88	1988	Napa Valley	13,200	20	20	1993-2000	7/90
68	1987	Napa Valley	12,500	20	25	Avoid	2/90
91	1986	Napa Valley	12,800	18	25	1991-1998	2/90
90	1985	Napa Valley	9,000	18	25	1991-1998	2/90
88	1984	Napa Valley	8,400	18	28	1991-1995	2/90
85	1983	Napa Valley	6,600	16	32	1991-1994	2/90
85	1982	Napa Valley	6,900	16	32	1991-1994	2/90
88	1981	Napa Valley	7,900	16	32	1991-1994	2/90
79	1980	Napa Valley	7,000	16	38	1991	2/90
78	1979	Napa Valley	7,800	16	38	1991	2/90
77	1978	Napa Valley	7,100	15	45	1991	2/90
85	1977	Napa Valley	6,000	15	60	1991-1993	2/90
77	1976	Napa and Alexander Valleys	2,500	11	50	1991	2/90
87	1975	Napa Valley	3,300	9	65	1991-1993	2/90
88	1974	Napa and Alexander Valleys	2,200	8	70	1991-1996	2/90
93	1973	Napa and Alexander Valleys	2,000	6.50	100	1991-1998	2/90
95	1972	Napa and Alexander Valleys	2,000	6	110	1991-1997	2/90
CHATEAU ST. JEAN							
96	1987	Alexander Valley Robert Young Vineyards Reserve 1.5L	112	NR	NR	1993-2000	7/90
91	1986	Alexander Valley Robert Young Vineyards Reserve 1.5L	507	NR	NR	1992-2000	7/90
95	1985	Alexander Valley Robert Young Vineyards Reserve 1.5L	978	40	40	1992-1998	7/90
87	1984	Alexander Valley Robert Young Vineyards Reserve 1.5L	918	40	50	1991-1993	3/90
91	1988	Alexander Valley Robert Young Vineyards	13,638	18	18	1992-1998	3/90
91	1987	Alexander Valley Robert Young Vineyards	13,108	18	25	1992-1999	3/90
92	1986	Alexander Valley Robert Young Vineyards	13,007	18	25	1992-1998	3/90
91	1985	Alexander Valley Robert Young Vineyards	13,613	18	26	1992-1998	3/90
88	1984	Alexander Valley Robert Young Vineyards	13,513	20	30	1991-1995	3/90
88	1983	Alexander Valley Robert Young Vineyards	7,697	18	33	1991-1994	3/90
75	1982	Alexander Valley Robert Young Vineyards	8,645	18	20	1991-1993	3/90
86	1981	Alexander Valley Robert Young Vineyards	8,586	18	25	1991-1993	3/90
85	1980	Alexander Valley Robert Young Vineyards	6,832	18	30	1991-1993	3/90
85	1979	Alexander Valley Robert Young Vineyards	5,344	17	30	1991-1994	3/90
84	1978	Alexander Valley Robert Young Vineyards	1,099	17	25	1991-1993	3/90
68	1977	Alexander Valley Robert Young Vineyards	1,597	17	22	Avoid	3/90
92	1976	Alexander Valley Robert Young Vineyards	1,400	8.75	25	1991-1994	7/90
63	1975	Alexander Valley Robert Young Vineyards	900	7.75	22	Avoid	7/90
90	1988	Alexander Valley Belle Terre Vineyards	8,848	16	16	1993-1998	3/90
91	1987	Alexander Valley Belle Terre Vineyards	2,590	16	22	1992-1998	3/90
90	1986	Alexander Valley Belle Terre Vineyards	3,625	16	20	1992-1997	3/90
92	1985	Alexander Valley Belle Terre Vineyards	3,371	16	25	1992-1996	3/90
85	1984	Alexander Valley Belle Terre Vineyards	6,384	16	27	1991-1995	3/90
89	1983	Alexander Valley Belle Terre Vineyards	1,281	16.75	30	1991-1995	3/90
86	1982	Alexander Valley Belle Terre Vineyards	4,735	15.50	20	1991-1995	3/90
83	1981	Alexander Valley Belle Terre Vineyards	3,847	15	18	1991-1995	3/90
88	1980	Alexander Valley Belle Terre Vineyards	4,427	15	24	1991-1994	3/90
84	1979	Alexander Valley Belle Terre Vineyards	3,668	12	22	1991-1993	3/90
73	1978	Alexander Valley Belle Terre Vineyards	2,194	14	20	1991	3/90
80	1977	Alexander Valley Belle Terre Vineyards	799	12	22	1991	3/90
77	1976	Alexander Valley Belle Terre Vineyards	1,100	7.50	22	1991-1992	7/90
88	1975	Alexander Valley Belle Terre Vineyards	800	7.50	22	1991-1993	7/90
89	1986	Dry Creek Valley Frank Johnson Vineyards	2,115	14	19	1991-1995	7/90
87	1985	Dry Creek Valley Frank Johnson Vineyards	1,517	14	14	1993-1997	3/90

NR — Not released.

Score	Vintage	Appellation / Vineyard	Case Production	Release Price	Current Price	Drink	Last Tasted
88	1984	Dry Creek Valley Frank Johnson Vineyards	3,100	$14	$20	1991-1995	7/90
79	1980	Dry Creek Valley Frank Johnson Vineyards	1,257	14	16	1991-1992	3/90
78	1979	Dry Creek Valley Frank Johnson Vineyards	349	13.50	15	1991	3/90
88	1988	Alexander Valley Jimtown Ranch	700	NR		1992-1998	7/90
87	1987	Alexander Valley Jimtown Ranch	689	15	15	1993-1997	3/90
87	1983	Alexander Valley Jimtown Ranch	1,166	16	20	1991-1996	7/90
87	1981	Alexander Valley Jimtown Ranch	1,720	14.75	22	1991-1995	3/90
77	1980	Alexander Valley Jimtown Ranch	864	14	16	1991	3/90
88	1987	Sonoma Valley McCrea Vineyards	364	15	15	1992-1996	3/90
87	1986	Sonoma Valley McCrea Vineyards	163	15	17	1992-1996	3/90
86	1985	Sonoma Valley McCrea Vineyards	1,543	14.25	17	1991-1996	7/90
87	1984	Sonoma Valley McCrea Vineyards	1,601	14.25	17	1991-1995	3/90
85	1983	Sonoma Valley McCrea Vineyards	1,009	15.25	18	1991-1995	7/90
88	1982	Sonoma Valley McCrea Vineyards	501	13	18	1991-1995	7/90
75	1981	Sonoma Valley McCrea Vineyards	846	15	18	1991-1992	3/90
70	1980	Sonoma Valley McCrea Vineyards	465	15	18	1991-1992	3/90
70	1979	Sonoma Valley McCrea Vineyards	325	14	18	1991	3/90
70	1978	Sonoma Valley McCrea Vineyards	309	12	20	1991	3/90
85	1977	Sonoma Valley McCrea Vineyards	346	10.25	25	1991	3/90
75	1976	Sonoma Valley McCrea Vineyards	300	9.25	20	1991-1992	7/90
78	1975	Sonoma Valley McCrea Vineyards	250	8.75	20	1991-1993	7/90
81	1981	Sonoma Valley Hunter Ranch	1,221	14.75	19	1991-1993	3/90
74	1980	Alexander Valley Gauer Ranch	2,614	14	18	1991	3/90
67	1980	Sonoma Valley Hunter Ranch	1,355	14	17	Avoid	3/90
71	1980	Sonoma Valley Wildwood Vineyards	1,853	13	19	1991-1992	7/90
70	1979	Alexander Valley Gauer Ranch	2,725	14	18	1991	3/90
80	1979	Sonoma Valley Hunter Farms	1,010	14	20	1991	3/90
65	1978	Sonoma Valley Hunter Farms	528	11.25	18	Avoid	3/90
81	1978	Sonoma Valley Les Pierres	729	13.75	22	1991	3/90
65	1978	Sonoma Valley Wildwood Vineyards	480	12	19	Avoid	3/90
81	1977	Sonoma Valley Hunter Farms	482	10.25	25	1991-1992	3/90
79	1977	Sonoma Valley Les Pierres	308	13.75	21	1991	3/90
73	1977	Sonoma Valley Wildwood Vineyards	492	15	22	1991	3/90
69	1976	Sonoma County Beltane Ranch	375	7.75	18	Avoid	7/90
88	1976	Alexander Valley Riverview Vineyards	600	9.50	22	1991-1994	7/90
82	1976	Sonoma Valley Wildwood Vineyards	402	10	20	1991-1993	7/90
86	1975	Sonoma County Bacigalupi	800	10	21	1991-1995	7/90
88	1975	Sonoma County Beltane Ranch	500	12.50	21	1991-1994	7/90
70	1975	Sonoma Valley Wildwood Vineyards	350	9.50	20	1991	7/90

CHATEAU WOLTNER

Score	Vintage	Appellation / Vineyard	Case Production	Release Price	Current Price	Drink	Last Tasted
86	1988	Howell Mountain Estate Reserve	1,645	24	24	1992-1998	4/90
88	1987	Howell Mountain Estate Reserve	2,151	24	24	1991-1997	4/90
91	1986	Howell Mountain Estate Reserve	1,228	24	24	1991-1997	4/90
86	1988	Howell Mountain St. Thomas Vineyard	617	36	36	1993-1998	4/90
87	1987	Howell Mountain St. Thomas Vineyard	883	36	36	1993-1998	4/90
89	1986	Howell Mountain St. Thomas Vineyard	747	36	37	1991-1997	4/90
86	1988	Howell Mountain Titus Vineyard	147	54	54	1993-1999	4/90
85	1987	Howell Mountain Titus Vineyard	309	54	54	1992-1998	4/90
88	1986	Howell Mountain Titus Vineyard	179	54	54	1993-1998	4/90
87	1988	Howell Mountain Frederique Vineyard	210	54	54	1993-1998	4/90

NR — Not released.

Score	Vintage	Appellation / Vineyard	Case Production	Release Price	Current Price	Drink	Last Tasted
CLOS DU BOIS WINERY							
89	1988	Alexander Valley Calcaire Vineyard	7,334	$17	$17	1992-1997	2/90
88	1987	Alexander Valley Calcaire Vineyard	6,593	20	20	1992-1996	2/90
85	1986	Alexander Valley Calcaire Vineyard	5,096	16	22	1992-1996	2/90
83	1985	Alexander Valley Calcaire Vineyard	4,208	18	28	1991-1994	2/90
90	1984	Alexander Valley Calcaire Vineyard	1,590	12	30	1991-1994	2/90
91	1983	Alexander Valley Calcaire Vineyard	905	12	30	1991-1996	2/90
90	1988	Dry Creek Valley Flintwood Vineyard	5,469	18	18	1992-1997	2/90
87	1987	Dry Creek Valley Flintwood Vineyard	4,217	20	20	1992-1997	2/90
88	1986	Dry Creek Valley Flintwood Vineyard	4,911	19.50	25	1992-1996	2/90
70	1985	Dry Creek Valley Flintwood Vineyard	1,535	18	29	1991-1993	5/90
74	1984	Dry Creek Valley Flintwood Vineyard	1,231	11.25	30	1991-1992	5/90
69	1983	Dry Creek Valley Flintwood Vineyard	634	10.50	30	Avoid	5/90
87	1980	Dry Creek Valley Flintwood Vineyard	977	17	32	1991-1994	2/90
89	1988	Russian River Valley Winemaker's Reserve	3807	NR		1993-1999	5/90
92	1987	Alexander Valley Winemaker's Reserve	3,565	24	24	1991-1995	2/90
78	1986	Alexander Valley Proprietor's Reserve	4,097	22.50	23	1991-1994	5/90
85	1985	Alexander Valley Proprietor's Reserve	1,762	22	25	1991-1995	5/90
70	1981	Alexander Valley Proprietor's Reserve	1,341	15	22	1991-1992	5/90
85	1988	Alexander Valley Barrel Fermented	89,600	11	11	1991-1995	2/90
87	1987	Alexander Valley Barrel Fermented	81,650	11	11	1991-1995	2/90
80	1986	Alexander Valley Barrel Fermented	81,616	10	12	1991-1992	12/89
84	1985	Alexander Valley Barrel Fermented	47,082	9	12	1991-1993	2/90
84	1984	Alexander Valley Barrel Fermented	34,827	8	12	1991-1994	2/90
CLOS DU VAL WINE CO.							
88	1988	Carneros	15,000	16	16	1992-1997	6/90
89	1987	Carneros	13,000	13	13	1991-1995	6/90
84	1986	Carneros	12,000	12	14	1991-1995	6/90
87	1987	Napa Valley	9,000	12	12	1991-1996	6/90
87	1985	Napa Valley	14,000	11.50	17	1991-1997	6/90
85	1984	Napa Valley	12,000	11.50	15	1991-1995	6/90
82	1983	Napa Valley	1,0000	11.50	15	1991-1996	6/90
78	1982	California	4,700	11.50	16	1992-1996	6/90
78	1981	Napa Valley	2,700	12.50	18	1991-1994	6/90
80	1980	Napa Valley	24,000	12.50	18	1991-1994	6/90
CLOS PEGASE							
89	1988	Carneros	5,128	16.50	16.50	1991-1997	3/90
90	1987	Carneros	4,402	15.50	17	1991-1995	3/90
89	1986	Carneros	2,825	15.50	17	1991-1996	3/90
88	1988	Napa Valley	13,681	12	12	1991-1996	3/90
86	1987	Napa Valley	11,131	12	12	1991-1995	3/90
85	1986	Napa Valley	6,689	12	14	1991-1995	3/90
87	1985	Alexander Valley	3,100	13	15	1991-1995	3/90

NR — Not released.

Score	Vintage	Appellation / Vineyard	Case Production	Release Price	Current Price	Drink	Last Tasted
CONGRESS SPRINGS VINEYARDS							
86	1988	Santa Clara County San Ysidro Reserve	2,682	$20	$20	1991-1994	4/90
90	1987	Santa Clara County San Ysidro Reserve	2,000	16	23	1991-1995	4/90
85	1986	Santa Clara County San Ysidro Reserve	2,275	15	22	1991-1994	4/90
88	1988	Santa Cruz Mountains Monmartre	224	30	30	1991-1996	4/90
87	1987	Santa Cruz Mountains Monmartre	770	28	30	1991-1995	4/90
85	1986	Santa Cruz Mountains Private Reserve	552	20	23	1991-1994	4/90
84	1985	Santa Cruz Mountains Private Reserve	431	16	27	1991-1994	4/90
80	1984	Santa Cruz Mountains Private Reserve	420	16	27	1991-1992	4/90
74	1983	Santa Cruz Mountains Private Reserve	328	15	28	1991-1992	4/90
87	1982	Santa Cruz Mountains Private Reserve	310	15	28	1991-1994	4/90
86	1988	Santa Clara County Barrel Fermented	13,431	14	14	1991-1995	4/90
84	1987	Santa Clara County	12,500	12	18	1991-1994	4/90
83	1986	Santa Clara County	4,900	12	18	1991-1994	4/90
87	1985	Santa Clara County	2,500	12	20	1991-1994	4/90
90	1984	Santa Clara County	2,053	11	25	1991-1994	4/90
85	1983	Santa Clara County Barrel Fermented	1,102	10	25	1991-1994	4/90
79	1982	Santa Clara County	957	10	20	1991-1992	4/90
CUVAISON WINERY							
92	1988	Carneros Reserve	2,400	NR	NR	1993-2001	6/90
91	1987	Carneros Reserve	1,260	22	22	1992-1998	7/90
94	1986	Carneros Reserve	1,800	20	28	1992-1996	6/90
91	1988	Carneros	34,000	15	15	1993-1999	4/90
90	1987	Napa Valley	31,000	13.50	16	1993-1998	4/90
89	1986	Napa Valley	22,000	12.75	18	1992-1998	4/90
93	1985	Napa Valley	6,000	12	20	1991-1996	4/90
82	1984	Napa Valley	5,000	12	20	1991-1995	4/90
62	1983	Napa Valley	21,000	12	17	Avoid	4/90
61	1982	Napa Valley	14,000	12	17	Avoid	4/90
75	1981	Napa Valley	1,0000	12	18	1991-1995	4/90
87	1980	Napa Valley	1,0000	11	26	1991-1995	4/90
84	1979	Napa Valley	1,0000	10	26	1991-1995	4/90
81	1978	Napa Valley	1,0000	10	28	1991-1995	4/90
DE LOACH VINEYARDS							
87	1988	Russian River Valley O.F.S	3,200	22	22	1992-1996	5/90
92	1987	Russian River Valley O.F.S	2,400	22	25	1991-1995	5/90
86	1986	Russian River Valley O.F.S	1,800	22	26	1991-1995	2/90
79	1985	Russian River Valley O.F.S	1,200	20	22	1991-1995	2/90
90	1984	Russian River Valley O.F.S	600	20	28	1991-1995	2/90
87	1988	Russian River Valley	26,000	15	15	1992-1996	5/90
87	1987	Russian River Valley	24,000	15	20	1991-1995	2/90
89	1986	Russian River Valley	18,000	14	20	1991-1994	2/90
90	1985	Russian River Valley	12,000	14	23	1991-1994	2/90
88	1984	Russian River Valley	8,000	12.50	24	1991-1994	2/90
83	1983	Russian River Valley	8,000	12	22	1991-1993	2/90
74	1982	Russian River Valley	3,900	12	20	1991	2/90
72	1981	Russian River Valley	2,800	10	18	1991	2/90
62	1980	Russian River Valley	2,000	10	18	Aviod	2/90
DEHLINGER WINERY							
91	1988	Russian River Valley	4,000	12	12	1991-1996	4/90
90	1987	Russian River Valley	4,900	11.50	12	1991-1996	4/90
87	1986	Russian River Valley	3,200	11	14	1991-1995	4/90
86	1985	Russian River Valley	2,000	10	14	1991-1998	5/90
86	1984	Russian River Valley	2,300	10	14	1991-1996	4/90
85	1983	Russian River Valley	1,400	10	15	1991-1995	4/90

NR — Not released.

Score	Vintage	Appellation / Vineyard	Case Production	Release Price	Current Price	Drink	Last Tasted
EDNA VALLEY VINEYARD							
89	1988	Edna Valley	46,500	$14.75	$16	1992-1997	3/90
91	1987	Edna Valley	41,000	14	20	1991-1996	3/90
88	1986	Edna Valley	36,000	13.50	20	1991-1995	3/90
85	1985	Edna Valley	31,000	13	25	1991-1994	3/90
86	1984	Edna Valley	23,800	12.50	24	1991-1995	6/90
76	1983	Edna Valley	15,500	12.50	20	1991-1993	3/90
70	1982	Edna Valley	17,400	12	20	1991	3/90
94	1981	Edna Valley	11,000	12	25	1991-1995	3/90
87	1980	Edna Valley	5,200	12	25	1991-1994	3/90
FAR NIENTE WINERY							
91	1988	Napa Valley	24,000	26	28	1992-1998	2/90
91	1987	Napa Valley	20,000	26	30	1992-1998	2/90
88	1986	Napa Valley	18,000	24	31	1991-1997	2/90
90	1985	Napa Valley	14,300	24	33	1992-1998	2/90
86	1984	Napa Valley	11,000	22	36	1991-1996	2/90
87	1983	Napa Valley	8,000	22	38	1991-1995	2/90
89	1983	Napa Valley Estate	2,000	22	38	1991-1995	2/90
86	1982	Napa Valley	7,000	18	38	1991-1996	2/90
91	1982	Napa Valley Estate	2,000	18	38	1991-1996	2/90
88	1981	Napa Valley	7,000	16.50	40	1991-1996	2/90
93	1980	Napa Valley	6,500	16.50	45	1991-1997	2/90
92	1979	Napa Valley	3,700	15	45	1991-1996	2/90
FERRARI-CARANO VINEYARD & WINERY							
93	1988	California Reserve	1,200	NR	NR	1992-1998	6/90
89	1987	California Reserve	780	28	28	1992-1998	5/90
93	1986	California Reserve	300	28	42	1991-1997	5/90
93	1988	Alexander Valley	22,000	18	18	1991-1995	5/90
94	1987	Alexander Valley	14,000	16	23	1991-1997	5/90
92	1986	Alexander Valley	7,200	16	28	1991-1996	5/90
91	1985	Alexander Valley	2,500	14	30	1991-1996	5/90
FISHER VINEYARDS							
88	1988	Sonoma County Whitney's Vineyard	65	NR	NR	1992-1997	2/90
86	1987	Sonoma County Whitney's Vineyard	48	24	24	1991-1995	2/90
84	1985	Sonoma County Whitney's Vineyard	48	24	30	1991-1994	2/90
90	1984	Sonoma County Whitney's Vineyard	48	20	30	1991-1995	2/90
78	1983	Sonoma County Whitney's Vineyard	24	20	30	1991-1993	2/90
78	1982	Sonoma County Whitney's Vineyard	24	20	25	1991-1993	6/90
85	1981	Sonoma County Whitney's Vineyard	24	20	25	1991-1994	2/90
92	1980	Sonoma County Whitney's Vineyard	24	20	30	1991-1996	2/90
87	1988	Sonoma County Coach Insignia	6,000	18	18	1991-1996	2/90
84	1987	Sonoma County Coach Insignia	5,000	18	18	1991-1995	2/90
90	1986	Sonoma County Coach Insignia	3,000	17	20	1991-1997	2/90
84	1985	Sonoma County Coach Insignia	3,000	16	20	1991-1993	2/90
82	1984	Sonoma County Coach Insignia	2,500	15	20	1991-1994	2/90
82	1983	Sonoma and Napa Counties	3,000	14	18	1991-1994	6/90
81	1982	Sonoma County	2,200	14	22	1991-1993	2/90
88	1981	Sonoma County	2,000	14	25	1990-1993	2/90
85	1980	Sonoma County	1,200	14	22	1990-1993	2/90

NR — Not released.

Score	Vintage	Appellation/Vineyard	Case Production	Release Price	Current Price	Drink	Last Tasted
FLORA SPRINGS WINE CO.							
92	1988	Napa Valley Barrel Fermented	4,700	$24	$24	1993-1997	4/90
95	1987	Napa Valley Barrel Fermented	3,400	20	24	1992-1997	1/90
87	1986	Napa Valley Barrel Fermented	2,800	20	24	1992-1996	1/90
85	1985	Napa Valley Barrel Fermented	2,100	18	27	1992-1996	1/90
88	1984	Napa Valley Barrel Fermented	1,800	18	28	1991-1994	1/90
94	1983	Napa Valley Barrel Fermented	1,200	18	28	1991-1996	1/90
70	1982	Napa Valley Barrel Fermented	700	15	15	1991-1992	6/88
89	1981	Napa Valley Special Selection	1500	12	25	1991-1995	1/90
88	1980	Napa Valley Special Selection	300	12	25	1991-1993	1/90
91	1979	Napa Valley	200	9	25	1991-1994	1/90
FOLIE A DEUX WINERY							
87	1988	Napa Valley	6,900	16	16	1991-1997	6/90
90	1987	Napa Valley	5,300	15	16	1992-1997	6/90
88	1986	Napa Valley	2,600	15	18	1991-1997	6/90
88	1985	Napa Valley	1,200	14.50	18	1991-1995	6/90
87	1984	Napa Valley	1,100	14	18	1991-1996	6/90
78	1982	Napa Valley	500	12.50	17	1991-1992	7/90
FORMAN VINEYARD							
92	1988	Napa Valley	1,400	20	27	1991-1994	2/90
89	1987	Napa Valley	1,400	18	35	1991-1994	2/90
92	1986	Napa Valley	1,000	18	45	1991-1994	2/90
93	1985	Napa Valley	800	15	45	1991-1995	2/90
86	1984	Napa Valley	400	15	45	1991-1994	2/90
FRANCISCAN VINEYARDS							
94	1988	Napa Valley Cuvée Sauvage	300	20	20	1991-1996	7/90
91	1987	Napa Valley Cuvée Sauvage	400	20	20	1991-1996	6/90
86	1987	Napa Valley Reserve	600	15	15	1992-1997	6/90
91	1986	Napa Valley Reserve	3,000	14	15	1991-1997	4/90
86	1984	Napa Valley Reserve	2,000	12	16	1991-1995	4/90
82	1983	Napa Valley Reserve	1,500	12	14	1991-1996	4/90
84	1982	Carneros Reserve	2,000	12	20	1991-1994	4/90
FREEMARK ABBEY WINERY							
89	1988	Napa Valley	19,200	15	15	1991-1997	2/90
84	1987	Napa Valley	16,500	15	15	1992-1996	2/90
86	1986	Napa Valley	16,997	15	15	1991-1996	2/90
80	1985	Napa Valley	15,787	14	16	1991-1995	2/90
87	1984	Napa Valley	15,500	14	17	1991-1994	2/90
85	1983	Napa Valley	13,000	14	18	1991-1995	2/90
72	1982	Napa Valley	13,085	12.75	18	1991-1993	2/90
81	1981	Napa Valley	13,183	13.50	20	1991-1994	2/90
84	1980	Napa Valley	10,771	13.50	24	1991-1993	2/90
76	1979	Napa Valley	10,935	13.25	25	1991	2/90
70	1978	Napa Valley	9,894	10	26	1991	2/90
58	1977	Napa Valley	10,901	10	36	Avoid	2/90
62	1976	Napa Valley	4,802	9.75	26	Avoid	2/90
82	1975	Napa Valley	7,100	9	45	1991	2/90
74	1974	Napa Valley	4,110	7.95	42	1991	2/90
77	1973	Napa Valley	6,117	6.50	32	1991	2/90
77	1972	Napa Valley	3,984	6.50	48	1991	2/90
70	1971	Napa Valley	3,959	7	40	1991	2/90
55	1970	Napa Valley	2,698	7	35	Avoid	2/90
60	1969	Napa Valley	2,307	6	37	Avoid	2/90
73	1968	Napa Valley	996	5	40	1991	2/90
86	1988	Napa Valley Carpy Ranch	566	20	20	1991-1996	2/90

NR — Not released.

Score	Vintage	Appellation/Vineyard	Case Production	Release Price	Current Price	Drink	Last Tasted
FROG'S LEAP WINERY							
87	1988	Napa Valley	2,500	$15	$15	1991-1996	3/90
88	1987	Napa Valley	1,800	14	16	1991-1995	3/90
90	1986	Napa Valley	1,500	12	18	1991-1995	3/90
84	1985	Napa Valley	1,100	12	16	1991-1995	6/90
91	1984	Napa Valley	1,100	12	23	1991-1995	3/90
91	1988	Carneros	1,200	16	16	1992-1997	3/90
86	1987	Carneros	1,500	15	17	1991-1996	3/90
87	1986	Carneros	1,300	14	18	1991-1995	6/90
GIRARD WINERY							
91	1988	Napa Valley Reserve	700	NR	NR	1992-2000	6/90
87	1987	Napa Valley Reserve	700	25	25	1993-1996	6/90
92	1986	Napa Valley Reserve	701	25	25	1991-1996	3/90
91	1985	Napa Valley Reserve	242	25	35	1991-1995	3/90
88	1988	Napa Valley Estate	4,800	16	16	1991-1997	6/90
81	1987	Napa Valley Estate	5,757	14.50	16	1992-1995	3/90
92	1986	Napa Valley Estate	5,297	13.50	28	1991-1996	3/90
90	1985	Napa Valley Estate	4,740	13.50	25	1991-1996	3/90
80	1984	Napa Valley Estate	7,123	13.50	22	1991-1993	3/90
76	1983	Napa Valley Estate	5,741	12.50	22	1991	3/90
76	1982	Napa Valley Estate	4,228	12.50	21	1991	3/90
90	1981	Napa Valley Estate	4,736	12.50	35	1991-1995	3/90
85	1980	Napa Valley Estate	2,100	11	25	1991-1994	3/90
GRGICH HILLS CELLAR							
93	1988	Napa Valley	20,000	22	22	1992-1999	7/90
90	1987	Napa Valley	33,000	22	28	1992-1997	6/90
91	1986	Napa Valley	25,000	22	33	1991-1996	3/90
92	1985	Napa Valley	25,000	22	33	1991-1995	3/90
90	1984	Napa Valley	24,000	18	33	1991-1995	3/90
92	1983	Napa Valley	15,000	17	33	1991-1995	3/90
87	1982	Napa Valley	15,000	17	36	1991-1994	3/90
88	1981	Napa Valley	16,000	17	45	1991-1995	3/90
88	1980	Napa Valley	15,000	17	50	1991-1994	3/90
95	1979	Napa Valley	10,000	16	55	1991-1994	3/90
92	1978	Napa Valley	6,000	13.75	60	1991-1996	3/90
89	1977	Sonoma County	6,000	11	65	1991-1993	3/90
85	1976	Napa Valley (Hills Cellars)	2,500	8	50	1991-1995	3/90
HACIENDA WINERY							
85	1988	Sonoma County Clair de Lune	10,500	15	15	1991-1996	6/90
72	1987	Sonoma County Clair de Lune	9,600	12	15	1991-1993	4/90
89	1986	Sonoma County Clair de Lune	7,000	12	18	1991-1995	4/90
87	1985	Sonoma County Clair de Lune	7,000	11	20	1991-1995	4/90
88	1984	Sonoma County Clair de Lune	4,285	10	18	1991-1994	4/90
83	1983	Sonoma County Clair de Lune	4,200	10	22	1991-1993	4/90
78	1982	Sonoma County Clair de Lune	7,200	9	20	1991-1993	4/90
74	1981	Sonoma County Clair de Lune	4,600	12	20	1991-1992	4/90
80	1980	Sonoma County Clair de Lune	3,400	10.50	22	1991-1993	4/90
86	1979	Sonoma County Clair de Lune	2,900	9	25	1991-1993	4/90
73	1978	Sonoma County Clair de Lune	3,000	9	25	1991	4/90
76	1977	Sonoma County Clair de Lune	1,000	8	23	1991-1993	4/90
85	1976	Sonoma County Clair de Lune	750	7	40	1991-1994	4/90
80	1974	Sonoma County Clair de Lune	675	5	40	1991-1992	4/90
91	1973	Sonoma County Clair de Lune	495	5	50	1991-1994	4/90

NR — Not released.

Score	Vintage	Appellation/Vineyard	Case Production	Release Price	Current Price	Drink	Last Tasted
HANZELL VINEYARDS							
90	1988	Sonoma Valley	750	$24	$24	1993-2000	5/90
90	1987	Sonoma Valley	1,050	24	28	1993-2000	1/90
87	1986	Sonoma Valley	1,070	22	32	1993-1998	1/90
90	1985	Sonoma Valley	830	22	35	1991-1999	1/90
84	1984	Sonoma Valley	980	20	36	1991-1996	1/90
84	1983	Sonoma Valley	930	20	45	1991-1996	1/90
89	1982	Sonoma Valley	940	19	45	1991-1996	1/90
86	1981	Sonoma Valley	650	18	50	1991-1997	1/90
90	1980	Sonoma Valley	740	17	60	1991-1998	1/90
85	1979	Sonoma Valley	460	16	70	1991-1995	1/90
95	1978	Sonoma Valley	310	13	80	1991-1998	1/90
88	1977	Sonoma Valley	260	12	85	1991-1994	1/90
91	1976	Sonoma Valley	210	12	90	1991-1995	1/90
86	1975	Sonoma Valley	310	10	70	1991-1994	1/90
88	1974	Sonoma Valley	300	9	75	1991-1995	1/90
85	1973	Sonoma Valley	310	8	100	1991-1995	1/90
90	1972	Sonoma Valley	170	7	75	1991-1995	1/90
85	1971	Sonoma Valley	160	7	120	1991-1994	1/90
84	1970	Sonoma Valley	220	7	120	1991-1994	1/90
90	1969	Sonoma Valley	220	6	140	1991-1995	1/90
91	1968	Sonoma Valley	240	6	140	1991-1995	1/90
89	1967	Sonoma Valley	330	6	140	1991-1994	1/90
94	1966	Sonoma Valley	260	6	170	1991-2000	1/90
84	1965	Sonoma Valley	190	6	180	1991-1995	1/90
87	1962	Napa Valley (Heitz Wine Cellar)	250	6	150	1991-1997	6/90
93	1961	Napa Valley (Heitz Wine Cellar)	250	6	150	1991-2000	6/90
88	1959	California	120	4	200	1991-1995	12/89
90	1957	California	240	4	240	1991-1993	12/89
HESS COLLECTION WINERY							
88	1988	Napa Valley	10,000	13.75	13.75	1992-1998	4/90
91	1987	Napa Valley	4,100	13.25	15	1991-1997	4/90
88	1986	Napa Valley	4,285	12.75	16	1991-1996	4/90
WILLIAM HILL WINERY							
88	1988	Napa Valley Reserve	30,088	18	18	1992-1998	3/90
91	1987	Napa Valley Reserve	21,042	18	18	1992-1998	3/90
91	1986	Napa Valley Reserve	18,228	17	20	1991-1995	3/90
90	1985	Napa Valley Reserve	16,313	16	24	1991-1997	3/90
88	1984	Napa Valley Reserve	652	20	24	1991-1996	3/90
85	1983	Napa Valley Reserve	1,428	22	28	1991-1994	3/90
86	1982	Napa Valley Reserve	1,427	24	28	1991-1995	3/90
70	1980	Napa Valley Gold Label	775	16	30	1991	3/90
INGLENOOK-NAPA VALLEY							
88	1988	Napa Valley Reserve	2,000	NR	NR	1992-1998	4/90
86	1987	Napa Valley Reserve	6,000	14	14	1992-1997	4/90
88	1986	Napa Valley Reserve	6,135	14.50	14.50	1991-1996	4/90
78	1985	Napa Valley Reserve	2,500	14.50	15	1991-1994	4/90
86	1984	Napa Valley Reserve	2,200	12.50	18	1991-1995	4/90
82	1983	Napa Valley Reserve	1,500	16	19	1991-1994	4/90

NR — Not released.

Score	Vintage	Appellation/Vineyard	Production	Release Price	Current Price	Drink	Last Tasted
KENDALL-JACKSON VINEYARDS							
85	1988	Anderson Valley Du Pratt Vineyard	200	$14	$14	1991-1994	4/90
85	1988	Redwood Valley Lolonis Vineyard	100	NR	NR	1991-1994	4/90
87	1988	California The Proprietor's	25,000	24.50	25	1991-1995	4/90
89	1987	Anderson Valley De Patie Vineyard	200	14	14	1991-1995	4/90
82	1987	Anderson Valley Dennison Vineyard	200	14	14	1991-1993	4/90
86	1987	Sonoma Valley Durell Vineyard	500	14	14	1991-1994	4/90
92	1987	California The Proprietor's	11,000	20	20	1991-1995	4/90
91	1986	Sonoma Valley Durell Vineyard	500	14	16	1991-1996	6/90
86	1986	California The Proprietor's	5,000	17	20	1991-1994	4/90
85	1985	Anderson Valley Dennison Vineyard	200	14	20	1991-1993	4/90
87	1985	Sonoma Valley Durell Vineyard	500	14	20	1991-1995	4/90
KENWOOD VINEYARDS							
89	1988	Sonoma Valley Beltane Ranch	3,000	15	15	1992-1998	7/90
87	1987	Sonoma Valley Beltane Ranch	3,000	15	17	1992-1997	7/90
85	1986	Sonoma Valley Beltane Ranch	2,500	14	18	1991-1995	7/90
84	1985	Sonoma Valley Beltane Ranch	2,200	14	18	1991-1995	7/90
87	1988	Sonoma Valley Yulupa Vineyard	3,000	14	14	1991-1996	7/90
85	1987	Sonoma Valley Yulupa Vineyard	3,000	14	16	1992-1996	7/90
82	1986	Sonoma Valley Yulupa Vineyard	6,000	12	17	1991-1995	7/90
84	1985	Sonoma Valley Yulupa Vineyard	3,000	12	17	1991-1994	7/90
85	1983	Sonoma Valley Yulupa Vineyard	1,000	11	18	1991-1994	7/90
KISTLER VINEYARDS							
92	1988	Russian River Valley Dutton Ranch	4,987	22	22	1991-1995	2/90
93	1987	Russian River Valley Dutton Ranch	4,020	18	24	1991-1993	2/90
90	1986	Russian River Valley Dutton Ranch	3,151	16.50	28	1991-1997	2/90
88	1985	California Dutton Ranch/Winery Lake	5251	15	30	1991-1994	2/90
89	1984	Russian River Valley Dutton Ranch	3,911	15	30	1991-1995	2/90
95	1988	Sonoma Valley Kistler Estate Vineyard	507	26	26	1991-1996	2/90
90	1987	Sonoma Valley Kistler Estate Vineyard	866	22	26	1991-1996	2/90
92	1986	Sonoma Valley Kistler Estate Vineyard	397	18	35	1991-1997	2/90
91	1988	Sonoma Valley Durell Vineyard	2,337	17	17	1992-1998	2/90
93	1987	Sonoma Valley Durell Vineyard	1,300	16	20	1991-1997	2/90
89	1986	Sonoma Valley Durell Vineyard	620	16	25	1991-1997	2/90
92	1988	Sonoma Valley McCrea Vineyard	1,010	24	24	1991-1996	2/90
LA CREMA							
91	1988	California Reserve	5,000	22	22	1991-1999	6/90
83	1987	California Reserve	2,900	22	22	1993-1999	6/90
85	1986	California Reserve	1,200	18	22	1991-1996	6/90
86	1985	California Reserve	1,200	18	22	1991-1995	6/90
88	1984	Monterey County Reserve Ventana Vineyard	2,000	18	22	1991-1998	6/90
LONG VINEYARDS							
93	1988	Napa Valley	900	27.50	30	1991-1998	4/90
90	1987	Napa Valley	900	27.50	35	1991-1998	4/90
92	1986	Napa Valley	800	27.50	45	1991-1997	4/90
91	1985	Napa Valley	850	27.50	45	1991-1996	4/90
88	1984	Napa Valley	600	27.50	45	1991-1995	4/90
MARKHAM VINEYARDS							
89	1988	Napa Valley	8,026	12	12	1991-1997	2/90
87	1987	Napa Valley	4,720	12	12	1991-1996	2/90
84	1986	Napa Valley Estate	4,649	12	14	1991-1994	2/90
86	1985	Napa Valley Estate	2,843	12	16	1991-1995	2/90
85	1984	Napa Valley	2,955	12	16	1991-1995	2/90
81	1983	Napa Valley Estate	860	11.50	16	1991-1992	2/90
83	1982	Napa Valley Estate	531	12	17	1991-1993	2/90

NR — Not released.

Score	Vintage	Appellation/Vineyard	Production	Release Price	Current Price	Drink	Last Tasted
MATANZAS CREEK WINERY							
89	1988	Sonoma County	17,165	$18.75	$18.75	1991-1996	2/90
90	1987	Sonoma County	13,506	18	20	1991-1996	2/90
89	1986	Sonoma County	8,817	17.50	22	1991-1994	2/90
88	1985	Sonoma County	6,221	16.50	28	1991-1994	2/90
89	1984	Sonoma County	3,717	15	28	1991-1994	2/90
85	1983	Sonoma County	1,788	15	28	1991-1993	2/90
78	1982	Sonoma County	1,735	15	25	1991	2/90
85	1981	Sonoma County	1,925	15	28	1991-1993	2/90
82	1980	Sonoma County	1,700	15	25	1991-1992	2/90
80	1979	Sonoma and Napa Counties	1,650	14.50	40	1991	2/90
79	1978	Sonoma County	1,230	12.50	40	1991	2/90
86	1985	Sonoma Valley Estate	380	18	31	1991-1994	2/90
80	1984	Sonoma Valley Estate	830	18	28	1991-1993	2/90
68	1983	Sonoma Valley Estate	516	18	18	Avoid	2/90
88	1982	Sonoma Valley Estate	700	18	25	1991-1994	2/90
70	1980	Sonoma County Estate	85	18	18	1991	2/90
MAYACAMAS VINEYARDS							
89	1988	Napa Valley	1,427	NR	NR	1992-1997	6/90
87	1987	Napa Valley	2,640	20	20	1991-1996	1/90
87	1986	Napa Valley	1,860	20	20	1991-1996	3/90
90	1985	Napa Valley	1,415	20	25	1991-1998	1/90
88	1984	Napa Valley	1,715	18	25	1991-1998	3/90
86	1983	Napa Valley	1,775	16	25	1991-1996	1/90
85	1982	Napa Valley	2,215	16	30	1991-1997	1/90
78	1981	Napa Valley	1,955	16	35	1991-1994	1/90
74	1980	Napa Valley	1,480	16	35	1991	1/90
70	1979	Napa Valley	1,220	15	35	1991	1/90
75	1978	Napa Valley	1,233	13	30	1991	1/90
70	1977	Napa Valley	1,520	12	35	1991	1/90
81	1976	Napa Valley	1,255	11	45	1991-1994	1/90
78	1975	Napa Valley	1,464	9	50	1991	1/90
70	1974	Napa Valley	1,257	7.50	50	1991	1/90
60	1973	Napa Valley	1,082	7	50	Avoid	1/90
59	1972	Napa Valley	704	7	50	Avoid	1/90
58	1965	Napa Valley	500	2.50	125	Avoid	1/90
92	1964	Napa Valley	500	1.75	200	1991-1994	1/90
58	1963	Napa Valley	400	1.75	150	Avoid	1/90
58	1962	Napa Valley	400	1.75	150	Avoid	1/90
60	1958	Napa Valley	500	1	200	Avoid	1/90
88	1955	Napa Valley	250	1	325	1991-1995	1/90
ROBERT MONDAVI WINERY							
91	1988	Napa Valley Reserve	12,000	26	26	1992-1997	6/90
92	1987	Napa Valley Reserve	10,000	26	26	1991-1997	6/90
89	1986	Napa Valley Reserve	11,000	25	28	1991-1995	3/90
88	1985	Napa Valley Reserve	13,000	25	27	1991-1995	3/90
87	1984	Napa Valley Reserve	9,000	22	24	1991-1994	3/90
88	1983	Napa Valley Reserve	7,800	20	25	1991-1995	3/90
81	1982	Napa Valley Reserve	6,000	20	25	1991	3/90
86	1981	Napa Valley Reserve	6,800	20	24	1991-1993	3/90
69	1980	Napa Valley Reserve	3,500	20	30	Avoid	3/90
79	1979	Napa Valley Reserve	8,700	20	27	1991	3/90
69	1978	Napa Valley Reserve	5,100	20	24	Avoid	3/90
68	1977	Napa Valley Reserve	2,600	14	32	Avoid	3/90
78	1976	Napa Valley Reserve	1,450	12	32	1991	3/90
75	1975	Napa Valley Reserve	1,500	10	35	1991	3/90
88	1974	Napa Valley Reserve	1,000	10	45	1991-1994	3/90

NR — Not released.

Score	Vintage	Appellation / Vineyard	Production	Release Price	Current Price	Drink	Last Tasted
MONTICELLO CELLARS							
94	1988	Napa Valley Corley Reserve	4,000	$17.25	$17.25	1991-1997	2/90
86	1987	Napa Valley Corley Reserve	4,400	17.25	18	1992-1997	6/90
89	1986	Napa Valley Corley Reserve	3,200	16.50	18	1991-1996	2/90
85	1985	Napa Valley Corley Reserve	2,200	14	20	1991-1994	2/90
94	1984	Napa Valley Corley Reserve	860	12.50	25	1991-1995	2/90
80	1983	Napa Valley Barrel Fermented	720	12.50	20	1991-1993	2/90
84	1982	Napa Valley Barrel Fermented	800	14	20	1991-1992	2/90
90	1988	Napa Valley Jefferson Ranch	7,500	12.25	12.25	1991-1997	2/90
86	1987	Napa Valley Jefferson Ranch	8,100	12.25	13	1991-1995	2/90
86	1986	Napa Valley Jefferson Ranch	5,700	11	14	1991-1995	2/90
82	1985	Napa Valley Jefferson Ranch	4,000	11	16	1991-1993	2/90
86	1984	Napa Valley Jefferson Ranch	2,450	10	18	1991-1994	2/90
93	1983	Napa Valley Jefferson Ranch	1,200	10	20	1991-1995	2/90
82	1982	Napa Valley	4,000	13.50	20	1991-1993	2/90
76	1981	Napa Valley	2,700	12	20	1991	2/90
86	1980	Napa Valley	1,250	12	20	1991-1993	2/90
MORGAN WINERY							
92	1988	Monterey Reserve	1,500	20	20	1991-1997	6/90
85	1987	Monterey Reserve	1,500	19	19	1991-1994	6/90
89	1988	Monterey	8,500	15	16	1991-1996	5/90
84	1987	Monterey	8,500	15	16	1991-1994	5/90
89	1986	Monterey	6,000	14	20	1991-1995	5/90
86	1985	Monterey County	5,000	14	25	1991-1996	7/90
86	1984	Monterey County	5,000	12.75	25	1991-1995	5/90
80	1983	Monterey County	3,000	12.50	25	1991-1993	5/90
89	1982	Monterey County	2,000	12	28	1991-1995	5/90
MOUNT EDEN VINEYARDS							
88	1988	Santa Cruz Mountains	715	30	30	1992-1997	3/90
90	1987	Santa Cruz Mountains	1,348	28	32	1992-1997	3/90
88	1986	Santa Cruz Mountains	677	25	42	1991-1996	3/90
87	1985	Santa Cruz Mountains	540	25	40	1991-1996	3/90
85	1984	Santa Cruz Mountains	756	23	45	1991-1995	3/90
84	1983	Santa Cruz Mountains	455	20	35	1991-1994	3/90
76	1982	Santa Cruz Mountains	500	18	40	1991-1994	3/90
89	1981	Santa Cruz Mountains	445	18	60	1991-1995	3/90
87	1980	Santa Cruz Mountains	245	30	50	1991-1995	3/90
90	1979	Santa Cruz Mountains	495	16	60	1991-1996	3/90
66	1978	Santa Cruz Mountains	400	16	50	Avoid	3/90
85	1977	Santa Cruz Mountains	150	16	50	1991-1995	8/90
78	1976	Santa Cruz Mountains	200	16	50	1991	3/90
60	1975	Santa Cruz Mountains	108	14	45	Avoid	3/90
59	1974	Santa Cruz Mountains	170	14	45	Avoid	3/90
82	1973	Santa Cruz Mountains	281	12	55	1991	3/90
80	1972	Santa Cruz Mountains	210	20	50	1991-1993	3/90
88	1988	Edna Valley MacGregor Vineyard	1,551	14	14	1991-1996	6/90
94	1987	Edna Valley MEV MacGregor Vineyard	1,500	14	18	1991-1997	3/90
81	1986	Edna Valley MEV MacGregor Vineyard	1,200	13	16	1991-1995	3/90
87	1985	Edna Valley MEV MacGregor Vineyard	1,100	12.50	14	1991-1995	3/90
MURPHY-GOODE							
88	1988	Alexander Valley	12,000	11.50	11.50	1991-1995	4/90
87	1987	Alexander Valley Premier Vineyard	7,000	11	11	1991-1996	4/90
86	1986	Alexander Valley	7,000	10	12	1991-1995	4/90
85	1985	Alexander Valley	5,000	9	12	1991-1995	4/90

NR — Not released.

Score	Vintage	Appellation/Vineyard	Production	Release Price	Current Price	Drink	Last Tasted
NAVARRO VINEYARDS							
91	1988	Anderson Valley Première Reserve	3,596	$14	$14	1991-1998	5/90
87	1987	Anderson Valley Première Reserve	1,813	14	14	1992-1996	3/90
87	1986	Anderson Valley Première Reserve	1,555	14	18	1991-1996	3/90
89	1985	Anderson Valley Première Reserve	1,331	12	18	1991-1995	3/90
91	1984	Anderson Valley Première Reserve	856	12	22	1991-1995	3/90
NEWTON VINEYARD							
88	1988	Napa Valley	5,546	14.50	14.50	1991-1997	3/90
88	1987	Napa Valley	6,000	14	14	1991-1997	3/90
85	1986	Napa Valley	5,000	14	14	1992-1997	3/90
85	1985	Napa Valley	3,100	12.75	19	1991-1996	3/90
86	1984	Napa Valley	3,900	11.50	18	1991-1998	5/90
89	1983	Napa Valley	2,000	12	19	1991-1998	5/90
ROBERT PECOTA WINERY							
87	1988	Alexander Valley Canepa Vineyard	800	16	16	1991-1995	4/90
91	1987	Alexander Valley Canepa Vineyard	800	16	18	1991-1996	4/90
85	1986	Alexander Valley Canepa Vineyard	800	16	19	1991-1995	4/90
89	1985	Alexander Valley Canepa Vineyard	800	16	18	1991-1996	7/90
83	1984	Alexander Valley Canepa Vineyard	600	14	18	1991-1993	4/90
79	1983	Alexander Valley Canepa Vineyard	600	14	18	1990-1991	4/90
75	1981	Alexander Valley Canepa Vineyard	425	12	20	1990-1991	4/90
89	1980	Alexander Valley Canepa Vineyard	325	12	20	1990-1994	4/90
PINE RIDGE WINERY							
88	1988	Stags Leap District Pine Ridge Stags Leap Vineyard	2,063	20	20	1991-1996	7/90
91	1987	Stags Leap District Pine Ridge Stags Leap Vineyard	2,765	20	20	1991-1996	4/90
88	1986	Stags Leap District Pine Ridge Stags Leap Vineyard	2,215	19	23	1991-1996	4/90
85	1985	Stags Leap District Pine Ridge Stags Leap Vineyard	1,793	18	23	1991-1995	4/90
84	1984	Stags Leap District Pine Ridge Stags Leap Vineyard	1,405	18	25	1991-1994	4/90
86	1983	Stags Leap District Pine Ridge Stags Leap Vineyard	1,199	16	25	1991-1994	4/90
82	1982	Stags Leap District Stags Leap Vineyard	780	15	27	1991-1994	4/90
86	1981	Stags Leap District Stags Leap Vineyard	1,114	15	31	1991-1994	4/90
82	1979	Stags Leap District Stags Leap Vineyard	588	9.50	32	1991-1992	4/90
88	1988	Napa Valley Knollside Cuvée	11,062	15	15	1991-1995	7/90
90	1987	Napa Valley Knollside Cuvée	9,854	15	16	1991-1995	4/90
88	1986	Napa Valley Knollside Cuvée	7,918	14	16	1991-1995	4/90
87	1985	Napa Valley Knollside Cuvée	6,869	14	16	1991-1995	4/90
85	1984	Napa Valley Knollside Cuvée	4,285	14	17	1991-1995	4/90
88	1983	Napa Valley Oak Knoll Cuvée	3,685	13	18	1991-1994	4/90
78	1982	Napa Valley Oak Knoll Cuvée	2,026	13	19	1991-1993	4/90
84	1981	Napa Valley Oak Knoll Cuvée	1,168	13	20	1991-1994	4/90
RAYMOND VINEYARD & CELLAR							
90	1988	Napa Valley Private Reserve	4,434	NR	NR	1991-1997	5/90
88	1987	Napa Valley Private Reserve	4,404	22	22	1991-1996	5/90
87	1986	Napa Valley Private Reserve	1,842	18	21	1991-1995	5/90
91	1985	Napa Valley Private Reserve	1,720	18	21	1991-1995	5/90
70	1981	Napa Valley Private Reserve	500	15	25	1991	6/90
REVERE WINERY							
87	1988	Napa Valley Reserve	366	NR	NR	1992-1998	4/90
83	1987	Napa Valley Reserve	101	25	25	1991-1995	4/90
87	1986	Napa Valley Reserve	206	22	25	1991-1996	4/90
85	1986	Napa Valley	1,375	15	15	1991-1996	4/90
85	1985	Napa Valley	1,052	15	20	1991-1995	4/90

NR — Not released.

Score	Vintage	Appellation/Vineyard	Production	Release Price	Current Price	Drink	Last Tasted
ROMBAUER VINEYARDS							
89	1988	Napa Valley Reserve	330	NR	NR	1992-1997	6/90
87	1987	Napa Valley Reserve	200	25	25	1991-1995	6/90
86	1986	Napa Valley Reserve	200	24	26	1991-1995	6/90
88	1988	Napa Valley	4,014	15	15	1991-1996	6/90
86	1987	Napa Valley	4,300	14.50	15	1991-1996	6/90
85	1986	Napa Valley	3,815	14.50	16	1991-1995	6/90
84	1985	Napa Valley	1,337	14.50	18	1991-1994	6/90
78	1984	Napa Valley	1,337	14.50	20	1991-1994	6/90
87	1983	Napa Valley	1,010	14.50	25	1991-1995	7/90
84	1982	Napa Valley	382	14.50	25	1991-1994	6/90
SAINTSBURY							
90	1988	Carneros	14,750	14	14	1992-1997	2/90
90	1987	Carneros	13,150	13	15	1992-1997	2/90
88	1986	Carneros	10,075	12	17	1992-1997	2/90
90	1985	Carneros	6,600	11	19	1991-1996	2/90
92	1984	Carneros	6,400	11	25	1991-1994	2/90
80	1983	Carneros	6,550	11	20	1991-1994	2/90
65	1982	Sonoma County	3,750	11	14	Avoid	2/90
87	1981	Sonoma County	950	10	25	1991-1994	2/90
92	1988	Carneros Reserve	1,800	20	20	1992-1998	2/90
89	1987	Carneros Reserve	1,450	20	20	1992-1997	2/90
84	1986	Carneros Reserve	1,015	20	25	1992-1996	2/90
SANFORD WINERY							
94	1988	Santa Barbara County Barrel Select	1,000	25	25	1991-1997	6/90
91	1987	Santa Barbara County Barrel Select	300	24	30	1991-1997	2/90
92	1985	Santa Barbara County Barrel Select	150	20	30	1991-1996	2/90
92	1988	Santa Barbara County	18,000	16	16	1991-1997	6/90
92	1987	Santa Barbara County	18,000	15	16	1991-1996	2/90
88	1986	Santa Barbara County	6,000	14	16	1991-1995	2/90
90	1985	Santa Barbara County	5,000	13.50	20	1991-1997	2/90
78	1984	Central Coast	4,000	12.50	15	1991-1993	2/90
88	1983	Central Coast	3,000	12	15	1991-1995	2/90
68	1982	Santa Maria Valley	2,500	12	20	Avoid	2/90
74	1981	Santa Maria Valley	1,000	11	20	1991	2/90
SEQUOIA GROVE VINEYARDS							
92	1988	Napa Valley Estate	4,228	16	16	1991-1996	5/90
88	1987	Napa Valley Estate	2,167	16	16	1991-1996	5/90
88	1986	Napa Valley Estate	2,064	15	18	1991-1994	5/90
89	1985	Napa Valley Estate	4,981	16	20	1991-1995	5/90
89	1984	Napa Valley Estate	1,808	14	20	1991-1994	5/90
87	1983	Napa Valley Estate	1,639	12	20	1991-1996	5/90
72	1982	Napa Valley Estate	880	12	20	1991	5/90
88	1981	Napa Valley Estate	952	12	20	1991-1995	7/90
87	1980	Napa Valley Estate	1,500	10	18	1991-1994	5/90
86	1988	Carneros	6,978	14	14	1991-1996	5/90
83	1987	Carneros	5,530	14	14	1991-1995	5/90
78	1986	Carneros	4,880	13	16	1991-1995	5/90
88	1985	Carneros	4,976	12	16	1991-1995	5/90
CHARLES F. SHAW VINEYARD							
86	1988	Napa Valley	10,500	11	11	1991-1995	5/90
85	1987	Napa Valley	7,500	11	11	1992-1997	5/90
85	1986	Napa Valley	7,500	11	11	1991-1995	5/90
87	1985	Napa Valley	5,000	12	15	1991-1994	5/90
82	1984	Napa Valley	5,000	12	15	1991-1993	5/90
84	1983	Napa Valley	5,000	12	16	1991-1993	5/90

NR — Not released.

Score	Vintage	Appellation/Vineyard	Production	Release Price	Current Price	Drink	Last Tasted
SILVERADO VINEYARDS							
88	1988	Napa Valley	41,000	$14	$14	1991-1996	3/90
88	1987	Napa Valley	30,000	13.50	15	1991-1996	3/90
90	1986	Napa Valley	22,000	12	16	1991-1996	3/90
87	1985	Napa Valley	17,000	11.50	17	1991-1995	3/90
81	1984	Napa Valley	11,000	11	18	1991-1994	3/90
84	1983	Napa Valley	5,000	11	20	1991-1993	3/90
73	1982	Napa Valley	4,500	10	20	1991	3/90
70	1981	Napa Valley	1,800	10	20	1991	3/90
92	1987	Napa Valley Limited Reserve	1,300	NR	NR	1993-2000	7/90
90	1986	Napa Valley Limited Reserve	650	25	25	1992-1997	7/90
SIMI WINERY							
91	1988	Sonoma County Reserve	2,300	NR	NR	1992-1998	7/90
94	1987	Sonoma County Reserve	2,000	NR	NR	1991-1997	4/90
92	1986	Sonoma County Reserve	1,600	28	32	1991-1998	4/90
91	1985	Sonoma County Reserve	1,200	28	32	1991-1996	4/90
89	1984	Sonoma County Reserve	1,100	28	32	1991-1996	4/90
88	1983	Sonoma County Reserve	1,000	22	32	1991-1995	4/90
94	1982	Sonoma County Reserve	1,000	22	40	1991-1995	4/90
91	1981	Sonoma County Reserve	1,600	20	40	1991-1996	4/90
94	1980	Mendocino County Reserve	1,100	20	40	1991-1997	4/90
SMITH-MADRONE VINEYARD							
88	1988	Napa Valley	1980	13	13	1993-2000	5/90
91	1987	Napa Valley	2,542	13	13	1993-2000	5/90
89	1986	Napa Valley	2,375	12.50	16	1990-1998	5/90
87	1985	Napa Valley	1,832	12.50	16	1990-1996	5/90
80	1984	Napa Valley	1,606	12	16	1991-1996	5/90
71	1983	Napa Valley	1,473	12	15	1991-1994	5/90
86	1982	Napa Valley	1,004	12	18	1990-1998	5/90
81	1981	Napa Valley	650	12	18	1990-1993	5/90
85	1980	Napa Valley	450	11	20	1990-1995	5/90
92	1979	Napa Valley	580	10	28	1990-2000	5/90
86	1978	Napa Valley	375	10	30	1990-1997	5/90
SONOMA-CUTRER VINEYARDS							
93	1988	Sonoma Valley Les Pierres	11,075	22.50	22.50	1992-2001	7/90
92	1987	Sonoma Valley Les Pierres	11,510	22.50	26	1992-1997	3/90
88	1986	Sonoma Valley Les Pierres	9,125	19.50	27	1992-1997	3/90
92	1985	Sonoma Valley Les Pierres	8,500	17.50	30	1991-1997	3/90
89	1984	Sonoma Valley Les Pierres	7,000	16.50	30	1991-1995	3/90
86	1983	Sonoma Valley Les Pierres	7,000	15.50	30	1991-1994	3/90
88	1982	Sonoma Valley Les Pierres	2,500	15	35	1991-1994	3/90
94	1981	Sonoma Valley Les Pierres	850	14.50	40	1991-1997	3/90
92	1988	Russian River Valley Cutrer Vineyard	10,010	17.50	17.50	1992-2000	7/90
91	1987	Russian River Valley Cutrer Vineyard	9,840	17.50	18	1991-1996	3/90
89	1986	Russian River Valley Cutrer Vineyard	7,100	16	20	1992-1997	3/90
87	1985	Russian River Valley Cutrer Vineyard	6,000	14.75	23	1991-1996	3/90
87	1984	Russian River Valley Cutrer Vineyard	6,000	14.25	25	1991-1995	3/90
86	1983	Russian River Valley Cutrer Vineyard	3,000	13.75	25	1991-1994	3/90
87	1982	Russian River Valley Cutrer Vineyard	5,000	13	25	1991-1994	3/90
91	1981	Russian River Valley Cutrer Vineyard	2,500	12.50	30	1991-1995	3/90
91	1988	Russian River Valley Russian River Ranches	51,900	13.25	14	1992-1998	3/90
88	1987	Russian River Valley Russian River Ranches	53,055	12	16	1991-1995	3/90
86	1986	Russian River Valley Russian River Ranches	41,725	12	18	1992-1996	3/90
88	1985	Russian River Valley Russian River Ranches	28,256	11.50	22	1991-1995	3/90
85	1983	Russian River Valley Russian River Ranches	9,900	10.50	22	1991-1994	3/90
87	1982	Russian River Valley Russian River Ranches	5,200	10	24	1991-1994	3/90
82	1981	Russian River Valley Russian River Ranches	1,250	9.35	30	1991-1994	3/90

NR — Not released.

Score	Vintage	Appellation/Vineyard	Production	Release Price	Current Price	Drink	Last Tasted
ST. CLEMENT VINEYARDS							
88	1988	Napa Valley	3,683	$15	$15	1992-1998	3/90
86	1987	Napa Valley	3,500	15	15	1992-1997	3/90
89	1986	Napa Valley	1,450	15	15	1992-1997	3/90
85	1985	Napa Valley	3,700	14.50	16	1991-1995	3/90
88	1984	Napa Valley	4,000	14.50	17	1991-1996	3/90
76	1983	Napa Valley	4,500	14.50	17	1991	3/90
73	1982	Napa Valley	4,600	14.50	20	1991	3/90
75	1981	Napa Valley	3,000	13.50	25	1991	3/90
83	1980	Napa Valley	3,200	12	25	1991-1992	3/90
93	1979	Napa Valley	3,000	12	27	1991-1996	3/90
91	1987	Carneros Abbott's Vineyard	500	17	17	1992-1997	3/90
STAG'S LEAP WINE CELLARS							
90	1988	Napa Valley Reserve	335	28	28	1993-1998	3/90
89	1987	Napa Valley Reserve	1,172	28	28	1992-1997	3/90
88	1986	Napa Valley Reserve	480	26	26	1991-1994	6/90
85	1985	Napa Valley Reserve	1,214	22	26	1991-1995	3/90
87	1988	Napa Valley	15,500	18	18	1993-1997	3/90
89	1987	Napa Valley	17,710	18	18	1992-1997	3/90
86	1986	Napa Valley	8,166	17	20	1991-1995	3/90
83	1985	Napa Valley	7,002	16	18	1991-1994	3/90
77	1984	Napa Valley	5,861	14	17	1991-1992	6/90
62	1983	Napa Valley	4,582	13.50	17	Avoid	3/90
70	1982	Napa Valley	3,874	13.50	17	1991	3/90
79	1981	Napa Valley	4,760	13.50	17	1991-1993	3/90
78	1980	Napa Valley	2,194	10.50	17	1991-1992	3/90
59	1977	Napa Valley	2,452	8	17	Avoid	3/90
58	1976	Napa Valley	335	8	17	Avoid	3/90
82	1979	Napa Valley Haynes	2,000	12.50	20	1991-1992	3/90
74	1978	Napa Valley Haynes	1,815	10	20	1991	3/90
67	1977	Napa Valley Haynes	1,752	9	20	Avoid	3/90
70	1982	Napa Valley Mirage	3,564	11.50	18	1991	3/90
STERLING VINEYARDS							
90	1988	Carneros Winery Lake	8,000	20	20	1992-1996	4/90
89	1987	Carneros Winery Lake	7,000	20	20	1991-1996	4/90
89	1986	Carneros Winery Lake	3,000	20	23	1991-1994	4/90
91	1988	Napa Valley Diamond Mountain Ranch	2,000	NR	NR	1993-2000	7/90
88	1987	Napa Valley Diamond Mountain Ranch	6,000	NR	NR	1993-1999	7/90
86	1986	Napa Valley Diamond Mountain Ranch	7,500	15	15	1991-1996	4/90
87	1985	Napa Valley Diamond Mountain Ranch	5,400	15	17	1993-1999	7/90
86	1984	Napa Valley Diamond Mountain Ranch	3,000	15	17	1991-1995	4/90
86	1983	Napa Valley Diamond Mountain Ranch	1,400	15	18	1991-1994	4/90
73	1982	Napa Valley Estate	10,000	14	17	1991	4/90
71	1981	Napa Valley Estate	4,000	14	17	1991	4/90
70	1980	Napa Valley Estate	4,000	13	17	1991	4/90
73	1979	Napa Valley Estate	2,800	13	17	1991	4/90
70	1977	Napa Valley Estate	4,000	10	20	1991	4/90
59	1976	Napa Valley Estate	2,600	5.25	18	Avoid	4/90
78	1974	Napa Valley Estate	3,000	4.75	35	1991-1993	4/90

NR — Not released.

Score	Vintage	Appellation/Vineyard	Production	Release Price	Current Price	Drink	Last Tasted
STONY HILL VINEYARD							
90	1988	Napa Valley	960	$18	$18	1992-2002	6/90
87	1987	Napa Valley	1,195	18	35	1991-1997	5/90
87	1986	Napa Valley	1,420	16	55	1992-1999	7/90
92	1985	Napa Valley	1947	16	61	1991-2000	5/90
90	1984	Napa Valley	1,820	13	70	1991-1998	5/90
85	1983	Napa Valley	1934	13	70	1991-1996	5/90
85	1982	Napa Valley	2,747	12	63	1991-1994	5/90
86	1981	Napa Valley	2,137	12	68	1991-1996	5/90
86	1980	Napa Valley	2,220	12	72	1991-1998	5/90
81	1979	Napa Valley	2,250	12	95	1991-1994	5/90
85	1978	Napa Valley	1,750	10	90	1991-1996	5/90
91	1977	Napa Valley	1,032	9	95	1991-1999	6/90
88	1976	Napa Valley	670	9	120	1991-1997	6/90
75	1975	Napa Valley	855	9	125	1991-1993	5/90
73	1974	Napa Valley	1,280	7	110	1991-1993	5/90
79	1973	Napa Valley	1,250	7	120	1991-1992	5/90
83	1972	Napa Valley	645	7	110	1991-1992	5/90
80	1971	Napa Valley	580	6	110	1991-1992	5/90
92	1970	Napa Valley	685	6	175	1991-1996	5/90
85	1969	Napa Valley	750	5	175	1991-1993	5/90
93	1968	Napa Valley	750	5	250	1991-1996	5/90
83	1967	Napa Valley	700	4.50	250	1991-1992	5/90
91	1966	Napa Valley	150	4.50	300	1991-1995	5/90
90	1965	Napa Valley	300	4	400	1991-1994	5/90
98	1964	Napa Valley	300	4	450	1991-2000	5/90
87	1963	Napa Valley	160	4	450	1991-1993	5/90
96	1962	Napa Valley	275	3.25	450	1991-1998	5/90
88	1960	Napa Valley	200	3	430	1991-1995	5/90
TREFETHEN VINEYARDS							
90	1988	Napa Valley	28,000	NR	NR	1992-1997	3/90
88	1987	Napa Valley	29,115	16.75	16.75	1992-1996	3/90
87	1986	Napa Valley	26,595	16.25	19	1992-1996	3/90
88	1985	Napa Valley	23,016	15.25	24	1991-1995	3/90
86	1984	Napa Valley	20,291	14.25	25	1991-1993	3/90
77	1983	Napa Valley	18,942	13.75	27	1991	3/90
73	1982	Napa Valley	15,318	13.50	28	1991	3/90
83	1981	Napa Valley	12,933	13	28	1991-1992	3/90
86	1980	Napa Valley	9,369	13	30	1991-1993	3/90
73	1979	Napa Valley	9,486	12	30	1991	3/90
90	1978	Napa Valley	6,352	10	40	1991-1994	3/90
81	1977	Napa Valley	3,966	8.50	40	1991	3/90
74	1976	Napa Valley	3,358	7	40	1991	3/90
73	1975	Napa Valley	1,449	6.50	45	1991	3/90
80	1974	Napa Valley	1,294	5.75	50	1991-1993	3/90
85	1973	Napa Valley	643	6.50	50	1991-1993	3/90
VICHON WINERY							
88	1988	Napa Valley	25,800	17	17	1991-1996	3/90
87	1987	Napa Valley	13,500	16	16	1991-1996	3/90
90	1986	Napa Valley	8,000	15	17	1991-1996	3/90
88	1985	Napa Valley	20,900	15	17	1991-1995	3/90
86	1984	Napa Valley	17,600	15	17	1991-1994	3/90
71	1983	Napa Valley	14,900	15	18	1991	3/90
66	1982	Napa Valley	9,500	15	20	Avoid	3/90
76	1981	Napa Valley	7,000	15	25	1991-1993	3/90
87	1980	Napa Valley	3,800	15	25	1991-1995	3/90

NR — Not released.

Score	Vintage	Appellation/Vineyard	Production	Release Price	Current Price	Drink	Last Tasted
WHITE OAK VINEYARDS & WINERY							
88	1988	Sonoma County Myers Limited Release	988	$18	$20	1992-1997	5/90
81	1987	Sonoma County Myers Limited Release	843	18	20	1991-1994	5/90
87	1986	Sonoma County Myers Limited Release	621	16	20	1991-1996	5/90
90	1985	Alexander Valley Myers Limited Release	237	14.50	22	1991-1996	5/90
88	1988	Sonoma County	6,000	12	12	1991-1996	5/90
85	1987	Sonoma County	4,000	11	16	1991-1996	5/90
86	1986	Sonoma County	3,500	11	16	1991-1995	5/90
89	1985	Sonoma County	3,000	10.50	16	1991-1996	5/90
86	1984	Sonoma County	3,000	10	16	1991-1996	5/90
ZD WINES							
89	1988	California	18,418	20	20	1992-1996	3/90
85	1987	California	15,203	18.50	25	1991-1995	3/90
85	1986	California	15,773	18	25	1991-1997	6/90
90	1985	California	9,639	16	28	1992-1996	3/90
90	1984	California	7,631	15	30	1991-1995	3/90
74	1983	California	5,369	14	25	1991-1994	3/90
76	1982	California	5,506	14	30	1991-1993	3/90
87	1981	California	5,742	13	28	1991-1994	3/90
81	1980	California	4,005	13	28	1991-1994	3/90

NR — Not released.

APPENDIX 2
All Wines Tasted, Listed By Score

Vintage	Winery	Appellation/Vineyard	Case Production	Release Price	Current Price	Drink	Last Tasted
SCORE: 98							
1964	STONY HILL VINEYARD	Napa Valley	300	$4	$450	1991-2000	5/90
SCORE: 96							
1987	CHATEAU ST. JEAN	Alexander Valley Robert Young Vineyards Reserve 1.5L	112	NR	NR	1993-2000	7/90
1962	STONY HILL VINEYARD	Napa Valley	275	3.25	450	1991-1998	5/90
SCORE: 95							
1982	CHALONE VINEYARD	Chalone	5,125	18	53	1991-1996	1/90
1972	CHATEAU MONTELENA WINERY	Napa and Alexander Valleys	2,000	6	110	1991-1997	2/90
1985	CHATEAU ST. JEAN	Alexander Valley Robert Young Vineyards Reserve 1.5L	978	40	40	1992-1998	7/90
1987	FLORA SPRINGS WINE CO.	Napa Valley Barrel Fermented	3,400	20	24	1992-1997	1/90
1979	GRGICH HILLS CELLAR	Napa Valley	10,000	16	55	1991-1994	3/90
1978	HANZELL VINEYARDS	Sonoma Valley	310	13	80	1991-1998	1/90
1988	KISTLER VINEYARDS	Sonoma Valley Kistler Estate Vineyard	507	26	26	1991-1996	2/90
SCORE: 94							
1985	CHALONE VINEYARD	Chalone Reserve	308	28	42	1991-1998	6/90
1980	CHALONE VINEYARD	Chalone Reserve	166	18	55	1991-1997	5/90
1986	CHALONE VINEYARD	Chalone	4,768	22	48	1991-1998	1/90
1986	CUVAISON WINERY	Carneros Reserve	1,800	20	28	1992-1996	6/90
1981	EDNA VALLEY VINEYARD	Edna Valley	11,000	12	25	1991-1995	3/90
1987	FERRARI-CARANO VINEYARD & WINERY	Alexander Valley	14,000	16	23	1991-1997	5/90
1983	FLORA SPRINGS WINE CO.	Napa Valley Barrel Fermented	1,200	18	28	1991-1996	1/90
1988	FRANCISCAN VINEYARDS	Napa Valley Cuvée Sauvage	300	20	20	1991-1996	7/90
1966	HANZELL VINEYARDS	Sonoma Valley	260	6	170	1991-2000	1/90
1988	MONTICELLO CELLARS	Napa Valley Corley Reserve	4,000	17.25	17.25	1991-1997	2/90
1984	MONTICELLO CELLARS	Napa Valley Corley Reserve	860	12.50	25	1991-1995	2/90
1987	MOUNT EDEN VINEYARDS	Edna Valley MEV MacGregor Vineyard	1,500	14	18	1991-1997	3/90
1988	SANFORD WINERY	Santa Barbara County Barrel Select	1,000	25	25	1991-1997	6/90
1987	SIMI WINERY	Sonoma County Reserve	2,000	NR	NR	1991-1997	4/90
1982	SIMI WINERY	Sonoma County Reserve	1,000	22	40	1991-1995	4/90
1980	SIMI WINERY	Mendocino County Reserve	1,100	20	40	1991-1997	4/90
1981	SONOMA-CUTRER VINEYARDS	Sonoma Valley Les Pierres	850	14.50	40	1991-1997	3/90
SCORE: 93							
1982	CHALONE VINEYARD	Chalone Reserve	498	25	48	1991-1996	5/90
1981	CHALONE VINEYARD	Chalone	3,545	17	53	1991-1996	4/90
1973	CHATEAU MONTELENA WINERY	Napa and Alexander Valleys	2,000	6.50	100	1991-1998	2/90
1985	CUVAISON WINERY	Napa Valley	6,000	12	20	1991-1996	4/90
1980	FAR NIENTE WINERY	Napa Valley	6,500	16.50	45	1991-1997	2/90
1988	FERRARI-CARANO VINEYARD & WINERY	Alexander Valley	22,000	18	18	1991-1995	5/90
1988	FERRARI-CARANO VINEYARD & WINERY	California Reserve	1,200	NR	NR	1992-1998	6/90
1986	FERRARI-CARANO VINEYARD & WINERY	California Reserve	300	28	42	1991-1997	5/90
1985	FORMAN VINEYARD	Napa Valley	800	15	45	1991-1995	2/90
1988	GRGICH HILLS CELLAR	Napa Valley	20,000	22	22	1992-1999	7/90
1961	HEITZ WINE CELLAR	Napa Valley	250	6	150	1991-2000	6/90
1987	KISTLER VINEYARDS	Russian River Valley Dutton Ranch	4,020	18	24	1991-1993	2/90

NR — Not released.

Vintage	Winery	Appellation / Vineyard	Case Production	Release Price	Current Price	Drink	Last Tasted
1987	KISTLER VINEYARDS	Sonoma Valley Durell Vineyard	1,300	$16	$20	1991-1997	2/90
1988	LONG VINEYARDS	Napa Valley	900	27.50	30	1991-1998	4/90
1983	MONTICELLO CELLARS	Napa Valley Jefferson Ranch	1,200	10	20	1991-1995	7/90
1988	SONOMA-CUTRER VINEYARDS	Sonoma Valley Les Pierres	11,075	22.50	22.50	1992-2001	7/90
1979	ST. CLEMENT VINEYARDS	Napa Valley	3,000	12	27	1991-1996	3/90
1968	STONY HILL VINEYARD	Napa Valley	750	5	250	1991-1996	5/90

SCORE: 92

Vintage	Winery	Appellation / Vineyard	Case Production	Release Price	Current Price	Drink	Last Tasted
1985	S. ANDERSON VINEYARD	Stags Leap District Estate	3,500	14	25	1991-1995	3/90
1988	ARROWOOD VINEYARDS & WINERY	Sonoma County	6,300	18	18	1992-1997	4/90
1987	ARROWOOD VINEYARDS & WINERY	Sonoma County Réserve Spéciale 1.5L	57	50	50	1991-1997	4/90
1980	CHALONE VINEYARD	Chalone	3,510	17	53	1991-1995	1/90
1982	CHATEAU MONTELENA WINERY	Alexander Valley	5,800	14	36	1991-1996	2/90
1986	CHATEAU ST. JEAN	Alexander Valley Robert Young Vineyards	13,007	18	25	1992-1998	3/90
1976	CHATEAU ST. JEAN	Alexander Valley Robert Young Vineyards	1,400	8.75	25	1991-1994	7/90
1985	CHATEAU ST. JEAN	Alexander Valley Belle Terre Vineyards	3,371	16	25	1992-1996	3/90
1987	CLOS DU BOIS WINERY	Alexander Valley Winemaker's Reserve	3,565	24	24	1991-1995	2/90
1988	CUVAISON WINERY	Carneros Reserve	2,400	NR	NR	1993-2001	6/90
1987	DE LOACH VINEYARDS	Russian River Valley O.F.S	2,400	22	25	1991-1995	5/90
1979	FAR NIENTE WINERY	Napa Valley	3,700	15	45	1991-1996	2/90
1986	FERRARI-CARANO VINEYARD & WINERY	Alexander Valley	7,200	16	28	1991-1996	5/90
1980	FISHER VINEYARDS	Sonoma County Whitney's Vineyard	24	20	30	1991-1996	2/90
1988	FLORA SPRINGS WINE CO.	Napa Valley Barrel Fermented	4,700	24	24	1993-1997	4/90
1988	FORMAN VINEYARD	Napa Valley	1,400	20	27	1991-1994	2/90
1986	FORMAN VINEYARD	Napa Valley	1,000	18	45	1991-1994	2/90
1986	GIRARD WINERY	Napa Valley Reserve	701	25	25	1991-1996	3/90
1986	GIRARD WINERY	Napa Valley Estate	5,297	13.50	28	1991-1996	3/90
1985	GRGICH HILLS CELLAR	Napa Valley	25,000	22	33	1991-1995	3/90
1983	GRGICH HILLS CELLAR	Napa Valley	15,000	17	33	1991-1995	3/90
1978	GRGICH HILLS CELLAR	Napa Valley	6,000	13.75	60	1991-1996	3/90
1987	KENDALL-JACKSON VINEYARDS	California The Proprietor's	11,000	20	20	1991-1995	4/90
1988	KISTLER VINEYARDS	Russian River Valley Dutton Ranch	4,987	22	22	1991-1995	2/90
1986	KISTLER VINEYARDS	Sonoma Valley Kistler Estate Vineyard	397	18	35	1991-1997	2/90
1988	KISTLER VINEYARDS	Sonoma Valley McCrea Vineyard	1,010	24	24	1991-1996	2/90
1986	LONG VINEYARDS	Napa Valley	800	27.50	45	1991-1997	4/90
1964	MAYACAMAS VINEYARDS	Napa Valley	500	1.75	200	1991-1994	1/90
1987	ROBERT MONDAVI WINERY	Napa Valley Reserve	10,000	26	26	1991-1997	6/90
1988	MORGAN WINERY	Monterey Reserve	1,500	20	20	1991-1997	6/90
1984	SAINTSBURY	Carneros	6,400	11	25	1991-1994	2/90
1988	SAINTSBURY	Carneros Reserve	1,800	20	20	1992-1998	2/90
1985	SANFORD WINERY	Santa Barbara County Barrel Select	150	20	30	1991-1996	2/90
1988	SANFORD WINERY	Santa Barbara County	18,000	16	16	1991-1997	6/90
1987	SANFORD WINERY	Santa Barbara County	18,000	15	16	1991-1996	2/90
1988	SEQUOIA GROVE VINEYARDS	Napa Valley Estate	4,228	16	16	1991-1996	5/90
1987	SILVERADO VINEYARDS	Napa Valley Limited Reserve	1,300	NR	NR	1993-2000	7/90
1986	SIMI WINERY	Sonoma County Reserve	1,600	28	32	1991-1998	4/90
1979	SMITH-MADRONE VINEYARD	Napa Valley	580	10	28	1990-2000	5/90
1987	SONOMA-CUTRER VINEYARDS	Sonoma Valley Les Pierres	11,510	22.50	26	1992-1997	3/90
1985	SONOMA-CUTRER VINEYARDS	Sonoma Valley Les Pierres	8,500	17.50	30	1991-1997	3/90
1988	SONOMA-CUTRER VINEYARDS	Russian River Valley Cutrer Vineyard	10,010	17.50	17.50	1992-2000	7/90

NR — Not released.

Vintage	Winery	Appellation/Vineyard	Case Production	Release Price	Current Price	Drink	Last Tasted
1985	STONY HILL VINEYARD	Napa Valley	1,947	$16	$61	1991-2000	5/90
1970	STONY HILL VINEYARD	Napa Valley	685	6	175	1991-1996	5/90

SCORE: 91

Vintage	Winery	Appellation/Vineyard	Case Production	Release Price	Current Price	Drink	Last Tasted
1985	ALTAMURA WINERY & VINEYARDS	Napa Valley	600	14	21	1991-1996	1/90
1986	BUENA VISTA WINERY	Carneros Private Reserve	3,700	16.50	17	1991-1996	3/90
1973	CHAPPELLET VINEYARD	Napa Valley	400	6.75	50	1991-1994	3/90
1988	CHATEAU MONTELENA WINERY	Alexander Valley	3,100	20	20	1992-2000	2/90
1986	CHATEAU MONTELENA WINERY	Alexander Valley	5,700	18	26	1991-1997	2/90
1985	CHATEAU MONTELENA WINERY	Alexander Valley	8,600	16	28	1991-1997	2/90
1981	CHATEAU MONTELENA WINERY	Alexander Valley	2,600	14	36	1991-1997	2/90
1986	CHATEAU MONTELENA WINERY	Napa Valley	12,800	18	25	1991-1998	2/90
1986	CHATEAU ST. JEAN	Alexander Valley Robert Young Vineyards Reserve 1.5L	507	NR	NR	1992-2000	7/90
1988	CHATEAU ST. JEAN	Alexander Valley Robert Young Vineyards	13,638	18	18	1992-1998	3/90
1987	CHATEAU ST. JEAN	Alexander Valley Robert Young Vineyards	13,108	18	25	1992-1999	3/90
1985	CHATEAU ST. JEAN	Alexander Valley Robert Young Vineyards	13,613	18	26	1992-1998	3/90
1987	CHATEAU ST. JEAN	Alexander Valley Belle Terre Vineyards	2,590	16	22	1992-1998	3/90
1986	CHATEAU WOLTNER	Howell Mountain Estate Reserve	1228	24	24	1991-1997	4/90
1983	CLOS DU BOIS WINERY	Alexander Valley Calcaire Vineyard	905	12	30	1991-1996	2/90
1987	CUVAISON WINERY	Carneros Reserve	1,260	22	22	1992-1998	7/90
1988	CUVAISON WINERY	Carneros	34,000	15	15	1993-1999	4/90
1988	DEHLINGER WINERY	Russian River Valley	4,000	12	12	1991-1996	4/90
1987	EDNA VALLEY VINEYARD	Edna Valley	41,000	14	20	1991-1996	3/90
1988	FAR NIENTE WINERY	Napa Valley	24,000	26	28	1992-1998	2/90
1987	FAR NIENTE WINERY	Napa Valley	20,000	26	30	1992-1998	2/90
1982	FAR NIENTE WINERY	Napa Valley Estate	2,000	18	38	1991-1996	2/90
1985	FERRARI-CARANO VINEYARD & WINERY	Alexander Valley	2,500	14	30	1991-1996	5/90
1979	FLORA SPRINGS WINE CO.	Napa Valley	200	9	25	1991-1994	1/90
1987	FRANCISCAN VINEYARDS	Napa Valley Cuvée Sauvage	400	20	20	1991-1996	6/90
1986	FRANCISCAN VINEYARDS	Napa Valley Reserve	3,000	14	15	1991-1997	4/90
1984	FROG'S LEAP WINERY	Napa Valley	1,100	12	23	1991-1995	3/90
1988	FROG'S LEAP WINERY	Carneros	1,200	16	16	1992-1997	3/90
1988	GIRARD WINERY	Napa Valley Reserve	700	NR	NR	1992-2000	6/90
1985	GIRARD WINERY	Napa Valley Reserve	242	25	35	1991-1995	3/90
1986	GRGICH HILLS CELLAR	Napa Valley	25,000	22	33	1991-1996	3/90
1973	HACIENDA WINERY	Sonoma County Clair de Lune	495	5	50	1991-1994	4/90
1976	HANZELL VINEYARDS	Sonoma Valley	210	12	90	1991-1995	1/90
1968	HANZELL VINEYARDS	Sonoma Valley	240	6	140	1991-1995	1/90
1987	HESS COLLECTION WINERY	Napa Valley	4,100	13.25	15	1991-1997	4/90
1987	WILLIAM HILL WINERY	Napa Valley Reserve	21,042	18	18	1992-1998	3/90
1986	WILLIAM HILL WINERY	Napa Valley Reserve	18,228	17	20	1991-1995	3/90
1986	KENDALL-JACKSON VINEYARDS	Sonoma Valley Durell Vineyard	500	14	16	1991-1996	6/90
1988	KISTLER VINEYARDS	Sonoma Valley Durell Vineyard	2,337	17	17	1992-1998	2/90
1988	LA CREMA	California Reserve	5,000	22	22	1991-1999	6/90
1985	LONG VINEYARDS	Napa Valley	850	27.50	45	1991-1996	4/90
1988	ROBERT MONDAVI WINERY	Napa Valley Reserve	12,000	26	26	1992-1997	6/90
1988	NAVARRO VINEYARDS	Anderson Valley Première Reserve	3,596	14	14	1991-1998	5/90
1984	NAVARRO VINEYARDS	Anderson Valley Première Reserve	856	12	22	1991-1995	3/90
1987	ROBERT PECOTA WINERY	Alexander Valley Canepa Vineyard	800	16	18	1991-1996	4/90
1987	PINE RIDGE WINERY	Stags Leap District Pine Ridge Stags Leap Vineyard	2,765	20	20	1991-1996	4/90
1985	RAYMOND VINEYARD & CELLAR	Napa Valley Private Reserve	1,720	18	21	1991-1995	5/90

NR — Not released.

Vintage	Winery	Appellation / Vineyard	Case Production	Release Price	Current Price	Drink	Last Tasted
1987	SANFORD WINERY	Santa Barbara County Barrel Select	300	$24	$30	1991-1997	2/90
1988	SIMI WINERY	Sonoma County Reserve	2,300	NR	NR	1992-1998	7/90
1985	SIMI WINERY	Sonoma County Reserve	1,200	28	32	1991-1996	4/90
1981	SIMI WINERY	Sonoma County Reserve	1,600	20	40	1991-1996	4/90
1987	SMITH-MADRONE VINEYARD	Napa Valley	2,542	13	13	1993-2000	5/90
1987	SONOMA-CUTRER VINEYARDS	Russian River Valley Cutrer Vineyard	9,840	17.50	18	1991-1996	3/90
1981	SONOMA-CUTRER VINEYARDS	Russian River Valley Cutrer Vineyard	2,500	12.50	30	1991-1995	3/90
1988	SONOMA-CUTRER VINEYARDS	Russian River Valley Russian River Ranches	51,900	13.25	14	1992-1998	3/90
1987	ST. CLEMENT VINEYARDS	Napa Valley Abbott's Vineyard	500	17	17	1992-1997	3/90
1988	STERLING VINEYARDS	Napa Valley Diamond Mountain Ranch	2,000	NR	NR	1993-2000	7/90
1977	STONY HILL VINEYARD	Napa Valley	1,032	9	95	1991-1999	6/90
1966	STONY HILL VINEYARD	Napa Valley	150	4.50	300	1991-1995	5/90

SCORE: 90

Vintage	Winery	Appellation / Vineyard	Case Production	Release Price	Current Price	Drink	Last Tasted
1988	ALTAMURA WINERY & VINEYARDS	Napa Valley	2,000	NR	NR	1992-1997	1/90
1986	BERINGER VINEYARDS	Napa Valley Private Reserve	6,747	16	22	1991-1995	4/90
1988	CHALONE VINEYARD	Chalone	8,003	22	27	1992-1999	6/90
1983	CHALONE VINEYARD	Chalone	6,669	18	50	1991-1998	1/90
1986	CHAPPELLET VINEYARD	Napa Valley	4,500	14	14	1991-1997	3/90
1977	CHAPPELLET VINEYARD	Napa Valley	1,500	11.75	40	1991-1998	6/90
1984	CHATEAU MONTELENA WINERY	Alexander Valley	5,600	16	32	1991-1997	2/90
1985	CHATEAU MONTELENA WINERY	Napa Valley	9,000	18	25	1991-1998	2/90
1988	CHATEAU ST. JEAN	Alexander Valley Belle Terre Vineyards	8,848	16	16	1993-1998	3/90
1986	CHATEAU ST. JEAN	Alexander Valley Belle Terre Vineyards	3,625	16	20	1992-1997	3/90
1984	CLOS DU BOIS WINERY	Alexander Valley Calcaire Vineyard	1,590	12	30	1991-1994	2/90
1988	CLOS DU BOIS WINERY	Dry Creek Valley Flintwood Vineyard	5,469	18	18	1992-1997	2/90
1987	CLOS PEGASE	Carneros	4,402	15.50	17	1991-1995	3/90
1987	CONGRESS SPRINGS VINEYARDS	Santa Clara County San Ysidro Reserve	2,000	16	23	1991-1995	4/90
1984	CONGRESS SPRINGS VINEYARDS	Santa Clara County	2,053	11	25	1991-1994	4/90
1987	CUVAISON WINERY	Napa Valley	31,000	13.50	16	1993-1998	4/90
1984	DE LOACH VINEYARDS	Russian River Valley O.F.S	600	20	28	1991-1995	2/90
1985	DE LOACH VINEYARDS	Russian River Valley	12,000	14	23	1991-1994	2/90
1987	DEHLINGER WINERY	Russian River Valley	4,900	11.50	12	1991-1996	4/90
1985	FAR NIENTE WINERY	Napa Valley	14,300	24	33	1992-1998	2/90
1984	FISHER VINEYARDS	Sonoma County Whitney's Vineyard	48	20	30	1991-1995	2/90
1986	FISHER VINEYARDS	Sonoma County Coach Insignia	3,000	17	20	1991-1997	2/90
1987	FOLIE A DEUX WINERY	Napa Valley	5,300	15	16	1992-1997	6/90
1986	FROG'S LEAP WINERY	Napa Valley	1,500	12	18	1991-1995	3/90
1985	GIRARD WINERY	Napa Valley Estate	4,740	13.50	25	1991-1996	3/90
1981	GIRARD WINERY	Napa Valley Estate	4,736	12.50	35	1991-1995	3/90
1987	GRGICH HILLS CELLAR	Napa Valley	33,000	22	28	1992-1997	6/90
1984	GRGICH HILLS CELLAR	Napa Valley	24,000	18	33	1991-1995	3/90
1988	HANZELL VINEYARDS	Sonoma Valley	750	24	24	1993-2000	5/90
1987	HANZELL VINEYARDS	Sonoma Valley	1,050	24	28	1993-2000	1/90
1985	HANZELL VINEYARDS	Sonoma Valley	830	22	35	1991-1999	1/90
1980	HANZELL VINEYARDS	Sonoma Valley	740	17	60	1991-1998	1/90
1972	HANZELL VINEYARDS	Sonoma Valley	170	7	75	1991-1995	1/90
1969	HANZELL VINEYARDS	Sonoma Valley	220	6	140	1991-1995	1/90
1957	HANZELL VINEYARDS	California	240	4	240	1991-1993	12/89
1985	WILLIAM HILL WINERY	Napa Valley Reserve	16,313	16	24	1991-1997	3/90

NR — Not released.

Vintage	Winery	Appellation/Vineyard	Case Production	Release Price	Current Price	Drink	Last Tasted
1986	KISTLER VINEYARDS	Russian River Valley Dutton Ranch	3,151	$16.50	$28	1991-1997	2/90
1987	KISTLER VINEYARDS	Sonoma Valley Kistler Estate Vineyard	866	22	26	1991-1996	2/90
1987	LONG VINEYARDS	Napa Valley	900	27.50	35	1991-1998	4/90
1987	MATANZAS CREEK WINERY	Sonoma County	13,506	18	20	1991-1996	2/90
1985	MAYACAMAS VINEYARDS	Napa Valley	1,415	20	25	1991-1998	1/90
1988	MONTICELLO CELLARS	Napa Valley Jefferson Ranch	7,500	12.25	12.25	1991-1997	2/90
1987	MOUNT EDEN VINEYARDS	Santa Cruz Mountains	1,348	28	32	1992-1997	3/90
1979	MOUNT EDEN VINEYARDS	Santa Cruz Mountains	495	16	60	1991-1996	3/90
1987	PINE RIDGE WINERY	Napa Valley Knollside Cuvée	9,854	15	16	1991-1995	4/90
1988	RAYMOND VINEYARD & CELLAR	Napa Valley Private Reserve	4,434	NR	NR	1991-1997	5/90
1988	SAINTSBURY	Carneros	14,750	14	14	1992-1997	2/90
1987	SAINTSBURY	Carneros	13,150	13	15	1992-1997	2/90
1985	SAINTSBURY	Carneros	6,600	11	19	1991-1996	2/90
1985	SANFORD WINERY	Santa Barbara County	5,000	13.50	20	1991-1997	2/90
1986	SILVERADO VINEYARDS	Napa Valley	22,000	12	16	1991-1996	3/90
1986	SILVERADO VINEYARDS	Napa Valley Limited Reserve	650	25	25	1992-1997	7/90
1988	STAG'S LEAP WINE CELLARS	Napa Valley Reserve	335	28	28	1993-1998	3/90
1988	STERLING VINEYARDS	Carneros Winery Lake	8,000	20	20	1992-1996	4/90
1988	STONY HILL VINEYARD	Napa Valley	960	18	18	1992-2002	6/90
1984	STONY HILL VINEYARD	Napa Valley	1,820	13	70	1991-1998	5/90
1965	STONY HILL VINEYARD	Napa Valley	300	4	400	1991-1994	5/90
1988	TREFETHEN VINEYARDS	Napa Valley	28,000	NR	NR	1992-1997	3/90
1978	TREFETHEN VINEYARDS	Napa Valley	6,352	10	40	1991-1994	3/90
1986	VICHON WINERY	Napa Valley	8,000	15	17	1991-1996	3/90
1985	WHITE OAK VINEYARDS & WINERY	Alexander Valley Myers Limited Release	237	14.50	22	1991-1996	5/90
1985	ZD WINES	California	9,639	16	28	1992-1996	3/90
1984	ZD WINES	California	7,631	15	30	1991-1995	3/90

SCORE: 89

Vintage	Winery	Appellation/Vineyard	Case Production	Release Price	Current Price	Drink	Last Tasted
1988	ACACIA WINERY	Carneros Marina Vineyard	7,133	20	20	1991-1996	1/90
1984	ACACIA WINERY	Napa Valley	7,000	12.50	16	1991-1996	7/90
1987	S. ANDERSON VINEYARD	Stags Leap District Proprietor's Reserve	480	20	20	1991-1996	3/90
1984	S. ANDERSON VINEYARD	Stags Leap District Estate	1,770	12.50	25	1991-1994	3/90
1987	ARROWOOD VINEYARDS & WINERY	Sonoma County	6,000	18	18	1991-1995	4/90
1986	ARROWOOD VINEYARDS & WINERY	Sonoma County	4,600	18	25	1991-1995	4/90
1988	BEAULIEU VINEYARD	Carneros Carneros Reserve	10,000	14	14	1992-1994	6/90
1988	CHALONE VINEYARD	Chalone Reserve	217	NR	NR	1992-2000	6/90
1979	CHALONE VINEYARD	Chalone	3,728	14	55	1991-1994	1/90
1988	CHAPPELLET VINEYARD	Napa Valley	4,500	NR	NR	1991-1998	6/90
1987	CHATEAU MONTELENA WINERY	Alexander Valley	5,400	20	24	1992-1998	2/90
1983	CHATEAU ST. JEAN	Alexander Valley Belle Terre Vineyards	1,281	16.75	30	1991-1995	3/90
1986	CHATEAU ST. JEAN	Dry Creek Valley Frank Johnson Vineyards	2,115	14	19	1991-1995	7/90
1986	CHATEAU WOLTNER	Howell Mountain St. Thomas Vineyard	747	36	37	1991-1997	4/90
1988	CLOS DU BOIS WINERY	Alexander Valley Calcaire Vineyard	7,334	17	17	1992-1997	2/90
1988	CLOS DU BOIS WINERY	Russian River Valley Winemaker's Reserve	3,807	NR	NR	1993-1999	5/90
1987	CLOS DU VAL WINE CO.	Carneros	13,000	13	13	1991-1995	6/90
1988	CLOS PEGASE	Carneros	5,128	16.50	16.50	1991-1997	3/90
1986	CLOS PEGASE	Carneros	2,825	15.50	17	1991-1996	3/90
1986	CUVAISON WINERY	Napa Valley	22,000	12.75	18	1992-1998	4/90
1986	DE LOACH VINEYARDS	Russian River Valley	18,000	14	20	1991-1994	2/90
1988	EDNA VALLEY VINEYARD	Edna Valley	46,500	14.75	16	1992-1997	3/90
1983	FAR NIENTE WINERY	Napa Valley Estate	2,000	22	38	1991-1995	2/90

NR — Not released.

Vintage	Winery	Appellation / Vineyard	Case Production	Release Price	Current Price	Drink	Last Tasted
1987	FERRARI-CARANO VINEYARD & WINERY	California Reserve	780	$28	$28	1992-1998	5/90
1981	FLORA SPRINGS WINE CO.	Napa Valley Special Selection	1,500	12	25	1991-1995	1/90
1987	FORMAN VINEYARD	Napa Valley	1,400	18	35	1991-1994	2/90
1988	FREEMARK ABBEY WINERY	Napa Valley	19,200	15	15	1991-1997	2/90
1977	GRGICH HILLS CELLAR	Sonoma County	6,000	11	65	1991-1993	3/90
1986	HACIENDA WINERY	Sonoma County Clair de Lune	7,000	12	18	1991-1995	4/90
1982	HANZELL VINEYARDS	Sonoma Valley	940	19	45	1991-1996	1/90
1967	HANZELL VINEYARDS	Sonoma Valley	330	6	140	1991-1994	1/90
1987	KENDALL-JACKSON VINEYARDS	Anderson Valley De Patie Vineyard	200	14	14	1991-1995	4/90
1988	KENWOOD VINEYARDS	Sonoma Valley Beltane Ranch	3,000	15	15	1992-1998	7/90
1984	KISTLER VINEYARDS	Russian River Valley Dutton Ranch	3,911	15	30	1991-1995	2/90
1986	KISTLER VINEYARDS	Sonoma Valley Durell Vineyard	620	16	25	1991-1997	2/90
1988	MARKHAM VINEYARDS	Napa Valley	8,026	12	12	1991-1997	2/90
1988	MATANZAS CREEK WINERY	Sonoma County	17,165	18.75	18.75	1991-1996	2/90
1986	MATANZAS CREEK WINERY	Sonoma County	8,817	17.50	22	1991-1994	2/90
1984	MATANZAS CREEK WINERY	Sonoma County	3,717	15	28	1991-1994	2/90
1988	MAYACAMAS VINEYARDS	Napa Valley	1,427	NR	NR	1992-1997	6/90
1986	ROBERT MONDAVI WINERY	Napa Valley Reserve	11,000	25	28	1991-1995	3/90
1986	MONTICELLO CELLARS	Napa Valley Corley Reserve	3,200	16.50	18	1991-1996	2/90
1988	MORGAN WINERY	Monterey	8,500	15	16	1991-1996	5/90
1986	MORGAN WINERY	Monterey	6,000	14	20	1991-1995	5/90
1982	MORGAN WINERY	Monterey County	2,000	12	28	1991-1995	5/90
1981	MOUNT EDEN VINEYARDS	Santa Cruz Mountains	445	18	60	1991-1995	3/90
1985	NAVARRO VINEYARDS	Anderson Valley Première Reserve	1,331	12	18	1991-1995	3/90
1983	NEWTON VINEYARD	Napa Valley	2,000	12	19	1991-1998	5/90
1985	ROBERT PECOTA WINERY	Alexander Valley Canepa Vineyard	800	16	18	1991-1996	7/90
1980	ROBERT PECOTA WINERY	Alexander Valley Canepa Vineyard	325	12	20	1990-1994	4/90
1988	ROMBAUER VINEYARDS	Napa Valley Reserve	330	NR	NR	1992-1997	6/90
1987	SAINTSBURY	Carneros Reserve	1,450	20	20	1992-1997	2/90
1985	SEQUOIA GROVE VINEYARDS	Napa Valley Estate	4,981	$16	$20	1991-1995	5/90
1984	SEQUOIA GROVE VINEYARDS	Napa Valley Estate	1,808	$14	$20	1991-1994	5/90
1984	SIMI WINERY	Sonoma County Reserve	1,100	28	32	1991-1996	4/90
1986	SMITH-MADRONE VINEYARD	Napa Valley	2,375	12.50	16	1990-1998	5/90
1984	SONOMA-CUTRER VINEYARDS	Sonoma Valley Les Pierres	7,000	16.50	30	1991-1995	3/90
1986	SONOMA-CUTRER VINEYARDS	Russian River Valley Cutrer Vineyard	7,100	16	20	1992-1997	3/90
1986	ST. CLEMENT VINEYARDS	Napa Valley	1,450	15	15	1992-1997	3/90
1987	STAG'S LEAP WINE CELLARS	Napa Valley Reserve	1,172	28	28	1992-1997	3/90
1987	STAG'S LEAP WINE CELLARS	Napa Valley	17,710	18	18	1992-1997	3/90
1987	STERLING VINEYARDS	Carneros Winery Lake	7,000	20	20	1991-1996	4/90
1986	STERLING VINEYARDS	Carneros Winery Lake	3,000	20	23	1991-1994	4/90
1985	WHITE OAK VINEYARDS & WINERY	Sonoma County	3,000	10.50	16	1991-1996	5/90
1988	ZD WINES	California	18,418	20	20	1992-1996	3/90

SCORE: 88

Vintage	Winery	Appellation / Vineyard	Case Production	Release Price	Current Price	Drink	Last Tasted
1984	ACACIA WINERY	Carneros Winery Lake Vineyard	2,100	18	25	1991-1994	1/90
1986	ALTAMURA WINERY & VINEYARDS	Napa Valley	1,500	15	21	1993-1997	1/90
1988	S. ANDERSON VINEYARD	Stags Leap District Estate	4,388	18	18	1992-1997	3/90
1984	BERINGER VINEYARDS	Napa Valley Private Reserve	4,102	15	24	1991-1994	4/90
1974	BERINGER VINEYARDS	Santa Barbara County	1,000	5	45	1991-1993	4/90
1988	BOUCHAINE VINEYARDS	Carneros Estate Reserve	1,600	NR	NR	1993-1998	6/90
1986	BOUCHAINE VINEYARDS	Carneros Estate Reserve	1,500	19	19	1991-1995	2/90
1986	BOUCHAINE VINEYARDS	Napa Valley	7,000	13	17	1991-1995	2/90
1988	BURGESS CELLARS	Napa Valley Triere Vineyard	18,000	16	16	1991-1996	12/89

NR — Not released.

Vintage	Winery	Appellation / Vineyard	Case Production	Release Price	Current Price	Drink	Last Tasted
1985	BURGESS CELLARS	Napa Valley Vintage Reserve	17,000	$13	$16	1990-1995	12/89
1984	CHALONE VINEYARD	Chalone	2,885	18	45	1991-1998	1/90
1988	CHATEAU MONTELENA WINERY	Napa Valley	13,200	20	20	1993-2000	7/90
1984	CHATEAU MONTELENA WINERY	Napa Valley	8,400	18	28	1991-1995	2/90
1981	CHATEAU MONTELENA WINERY	Napa Valley	7,900	16	32	1991-1994	2/90
1974	CHATEAU MONTELENA WINERY	Napa and Alexander Valleys	2,200	8	70	1991-1996	2/90
1984	CHATEAU ST. JEAN	Alexander Valley Robert Young Vineyards	13,513	20	30	1991-1995	3/90
1983	CHATEAU ST. JEAN	Alexander Valley Robert Young Vineyards	7,697	18	33	1991-1994	3/90
1980	CHATEAU ST. JEAN	Alexander Valley Belle Terre Vineyards	4,427	15	24	1991-1994	3/90
1975	CHATEAU ST. JEAN	Alexander Valley Belle Terre Vineyards	800	7.50	22	1991-1993	7/90
1984	CHATEAU ST. JEAN	Dry Creek Valley Frank Johnson Vineyards	3,100	14	20	1991-1995	7/90
1988	CHATEAU ST. JEAN	Alexander Valley Jimtown Ranch	700	NR	NR	1992-1998	7/90
1987	CHATEAU ST. JEAN	Sonoma Valley McCrea Vineyards	364	15	15	1992-1996	3/90
1982	CHATEAU ST. JEAN	Sonoma Valley McCrea Vineyards	501	13	18	1991-1995	7/90
1975	CHATEAU ST. JEAN	Sonoma County Beltane Ranch	500	12.50	21	1991-1994	7/90
1976	CHATEAU ST. JEAN	Alexander Valley Riverview Vineyards	600	9.50	22	1991-1994	7/90
1987	CHATEAU WOLTNER	Howell Mountain Estate Reserve	2,151	24	24	1991-1997	4/90
1986	CHATEAU WOLTNER	Howell Mountain Titus Vineyard	179	54	54	1993-1998	4/90
1987	CLOS DU BOIS WINERY	Alexander Valley Calcaire Vineyard	6,593	20	20	1992-1996	2/90
1986	CLOS DU BOIS WINERY	Dry Creek Valley Flintwood Vineyard	4,911	19.50	25	1992-1996	2/90
1988	CLOS DU VAL WINE CO.	Carneros	15,000	16	16	1992-1997	6/90
1988	CLOS PEGASE	Napa Valley	13,681	12	12	1991-1996	3/90
1988	CONGRESS SPRINGS VINEYARDS	Santa Cruz Mountains Monmartre	224	30	30	1991-1996	4/90
1984	DE LOACH VINEYARDS	Russian River Valley	8,000	12.50	24	1991-1994	2/90
1986	EDNA VALLEY VINEYARD	Edna Valley	36,000	13.50	20	1991-1995	3/90
1986	FAR NIENTE WINERY	Napa Valley	18,000	24	31	1991-1997	2/90
1981	FAR NIENTE WINERY	Napa Valley	7,000	16.50	40	1991-1996	2/90
1988	FISHER VINEYARDS	Sonoma County Whitney's Vineyard	65	NR	NR	1992-1997	2/90
1981	FISHER VINEYARDS	Sonoma County	2,000	14	25	1990-1993	2/90
1984	FLORA SPRINGS WINE CO.	Napa Valley Barrel Fermented	1,800	18	28	1991-1994	1/90
1980	FLORA SPRINGS WINE CO.	Napa Valley Special Selection	300	12	25	1991-1993	1/90
1986	FOLIE A DEUX WINERY	Napa Valley	2,600	15	18	1991-1997	6/90
1985	FOLIE A DEUX WINERY	Napa Valley	1,200	14.50	18	1991-1995	6/90
1987	FROG'S LEAP WINERY	Napa Valley	1,800	14	16	1991-1995	3/90
1988	GIRARD WINERY	Napa Valley Estate	4,800	16	16	1991-1997	6/90
1981	GRGICH HILLS CELLAR	Napa Valley	16,000	17	45	1991-1995	3/90
1980	GRGICH HILLS CELLAR	Napa Valley	15,000	17	50	1991-1994	3/90
1984	HACIENDA WINERY	Sonoma County Clair de Lune	4,285	10	18	1991-1994	4/90
1977	HANZELL VINEYARDS	Sonoma Valley	260	12	85	1991-1994	1/90
1974	HANZELL VINEYARDS	Sonoma Valley	300	9	75	1991-1995	1/90
1959	HANZELL VINEYARDS	California	120	4	200	1991-1995	12/89
1988	HESS COLLECTION WINERY	Napa Valley	10,000	13.75	13.75	1992-1998	4/90
1986	HESS COLLECTION WINERY	Napa Valley	4,285	12.75	16	1991-1996	4/90
1988	WILLIAM HILL WINERY	Napa Valley Reserve	30,088	18	18	1992-1998	3/90
1984	WILLIAM HILL WINERY	Napa Valley Reserve	652	20	24	1991-1996	3/90
1988	INGLENOOK-NAPA VALLEY	Napa Valley Reserve	2,000	NR	NR	1992-1998	4/90

NR — Not released.

Vintage	Winery	Appellation/Vineyard	Case Production	Release Price	Current Price	Drink	Last Tasted
1986	INGLENOOK-NAPA VALLEY	Napa Valley Reserve	6,135	$14.50	$14.50	1991-1996	4/90
1985	KISTLER VINEYARDS	California Dutton Ranch/ Winery Lake	5,251	15	30	1991-1994	2/90
1984	LA CREMA	Monterey County Ventana Vineyard	2,000	18	22	1991-1998	6/90
1984	LONG VINEYARDS	Napa Valley	600	27.50	45	1991-1995	4/90
1985	MATANZAS CREEK WINERY	Sonoma County	6,221	16.50	28	1991-1994	2/90
1982	MATANZAS CREEK WINERY	Sonoma Valley Estate	700	18	25	1991-1994	2/90
1984	MAYACAMAS VINEYARDS	Napa Valley	1,715	18	25	1991-1998	3/90
1955	MAYACAMAS VINEYARDS	Napa Valley	250	1	325	1991-1995	1/90
1985	ROBERT MONDAVI WINERY	Napa Valley Reserve	13,000	25	27	1991-1995	3/90
1983	ROBERT MONDAVI WINERY	Napa Valley Reserve	7,800	20	25	1991-1995	3/90
1974	ROBERT MONDAVI WINERY	Napa Valley Reserve	1,000	10	45	1991-1994	3/90
1988	MOUNT EDEN VINEYARDS	Santa Cruz Mountains	715	30	30	1992-1997	3/90
1986	MOUNT EDEN VINEYARDS	Santa Cruz Mountains	677	25	42	1991-1996	3/90
1988	MOUNT EDEN VINEYARDS	Edna Valley MacGregor Vineyard	1,551	14	14	1991-1996	6/90
1988	MURPHY-GOODE	Alexander Valley	12,000	11.50	11.50	1991-1995	4/90
1988	NEWTON VINEYARD	Napa Valley	5,546	14.50	14.50	1991-1997	3/90
1987	NEWTON VINEYARD	Napa Valley	6,000	14	14	1991-1997	3/90
1988	PINE RIDGE WINERY	Stags Leap District Pine Ridge Stags Leap Vineyard	2,063	20	20	1991-1996	7/90
1986	PINE RIDGE WINERY	Stags Leap District Pine Ridge Stags Leap Vineyard	2,215	19	23	1991-1996	4/90
1988	PINE RIDGE WINERY	Napa Valley Knollside Cuvée	11,062	15	15	1991-1995	7/90
1986	PINE RIDGE WINERY	Napa Valley Knollside Cuvée	7,918	14	16	1991-1995	4/90
1983	PINE RIDGE WINERY	Napa Valley Oak Knoll Cuvée	3,685	13	18	1991-1994	4/90
1987	RAYMOND VINEYARD & CELLAR	Napa Valley Private Reserve	4,404	22	22	1991-1996	5/90
1988	ROMBAUER VINEYARDS	Napa Valley	4,014	15	15	1991-1996	6/90
1986	SAINTSBURY	Carneros	10,075	12	17	1992-1997	2/90
1986	SANFORD WINERY	Santa Barbara County	6,000	14	16	1991-1995	2/90
1983	SANFORD WINERY	Central Coast	3,000	12	15	1991-1995	2/90
1987	SEQUOIA GROVE VINEYARDS	Napa Valley Estate	2,167	16	16	1991-1996	5/90
1986	SEQUOIA GROVE VINEYARDS	Napa Valley Estate	2,064	15	18	1991-1994	5/90
1981	SEQUOIA GROVE VINEYARDS	Napa Valley Estate	952	12	20	1991-1995	7/90
1985	SEQUOIA GROVE VINEYARDS	Carneros	4,976	12	16	1991-1995	5/90
1988	SILVERADO VINEYARDS	Napa Valley	41,000	14	14	1991-1996	3/90
1987	SILVERADO VINEYARDS	Napa Valley	30,000	13.50	15	1991-1996	3/90
1983	SIMI WINERY	Sonoma County Reserve	1,000	22	32	1991-1995	4/90
1988	SMITH-MADRONE VINEYARD	Napa Valley	1980	13	13	1993-2000	5/90
1986	SONOMA-CUTRER VINEYARDS	Sonoma Valley Les Pierres	9,125	19.50	27	1992-1997	3/90
1982	SONOMA-CUTRER VINEYARDS	Sonoma Valley Les Pierres	2,500	15	35	1991-1994	3/90
1987	SONOMA-CUTRER VINEYARDS	Russian River Valley Russian River Ranches	53,055	12	16	1991-1995	3/90
1985	SONOMA-CUTRER VINEYARDS	Russian River Valley Russian River Ranches	28,256	11.50	22	1991-1995	3/90
1988	ST. CLEMENT VINEYARDS	Napa Valley	3,683	15	15	1992-1998	3/90
1984	ST. CLEMENT VINEYARDS	Napa Valley	4,000	14.50	17	1991-1996	3/90
1986	STAG'S LEAP WINE CELLARS	Napa Valley Reserve	480	26	26	1991-1994	6/90
1987	STERLING VINEYARDS	Napa Valley Diamond Mountain Ranch	6,000	NR	NR	1993-1999	7/90
1976	STONY HILL VINEYARD	Napa Valley	670	9	120	1991-1997	6/90
1960	STONY HILL VINEYARD	Napa Valley	200	3	430	1991-1995	5/90
1987	TREFETHEN VINEYARDS	Napa Valley	29,115	16.75	16.75	1992-1996	3/90
1985	TREFETHEN VINEYARDS	Napa Valley	23,016	15.25	24	1991-1995	3/90
1988	VICHON WINERY	Napa Valley	25,800	17	17	1991-1996	3/90
1985	VICHON WINERY	Napa Valley	20,900	15	17	1991-1995	3/90
1988	WHITE OAK VINEYARDS & WINERY	Sonoma County Myers Limited Release	988	18	20	1992-1997	5/90
1988	WHITE OAK VINEYARDS & WINERY	Sonoma County	6,000	12	12	1991-1996	5/90

NR — Not released.

Vintage	Winery	Appellation/Vineyard	Case Production	Release Price	Current Price	Drink	Last Tasted
SCORE: 87							
1986	ACACIA WINERY	Carneros	11,500	$15	$18	1991-1993	1/90
1983	ACACIA WINERY	Carneros Winery Lake Vineyard	2,460	18	25	1991-1994	1/90
1987	ALTAMURA WINERY & VINEYARDS	Napa Valley	1,800	16.50	16.50	1993-1998	1/90
1983	S. ANDERSON VINEYARD	Stags Leap District Proprietor's Selection	100	16	40	1991-1993	3/90
1987	BEAULIEU VINEYARD	Carneros Los Carneros Reserve	10,000	14	16	1992-1998	5/90
1988	BERINGER VINEYARDS	Napa Valley Private Reserve	14,665	19	19	1992-1996	4/90
1985	BOUCHAINE VINEYARDS	Carneros	2,250	15	20	1991-1993	2/90
1985	BOUCHAINE VINEYARDS	Napa Valley	10,100	13	17	1991-1994	2/90
1986	BURGESS CELLARS	Napa Valley Triere Vineyard	17,000	14	16	1991-1994	12/89
1987	CHALONE VINEYARD	Chalone Reserve	727	NR	NR	1992-2000	5/90
1983	CHALONE VINEYARD	Chalone Reserve	617	25	45	1991-1997	5/90
1987	CHAPPELLET VINEYARD	Napa Valley	3,817	14	14	1993-2000	3/90
1985	CHAPPELLET VINEYARD	Napa Valley	3,300	12.50	15	1991-1996	3/90
1984	CHAPPELLET VINEYARD	Napa Valley	4,500	12	20	1991-1995	3/90
1975	CHATEAU MONTELENA WINERY	Napa Valley	3,300	9	65	1991-1993	2/90
1984	CHATEAU ST. JEAN	Alexander Valley Robert Young Vineyards Reserve 1.5L	918	40	50	1991-1993	3/90
1985	CHATEAU ST. JEAN	Dry Creek Valley Frank Johnson Vineyards	1,517	14	14	1993-1997	3/90
1987	CHATEAU ST. JEAN	Alexander Valley Jimtown Ranch	689	15	15	1993-1997	3/90
1983	CHATEAU ST. JEAN	Alexander Valley Jimtown Ranch	1,166	16	20	1991-1996	7/90
1981	CHATEAU ST. JEAN	Alexander Valley Jimtown Ranch	1,720	14.75	22	1991-1995	3/90
1986	CHATEAU ST. JEAN	Sonoma Valley McCrea Vineyards	163	15	17	1992-1996	3/90
1984	CHATEAU ST. JEAN	Sonoma Valley McCrea Vineyards	1601	14.25	17	1991-1995	3/90
1987	CHATEAU WOLTNER	Howell Mountain St. Thomas Vineyard	883	36	36	1993-1998	4/90
1988	CHATEAU WOLTNER	Howell Mountain Frederique Vineyard	210	54	54	1993-1998	4/90
1987	CLOS DU BOIS WINERY	Dry Creek Valley Flintwood Vineyard	4,217	20	20	1992-1997	2/90
1980	CLOS DU BOIS WINERY	Dry Creek Valley Flintwood Vineyard	977	17	32	1991-1994	2/90
1987	CLOS DU BOIS WINERY	Alexander Valley Barrel Fermented	81,650	11	11	1991-1995	2/90
1985	CLOS DU VAL WINE CO.	Napa Valley	14,000	11.50	17	1991-1997	6/90
1987	CLOS DU VAL WINE CO.	Napa Valley	9,000	12	12	1991-1996	6/90
1985	CLOS PEGASE	Alexander Valley	3,100	13	15	1991-1995	3/90
1987	CONGRESS SPRINGS VINEYARDS	Santa Cruz Mountains Monmartre	770	28	30	1991-1995	4/90
1982	CONGRESS SPRINGS VINEYARDS	Santa Cruz Mountains Private Reserve	310	15	28	1991-1994	4/90
1985	CONGRESS SPRINGS VINEYARDS	Santa Clara County	2,500	12	20	1991-1994	4/90
1980	CUVAISON WINERY	Napa Valley	10,000	11	26	1991-1995	4/90
1988	DE LOACH VINEYARDS	Russian River Valley O.F.S	3,200	22	22	1992-1996	5/90
1988	DE LOACH VINEYARDS	Russian River Valley	26,000	15	15	1992-1996	5/90
1987	DE LOACH VINEYARDS	Russian River Valley	24,000	15	20	1991-1995	2/90
1986	DEHLINGER WINERY	Russian River Valley	3,200	11	14	1991-1995	4/90
1980	EDNA VALLEY VINEYARD	Edna Valley	5,200	12	25	1991-1994	3/90
1983	FAR NIENTE WINERY	Napa Valley	8,000	22	38	1991-1995	2/90
1988	FISHER VINEYARDS	Sonoma County Coach Insignia	6,000	18	18	1991-1996	2/90
1986	FLORA SPRINGS WINE CO.	Napa Valley Barrel Fermented	2,800	20	24	1992-1996	1/90
1988	FOLIE A DEUX WINERY	Napa Valley	6,900	16	16	1991-1997	6/90

NR — Not released.

Vintage	Winery	Appellation / Vineyard	Case Production	Release Price	Current Price	Drink	Last Tasted
1984	FOLIE A DEUX WINERY	Napa Valley	1,100	$14	$18	1991-1996	6/90
1984	FREEMARK ABBEY WINERY	Napa Valley	15,500	14	17	1991-1994	2/90
1988	FROG'S LEAP WINERY	Napa Valley	2,500	15	15	1991-1996	3/90
1986	FROG'S LEAP WINERY	Carneros	1,300	14	18	1991-1995	6/90
1987	GIRARD WINERY	Napa Valley Reserve	700	25	25	1993-1996	6/90
1982	GRGICH HILLS CELLAR	Napa Valley	15,000	17	36	1991-1994	3/90
1985	HACIENDA WINERY	Sonoma County Clair de Lune	7,000	11	20	1991-1995	4/90
1986	HANZELL VINEYARDS	Sonoma Valley	1,070	22	32	1993-1998	1/90
1962	HEITZ WINE CELLAR	Napa Valley	250	6	150	1991-1997	6/90
1988	KENDALL-JACKSON VINEYARDS	California The Proprietor's	25,000	24.50	25	1991-1995	4/90
1985	KENDALL-JACKSON VINEYARDS	Sonoma Valley Durell Vineyard	500	14	20	1991-1995	4/90
1987	KENWOOD VINEYARDS	Sonoma Valley Beltane Ranch	3,000	15	17	1992-1997	7/90
1988	KENWOOD VINEYARDS	Sonoma Valley Yulupa Vineyard	3,000	14	14	1991-1996	7/90
1987	MARKHAM VINEYARDS	Napa Valley	4,720	12	12	1991-1996	2/90
1987	MAYACAMAS VINEYARDS	Napa Valley	2,640	20	20	1991-1996	1/90
1986	MAYACAMAS VINEYARDS	Napa Valley	1,860	20	20	1991-1996	3/90
1984	ROBERT MONDAVI WINERY	Napa Valley Reserve	9,000	22	24	1991-1994	3/90
1985	MOUNT EDEN VINEYARDS	Santa Cruz Mountains	540	25	40	1991-1996	3/90
1980	MOUNT EDEN VINEYARDS	Santa Cruz Mountains	245	30	50	1991-1995	3/90
1985	MOUNT EDEN VINEYARDS	Edna Valley MEV MacGregor Vineyard	1,100	12.50	14	1991-1995	3/90
1987	MURPHY-GOODE	Alexander Valley Premier Vineyard	7,000	11	11	1991-1996	4/90
1987	NAVARRO VINEYARDS	Anderson Valley Première Reserve	1813	14	14	1992-1996	3/90
1986	NAVARRO VINEYARDS	Anderson Valley Première Reserve	1,555	14	18	1991-1996	3/90
1988	ROBERT PECOTA WINERY	Alexander Valley Canepa Vineyard	800	16	16	1991-1995	4/90
1985	PINE RIDGE WINERY	Napa Valley Knollside Cuvée	6,869	14	16	1991-1995	4/90
1986	RAYMOND VINEYARD & CELLAR	Napa Valley Private Reserve	1,842	18	21	1991-1995	5/90
1988	REVERE WINERY	Napa Valley Reserve	366	NR	NR	1992-1998	4/90
1986	REVERE WINERY	Napa Valley Reserve	206	22	25	1991-1996	4/90
1987	ROMBAUER VINEYARDS	Napa Valley Reserve	200	25	25	1991-1995	6/90
1983	ROMBAUER VINEYARDS	Napa Valley	1,010	14.50	25	1991-1995	7/90
1981	SAINTSBURY	Sonoma County	950	10	25	1991-1994	2/90
1983	SEQUOIA GROVE VINEYARDS	Napa Valley Estate	1,639	12	20	1991-1996	5/90
1980	SEQUOIA GROVE VINEYARDS	Napa Valley Estate	1,500	10	18	1991-1994	5/90
1985	CHARLES F. SHAW VINEYARD	Napa Valley	5,000	12	15	1991-1994	5/90
1985	SILVERADO VINEYARDS	Napa Valley	17,000	11.50	17	1991-1995	3/90
1985	SMITH-MADRONE VINEYARD	Napa Valley	1,832	12.50	16	1990-1996	5/90
1985	SONOMA-CUTRER VINEYARDS	Russian River Valley Cutrer Vineyard	6,000	14.75	23	1991-1996	3/90
1984	SONOMA-CUTRER VINEYARDS	Russian River Valley Cutrer Vineyard	6,000	14.25	25	1991-1995	3/90
1982	SONOMA-CUTRER VINEYARDS	Russian River Valley Cutrer Vineyard	5,000	13	25	1991-1994	3/90
1982	SONOMA-CUTRER VINEYARDS	Russian River Valley Russian River Ranches	5,200	10	24	1991-1994	3/90
1988	STAG'S LEAP WINE CELLARS	Napa Valley	15,500	18	18	1993-1997	3/90
1985	STERLING VINEYARDS	Napa Valley Diamond Mountain Ranch	5,400	15	17	1993-1999	7/90
1987	STONY HILL VINEYARD	Napa Valley	1,195	18	35	1991-1997	5/90
1986	STONY HILL VINEYARD	Napa Valley	1,420	16	55	1992-1999	7/90
1963	STONY HILL VINEYARD	Napa Valley	160	4	450	1991-1993	5/90
1986	TREFETHEN VINEYARDS	Napa Valley	26,595	16.25	19	1992-1996	3/90
1987	VICHON WINERY	Napa Valley	13,500	16	16	1991-1996	3/90

NR — Not released.

Vintage	Winery	Appellation / Vineyard	Case Production	Release Price	Current Price	Drink	Last Tasted
1980	VICHON WINERY	Napa Valley	3,800	$15	$25	1991-1995	3/90
1986	WHITE OAK VINEYARDS & WINERY	Sonoma County Myers Limited Release	621	16	20	1991-1996	5/90
1981	ZD WINES	California	5,742	13	28	1991-1994	3/90

SCORE: 86

Vintage	Winery	Appellation / Vineyard	Case Production	Release Price	Current Price	Drink	Last Tasted
1986	ACACIA WINERY	Carneros Marina Vineyard	6,950	18	22	1991-1994	1/90
1984	ACACIA WINERY	Carneros Marina Vineyard	5,600	16	22	1991-1994	1/90
1983	S. ANDERSON VINEYARD	Stags Leap District Estate	1,415	12.50	25	1991-1993	3/90
1986	BEAULIEU VINEYARD	Carneros Los Carneros Reserve	10,000	12	15	1991-1996	6/90
1985	BERINGER VINEYARDS	Napa Valley Private Reserve	4,096	15	24	1991-1994	4/90
1981	BERINGER VINEYARDS	Napa Valley Private Reserve	4,784	15	28	1991-1993	4/90
1987	BOUCHAINE VINEYARDS	Carneros Estate Reserve	1,600	19	19	1991-1995	2/90
1988	BUENA VISTA WINERY	Carneros Private Reserve	6,150	16.50	17	1993-1999	6/90
1985	BUENA VISTA WINERY	Carneros Private Reserve	2,700	16.50	17	1991-1995	3/90
1981	CHALONE VINEYARD	Chalone Reserve	400	20	55	1991-1996	5/90
1981	CHATEAU ST. JEAN	Alexander Valley Robert Young Vineyards	8,586	18	25	1991-1993	3/90
1982	CHATEAU ST. JEAN	Alexander Valley Belle Terre Vineyards	4,735	15.50	20	1991-1995	3/90
1985	CHATEAU ST. JEAN	Sonoma Valley McCrea Vineyards	1,543	14.25	17	1991-1996	7/90
1975	CHATEAU ST. JEAN	Sonoma County Bacigalupi	800	10	21	1991-1995	7/90
1988	CHATEAU WOLTNER	Howell Mountain Estate Reserve	1,645	24	24	1992-1998	4/90
1988	CHATEAU WOLTNER	Howell Mountain St. Thomas Vineyard	617	36	36	1993-1998	4/90
1988	CHATEAU WOLTNER	Howell Mountain Titus Vineyard	147	54	54	1993-1999	4/90
1987	CLOS PEGASE	Napa Valley	11,131	12	12	1991-1995	3/90
1988	CONGRESS SPRINGS VINEYARDS	Santa Clara County San Ysidro Reserve	2,682	20	20	1991-1994	4/90
1988	CONGRESS SPRINGS VINEYARDS	Santa Clara County Barrel Fermented	13,431	14	14	1991-1995	4/90
1986	DE LOACH VINEYARDS	Russian River Valley O.F.S	1,800	22	26	1991-1995	2/90
1985	DEHLINGER WINERY	Russian River Valley	2,000	10	14	1991-1998	5/90
1984	DEHLINGER WINERY	Russian River Valley	2,300	10	14	1991-1996	4/90
1984	EDNA VALLEY VINEYARD	Edna Valley	23,800	12.50	24	1991-1995	6/90
1984	FAR NIENTE WINERY	Napa Valley	11,000	22	36	1991-1996	2/90
1982	FAR NIENTE WINERY	Napa Valley	7,000	18	38	1991-1996	2/90
1987	FISHER VINEYARDS	Sonoma County Whitney's Vineyard	48	24	24	1991-1995	2/90
1984	FORMAN VINEYARD	Napa Valley	400	15	45	1991-1994	2/90
1987	FRANCISCAN VINEYARDS	Napa Valley Reserve	600	15	15	1992-1997	6/90
1984	FRANCISCAN VINEYARDS	Napa Valley Reserve	2,000	12	16	1991-1995	4/90
1986	FREEMARK ABBEY WINERY	Napa Valley	16,997	15	15	1991-1996	2/90
1988	FREEMARK ABBEY WINERY	Napa Valley Carpy Ranch	566	20	20	1991-1996	2/90
1987	FROG'S LEAP WINERY	Carneros	1,500	15	17	1991-1996	3/90
1979	HACIENDA WINERY	Sonoma County Clair de Lune	2,900	9	25	1991-1993	4/90
1981	HANZELL VINEYARDS	Sonoma Valley	650	18	50	1991-1997	1/90
1975	HANZELL VINEYARDS	Sonoma Valley	310	10	70	1991-1994	1/90
1982	WILLIAM HILL WINERY	Napa Valley Reserve	1,427	24	28	1991-1995	3/90
1987	INGLENOOK-NAPA VALLEY	Napa Valley Reserve	6,000	14	14	1992-1997	4/90
1984	INGLENOOK-NAPA VALLEY	Napa Valley Reserve	2,200	12.50	18	1991-1995	4/90
1986	KENDALL-JACKSON VINEYARDS	California The Proprietor's	5,000	17	20	1991-1994	4/90
1987	KENDALL-JACKSON VINEYARDS	Sonoma Valley Durell Vineyard	500	14	14	1991-1994	4/90
1985	LA CREMA	California Reserve	1,200	18	22	1991-1995	6/90
1985	MARKHAM VINEYARDS	Napa Valley Estate	2,843	12	16	1991-1995	2/90
1985	MATANZAS CREEK WINERY	Sonoma Valley Estate	380	18	31	1991-1994	2/90
1983	MAYACAMAS VINEYARDS	Napa Valley	1,775	16	25	1991-1996	1/90
1981	ROBERT MONDAVI WINERY	Napa Valley Reserve	6,800	20	24	1991-1993	3/90

NR — Not released.

Vintage	Winery	Appellation / Vineyard	Case Production	Release Price	Current Price	Drink	Last Tasted
1987	MONTICELLO CELLARS	Napa Valley Corley Reserve	4,400	$17.25	$18	1992-1997	6/90
1987	MONTICELLO CELLARS	Napa Valley Jefferson Ranch	8,100	12.25	13	1991-1995	2/90
1986	MONTICELLO CELLARS	Napa Valley Jefferson Ranch	5,700	11	14	1991-1995	2/90
1984	MONTICELLO CELLARS	Napa Valley Jefferson Ranch	2,450	10	18	1991-1994	2/90
1980	MONTICELLO CELLARS	Napa Valley	1,250	12	20	1991-1993	2/90
1985	MORGAN WINERY	Monterey County	5,000	14	25	1991-1996	7/90
1984	MORGAN WINERY	Monterey County	5,000	12.75	25	1991-1995	5/90
1986	MURPHY-GOODE	Alexander Valley	7,000	10	12	1991-1995	4/90
1984	NEWTON VINEYARD	Napa Valley	3,900	11.50	18	1991-1998	5/90
1983	PINE RIDGE WINERY	Stags Leap District Pine Ridge Stags Leap Vineyard	1,199	16	25	1991-1994	4/90
1981	PINE RIDGE WINERY	Stags Leap District Stags Leap Vineyard	1,114	15	31	1991-1994	4/90
1986	ROMBAUER VINEYARDS	Napa Valley Reserve	200	24	26	1991-1995	6/90
1987	ROMBAUER VINEYARDS	Napa Valley	4,300	14.50	15	1991-1996	6/90
1988	SEQUOIA GROVE VINEYARDS	Carneros	6,978	14	14	1991-1996	5/90
1988	CHARLES F. SHAW VINEYARD	Napa Valley	10,500	11	11	1991-1995	5/90
1982	SMITH-MADRONE VINEYARD	Napa Valley	1,004	12	18	1990-1998	5/90
1978	SMITH-MADRONE VINEYARD	Napa Valley	375	10	30	1990-1997	5/90
1983	SONOMA-CUTRER VINEYARDS	Sonoma Valley Les Pierres	7,000	15.50	30	1991-1994	3/90
1983	SONOMA-CUTRER VINEYARDS	Russian River Valley Cutrer Vineyard	3,000	13.75	25	1991-1994	3/90
1986	SONOMA-CUTRER VINEYARDS	Russian River Valley Russian River Ranches	41,725	12	18	1992-1996	3/90
1987	ST. CLEMENT VINEYARDS	Napa Valley	3,500	15	15	1992-1997	3/90
1986	STAG'S LEAP WINE CELLARS	Napa Valley	8,166	17	20	1991-1995	3/90
1986	STERLING VINEYARDS	Napa Valley Diamond Mountain Ranch	7,500	15	15	1991-1996	4/90
1984	STERLING VINEYARDS	Napa Valley Diamond Mountain Ranch	3,000	15	17	1991-1995	4/90
1983	STERLING VINEYARDS	Napa Valley Diamond Mountain Ranch	1,400	15	18	1991-1994	4/90
1981	STONY HILL VINEYARD	Napa Valley	2,137	12	68	1991-1996	5/90
1980	STONY HILL VINEYARD	Napa Valley	2,220	12	72	1991-1998	5/90
1984	TREFETHEN VINEYARDS	Napa Valley	20,291	14.25	25	1991-1993	3/90
1980	TREFETHEN VINEYARDS	Napa Valley	9,369	13	30	1991-1993	3/90
1984	VICHON WINERY	Napa Valley	17,600	15	17	1991-1994	3/90
1986	WHITE OAK VINEYARDS & WINERY	Sonoma County	3,500	11	16	1991-1995	5/90
1984	WHITE OAK VINEYARDS & WINERY	Sonoma County	3,000	10	16	1991-1996	5/90

SCORE: 85

Vintage	Winery	Appellation / Vineyard	Case Production	Release Price	Current Price	Drink	Last Tasted
1987	ACACIA WINERY	Carneros Marina Vineyard	8,600	18	19	1991-1995	1/90
1988	ACACIA WINERY	Carneros	22,300	16	16	1991-1993	1/90
1987	S. ANDERSON VINEYARD	Stags Leap District Estate	3,798	16	18	1993-1998	6/90
1988	BOUCHAINE VINEYARDS	Carneros	8,400	15	15	1993-1997	6/90
1984	BOUCHAINE VINEYARDS	Carneros	3,400	14	20	1991-1993	2/90
1987	BURGESS CELLARS	Napa Valley Triere Vineyard	18,000	14.50	15	1991-1996	12/89
1973	BURGESS CELLARS	Napa Valley	400	6	30	1991-1993	12/89
1986	CHALONE VINEYARD	Chalone Reserve	379	28	38	1991-1995	5/90
1982	CHAPPELLET VINEYARD	Napa Valley	7,200	12.50	20	1991-1993	3/90
1983	CHATEAU MONTELENA WINERY	Napa Valley	6,600	16	32	1991-1994	2/90
1982	CHATEAU MONTELENA WINERY	Napa Valley	6,900	16	32	1991-1994	2/90
1977	CHATEAU MONTELENA WINERY	Napa Valley	6,000	15	60	1991-1993	2/90
1980	CHATEAU ST. JEAN	Alexander Valley Robert Young Vineyards	6,832	18	30	1991-1993	3/90
1979	CHATEAU ST. JEAN	Alexander Valley Robert Young Vineyards	5,344	17	30	1991-1994	3/90
1984	CHATEAU ST. JEAN	Alexander Valley Belle Terre Vineyards	6,384	16	27	1991-1995	3/90
1983	CHATEAU ST. JEAN	Sonoma Valley McCrea Vineyards	1,009	15.25	18	1991-1995	7/90

NR — Not released.

Vintage	Winery	Appellation/Vineyard	Case Production	Release Price	Current Price	Drink	Last Tasted
1977	CHATEAU ST. JEAN	Sonoma Valley McCrea Vineyards	346	$10.25	$25	1991	3/90
1987	CHATEAU WOLTNER	Howell Mountain Titus Vineyard	309	54	54	1992-1998	4/90
1986	CLOS DU BOIS WINERY	Alexander Valley Calcaire Vineyard	5,096	16	22	1992-1996	2/90
1985	CLOS DU BOIS WINERY	Alexander Valley Proprietor's Reserve	1,762	22	25	1991-1995	5/90
1988	CLOS DU BOIS WINERY	Alexander Valley Barrel Fermented	89,600	11	11	1991-1995	2/90
1984	CLOS DU VAL WINE CO.	Napa Valley	12,000	11.50	15	1991-1995	6/90
1986	CLOS PEGASE	Napa Valley	6,689	12	14	1995	3/90
1986	CONGRESS SPRINGS VINEYARDS	Santa Clara County San Ysidro Reserve	2,275	15	22	1991-1994	4/90
1986	CONGRESS SPRINGS VINEYARDS	Santa Cruz Mountains Private Reserve	552	20	23	1991-1994	4/90
1983	CONGRESS SPRINGS VINEYARDS	Santa Clara County Barrel Fermented	1,102	10	25	1991-1994	4/90
1983	DEHLINGER WINERY	Russian River Valley	1,400	10	15	1991-1995	4/90
1985	EDNA VALLEY VINEYARD	Edna Valley	31,000	13	25	1991-1994	3/90
1981	FISHER VINEYARDS	Sonoma County Whitney's Vineyard	24	20	25	1991-1994	2/90
1980	FISHER VINEYARDS	Sonoma County	1,200	14	22	1990-1993	2/90
1985	FLORA SPRINGS WINE CO.	Napa Valley Barrel Fermented	2,100	18	27	1992-1996	1/90
1983	FREEMARK ABBEY WINERY	Napa Valley	13,000	14	18	1991-1995	2/90
1980	GIRARD WINERY	Napa Valley Estate	2,100	11	25	1991-1994	3/90
1976	HILLS CELLARS	Napa Valley	2,500	8	50	1991-1995	3/90
1988	HACIENDA WINERY	Sonoma County Clair de Lune	10,500	15	15	1991-1996	6/90
1976	HACIENDA WINERY	Sonoma County Clair de Lune	750	7	40	1991-1994	4/90
1979	HANZELL VINEYARDS	Sonoma Valley	460	16	70	1991-1995	1/90
1973	HANZELL VINEYARDS	Sonoma Valley	310	8	100	1991-1995	1/90
1971	HANZELL VINEYARDS	Sonoma Valley	160	7	120	1991-1994	1/90
1983	WILLIAM HILL WINERY	Napa Valley Reserve	1,428	22	28	1991-1994	3/90
1985	KENDALL-JACKSON VINEYARDS	Anderson Valley Dennison Vineyard	200	14	20	1991-1993	4/90
1988	KENDALL-JACKSON VINEYARDS	Anderson Valley Du Pratt Vineyard	200	14	14	1991-1994	4/90
1988	KENDALL-JACKSON VINEYARDS	Redwood Valley Lolonis Vineyard	100	NR	NR	1991-1994	4/90
1986	KENWOOD VINEYARDS	Sonoma Valley Beltane Ranch	2,500	14	18	1991-1995	7/90
1987	KENWOOD VINEYARDS	Sonoma Valley Yulupa Vineyard	3,000	14	16	1992-1996	7/90
1983	KENWOOD VINEYARDS	Sonoma Valley Yulupa Vineyard	1,000	11	18	1991-1994	7/90
1986	LA CREMA	California Reserve	1,200	18	22	1991-1996	6/90
1984	MARKHAM VINEYARDS	Napa Valley	2,955	12	16	1991-1995	2/90
1983	MATANZAS CREEK WINERY	Sonoma County	1,788	15	28	1991-1993	2/90
1981	MATANZAS CREEK WINERY	Sonoma County	1925	15	28	1991-1993	2/90
1982	MAYACAMAS VINEYARDS	Napa Valley	2,215	16	30	1991-1997	1/90
1985	MONTICELLO CELLARS	Napa Valley Corley Reserve	2,200	14	20	1991-1994	2/90
1987	MORGAN WINERY	Monterey Reserve	1,500	19*	19	1991-1994	6/90
1984	MOUNT EDEN VINEYARDS	Santa Cruz Mountains	756	23	45	1991-1995	3/90
1977	MOUNT EDEN VINEYARDS	Santa Cruz Mountains	150	16	50	1991-1995	8/90
1985	MURPHY-GOODE	Alexander Valley	5,000	9	12	1991-1995	4/90
1986	NEWTON VINEYARD	Napa Valley	5,000	14	14	1992-1997	3/90
1985	NEWTON VINEYARD	Napa Valley	3,100	12.75	19	1991-1996	3/90
1986	ROBERT PECOTA WINERY	Alexander Valley Canepa Vineyard	800	16	19	1991-1995	4/90
1985	PINE RIDGE WINERY	Stags Leap District Pine Ridge Stags Leap Vineyard	1,793	18	23	1991-1995	4/90
1984	PINE RIDGE WINERY	Napa Valley Knollside Cuvée	4,285	14	17	1991-1995	4/90

NR — Not released.

Vintage	Winery	Appellation / Vineyard	Case Production	Release Price	Current Price	Drink	Last Tasted
1986	REVERE WINERY	Napa Valley	1,375	$15	$15	1991-1996	4/90
1985	REVERE WINERY	Napa Valley	1,052	15	20	1991-1995	4/90
1986	ROMBAUER VINEYARDS	Napa Valley	3,815	14.50	16	1991-1995	6/90
1987	CHARLES F. SHAW VINEYARD	Napa Valley	7,500	11	11	1992-1997	5/90
1986	CHARLES F. SHAW VINEYARD	Napa Valley	7,500	11	11	1991-1995	5/90
1980	SMITH-MADRONE VINEYARD	Napa Valley	450	11	20	1990-1995	5/90
1983	SONOMA-CUTRER VINEYARDS	Russian River Valley Russian River Ranches	9,900	10.50	22	1991-1994	3/90
1985	ST. CLEMENT VINEYARDS	Napa Valley	3,700	14.50	16	1991-1995	3/90
1985	STAG'S LEAP WINE CELLARS	Napa Valley Reserve	1,214	22	26	1991-1995	3/90
1983	STONY HILL VINEYARD	Napa Valley	1934	13	70	1991-1996	5/90
1982	STONY HILL VINEYARD	Napa Valley	2,747	12	63	1991-1994	5/90
1978	STONY HILL VINEYARD	Napa Valley	1,750	10	90	1991-1996	5/90
1969	STONY HILL VINEYARD	Napa Valley	750	5	175	1991-1993	5/90
1973	TREFETHEN VINEYARDS	Napa Valley	643	6.50	50	1991-1993	3/90
1987	WHITE OAK VINEYARDS & WINERY	Sonoma County	4,000	11	16	1991-1996	5/90
1987	ZD WINES	California	15,203	18.50	25	1991-1995	3/90
1986	ZD WINES	California	15,773	18	25	1991-1997	6/90

SCORE: 84

Vintage	Winery	Appellation / Vineyard	Case Production	Release Price	Current Price	Drink	Last Tasted
1987	ACACIA WINERY	Carneros	17,700	17	17	1991-1995	1/90
1984	ACACIA WINERY	Carneros	7,800	14	20	1991-1993	1/90
1985	BEAULIEU VINEYARD	Carneros Los Carneros Reserve	10,000	12	16	1991-1995	6/90
1983	BUENA VISTA WINERY	Carneros Private Reserve	1,000	14.50	18	1991-1994	3/90
1975	BURGESS CELLARS	Carneros Winery Lake Vineyard	770	9	28	1991-1994	12/89
1980	CHAPPELLET VINEYARD	Napa Valley	4,000	14	25	1991-1992	3/90
1983	CHATEAU MONTELENA WINERY	Alexander Valley	5,600	14	32	1991-1994	2/90
1978	CHATEAU ST. JEAN	Alexander Valley Robert Young Vineyards	1,099	17	25	1991-1993	3/90
1979	CHATEAU ST. JEAN	Alexander Valley Belle Terre Vineyards	3,668	12	22	1991-1993	3/90
1985	CLOS DU BOIS WINERY	Alexander Valley Barrel Fermented	47,082	9	12	1991-1993	2/90
1984	CLOS DU BOIS WINERY	Alexander Valley Barrel Fermented	34,827	8	12	1991-1994	2/90
1986	CLOS DU VAL WINE CO.	Carneros	12,000	12	14	1991-1995	6/90
1985	CONGRESS SPRINGS VINEYARDS	Santa Cruz Mountains Private Reserve	431	16	27	1991-1994	4/90
1987	CONGRESS SPRINGS VINEYARDS	Santa Clara County	12,500	12	18	1991-1994	4/90
1979	CUVAISON WINERY	Napa Valley	10,000	10	26	1991-1995	4/90
1985	FISHER VINEYARDS	Sonoma County Whitney's Vineyard	48	24	30	1991-1994	2/90
1987	FISHER VINEYARDS	Sonoma County Coach Insignia	5,000	18	18	1991-1995	2/90
1985	FISHER VINEYARDS	Sonoma County Coach Insignia	3,000	16	20	1991-1993	2/90
1982	FRANCISCAN VINEYARDS	Carneros Reserve	2,000	12	20	1991-1994	4/90
1987	FREEMARK ABBEY WINERY	Napa Valley	16,500	15	15	1992-1996	2/90
1980	FREEMARK ABBEY WINERY	Napa Valley	10,771	13.50	24	1991-1993	2/90
1985	FROG'S LEAP WINERY	Napa Valley	1,100	12	16	1991-1995	6/90
1984	HANZELL VINEYARDS	Sonoma Valley	980	20	36	1991-1996	1/90
1983	HANZELL VINEYARDS	Sonoma Valley	930	20	45	1991-1996	1/90
1970	HANZELL VINEYARDS	Sonoma Valley	220	7	120	1991-1994	1/90
1965	HANZELL VINEYARDS	Sonoma Valley	190	6	180	1991-1995	1/90
1985	KENWOOD VINEYARDS	Sonoma Valley Beltane Ranch	2,200	14	18	1991-1995	7/90
1985	KENWOOD VINEYARDS	Sonoma Valley Yulupa Vineyard	3,000	12	17	1991-1994	7/90
1986	MARKHAM VINEYARDS	Napa Valley Estate	4,649	12	14	1991-1994	2/90
1982	MONTICELLO CELLARS	Napa Valley Barrel Fermented	800	14	20	1991-1992	2/90
1987	MORGAN WINERY	Monterey	8,500	15	16	1991-1994	5/90

NR — Not released.

Vintage	Winery	Appellation/Vineyard	Case Production	Release Price	Current Price	Drink	Last Tasted
1983	MOUNT EDEN VINEYARDS	Santa Cruz Mountains	455	$20	$35	1991-1994	3/90
1984	PINE RIDGE WINERY	Stags Leap District Pine Ridge Stags Leap Vineyard	1,405	18	25	1991-1994	4/90
1981	PINE RIDGE WINERY	Napa Valley Oak Knoll Cuvée	1,168	13	20	1991-1994	4/90
1985	ROMBAUER VINEYARDS	Napa Valley	1,337	14.50	18	1991-1994	6/90
1982	ROMBAUER VINEYARDS	Napa Valley	382	14.50	25	1991-1994	6/90
1986	SAINTSBURY	Carneros Reserve	1,015	20	25	1992-1996	2/90
1983	CHARLES F. SHAW VINEYARD	Napa Valley	5,000	12	16	1991-1993	5/90
1983	SILVERADO VINEYARDS	Napa Valley	5,000	11	20	1991-1993	3/90

SCORE: 83

Vintage	Winery	Appellation/Vineyard	Case Production	Release Price	Current Price	Drink	Last Tasted
1980	S. ANDERSON VINEYARD	Stags Leap District Estate	1,545	12.50	30	1991-1993	3/90
1987	BOUCHAINE VINEYARDS	Carneros	7,400	14	14	1991-1994	2/90
1981	CHATEAU ST. JEAN	Alexander Valley Belle Terre Vineyards	3,847	15	18	1991-1995	3/90
1985	CLOS DU BOIS WINERY	Alexander Valley Calcaire Vineyard	4,208	18	28	1991-1994	2/90
1986	CONGRESS SPRINGS VINEYARDS	Santa Clara County	4,900	12	18	1991-1994	4/90
1983	DE LOACH VINEYARDS	Russian River Valley	8,000	12	22	1991-1993	2/90
1983	HACIENDA WINERY	Sonoma County Clair de Lune	4,200	10	22	1991-1993	4/90
1987	LA CREMA	California Reserve	2,900	22	22	1993-1999	6/90
1982	MARKHAM VINEYARDS	Napa Valley Estate	531	12	17	1991-1993	2/90
1984	ROBERT PECOTA WINERY	Alexander Valley Canepa Vineyard	600	14	18	1991-1993	4/90
1987	REVERE WINERY	Napa Valley Reserve	101	25	25	1991-1995	4/90
1987	SEQUOIA GROVE VINEYARDS	Carneros	5,530	14	14	1991-1995	5/90
1980	ST. CLEMENT VINEYARDS	Napa Valley	3,200	12	25	1991-1992	3/90
1985	STAG'S LEAP WINE CELLARS	Napa Valley	7,002	16	18	1991-1994	3/90
1972	STONY HILL VINEYARD	Napa Valley	645	7	110	1991-1992	5/90
1967	STONY HILL VINEYARD	Napa Valley	700	4.50	250	1991-1992	5/90
1981	TREFETHEN VINEYARDS	Napa Valley	12,933	13	28	1991-1992	3/90

SCORE: 82

Vintage	Winery	Appellation/Vineyard	Case Production	Release Price	Current Price	Drink	Last Tasted
1985	ACACIA WINERY	Carneros Winery Lake Vineyard	3,700	18	25	1991-1994	1/90
1987	BUENA VISTA WINERY	Carneros Private Reserve	5,500	16.50	17	1991-1994	3/90
1975	CHAPPELLET VINEYARD	Napa Valley	800	6.75	40	1991	3/90
1976	CHATEAU ST. JEAN	Sonoma Valley Wildwood Vineyards	402	10	20	1991-1993	7/90
1983	CLOS DU VAL WINE CO.	Napa Valley	10,000	11.50	15	1991-1996	6/90
1984	CUVAISON WINERY	Napa Valley	3,600	13	20	1991-1995	4/90
1984	FISHER VINEYARDS	Sonoma County Coach Insignia					
1983	FISHER VINEYARDS	Sonoma and Napa Counties	3,000	14	18	1991-1994	6/90
1983	FRANCISCAN VINEYARDS	Napa Valley Reserve	1,500	12	14	1991-1996	4/90
1975	FREEMARK ABBEY WINERY	Napa Valley	7,100	9	45	1991	2/90
1983	INGLENOOK-NAPA VALLEY	Napa Valley Reserve	1,500	16	19	1991-1994	4/90
1987	KENDALL-JACKSON VINEYARDS	Anderson Valley Dennison Vineyard	200	14	14	1991-1993	4/90
1986	KENWOOD VINEYARDS	Sonoma Valley Yulupa Vineyard	6,000	12	17	1991-1995	7/90
1980	MATANZAS CREEK WINERY	Sonoma County	1,700	15	25	1991-1992	2/90
1985	MONTICELLO CELLARS	Napa Valley Jefferson Ranch	4,000	11	16	1991-1993	2/90
1982	MONTICELLO CELLARS	Napa Valley	4,000	13.50	20	1991-1993	2/90
1973	MOUNT EDEN VINEYARDS	Santa Cruz Mountains	281	12	55	1991	3/90
1982	PINE RIDGE WINERY	Stags Leap District Stags Leap Vineyard	780	15	27	1991-1994	4/90
1979	PINE RIDGE WINERY	Stags Leap District Stags Leap Vineyard	588	9.50	32	1991-1992	4/90

NR — Not released.

Vintage	Winery	Appellation/Vineyard	Case Production	Release Price	Current Price	Drink	Last Tasted
1984	CHARLES F. SHAW VINEYARD	Napa Valley	5,000	$12	$15	1991-1993	5/90
1981	SONOMA-CUTRER VINEYARDS	Russian River Valley Russian River Ranches	1,250	9.35	30	1991-1994	3/90
1979	STAG'S LEAP WINE CELLARS	Napa Valley Haynes	2,000	12.50	20	1991-1992	3/90

SCORE: 81

Vintage	Winery	Appellation/Vineyard	Case Production	Release Price	Current Price	Drink	Last Tasted
1986	ACACIA WINERY	Napa Valley	6,700	15	17	1991-1993	1/90
1986	S. ANDERSON VINEYARD	Stags Leap District Estate	4,792	16	18	1991-1994	3/90
1981	CHATEAU ST. JEAN	Sonoma Valley Hunter Ranch	1,221	14.75	19	1991-1993	3/90
1977	CHATEAU ST. JEAN	Sonoma Valley Hunter Farms	482	10.25	25	1991-1992	3/90
1978	CHATEAU ST. JEAN	Sonoma Valley Les Pierres	729	13.75	22	1991	3/90
1978	CUVAISON WINERY	Napa Valley	10,000	10	28	1991-1995	4/90
1982	FISHER VINEYARDS	Sonoma County	2,200	14	22	1991-1993	2/90
1981	FREEMARK ABBEY WINERY	Napa Valley	13,183	13.50	20	1991-1994	2/90
1987	GIRARD WINERY	Napa Valley Estate	5,757	14.50	16	1992-1995	3/90
1983	MARKHAM VINEYARDS	Napa Valley Estate	860	11.50	16	1991-1992	2/90
1976	MAYACAMAS VINEYARDS	Napa Valley	1,255	11	45	1991-1994	1/90
1982	ROBERT MONDAVI WINERY	Napa Valley Reserve	6,000	20	25	1991	3/90
1986	MOUNT EDEN VINEYARDS	Edna Valley MEV MacGregor Vineyard	1,200	13	16	1991-1995	3/90
1984	SILVERADO VINEYARDS	Napa Valley	11,000	11	18	1991-1994	3/90
1981	SMITH-MADRONE VINEYARD	Napa Valley	650	12	18	1990-1993	5/90
1979	STONY HILL VINEYARD	Napa Valley	2,250	12	95	1991-1994	5/90
1977	TREFETHEN VINEYARDS	Napa Valley	3,966	8.50	40	1991	3/90
1987	WHITE OAK VINEYARDS & WINERY	Sonoma County Myers Limited Release	843	18	20	1991-1994	5/90
1980	ZD WINES	California	4,005	13	28	1991-1994	3/90

SCORE: 80

Vintage	Winery	Appellation/Vineyard	Case Production	Release Price	Current Price	Drink	Last Tasted
1985	ACACIA WINERY	Carneros Marina Vineyard	5,000	18	19	1991-1993	1/90
1985	ACACIA WINERY	Carneros	10,000	15	20	1991-1993	1/90
1983	ACACIA WINERY	Napa Valley	4,300	12	18	1991-1993	1/90
1982	ACACIA WINERY	Napa Valley	4,900	12	20	1991-1993	1/90
1981	S. ANDERSON VINEYARD	Stags Leap District Estate	1,835	12.50	25	1991-1993	3/90
1977	BURGESS CELLARS	Napa Valley	4,000	11	23	1991-1992	12/89
1985	CHALONE VINEYARD	Chalone	3,686	22	45	1991-1994	4/90
1981	CHAPPELLET VINEYARD	Napa Valley	3,947	14	22	1991	3/90
1977	CHATEAU ST. JEAN	Alexander Valley Belle Terre Vineyards	799	12	22	1991	3/90
1979	CHATEAU ST. JEAN	Sonoma Valley Hunter Farms	1,010	14	20	1991	3/90
1986	CLOS DU BOIS WINERY	Alexander Valley Barrel Fermented	81,616	10	12	1991-1992	12/89
1980	CLOS DU VAL WINE CO.	Napa Valley	24,000	12.50	18	1991-1994	6/90
1984	CONGRESS SPRINGS VINEYARDS	Santa Cruz Mountains Private Reserve	420	16	27	1991-1992	4/90
1985	FREEMARK ABBEY WINERY	Napa Valley	15,787	14	16	1991-1995	2/90
1984	GIRARD WINERY	Napa Valley Estate	7,123	13.50	22	1991-1993	3/90
1980	HACIENDA WINERY	Sonoma County Clair de Lune	3,400	10.50	22	1991-1993	4/90
1974	HACIENDA WINERY	Sonoma County Clair de Lune	675	5	40	1991-1992	4/90
1979	MATANZAS CREEK WINERY	Sonoma and Napa Counties	1,650	14.50	40	1991	2/90
1984	MATANZAS CREEK WINERY	Sonoma Valley Estate	830	18	28	1991-1993	2/90
1983	MONTICELLO CELLARS	Napa Valley Barrel Fermented	720	12.50	20	1991-1993	2/90
1983	MORGAN WINERY	Monterey County	3,000	12.50	25	1991-1993	5/90
1972	MOUNT EDEN VINEYARDS	Santa Cruz Mountains	210	20	50	1991-1993	3/90
1983	SAINTSBURY	Carneros	6,550	11	20	1991-1994	2/90
1984	SMITH-MADRONE VINEYARD	Napa Valley	1,606	12	16	1991-1996	5/90
1971	STONY HILL VINEYARD	Napa Valley	580	6	110	1991-1992	5/90
1974	TREFETHEN VINEYARDS	Napa Valley	1,294	5.75	50	1991-1993	3/90

NR — Not released.

Vintage	Winery	Appellation / Vineyard	Case Production	Release Price	Current Price	Drink	Last Tasted
SCORE: 79							
1983	ACACIA WINERY	Carneros Marina Vineyard	5,300	$16	$23	1991-1993	1/90
1985	ACACIA WINERY	Napa Valley	4,900	12.50	16	1991-1992	1/90
1984	BEAULIEU VINEYARD	Carneros Los Carneros Reserve	10,000	10	16	1991-1992	4/90
1987	BERINGER VINEYARDS	Napa Valley Private Reserve	12,159	17	19	1991-1993	4/90
1982	BOUCHAINE VINEYARDS	Alexander Valley	2,000	14	18	1991-1993	2/90
1984	BURGESS CELLARS	Napa Valley Vintage Reserve	17,000	13	17	1991-1994	12/89
1974	BURGESS CELLARS	Carneros Winery Lake Vineyard	700	6	25	1991	12/89
1983	CHAPPELLET VINEYARD	Napa Valley	6,000	12	18	1991	3/90
1979	CHAPPELLET VINEYARD	Napa Valley	3,000	12	30	1991	3/90
1980	CHATEAU MONTELENA WINERY	Napa Valley	7,000	16	38	1991	2/90
1980	CHATEAU ST. JEAN	Dry Creek Valley Frank Johnson Vineyards	1,257	14	16	1991-1992	3/90
1977	CHATEAU ST. JEAN	Sonoma Valley Les Pierres Vineyards	308	13.75	21	1991	3/90
1982	CONGRESS SPRINGS VINEYARDS	Santa Clara County	957	10	20	1991-1992	4/90
1985	DE LOACH VINEYARDS	Russian River Valley O.F.S	1,200	20	22	1991-1995	2/90
1978	MATANZAS CREEK WINERY	Sonoma County	1,230	12.50	40	1991	2/90
1979	ROBERT MONDAVI WINERY	Napa Valley Reserve	8,700	20	27	1991	3/90
1983	ROBERT PECOTA WINERY	Alexander Valley Canepa Vineyard	600	14	18	1990-1991	4/90
1981	STAG'S LEAP WINE CELLARS	Napa Valley	4,760	13.50	17	1991-1993	3/90
1973	STONY HILL VINEYARD	Napa Valley	1,250	7	120	1991-1992	5/90
SCORE: 78							
1979	BERINGER VINEYARDS	Napa Valley Private Reserve	3,228	14	25	1991-1992	4/90
1979	BURGESS CELLARS	Napa Valley	5,500	11	18	1991-1994	12/89
1979	CHATEAU MONTELENA WINERY	Napa Valley	7,800	16	38	1991	2/90
1979	CHATEAU ST. JEAN	Dry Creek Valley Frank Johnson Vineyards	349	13.50	15	1991	3/90
1975	CHATEAU ST. JEAN	Sonoma Valley McCrea Vineyards	250	8.75	20	1991-1993	7/90
1986	CLOS DU BOIS WINERY	Alexander Valley Proprietor's Reserve	4,097	22.50	23	1991-1994	5/90
1982	CLOS DU VAL WINE CO.	California	4,700	11.50	16	1992-1996	6/90
1981	CLOS DU VAL WINE CO.	Napa Valley	2,700	12.50	18	1991-1994	6/90
1983	FISHER VINEYARDS	Sonoma County Whitney's Vineyard	24	20	30	1991-1993	2/90
1982	FISHER VINEYARDS	Sonoma County Whitney's Vineyard	24	20	25	1991-1993	6/90
1982	FOLIE A DEUX WINERY	Napa Valley	500	NR	NR	1991-1992	7/90
1982	HACIENDA WINERY	Sonoma County Clair de Lune	7,200	9	20	1991-1993	4/90
1985	INGLENOOK-NAPA VALLEY	Napa Valley Reserve	2,500	14.50	15	1991-1994	4/90
1982	MATANZAS CREEK WINERY	Sonoma County	1,735	15	25	1991	2/90
1981	MAYACAMAS VINEYARDS	Napa Valley	1955	16	35	1991-1994	1/90
1975	MAYACAMAS VINEYARDS	Napa Valley	1,464	9	50	1991	1/90
1976	ROBERT MONDAVI WINERY	Napa Valley Reserve	1,450	12	32	1991	3/90
1976	MOUNT EDEN VINEYARDS	Santa Cruz Mountains	200	16	50	1991	3/90
1982	PINE RIDGE WINERY	Napa Valley Oak Knoll Cuvée	2,026	13	19	1991-1993	4/90
1984	ROMBAUER VINEYARDS	Napa Valley	1,337	14.50	20	1991-1994	6/90
1984	SANFORD WINERY	Central Coast	4,000	12.50	15	1991-1993	2/90
1986	SEQUOIA GROVE VINEYARDS	Carneros	4,880	13	16	1991-1995	5/90
1980	STAG'S LEAP WINE CELLARS	Napa Valley	2,194	10.50	17	1991-1992	3/90
1974	STERLING VINEYARDS	Napa Valley Estate	3,000	4.75	35	1991-1993	4/90
SCORE: 77							
1983	BOUCHAINE VINEYARDS	Carneros	2,200	14	20	1991-1993	2/90
1978	BURGESS CELLARS	Napa Valley	4,200	11	18	1991-1994	12/89
1978	CHATEAU MONTELENA WINERY	Napa Valley	7,100	15	45	1991	2/90
1976	CHATEAU MONTELENA WINERY	Napa and Alexander Valleys	2,500	11	50	1991	2/90

NR — Not released.

Vintage	Winery	Appellation / Vineyard	Case Production	Release Price	Current Price	Drink	Last Tasted
1976	CHATEAU ST. JEAN	Alexander Valley Belle Terre Vineyards	1,100	$7.50	$22	1991-1992	7/90
1980	CHATEAU ST. JEAN	Alexander Valley Jimtown Ranch	864	14	16	1991	3/90
1973	FREEMARK ABBEY WINERY	Napa Valley	6,117	6.50	32	1991	2/90
1972	FREEMARK ABBEY WINERY	Napa Valley	3,984	6.50	48	1991	2/90
1984	STAG'S LEAP WINE CELLARS	Napa Valley	5,861	14	17	1991-1992	6/90
1983	TREFETHEN VINEYARDS	Napa Valley	18,942	13.75	27	1991	3/90

SCORE: 76

Vintage	Winery	Appellation / Vineyard	Case Production	Release Price	Current Price	Drink	Last Tasted
1979	ACACIA WINERY	Carneros Winery Lake Vineyard	1,400	16	25	1991	1/90
1983	BERINGER VINEYARDS	Napa Valley Private Reserve	7,445	15	24	1991-1993	4/90
1978	CHAPPELLET VINEYARD	Napa Valley	1,500	11.75	40	1991	3/90
1983	EDNA VALLEY VINEYARD	Edna Valley	15,500	12.50	20	1991-1993	3/90
1979	FREEMARK ABBEY WINERY	Napa Valley	10,935	13.25	25	1991	2/90
1983	GIRARD WINERY	Napa Valley Estate	5,741	12.50	22	1991	3/90
1982	GIRARD WINERY	Napa Valley Estate	4,228	12.50	21	1991	3/90
1977	HACIENDA WINERY	Sonoma County Clair de Lune	1,000	8	23	1991-1993	4/90
1981	MONTICELLO CELLARS	Napa Valley	2,700	12	20	1991	2/90
1982	MOUNT EDEN VINEYARDS	Santa Cruz Mountains	500	18	40	1991-1994	3/90
1983	ST. CLEMENT VINEYARDS	Napa Valley	4,500	14.50	17	1991	3/90
1981	VICHON WINERY	Napa Valley	7,000	15	25	1991-1993	3/90
1982	ZD WINES	California	5,506	14	30	1991-1993	3/90

SCORE: 75

Vintage	Winery	Appellation / Vineyard	Case Production	Release Price	Current Price	Drink	Last Tasted
1980	BERINGER VINEYARDS	Napa Valley Private Reserve	4,576	15	25	1991-1992	4/90
1983	BOUCHAINE VINEYARDS	Napa Valley	10,000	12.50	18	1991-1992	2/90
1984	BUENA VISTA WINERY	Carneros Private Reserve	3,000	14.50	16	1991-1992	6/90
1980	BURGESS CELLARS	Napa Valley	5,500	11	18	1991-1992	12/89
1982	CHATEAU ST. JEAN	Alexander Valley Robert Young Vineyards	8,645	18	20	1991-1993	3/90
1981	CHATEAU ST. JEAN	Sonoma Valley McCrea Vineyards	846	15	18	1991-1992	3/90
1976	CHATEAU ST. JEAN	Sonoma Valley McCrea Vineyards	300	9.25	20	1991-1992	7/90
1981	CUVAISON WINERY	Napa Valley	10,000	12	18	1991-1995	4/90
1978	MAYACAMAS VINEYARDS	Napa Valley	1,233	13	30	1991	1/90
1975	ROBERT MONDAVI WINERY	Napa Valley Reserve	1,500	10	35	1991	3/90
1981	ROBERT PECOTA WINERY	Alexander Valley Canepa Vineyard	425	12	20	1990-1991	4/90
1981	ST. CLEMENT VINEYARDS	Napa Valley	3,000	13.50	25	1991	3/90
1975	STONY HILL VINEYARD	Napa Valley	855	9	125	1991-1993	5/90

SCORE: 74

Vintage	Winery	Appellation / Vineyard	Case Production	Release Price	Current Price	Drink	Last Tasted
1983	BEAULIEU VINEYARD	Carneros Los Carneros Reserve	5,000	10	15	1991-1992	4/90
1982	BERINGER VINEYARDS	Napa Valley Private Reserve	7,077	15	22	1991-1993	4/90
1981	BURGESS CELLARS	Napa Valley	15,000	11	16	1991-1992	12/89
1980	CHATEAU ST. JEAN	Alexander Valley Gauer Ranch	2,614	14	18	1991	3/90
1984	CLOS DU BOIS WINERY	Dry Creek Valley Flintwood Vineyard	1,231	11.25	30	1991-1992	5/90
1983	CONGRESS SPRINGS VINEYARDS	Santa Cruz Mountains Private Reserve	328	15	28	1991-1992	4/90
1982	DE LOACH VINEYARDS	Russian River Valley	3,900	12	20	1991	2/90
1974	FREEMARK ABBEY WINERY	Napa Valley	4,110	7.95	42		2/90
1981	HACIENDA WINERY	Sonoma County Clair de Lune	4,600	12	20	1991-1992	4/90
1980	MAYACAMAS VINEYARDS	Napa Valley	1,480	16	35	1991	1/90
1981	SANFORD WINERY	Santa Maria Valley	1,000	11	20	1991	2/90
1978	STAG'S LEAP WINE CELLARS	Napa Valley Haynes	1,815	10	20	1991	3/90
1976	TREFETHEN VINEYARDS	Napa Valley	3,358	7	40	1991	3/90
1983	ZD WINES	California	5,369	14	25	1991-1994	3/90

NR — Not released.

Vintage	Winery	Appellation / Vineyard	Case Production	Release Price	Current Price	Drink	Last Tasted
SCORE: 73							
1978	CHATEAU ST. JEAN	Alexander Valley Belle Terre Vineyards	2,194	$14	$20	1991	3/90
1977	CHATEAU ST. JEAN	Sonoma Valley Wildwood Vineyards	492	15	22	1991	3/90
1968	FREEMARK ABBEY WINERY	Napa Valley	996	5	40	1991	2/90
1978	HACIENDA WINERY	Sonoma County Clair de Lune	3,000	9	25	1991	4/90
1982	SILVERADO VINEYARDS	Napa Valley	4,500	10	20	1991	3/90
1982	ST. CLEMENT VINEYARDS	Napa Valley	4,600	14.50	20	1991	3/90
1982	STERLING VINEYARDS	Napa Valley Estate	10,000	14	17	1991	4/90
1979	STERLING VINEYARDS	Napa Valley Estate	2,800	13	17	1991	4/90
1974	STONY HILL VINEYARD	Napa Valley	1,280	7	110	1991-1993	5/90
1982	TREFETHEN VINEYARDS	Napa Valley	15,318	13.50	28	1991	3/90
1979	TREFETHEN VINEYARDS	Napa Valley	9,486	12	30	1991	3/90
1975	TREFETHEN VINEYARDS	Napa Valley	1,449	6.50	45	1991	3/90
SCORE: 72							
1982	S. ANDERSON VINEYARD	Stags Leap District Estate	1,412	12.50	21	1991	3/90
1982	BEAULIEU VINEYARD	Carneros Los Carneros Reserve	5,000	10	16	1991-1992	4/90
1974	CHAPPELLET VINEYARD	Napa Valley	600	6.75	45	1991	3/90
1981	DE LOACH VINEYARDS	Russian River Valley	2,800	10	18	1991	2/90
1982	FREEMARK ABBEY WINERY	Napa Valley	13,085	12.75	18	1991-1993	2/90
1987	HACIENDA WINERY	Sonoma County Clair de Lune	9,600	12	15	1991-1993	4/90
1982	SEQUOIA GROVE VINEYARDS	Napa Valley Estate	880	12	20	1991	5/90
SCORE: 71							
1984	BOUCHAINE VINEYARDS	Carneros Winery Lake	2,200	22	22	1991	2/90
1976	CHAPPELLET VINEYARD	Napa Valley	1,000	9.75	30	1991	3/90
1980	CHATEAU ST. JEAN	Sonoma Valley Wildwood Vineyards	1,853	13	19	1991-1992	7/90
1983	SMITH-MADRONE VINEYARD	Napa Valley	1,473	12	15	1991-1994	5/90
1981	STERLING VINEYARDS	Napa Valley Estate	4,000	14	17	1991	4/90
1983	VICHON WINERY	Napa Valley	14,900	15	18	1991	3/90
SCORE: 70							
1981	BEAULIEU VINEYARD	Carneros Los Carneros Reserve	5,000	10	18	1991-1992	4/90
1979	BEAULIEU VINEYARD	Napa Valley Beaufort	30,000	6	20	1991-1992	4/90
1978	BEAULIEU VINEYARD	Napa Valley Beaufort	30,000	6	22	1991	4/90
1978	BERINGER VINEYARDS	Napa Valley Private Reserve	1,878	12	15	1991	4/90
1974	BERINGER VINEYARDS	Napa Valley Centennial Cask Selection	1,000	5	40	1991-1992	4/90
1976	BURGESS CELLARS	Carneros Winery Lake Vineyard	1,300	10	20	1991	12/89
1980	CHATEAU ST. JEAN	Sonoma Valley McCrea Vineyards	465	15	18	1991-1992	3/90
1979	CHATEAU ST. JEAN	Sonoma Valley McCrea Vineyards	325	14	18	1991	3/90
1978	CHATEAU ST. JEAN	Sonoma Valley McCrea Vineyards	309	12	20	1991	3/90
1975	CHATEAU ST. JEAN	Sonoma Valley Wildwood Vineyards	350	9.50	20	1991	7/90
1979	CHATEAU ST. JEAN	Alexander Valley Gauer Ranch	2,725	14	18	1991	3/90
1985	CLOS DU BOIS WINERY	Dry Creek Valley Flintwood Vineyard	1,535	18	29	1991-1993	5/90
1981	CLOS DU BOIS WINERY	Alexander Valley Proprietor's Reserve	1,341	15	22	1991-1992	5/90
1982	EDNA VALLEY VINEYARD	Edna Valley	17,400	12	20	1991	3/90
1982	FLORA SPRINGS WINE CO.	Napa Valley Barrel Fermented	700	15	15	1991-1992	6/88
1978	FREEMARK ABBEY WINERY	Napa Valley	9,894	10	26	1991	2/90
1971	FREEMARK ABBEY WINERY	Napa Valley	3,959	7	40	1991	2/90
1980	WILLIAM HILL WINERY	Napa Valley Gold Label	775	16	30	1991	3/90
1980	MATANZAS CREEK WINERY	Sonoma County Estate	85	18	18	1991	2/90
1979	MAYACAMAS VINEYARDS	Napa Valley	1,220	15	35	1991	1/90

NR — Not released.

Vintage	Winery	Appellation/Vineyard	Case Production	Release Price	Current Price	Drink	Last Tasted
1977	MAYACAMAS VINEYARDS	Napa Valley	1,520	$12	$35	1991	1/90
1974	MAYACAMAS VINEYARDS	Napa Valley	1,257	7.50	50	1991	1/90
1981	RAYMOND VINEYARD & CELLAR	Napa Valley Private Reserve	500	15	25	1991	6/90
1981	SILVERADO VINEYARDS	Napa Valley	1,800	10	20	1991	3/90
1982	STAG'S LEAP WINE CELLARS	Napa Valley	3,874	13.50	17	1991	3/90
1982	STAG'S LEAP WINE CELLARS	Napa Valley Mirage	3,564	11.50	18	1991	3/90
1980	STERLING VINEYARDS	Napa Valley Estate	4,000	13	17	1991	4/90
1977	STERLING VINEYARDS	Napa Valley Estate	4,000	10	20	1991	4/90

SCORE: 69

Vintage	Winery	Appellation/Vineyard	Case Production	Release Price	Current Price	Drink	Last Tasted
1983	BURGESS CELLARS	Napa Valley Vintage Reserve	16,000	12	18	Avoid	12/89
1976	CHATEAU ST. JEAN	Sonoma County Beltane Ranch					
1983	CLOS DU BOIS WINERY	Dry Creek Valley Flintwood Vineyard	634	10.50	30	Avoid	5/90
1980	ROBERT MONDAVI WINERY	Napa Valley Reserve	3,500	20	30	Avoid	3/90
1978	ROBERT MONDAVI WINERY	Napa Valley Reserve	5,100	20	24	Avoid	3/90

SCORE: 68

Vintage	Winery	Appellation/Vineyard	Case Production	Release Price	Current Price	Drink	Last Tasted
1982	BURGESS CELLARS	Napa Valley Vintage Reserve	16,000	12	12	Avoid	12/89
1987	CHATEAU MONTELENA WINERY	Napa Valley	12,500	20	25	Avoid	2/90
1977	CHATEAU ST. JEAN	Alexander Valley Robert Young Vineyards	1,597	17	22	Avoid	3/90
1983	MATANZAS CREEK WINERY	Sonoma Valley Estate	516	18	18	Avoid	2/90
1977	ROBERT MONDAVI WINERY	Napa Valley Reserve	2,600	14	32	1991	3/90
1982	SANFORD WINERY	Santa Maria Valley	2,500	12	20	Avoid	2/90

SCORE: 67

Vintage	Winery	Appellation/Vineyard	Case Production	Release Price	Current Price	Drink	Last Tasted
1980	CHATEAU ST. JEAN	Sonoma Valley Hunter Ranch	1,355	14	17	Avoid	3/90
1977	STAG'S LEAP WINE CELLARS	Napa Valley Haynes	1,752	9	20	Avoid	3/90

SCORE: 66

Vintage	Winery	Appellation/Vineyard	Case Production	Release Price	Current Price	Drink	Last Tasted
1984	BOUCHAINE VINEYARDS	Napa Valley	9,400	12.50	15	Avoid	2/90
1978	MOUNT EDEN VINEYARDS	Santa Cruz Mountains	400	16	50	Avoid	3/90
1982	VICHON WINERY	Napa Valley	9,500	15	20	Avoid	3/90

SCORE: 65

Vintage	Winery	Appellation/Vineyard	Case Production	Release Price	Current Price	Drink	Last Tasted
1978	CHATEAU ST. JEAN	Sonoma Valley Wildwood Vineyards	480	12	19	Avoid	3/90
1978	CHATEAU ST. JEAN	Sonoma Valley Hunter Farms	528	11.25	18	Avoid	3/90
1982	SAINTSBURY	Sonoma County	3,750	11	14	Avoid	2/90

SCORE: 64

Vintage	Winery	Appellation/Vineyard	Case Production	Release Price	Current Price	Drink	Last Tasted
1977	BEAULIEU VINEYARD	Napa Valley Beaufort	25,000	6	22	Avoid	4/90

SCORE: 63

Vintage	Winery	Appellation/Vineyard	Case Production	Release Price	Current Price	Drink	Last Tasted
1975	CHATEAU ST. JEAN	Alexander Valley Robert Young Vineyards	900	7.75	22	Avoid	7/90

SCORE: 62

Vintage	Winery	Appellation/Vineyard	Case Production	Release Price	Current Price	Drink	Last Tasted
1976	BEAULIEU VINEYARD	Napa Valley Beaufort	20,000	6	22	Avoid	4/90
1974	BEAULIEU VINEYARD	Napa Valley Beaufort	15,000	5	25	Avoid	4/90
1983	CUVAISON WINERY	Napa Valley	21,000	12	17	Avoid	4/90
1980	DE LOACH VINEYARDS	Russian River Valley	2,000	10	18	Aviod	2/90
1976	FREEMARK ABBEY WINERY	Napa Valley	4,802	9.75	26	Avoid	2/90
1983	STAG'S LEAP WINE CELLARS	Napa Valley	4,582	13.50	17	Avoid	3/90

SCORE: 61

Vintage	Winery	Appellation/Vineyard	Case Production	Release Price	Current Price	Drink	Last Tasted
1975	BEAULIEU VINEYARD	Napa Valley Beaufort	20,000	5	28	Avoid	4/90
1982	CUVAISON WINERY	Napa Valley	14,000	12	17	Avoid	4/90

SCORE: 60

Vintage	Winery	Appellation/Vineyard	Case Production	Release Price	Current Price	Drink	Last Tasted
1973	BEAULIEU VINEYARD	Napa Valley Beaufort	15,000	5	30	Avoid	4/90
1972	BEAULIEU VINEYARD	Napa Valley Beaufort	12,000	5	30	Avoid	4/90
1969	FREEMARK ABBEY WINERY	Napa Valley	2,307	6	37	Avoid	2/90

NR — Not released.

Vintage	Winery	Appellation / Vineyard	Case Production	Release Price	Current Price	Drink	Last Tasted
1973	MAYACAMAS VINEYARDS	Napa Valley	1,082	$7	$50	Avoid	1/90
1958	MAYACAMAS VINEYARDS	Napa Valley	500	1	200	Avoid	1/90
1975	MOUNT EDEN VINEYARDS	Santa Cruz Mountains	108	14	45	Avoid	3/90

SCORE: 59

Vintage	Winery	Appellation / Vineyard	Case Production	Release Price	Current Price	Drink	Last Tasted
1970	BEAULIEU VINEYARD	Napa Valley Beaufort	3,000	4	32	Avoid	4/90
1968	BEAULIEU VINEYARD	Napa Valley Beaufort	2,000	2	35	Avoid	4/90
1972	MAYACAMAS VINEYARDS	Napa Valley	704	7	50	Avoid	1/90
1974	MOUNT EDEN VINEYARDS	Santa Cruz Mountains	170	14	45	Avoid	3/90
1977	STAG'S LEAP WINE CELLARS	Napa Valley	2,452	8	17	Avoid	3/90
1976	STERLING VINEYARDS	Napa Valley Estate	2,600	5.25	18	Avoid	4/90

SCORE: 58

Vintage	Winery	Appellation / Vineyard	Case Production	Release Price	Current Price	Drink	Last Tasted
1971	BEAULIEU VINEYARD	Napa Valley Beaufort	10,000	4	30	Avoid	4/90
1987	CHALONE VINEYARD	Chalone	5,442	22	30	Avoid	1/90
1977	FREEMARK ABBEY WINERY	Napa Valley	10,901	10	36	Avoid	2/90
1965	MAYACAMAS VINEYARDS	Napa Valley	500	2.50	125	Avoid	1/90
1963	MAYACAMAS VINEYARDS	Napa Valley	400	1.75	150	Avoid	1/90
1962	MAYACAMAS VINEYARDS	Napa Valley	400	1.75	150	Avoid	1/90
1976	STAG'S LEAP WINE CELLARS	Napa Valley	335	8	17	Avoid	3/90

SCORE: 57

Vintage	Winery	Appellation / Vineyard	Case Production	Release Price	Current Price	Drink	Last Tasted
1969	BEAULIEU VINEYARD	Napa Valley Beaufort	3,000	2	35	Avoid	4/90

SCORE: 55

Vintage	Winery	Appellation / Vineyard	Case Production	Release Price	Current Price	Drink	Last Tasted
1970	FREEMARK ABBEY WINERY	Napa Valley	2,698	7	35	Avoid	2/90

NR — Not released.

APPENDIX 3
All Wines Tasted, Listed By Vintage, Score and Winery

Score	Winery	Appellation / Vineyard	Case Production	Release Price	Current Price	Drink	Last Tasted
VINTAGE: 1988							
95	KISTLER VINEYARDS	Sonoma Valley Kistler Estate Vineyard	507	$26	$26	1991-1996	2/90
94	FRANCISCAN VINEYARDS	Napa Valley Cuvée Sauvage	300	20	20	1991-1996	7/90
94	MONTICELLO CELLARS	Napa Valley Corley Reserve	4,000	17.25	17.25	1991-1997	2/90
94	SANFORD WINERY	Santa Barbara County Barrel Select	1,000	25	25	1991-1997	6/90
93	FERRARI-CARANO VINEYARD & WINERY	Alexander Valley	22,000	18	18	1991-1995	5/90
93	FERRARI-CARANO VINEYARD & WINERY	California Reserve	1,200	NR	NR	1992-1998	6/90
93	GRGICH HILLS CELLAR	Napa Valley	20,000	22	22	1992-1999	7/90
93	LONG VINEYARDS	Napa Valley	900	27.50	30	1991-1998	4/90
93	SONOMA-CUTRER VINEYARDS	Sonoma Valley Les Pierres	11,075	22.50	22.50	1992-2001	7/90
92	ARROWOOD VINEYARDS & WINERY	Sonoma County	6,300	18	18	1992-1997	4/90
92	CUVAISON WINERY	Carneros Reserve	2,400	NR	NR	1993-2001	6/90
92	FLORA SPRINGS WINE CO.	Napa Valley Barrel Fermented	4,700	24	24	1993-1997	4/90
92	FORMAN VINEYARD	Napa Valley	1,400	20	27	1991-1994	2/90
92	KISTLER VINEYARDS	Russian River Valley Dutton Ranch	4,987	22	22	1991-1995	2/90
92	KISTLER VINEYARDS	Sonoma Valley McCrea Vineyard	1,010	24	24	1991-1996	2/90
92	MORGAN WINERY	Monterey Reserve	1,500	20	20	1991-1997	6/90
92	SAINTSBURY	Carneros Reserve	1,800	20	20	1992-1998	2/90
92	SANFORD WINERY	Santa Barbara County	18,000	16	16	1991-1997	6/90
92	SEQUOIA GROVE VINEYARDS	Napa Valley Estate	4,228	16	16	1991-1996	5/90
92	SONOMA-CUTRER VINEYARDS	Russian River Valley Cutrer Vineyard	10,010	17.50	17.50	1992-2000	7/90
91	CHATEAU MONTELENA WINERY	Alexander Valley	3,100	20	20	1992-2000	2/90
91	CHATEAU ST. JEAN	Alexander Valley Robert Young Vineyards	13,638	18	18	1992-1998	3/90
91	CUVAISON WINERY	Carneros	34,000	15	15	1993-1999	4/90
91	DEHLINGER WINERY	Russian River Valley	4,000	12	12	1991-1996	4/90
91	FAR NIENTE WINERY	Napa Valley	24,000	26	28	1992-1998	2/90
91	FROG'S LEAP WINERY	Carneros	1,200	16	16	1992-1997	3/90
91	GIRARD WINERY	Napa Valley Reserve	700	NR	NR	1992-2000	6/90
91	KISTLER VINEYARDS	Sonoma Valley Durell Vineyard	2,337	17	17	1992-1998	2/90
91	LA CREMA	California Reserve	5,000	22	22	1991-1999	6/90
91	ROBERT MONDAVI WINERY	Napa Valley Reserve	12,000	26	26	1992-1997	6/90
91	NAVARRO VINEYARDS	Anderson Valley Première Reserve	3,596	14	14	1991-1998	5/90
91	SIMI WINERY	Sonoma County Reserve	2,300	NR	NR	1992-1998	7/90
91	SONOMA-CUTRER VINEYARDS	Russian River Valley Russian River Ranches	51,900	13.25	14	1992-1998	3/90
91	STERLING VINEYARDS	Napa Valley Diamond Mountain Ranch	2,000	NR	NR	1993-2000	7/90
90	ALTAMURA WINERY & VINEYARDS	Napa Valley	2,000	NR	NR	1992-1997	1/90
90	CHALONE VINEYARD	Chalone	8,003	22	27	1992-1999	6/90
90	CHATEAU ST. JEAN	Alexander Valley Belle Terre Vineyards	8,848	16	16	1993-1998	3/90
90	CLOS DU BOIS WINERY	Dry Creek Valley Flintwood Vineyard	5,469	18	18	1992-1997	2/90
90	HANZELL VINEYARDS	Sonoma Valley	750	24	24	1993-2000	5/90
90	MONTICELLO CELLARS	Napa Valley Jefferson Ranch	7,500	12.25	12.25	1991-1997	2/90
90	RAYMOND VINEYARD & CELLAR	Napa Valley Private Reserve	4,434	NR	NR	1991-1997	5/90
90	SAINTSBURY	Carneros	14,750	14	14	1992-1997	2/90

NR — Not released.

Score	Winery	Appellation / Vineyard	Production	Release Price	Current Price	Drink	Last Tasted
90	STAG'S LEAP WINE CELLARS	Napa Valley Reserve	335	$28	$28	1993-1998	3/90
90	STERLING VINEYARDS	Carneros Winery Lake	8,000	20	20	1992-1996	4/90
90	STONY HILL VINEYARD	Napa Valley	960	18	18	1992-2002	6/90
90	TREFETHEN VINEYARDS	Napa Valley	28,000	NR	NR	1992-1997	3/90
89	ACACIA WINERY	Carneros Marina Vineyard	7,133	20	20	1991-1996	1/90
89	BEAULIEU VINEYARD	Carneros Carneros Reserve	10,000	14	14	1992-1998	6/90
89	CHALONE VINEYARD	Chalone Reserve	217	NR	NR	1992-2000	6/90
89	CHAPPELLET VINEYARD	Napa Valley	4,500	NR	NR	1991-1998	6/90
89	CLOS DU BOIS WINERY	Alexander Valley Calcaire Vineyard	7,334	17	17	1992-1997	2/90
89	CLOS DU BOIS WINERY	Russian River Valley Winemaker's Reserve	3,807	NR	NR	1993-1999	5/90
89	CLOS PEGASE	Carneros	5,128	16.50	16.50	1991-1997	3/90
89	EDNA VALLEY VINEYARD	Edna Valley	46,500	14.75	16	1992-1997	3/90
89	FREEMARK ABBEY WINERY	Napa Valley	19,200	15	15	1991-1997	2/90
89	KENWOOD VINEYARDS	Sonoma Valley Beltane Ranch	3,000	15	15	1992-1998	7/90
89	MARKHAM VINEYARDS	Napa Valley	8,026	12	12	1991-1997	2/90
89	MATANZAS CREEK WINERY	Sonoma County	17,165	18.75	18.75	1991-1996	2/90
89	MAYACAMAS VINEYARDS	Napa Valley	1,427	NR	NR	1992-1997	6/90
89	MORGAN WINERY	Monterey	8,500	15	16	1991-1996	5/90
89	ROMBAUER VINEYARDS	Napa Valley Reserve	330	NR	NR	1992-1997	6/90
89	ZD WINES	California	18,418	20	20	1992-1996	3/90
88	S. ANDERSON VINEYARD	Stags Leap District Estate	4,388	18	18	1992-1997	3/90
88	BOUCHAINE VINEYARDS	Carneros Estate Reserve	1,600	NR	NR	1993-1998	6/90
88	BURGESS CELLARS	Napa Valley Triere Vineyard	18,000	16	16	1991-1996	12/89
88	CHATEAU MONTELENA WINERY	Napa Valley	13,200	20	20	1993-2000	7/90
88	CHATEAU ST. JEAN	Alexander Valley Jimtown Ranch	700	NR	NR	1992-1998	7/90
88	CLOS DU VAL WINE CO.	Carneros	15,000	16	16	1992-1997	6/90
88	CLOS PEGASE	Napa Valley	13,681	12	12	1991-1996	3/90
88	CONGRESS SPRINGS VINEYARDS	Santa Cruz Mountains Monmartre	224	30	30	1991-1996	4/90
88	FISHER VINEYARDS	Sonoma County Whitney's Vineyard	65	NR	NR	1992-1997	2/90
88	GIRARD WINERY	Napa Valley Estate	4,800	16	16	1991-1997	6/90
88	HESS COLLECTION WINERY	Napa Valley	10,000	13.75	13.75	1992-1998	4/90
88	WILLIAM HILL WINERY	Napa Valley Reserve	30,088	18	18	1992-1998	3/90
88	INGLENOOK-NAPA VALLEY	Napa Valley Reserve	2,000	NR	NR	1992-1998	4/90
88	MOUNT EDEN VINEYARDS	Santa Cruz Mountains	715	30	30	1992-1997	3/90
88	MOUNT EDEN VINEYARDS	Edna Valley MacGregor Vineyard	1,551	14	14	1991-1996	6/90
88	MURPHY-GOODE	Alexander Valley	12,000	11.50	11.50	1991-1995	4/90
88	NEWTON VINEYARD	Napa Valley	5,546	14.50	14.50	1991-1997	3/90
88	PINE RIDGE WINERY	Stags Leap District Pine Ridge Stags Leap Vineyard	2,063	20	20	1991-1996	7/90
88	PINE RIDGE WINERY	Napa Valley Knollside Cuvée	11,062	15	15	1991-1995	7/90
88	ROMBAUER VINEYARDS	Napa Valley	4,014	15	15	1991-1996	6/90
88	SILVERADO VINEYARDS	Napa Valley	41,000	14	14	1991-1996	3/90
88	SMITH-MADRONE VINEYARD	Napa Valley	1980	13	13	1993-2000	5/90
88	ST. CLEMENT VINEYARDS	Napa Valley	3,683	15	15	1992-1998	3/90
88	VICHON WINERY	Napa Valley	25,800	17	17	1991-1996	3/90
88	WHITE OAK VINEYARDS & WINERY	Sonoma County Myers Limited Release	988	18	20	1992-1997	5/90
88	WHITE OAK VINEYARDS & WINERY	Sonoma County	6,000	12	12	1991-1996	5/90
87	BERINGER VINEYARDS	Napa Valley Private Reserve	14,665	19	19	1992-1996	4/90
87	CHATEAU WOLTNER	Howell Mountain Frederique Vineyard	210	54	54	1993-1998	4/90
87	DE LOACH VINEYARDS	Russian River Valley O.F.S	3,200	22	22	1992-1996	5/90
87	DE LOACH VINEYARDS	Russian River Valley	26,000	15	15	1992-1996	5/90
87	FISHER VINEYARDS	Sonoma County Coach Insignia	6,000	18	18	1991-1996	2/90
87	FOLIE A DEUX WINERY	Napa Valley	6,900	16	16	1991-1997	6/90
87	FROG'S LEAP WINERY	Napa Valley	2,500	15	15	1991-1996	3/90

NR — Not released.

Score	Winery	Appellation/Vineyard	Case Production	Release Price	Current Price	Drink	Last Tasted
87	KENDALL-JACKSON VINEYARDS	California The Proprietor's	25,000	$24.50	$25	1991-1995	4/90
87	KENWOOD VINEYARDS	Sonoma Valley Yulupa Vineyard	3,000	14	14	1991-1996	7/90
87	ROBERT PECOTA WINERY	Alexander Valley Canepa Vineyard	800	16	16	1991-1995	4/90
87	REVERE WINERY	Napa Valley Reserve	366	NR	NR	1992-1998	4/90
87	STAG'S LEAP WINE CELLARS	Napa Valley	15,500	18	18	1993-1997	3/90
86	BUENA VISTA WINERY	Carneros Private Reserve	6,150	16.50	17	1993-1999	6/90
86	CHATEAU WOLTNER	Howell Mountain Estate Reserve	1,645	24	24	1992-1998	4/90
86	CHATEAU WOLTNER	Howell Mountain St. Thomas Vineyard	617	36	36	1993-1998	4/90
86	CHATEAU WOLTNER	Howell Mountain Titus Vineyard	147	54	54	1993-1999	4/90
86	CONGRESS SPRINGS VINEYARDS	Santa Clara County San Ysidro Reserve	2,682	20	20	1991-1994	4/90
86	CONGRESS SPRINGS VINEYARDS	Santa Clara County Barrel Fermented	13,431	14	14	1991-1995	4/90
86	FREEMARK ABBEY WINERY	Napa Valley Carpy Ranch	566	20	20	1991-1996	2/90
86	SEQUOIA GROVE VINEYARDS	Carneros	6,978	14	14	1991-1996	5/90
86	CHARLES F. SHAW VINEYARD	Napa Valley	10,500	11	11	1991-1995	5/90
85	ACACIA WINERY	Carneros	22,300	16	16	1991-1993	1/90
85	BOUCHAINE VINEYARDS	Carneros	8,400	15	15	1993-1997	6/90
85	CLOS DU BOIS WINERY	Alexander Valley Barrel Fermented	89,600	11	11	1991-1995	2/90
85	HACIENDA WINERY	Sonoma County Clair de Lune	10,500	15	15	1991-1996	6/90
85	KENDALL-JACKSON VINEYARDS	Anderson Valley Du Pratt Vineyard	200	14	14	1991-1994	4/90
85	KENDALL-JACKSON VINEYARDS	Redwood Valley Lolonis Vineyard	100	NR	NR	1991-1994	4/90

VINTAGE: 1987

Score	Winery	Appellation/Vineyard	Case Production	Release Price	Current Price	Drink	Last Tasted
96	CHATEAU ST. JEAN	Alexander Valley Robert Young Vineyards Reserve 1.5L	112	NR	NR	1993-2000	7/90
95	FLORA SPRINGS WINE CO.	Napa Valley Barrel Fermented	3,400	20	24	1992-1997	1/90
94	FERRARI-CARANO VINEYARD & WINERY	Alexander Valley	14,000	16	23	1991-1997	5/90
94	MOUNT EDEN VINEYARDS	Edna Valley MEV MacGregor Vineyard	1,500	14	18	1991-1997	3/90
94	SIMI WINERY	Sonoma County Reserve	2,000	NR	NR	1991-1997	4/90
93	KISTLER VINEYARDS	Russian River Valley Dutton Ranch	4,020	18	24	1991-1993	2/90
93	KISTLER VINEYARDS	Sonoma Valley Durell Vineyard	1,300	16	20	1991-1997	2/90
92	ARROWOOD VINEYARDS & WINERY	Sonoma County Réserve Spéciale 1.5L	57	50	50	1991-1997	4/90
92	CLOS DU BOIS WINERY	Alexander Valley Winemaker's Reserve	3,565	24	24	1991-1995	2/90
92	DE LOACH VINEYARDS	Russian River Valley O.F.S	2,400	22	25	1991-1995	5/90
92	KENDALL-JACKSON VINEYARDS	California The Proprietor's	11,000	20	20	1991-1995	4/90
92	ROBERT MONDAVI WINERY	Napa Valley Reserve	10,000	26	26	1991-1997	6/90
92	SANFORD WINERY	Santa Barbara County	18,000	15	16	1991-1996	2/90
92	SILVERADO VINEYARDS	Napa Valley Limited Reserve	1,300	NR	NR	1993-2000	7/90
92	SONOMA-CUTRER VINEYARDS	Sonoma Valley Les Pierres	11,510	22.50	26	1992-1997	3/90
91	CHATEAU ST. JEAN	Alexander Valley Robert Young Vineyards	13,108	18	25	1992-1999	3/90
91	CHATEAU ST. JEAN	Alexander Valley Belle Terre Vineyards	2,590	16	22	1992-1998	3/90
91	CUVAISON WINERY	Carneros Reserve	1,260	22	22	1992-1998	7/90
91	EDNA VALLEY VINEYARD	Edna Valley	41,000	14	20	1991-1996	3/90
91	FAR NIENTE WINERY	Napa Valley	20,000	26	30	1992-1998	2/90
91	FRANCISCAN VINEYARDS	Napa Valley Cuvée Sauvage	400	20	20	1991-1996	6/90
91	HESS COLLECTION WINERY	Napa Valley	4,100	13.25	15	1991-1997	4/90
91	WILLIAM HILL WINERY	Napa Valley Reserve	21,042	18	18	1992-1998	3/90
91	ROBERT PECOTA WINERY	Alexander Valley Canepa Vineyard	800	16	18	1991-1996	4/90
91	PINE RIDGE WINERY	Stags Leap District Pine Ridge Stags Leap Vineyard	2,765	20	20	1991-1996	4/90

NR — Not released.

Score	Winery	Appellation/Vineyard	Case Production	Release Price	Current Price	Drink	Last Tasted
91	SANFORD WINERY	Santa Barbara County Barrel Select	300	$24	$30	1991-1997	2/90
91	SMITH-MADRONE VINEYARD	Napa Valley	2,542	13	13	1993-2000	5/90
91	SONOMA-CUTRER VINEYARDS	Russian River Valley Cutrer Vineyard	9,840	17.50	18	1991-1996	3/90
91	ST. CLEMENT VINEYARDS	Napa Valley Abbott's Vineyard	500	17	17	1992-1997	3/90
90	CLOS PEGASE	Carneros	4,402	15.50	17	1991-1995	3/90
90	CONGRESS SPRINGS VINEYARDS	Santa Clara County San Ysidro Reserve	2,000	16	23	1991-1995	4/90
90	CUVAISON WINERY	Napa Valley	31,000	13.50	16	1993-1998	4/90
90	DEHLINGER WINERY	Russian River Valley	4,900	11.50	12	1991-1996	4/90
90	FOLIE A DEUX WINERY	Napa Valley	5,300	15	16	1992-1997	6/90
90	GRGICH HILLS CELLAR	Napa Valley	33,000	22	28	1992-1997	6/90
90	HANZELL VINEYARDS	Sonoma Valley	1,050	24	28	1993-2000	1/90
90	KISTLER VINEYARDS	Sonoma Valley Kistler Estate Vineyard	866	22	26	1991-1996	2/90
90	LONG VINEYARDS	Napa Valley	900	27.50	35	1991-1998	4/90
90	MATANZAS CREEK WINERY	Sonoma County	13,506	18	20	1991-1996	2/90
90	MOUNT EDEN VINEYARDS	Santa Cruz Mountains	1,348	28	32	1992-1997	3/90
90	PINE RIDGE WINERY	Napa Valley Knollside Cuvée	9,854	15	16	1991-1995	4/90
90	SAINTSBURY	Carneros	13,150	13	15	1992-1997	2/90
89	S. ANDERSON VINEYARD	Stags Leap District Proprietor's Reserve	480	20	20	1991-1996	3/90
89	ARROWOOD VINEYARDS & WINERY	Sonoma County	6,000	18	18	1991-1995	4/90
89	CHATEAU MONTELENA WINERY	Alexander Valley	5,400	20	24	1992-1998	2/90
89	CLOS DU VAL WINE CO.	Carneros	13,000	13	13	1991-1995	6/90
89	FERRARI-CARANO VINEYARD & WINERY	California Reserve	780	28	28	1992-1998	5/90
89	FORMAN VINEYARD	Napa Valley	1,400	18	35	1991-1994	2/90
89	KENDALL-JACKSON VINEYARDS	Anderson Valley De Patie Vineyard	200	14	14	1991-1995	4/90
89	SAINTSBURY	Carneros Reserve	1,450	20	20	1992-1997	2/90
89	STAG'S LEAP WINE CELLARS	Napa Valley Reserve	1,172	28	28	1992-1997	3/90
89	STAG'S LEAP WINE CELLARS	Napa Valley	17,710	18	18	1992-1997	3/90
89	STERLING VINEYARDS	Carneros Winery Lake	7,000	20	20	1991-1996	4/90
88	CHATEAU ST. JEAN	Sonoma Valley McCrea Vineyards	364	15	15	1992-1996	3/90
88	CHATEAU WOLTNER	Howell Mountain Estate Reserve	2,151	24	24	1991-1997	4/90
88	CLOS DU BOIS WINERY	Alexander Valley Calcaire Vineyard	6,593	20	20	1992-1996	2/90
88	FROG'S LEAP WINERY	Napa Valley	1,800	14	16	1991-1995	3/90
88	NEWTON VINEYARD	Napa Valley	6,000	14	14	1991-1997	3/90
88	RAYMOND VINEYARD & CELLAR	Napa Valley Private Reserve	4,404	22	22	1991-1996	5/90
88	SEQUOIA GROVE VINEYARDS	Napa Valley Estate	2,167	16	16	1991-1996	5/90
88	SILVERADO VINEYARDS	Napa Valley	30,000	13.50	15	1991-1996	3/90
88	SONOMA-CUTRER VINEYARDS	Russian River Valley Russian River Ranches	53,055	12	16	1991-1995	3/90
88	STERLING VINEYARDS	Napa Valley Diamond Mountain Ranch	6,000	NR	NR	1993-1999	7/90
88	TREFETHEN VINEYARDS	Napa Valley	29,115	16.75	16.75	1992-1996	3/90
87	ALTAMURA WINERY & VINEYARDS	Napa Valley	1,800	16.50	16.50	1993-1998	1/90
87	BEAULIEU VINEYARD	Carneros Los Carneros Reserve	10,000	14	16	1992-1998	5/90
87	CHALONE VINEYARD	Chalone Reserve	727	NR	NR	1992-2000	5/90
87	CHAPPELLET VINEYARD	Napa Valley	3,817	14	14	1993-2000	3/90
87	CHATEAU ST. JEAN	Alexander Valley Jimtown Ranch	689	15	15	1993-1997	3/90
87	CHATEAU WOLTNER	Howell Mountain St. Thomas Vineyard	883	36	36	1993-1998	4/90
87	CLOS DU BOIS WINERY	Dry Creek Valley Flintwood Vineyard	4,217	20	20	1992-1997	2/90
87	CLOS DU BOIS WINERY	Alexander Valley Barrel Fermented	81,650	11	11	1991-1995	2/90

NR — Not released.

Score	Winery	Appellation / Vineyard	Case Production	Release Price	Current Price	Drink	Last Tasted
87	CLOS DU VAL WINE CO.	Napa Valley	9,000	$12	$12	1991-1996	6/90
87	CONGRESS SPRINGS VINEYARDS	Santa Cruz Mountains Monmartre	770	28	30	1991-1995	4/90
87	DE LOACH VINEYARDS	Russian River Valley	24,000	15	20	1991-1995	2/90
87	GIRARD WINERY	Napa Valley Reserve	700	25	25	1993-1996	6/90
87	KENWOOD VINEYARDS	Sonoma Valley Beltane Ranch	3,000	15	17	1992-1997	7/90
87	MARKHAM VINEYARDS	Napa Valley	4,720	12	12	1991-1996	2/90
87	MAYACAMAS VINEYARDS	Napa Valley	2,640	20	20	1991-1996	1/90
87	MURPHY-GOODE	Alexander Valley Premier Vineyard	7,000	11	11	1991-1996	4/90
87	NAVARRO VINEYARDS	Anderson Valley Première Reserve	1,813	14	14	1992-1996	3/90
87	ROMBAUER VINEYARDS	Napa Valley Reserve	200	25	25	1991-1995	6/90
87	STONY HILL VINEYARD	Napa Valley	1,195	18	35	1991-1997	5/90
87	VICHON WINERY	Napa Valley	13,500	16	16	1991-1996	3/90
86	BOUCHAINE VINEYARDS	Carneros Estate Reserve	1,600	19	19	1991-1995	2/90
86	CLOS PEGASE	Napa Valley	11,131	12	12	1991-1995	3/90
86	FISHER VINEYARDS	Sonoma County Whitney's Vineyard	48	24	24	1991-1995	2/90
86	FRANCISCAN VINEYARDS	Napa Valley Reserve	600	15	15	1992-1997	6/90
86	FROG'S LEAP WINERY	Carneros	1,500	15	17	1991-1996	3/90
86	INGLENOOK-NAPA VALLEY	Napa Valley Reserve	6,000	14	14	1992-1997	4/90
86	KENDALL-JACKSON VINEYARDS	Sonoma Valley Durell Vineyard	500	14	14	1991-1994	4/90
86	MONTICELLO CELLARS	Napa Valley Corley Reserve	4,400	17.25	18	1992-1997	6/90
86	MONTICELLO CELLARS	Napa Valley Jefferson Ranch	8,100	12.25	13	1991-1995	2/90
86	ROMBAUER VINEYARDS	Napa Valley	4,300	14.50	15	1991-1996	6/90
86	ST. CLEMENT VINEYARDS	Napa Valley	3,500	15	15	1992-1997	3/90
85	ACACIA WINERY	Carneros Marina Vineyard	8,600	18	19	1991-1995	1/90
85	S. ANDERSON VINEYARD	Stags Leap District Estate	3,798	16	18	1993-1998	6/90
85	BURGESS CELLARS	Napa Valley Triere Vineyard	18,000	14.50	15	1991-1996	12/89
85	CHATEAU WOLTNER	Howell Mountain Titus Vineyard	309	54	54	1992-1998	4/90
85	KENWOOD VINEYARDS	Sonoma Valley Yulupa Vineyard	3,000	14	16	1992-1996	7/90
85	MORGAN WINERY	Monterey Reserve	1,500	19	19	1991-1994	6/90
85	CHARLES F. SHAW VINEYARD	Napa Valley	7,500	11	11	1992-1997	5/90
85	WHITE OAK VINEYARDS & WINERY	Sonoma County	4,000	11	16	1991-1996	5/90
85	ZD WINES	California	15,203	18.50	25	1991-1995	3/90
84	ACACIA WINERY	Carneros	17,700	17	17	1991-1995	1/90
84	CONGRESS SPRINGS VINEYARDS	Santa Clara County	12,500	12	18	1991-1994	4/90
84	FISHER VINEYARDS	Sonoma County Coach Insignia	5,000	18	18	1991-1995	2/90
84	FREEMARK ABBEY WINERY	Napa Valley	16,500	15	15	1992-1996	2/90
84	MORGAN WINERY	Monterey	8,500	15	16	1991-1994	5/90
83	BOUCHAINE VINEYARDS	Carneros	7,400	14	14	1991-1994	2/90
83	LA CREMA	California Reserve	2,900	22	22	1993-1999	6/90
83	REVERE WINERY	Napa Valley Reserve	101	25	25	1991-1995	4/90
83	SEQUOIA GROVE VINEYARDS	Carneros	5,530	14	14	1991-1995	5/90
82	BUENA VISTA WINERY	Carneros Private Reserve	5,500	16.50	17	1991-1994	3/90
82	KENDALL-JACKSON VINEYARDS	Anderson Valley Dennison Vineyard	200	14	14	1991-1993	4/90
81	GIRARD WINERY	Napa Valley Estate	5,757	14.50	16	1992-1995	3/90
81	WHITE OAK VINEYARDS & WINERY	Sonoma County Myers Limited Release	843	18	20	1991-1994	5/90
79	BERINGER VINEYARDS	Napa Valley Private Reserve	12,159	17	19	1991-1993	4/90
72	HACIENDA WINERY	Sonoma County Clair de Lune	9,600	12	15	1991-1993	4/90
68	CHATEAU MONTELENA WINERY	Napa Valley	12,500	20	25	Avoid	2/90
58	CHALONE VINEYARD	Chalone	5,442	22	30	Avoid	1/90

NR — Not released

Score	Winery	Appellation / Vineyard	Case Production	Release Price	Current Price	Drink	Last Tasted
VINTAGE: 1986							
94	CHALONE VINEYARD	Chalone	4,768	$22	$48	1991-1998	1/90
94	CUVAISON WINERY	Carneros Reserve	1,800	20	28	1992-1996	6/90
93	FERRARI-CARANO VINEYARD & WINERY	California Reserve	300	28	42	1991-1997	5/90
92	CHATEAU ST. JEAN	Alexander Valley Robert Young Vineyards	13,007	18	25	1992-1998	3/90
92	FERRARI-CARANO VINEYARD & WINERY	Alexander Valley	7,200	16	28	1991-1996	5/90
92	FORMAN VINEYARD	Napa Valley	1,000	18	45	1991-1994	2/90
92	GIRARD WINERY	Napa Valley Reserve	701	25	25	1991-1996	3/90
92	GIRARD WINERY	Napa Valley Estate	5,297	13.50	28	1991-1996	3/90
92	KISTLER VINEYARDS	Sonoma Valley Kistler Estate Vineyard	397	18	35	1991-1997	2/90
92	LONG VINEYARDS	Napa Valley	800	27.50	45	1991-1997	4/90
92	SIMI WINERY	Sonoma County Reserve	1,600	28	32	1991-1998	4/90
91	BUENA VISTA WINERY	Carneros Private Reserve	3,700	16.50	17	1991-1996	3/90
91	CHATEAU MONTELENA WINERY	Alexander Valley	5,700	18	26	1991-1997	2/90
91	CHATEAU MONTELENA WINERY	Napa Valley	12,800	18	25	1991-1998	2/90
91	CHATEAU ST. JEAN	Alexander Valley Robert Young Vineyards Reserve 1.5L	507	NR	NR	1992-2000	7/90
91	CHATEAU WOLTNER	Howell Mountain Estate Reserve	1,228	24	24	1991-1997	4/90
91	FRANCISCAN VINEYARDS	Napa Valley Reserve	3,000	14	15	1991-1997	4/90
91	GRGICH HILLS CELLAR	Napa Valley	25,000	22	33	1991-1996	3/90
91	WILLIAM HILL WINERY	Napa Valley Reserve	18,228	17	20	1991-1995	3/90
91	KENDALL-JACKSON VINEYARDS	Sonoma Valley Durell Vineyard	500	14	16	1991-1996	6/90
90	BERINGER VINEYARDS	Napa Valley Private Reserve	6,747	16	22	1991-1995	4/90
90	CHAPPELLET VINEYARD	Napa Valley	4,500	14	14	1991-1997	3/90
90	CHATEAU ST. JEAN	Alexander Valley Belle Terre Vineyards	3,625	16	20	1992-1997	3/90
90	FISHER VINEYARDS	Sonoma County Coach Insignia	3,000	17	20	1991-1997	2/90
90	FROG'S LEAP WINERY	Napa Valley	1,500	12	18	1991-1995	3/90
90	KISTLER VINEYARDS	Russian River Valley Dutton Ranch	3,151	16.50	28	1991-1997	2/90
90	SILVERADO VINEYARDS	Napa Valley	22,000	12	16	1991-1996	3/90
90	SILVERADO VINEYARDS	Napa Valley Limited Reserve	650	25	25	1992-1997	7/90
90	VICHON WINERY	Napa Valley	8,000	15	17	1991-1996	3/90
89	ARROWOOD VINEYARDS & WINERY	Sonoma County	4,600	18	25	1991-1995	4/90
89	CHATEAU ST. JEAN	Dry Creek Valley Frank Johnson Vineyards	2,115	14	19	1991-1995	7/90
89	CHATEAU WOLTNER	Howell Mountain St. Thomas Vineyard	747	36	37	1991-1997	4/90
89	CLOS PEGASE	Carneros	2,825	15.50	17	1991-1996	3/90
89	CUVAISON WINERY	Napa Valley	22,000	12.75	18	1992-1998	4/90
89	DE LOACH VINEYARDS	Russian River Valley	18,000	14	20	1991-1994	2/90
89	HACIENDA WINERY	Sonoma County Clair de Lune	7,000	12	18	1991-1995	4/90
89	KISTLER VINEYARDS	Sonoma Valley Durell Vineyard	620	16	25	1991-1997	2/90
89	MATANZAS CREEK WINERY	Sonoma County	8,817	17.50	22	1991-1994	2/90
89	ROBERT MONDAVI WINERY	Napa Valley Reserve	11,000	25	28	1991-1995	3/90
89	MONTICELLO CELLARS	Napa Valley Corley Reserve	3,200	16.50	18	1991-1996	2/90
89	MORGAN WINERY	Monterey	6,000	14	20	1991-1995	5/90
89	SMITH-MADRONE VINEYARD	Napa Valley	2,375	12.50	16	1990-1998	5/90
89	SONOMA-CUTRER VINEYARDS	Russian River Valley Cutrer Vineyard	7,100	16	20	1992-1997	3/90
89	ST. CLEMENT VINEYARDS	Napa Valley	1,450	15	15	1992-1997	3/90
89	STERLING VINEYARDS	Carneros Winery Lake	3,000	20	23	1991-1994	4/90
88	ALTAMURA WINERY & VINEYARDS	Napa Valley	1,500	15	21	1993-1997	1/90

NR — Not released.

Score	Winery	Appellation / Vineyard	Case Production	Release Price	Current Price	Drink	Last Tasted
88	BOUCHAINE VINEYARDS	Carneros Estate Reserve	1,500	$19	$19	1991-1995	2/90
88	BOUCHAINE VINEYARDS	Napa Valley	7,000	13	17	1991-1995	2/90
88	CHATEAU WOLTNER	Howell Mountain Titus Vineyard	179	54	54	1993-1998	4/90
88	CLOS DU BOIS WINERY	Dry Creek Valley Flintwood Vineyard	4,911	19.50	25	1992-1996	2/90
88	EDNA VALLEY VINEYARD	Edna Valley	36,000	13.50	20	1991-1995	3/90
88	FAR NIENTE WINERY	Napa Valley	18,000	24	31	1991-1997	2/90
88	FOLIE A DEUX WINERY	Napa Valley	2,600	15	18	1991-1997	6/90
88	HESS COLLECTION WINERY	Napa Valley	4,285	12.75	16	1991-1996	4/90
88	INGLENOOK-NAPA VALLEY	Napa Valley Reserve	6,135	14.50	14.50	1991-1996	4/90
88	MOUNT EDEN VINEYARDS	Santa Cruz Mountains	677	25	42	1991-1996	3/90
88	PINE RIDGE WINERY	Stags Leap District Pine Ridge Stags Leap Vineyard	2,215	19	23	1991-1996	4/90
88	PINE RIDGE WINERY	Napa Valley Knollside Cuvée	7,918	14	16	1991-1995	4/90
88	SAINTSBURY	Carneros	10,075	12	17	1992-1997	2/90
88	SANFORD WINERY	Santa Barbara County	6,000	14	16	1991-1995	2/90
88	SEQUOIA GROVE VINEYARDS	Napa Valley Estate	2,064	15	18	1991-1994	5/90
88	SONOMA-CUTRER VINEYARDS	Sonoma Valley Les Pierres	9,125	19.50	27	1992-1997	3/90
88	STAG'S LEAP WINE CELLARS	Napa Valley Reserve	480	26	26	1991-1994	6/90
87	ACACIA WINERY	Carneros	11,500	15	18	1991-1993	1/90
87	BURGESS CELLARS	Napa Valley Triere Vineyard	17,000	14	16	1991-1994	12/89
87	CHATEAU ST. JEAN	Sonoma Valley McCrea Vineyards	163	15	17	1992-1996	3/90
87	DEHLINGER WINERY	Russian River Valley	3,200	11	14	1991-1995	4/90
87	FLORA SPRINGS WINE CO.	Napa Valley Barrel Fermented	2,800	20	24	1992-1996	1/90
87	FROG'S LEAP WINERY	Carneros	1,300	14	18	1991-1995	6/90
87	HANZELL VINEYARDS	Sonoma Valley	1,070	22	32	1993-1998	1/90
87	MAYACAMAS VINEYARDS	Napa Valley	1,860	20	20	1991-1996	3/90
87	NAVARRO VINEYARDS	Anderson Valley Première Reserve	1,555	14	18	1991-1996	3/90
87	RAYMOND VINEYARD & CELLAR	Napa Valley Private Reserve	1,842	18	21	1991-1995	5/90
87	REVERE WINERY	Napa Valley Reserve	206	22	25	1991-1996	4/90
87	STONY HILL VINEYARD	Napa Valley	1,420	16	55	1992-1999	7/90
87	TREFETHEN VINEYARDS	Napa Valley	26,595	16.25	19	1992-1996	3/90
87	WHITE OAK VINEYARDS & WINERY	Sonoma County Myers Limited Release	621	16	20	1991-1996	5/90
86	ACACIA WINERY	Carneros Marina Vineyard	6,950	18	22	1991-1994	1/90
86	BEAULIEU VINEYARD	Carneros Los Carneros Reserve	10,000	12	15	1991-1996	6/90
86	DE LOACH VINEYARDS	Russian River Valley O.F.S	1,800	22	26	1991-1995	2/90
86	FREEMARK ABBEY WINERY	Napa Valley	16,997	15	15	1991-1996	2/90
86	KENDALL-JACKSON VINEYARDS	California The Proprietor's	5,000	17	20	1991-1994	4/90
86	MONTICELLO CELLARS	Napa Valley Jefferson Ranch	5,700	11	14	1991-1995	2/90
86	MURPHY-GOODE	Alexander Valley	7,000	10	12	1991-1995	4/90
86	ROMBAUER VINEYARDS	Napa Valley Reserve	200	24	26	1991-1995	6/90
86	SONOMA-CUTRER VINEYARDS	Russian River Valley Russian River Ranches	41,725	12	18	1992-1996	3/90
86	STAG'S LEAP WINE CELLARS	Napa Valley	8,166	17	20	1991-1995	3/90
86	STERLING VINEYARDS	Napa Valley Diamond Mountain Ranch	7,500	15	15	1991-1996	4/90
86	WHITE OAK VINEYARDS & WINERY	Sonoma County	3,500	11	16	1991-1995	5/90
85	CHALONE VINEYARD	Chalone Reserve	379	28	38	1991-1995	5/90
85	CLOS DU BOIS WINERY	Alexander Valley Calcaire Vineyard	5,096	16	22	1992-1996	2/90
85	CLOS PEGASE	Napa Valley	6,689	12	14	1991-1995	3/90
85	CONGRESS SPRINGS VINEYARDS	Santa Clara County San Ysidro Reserve	2,275	15	22	1991-1994	4/90
85	CONGRESS SPRINGS VINEYARDS	Santa Cruz Mountains Private Reserve	552	20	23	1991-1994	4/90
85	KENWOOD VINEYARDS	Sonoma Valley Beltane Ranch	2,500	14	18	1991-1995	7/90
85	LA CREMA	California Reserve	1,200	18	22	1991-1996	6/90
85	NEWTON VINEYARD	Napa Valley	5,000	14	14	1992-1997	3/90

NR — Not released.

Score	Winery	Appellation / Vineyard	Case Production	Release Price	Current Price	Drink	Last Tasted
85	ROBERT PECOTA WINERY	Alexander Valley Canepa Vineyard	800	$16	$19	1991-1995	4/90
85	REVERE WINERY	Napa Valley	1,375	15	15	1991-1996	4/90
85	ROMBAUER VINEYARDS	Napa Valley	3,815	14.50	16	1991-1995	6/90
85	CHARLES F. SHAW VINEYARD	Napa Valley	7,500	11	11	1991-1995	5/90
85	ZD WINES	California	15,773	18	25	1991-1997	6/90
84	CLOS DU VAL WINE CO.	Carneros	12,000	12	14	1991-1995	6/90
84	MARKHAM VINEYARDS	Napa Valley Estate	4,649	12	14	1991-1994	2/90
84	SAINTSBURY	Carneros Reserve	1,015	20	25	1992-1996	2/90
83	CONGRESS SPRINGS VINEYARDS	Santa Clara County	4,900	12	18	1991-1994	4/90
82	KENWOOD VINEYARDS	Sonoma Valley Yulupa Vineyard	6,000	12	17	1991-1995	7/90
81	ACACIA WINERY	Napa Valley	6,700	15	17	1991-1993	1/90
81	S. ANDERSON VINEYARD	Stags Leap District Estate	4,792	16	18	1991-1994	3/90
81	MOUNT EDEN VINEYARDS	Edna Valley MEV MacGregor Vineyard	1,200	13	16	1991-1995	3/90
80	CLOS DU BOIS WINERY	Sonoma Valley Barrel Fermented	81,616	10	12	1991-1992	12/89
78	CLOS DU BOIS WINERY	Alexander Valley Proprietor's Reserve	4,097	22.50	23	1991-1994	5/90
78	SEQUOIA GROVE VINEYARDS	Carneros	4,880	13	16	1991-1995	5/90

VINTAGE: 1985

Score	Winery	Appellation / Vineyard	Case Production	Release Price	Current Price	Drink	Last Tasted
95	CHATEAU ST. JEAN	Alexander Valley Robert Young Vineyards Reserve 1.5L	978	40	40	1992-1998	7/90
94	CHALONE VINEYARD	Chalone Reserve	308	28	42	1991-1998	6/90
93	CUVAISON WINERY	Napa Valley	6,000	12	20	1991-1996	4/90
93	FORMAN VINEYARD	Napa Valley	800	15	45	1991-1995	2/90
92	S. ANDERSON VINEYARD	Stags Leap District Estate	3,500	14	25	1991-1995	3/90
92	CHATEAU ST. JEAN	Alexander Valley Belle Terre Vineyards	3,371	16	25	1992-1996	3/90
92	GRGICH HILLS CELLAR	Napa Valley	25,000	22	33	1991-1995	3/90
92	SANFORD WINERY	Santa Barbara County Barrel Select	150	20	30	1991-1996	2/90
92	SONOMA-CUTRER VINEYARDS	Sonoma Valley Les Pierres	8,500	17.50	30	1991-1997	3/90
92	STONY HILL VINEYARD	Napa Valley	1947	16	61	1991-2000	5/90
91	ALTAMURA WINERY & VINEYARDS	Napa Valley	600	14	21	1991-1996	1/90
91	CHATEAU MONTELENA WINERY	Alexander Valley	8,600	16	28	1991-1997	2/90
91	CHATEAU ST. JEAN	Alexander Valley Robert Young Vineyards	13,613	18	26	1992-1998	3/90
91	FERRARI-CARANO VINEYARD & WINERY	Alexander Valley	2,500	14	30	1991-1996	5/90
91	GIRARD WINERY	Napa Valley Reserve	242	25	35	1991-1995	3/90
91	LONG VINEYARDS	Napa Valley	850	27.50	45	1991-1996	4/90
91	RAYMOND VINEYARD & CELLAR	Napa Valley Private Reserve	1,720	18	21	1991-1995	5/90
91	SIMI WINERY	Sonoma County Reserve	1,200	28	32	1991-1996	4/90
90	CHATEAU MONTELENA WINERY	Napa Valley	9,000	18	25	1991-1998	2/90
90	DE LOACH VINEYARDS	Russian River Valley	12,000	14	23	1991-1994	2/90
90	FAR NIENTE WINERY	Napa Valley	14,300	24	33	1992-1998	2/90
90	GIRARD WINERY	Napa Valley Estate	4,740	13.50	25	1991-1996	3/90
90	HANZELL VINEYARDS	Sonoma Valley	830	22	35	1991-1999	1/90
90	WILLIAM HILL WINERY	Napa Valley Reserve	16,313	16	24	1991-1997	3/90
90	MAYACAMAS VINEYARDS	Napa Valley	1,415	20	25	1991-1998	1/90
90	SAINTSBURY	Carneros	6,600	11	19	1991-1996	2/90
90	SANFORD WINERY	Santa Barbara County	5,000	13.50	20	1991-1997	2/90
90	WHITE OAK VINEYARDS & WINERY	Alexander Valley Myers Limited Release	237	14.50	22	1991-1996	5/90
90	ZD WINES	California	9,639	16	28	1992-1996	3/90
89	NAVARRO VINEYARDS	Anderson Valley Première Reserve	1,331	12	18	1991-1995	3/90
89	ROBERT PECOTA WINERY	Alexander Valley Canepa Vineyard	800	16	18	1991-1996	7/90
89	SEQUOIA GROVE VINEYARDS	Napa Valley Estate	4,981	16	20	1991-1995	5/90

NR — Not released.

Score	Winery	Appellation / Vineyard	Case Production	Release Price	Current Price	Drink	Last Tasted
89	WHITE OAK VINEYARDS & WINERY	Sonoma County	3,000	$10.50	$16	1991-1996	5/90
88	BURGESS CELLARS	Napa Valley Vintage Reserve	17,000	13	16	1990-1995	12/89
88	FOLIE A DEUX WINERY	Napa Valley	1,200	14.50	18	1991-1995	6/90
88	KISTLER VINEYARDS	California Dutton Ranch/Winery Lake	5,251	15	30	1991-1994	2/90
88	MATANZAS CREEK WINERY	Sonoma County	6,221	16.50	28	1991-1994	2/90
88	ROBERT MONDAVI WINERY	Napa Valley Reserve	13,000	25	27	1991-1995	3/90
88	SEQUOIA GROVE VINEYARDS	Carneros	4,976	12	16	1991-1995	5/90
88	SONOMA-CUTRER VINEYARDS	Russian River Valley Russian River Ranches	28,256	11.50	22	1991-1995	3/90
88	TREFETHEN VINEYARDS	Napa Valley	23,016	15.25	24	1991-1995	3/90
88	VICHON WINERY	Napa Valley	20,900	15	17	1991-1995	3/90
87	BOUCHAINE VINEYARDS	Carneros	2,250	15	20	1991-1993	2/90
87	BOUCHAINE VINEYARDS	Napa Valley	10,100	13	17	1991-1994	2/90
87	CHAPPELLET VINEYARD	Napa Valley	3,300	12.50	15	1991-1996	3/90
87	CHATEAU ST. JEAN	Dry Creek Valley Frank Johnson Vineyards	1,517	14	14	1993-1997	3/90
87	CLOS DU VAL WINE CO.	Napa Valley	14,000	11.50	17	1991-1997	6/90
87	CLOS PEGASE	Alexander Valley	3,100	13	15	1991-1995	3/90
87	CONGRESS SPRINGS VINEYARDS	Santa Clara County	2,500	12	20	1991-1994	4/90
87	HACIENDA WINERY	Sonoma County Clair de Lune	7,000	11	20	1991-1995	4/90
87	KENDALL-JACKSON VINEYARDS	Sonoma Valley Durell Vineyard	500	14	20	1991-1995	4/90
87	MOUNT EDEN VINEYARDS	Santa Cruz Mountains	540	25	40	1991-1996	3/90
87	MOUNT EDEN VINEYARDS	Edna Valley MEV MacGregor Vineyard	1,100	12.50	14	1991-1995	3/90
87	PINE RIDGE WINERY	Napa Valley Knollside Cuvée	6,869	14	16	1991-1995	4/90
87	CHARLES F. SHAW VINEYARD	Napa Valley	5,000	12	15	1991-1994	5/90
87	SILVERADO VINEYARDS	Napa Valley	17,000	11.50	17	1991-1995	3/90
87	SMITH-MADRONE VINEYARD	Napa Valley	1,832	12.50	16	1990-1996	5/90
87	SONOMA-CUTRER VINEYARDS	Russian River Valley Cutrer Vineyard	6,000	14.75	23	1991-1996	3/90
87	STERLING VINEYARDS	Napa Valley Diamond Mountain Ranch	5,400	15	17	1993-1999	7/90
86	BERINGER VINEYARDS	Napa Valley Private Reserve	4,096	15	24	1991-1994	4/90
86	BUENA VISTA WINERY	Carneros Private Reserve	2,700	16.50	17	1991-1995	3/90
86	CHATEAU ST. JEAN	Sonoma Valley McCrea Vineyards	1,543	14.25	17	1991-1996	7/90
86	DEHLINGER WINERY	Russian River Valley	2,000	10	14	1991-1998	5/90
86	LA CREMA	California Reserve	1,200	18	22	1991-1995	6/90
86	MARKHAM VINEYARDS	Napa Valley Estate	2,843	12	16	1991-1995	2/90
86	MATANZAS CREEK WINERY	Sonoma Valley Estate	380	18	31	1991-1994	2/90
86	MORGAN WINERY	Monterey County	5,000	14	25	1991-1996	7/90
85	CLOS DU BOIS WINERY	Alexander Valley Proprietor's Reserve	1,762	22	25	1991-1995	5/90
85	EDNA VALLEY VINEYARD	Edna Valley	31,000	13	25	1991-1994	3/90
85	FLORA SPRINGS WINE CO.	Napa Valley Barrel Fermented	2,100	18	27	1992-1996	1/90
85	KENDALL-JACKSON VINEYARDS	Anderson Valley Dennison Vineyard	200	14	20	1991-1993	4/90
85	MONTICELLO CELLARS	Napa Valley Corley Reserve	2,200	14	20	1991-1994	2/90
85	MURPHY-GOODE	Alexander Valley	5,000	9	12	1991-1995	4/90
85	NEWTON VINEYARD	Napa Valley	3,100	12.75	19	1991-1996	3/90
85	PINE RIDGE WINERY	Stags Leap District Pine Ridge Stags Leap Vineyard	1,793	18	23	1991-1995	4/90
85	REVERE WINERY	Napa Valley	1,052	15	20	1991-1995	4/90
85	ST. CLEMENT VINEYARDS	Napa Valley	3,700	14.50	16	1991-1995	3/90
85	STAG'S LEAP WINE CELLARS	Napa Valley Reserve	1,214	22	26	1991-1995	3/90
84	BEAULIEU VINEYARD	Carneros Los Carneros Reserve	10,000	12	16	1991-1995	6/90
84	CLOS DU BOIS WINERY	Alexander Valley Barrel Fermented	47,082	9	12	1991-1993	2/90

NR — Not released.

Score	Winery	Appellation / Vineyard	Case Production	Release Price	Current Price	Drink	Last Tasted
84	CONGRESS SPRINGS VINEYARDS	Santa Cruz Mountains Private Reserve	431	$16	$27	1991-1994	4/90
84	FISHER VINEYARDS	Sonoma County Whitney's Vineyard	48	24	30	1991-1994	2/90
84	FISHER VINEYARDS	Sonoma County Coach Insignia	3,000	16	20	1991-1993	2/90
84	FROG'S LEAP WINERY	Napa Valley	1,100	12	16	1991-1995	6/90
84	KENWOOD VINEYARDS	Sonoma Valley Beltane Ranch	2,200	14	18	1991-1995	7/90
84	KENWOOD VINEYARDS	Sonoma Valley Yulupa Vineyard	3,000	12	17	1991-1994	7/90
84	ROMBAUER VINEYARDS	Napa Valley	1,337	14.50	18	1991-1994	6/90
83	CLOS DU BOIS WINERY	Alexander Valley Calcaire Vineyard	4,208	18	28	1991-1994	2/90
83	STAG'S LEAP WINE CELLARS	Napa Valley	7,002	16	18	1991-1994	3/90
82	ACACIA WINERY	Carneros Winery Lake Vineyard	3,700	18	25	1991-1994	1/90
82	MONTICELLO CELLARS	Napa Valley Jefferson Ranch	4,000	11	16	1991-1993	2/90
80	ACACIA WINERY	Carneros Marina Vineyard	5,000	18	19	1991-1993	1/90
80	ACACIA WINERY	Carneros	10,000	15	20	1991-1993	1/90
80	CHALONE VINEYARD	Chalone	3,686	22	45	1991-1994	4/90
80	FREEMARK ABBEY WINERY	Napa Valley	15,787	14	16	1991-1995	2/90
79	ACACIA WINERY	Napa Valley	4,900	12.50	16	1991-1992	1/90
79	DE LOACH VINEYARDS	Russian River Valley O.F.S	1,200	20	22	1991-1995	2/90
78	INGLENOOK-NAPA VALLEY	Napa Valley Reserve	2,500	14.50	15	1991-1994	4/90
70	CLOS DU BOIS WINERY	Dry Creek Valley Flintwood Vineyard	1,535	18	29	1991-1993	5/90

VINTAGE: 1984

Score	Winery	Appellation / Vineyard	Case Production	Release Price	Current Price	Drink	Last Tasted
94	MONTICELLO CELLARS	Napa Valley Corley Reserve	860	12.50	25	1991-1995	2/90
92	SAINTSBURY	Carneros	6,400	11	25	1991-1994	2/90
91	FROG'S LEAP WINERY	Napa Valley	1,100	12	23	1991-1995	3/90
91	NAVARRO VINEYARDS	Anderson Valley Première Reserve	856	12	22	1991-1995	3/90
90	CHATEAU MONTELENA WINERY	Alexander Valley	5,600	16	32	1991-1997	2/90
90	CLOS DU BOIS WINERY	Alexander Valley Calcaire Vineyard	1,590	12	30	1991-1994	2/90
90	CONGRESS SPRINGS VINEYARDS	Santa Clara County	2,053	11	25	1991-1994	4/90
90	DE LOACH VINEYARDS	Russian River Valley O.F.S	600	20	28	1991-1995	2/90
90	FISHER VINEYARDS	Sonoma County Whitney's Vineyard	48	20	30	1991-1995	2/90
90	GRGICH HILLS CELLAR	Napa Valley	24,000	18	33	1991-1995	3/90
90	STONY HILL VINEYARD	Napa Valley	1,820	13	70	1991-1998	5/90
90	ZD WINES	California	7,631	15	30	1991-1995	3/90
89	ACACIA WINERY	Napa Valley	7,000	12.50	16	1991-1996	7/90
89	S. ANDERSON VINEYARD	Stags Leap District Estate	1,770	12.50	25	1991-1994	3/90
89	KISTLER VINEYARDS	Russian River Valley Dutton Ranch	3,911	15	30	1991-1995	2/90
89	MATANZAS CREEK WINERY	Sonoma County	3,717	15	28	1991-1994	2/90
89	SEQUOIA GROVE VINEYARDS	Napa Valley Estate	1,808	14	20	1991-1994	5/90
89	SIMI WINERY	Sonoma County Reserve	1,100	28	32	1991-1996	4/90
89	SONOMA-CUTRER VINEYARDS	Sonoma Valley Les Pierres	7,000	16.50	30	1991-1995	3/90
88	ACACIA WINERY	Carneros Winery Lake Vineyard	2,100	18	25	1991-1994	1/90
88	BERINGER VINEYARDS	Napa Valley Private Reserve	4,102	15	24	1991-1994	4/90
88	CHALONE VINEYARD	Chalone	2,885	18	45	1991-1998	1/90
88	CHATEAU MONTELENA WINERY	Napa Valley	8,400	18	28	1991-1995	2/90
88	CHATEAU ST. JEAN	Alexander Valley Robert Young Vineyards	13,513	20	30	1991-1995	3/90
88	CHATEAU ST. JEAN	Dry Creek Valley Frank Johnson Vineyards	3,100	14	20	1991-1995	7/90
88	DE LOACH VINEYARDS	Russian River Valley	8,000	12.50	24	1991-1994	2/90
88	FLORA SPRINGS WINE CO.	Napa Valley Barrel Fermented	1,800	18	28	1991-1994	1/90
88	HACIENDA WINERY	Sonoma County Clair de Lune	4,285	10	18	1991-1994	4/90
88	WILLIAM HILL WINERY	Napa Valley Reserve	652	20	24	1991-1996	3/90
88	LA CREMA	Monterey County Ventana Vineyard	2,000	18	22	1991-1998	6/90
88	LONG VINEYARDS	Napa Valley	600	27.50	45	1991-1995	4/90

NR — Not released.

Score	Winery	Appellation / Vineyard	Case Production	Release Price	Current Price	Drink	Last Tasted
88	MAYACAMAS VINEYARDS	Napa Valley	1,715	$18	$25	1991-1998	3/90
88	ST. CLEMENT VINEYARDS	Napa Valley	4,000	14.50	17	1991-1996	3/90
87	CHAPPELLET VINEYARD	Napa Valley	4,500	12	20	1991-1995	3/90
87	CHATEAU ST. JEAN	Alexander Valley Robert Young Vineyards Reserve 1.5L	918	40	50	1991-1993	3/90
87	CHATEAU ST. JEAN	Sonoma Valley McCrea Vineyards	1,601	14.25	17	1991-1995	3/90
87	FOLIE A DEUX WINERY	Napa Valley	1,100	14	18	1991-1996	6/90
87	FREEMARK ABBEY WINERY	Napa Valley	15,500	14	17	1991-1994	2/90
87	ROBERT MONDAVI WINERY	Napa Valley Reserve	9,000	22	24	1991-1994	3/90
87	SONOMA-CUTRER VINEYARDS	Russian River Valley Cutrer Vineyard	6,000	14.25	25	1991-1995	3/90
86	ACACIA WINERY	Carneros Marina Vineyard	5,600	16	22	1991-1994	1/90
86	DEHLINGER WINERY	Russian River Valley	2,300	10	14	1991-1996	4/90
86	EDNA VALLEY VINEYARD	Edna Valley	23,800	12.50	24	1991-1995	6/90
86	FAR NIENTE WINERY	Napa Valley	11,000	22	36	1991-1996	2/90
86	FORMAN VINEYARD	Napa Valley	400	15	45	1991-1994	2/90
86	FRANCISCAN VINEYARDS	Napa Valley Reserve	2,000	12	16	1991-1995	4/90
86	INGLENOOK-NAPA VALLEY	Napa Valley Reserve	2,200	12.50	18	1991-1995	4/90
86	MONTICELLO CELLARS	Napa Valley Jefferson Ranch	2,450	10	18	1991-1994	2/90
86	MORGAN WINERY	Monterey County	5,000	12.75	25	1991-1995	5/90
86	NEWTON VINEYARD	Napa Valley	3,900	11.50	18	1991-1998	5/90
86	STERLING VINEYARDS	Napa Valley Diamond Mountain Ranch	3,000	15	17	1991-1995	4/90
86	TREFETHEN VINEYARDS	Napa Valley	20,291	14.25	25	1991-1993	3/90
86	VICHON WINERY	Napa Valley	17,600	15	17	1991-1994	3/90
86	WHITE OAK VINEYARDS & WINERY	Sonoma County	3,000	10	16	1991-1996	5/90
85	BOUCHAINE VINEYARDS	Carneros	3,400	14	20	1991-1993	2/90
85	CHATEAU ST. JEAN	Alexander Valley Belle Terre Vineyards	6,384	16	27	1991-1995	3/90
85	CLOS DU VAL WINE CO.	Napa Valley	12,000	11.50	15	1991-1995	6/90
85	MARKHAM VINEYARDS	Napa Valley	2,955	12	16	1991-1995	2/90
85	MOUNT EDEN VINEYARDS	Santa Cruz Mountains	756	23	45	1991-1995	3/90
85	PINE RIDGE WINERY	Napa Valley Knollside Cuvée	4,285	14	17	1991-1995	4/90
84	ACACIA WINERY	Carneros	7,800	14	20	1991-1993	1/90
84	CLOS DU BOIS WINERY	Alexander Valley Barrel Fermented	34,827	8	12	1991-1994	2/90
84	HANZELL VINEYARDS	Sonoma Valley	980	20	36	1991-1996	1/90
84	PINE RIDGE WINERY	Stags Leap District Pine Ridge Stags Leap Vineyard	1,405	18	25	1991-1994	4/90
83	ROBERT PECOTA WINERY	Alexander Valley Canepa Vineyard	600	14	18	1991-1993	4/90
82	CUVAISON WINERY	Napa Valley	5,000	12	20	1991-1995	4/90
82	FISHER VINEYARDS	Sonoma County Coach Insignia	2,500	15	20	1991-1994	2/90
82	CHARLES F. SHAW VINEYARD	Napa Valley	5,000	12	15	1991-1993	5/90
81	SILVERADO VINEYARDS	Napa Valley	11,000	11	18	1991-1994	3/90
80	CONGRESS SPRINGS VINEYARDS	Santa Cruz Mountains Private Reserve	420	16	27	1991-1992	4/90
80	GIRARD WINERY	Napa Valley Estate	7,123	13.50	22	1991-1993	3/90
80	MATANZAS CREEK WINERY	Sonoma Valley Estate	830	18	28	1991-1993	2/90
80	SMITH-MADRONE VINEYARD	Napa Valley	1,606	12	16	1991-1996	5/90
79	BEAULIEU VINEYARD	Carneros Los Carneros Reserve	10,000	10	16	1991-1992	4/90
79	BURGESS CELLARS	Napa Valley Vintage Reserve	17,000	13	17	1991-1994	12/89
78	ROMBAUER VINEYARDS	Napa Valley	1,337	14.50	20	1991-1994	6/90
78	SANFORD WINERY	Central Coast	4,000	12.50	15	1991-1993	2/90
77	STAG'S LEAP WINE CELLARS	Napa Valley	5,861	14	17	1991-1992	6/90
75	BUENA VISTA WINERY	Carneros Private Reserve	3,000	14.50	16	1991-1992	6/90
74	CLOS DU BOIS WINERY	Dry Creek Valley Flintwood Vineyard	1,231	11.25	30	1991-1992	5/90
71	BOUCHAINE VINEYARDS	Carneros Winery Lake	2,200	22	22	1991	2/90
66	BOUCHAINE VINEYARDS	Napa Valley	9,400	12.50	15	Avoid	2/90

NR — Not released.

Score	Winery	Appellation/Vineyard	Case Production	Release Price	Current Price	Drink	Last Tasted
VINTAGE: 1983							
94	FLORA SPRINGS WINE CO.	Napa Valley Barrel Fermented	1,200	$18	$28	1991-1996	1/90
93	MONTICELLO CELLARS	Napa Valley Jefferson Ranch	1,200	10	20	1991-1995	2/90
92	GRGICH HILLS CELLAR	Napa Valley	15,000	17	33	1991-1995	3/90
91	CLOS DU BOIS WINERY	Alexander Valley Calcaire Vineyard	905	12	30	1991-1996	2/90
90	CHALONE VINEYARD	Chalone	6,669	18	50	1991-1998	1/90
89	CHATEAU ST. JEAN	Alexander Valley Belle Terre Vineyards	1,281	16.75	30	1991-1995	3/90
89	FAR NIENTE WINERY	Napa Valley Estate	2,000	22	38	1991-1995	2/90
89	NEWTON VINEYARD	Napa Valley	2,000	12	19	1991-1998	5/90
88	CHATEAU ST. JEAN	Alexander Valley Robert Young Vineyards	7,697	18	33	1991-1994	3/90
88	ROBERT MONDAVI WINERY	Napa Valley Reserve	7,800	20	25	1991-1995	3/90
88	PINE RIDGE WINERY	Napa Valley Oak Knoll Cuvée	3,685	13	18	1991-1994	4/90
88	SANFORD WINERY	Central Coast	3,000	12	15	1991-1995	2/90
88	SIMI WINERY	Sonoma County Reserve	1,000	22	32	1991-1995	4/90
87	ACACIA WINERY	Carneros Winery Lake Vineyard	2,460	18	25	1991-1994	1/90
87	S. ANDERSON VINEYARD	Stags Leap District Proprietor's Selection	100	16	40	1991-1993	3/90
87	CHALONE VINEYARD	Chalone Reserve	617	25	45	1991-1997	5/90
87	CHATEAU ST. JEAN	Alexander Valley Jimtown Ranch	1,166	16	20	1991-1996	7/90
87	FAR NIENTE WINERY	Napa Valley	8,000	22	38	1991-1995	2/90
87	ROMBAUER VINEYARDS	Napa Valley	1,010	14.50	25	1991-1995	7/90
87	SEQUOIA GROVE VINEYARDS	Napa Valley Estate	1,639	12	20	1991-1996	5/90
86	S. ANDERSON VINEYARD	Stags Leap District Estate	1,415	12.50	25	1991-1993	3/90
86	MAYACAMAS VINEYARDS	Napa Valley	1,775	16	25	1991-1996	1/90
86	PINE RIDGE WINERY	Stags Leap District Pine Ridge Stags Leap Vineyard	1,199	16	25	1991-1994	4/90
86	SONOMA-CUTRER VINEYARDS	Sonoma Valley Les Pierres	7,000	15.50	30	1991-1994	3/90
86	SONOMA-CUTRER VINEYARDS	Russian River Valley Cutrer Vineyard	3,000	13.75	25	1991-1994	3/90
86	STERLING VINEYARDS	Napa Valley Diamond Mountain Ranch	1,400	15	18	1991-1994	4/90
85	CHATEAU MONTELENA WINERY	Napa Valley	6,600	16	32	1991-1994	2/90
85	CHATEAU ST. JEAN	Sonoma Valley McCrea Vineyards	1,009	15.25	18	1991-1995	7/90
85	CONGRESS SPRINGS VINEYARDS	Santa Clara County Barrel Fermented	1,102	10	25	1991-1994	4/90
85	DEHLINGER WINERY	Russian River Valley	1,400	10	15	1991-1995	4/90
85	FREEMARK ABBEY WINERY	Napa Valley	13,000	14	18	1991-1995	2/90
85	WILLIAM HILL WINERY	Napa Valley Reserve	1,428	22	28	1991-1994	3/90
85	KENWOOD VINEYARDS	Sonoma Valley Yulupa Vineyard	1,000	11	18	1991-1994	7/90
85	MATANZAS CREEK WINERY	Sonoma County	1,788	15	28	1991-1993	2/90
85	SONOMA-CUTRER VINEYARDS	Russian River Valley Russian River Ranches	9,900	10.50	22	1991-1994	3/90
85	STONY HILL VINEYARD	Napa Valley	1934	13	70	1991-1996	5/90
84	BUENA VISTA WINERY	Carneros Private Reserve	1,000	14.50	18	1991-1994	3/90
84	CHATEAU MONTELENA WINERY	Alexander Valley	5,600	14	32	1991-1994	2/90
84	HANZELL VINEYARDS	Sonoma Valley	930	20	45	1991-1996	1/90
84	MOUNT EDEN VINEYARDS	Santa Cruz Mountains	455	20	35	1991-1994	3/90
84	CHARLES F. SHAW VINEYARD	Napa Valley	5,000	12	16	1991-1993	5/90
84	SILVERADO VINEYARDS	Napa Valley	5,000	11	20	1991-1993	3/90
83	DE LOACH VINEYARDS	Russian River Valley	8,000	12	22	1991-1993	2/90
83	HACIENDA WINERY	Sonoma County Clair de Lune	4,200	10	22	1991-1993	4/90
82	CLOS DU VAL WINE CO.	Napa Valley	10,000	11.50	15	1991-1996	6/90
82	FISHER VINEYARDS	Sonoma and Napa Counties	3,000	14	18	1991-1994	6/90
82	FRANCISCAN VINEYARDS	Napa Valley Reserve	1,500	12	14	1991-1996	4/90
82	INGLENOOK-NAPA VALLEY	Napa Valley Reserve	1,500	16	19	1991-1994	4/90
81	MARKHAM VINEYARDS	Napa Valley Estate	860	11.50	16	1991-1992	2/90
80	ACACIA WINERY	Napa Valley	4,300	12	18	1991-1993	1/90

NR — Not released.

Score	Winery	Appellation / Vineyard	Case Production	Release Price	Current Price	Drink	Last Tasted
80	MONTICELLO CELLARS	Napa Valley Barrel Fermented	720	$12.50	$20	1991-1993	2/90
80	MORGAN WINERY	Monterey County	3,000	12.50	25	1991-1993	5/90
80	SAINTSBURY	Carneros	6,550	11	20	1991-1994	2/90
79	ACACIA WINERY	Carneros Marina Vineyard	5,300	16	23	1991-1993	1/90
79	CHAPPELLET VINEYARD	Napa Valley	6,000	12	18	1991	3/90
79	ROBERT PECOTA WINERY	Alexander Valley Canepa Vineyard	600	14	18	1990-1991	4/90
78	FISHER VINEYARDS	Sonoma County Whitney's Vineyard	24	20	30	1991-1993	2/90
77	BOUCHAINE VINEYARDS	Carneros	2,200	14	20	1991-1993	2/90
77	TREFETHEN VINEYARDS	Napa Valley	18,942	13.75	27	1991	3/90
76	BERINGER VINEYARDS	Napa Valley Private Reserve	7,445	15	24	1991-1993	4/90
76	EDNA VALLEY VINEYARD	Edna Valley	15,500	12.50	20	1991-1993	3/90
76	GIRARD WINERY	Napa Valley Estate	5,741	12.50	22	1991	3/90
76	ST. CLEMENT VINEYARDS	Napa Valley	4,500	14.50	17	1991	3/90
75	BOUCHAINE VINEYARDS	Napa Valley	10,000	12.50	18	1991-1992	2/90
74	BEAULIEU VINEYARD	Carneros Los Carneros Reserve	5,000	10	15	1991-1992	4/90
74	CONGRESS SPRINGS VINEYARDS	Santa Cruz Mountains Private Reserve	328	15	28	1991-1992	4/90
74	ZD WINES	California	5,369	14	25	1991-1994	3/90
71	SMITH-MADRONE VINEYARD	Napa Valley	1,473	12	15	1991-1994	5/90
71	VICHON WINERY	Napa Valley	14,900	15	18	1991	3/90
69	BURGESS CELLARS	Napa Valley Vintage Reserve	16,000	12	14	1991	12/89
69	CLOS DU BOIS WINERY	Dry Creek Valley Flintwood Vineyard	634	10.50	30	Avoid	5/90
68	MATANZAS CREEK WINERY	Sonoma Valley Estate	516	18	18	Avoid	2/90
62	CUVAISON WINERY	Napa Valley	21,000	12	17	Avoid	4/90
62	STAG'S LEAP WINE CELLARS	Napa Valley	4,582	13.50	17	Avoid	3/90

VINTAGE: 1982

Score	Winery	Appellation / Vineyard	Case Production	Release Price	Current Price	Drink	Last Tasted
95	CHALONE VINEYARD	Chalone	5,125	18	53	1991-1996	1/90
94	SIMI WINERY	Sonoma County Reserve	1,000	22	40	1991-1995	4/90
93	CHALONE VINEYARD	Chalone Reserve	498	25	48	1991-1996	5/90
92	CHATEAU MONTELENA WINERY	Alexander Valley	5,800	14	36	1991-1996	2/90
91	FAR NIENTE WINERY	Napa Valley Estate	2,000	18	38	1991-1996	2/90
89	HANZELL VINEYARDS	Sonoma Valley	940	19	45	1991-1996	1/90
89	MORGAN WINERY	Monterey County	2,000	12	28	1991-1995	5/90
88	CHATEAU ST. JEAN	Sonoma Valley McCrea Vineyards	501	13	18	1991-1995	7/90
88	MATANZAS CREEK WINERY	Sonoma Valley Estate	700	18	25	1991-1994	2/90
88	SONOMA-CUTRER VINEYARDS	Sonoma Valley Les Pierres	2,500	15	35	1991-1994	3/90
87	CONGRESS SPRINGS VINEYARDS	Santa Cruz Mountains Private Reserve	310	15	28	1991-1994	4/90
87	GRGICH HILLS CELLAR	Napa Valley	15,000	17	36	1991-1994	3/90
87	SONOMA-CUTRER VINEYARDS	Russian River Valley Cutrer Vineyard	5,000	13	25	1991-1994	3/90
87	SONOMA-CUTRER VINEYARDS	Russian River Valley Russian River Ranches	5,200	10	24	1991-1994	3/90
86	CHATEAU ST. JEAN	Alexander Valley Belle Terre Vineyards	4,735	15.50	20	1991-1995	3/90
86	FAR NIENTE WINERY	Napa Valley	7,000	18	38	1991-1996	2/90
86	WILLIAM HILL WINERY	Napa Valley Reserve	1,427	24	28	1991-1995	3/90
86	SMITH-MADRONE VINEYARD	Napa Valley	1,004	12	18	1990-1998	5/90
85	CHAPPELLET VINEYARD	Napa Valley	7,200	12.50	20	1991-1993	3/90
85	CHATEAU MONTELENA WINERY	Napa Valley	6,900	16	32	1991-1994	2/90
85	MAYACAMAS VINEYARDS	Napa Valley	2,215	16	30	1991-1997	1/90
85	STONY HILL VINEYARD	Napa Valley	2,747	12	63	1991-1994	5/90
84	FRANCISCAN VINEYARDS	Carneros Reserve	2,000	12	20	1991-1994	4/90
84	MONTICELLO CELLARS	Napa Valley Barrel Fermented	800	14	20	1991-1992	2/90
84	ROMBAUER VINEYARDS	Napa Valley	382	14.50	25	1991-1994	6/90

NR — Not released.

Score	Winery	Appellation/Vineyard	Production	Release Price	Current Price	Drink	Last Tasted
83	MARKHAM VINEYARDS	Napa Valley Estate	531	$12	$17	1991-1993	2/90
82	MONTICELLO CELLARS	Napa Valley	4,000	13.50	20	1991-1993	2/90
82	PINE RIDGE WINERY	Stags Leap District Stags Leap Vineyard	780	15	27	1991-1994	4/90
81	FISHER VINEYARDS	Sonoma County	2,200	14	22	1991-1993	2/90
81	ROBERT MONDAVI WINERY	Napa Valley Reserve	6,000	20	25	1991	3/90
80	ACACIA WINERY	Napa Valley	4,900	12	20	1991-1993	1/90
79	BOUCHAINE VINEYARDS	Alexander Valley	2,000	14	18	1991-1993	2/90
79	CONGRESS SPRINGS VINEYARDS	Santa Clara County	957	10	20	1991-1992	4/90
78	CLOS DU VAL WINE CO.	California	4,700	11.50	16	1992-1996	6/90
78	FISHER VINEYARDS	Sonoma County Whitney's Vineyard	24	20	25	1991-1993	6/90
78	FOLIE A DEUX WINERY	Napa Valley	50	12.50	17	1991-1992	7/90
78	HACIENDA WINERY	Sonoma County Clair de Lune	7,200	9	20	1991-1993	4/90
78	MATANZAS CREEK WINERY	Sonoma County	1,735	15	25	1991	2/90
78	PINE RIDGE WINERY	Napa Valley Oak Knoll Cuvée	2,026	13	19	1991-1993	4/90
76	GIRARD WINERY	Napa Valley Estate	4,228	12.50	21	1991	3/90
76	MOUNT EDEN VINEYARDS	Santa Cruz Mountains	500	18	40	1991-1994	3/90
76	ZD WINES	California	5,506	14	30	1991-1993	3/90
75	CHATEAU ST. JEAN	Alexander Valley Robert Young Vineyards	8,645	18	20	1991-1993	3/90
74	BERINGER VINEYARDS	Napa Valley Private Reserve	7,077	15	22	1991-1993	4/90
74	DE LOACH VINEYARDS	Russian River Valley	3,900	12	20	1991	2/90
73	SILVERADO VINEYARDS	Napa Valley	4,500	10	20	1991	3/90
73	ST. CLEMENT VINEYARDS	Napa Valley	4,600	14.50	20	1991	3/90
73	STERLING VINEYARDS	Napa Valley Estate	10,000	14	17	1991	4/90
73	TREFETHEN VINEYARDS	Napa Valley	15,318	13.50	28	1991	3/90
72	S. ANDERSON VINEYARD	Stags Leap District Estate	1,412	12.50	21	1991	3/90
72	BEAULIEU VINEYARD	Carneros Los Carneros Reserve	5,000	10	16	1991-1992	4/90
72	FREEMARK ABBEY WINERY	Napa Valley	13,085	12.75	18	1991-1993	2/90
72	SEQUOIA GROVE VINEYARDS	Napa Valley Estate	880	12	20	1991	5/90
70	EDNA VALLEY VINEYARD	Edna Valley	17,400	12	20	1991	3/90
70	FLORA SPRINGS WINE CO.	Napa Valley Barrel Fermented	700	15	15	1991-1992	6/88
70	STAG'S LEAP WINE CELLARS	Napa Valley	3,874	13.50	17	1991	3/90
70	STAG'S LEAP WINE CELLARS	Napa Valley Mirage	3,564	11.50	18	1991	3/90
68	BURGESS CELLARS	Napa Valley Vintage Reserve	16,000	12	12	Avoid	12/89
68	SANFORD WINERY	Santa Maria Valley	2,500	12	20	Avoid	2/90
66	VICHON WINERY	Napa Valley	9,500	15	20	Avoid	3/90
65	SAINTSBURY	Sonoma County	3,750	11	14	Avoid	2/90
61	CUVAISON WINERY	Napa Valley	14,000	12	17	Avoid	4/90

VINTAGE: 1981

Score	Winery	Appellation/Vineyard	Production	Release Price	Current Price	Drink	Last Tasted
94	EDNA VALLEY VINEYARD	Edna Valley	11,000	12	25	1991-1995	3/90
94	SONOMA-CUTRER VINEYARDS	Sonoma Valley Les Pierres	850	14.50	40	1991-1997	3/90
93	CHALONE VINEYARD	Chalone	3,545	17	53	1991-1996	4/90
91	CHATEAU MONTELENA WINERY	Alexander Valley	2,600	14	36	1991-1997	2/90
91	SIMI WINERY	Sonoma County Reserve	1,600	20	40	1991-1996	4/90
91	SONOMA-CUTRER VINEYARDS	Russian River Valley Cutrer Vineyard	2,500	12.50	30	1991-1995	3/90
90	GIRARD WINERY	Napa Valley Estate	4,736	12.50	35	1991-1995	3/90
89	FLORA SPRINGS WINE CO.	Napa Valley Special Selection	1,500	12	25	1991-1995	1/90
89	MOUNT EDEN VINEYARDS	Santa Cruz Mountains	445	18	60	1991-1995	3/90
88	CHATEAU MONTELENA WINERY	Napa Valley	7,900	16	32	1991-1994	2/90
88	FAR NIENTE WINERY	Napa Valley	7,000	16.50	40	1991-1996	2/90
88	FISHER VINEYARDS	Sonoma County	2,000	14	25	1990-1993	2/90
88	GRGICH HILLS CELLAR	Napa Valley	16,000	17	45	1991-1995	3/90
88	SEQUOIA GROVE VINEYARDS	Napa Valley Estate	952	12	20	1991-1995	7/90
87	CHATEAU ST. JEAN	Alexander Valley Jimtown Ranch	1,720	14.75	22	1991-1995	3/90

NR — Not released

Score	Winery	Appellation/Vineyard	Production	Release Price	Current Price	Drink	Last Tasted
87	SAINTSBURY	Sonoma County	950	$10	$25	1991-1994	2/90
87	ZD WINES	California	5,742	13	28	1991-1994	3/90
86	BERINGER VINEYARDS	Napa Valley Private Reserve	4,784	15	28	1991-1993	4/90
86	CHALONE VINEYARD	Chalone Reserve	400	20	55	1991-1996	5/90
86	CHATEAU ST. JEAN	Alexander Valley Robert Young Vineyards	8,586	18	25	1991-1993	3/90
86	HANZELL VINEYARDS	Sonoma Valley	650	18	50	1991-1997	1/90
86	ROBERT MONDAVI WINERY	Napa Valley Reserve	6,800	20	24	1991-1993	3/90
86	PINE RIDGE WINERY	Stags Leap District Stags Leap Vineyard	1,114	15	31	1991-1994	4/90
86	STONY HILL VINEYARD	Napa Valley	2,137	12	68	1991-1996	5/90
85	FISHER VINEYARDS	Sonoma County Whitney's Vineyard	24	20	25	1991-1994	2/90
85	MATANZAS CREEK WINERY	Sonoma County	1925	15	28	1991-1993	2/90
84	PINE RIDGE WINERY	Napa Valley Oak Knoll Cuvée	1,168	13	20	1991-1994	4/90
83	CHATEAU ST. JEAN	Alexander Valley Belle Terre Vineyards	3,847	15	18	1991-1995	3/90
83	TREFETHEN VINEYARDS	Napa Valley	12,933	13	28	1991-1992	3/90
82	SONOMA-CUTRER VINEYARDS	Russian River Valley Russian River Ranches	1,250	9.35	30	1991-1994	3/90
81	CHATEAU ST. JEAN	Sonoma Valley Hunter Ranch	1,221	14.75	19	1991-1993	3/90
81	FREEMARK ABBEY WINERY	Napa Valley	13,183	13.50	20	1991-1994	2/90
81	SMITH-MADRONE VINEYARD	Napa Valley	650	12	18	1990-1993	5/90
80	S. ANDERSON VINEYARD	Stags Leap District Estate	1,835	12.50	25	1991-1993	3/90
80	CHAPPELLET VINEYARD	Napa Valley	3,947	14	22	1991	3/90
79	STAG'S LEAP WINE CELLARS	Napa Valley	4,760	13.50	17	1991-1993	3/90
78	CLOS DU VAL WINE CO.	Napa Valley	2,700	12.50	18	1991-1994	6/90
78	MAYACAMAS VINEYARDS	Napa Valley	1955	16	35	1991-1994	1/90
76	MONTICELLO CELLARS	Napa Valley	2,700	12	20	1991	2/90
76	VICHON WINERY	Napa Valley	7,000	15	25	1991-1993	3/90
75	CHATEAU ST. JEAN	Sonoma Valley McCrea Vineyards	846	15	18	1991-1992	3/90
75	CUVAISON WINERY	Napa Valley	10,000	12	18	1991-1995	4/90
75	ROBERT PECOTA WINERY	Alexander Valley Canepa Vineyard	425	12	20	1990-1991	4/90
75	ST. CLEMENT VINEYARDS	Napa Valley	3,000	13.50	25	1991	3/90
74	BURGESS CELLARS	Napa Valley	15,000	11	16	1991-1992	12/89
74	HACIENDA WINERY	Sonoma County Clair de Lune	4,600	12	20	1991-1992	4/90
74	SANFORD WINERY	Santa Maria Valley	1,000	11	20	1991	2/90
72	DE LOACH VINEYARDS	Russian River Valley	2,800	10	18	1991	2/90
71	STERLING VINEYARDS	Napa Valley Estate	4,000	14	17	1991	4/90
70	BEAULIEU VINEYARD	Carneros Los Carneros Reserve	5,000	10	18	1991-1992	4/90
70	CLOS DU BOIS WINERY	Alexander Valley Proprietor's Reserve	1,341	15	22	1991-1992	5/90
70	RAYMOND VINEYARD & CELLAR	Napa Valley Private Reserve	500	15	25	1991	6/90
70	SILVERADO VINEYARDS	Napa Valley	1,800	10	20	1991	3/90

VINTAGE: 1980

Score	Winery	Appellation/Vineyard	Production	Release Price	Current Price	Drink	Last Tasted
94	CHALONE VINEYARD	Chalone Reserve	166	18	55	1991-1997	5/90
94	SIMI WINERY	Mendocino County Reserve	1,100	20	40	1991-1997	4/90
93	FAR NIENTE WINERY	Napa Valley	6,500	16.50	45	1991-1997	2/90
92	CHALONE VINEYARD	Chalone	3,510	17	53	1991-1995	1/90
92	FISHER VINEYARDS	Sonoma County Whitney's Vineyard	24	20	30	1991-1996	2/90
90	HANZELL VINEYARDS	Sonoma Valley	740	17	60	1991-1998	1/90
89	ROBERT PECOTA WINERY	Alexander Valley Canepa Vineyard	325	12	20	1990-1994	4/90
88	CHATEAU ST. JEAN	Alexander Valley Belle Terre Vineyards	4,427	15	24	1991-1994	3/90
88	FLORA SPRINGS WINE CO.	Napa Valley Special Selection	300	12	25	1991-1993	1/90
88	GRGICH HILLS CELLAR	Napa Valley	15,000	17	50	1991-1994	3/90
87	CLOS DU BOIS WINERY	Dry Creek Valley Flintwood Vineyard	977	17	32	1991-1994	2/90
87	CUVAISON WINERY	Napa Valley	10,000	11	26	1991-1995	4/90

NR — Not released.

Score	Winery	Appellation/Vineyard	Production	Release Price	Current Price	Drink	Last Tasted
87	EDNA VALLEY VINEYARD	Edna Valley	5,200	$12	$25	1991-1994	3/90
87	MOUNT EDEN VINEYARDS	Santa Cruz Mountains	245	30	50	1991-1995	3/90
87	SEQUOIA GROVE VINEYARDS	Napa Valley Estate	1,500	10	18	1991-1994	5/90
87	VICHON WINERY	Napa Valley	3,800	15	25	1991-1995	3/90
86	MONTICELLO CELLARS	Napa Valley	1,250	12	20	1991-1993	2/90
86	STONY HILL VINEYARD	Napa Valley	2,220	12	72	1991-1998	5/90
86	TREFETHEN VINEYARDS	Napa Valley	9,369	13	30	1991-1993	3/90
85	CHATEAU ST. JEAN	Alexander Valley Robert Young Vineyards	6,832	18	30	1991-1993	3/90
85	FISHER VINEYARDS	Sonoma County	1,200	14	22	1990-1993	2/90
85	GIRARD WINERY	Napa Valley Estate	2,100	11	25	1991-1994	3/90
85	SMITH-MADRONE VINEYARD	Napa Valley	450	11	20	1990-1995	5/90
84	CHAPPELLET VINEYARD	Napa Valley	4,000	14	25	1991-1992	3/90
84	FREEMARK ABBEY WINERY	Napa Valley	10,771	13.50	24	1991-1993	2/90
83	S. ANDERSON VINEYARD	Stags Leap District Estate	1,545	12.50	30	1991-1993	3/90
83	ST. CLEMENT VINEYARDS	Napa Valley	3,200	12	25	1991-1992	3/90
82	MATANZAS CREEK WINERY	Sonoma County	1,700	15	25	1991-1992	2/90
81	ZD WINES	California	4,005	13	28	1991-1994	3/90
80	CLOS DU VAL WINE CO.	Napa Valley	24,000	12.50	18	1991-1994	6/90
80	HACIENDA WINERY	Sonoma County Clair de Lune	3,400	10.50	22	1991-1993	4/90
79	CHATEAU MONTELENA WINERY	Napa Valley	7,000	16	38	1991	2/90
79	CHATEAU ST. JEAN	Dry Creek Valley Frank Johnson Vineyards	1,257	14	16	1991-1992	3/90
78	STAG'S LEAP WINE CELLARS	Napa Valley	2,194	10.50	17	1991-1992	3/90
77	CHATEAU ST. JEAN	Alexander Valley Jimtown Ranch	864	14	16	1991	3/90
75	BERINGER VINEYARDS	Napa Valley Private Reserve	4,576	15	25	1991-1992	4/90
75	BURGESS CELLARS	Napa Valley	5,500	11	18	1991-1992	12/89
74	CHATEAU ST. JEAN	Alexander Valley Gauer Ranch	2,614	14	18	1991	3/90
74	MAYACAMAS VINEYARDS	Napa Valley	1,480	16	35	1991	1/90
71	CHATEAU ST. JEAN	Sonoma Valley Wildwood Vineyards	1,853	13	19	1991-1992	7/90
70	CHATEAU ST. JEAN	Sonoma Valley McCrea Vineyards	465	15	18	1991-1992	3/90
70	WILLIAM HILL WINERY	Napa Valley Gold Label	775	16	30	1991	3/90
70	MATANZAS CREEK WINERY	Sonoma County Estate	85	18	18	1991	2/90
70	STERLING VINEYARDS	Napa Valley Estate	4,000	13	17	1991	4/90
69	ROBERT MONDAVI WINERY	Napa Valley Reserve	3,500	20	30	Avoid	3/90
67	CHATEAU ST. JEAN	Sonoma Valley Hunter Ranch	1,355	14	17	Avoid	3/90
62	DE LOACH VINEYARDS	Russian River Valley	2,000	10	18	Aviod	2/90

VINTAGE: 1979

Score	Winery	Appellation/Vineyard	Production	Release Price	Current Price	Drink	Last Tasted
95	GRGICH HILLS CELLAR	Napa Valley	10,000	16	55	1991-1994	3/90
93	ST. CLEMENT VINEYARDS	Napa Valley	3,000	12	27	1991-1996	3/90
92	FAR NIENTE WINERY	Napa Valley	3,700	15	45	1991-1996	2/90
92	SMITH-MADRONE VINEYARD	Napa Valley	580	10	28	1990-2000	5/90
91	FLORA SPRINGS WINE CO.	Napa Valley	200	9	25	1991-1994	1/90
90	MOUNT EDEN VINEYARDS	Santa Cruz Mountains	495	16	60	1991-1996	3/90
89	CHALONE VINEYARD	Chalone	3,728	14	55	1991-1994	1/90
86	HACIENDA WINERY	Sonoma County Clair de Lune	2,900	9	25	1991-1993	4/90
85	CHATEAU ST. JEAN	Alexander Valley Robert Young Vineyards	5,344	17	30	1991-1994	3/90
85	HANZELL VINEYARDS	Sonoma Valley	460	16	70	1991-1995	1/90
84	CHATEAU ST. JEAN	Alexander Valley Belle Terre Vineyards	3,668	12	22	1991-1993	3/90
84	CUVAISON WINERY	Napa Valley	10,000	10	26	1991-1995	4/90
82	PINE RIDGE WINERY	Stags Leap District Stags Leap Vineyard	588	9.50	32	1991-1992	4/90
82	STAG'S LEAP WINE CELLARS	Napa Valley Haynes	2,000	12.50	20	1991-1992	3/90
81	STONY HILL VINEYARD	Napa Valley	2,250	12	95	1991-1994	5/90
80	CHATEAU ST. JEAN	Sonoma Valley Hunter Farms	1,010	14	20	1991	3/90
80	MATANZAS CREEK WINERY	Sonoma and Napa Counties	1,650	14.50	40	1991	2/90

NR — Not released.

Score	Winery	Appellation / Vineyard	Production	Release Price	Current Price	Drink	Last Tasted
79	CHAPPELLET VINEYARD	Napa Valley	3,000	$12	$30	1991	3/90
79	ROBERT MONDAVI WINERY	Napa Valley Reserve	8,700	20	27	1991	3/90
78	BERINGER VINEYARDS	Napa Valley Private Reserve	3,228	14	25	1991-1992	4/90
78	BURGESS CELLARS	Napa Valley	5,500	11	18	1991-1994	12/89
78	CHATEAU MONTELENA WINERY	Napa Valley	7,800	16	38	1991	2/90
78	CHATEAU ST. JEAN	Dry Creek Valley Frank Johnson Vineyards	349	13.50	15	1991	3/90
76	ACACIA WINERY	Carneros Winery Lake Vineyard	1,400	16	25	1991	1/90
76	FREEMARK ABBEY WINERY	Napa Valley	10,935	13.25	25	1991	2/90
73	STERLING VINEYARDS	Napa Valley Estate	2,800	13	17	1991	4/90
73	TREFETHEN VINEYARDS	Napa Valley	9,486	12	30	1991	3/90
70	BEAULIEU VINEYARD	Napa Valley Beaufort	30,000	6	20	1991-1992	4/90
70	CHATEAU ST. JEAN	Sonoma Valley McCrea Vineyards	325	14	18	1991	3/90
70	CHATEAU ST. JEAN	Alexander Valley Gauer Ranch	2,725	14	18	1991	3/90
70	MAYACAMAS VINEYARDS	Napa Valley	1,220	15	35	1991	1/90

VINTAGE: 1978

Score	Winery	Appellation / Vineyard	Production	Release Price	Current Price	Drink	Last Tasted
95	HANZELL VINEYARDS	Sonoma Valley	310	13	80	1991-1998	1/90
92	GRGICH HILLS CELLAR	Napa Valley	6,000	13.75	60	1991-1996	3/90
90	TREFETHEN VINEYARDS	Napa Valley	6,352	10	40	1991-1994	3/90
86	SMITH-MADRONE VINEYARD	Napa Valley	375	10	30	1990-1997	5/90
85	STONY HILL VINEYARD	Napa Valley	1,750	10	90	1991-1996	5/90
84	CHATEAU ST. JEAN	Alexander Valley Robert Young Vineyards	1,099	17	25	1991-1993	3/90
81	CHATEAU ST. JEAN	Sonoma Valley Les Pierres Vineyards	729	13.75	22	1991	3/90
81	CUVAISON WINERY	Napa Valley	10,000	10	28	1991-1995	4/90
79	MATANZAS CREEK WINERY	Sonoma County	1,230	12.50	40	1991	2/90
77	BURGESS CELLARS	Napa Valley	4,200	11	18	1991-1994	12/89
77	CHATEAU MONTELENA WINERY	Napa Valley	7,100	15	45	1991	2/90
76	CHAPPELLET VINEYARD	Napa Valley	1,500	11.75	40	1991	3/90
75	MAYACAMAS VINEYARDS	Napa Valley	1,233	13	30	1991	1/90
74	STAG'S LEAP WINE CELLARS	Napa Valley Haynes	1,815	10	20	1991	3/90
73	CHATEAU ST. JEAN	Alexander Valley Belle Terre Vineyards	2,194	14	20	1991	3/90
73	HACIENDA WINERY	Sonoma County Clair de Lune	3,000	9	25	1991	4/90
70	BEAULIEU VINEYARD	Napa Valley Beaufort	30,000	6	22	1991	4/90
70	BERINGER VINEYARDS	Napa Valley Private Reserve	1,878	12	15	1991	4/90
70	CHATEAU ST. JEAN	Sonoma Valley McCrea Vineyards	309	12	20	1991	3/90
70	FREEMARK ABBEY WINERY	Napa Valley	9,894	10	26	1991	2/90
69	ROBERT MONDAVI WINERY	Napa Valley Reserve	5,100	20	24	Avoid	3/90
66	MOUNT EDEN VINEYARDS	Santa Cruz Mountains	400	16	50	Avoid	3/90
65	CHATEAU ST. JEAN	Sonoma Valley Wildwood Vineyards	480	12	19	Avoid	3/90
65	CHATEAU ST. JEAN	Sonoma Valley Hunter Farms	528	11.25	18	Avoid	3/90

VINTAGE: 1977

Score	Winery	Appellation / Vineyard	Production	Release Price	Current Price	Drink	Last Tasted
91	STONY HILL VINEYARD	Napa Valley	1,032	9	95	1991-1999	6/90
90	CHAPPELLET VINEYARD	Napa Valley	1,500	11.75	40	1991-1998	6/90
89	GRGICH HILLS CELLAR	Sonoma County	6,000	11	65	1991-1993	3/90
88	HANZELL VINEYARDS	Sonoma Valley	260	12	85	1991-1994	1/90
85	CHATEAU MONTELENA WINERY	Napa Valley	6,000	15	60	1991-1993	2/90
85	CHATEAU ST. JEAN	Sonoma Valley McCrea Vineyards	346	10.25	25	1991	3/90
85	MOUNT EDEN VINEYARDS	Santa Cruz Mountains	150	16	50	1991-1995	8/90
81	CHATEAU ST. JEAN	Sonoma Valley Hunter Farms	482	10.25	25	1991-1992	3/90
81	TREFETHEN VINEYARDS	Napa Valley	3,966	8.50	40	1991	3/90
80	BURGESS CELLARS	Napa Valley	4,000	11	23	1991-1992	12/89
80	CHATEAU ST. JEAN	Alexander Valley Belle Terre Vineyards	799	12	22	1991	3/90

NR — Not released.

Score	Winery	Appellation / Vineyard	Production	Release Price	Current Price	Drink	Last Tasted
79	CHATEAU ST. JEAN	Sonoma Valley Les Pierres Vineyards	308	$13.75	$21	1991	3/90
76	HACIENDA WINERY	Sonoma County Clair de Lune	1,000	8	23	1991-1993	4/90
73	CHATEAU ST. JEAN	Sonoma Valley Wildwood Vineyards	492	15	22	1991	3/90
70	MAYACAMAS VINEYARDS	Napa Valley	1,520	12	35	1991	1/90
70	STERLING VINEYARDS	Napa Valley Estate	4,000	10	20	1991	4/90
68	CHATEAU ST. JEAN	Alexander Valley Robert Young Vineyards	1,597	17	22	Avoid	3/90
68	ROBERT MONDAVI WINERY	Napa Valley Reserve	2,600	14	32	1991	3/90
67	STAG'S LEAP WINE CELLARS	Napa Valley Haynes	1,752	9	20	Avoid	3/90
64	BEAULIEU VINEYARD	Napa Valley Beaufort	25,000	6	22	Avoid	4/90
59	STAG'S LEAP WINE CELLARS	Napa Valley	2,452	8	17	Avoid	3/90
58	FREEMARK ABBEY WINERY	Napa Valley	10,901	10	36	Avoid	2/90

VINTAGE: 1976

Score	Winery	Appellation / Vineyard	Production	Release Price	Current Price	Drink	Last Tasted
92	CHATEAU ST. JEAN	Alexander Valley Robert Young Vineyards	1,400	8.75	25	1991-1994	7/90
91	HANZELL VINEYARDS	Sonoma Valley	210	12	90	1991-1995	1/90
88	CHATEAU ST. JEAN	Alexander Valley Riverview Vineyards	600	9.50	22	1991-1994	7/90
88	STONY HILL VINEYARD	Napa Valley	670	9	120	1991-1997	6/90
85	HILLS CELLARS	Napa Valley	2,500	8	50	1991-1995	3/90
85	HACIENDA WINERY	Sonoma County Clair de Lune	750	7	40	1991-1994	4/90
82	CHATEAU ST. JEAN	Sonoma Valley Wildwood Vineyards	402	10	20	1991-1993	7/90
81	MAYACAMAS VINEYARDS	Napa Valley	1,255	11	45	1991-1994	1/90
78	ROBERT MONDAVI WINERY	Napa Valley Reserve	1,450	12	32	1991	3/90
78	MOUNT EDEN VINEYARDS	Santa Cruz Mountains	200	16	50	1991	3/90
77	CHATEAU MONTELENA WINERY	Napa and Alexander Valleys	2,500	11	50	1991	2/90
77	CHATEAU ST. JEAN	Alexander Valley Belle Terre Vineyards	1,100	7.50	22	1991-1992	7/90
75	CHATEAU ST. JEAN	Sonoma Valley McCrea Vineyards	300	9.25	20	1991-1992	7/90
74	TREFETHEN VINEYARDS	Napa Valley	3,358	7	40	1991	3/90
71	CHAPPELLET VINEYARD	Napa Valley	1,000	9.75	30	1991	3/90
70	BURGESS CELLARS	Carneros Winery Lake Vineyard	1,300	10	20	1991	12/89
69	CHATEAU ST. JEAN	Sonoma County Beltane Ranch	375	7.75	18	Avoid	7/90
62	BEAULIEU VINEYARD	Napa Valley Beaufort	20,000	6	22	Avoid	4/90
62	FREEMARK ABBEY WINERY	Napa Valley	4,802	9.75	26	Avoid	2/90
59	STERLING VINEYARDS	Napa Valley Estate	2,600	5.25	18	Avoid	4/90
58	STAG'S LEAP WINE CELLARS	Napa Valley	335	8	17	Avoid	3/90

VINTAGE: 1975

Score	Winery	Appellation / Vineyard	Production	Release Price	Current Price	Drink	Last Tasted
88	CHATEAU ST. JEAN	Alexander Valley Belle Terre Vineyards	800	7.50	22	1991-1993	7/90
88	CHATEAU ST. JEAN	Sonoma County Beltane Ranch	500	12.50	21	1991-1994	7/90
87	CHATEAU MONTELENA WINERY	Napa Valley	3,300	9	65	1991-1993	2/90
86	CHATEAU ST. JEAN	Sonoma County Bacigalupi	800	10	21	1991-1995	7/90
86	HANZELL VINEYARDS	Sonoma Valley	310	10	70	1991-1994	1/90
84	BURGESS CELLARS	Carneros Winery Lake Vineyard	770	9	28	1991-1994	12/89
82	CHAPPELLET VINEYARD	Napa Valley	800	6.75	40	1991	3/90
82	FREEMARK ABBEY WINERY	Napa Valley	7,100	9	45	1991	2/90
78	CHATEAU ST. JEAN	Sonoma Valley McCrea Vineyards	250	8.75	20	1991-1993	7/90
78	MAYACAMAS VINEYARDS	Napa Valley	1,464	9	50	1991	1/90
75	ROBERT MONDAVI WINERY	Napa Valley Reserve	1,500	10	35	1991	3/90
75	STONY HILL VINEYARD	Napa Valley	855	9	125	1991-1993	5/90
73	TREFETHEN VINEYARDS	Napa Valley	1,449	6.50	45	1991	3/90
70	CHATEAU ST. JEAN	Sonoma Valley Wildwood Vineyards	350	9.50	20	1991	7/90
63	CHATEAU ST. JEAN	Alexander Valley Robert Young Vineyards	900	7.75	22	Avoid	7/90

NR — Not released.

Score	Winery	Appellation/Vineyard	Production	Release Price	Current Price	Drink	Last Tasted
61	BEAULIEU VINEYARD	Napa Valley Beaufort	20,000	$5	$28	Avoid	4/90
60	MOUNT EDEN VINEYARDS	Santa Cruz Mountains	108	14	45	Avoid	3/90
VINTAGE: 1974							
88	BERINGER VINEYARDS	Santa Barbara County	1,000	5	45	1991-1993	4/90
88	CHATEAU MONTELENA WINERY	Napa and Alexander Valleys	2,200	8	70	1991-1996	2/90
88	HANZELL VINEYARDS	Sonoma Valley	300	9	75	1991-1995	1/90
88	ROBERT MONDAVI WINERY	Napa Valley Reserve	1,000	10	45	1991-1994	3/90
80	HACIENDA WINERY	Sonoma County Clair de Lune	675	5	40	1991-1992	4/90
80	TREFETHEN VINEYARDS	Napa Valley	1,294	5.75	50	1991-1993	3/90
79	BURGESS CELLARS	Carneros Winery Lake Vineyard	700	$6	$25	1991	12/89
78	STERLING VINEYARDS	Napa Valley Estate	3,000	4.75	35	1991-1993	4/90
74	FREEMARK ABBEY WINERY	Napa Valley	4,110	7.95	42	1991	2/90
73	STONY HILL VINEYARD	Napa Valley	1,280	7	110	1991-1993	5/90
72	CHAPPELLET VINEYARD	Napa Valley	600	6.75	45	1991	3/90
70	BERINGER VINEYARDS	Napa Valley Centennial Cask Selection	1,000	5	40	1991-1992	4/90
70	MAYACAMAS VINEYARDS	Napa Valley	1,257	7.50	50	1991	1/90
62	BEAULIEU VINEYARD	Napa Valley Beaufort	15,000	5	25	Avoid	4/90
59	MOUNT EDEN VINEYARDS	Santa Cruz Mountains	170	14	45	Avoid	3/90
VINTAGE: 1973							
93	CHATEAU MONTELENA WINERY	Napa and Alexander Valleys	2,000	6.50	100	1991-1998	2/90
91	CHAPPELLET VINEYARD	Napa Valley	400	6.75	50	1991-1994	3/90
91	HACIENDA WINERY	Sonoma County Clair de Lune	495	5	50	1991-1994	4/90
85	BURGESS CELLARS	Napa Valley	400	6	30	1991-1993	12/89
85	HANZELL VINEYARDS	Sonoma Valley	310	8	100	1991-1995	1/90
85	TREFETHEN VINEYARDS	Napa Valley	643	6.50	50	1991-1993	3/90
82	MOUNT EDEN VINEYARDS	Santa Cruz Mountains	281	12	55	1991	3/90
79	STONY HILL VINEYARD	Napa Valley	1,250	7	120	1991-1992	5/90
77	FREEMARK ABBEY WINERY	Napa Valley	6,117	6.50	32	1991	2/90
60	BEAULIEU VINEYARD	Napa Valley Beaufort	15,000	5	30	Avoid	4/90
60	MAYACAMAS VINEYARDS	Napa Valley	1,082	7	50	Avoid	1/90
VINTAGE: 1972							
95	CHATEAU MONTELENA WINERY	Napa and Alexander Valleys	2,000	6	110	1991-1997	2/90
90	HANZELL VINEYARDS	Sonoma Valley	170	7	75	1991-1995	1/90
83	STONY HILL VINEYARD	Napa Valley	645	7	110	1991-1992	5/90
80	MOUNT EDEN VINEYARDS	Santa Cruz Mountains	210	20	50	1991-1993	3/90
77	FREEMARK ABBEY WINERY	Napa Valley	3,984	6.50	48	1991	2/90
60	BEAULIEU VINEYARD	Napa Valley Beaufort	12,000	5	30	Avoid	4/90
59	MAYACAMAS VINEYARDS	Napa Valley	704	7	50	Avoid	1/90
VINTAGE: 1971							
85	HANZELL VINEYARDS	Sonoma Valley	160	7	120	1991-1994	1/90
80	STONY HILL VINEYARD	Napa Valley	580	6	110	1991-1992	5/90
70	FREEMARK ABBEY WINERY	Napa Valley	3,959	7	40	1991	2/90
58	BEAULIEU VINEYARD	Napa Valley Beaufort	10,000	4	30	Avoid	4/90
VINTAGE: 1970							
92	STONY HILL VINEYARD	Napa Valley	685	6	175	1991-1996	5/90
84	HANZELL VINEYARDS	Sonoma Valley	220	7	120	1991-1994	1/90
59	BEAULIEU VINEYARD	Napa Valley Beaufort	3,000	4	32	Avoid	4/90
55	FREEMARK ABBEY WINERY	Napa Valley	2,698	7	35	Avoid	2/90
VINTAGE: 1969							
90	HANZELL VINEYARDS	Sonoma Valley	220	6	140	1991-1995	1/90
85	STONY HILL VINEYARD	Napa Valley	750	5	175	1991-1993	5/90
60	FREEMARK ABBEY WINERY	Napa Valley	2,307	6	37	Avoid	2/90
57	BEAULIEU VINEYARD	Napa Valley Beaufort	3,000	2	35	Avoid	4/90

NR — Not released.

Score	Winery	Appellation/Vineyard	Production	Release Price	Current Price	Drink	Last Tasted
VINTAGE: 1968							
93	STONY HILL VINEYARD	Napa Valley	750	$5	$250	1991-1996	5/90
91	HANZELL VINEYARDS	Sonoma Valley	240	6	140	1991-1995	1/90
73	FREEMARK ABBEY WINERY	Napa Valley	996	5	40	1991	2/90
59	BEAULIEU VINEYARD	Napa Valley Beaufort	2,000	2	35	Avoid	4/90
VINTAGE: 1967							
89	HANZELL VINEYARDS	Sonoma Valley	330	6	140	1991-1994	1/90
83	STONY HILL VINEYARD	Napa Valley	700	4.50	250	1991-1992	5/90
VINTAGE: 1966							
94	HANZELL VINEYARDS	Sonoma Valley	260	6	170	1991-2000	1/90
91	STONY HILL VINEYARD	Napa Valley	150	4.50	300	1991-1995	5/90
VINTAGE: 1965							
90	STONY HILL VINEYARD	Napa Valley	300	4	400	1991-1994	5/90
84	HANZELL VINEYARDS	Sonoma Valley	190	6	180	1991-1995	1/90
58	MAYACAMAS VINEYARDS	Napa Valley	500	2.50	125	Avoid	1/90
VINTAGE: 1964							
98	STONY HILL VINEYARD	Napa Valley	300	4	450	1991-2000	5/90
92	MAYACAMAS VINEYARDS	Napa Valley	500	1.75	200	1991-1994	1/90
VINTAGE: 1963							
87	STONY HILL VINEYARD	Napa Valley	160	4	450	1991-1993	5/90
58	MAYACAMAS VINEYARDS	Napa Valley	400	1.75	150	Avoid	1/90
VINTAGE: 1962							
96	STONY HILL VINEYARD	Napa Valley	275	3.25	450	1991-1998	5/90
87	HEITZ WINE CELLAR	Napa Valley	250	6	150	1991-1997	6/90
58	MAYACAMAS VINEYARDS	Napa Valley	400	1.75	150	Avoid	1/90
VINTAGE: 1961							
93	HEITZ WINE CELLAR	Napa Valley	250	6	150	1991-2000	6/90
VINTAGE: 1960							
88	STONY HILL VINEYARD	Napa Valley	200	3	430	1991-1995	5/90
VINTAGE: 1959							
88	HANZELL VINEYARDS	California	120	4	200	1991-1995	12/89
VINTAGE: 1958							
60	MAYACAMAS VINEYARDS	Napa Valley	500	1	200	Avoid	1/90
VINTAGE: 1957							
90	HANZELL VINEYARDS	California	240	4	240	1991-1993	12/89
VINTAGE: 1955							
88	MAYACAMAS VINEYARDS	Napa Valley	250	1	325	1991-1995	1/90

NR — Not released.

APPENDIX 4
Chardonnay Vintage Chart, 1989-1970

The following is a list of all vintages reviewed between 1989 and 1970 in chronological order. The number next to the vintage is its score based on *The Wine Spectator's* 100-point scale.

1980s

1989	86	Very Good	Rainy, Uneven Quality, Some Outstanding
1988	92	Outstanding	Delicate, Ripe, Forward, Balanced
1987	87	Very Good	Austere, Tart, Ageworthy, Concentrated
1986	91	Outstanding	Deep, Rich, Concentrated, Complex
1985	94	Outstanding	Ripe, Elegant, Concentrated, Harmonious
1984	88	Very Good	Very Ripe, Bold, Fleshy, Early Maturing
1983	81	Good	Austere Style, Uneven Quality, "Food Wines"
1982	78	Average	Huge Crop, Very Ripe, Unbalanced
1981	86	Very Good	Ripe, Forward, Fleshy, Charming
1980	85	Very Good	Huge Crop, Very Ripe, Full-Bodied

1970s

1979	89	Very Good	Austere, Elegant, Balanced, Ageworthy
1978	85	Very Good	Ripe, Intense, Powerful
1977	84	Good	Drought Year, Elegant, Balanced, Charming
1976	77	Average	Drought Year, Very Ripe, Unbalanced
1975	85	Very Good	Ripe, Elegant, Balanced, Charming
1974	88	Very Good	Ripe, Rich, Bold, Balanced
1973	85	Very Good	Elegant, Subtle, Balanced, Charming
1972	67	Below Average	Rainy, Simple, Watery, Uninspired
1971	68	Below Average	Rainy Harvest, Poor Quality
1970	89	Very Good	Complex, Elegant, Balanced

Classic	**(95-100 points)**
Outstanding	**(90-94)**
Good to Very Good	**(80-89)**
Average	**(70-79)**
Below Average	**(60-69)**
Poor	**(50-59)**

APPENDIX 5
Chardonnay Vintages by Score

The following is a list of all vintages reviewed between 1989 and 1970 and ranks them in order by score. The number next to the vintage is its score based on *The Wine Spectator's* 100-point scale.

Outstanding (90-94)
1. 1985 94 Outstanding — Ripe, Elegant, Concentrated, Harmonious
2. 1988 92 Outstanding — Delicate, Ripe, Forward, Balanced
3. 1986 91 Outstanding — Deep, Rich, Concentrated, Complex

Good to Very Good (80-89)
4. 1970 89 Very Good — Complex, Elegant, Balanced
5. 1979 89 Very Good — Austere, Elegant, Balanced, Ageworthy
6. 1984 88 Very Good — Very Ripe, Bold, Fleshy, Early Maturing
7. 1974 88 Very Good — Ripe, Rich, Bold, Balanced
8. 1987 87 Very Good — Austere, Tart, Ageworthy, Concentrated
9. 1981 86 Very Good — Ripe, Forward, Fleshy, Charming
10. 1989 86 Very Good — Rainy, Uneven Quality, Some Outstanding
11. 1980 85 Very Good — Huge Crop, Very Ripe, Full-Bodied
12. 1978 85 Very Good — Ripe, Intense, Powerful
13. 1975 85 Very Good — Ripe, Elegant, Balanced, Charming
14. 1973 85 Very Good — Elegant, Subtle, Balanced, Charming
15. 1977 84 Good — Drought Year, Elegant, Balanced, Charming
16. 1983 81 Good — Austere Style, Uneven Quality, "Food Wines"

Average (70-79)
17. 1982 78 Average — Huge Crop, Very Ripe, Unbalanced
18. 1976 77 Average — Drought Year, Very Ripe, Unbalanced

Below Average (60-69)
19. 1971 68 Below Average — Rainy Harvest, Poor Quality
20. 1972 67 Below Average — Rainy, Simple, Watery, Uninspired

Classic	(95-100 points)
Outstanding	(90-94)
Good to Very Good	(80-89)
Average	(70-79)
Below Average	(60-69)
Poor	(50-59)

APPENDIX 6
Chardonnay Producers Considered For This Book

The following is a list of all Chardonnay producers considered for inclusion in *California's Great Chardonnays*.

Acacia Winery
Adelaida Cellars
Adler Fels
Ahern Winery
Alderbrook Winery
Alexander Valley Vineyards
Altamura Winery and Vineyards
S. Anderson Vineyard
Arciero Winery
Arrowood Vineyards & Winery
Arthur Vineyards
David Ashley Vineyard
Au Bon Climat
Babcock Vineyards
Baldinelli Vineyards
Ballard Canyon Winery
Balverne Winery and Vineyards
Bandiera Winery
Bargetto Winery
Barrow Green
Beaulieu Vineyard
Belvedere Winery
Beringer Vineyards
Black Mountain Vineyard
Boeger Winery
Bonny Doon Vineyard
Bouchaine
Brander Vineyard
Braren Pauli Winery
David Bruce Winery
Buena Vista Winery
Burgess Cellars
Davis Bynum Winery
Byron Vineyard & Winery
Cain Cellars
Cakebread Cellars
Calera Wine Co.
Callaway Vineyard and Winery
Cambria Winery & Vineyard
Canterbury
J. Carey Vineyards & Winery
Carneros Creek Winery
Caymus Vineyards
Cecchetti Sebastiani Cellar
Chalk Hill Winery
Chalone Vineyard
Chamisal Vineyard
Chappellet Vineyard
Chateau Chevalier
Chateau De Leu Winery
Chateau Julien Winery
Chateau Montelena Winery
Chateau Napa Beaucannon
Chateau Potelle

Chateau Souverain
Chateau St. Jean
Chateau Woltner
Chestnut Hill
Chimney Rock Winery
Christian Brothers
Christophe Vineyards
Clos du Bois Winery
Clos Du Val Wine Co.
Clos Pegase
B.R. Cohn
Colby Vineyards
Concannon Vineyard
Congress Springs Vineyards
Conn Creek Winery
Corbett Canyon Vineyards
Cosentino Winery
Creston Manor Vineyards & Winery
Crichton Hall
Cronin Vineyards
Cuvaison Winery
De Loach Vineyards
Dehlinger Winery
Delicato Vineyards
De Lorimier Winery
Dion Vineyard
Dolan Vineyards
Domaine De Napa Winery
Domaine Laurier
Domaine Michel
Domaine St. George Winery
Dry Creek Vineyard
Durney Vineyard
Eberle Winery
Edna Valley Vineyard
Estancia
Far Niente Winery
Gary Farrell
Ferrari-Carano Vineyards
Fetzer Vineyards
Firestone Vineyard
Fisher Vineyards
Fitch Mountain Cellars
Flax Vineyard
Flora Springs Wine Co.
Thomas Fogarty Winery
Folie à Deux Winery
Foppiano Vineyards
Forman Vineyard
Fox Mountain
Foxen Vineyard
Franciscan Vineyards
Freemark Abbey Winery
Fritz Cellars

Frog's Leap Winery
Gainey Vineyard
E. & J. Gallo Winery
Gan Eden
Gauer Estate
Geyser Peak Winery
Girard Winery
Glen Ellen Winery
Goosecross Cellars
Grand Cru Vineyards
Green and Red Vineyard
Grgich Hills Cellar
Groth Vineyards & Winery
Guenoc Winery
Gundlach-Bundschu Winery
Hacienda Winery
Hagafen Cellars
Hallcrest Vineyards
Handley Cellars
Hanna Winery
Hanzell Vineyards
Havens Wine Cellars
Haywood Winery
Hawk Crest
Heron Lake
Heitz Wine Cellars
Hess Collection Winery
Hidden Cellars Winery
William Hill Winery
Hop Kiln Winery
Houtz Vineyards
Husch Vineyards
Inglenook-Napa Valley
Innisfree
Iron Horse Vineyards
Jekel Vineyards
Jepson Vineyards
Johnson Turnbull Vineyards
Jordan Vineyard and Winery
Jory Winery
Kalin Cellars
Karly Wines
Robert Keenan Winery
Kendall-Jackson Vineyards
Kenwood Vineyards
Kistler Vineyards
Konocti Winery
Charles Krug Winery
La Crema
La Reina Winery
Lakespring Winery
Lambert Bridge
Landmark Vineyards
Lazy Creek Vineyards

Leeward Winery
Liberty School
Llords and Elwood Winery
J. Lohr Winery
Lolonis Winery
Long Vineyards
Macrostie Winery
Mariposa Cellars
Mark West Vineyards
Markham Vineyards
Martin Brothers Winery
Louis M. Martini Winery
Paul Masson
Matanzas Creek Winery
Mayacamas Vineyards
Mazzocco Vineyards
McDowell Valley Vineyards
Meeker Vineyard
Mendocino Estate
Meridian Vineyards
Merlion Winery
Merry Vintners
Merryvale Vineyards
Milano Winery
Mill Creek Vineyards
Mirassou Winery
Robert Mondavi Winery
Mont St. John Cellars
Monterey Peninsula Winery
The Monterey Vineyard
Montevina Wines
Monticello Cellars
Morgan Winery
Mount Eden Vineyards
Mount Veeder Winery
Mountain House Winery
Mountain View Vintners
Murphy-Goode Estate Winery
Napa Creek Winery
Navarro Vineyards
Newlan Vineyards and Winery
Newton Vineyard
Neyers Winery
Gustave Niebaum
Olson Vineyards Winery
Page Mill Winery
Parducci Wine Cellars

Parsons Creek Winery
Pat Paulsen
Robert Pecota Winery
J. Pedroncelli Winery
Perret Vineyards
Robert Pepi Winery
Joseph Phelps Vineyards
Phillips Vineyard
R.H. Phillips Winery
Pine Ridge Winery
Plam Vineyards
Bernard Pradel Cellars
Quail Ridge Cellars
Qupé
Rancho Sisquoc Winery
Kent Rasmussen Vineyards
Ravenswood
Raymond Vineyard and Cellar
Revere Vineyard and Winery
Ridge Vineyards
Roche Winery
Rochioli Vineyard/Winery
Rombauer Vineyards
Roudon-Smith Vineyards
Round Hill Cellars
Rutherford Estate
Rutherford Hill Winery
Rutherford Ranch Vineyards
Sage Creek Vineyard
Saintsbury
San Martin Winery
Sanford Winery
Santa Barbara Winery
Santa Ynez Winery
Sausal Winery
Schug Cellars
Sebastiani Vineyards
Seghesio Winery
Sequoia Grove Vineyards
Shafer Vineyards
Charles F. Shaw Vineyard
Signorello Vineyards
Silverado Vineyards
Simi Winery
Robert Sinskey Vineyards
Smith-Madrone Vineyard
Sonoma-Cutrer Vineyards

Spring Mountain Vineyards
St. Andrews Winery
St. Clement Vineyards
St. Francis Winery
St. Supery Vineyards & Winery
Stag's Leap Wine Cellars
Star Hill Wines
David S. Stare
Sterling Vineyards
Stevenot Winery
Stone Creek Cellars
Stonegate Winery
Stony Hill Vineyard
Stratford Winery
Rodney Strong Vineyards
Sunny St. Helena Winery
Joseph Swan Vineyards
Swanson Vineyards and Winery
Taft Street Winery
Robert Talbott Vineyards
Talley Vineyards
Iván Támas
Tiffany Hill Vineyards
Tijsseling Vineyards
Trefethen Vineyards
M.G. Vallejo
Vega Vineyards Winery
Ventana Vineyards
Viansa Winery
Vichon Winery
Villa Mt. Eden
Villa Zapu
Vita Nova
Wente Bros.
William Wheeler Winery
White Oak Vineyards & Winery
Whitehall Lane Winery
Wild Horse Winery
Willow Creek Vineyard
Windemere Wines
York Mountain Winery
Zaca Mesa Winery
ZD Wines
Z Moore Winery
Stephen Zellerbach Vineyards

INDEX

INDEX

THE
WINE SPECTATOR

Much of the research and tasting analysis in this book by James Laube has been done in conjunction with his duties as senior editor of *The Wine Spectator.*

The Wine Spectator, America's best-selling consumer wine magazine, is edited for those who are serious about wine. Published twice a month, each issue offers a unique "insider's view" of the world of wine, featuring current news, wine ratings, personality profiles and wine and food articles as well as pieces on entertainment and travel, all of which are written by the world's leading wine journalists.

A one-year subscription to *The Wine Spectator* is $35 for U.S. delivery, $45 for Canada, and $90 for delivery anywhere else in the world. To subscribe call 1-800-622-2062, or send your check, payable to *The Wine Spectator* in U.S. funds to *The Wine Spectator*, P.O. Box 1960, Marion, OH 43305.